Tolley's Estate Planning

2010–11

by

Sharon McKie LLB(Hons), Solicitor (non-practising), CTA, ACSI

and

Simon McKie MA(Oxon), FCA, CTA (Fellow), APFS, TEP,

Barrister-at-Law of Lincoln's Inn

both of McKie & Co (Advisory Services) LLP

LexisNexis®

Members of the LexisNexis Group worldwide

United Kingdom	LexisNexis, a Division of Reed Elsevier (UK) Ltd, Halsbury House, 35 Chancery Lane, London, WC2A 1EL, and London House, 20–22 East London Street, Edinburgh EH7 4BQ
Australia	LexisNexis Butterworths, Chatswood, New South Wales
Austria	LexisNexis Verlag ARD Orac GmbH & Co KG, Vienna
Benelux	LexisNexis Benelux, Amsterdam
Canada	LexisNexis Canada, Markham, Ontario
China	LexisNexis China, Beijing and Shanghai
France	LexisNexis SA, Paris
Germany	LexisNexis Deutschland GmbH, Munster
Hong Kong	LexisNexis Hong Kong, Hong Kong
India	LexisNexis India, New Delhi
Italy	Giuffrè Editore, Milan
Japan	LexisNexis Japan, Tokyo
Malaysia	Malayan Law Journal Sdn Bhd, Kuala Lumpur
New Zealand	LexisNexis NZ Ltd, Wellington
Poland	Wydawnictwo Prawnicze LexisNexis Sp, Warsaw
Singapore	LexisNexis Singapore, Singapore
South Africa	LexisNexis Butterworths, Durban
USA	LexisNexis, Dayton, Ohio

Published by LexisNexis

A CIP Catalogue record for this book is available from the British Library.

ISBN 978 0 7545 3895 0

Printed and bound in Great Britain by Hobbs the Printers Ltd, Totton, Hampshire

Visit LexisNexis at www.lexisnexis.co.uk

About the Authors

Sharon McKie is a designated member of McKie & Co (Advisory Services) LLP. She has specialised in private client taxation services since 1997, providing bespoke tax planning advice to private clients. She has particular expertise in Stamp Duty and SDLT issues as they affect the private client. She is a well-known authoress on capital tax planning issues and a member of the Succession Taxes Sub-Committee of the Chartered Institute of Taxation and is a former member of the Inheritance Tax & Trusts Sub-Committee of the Faculty of Taxation.

Simon McKie is a designated member of McKie & Co (Advisory Services) LLP. He is a member of the Technical Committee of the Society of Trust and Estate Practitioners, and also a member and former chairman of the Succession Taxes Sub-Committee, as well as a member of the Capital Gains and Investment Sub-Committee of the Chartered Institute of Taxation. He is a former chairman of the Faculty of Taxation and of the Faculty of Inheritance Tax and Trusts Technical Sub-Committee. Simon is a member of the editorial board of Taxation Magazine. He is an established tax author and has written and lectured widely on taxation.

McKie & Co (Advisory Services) LLP provides expert advice on matters of private client taxation to solicitors, accountants and other advisers. It also provides advice directly to individuals, trusts, companies and other entities. It won the Society of Trust and Estate Practitioners' award for 'Boutique Firm of the Year' in 2009/10. The judges said: 'McKie & Co offers the highest level of specialist trust and tax service. Their broad experience and clear, logically ordered and positive advice was reflected in positive client references.'

Preface

This year has once again seen the introduction of many small scale changes which have been reflected in the many detailed changes to the text.

We are grateful for the enormous help we have received from our specialist contributors – from Ken Chapman in relation to insurance and pensions; from Roger Maggs of Hampden Tax Consultants who has given expert advice in relation to Lloyds Underwriters; from Simon Rylatt, Anne Kay, Sharon Kenchington and Caroline Wright of Boodle Hatfield whose advice on matrimonial matters has been invaluable.

Our thanks are also due to the editorial staff at LexisNexis for entrusting us with this task and for their help and encouragement in bringing it to fruition.

Sharon McKie

Simon McKie
August 2010

Contents

Table of Statutes

Paragraph references printed in **bold** type indicate where the Statute is set out in part or in full.

Table of Statutory Instruments

Paragraph references printed in **bold** type indicate where the Statutory Instrument is set out in part or in full

Table of Cases

A

B

C

D

E

F

G

H

I

J

K

N

O

P

R

S

T

U

V

W

Y

Chapter 1

What is Estate Planning?

A science and an art

[1.1] This is a work on taxation but estate planning is not merely a sub-division of tax planning. Estate planning is planning to preserve, protect and devolve family wealth. If taxation did not exist, estate planning would still not be simple. An individual would still be faced with hard choices in protecting their wealth against investment risk and political interference and in balancing their children's need to gain experience in the management of wealth against the dangers of youthful improvidence.

In writing about taxation for estate planning, therefore, one needs to keep always in mind a variety of non-taxation considerations which define the problems to be solved as well as constraining the solutions.

One should take account of the client's wishes, expectations, opinions and prejudices and the nature of their relationships with their spouse, children, grandchildren and wider family. One needs to make informed guesses about the future; as to how their family relationships will develop, what will happen to their major assets, how they will want to live and how the political and economic environment will change.

Dealing with such subjective and uncertain matters, estate planning can never be either uniform or absolute; it is a bespoke service and not a retail product. It should be a continuing service rather than a once and for all event. The future becomes the present and then the past in ways which are never completely predictable. Our predictions must always be provisional; estate plans must be continually revised.

Perhaps it is only the saints who, in this life, are indifferent to protecting their wealth. The rest of mankind needs some form of estate planning. For many, the irreducible minimum is to make a will, to take some life insurance cover to protect one's dependants from the consequences of one's death and to write those insurance policies in trust so that the proceeds will be available to one's personal representatives before probate is granted. In addition, joint owners of property need to consider whether that property should be held as joint tenants or as tenants in common and members of pension schemes should ensure that the scheme trustees have been informed of their wishes for the application of death benefits. Readers of this book are, however, likely to have, or to advise clients who have, estates far more complex than that which require tax planning which is similarly more complex than this bare minimum.

Estate planning is essential to anyone who owns significant assets, from the moderately prosperous to the very rich, although not all estate planning techniques will be appropriate to every level of wealth. We attempt to cover estate planning as it is relevant to every level of wealth, however one describes holders of such wealth. Those with very substantial assets are often described by such terms as 'High Net Worth Individuals' or HNWIs or the 'super rich'. We eschew such unlovely jargon for it disguises the many other ways in which persons suitable for estate planning may be categorised. We keep in mind throughout, however, the differing characteristics of the moderately prosperous, the substantially wealthy and the very rich and **CHAPTER 21 A LIFETIME OF PLANNING**, gives an extended example of lifetime planning for a family with very substantial assets indeed.

Basic principles

[1.2] The basic principles of all estate planning, however, are simple.

First, one must determine the client's objectives. In order to do so one needs to explore the nature of their wealth, their relationships with their family, their expectations for the future and their attitudes towards financial risk and the devolution of wealth.

Secondly, as most estate planning involves making gifts of some sort, one should determine whether they currently have, or expect to have, a surplus of wealth over required expenditure. We deliberately express it in that way because often one of the greatest barriers to estate planning is an over-emphasis by clients on the need to preserve capital and to spend only income. A man of eighty with an annual expenditure of only £40,000 may yet have a portfolio of £1m. Whatever view one takes of his life expectancy he does not need to hold on to all of his capital in order to be quite secure that he will be able to continue to maintain his expenditure for the rest of his life. Holding on to wealth too long is far commoner than giving away too much too early.

Thirdly, in making gifts one must determine the appropriate assets to be given away. For example, it may be useful to give assets which have the prospect of substantial future capital growth to younger family members. One must also determine the appropriate form of the gift; should it be absolute or in trust? In coming to these decisions one must avoid creating unnecessary administrative difficulties but be careful to consider the effect of the gift on the recipient. It is usually unwise, for example, to give absolute control of a family company to a child who is just eighteen.

Fourthly, although most estate planning will be directed towards avoiding particular tax charges, it is important to keep in mind the whole range of taxes which can apply to family wealth.

Fifthly, one should aim for the greatest possible flexibility so that one can adapt the chosen strategy to changes in circumstances and expectations.

Finally, whatever plan is adopted, one needs to review it formally at regular intervals to determine changes in the client's intentions and expectations for the future and to adapt the plan to those changes.

A hostile environment

[1.3] In designing and implementing tax planning steps, an adviser should recognise that he is now operating in a very much more hostile environment than was the case just a few years ago. For some years the government and HMRC have conducted a campaign to vilify tax planners and tax planning and to blur the very clear dividing line between tax planning and tax evasion. HMRC's new litigation strategy has seen the government refusing to make sensible compromises in disputes with taxpayers; rather it has chosen to litigate aggressively, considerably increasing the number of cases coming to the courts. At the same time, the government has taken, without adequate consultation, new powers for HMRC to obtain information, to enter and search premises and to impose penalties. These powers allow HMRC to inconvenience and penalise taxpayers of whose activities it disapproves.

There has been an alarming decline in the precision with which tax legislation is drafted. This has diminished the taxpayers' ability to determine the scope of the law by which they are taxed, a situation which is made worse by the decline in the standard of HMRC's guidance on the law. In many instances that guidance has been criticised by the professional bodies as positively misleading and as an improper attempt to substitute administrative fiat for the rule of law. In the courts, the decision in *Barclays Mercantile Business Finance Ltd v Mawson (Inspector of Taxes)* [2004] UKHL 51, [2005] 1 AC 684, [2005] STC 1, a laudable attempt to bring some conceptual clarity to the line of cases which began with *WT Ramsey Ltd v IRC* [1982] AC 300, [1981] 1 All ER 865, [1981] STC 174, has encouraged some of the judiciary to take liberties with the language of tax legislation. They have gone beyond construing the words of legislation in the light of Parliament's intention to substituting provisions which the court considers Parliament should have enacted for the words which it actually did enact. Other members of the judiciary continue to apply themselves to construing the words enacted by Parliament (see *Revenue and Customs Comrs v D'Arcy* [2007] EWHC 163 (Ch), [2008] STC 1329). Hence the outcome of tax litigation has become heavily dependent upon which judge (or judges) is (or are) allocated to a particular case.

It does not appear, as yet, that a change of government has reversed any of these trends. Indeed, the proposal to extend the legislation requiring the notification to HMRC of arrangements which confer a tax advantage (which has done so much to undermine the relationship between HMRC and taxation advisers) to arrangements conferring an inheritance tax advantage on transfers into trust, is an ominous sign.

Of course these developments have disturbing implications for the essential freedoms and economic health of the nation but to the adviser they cause particular problems. He may not be able to determine how the law applies to particular transactions. Instead of relying entirely on the protection of the law he must calculate whether a particular course of action is likely to arouse the hostility of the Revenue authorities. He must consider what he must do where the law conflicts with HMRC's guidance on it. If he advises his client to take his case before the courts, he must ensure that the client understands that, however strong his case may appear to be, there will be a significant possibility of an adverse outcome.

If the current time is a difficult one for tax planning however, it is also one in which such planning is absolutely necessary. The previous government's colossal profligacy has created budget deficits of an unprecedented scale and the new government is now faced with having to raise money to reduce these deficits. The top rate of income tax has been raised this year to 50% and, whilst HMRC continues to caricature tax planning as a dishonest assault on the pockets of the many, it has resorted to strained constructions of the law amounting to artificial tax assessment in its efforts to maintain government revenues (see *Nason v Revenue and Customs Comrs* [2007] STC (SCD) 125, [2007] SWTI 200, *Revenue and Customs Comrs v William Grant & Sons Distillers Ltd* [2007] UKHL 15, [2007] 2 All ER 440, [2007] STC 680, *Postlethwaite's Executors v Revenue and Customs Comrs* [2007] STC (SCD) 83, [2007] SWTI 346, *Revenue and Customs Comrs v Valentine Marketing Holdings Ltd* [2006] EWHC 2820 (Ch), [2007] STC 1631, *Revenue and Customs Comrs v Smallwood* [2007] EWCA Civ 462, [2007] STC 1237, *Fenston Will Trusts (Trustees of) v Revenue and Customs Comrs* [2007] STC (SCD) 316), *Atkinson v Revenue and Customs Comrs* [2010] UKFTT 108 (TC), [2010] SWTI 2123 and *Pitt v Holt* [2010] EWHC 45 (Ch), [2010] 2 All ER 774, [2010] 1 WLR 1199). More than ever, clients need the ingenuity of their advisers to protect them from a department of government determined to maximise revenue in the short term regardless of the consequences for the long term integrity of the country's taxation system.

Chapter 2

Lifetime Planning

Introduction

[2.1] The purpose of this chapter is to give a general outline of the basic principles involved in lifetime estate planning. It will outline a number of matters which receive more detailed treatment in other chapters.

So: 'what is the primary purpose of lifetime planning?'. The traditional response will be the mitigation of inheritance tax payable on a person's death'. However, in today's world, consideration will also be given to the mitigation of capital gains tax and, in some cases, income tax. Tax saving is not the only purpose of estate planning. Whilst the deceased's heirs will usually regard the inheritance tax payable on death as being most instrumental in reducing their share of the estate, the legal and other costs of winding up the estate, which these days can be considerable, have the same effect. Therefore, one aspect of lifetime planning should be to organise your estate into a form which minimises the costs of administration after death.

Whilst one motive a client may have for passing assets on to his children may be to take a proportion of his estate out of the inheritance tax charge on his death, there are other motives for passing on assets. These include the desire to give children a 'start in life', by helping them, for example, to buy a flat or a car or set up their own business; or the desire to help with the cost of educating their grandchildren. The client will therefore be seeking advice on the most tax efficient ways of making such gifts; in particular, ways which give rise to minimum inheritance tax, capital gains tax, stamp duty land tax or income tax liabilities.

These three aspects of lifetime planning — the general mitigation of the inheritance tax charge on death, tax efficient ways of giving and the general organisation of an estate — are the subject matter of this chapter. There is a clear overlap between the first and second of these because one of the most obvious ways of mitigating inheritance tax on death is by immediate lifetime gifts. Thus, whilst a client may have differing motives for making a gift during his lifetime, the general principles involved will be the same and accordingly the second of these three aspects will be dealt with as part of the first.

Mitigation of inheritance tax

[2.2] Broadly, inheritance tax may be mitigated in one of the following four ways.

(a) Reducing the estate through immediate lifetime gifts, the intention being to take assets out of the inheritance tax charge on death. This is known as 'asset reduction'.
(b) Converting assets of the estate which do not qualify for any form of inheritance tax relief into assets which do (for example, agricultural property or business assets), the intention being to reduce the value of the assets when calculating the inheritance tax charge on death. This is known as 'asset conversion'.
(c) Freezing the value of assets in the estate so that any future growth in value will pass to the next generation, the intention being to take the 'growth element' out of the inheritance tax charge altogether. This is known as 'asset freezing'.
(d) Converting capital assets of the estate into high income producing assets. This is known as 'conversion of capital assets'.

Each of these headings will be dealt with in turn.

Asset reduction

[2.3] Inheritance tax is a tax both on lifetime gifts and on the ultimate gift a person is deemed to make on his death. The 2010/11 death rates are:

£0–£325,000	0%
Above £325,000	40%

The rate of inheritance tax on chargeable lifetime gifts is one half of that applicable on death, ie 20% (IHTA 1984, s 7(2)). Where a person dies within three years of a chargeable gift, then the tax payable is recomputed either at the death rates in force at the date of the gift or, if the rates have been reduced, at the rates applicable at the date of death, and the additional tax, if any, becomes payable (IHTA 1984, s 7(1), (4), Sch 2). Similarly, where a person dies more than 3 years after the chargeable gift, taper relief is available. The tax is recomputed at the tapering percentages of either the death rates in force at the date of the gift or, if the rates are lower, the death rates in force at the date of death. Again, any additional tax becomes payable (IHTA 1984, s 7(4), Sch 2).

Where the subject matter of the gift:

(a) is still in the hands of the transferee or his spouse at the date of death and has a lower value at that date than at the date of the gift; or
(b) has been sold on the open market before the death at a lower value,

then the additional tax payable on death is calculated by reference to the lower value (IHTA 1984, s 131). For this to apply, however, the gift must not comprise tangible movable property which are wasting assets (IHTA 1984, s 132).

Inheritance tax is a 'cumulative' tax in the sense that all chargeable gifts made within a 7-year period are aggregated in order to determine the rates of tax applicable to the latest chargeable gift.

Potentially exempt transfers

[2.4] Potentially exempt transfers enable an individual to make specified gifts of unlimited value which will escape tax completely if he survives for a period of 7 years following the gift (IHTA 1984, s 3A). A gift will only be a potentially exempt transfer if it is made by an individual to:

(i) another individual (including the creation of a transitional serial interest); or

(ii) the trustees of a disabled trust; or

(iii) the trustees of a bereaved minor's trust on the coming to the end of an immediate post-death interest.

This means that a gift to an accumulation and maintenance trust or an interest in possession trust (unless it falls within one of the special categories) will not be a potentially exempt transfer, instead it will be a lifetime chargeable transfer. The various types of trust above are discussed in more detail in **CHAPTER 4 CREATING SETTLEMENTS**.

Although it is no longer possible for transfers into trust to be potentially exempt transfers, it will not necessarily be a problem for all. Where an individual is going to make a transfer equal to or below the nil rate band but considers because of family circumstances that a trust is required, there is no immediate difference between making a chargeable transfer or a potentially exempt transfer.

Example

Mary's estate is worth £2m. She is 81 years of age and wishes to settle the sum of £325,000 on interest in possession trusts for the benefit of her 4 granddaughters. Mary will be excluded from benefiting under the terms of the trust. The money is settled on 1 October 2010. Mary is 'staunch' and outlives the 7-year period.

The transfer to the trust is a chargeable transfer which is taxed at 0%. As she survives the 7-year period there is no inheritance tax liability on that transfer. On 1 October 2017 a new full nil rate band is then available for use.

If she had made an absolute gift to her granddaughters, there would have been no inheritance tax paid on the gift. Having survived for the requisite 7-year period the potentially exempt transfer would be fully exempt.

In the event that she had not survived the 7-year period the chargeable transfer would remain a chargeable transfer and the potentially exempt transfer would have become chargeable. This would have resulted in the same consequences thus reducing the nil rate band available on death.

Where the transferor dies within 3 years of the gift, inheritance tax at the full death rates is charged unless those rates have increased in which case the rates at the time of the transfer are used. Where the gift is made more than 3 years before the death, the rates are 'tapered' as follows.

Years between transfer and death	*Percentage of full tax rate*
More than 3 but not more than 4	80%
More than 4 but not more than 5	60%
More than 5 but not more than 6	40%
More than 6 but not more than 7	20%

In addition, when calculating the inheritance tax payable on the transferor's estate, any potentially exempt transfers and chargeable transfers will be aggregated with the value of his estate. This may increase the amount of tax payable on death.

The potentially exempt transfer is still very important in estate planning. It is possible to make gifts without any charge to inheritance tax at all provided the transferor survives for the necessary period. The risk of the transferor dying within this period may be insured against at rates which, depending upon the age and state of health of the transferor, are often only a small percentage of the potential tax liability. This is considered in more detail in **CHAPTER 7 INSURANCE**.

Gifts within the nil rate tax band

[2.5] No tax is payable until the cumulative total of all gifts made within any 7-year period exceeds £325,000.

Although unlimited tax-free gifts can be made by way of potentially exempt transfers, in some circumstances it may be preferable to make gifts within the nil rate band to a discretionary trust. This would apply, for example, to individuals who prefer to have the flexibility of placing assets in a discretionary trust under which they are excluded as beneficiaries or to individuals who as yet have no children. This will allow further gifts to be made to the trust, or to another trust, 7 years after the initial gift.

Gifts to relevant property trusts have a significant advantage over outright gifts. An election may be made under TCGA 1992, s 260 to hold-over any chargeable gain which would otherwise arise on the gift to a trust from which the settlor is excluded from benefiting, provided that there is no arrangement subsisting under which the settlor may acquire an interest in the settlement (TCGA 1992, s 169B(2)). The held-over gains may be brought back into charge if the settlor acquires an interest in the settlement or arrangements subsist under which the settlor will, or may, acquire such an interest within a defined period. The clawback period begins immediately following the disposal and ends 6 years after the end of the year of assessment in which the disposal was made. (TCGA 1992, s 169C). In relation to gifts which are potentially exempt transfers, hold-over relief will only be available in relation to certain types of business assets (see **2.28** below).

Exemptions and quasi-exemptions

[2.6] Because inheritance tax is charged by reference to the reduction in value of a person's estate (IHTA 1984, s 3(1)), any gift will *prima facie* give rise to a tax charge. There are, however, a number of important exemptions and, what could be termed, 'quasi-exemptions' which enable a person to reduce his estate without giving rise to an immediate tax charge.

Some of the exemptions only apply to transactions made in a person's lifetime whilst others apply both to lifetime transfers and transfers on death. The lifetime exemptions are set out in **2.7–2.11**.

These exemptions and quasi-exemptions will now each be considered in turn.

Annual exemption

[2.7] A person may make gifts of up to £3,000 each year completely free of inheritance tax (IHTA 1984, s 19). Unlike the potentially exempt transfer, this exemption applies regardless of the nature of the recipient of the gift. In addition, there is no requirement for survival by the transferor. If this exemption is wholly or partly unused in any year, it or the balance may be carried forward to the next year. However, if it is not used in that year it will be lost.

Example

A transferor who makes a gift in year 1 of only £1,000 may make gifts within the annual exemption of up to £5,000 in year 2. If he only makes gifts of £3,000 in year 2, the £2,000 shortfall in year 1 will be lost forever.

It will be apparent that in the case of outright gifts either to an individual, or to trustees of privileged trusts, there is an overlap between this exemption and the potentially exempt transfer. Thus, a transferor who reasonably expects to survive for the next 7 years need not limit himself to annual gifts of only £3,000. He could give away significantly more each year. The existence of the annual exemption will only become material if the transferor dies within 7 years of one of these gifts.

Example

A father gives his son £49,428 in each of years 1 to 7. If the father then dies at the end of year 7, all the previous gifts will become chargeable but only as to £46,428 of each, because the annual exemption will be available to exempt the first £3,000 of each gift. As the chargeable gifts amount to £324,996, which is within the 2010/11 nil rate tax band, the lifetime gifts will not give rise to any tax charge. They will, however, be aggregated with the value of the deceased's free estate in calculating the inheritance tax due on the death.

If in the above example the father had survived for 7 years then the annual exemption is wasted on gifts that are subsequently exempt. To ensure that the annual exemption is fully utilised the father could have made a chargeable transfer before making a PET. The annual exemption is set against the first gift made (see Inheritance Tax Manual para 14143). Even with the existence of the potentially exempt transfer, the annual exemption is of importance.

The 'normal expenditure out of income' exemption

[2.8] This exemption applies to a gift if, or to the extent that, it is shown that:

(a) the gift is made as part of the normal expenditure of the transferor;
(b) taking one year with another, the gift is made out of his income; and
(c) after allowing for all other gifts or dispositions forming part of his normal expenditure, the transferor is left with sufficient income to maintain his usual standard of living. (IHTA 1984, s 21).

This exemption must be claimed and will not apply automatically. Whether a gift will qualify for this exemption will be a question of fact in each case.

Made as Part of the Normal Expenditure

[2.8A] According to the Revenue, 'normal' is considered to mean typical of the transferor, not those of the average or reasonable man (HMRC Inheritance Tax Manual, para 14243). So what may be 'normal expenditure' for a person with a net income of £150,000 is unlikely to be so for a person earning £30,000. On the other hand, a person who does earn £30,000 net, with no mortgage, wife, or children and a simple lifestyle may be able to make gifts, for example, to nieces and nephews, which qualify for this exemption to an extent which a person with a much higher income but with a wife and children and a high standard of living cannot.

To be normal, the gift does not necessarily have to be one of a series of regular payments but if not, it must be the type of payment which by its nature is likely to recur (as in the case of the examples given below). As it is essential that the gifts are made out of income, it is advisable that they are payments of cash.

The scope of IHTA 1984, s 21 was considered in the case of *Bennett v CIR* [1995] STC 54 (Ch D). The *Bennett* decision answered a number of key questions concerning the operation of the exemption. The term 'normal expenditure out of income' simply means expenditure which at the time it takes place accords with the settled pattern of expenditure adopted by the transferor. This pattern may be established in one of two ways, by reference to a sequence of payments by the transferor in the past, or by proof of some prior commitment or resolution adopted by him as regards future expenditure, and which he complied with thereafter.

The High Court affirmed that there is no fixed minimum period during which the expenditure must have been incurred. All that is necessary is for there to be evidence of a pattern of actual or intended regular payments, and that the payment in question falls within that category. This means that a single payment might qualify, provided sufficient resolution or commitment for future payments also exists. Where there is a commitment to make future expenditure the commitment must envisage that the payments will 'remain in place . . . for a sufficient period (barring unforeseen circumstances) . . . it need not be legally binding'. It is important that the prospect that the pattern of such gifts continues for more than simply a *de minimis* period of time, barring unforeseen circumstances. This effectively precludes death bed schemes. The Revenue considers that a reasonable period would normally be 3 to 4 years (HMRC Inheritance Tax Manual, para 14241). In the Revenue's view, the amount of the expenditure does not have to be fixed but must be comparable in size (HMRC Inheritance Tax Manual, para 14244). However, if the details provided over a given period do not illustrate normality, an individual may be asked to provide particulars over a longer period. This means that gifts to a discernible class, such as members of the same family could qualify. In the case of *Nadin v ICR* [1997] STC (SCD) 107, (SpC 112) the Special Commissioners held that irregular payments to close relatives did not constitute normal expenditure.

In *McDowall (McDowall's Executors) v CIR (and related appeal)* [2004] STC (SCD) 22, (SpC 382) the issue arose as to whether payments made by an attorney established a pattern of intended regular payments. It was held, in that particular case, that the attorney did not have the power to make the gifts. Had the gifts been valid, however, they would have been exempt under IHTA 1984, s 21.

Made out of Income

[2.8B] What does the phrase 'made out of income' mean? First, it is accepted that 'income' here, means income under the general meaning of that word, that is, income determined under normal accountancy principles, rather than amounts assessable to income tax under the Taxes Acts. Thus, it will not include amounts of capital such as gains arising on the surrender of life insurance policies or amounts received on the sale of government securities treated as income under the accrued income scheme. HMRC's guidance says:

> 'Income is not defined but should be determined; it does not necessarily coincide with income for Income Tax purposes.' (HMRC Inheritance Tax Manual, para 14250)

Does the requirement that the transfer be 'made out of the [transferor's] income' require one to undertake a tracing exercise such as is required to determine whether there has been a remittance of foreign income or capital gains under the remittance basis? The decided cases do not specifically deal with the problem.

Except where the remittance basis is in point, it is highly unusual for individuals to segregate their income from their capital and there is nothing in the decided cases which suggests that the individuals concerned in those cases did so.

HMRC guidance says that:

> ' . . . the transferor should have made the gift out of their income. Thus the gift of jewellery or securities does not qualify unless it was specifically purchased by the donor with the intention of making a gift.
>
> Repeated renunciations of bonus issues of shares do not qualify for exemption although purchases of rights issues in the names of donees may do so.
>
> Income is considered to refer to current income. Gifts will not normally satisfy the second condition if made from a source which, although originally income, has by

> retention over a period of time acquired the nature of capital. The fact that the retained income has been invested or saved in a form that itself yields income will normally show that it has become capital. However, invested funds may remain income if the transferor was really saving them temporarily in order to accumulate an amount sufficient for some expenditure specifically contemplated.' (HMRC Inheritance Tax Manual, para 14250)

This suggests that in HMRC's view a tracing exercise is required. If that is HMRC's view, it goes beyond what is justified by the legislation or the case law. Nonetheless, the cost and uncertainty of challenging HMRC's view on any matter are so great that it is prudent to fall within their published views rather than outside them if one can. A counsel of perfection would be to segregate funds in the way in which, for example, a non-domiciliary segregates his offshore accounts so as to clearly identify the regular payments as being amounts of income. In practice, few people would care to have their use of money restricted in this way. If there is a surplus of income over revenue expenditure it is unlikely that HMRC would be successful in asserting that a gift from a bank account which, although it also contained capital, contained sufficient income to make the gift, did not come wholly within s 21(1)(b).

Sufficient income to maintain his usual standard of living

[2.8C] How does one determine whether the transferor was 'left with sufficient income'? Of the three cases which have been decided on s 21, sub-section (c) was considered only in *Nadin v Inland Revenue Commissioners* [1997] STC (SCD) 107 (this was a case before the Special Commissioners which did not proceed to the High Court). In that case, in respect of certain years, the Special Commissioner found that the condition in sub-section (c) was not satisfied because the taxpayer's annual nursing home costs, personal expenditure and Income Tax exceeded her annual income. The decision does not record any argument on the construction of sub-section (c) except that the Appellant argued that capital sums on the sale of investments were income. What was not argued was whether sub-section (c) allows one to take into account the extent to which capital is available to supplement income and is actually applied to doing so.

HMRC assumes in its guidance, that the exemption will not apply to the extent that 'the transferor had to resort to capital for living expenses' (HMRC Inheritance Tax Manual, para 14251). It is arguable, however, that if one had such a large amount of capital that, on the basis of the most conservative estimates, it would be sufficient to fund one's living expenses for one's lifetime, even a small amount of income would be sufficient to maintain one's usual standard of living. People in that position, therefore, would have sufficient income to maintain their usual standard of living even if all but a minimal part of their income were expended in making gifts.

Uses

[2.8D] Normal expenditure out of income is an important exemption, which can be used in the following ways.

(a) Payments out of income by individuals.

Individuals with large net incomes or surplus incomes can make regular gifts out of that income free of inheritance tax to members of their families or to family trusts. In some instances this is done by way of deed of covenant but it is not necessary to do so.

(b) A parent takes out a 10-year endowment policy on his life and declares himself a bare trustee of the policy for the benefit of his children. He pays all the premiums under the policy out of his income. On the maturity of the policy the beneficiaries under the trust benefit from the proceeds. If the premiums are paid direct to the life assurance company, such payments will not be potentially exempt if the amount of the premium is not fully reflected in the increased value of the policy. However, provided the parent pays the premiums out of his income and is able to maintain his usual standard of living, such payments should fall within the normal expenditure out of income exemption. If an alternative investment vehicle is required, there seems no reason why the same arrangement could not be set up by means of a regular monthly savings contract with a unit trust or an investment company, the units and shares themselves being held in trust for the next generation. The disadvantage of this alternative is that it will be necessary for the trustees to make annual returns of trust income.

(c) Premiums on a life policy written in trust to fund all or part of any potential inheritance tax liability on lifetime transfers or on death.

(d) Annuities paid gratuitously by partners out of their trading profits to a retired partner or the spouse of a deceased partner.

(e) Where the nil rate band has already been utilised, payments out of income could be made to fund a discretionary trust.

It should be noted that the exemption does not apply where a policy is taken out in conjunction with the purchase of an annuity on the individual's life (IHTA 1984, s 21(2)).

Regular gifts out of income may also be made to help the transferee of an earlier chargeable gift pay the inheritance tax due where there is a facility to pay the tax by annual instalments — see **2.38** below

It is advisable that such payments made are documented to provide evidence of such gifts. The information retained should be the date of such a gift, the name of the transferee and the nature of his relationship with the transferor, a description of the gift (ie cash, the premia paid on an insurance policy) and the value of the gift. This information can then be used to complete Schedule IHT403 to the IHT Account form IHT400.

The above examples show how this exemption can be used to pass assets down to the next generation on a regular basis whilst still preserving the £3,000 annual exemption for other gifts. Ideally, both exemptions should be used in tandem.

Small gifts

[2.9] Gifts of up to £250 can be made to any one person in any one year free of inheritance tax (IHTA 1984, s 20). This exemption cannot be used in conjunction with another exemption, eg the annual exemption. It will be lost if the total annual gifts to any one person exceed £250. The gifts must be outright and therefore cannot be made to trustees. In an estate planning context the exemption is '*de minimis*'.

Gifts in consideration of marriage or registration of a civil partnership

[2.10] Gifts below a certain value that are made 'in consideration of marriage or of the registration of a civil partnership' are exempt from inheritance tax. A gift in consideration of marriage or civil partnership is not defined in the legislation. In the case of *Rennell v IRC* [1964] AC 173 which was an estate duty case, the House of Lords held that a gift had to satisfy three conditions to be accepted as 'made in consideration of marriage'. The conditions are that:

- the gift must be made on the occasion of the marriage or civil partnership;
- it must be conditional on the marriage or civil partnership taking place; and
- the gift must be made by a person for the purpose of, or with a view to encouraging or facilitating, the marriage or civil partnership.

Parents may each give outright gifts in consideration of marriage or of the registration of a civil partnership of up to £5,000 to the parties to the marriage or civil partnership completely free of inheritance tax. Grandparents and great grandparents may similarly make outright gifts of up to £2,500. Other persons may make such gifts of up to £1,000 (IHTA 1984, s 22).

The exemption applies not only to outright gifts but also to gifts into a settlement. The beneficiaries of such a settlement must, however, be limited to those persons specified in IHTA 1984, s 22(4) to which special reference should be made by anyone wishing to create such a settlement. Care should therefore be taken when defining the beneficiaries of such a trust.

To ensure that the gifts are made 'in consideration of the marriage or civil partnership', they must be made either before or at the date of the marriage or civil partnership. The gifts should also be accompanied by a suitable letter evidencing the fact that the gift is conditional on the marriage or civil partnership taking place.

Gifts for maintenance of family

[2.11] Under IHTA 1984, s 11 there are complete exemptions from inheritance tax for gifts made:

(a) by one party to a marriage or civil partnership in favour of the other party for his or her maintenance;
(b) by one party to a marriage or civil partnership in favour of a child of either party for the maintenance, education or training of the child and made up to the later of the year in which the child attains 18 or ceases full-time education or training. These provisions are important in that they exempt all expenditure by a parent on the education of his children;

(c) in favour of a child who is not in the care of his parent for his maintenance, education or training and made up to the later of the year in which the child attains 18 or ceases full-time education or training. Gifts made to such a child who is over 18 are only exempt if they are made by a person in whose care the child has been for substantial periods prior to attaining 18;

(d) in favour of an illegitimate child of the transferor for his maintenance, education or training and made up to the later of the year in which he attains 18 or ceases full-time education or training; and

(e) in favour of a 'dependent relative' which constitute reasonable provision for his or her care or maintenance. Unlike the situation with a spouse or civil partner and children the provision may be for 'care' or maintenance, but it must be reasonable. This is not defined in the legislation but it is the Revenue's view that 'care' is the provision of services, whether privately or in an institution. The Revenue considers that 'reasonable' is 'an amount as is reasonably necessary for the purpose of providing care and maintenance (but no more), having regard to the financial and other circumstances of the transferor and the relative and the degree of incapacity [and] infirmity of the [relative]' (HMRC Inheritance Tax Manual, para 4177). The Revenue consider that the incapacity needs to be both physical and financial (HMRC Inheritance Tax Manual, para 4179). A 'dependent relative' is defined as any relative of the transferor or of his spouse or civil partner who is incapacitated by old age or infirmity from maintaining himself; or his mother or father or his spouse's or civil partner's mother or father. By concession, a gift made by a child to his or her unmarried mother is also treated as an exempt transfer, whether or not the mother is incapacitated, provided she is genuinely financially dependent on the child (Revenue Extra-statutory Concession F12).

Traditionally, the Revenue has argued that IHTA 1984, s 11 only applied to income expenditure and did not apply to a gift of capital. In *McKelvey (personal representative of McKelvey, decd) v Revenue and Customs Comrs* [2008] STC (SCD) 944, [2008] SWTI 1752 it was held that the exemption could extend to a gift of capital in appropriate circumstances. The deceased ('D') lived with her mother ('M') who was in poor health. D had been diagnosed with cancer. She transferred two properties to M to provide for her maintenance, the intention was that the properties be sold, when necessary, to meet the costs of M's nursing care. In the meantime M had had the benefit of the rental income. The properties were not sold because of M's refusal to accept paid care. HMRC sought tax on the basis that the transfers were PETs. D's executors appealed arguing that the gifts were exempt transfers under s 11. The Special Commissioner held that the reasonableness of the provisions had to be considered in the light of the circumstances as they were reasonably believed to be at the time of the gift and not as they later turned out to be. However, the transferor's view of what was reasonable was not the standard by which the gift was to be judged. An objective standard had to be applied. The Commissioner in deciding what was reasonably required considered that 'the approach adopted in personal injury cases [was] appropriate'. Using a multiplier of 5.5 being the number of years M would on the evidence have required nursing care and an annual care cost he calculated what he considered to be reasonable. This amount was exempt under s 11 whilst the excess was subject to IHT.

Where a gift is made on the occasion of a divorce or annulment, 'marriage' includes a former marriage or civil partnership. Thus in the context of a divorce, this exemption covers gifts to a former spouse or civil partner.

Gifts between spouses or civil partners

[2.12] Gifts between spouses or civil partners are completely exempt from inheritance tax except where the transferor spouse or civil partner is domiciled in the UK for inheritance tax purposes but the transferee spouse or civil partner is not, in which case the exemption is limited to a cumulative total of £55,000 (IHTA 1984, s 18). It should be noted that the transferee spouse will be treated as being deemed domiciled in a country in the UK if he or she has been resident in the UK for 17 out of the previous 20 years. Therefore if a husband wishes to make a gift to his wife who has only been resident in the UK for 16 out of the previous 20 years it may be sensible to wait depending upon the value of the gift. This does not, however, preclude the treatment of such gifts as potentially exempt transfers in appropriate cases. The spouse exemption is not available for lifetime gifts into a trust of which the settlor's spouse or civil partner is the life tenant.

The spouse exemption will be available to couples who are separated and living apart. This is in contrast to capital gains tax and income tax where a husband and wife have to be living together to benefit from any spousal benefits. The spouse exemption is not available for cohabitees. There have been attempts to extend the spouse exemption by relying on the Human Rights Act 1998. The most recent case is that of *Burden v UK* [2008] STC 1305, [2008] 2 FCR 244 where two sisters living together claimed that their rights under the European Convention on Human Rights had been violated by the United Kingdom's restriction of the spouse exemption. The majority of the Grand Chamber held that the applicants as cohabiting sisters could not be compared to that of a married couple or civil partners and so their case failed.

For the purposes of the charge to income tax by reference to enjoyment of property previously owned (also referred to as tax on pre-owned assets), gifts between spouses or civil partners are excluded transactions (FA 2004, Sch 15 para 10(1)(b)). This is an important exemption as spouses or civil partners may continue to make gifts to one another without triggering an income tax charge. This charge to income tax is discussed in greater detail at **2.17** below.

This exemption was extremely important in the past in its use in equalising estates to ensure that each spouse utilised their nil rate band on death. Now, unused nil rate bands can be transferred between the estates of husband and wife or civil partners (IHTA 1984, s 8A). The effect of this is that when the surviving spouse or civil partner dies, the nil rate band available at their death would be increased by the proportion of the nil rate band that was not used on the death of their spouse or civil partner. This is discussed in **CHAPTER 16 PLANNING FOR DEATH**.

The equalisation of estates should be seen as part of an overall lifetime strategy designed to enable both spouses and civil partners to have sufficient assets which they can each use to make potentially exempt transfers and gifts within the annual exemption. Spouses and civil partners should consider the equalisation of their estates both when acquiring new assets and when deciding out of which estate an intended gift should be made. Where one spouse or civil partner has a significantly greater life expectancy than the other, then there is much to be said for keeping the bulk of their assets in the estate of the first spouse or civil partner to allow potentially exempt transfers to be made. On the other hand, any assets showing large unrealised gains should perhaps be kept in the estate of the other spouse or civil partner to get the benefit of the capital gains tax free base uplift on his or her death.

In addition, an equal distribution of assets between the spouses or civil partners may also result in capital gains tax savings. This may also confer income tax advantages but one needs to take account of the possibility that the government may introduce legislation at some point which negates any income tax savings (see para **2.16** below).

Another use of the spouse or civil partner exemption is to enable assets to be given by one spouse or civil partner to the other so that the other spouse or civil partner may then give away the assets and thereby use his or her annual exemption or make a potentially exempt transfer (on the basis that he or she may be the more likely of the two to survive for the necessary 7-year period). The danger of this type of 'channelling' exercise is that the Revenue may attempt to apply the 'associated operations' provisions contained in IHTA 1984, s 268 and tax the gift as if it had been made directly to the ultimate transferee by the first spouse or civil partner. The Revenue has indicated, however, that it would not regard the provisions as applicable unless in such circumstances it was a condition that the second gift was made (Revenue Press Release dated 8 April 1975). The Revenue still adopts this practice, although care should be taken over the timing of the gifts and the evidencing of them (HMRC Inheritance Tax Manual, para 14833).

Gifts to charities

[2.13] The making of gifts to charities may perhaps not be regarded as an aspect of estate planning by some, although such gifts will clearly reduce the amount of inheritance tax payable on a person's death. As many wealthy individuals feel a moral obligation to pass some of the benefit of their good fortune or hard work to those less fortunate than themselves, the subject is properly within the scope of this book. Immediate, unconditional and indefeasible gifts to charities are completely free of inheritance tax (IHTA 1984, s 23). Income tax relief is also available for single gifts made by individuals to charities. As charities may realise chargeable gains free of tax (TCGA 1992, s 256), a transferor proposing to give a capital sum to a charity should consider transferring over investments or property which show large unrealised gains rather than cash. The gift of the investments or the property will not give rise to a charge to capital gains tax (TCGA 1992, s 257). The value of listed shares, securities, certain collective investments and qualifying interests in land given to charities will be deductible from the transferor's income for income tax purposes (ITA 2007, ss 431–446). These reliefs, with some further restrictions, also apply to gifts to Community Amateur Sports Clubs.

Charities generally and Community Amateur Sports Clubs are dealt with in more detail in **Chapter 13 Gifts to Charities and Other Non-Profit Organisations.**

Gifts of 'excluded property'

[2.14] For the purposes of inheritance tax no account is taken of 'excluded property' which ceases to form part of a person's estate (IHTA 1984, s 3(2)). Thus, gifts of excluded property may be made completely free of inheritance tax.

Excluded property appears in two main situations. The first is in connection with property owned by, or settled in trust by, a person who is neither domiciled in the UK nor treated as being so domiciled for inheritance tax purposes. This aspect is considered further in **Chapter 19 The Internationally Mobile** and **Chapter 20 The Overseas Client.**

The other situation is in that of settlements and settled property. Broadly, any future interest under a settlement, which is called a 'reversionary interest' in IHTA 1984, s 47, is excluded property unless it has been acquired for a consideration in money or money's worth or is one to which the settlor of the settlement or his spouse or civil partner is or has been beneficially entitled (IHTA 1984, s 48(1)).

Example

Tatum is 87 years of age. The White Settlement provides that she is entitled to the income for her lifetime with the remainder to be divided between her two children Milly and Molly who have children of their own. Milly and Molly's interests are reversionary interests. As they are both financially secure they consider assigning their interests in remainder to their children. During Tatum's lifetime they are able to assign or re-settle their interests for the benefit of their children without incurring any inheritance tax charge.

This is considered in more detail in **Chapter 5 Existing Settlements.**

The type of settlement under which there is a life tenant with one or more remaindermen often arises under wills drawn up in estate duty days when an exemption applied on the death of a surviving spouse, where that spouse had been left a life interest in the estate of the deceased. In the case of property settled in this way by a person dying before 13 November 1974, the exemption continues to apply on the death of the surviving spouse or on any prior termination of the life interest (IHTA 1984, Sch 6 para 2).

This type of settlement can also arise from the intestacy rules where the deceased dies intestate leaving a spouse or civil partner and children: the spouse or civil partner will take absolutely the deceased's personal chattels and the first £250,000 and a life interest in one half of the residue of the deceased's estate with the children taking the interests in remainder on the statutory trusts (Administration of Estates Act 1925, s 46).

Gifts with reservation

General

[2.15] Having looked at the most important exemptions and quasi-exemptions from inheritance tax, and before dealing with some of the practical aspects of giving, consideration must first be given to the gifts with reservation rules contained in FA 1986, ss 102–102C and Sch 20. These rules are designed to prevent an individual giving away an asset whilst continuing to enjoy the benefit from it.

The legislation provides that a gift of property subject to a reservation is treated, so far as the transferor is concerned, as a partial nullity for inheritance tax purposes. This is achieved by deeming the relevant property still to form part of the transferor's estate on death. The rules apply where either:

(a) possession and enjoyment of the property is not *bona fide* assumed by the transferee at least 7 years before the transferor's death; or

(b) the property is not enjoyed to the entire exclusion, or virtually to the entire exclusion, of the transferor and of any benefit to him by contract or otherwise (or by virtue of any associated operations within the meaning of IHTA 1984, s 268) at any time within 7 years of the transferor's death.

In essence, this means that a gift of property may fall foul of these provisions if the transferor receives, or is capable of receiving, any direct or indirect benefit whatsoever which is in some way referable to the gift. The benefit does not have to be provided out of the donated property (*A-G v Worrall* [1895] 1 QB 99), nor does it have to be provided by the transferee. The benefit may be financial, such as an annuity (*A-G v Worrall*), a rent charge (*Grey (Earl) v A-G* [1900] AC 124, [1900–1903] All ER Rep 268) or a right to remuneration (*Oakes v Comr of Stamp Duties of New South Wales* [1954] AC 57). Equally, it may well be the use or occupation (even as a bare licensee) of, or the ability to use or occupy, the donated property (*Chick v Comr of Stamp Duties of New South Wales* [1958] AC 435, [1958] All ER 623).

There is a wealth of complicated and contradictory case law on the meaning of the original provisions contained in the estate duty legislation. As the current provisions are closely based on earlier estate duty sections, the principles that can be extracted from the cases are relevant to the current provisions. However, it should be remembered that inheritance tax is fundamentally different from estate duty so that old cases should be considered with a degree of circumspection. In the case of *Melville v CIR* [2000] STC 628 (Ch D) Lightman J in the High Court said at page 636:

> . . . I do not think that authorities on the estate duty legislation are helpful on the quite different legislation which replaced it.

Although that may be true of the relationship of estate duty and inheritance tax generally, it does not indicate that one cannot refer to estate duty cases on reservation of benefit where the old and new legislation have substantially similar wording.

It is beyond the scope of this book to provide a detailed analysis of the complexities of the current provisions and of the old case law. The following comments are, however, offered as a guide. It is paradoxical really that after 26 years of inheritance tax there is very little case law.

Property given away

In determining whether there has been any reservation of benefit, it is essential to first identify the property which has been given away by the transferor (see for example, *Munro v Comr of Stamp Duties of New South Wales* [1934] AC 61 (PC) and *St Aubyn v A-G (No 2)* [1952] AC 15, [1951] 2 All ER 473 (HL)). It is this property which the transferor has to continue to either possess or enjoy. Property in which the transferor retains no interest and does not possess or enjoy will not be subject to a reservation. A gift made to a spouse or civil partner after 20 June 2003 will be a gift with reservation where:

- the property becomes settled property by virtue of the gift;
- the trusts of the settlement give an interest in possession to the transferor's spouse or civil partner (who is defined as the 'relevant beneficiary'), so that the gift is exempt from inheritance tax by reason of the spouse or civil partner exemption and the rule which treats an interest in possession as equivalent to outright ownership (IHTA 1984, s 49(1));
- between the date of the gift and the transferor's death the interest in possession comes to an end; and
- when that interest in possession comes to an end, the transferor's spouse or civil partner does not become beneficially entitled to the settled property or to another interest in possession in it.

In applying s 102 in such circumstances, the original disposal by way of gift will be treated, where relevant, as having been made immediately after the beneficiary's interest in possession ends, so that the circumstances before that time will not be considered in determining whether the property given away is 'property subject to a reservation' for inheritance tax purposes. This followed the Court of Appeal's decision in *CIR v Eversden (Greenstock's Executors)* [2003] STC 822 (CA). These provisions are likely to be relevant only to trusts established before 22 March 2006 because for trusts made on or after that date the spouse or civil partner exemption is unlikely to be available because s 49 only applies to a very limited range of interest in possessions created *inter vivos*.

This concept of first carving a separate proprietary interest out of an asset to be given away and then giving away the remaining interest (often called 'shearing') was accepted practice in estate duty days and the Revenue appeared to accept its efficacy under the inheritance tax regime, subject to certain important qualifications.

A particular application of the shearing principle was the lease carve out scheme. This was commonly used by estate planners in relation to the family home. The House of Lords considered the scheme and found in favour of the taxpayer in *Ingram v CIR* [1999] STC 37 (HL). It was that case that led to the reservation of benefit provisions being extended to certain gifts of interests in land where the transferor continues to occupy, or enjoy some right in, the land after the gift (Finance Act 1986, ss 102A, 102C). These schemes are examined in more detail in **CHAPTER 9 THE FAMILY HOME** at **9.9**.

The shearing technique is of wider application than the family home and remains important in relation to estate planning.

Reservation

The provisions only catch benefits reserved to the transferor and not those reserved to his or her spouse or civil partner whereas the estate duty provisions caught both. Whilst this does give some scope for flexibility in estate planning — for example, the transferor's spouse or civil partner could be a discretionary beneficiary of a trust while the transferor may not be — great care must be taken to ensure that any benefit reserved to a spouse or civil partner cannot be treated as a benefit to the transferor including a benefit obtained by virtue of any associated operations (FA 1986, Sch 20 para 6(1)(c)). Thus, for example, a wife who receives a distribution of capital from a discretionary trust of which her husband was the settlor should not pay the money into a joint bank account or one on which her husband has drawing facilities. Nor should she use the money to maintain him or to discharge any liabilities which would normally be regarded as his responsibility. It should be borne in mind that the inclusion of the settlor's spouse or civil partner as a beneficiary under a trust can have adverse income tax and capital gains tax consequences for the settlor.

Possession and enjoyment

Where possession and enjoyment is not bona fide assumed by the transferee at or before the beginning of a relevant period or at any time in the relevant period the property is not enjoyed to the entire exclusion or virtually to the entire exclusion of the transferor and of any benefit to him by contract or otherwise, a benefit will have been reserved.

The gifts with reservation provisions do not apply where the transferor and transferee occupy the land and the transferor does not receive any benefit, other than a negligible one, which is provided by or at the expense of the transferee for some reason connected with the gift (FA 1986, s 102B(4)). The transferee must not pay more than his or her share of the outgoings. There is not, however, a requirement for the proportionate sharing of expenses. It would cover the situation where elderly parents make unconditional gifts of a share in their house to their children and the property is occupied by the parents and their children each bearing his or her pro rata share of the running costs. This is not a gift with reservation because the children have taken up occupation and the parents' occupation is referable to their joint ownership and not the gift. (HMRC Inheritance Tax Manual, para 14332). The scope for this type of arrangement is fairly limited and problems may arise if one or more of the children leave home but retain their interest.

It is unwise to assume, relying on the authority of *A-G v Seccombe* [1911] 2 KB 688, that the words 'by contract or otherwise' in FA 1986, s 102 will be construed in accordance with the '*ejusdem generis*' rule. It was categorically stated by the government spokesman in the Standing Committee G debates on the 1986 Finance Bill that the non-enforceable enjoyment or benefit of property is, in the Revenue's view, sufficient to bring the gifts with reservation provisions into play.

Continuation of reasonable commercial arrangements

A director or employee of a company who wishes to give away some or all of his shares in the company should beware of reserving any benefits. The continuation of reasonable commercial arrangements in the form of remuneration or other benefits for the transferor's services in the company entered into prior to the gift will not be considered by the Revenue to be a reservation of benefit provided the benefits were in no way linked to or affected by the gift (HMRC Inheritance Tax Manual, paras 14337 and 14395). What is reasonable will depend upon all the facts. Generally speaking, it will be determined by what might be reasonably expected under arm's length arrangements between unconnected persons (HMRC Inheritance Tax Manual, para 14337). However, if the transferor attempts to entrench his position and benefits, eg by way of a fixed term service contract, or if following the gift he receives remuneration or other benefits in excess of normal commercial rates, he will be running the risk of reserving a benefit.

If the transferor is the sole trustee, or one of the trustees, of the donated property, his interest as trustee will not amount to a reservation of a benefit. This was the position under the estate duty legislation (*Comr of Stamp Duties of New South Wales v Perpetual Trustee Co Ltd* [1943] AC 425 (PC)). The Revenue has confirmed that in its view, the transferor or his spouse or civil partner being a trustee of a settlement does not of itself give rise to a reservation of benefit (HMRC Inheritance Tax Manual, para 14394). The position is the same even if the transferor and spouse are entitled to payment for their services as trustees provided the remuneration is not excessive. This is despite the decision in the *Oakes* case.

Simply because a settlor is a trustee of a settlement established in favour of his or her minor children should not itself cause a reservation to arise. Yet where such settled funds are subsequently applied to meet a contractual liability of the parent which was incurred to maintain his children, a reservation would then arise.

The position is more complex in the case of a settlor who acts as trustee of shares in a company of which he or she is a director. Specific relieving provisions are generally required in the trust instrument if the trustee is to retain the remuneration received from that company, unless a timely application is made to the court for relief (*Re Keeler's Settlement Trust* [1981] 1 Ch 156, [1981] 1 All ER 888). In this type of situation, the Revenue accepts that the continuation of reasonably commercial arrangements governing remuneration and benefits entered into prior to the gift would not, by itself, amount to a reservation (HMRC Inheritance Tax Manual, para 14395). This assumes that the remuneration package was not linked to, or affected by, the gift.

However, it has been suggested that the transferor should enter into a legally binding long-term service agreement prior to settling the shares, whilst having due regard to company law considerations. The idea being for the transferor to 'carve out' rights in his favour, excluding those from the property gifted. Doubts have been expressed concerning this interpretation. The argument being that the associated operations provisions contained in FA 1986, Sch 20 para 6(1)(c) might be applied to link the contractual arrangements with the subsequent gift of shares.

As a result it may be generally prudent to dissuade an executive director from being a trustee when settling shares in his or her private company. As such settlors are often reluctant to relinquish control in this way it will be necessary to arrange matters within the published parameters. A further safety precaution might be for the transferor to enter into a suitable long-term service agreement prior to giving the shares away, albeit that doubts may exist over the degree of protection this may afford in some cases.

Exclusion or Virtual Exclusion

HMRC Inheritance Tax accepts that the word 'virtually' in FA 1986, s 102(1)(b) is not defined but according to it means 'to all intents' or 'as good as'. It interprets 'virtually to the entire exclusion' as covering cases in which 'the benefit obtained by the transferor is insignificant in relation to the gifted property'.

Whilst acknowledging that each case will turn on its own facts, HMRC accepts that it will not apply FA 1986, s 102(1)(b) in such a way that transferors are unreasonably prevented from having limited access to property they have given away and a measure of flexibility will be adopted in applying the test.

The Revenue outlines a number of situations where limited benefit could arise to a transferor without causing the reservation of benefit rules to come into play (HMRC Inheritance Tax Manual, para 14333). These are set out below.

(a) A house which becomes the transferee's residence but where the transferor subsequently stays, in the absence of the transferee, for not more than 2 weeks each year, or stays with the transferee for less than 1 month a year.
(b) Social visits, excluding overnight stays made by a transferor as a guest of the transferee, to a house which he had given away. The extent of the social visits should be no greater than the visits which the transferor might be expected to make to the transferee's house in the absence of any gifts by the transferor.
(c) A temporary stay for some short term purpose in a house the transferor had previously given away, for example, while the transferor convalesces after medical treatment or looks after a transferee convalescing after medical treatment or while the transferor's own home is being redecorated.
(d) Visits to a house for domestic reasons, for example, baby-sitting by the transferor for the transferee's children.
(e) A house together with a library of books which the transferor visits less than five times in any year to consult or borrow a book.

(f) A motor car which the transferee uses to give occasional (ie less than three times a month) lifts to the transferor.

(g) Land which the transferor uses to walk his dogs or for horseriding provided this does not restrict the transferee's use of the land.

The following are suggested as representing cases where the reservation rules are likely to apply.

(i) A house in which the transferor stays most weekends, or for a month or more each year.

(ii) A second home or holiday home which both the transferor and the transferee use on an occasional basis.

(iii) A house with a library in which the transferor continues to keep his own books, or which the transferor uses on a regular basis, for example, because it is necessary for his work.

(iv) A motor car which the transferee uses every day to take the transferor to work.

Gift exemption

Gifts which qualify for certain inheritance tax exemptions — in particular the exemption for gifts in consideration of marriage or civil partnership — cannot constitute a gift with reservation (FA 1986, s 102(5)). Gifts to charities are also outside their scope but this is not surprising as the charity exemption already contains its own reservation of benefit provisions in IHTA 1984, s 23(4). Potentially exempt transfers and gifts within the annual exemption or normal expenditure out of income can, however, be caught by the provisions.

Full consideration exemption

The underlying principle is that the reservation rules will not apply where an interest is given away and the transferor pays full consideration for the future use of the property.

Where a transferor gives full consideration, the retention or assumption by him of the actual occupation or enjoyment of land, or of a right over land, or the actual possession of a chattel, is to be disregarded in determining whether the property is enjoyed to his exclusion or virtual exclusion and of any benefit to him by contract or otherwise. What constitutes full consideration has always been of concern for those involved in estate planning because, taken literally, the failure to satisfy this requirement by however small a margin would be fatal. The Revenue's interpretation of full consideration in this context is given in the Revenue Interpretation 55 and HMRC Inheritance Tax Manual, para 14341.

The Revenue Interpretation represents a welcome pragmatic approach:

> 'While we take the view that such full consideration is required throughout the relevant period — and therefore consider that the rent paid should be reviewed at appropriate intervals to reflect market changes — we do recognise that there is no single value at which consideration can be fixed as 'full'. Rather we accept that what constitutes full consideration in any case lies within a range of values, reflecting normal valuation tolerances, and that any amount within that range, can be accepted as satisfying the para 6(1)(a) test.'

A difficulty arises in relation to establishing a rental value for assets where there is no meaningful rental market. The Revenue states that 'it is unlikely that any . . . arrangement could be overturned if the taxpayer can demonstrate that it resulted from a bargain negotiated at arms' length by parties who were independently advised and which followed the normal commercial criteria in force at the time it was negotiated' (HMRC Inheritance Tax Manual, para 14341). In relation to items such as country house chattels or valuable works of art where there may be no meaningful rental market the Revenue's accepted norm is 1% of capital value. It admits that this rate 'has no robust basis but is regularly accepted by HMRC on a without prejudice basis'. The Revenue has warned that where purely nominal rental rates are used taxpayers 'can expect them to be vigorously challenged'. With regard to chattels, the procedure in the Bills of Sale Acts should be followed.

Infirm relative exemption

There is an exemption of limited application which, broadly speaking, will cover the case where a transferor gives a house to a relative whose circumstances have changed since the original gift and who has become unable to maintain himself for reasons of old age or infirmity. This only applies if the transferee is a relative of the transferor or of the transferor's spouse or civil partner.

Interest in possession trusts

FA 1986, s 102ZA subjects the exercise of the trustees discretion in interest in possession trusts to the reservation of benefit rules. Where the section applies an individual is taken to dispose of property in which his interest in possession comes to an end. The section applies where an individual became beneficially entitled to the interest in possession before 22 March 2006 or did so after that date where the interest is an immediate post-death interest, a disabled person's trust or a transitional serial interest and the interest in possession comes to an end during the individual's lifetime. This section was introduced to prevent the re-organisation of trust interests resulting in passing interests to children without incurring tax charges, although HMRC claims it was to 'align the treatment of cases involving trust property formerly subject to an interest in possession . . . with the treatment of similar facts where the property was formerly owned outright'.

Tracing

FA 1986, Sch 20 contains various provisions enabling the property subject to the reservation to be 'traced' into other property. These provisions are necessary in order to ascertain the value and nature of the property which is to be treated as forming part of the transferor's estate immediately before his death. However, where the original gift is one of cash (and the gift is not to a settlement), it is arguable that the tracing provisions do not apply. This will effectively freeze the value of the property subject to the reservation, but in addition it raises the interesting argument, that if by the time of the death of the transferor, the cash has ceased to exist, then there will be nothing on which FA 1986, s 102 can bite. Thus, for example, if a transferor gives his son a cash gift and the son subsequently uses the money to buy a property which the transferor occupies until his death, it might be thought that there is a reservation of benefit by associated operations to the transferor (by virtue of his occupation of the property provided by his son). The Revenue considers this to be the case. However, one argument is that as the cash ceases to exist as from the date of the purchase of the property, and because there are no provisions tracing the cash into the property, it is difficult to see how there can be any property subject to a reservation at the transferor's death. The contrary argument is that by being expended the cash does not cease to exist but merely becomes the property of another (and so on *ad infinitum*) so that the property subject to the reservation continues to exist (although not in the hands of the transferee) until the transferor's death. Until such time as this matter is tested in the courts the uncertainty will remain. In any event, this kind of arrangement will be subject to an income tax charge on pre-owned assets which is discussed in greater detail in **2.17** below.

The effects of the gift with reservation provisions are far reaching. In the event of these provisions being of relevance when advising a client, one should consider whether the client is making a gift of the right property. One has to consider the wasted time and costs of not only implementing the transaction but any subsequent correspondence with the Revenue together with the uncertainty for the client as to whether he has a potential inheritance tax charge. If the reservation of benefit provisions are found to apply, the transferor will have to pay the inheritance tax on his death as if he still owned the property but will not benefit from any capital gains tax uplift.

Income tax: transfers between spouses

[2.16] The settlements legislation found in ITTOIA 2005, ss 624–628 provide that where during the life of a settlor any property subject to a settlement, or any derived property, can become payable to, or applicable for the benefit of, the settlor, or spouse or civil partner of the settlor in any circumstances whatsoever, the income of the settlement is treated as the settlor's income for all income tax purposes. This is a very broad definition. It covers both payment or use of money and the provision of non-cash benefits. There are a number of exemptions including a spouse exemption (ITTOIA 2005, s 625).

For the spouse exemption to apply there must be an outright gift. Section 626(4) provides that a gift is not an outright gift if it is conditional or there are any circumstances in which the property or related property is:

(i) payable to the giver;
(ii) applicable for the benefit of the giver; or
(iii) will, or may become, so payable or applicable.

(ii) and (iii) are not defined and there have been no cases where their scope has been considered.

Therefore, if school fees are paid by one spouse using money arising under a settlement where both parents are liable to pay, then property will be being applied for the benefit of the settlor spouse and the gift is not an outright gift. It is therefore important that evidence is kept as to the application of the funds in the event that HMRC raise an enquiry. Although a full discussion of this subject is beyond the scope of this work, set out below are the main considerations which should be borne in mind when considering the transfer of assets between spouses.

The Revenue's interest in applying the settlements provisions was prompted by what it perceived as the use of small companies and partnerships to divert income earned by one person to another. The Revenue attempted to apply these provisions where it considered that the transfer of assets between spouses had the effect of diverting income from one spouse to the other such as in *Jones v Garnett* [2007] UKHL 35, [2007] 1 WLR 2030, [2007] All ER (D) 390 (Jul). The House of Lords held that the arrangement entered into by Mr and Mrs Jones constituted a statutory settlement within the meaning of ITTOIA 2005, s 620 and therefore Mr Jones was subject to charge under s 625. However, it was held that Mr Jones' transfer to his wife was an outright gift and the spouse exemption in ITTOIA 2005, s 626 applied. Mr Jones was therefore not assessable on the dividends received by his wife. In the case of *Buck v Revenue and Customs Comrs* [2009] STC (SCD) 6 Mr Buck held all but one share in his company with his wife holding the remaining share. Mr Buck waived his entitlement to the declared dividends, with the effect that Mrs Buck received all the dividends. It was held by the Special Commissioner that the settlement provisions did apply and there was no outright gift in the broad sense of that suggested by the House of Lords in *Jones v Garnett*; there was merely a one-off dividend waiver.

Although the application of the settlements legislation is of primary importance for income tax planning between married couples, it should be borne in mind that transfers of interests in small family companies as between spouses for the purposes of capital tax planning, may bring these provisions into effect.

The previous government announced their intention to introduce legislation to prevent this, but it did not materialise. The Coalition government has not, to date, indicated any intention to introduce such legislation.

With the additional rate of income tax at 50% for 2010/11, income splitting is worth exploring where there is a spouse with little significant income of their own. Careful planning is, however, a pre-requisite.

Pre-owned assets

General

[2.17] The pre-owned asset charge is not a charge to inheritance tax but a charge to income tax.

A charge is imposed where assets have, broadly speaking, been given away by an individual but under such circumstances that the transferor has retained the right to use or enjoy the assets given away while circumventing the inheritance tax gift with reservation rules (see **2.15** above). Much capital tax planning has been designed to create situations which do not fall within the gifts with reservation rules. In the examples used in this section, for the sake of simplicity, it is assumed that the gifts with reservation rules have been circumvented unless otherwise stated.

The pre-owned assets provisions may be very unfortunate for those individuals who have owned assets which have been disposed of, in whole or in part, since 18 March 1986. Although an election to opt out of the pre-owned asset provisions is possible (see **21.24** below), such an election still does not put an individual who has undertaken tax planning in the same position as he would have been if the planning had never been implemented. It may be expensive to unwind the structures already put in place. In some cases, it may not be possible to do so at all or to do so only by incurring a further tax charge.

Since these rules were announced, the Revenue has issued various Guidance Notes. However, it should be noted that the Detailed Guidance contains a proviso that they 'do not take account of any proposals in the 2006 Finance Bill. As soon as any changes proposed by the Bill becomes law we will review the guidance to see if, and to what extent, amendments need to be made'. Care should therefore be taken when relying on the Revenue's Guidance.

The legislation relating to the pre-owned asset charge can be found in FA 2004, s 84 and Sch 15. Up-to-date guidance, legislation and regulations can be found at www.hmrc.gov.uk/poa.

There are three separate charges under the pre-owned assets charge as the legislation differentiates between land, chattels and intangible property in a settlor-interested settlement.

Land

[2.18] Under FA 2004, Sch 15 para 3, an income tax charge will arise where an individual (the chargeable person) occupies land (referred to as the 'relevant land'), whether alone or with other persons, and the 'disposal condition' or the 'contribution condition' is satisfied in relation to the land.

(i) Occupation

Occupation is not defined in the legislation and so one would apply its normal meaning, that of 'taking possession'. The Revenue states that 'in this context "occupation" is construed quite widely' (Revenue Guidance 'Income Tax and Pre-owned Assets', para 4.6). A person will be regarded by the Revenue as occupying a property if he is resident in a property or is using it for storage. A person will also be regarded by HMRC as occupying a property if he has sole possession of the property (ie he has the only set of keys) and uses it from time to time. It would not seem to matter as to the nature of the occupation, be it under a gratuitous licence or a rack rent lease: the key is the fact of occupation. A person is not regarded as occupying a property from which he receives rent from the actual occupier (Revenue Guidance 'Income Tax and Pre-owned Assets', para 4.6). The Revenue says that, where occupation or use is limited in nature or duration, it may not fall within FA 2004, Sch 15 para 3; each case will depend on its own facts. There is no provision providing exemption from charge where the taxpayer's occupation is limited. What the Revenue probably means is that limited periods of physical presence or limited usage will not amount to occupation. The Revenue will apply its interpretation of occupation found in RI 55 (in the context of the gifts with reservation) to the pre-owned assets regime (Revenue Guidance 'Income Tax and Pre-owned Assets', para 4.6). Be that as it may, the Revenue gives a number of examples of what it calls limited occupation which will not fall within FA 2004, Sch 15 para 3. One such example is a house which is the owner's residence but where the chargeable person, subsequently to the gift, stays in the house with the other person for less than 1 month each year or, in their absence, stays for not more than 2 weeks each year. (Revenue Guidance 'Income Tax and Pre-owned Assets', para 4.6).

Further examples have been provided by the professional bodies on which the Revenue has commented. The Revenue has confirmed that where an individual has a right to the property throughout the year but does not in fact use it 'it is unlikely that there would be a Schedule 15 charge'. The Revenue has declined to confirm that no charge would arise where there is a right to use the property throughout the year and the chargeable person uses the property but it falls within the *de minimis* limit set out in the guidance notes that there would be no charge. Where there is a right to use the property throughout the year and an individual uses the property, for example, for 3 months of the year, the charge will be based on the whole year, even where others have a right to use the property during that period. This is of particular relevance in relation to holiday homes.

Due to the lack of definition of occupation it will be necessary to judge each situation on its facts which will inevitably lead to some uncertainty for the taxpayer.

The question of 'what is occupation' was considered in the VAT case of *Principal and Fellows of Newnham College in the University of Cambridge v Revenue and Customs Comrs* [2008] UKHL 23, [2008] 2 All ER 863, [2008] STC 1225.

The House of Lords held that mere physical presence on land was not enough to constitute occupation. For a person to be in occupation they should have the right to occupy the property as if they are the owner and to exclude any other person from enjoyment of such a right in addition to physical presence. Following this decision, HMRC has revised its interpretation of 'occupation' in Revenue & Customs Brief 33/09. Whilst the Revenue states the clarification relates only to the test of occupation in VATA 1994, Sch 10 paras 12–17, it may nonetheless be useful.

(ii) Land

An 'interest in land' has the same meaning as that found in IHTA 1984, Pt VI Ch IV where it is defined by IHTA 1984, s 190 as not including any estate, interest or right by way of mortgage or other security.

(iii) The 'disposal condition'

The 'disposal condition' is satisfied where, at any time after 17 March 1986, a chargeable person has:

- owned an interest in the relevant land (or in other property the disposal proceeds of which were directly or indirectly applied by another person towards the acquisition of an interest in the relevant land); and
- disposed of all or part of his interest in the relevant land or the other property, otherwise than by an excluded transaction (see **2.21** below).

These provisions might apply where, for example, a father gives away a property he owns to his son and, sometime later, either the father moves back into the property or the son sells the property and buys a new property which the father later occupies. They can also apply in more complex situations.

Examples

Marjorie gave her shares worth £250,000 to her great granddaughter Jasmine who sold the shares and used the proceeds to purchase a house in which Marjorie now lives.

The disposal condition would be met because Marjorie once owned other property (ie the shares) the proceeds of which were used by Jasmine to acquire the house.

If Jasmine had used the sale proceeds to build a granny annex onto the house in which Marjorie lived, it would appear that the disposal condition is not met because the sale proceeds of the shares were not used to acquire an interest in land but to improve the land.

(iv) The 'contribution condition'

The 'contribution condition' is satisfied where, at any time after 17 March 1986, the chargeable person has provided (directly or indirectly), otherwise than by an excluded transaction, any of the consideration given by another person for the acquisition of:

- an interest in the relevant land; or
- an interest in any other property, the disposal proceeds of which were (directly or indirectly) applied by another person towards acquiring the relevant land.

Examples

A father gives his son £100,000 towards the purchase of a £200,000 flat. The son provides the rest of the consideration. The father later moves into the flat.

The contribution condition is satisfied and an income tax charge arises.

Gillian gives Maxwell Court to Barbara who exchanges it for Hill House. Gillian moves into Hill House.

The contribution condition is satisfied and an income tax charge arises.

The contribution condition is extremely wide. It has been said, however, that if the chargeable person was only entitled to a share of the proceeds of the other property, then only that share of the proceeds should be regarded as flowing through to the relevant land (Finance Bill Standing Committee, 18 May 2004 col 266). It should be noted that an outright gift of money made at least 7 years before the chargeable person occupies the relevant property will be excluded (FA 2004, Sch 15 para 10(2)(c)). The Revenue does not consider that the contribution condition is satisfied where a lender resides in property purchased by another with money loaned to him by the lender. It is the

Revenue's view that 'it would not be reasonable to consider that the loan falls within the contribution condition [and therefore not reasonably attributable to the consideration] even where the loan was interest free.' (Revenue Guidance para 1.2.1). It is clear that the contribution condition is satisfied. This places a taxpayer and his adviser in a difficult position as to whether or not to rely on guidance which is incorrect in law.

A disposition which creates a new interest in land out of an existing interest in land is treated as a part disposal of the existing interest. This is, of course, of relevance to lease carve-out cases.

(v) Excluded transactions

There are five excluded transactions in relation to both the disposal condition and the contribution condition (see **2.21** below).

(vi) The charge

Where the provisions apply, a taxpayer is deemed to receive an amount of income equal to the chargeable amount on which he will be liable to income tax. The valuation of property follows the rule in IHTA 1984, s 160. It is the price that the property might reasonably be expected to fetch if sold in the open market at that time, without any scope for a reduction on the grounds that the whole property is to be placed on the market at one and the same time. The chargeable amount is calculated using the formula (set out in FA 2004, Sch 15 para 4) shown below:

$$R \times \frac{DV}{V}$$

where

R = the rental value of the relevant land;

DV = the appropriate proportion of the value of the relevant land at the valuation date. The definition varies according to whether it is the disposal condition or contribution condition that is at issue; and

V = the value of the relevant land at the valuation date.

Broadly speaking, the chargeable amount will be the appropriate rental value of the relevant land less any moneys actually paid to the owners of the relevant land in pursuance of a legal obligation. In respect of the taxpayer's occupation of the land, the intention is that only payments that are taxable in the hands of the recipient should be allowed as a deduction from the pre-owned assets income tax charge (Finance Bill Standing Committee, 18 May 2004 col 269). So where a person decides to pay a full market rent for occupation of the property in order to eliminate the pre-owned assets charge, he should put in place a tenancy agreement under which the rent is paid. For a taxpayer who, for example, wishes to benefit his son, such an arrangement has the additional advantage that it passes further value to the son by way of rental payments. The payment must be made during the 'taxable period' which is defined as the year of assessment, or part of the year of assessment, during which a pre-owned asset charge applies to a chargeable person (FA 2004, Sch 15 para 4(6)). Payments made outside the taxable period are disregarded.

Example

> Robin gives his daughter a property but continues to stay at it when he wishes to do so with no further permission from his daughter. He actually stays at the property 12 weeks per year. Robin enters into a legal agreement to pay his daughter £200 per week for his accommodation whilst he stays with her during the year and so pays £2,400. The appropriate rental value is £5,000 and so he will pay income tax on £2,600.

The rental value is based on an annual value as defined in FA 2004, Sch 15 para 3. The annual value is the rent which might reasonably be expected to be obtained on a letting from year to year if:

- the tenant undertook to pay all taxes, rates and charges usually paid by a tenant; and
- the landlord undertook to bear the costs of the repairs and insurance and the other expenses necessary for maintaining the property in a state to command that rent (FA 2004, Sch 15 para 5).

This is a circular definition because, in order to know the rent which might reasonably be expected, one must know the repairs and other expenses that are necessary to maintain the property in a state to command that rent. In order to know the repairs that are required, one needs to know the rent. The formula could be described as a 'landlord's repairing lease' but the Treasury Notes state that the annual value is the rent which will be paid under a standard tenant's repairing lease. The sources from which the required valuation should be obtained have not been specified. The Revenue expects the chargeable person to take all reasonable steps to ascertain the valuations, as they would do, for example, if they were looking to let a property in the open market (Revenue Guidance 'Income Tax and Pre-owned Assets', para 2.1).

Where there has been a disposal of the original property or a cash gift has been used to acquire land, the chargeable person will only be assessed to tax on the portion of the value of the relevant land which can reasonably be attributed to the value of the original property or the cash originally given. The Revenue, in their Technical Guidance, has referred only to the need to make a reasoned judgement, on the basis of the facts, of the value of the land disposed of and its ultimate sale price, the consideration provided and the independent financial resources of the recipient (Revenue Guidance 'Income Tax and Pre-owned Assets', para 4.3). This so-called guidance does not assist a practitioner and is disappointing. The Revenue has given only one example of attribution and fail to deal with the situation where the purchase price is more than the value of the property originally disposed of.

Example adapting the Revenue's example

> Marjorie gave land worth £200,000 to her grandson Luke who sold it in 2003 for £500,000. He used the proceeds to buy a house for £300,000 in which his grandmother now lives.

In such a situation, the Revenue considers it reasonable to treat the whole value of a new property as attributable to the property originally disposed of. If the value of the new property exceeds the proceeds received from the sale of the original property the proportion of the value reasonably attributable to the original property would be reduced. The value reasonably attributable to the new property cannot exceed the final value of the property originally disposed of.

(vii) Sales

Where there is a sale of an entire interest in a property by the chargeable person for a consideration paid in money (sterling or other currency), other than as an excluded transaction, this is known as a 'non-exempt sale'. An example of a non-exempt sale is an outright sale of a property to a connected person at an undervalue. The legislation attempts to take account of the fact that the proceeds from the sale will be comprised in the value of the chargeable person's estate. In these circumstances the annual rent is reduced by multiplying the annual rent by the 'appropriate proportion' calculated by the following fraction:

$$\frac{MV - P}{MV}$$

where

MV = the value of the interest in land at the time of sale; and

P = the amount paid

Example

Barbara sold 50 acres of land (worth £2,000,000) to Gillian for £1,600,000. The rental value was £100,000.

The appropriate proportion is

$$\frac{£2{,}000{,}000 - £1{,}600{,}000}{£2{,}000{,}000} = \frac{£400{,}000}{£2{,}000{,}000} = \frac{1}{5}$$

The rental value is then multiplied by the appropriate proportion

$$\frac{1}{5} \times £100{,}000 = £20{,}000$$

In this way, the amount for the annual rent which is attributable to the sum paid to the chargeable person for his interest is removed from charge.

Chattels

General

[2.19] An income tax charge will arise under FA 2004, Sch 15 para 6 where a chargeable person is in possession of, or has the use of, a chattel, either alone or with others, and the 'disposal condition' or the 'contribution condition' is met.

(i) Use or possession

The terms 'use' and 'possession' are not defined in the legislation and will therefore have their normal meaning. The question arises as to whether a mere legal right to have possession of the chattel is enough. It is unlikely that it is; it is necessary for control to be assumed by the individual. The Revenue has stated that very limited or occasional use of a chattel will not incur an income tax charge. An example is given of a car used to give occasional lifts (less than three times a month) to the chargeable person will not be liable to an income tax charge whereas a lift to work every day will likely incur an income tax charge (Revenue Guidance 'Income Tax and Pre-Owned Assets' para 4.6).

(ii) The 'disposal condition'

The 'disposal condition' is satisfied where, at any time after 17 March 1986, the individual (whether alone or jointly with others)

- owned the chattel or any other property the disposal proceeds of which were (directly or indirectly) applied by another person to acquire the chattel; and
- disposed of all or part of his interest in the chattel or other property otherwise than by an excluded transaction.

Examples

A father gives a valuable painting to his son which hangs in the son's house and later the father resumes possession of the painting by hanging it in his dining room.

A father gives his valuable stamp collection to his son. The son sells the stamp collection and buys a painting. The father later hangs the painting in his dining room.

(iii) The 'contribution condition'

The 'contribution condition' is satisfied when, at any time after 17 March 1986, the chargeable person has provided (directly or indirectly), otherwise than by an excluded transaction, any of the consideration given by another person for the acquisition of

- the chattel; or
- any other property the disposal proceeds of which were (directly or indirectly) applied by another person towards acquiring the chattel.

Examples

> A father gives his son the sum of £100,000 towards buying a painting which is worth £200,000 and which the father later hangs in his dining room.
>
> The provisions will also apply to exchanges. For example, a father gives a painting to his son who exchanges it for a stamp collection which the father has at his house.
>
> A father gives his son £250,000 to acquire a painting which he does and then sells it for £300,000. He uses the proceeds to buy a vintage car which his father has at his house.

A disposition which creates a new interest in a chattel out of an existing interest in a chattel is to be taken to be a disposal of part of the existing interest (FA 2004 Sch 15 para 6(4)).

(iv) The charge

Where FA 2004 Sch 15 para 6 applies in respect of the whole or part of a year of assessment, an amount equal to the 'chargeable amount' is treated as income of the individual which is chargeable to income tax.

The chargeable amount is the 'appropriate amount' less any amounts paid to the owner by the chargeable person under a legal obligation in respect of the possession or use of the chattel. The 'appropriate amount' is calculated by using the formula in FA 2004, Sch 15 para 7. The appropriate amount varies according to whether the disposal or contribution condition applies. The formula is similar to that for land except that instead of the appropriate rental value, para 7 refers to the appropriate amount and the formula uses a notional interest rate which is prescribed by regulation (currently 4.75%) which can produce a substantial income tax charge.

If a full market rent is paid for the use of chattels then in straightforward circumstances there will be no reservation of benefit because of FA 1986, Sch 20 para 6(1)(a). This will also have the result that the pre-owned asset charge under FA 2004, Sch 15 para 6 will not apply because of FA 2004, Sch 15 para 11(5)(d). It is very important that there is a regular review of the rent to ensure a full market rent is being paid.

There is no *de minimis* value below which chattels may be disregarded. This means that there is no margin for error in determining a full market rent. As, by definition, chattels are movable it may be difficult to track them.

There are three matters to consider in relation to the formula.

First, the valuation date is prescribed by Regulations. It has been set as the 6 April in the relevant tax year or, if later, the first day of the taxable period.

Second, Regulations provide that the valuation before the first 5-year anniversary is to be made by reference to the first valuation date and thereafter by reference to the valuation at the last 5-year anniversary. This regime is compulsory, not optional, and may have an adverse effect in relation to fluctuating chattel values. If there is an interruption in the use or occupation of the property by the taxpayer so that a fifth-year anniversary does not fall in a taxable period, the relevant date in the year when the provisions of Sch 15 next apply will be treated as the next 5-year anniversary.

Where the chattel in question is the original gift so satisfying the disposal condition, the appropriate amount is computed by the following fraction:

$$\frac{DV}{V}$$

where

DV = the value at the valuation date of the interest in the chattel that was disposed of by the chargeable person; and

V = the value of the chattel at the valuation date.

Example

Bill grants his son a lease of a painting when the painting was worth £500,000 and the lease £400,000. In 2010/11 the painting is worth £3,000,000 and the lease £1,500,000

On the assumption that the prescribed rate is 4.75%, the appropriate rental value is:

$$£3{,}000{,}000 \times \frac{£1{,}500{,}000}{£3{,}000{,}000} \times 4.75\% = £71{,}250$$

(v) Sale of a chattel

To take account of the fact that, in cases of sales at an undervalue, the sale proceeds may be relevant property comprised in the estate of the chargeable person, the legislation provides that the sale of a whole interest in a chattel by a chargeable person for a consideration paid in money is a non-exempt sale. A proportion is then not subject to the charge. The appropriate amount is reduced by multiplying it by the following fraction:

$$\frac{\text{Appropriate proportion of the value of the interest on the chattel disposed of}}{\text{Value of the chattel}}$$

The appropriate proportion in such a case would be

$$\frac{MV - P}{MV}$$

where

MV = the value of the interest in the chattel at the time of sale; and

P = the amount paid

Example

A father sells to his son a painting worth £2,000,000 for £1,600,000.

The appropriate proportion is:

$$\frac{£2{,}000{,}000 - £1{,}600{,}000}{£2{,}000{,}000} = \frac{1}{5}$$

The appropriate amount is:

$$4.75\% \times £2{,}000{,}000 \times \frac{1}{5} = £19{,}000$$

It should be remembered that the non-exempt sale relief is only available in respect of cash sales. Also, the relief is only available if the transferor has disposed of his whole interest in the chattel.

The Revenue has confirmed that in relation to the carve out strategies involving chattels the provisions of FA 1986, s 102A do not apply (Revenue Guidance 'Income Tax and Pre-Owned Assets', Appendix 1).

Settlements

(i) General

[2.20] Under FA 2004, Sch 15 para 8, a charge to income tax will arise where:

(a) there is a settlement under which any income arising from the property would be treated under ITTOIA 2005, s 624 as income of the settlor;
(b) the income would still be deemed to be the income of the settlor even if ITTOIA 2005, s 625(1) did not include any reference to the spouse or civil partner of the settlor; and
(c) the property comprised in the settlement includes property which is, or represents, intangible property settled or added to the settlement after 17 March 1986.

The charge under para 8 adopts an entirely different approach to the provisions relating to land and chattels. Under those provisions the taxpayer must have actually benefited. Under para 8 what matters is the possibility of benefiting. In such a case it might be worth considering selling any intangible investments and purchasing tangible assets such as let land or chattels which are not occupied or used or enjoyed by the taxpayer.

(ii) Intangible property

Intangible property is widely defined and means any property other than chattels or interests in land. This will include cash and insurance policies.

(iii) The charge

The 'chargeable amount' is calculated by applying the prescribed notional rate of interest to the value of the relevant property at the valuation date. The notional rate is prescribed by Regulations and is currently 4.75%. Relief is given for any income tax or capital gains tax payable by the chargeable person under the following specified charging provisions so far as the tax is attributable to the relevant property.

(i) ITTOIA 2005, s 461 (income tax on chargeable event gains).
(ii) ITTOIA 2005, s 624 (income tax on income arising in settlor-interested trusts).
(iii) ITA 2007, ss 720–730 (income tax on income arising on assets transferred abroad).
(iv) TCGA 1992, s 86 (capital gains tax on gains attributed to settlor of a non-resident trusts).

Unlike under the charge on land and chattels, for a charge to arise there is no need for there to be any benefit arising to the chargeable person nor is there any requirement for there to be any income arising under the settlement.

Relief is only given for the amount of tax paid under the above provisions, and not for the sums charged to tax. This is a grossly inequitable provision.

Example

Malcolm settled a property on trust of which he is the life tenant. The property is sold for £500,000 and the moneys are held on deposit earning 2.75% per annum.

Malcolm is liable to income tax under ITTOIA 2005, s 624 on the income arising of £13,750.

Assuming a notional rate of interest of 4.75%, he is also assessable to income tax on notional income under FA 2004, Sch 15 of £23,750. Against this notional income, he can deduct the tax charged on his actual income of £6,875 (50% of £13,750). Therefore, he only receives credit for the tax paid against notional income and not against the tax charged on notional income assessed on him under ITTOIA 2005, s 624.

Excluded transactions

[2.21] FA 2004, Sch 15 para 10 contains a list of 'excluded transactions' which will not be subject to an income tax charge under the pre-owned assets rules. They have 'no application to the charge on intangible property' (Revenue Guidance 'Income Tax and Pre-Owned Assets', para 1.3.1) discussed in **2.20** above. That statement is rather misleading as an excluded transaction may involve any kind of property, including intangible property. For example, an excluded transaction could involve intangible property that was later replaced by land or chattels, thus removing the land or chattels in question from the scope of the pre-owned assets charge. There are different exclusions that apply to the different conditions.

Disposal condition

For the 'disposal condition' for land and chattels, the following disposals will be excluded transactions.

(a) The 'full consideration' exclusion. A disposal by a chargeable person of his whole interest in the property except for any right expressly reserved by him over the property either
   (i) by a transaction made at arm's length with an unconnected person; or
   (ii) by a transaction which might be expected to be made at arm's length between unconnected persons.

   This would include a third party sale or the sale of land between father and daughter on full commercial terms. If, however, there were any unusual contract terms (of the type a third party would be unlikely to accept), this is likely to prevent the transaction being an excluded transaction. It should be noted that a disposal of a part interest will not in most circumstances be an excluded transaction with the result that, in the original legislation, equity release schemes were subject to the charge. It has therefore been provided that disposals of part of an interest in any property by a transaction made at arm's length with a person not connected with the chargeable person is specifically exempted from charge (Charge to Income Tax by Reference to Enjoyment of Property Previously Owned Regulations 2005, SI 2005 No 724, reg 5). In addition, the exemption is extended to disposals of a part share to anyone provided that they were made on arm's length terms and either took place before 7 March 2005 or took place on or after that date for a consideration not in the form of money or readily convertible assets. It should be noted that equity release transactions between family members will often be caught by the charge.

(b) Spouse exemption. A transfer of property to the chargeable person's spouse or civil partner (or to a former spouse or civil partner where the transfer has been ordered by a court).

   This important exception preserves the ability of married taxpayers or those in civil partnerships to distribute capital assets between them. There is no requirement that the spouse be domiciled in the United Kingdom, so the exemption is wider than the corresponding inheritance tax exemption.

(c) A disposal by way of gift by virtue of which the property became settled property in which a spouse or civil partner (or former spouse or civil partner if done in accordance with a court order) is beneficially entitled provided such an interest in possession has not come to an end otherwise than on the death of the spouse or former spouse. This exemption mirrors the exemption from the reservation of benefit rules found in IHTA 1984 ss 5 and 5A.

(d) A disposition for the maintenance of a family within IHTA 1984, s 11.

(e) An outright gift to an individual which for inheritance tax purposes is a transfer of value which is wholly exempt because the annual exemption (see **2.7** above) or the small gifts exemption (see **2.9** above) applies.

Gifts covered by other exemptions (eg gifts in consideration of marriage) are not excluded transactions.

Contribution condition

Provision by the chargeable person of consideration for another's acquisition of any property will be an excluded transaction in any of the following circumstances.

(i) Spouse exemption. Where the other person was the chargeable person's spouse or civil partner (or, where the transfer has been ordered by the court, his former spouse or civil partner).

(ii) On acquisition, the property became settled property in which his spouse, civil partner or former spouse or civil partner is beneficially entitled to an interest in possession (provided that interest in possession has not come to an end otherwise than on the death of the spouse or civil partner or former spouse or civil partner).

(iii) The consideration provided was an outright gift of money (whether in sterling or foreign currency) by the chargeable person to the other person and was made at least seven years before the earliest date the chargeable person began occupation of the relevant land or obtained possession of the chattel.
This is important as it excludes from the charge all outright gifts of money which were made 7 or more years before the earliest date the chargeable person either entered occupation of the relevant land or obtained possession of the chattel. As the earliest date the conditions can be met is 6 April 2005, any provision of consideration by way of an outright gift of cash made before 6 April 1998 will be an excluded transaction. This will mean that taxpayers will only have to look back to the previous 7 years when tracing gifts of cash used to acquire land or chattels. A problem may still arise where inadequate records have been kept. There is, however, no 7-year limit for gifts of chattels and land which have subsequently been converted to cash. This creates a substantial administrative burden on taxpayers.

(iv) The provision of consideration falls within the exemption for dispositions for the maintenance of family under IHTA 1984, s 11.

(v) The provision of consideration is an outright gift to an individual which is wholly exempt because the annual exemption (see **2.7** above) or the small gifts exemption (see **2.9** above) applies.

Example

Rachel and Mark jointly purchased a property in 1995 for £200,000, funding £180,000 of the purchase price by raising a joint mortgage loan. Rachel gave Mark £10,000 which he used to fund his share of the cash funds required. They subsequently married and are still living in the same flat which is now worth £750,000.

The 'contribution condition' is met and Rachel's gift is not an excluded transaction between spouses as they were not married at the time that she made it. Mark will be subject to an income tax charge under FA 2004, Sch 15 based on the $^1/_{20}$th of the rental value of the property, a truly absurd result.

Exemptions from charge

[2.22] There are a number of exemptions from the charges on land, chattels and intangible property which are set out in FA 2004, Sch 15 paras 11–13.

(a) There will be no charge where
   (i) the relevant property, or
   (ii) other property which derives its value from the relevant property and whose value is not substantially less than the relevant property

   is either within the chargeable person's estate for inheritance tax purposes or would be treated as such by virtue of the gifts with reservation rules. Where the taxpayer's estate includes property whose value derives from the relevant property but whose value is substantially less than the value of the relevant property, then there will be a reduced charge to income tax, taking into account the inclusion of part of the value in the taxpayer's estate. Additional anti-avoidance provisions apply where the property concerned is subsequently treated as forming part of the original transferor's estate by virtue of his coming to have an interest in possession in the property (see **2.23**).

   In determining the value of property, a deduction is made for an 'excluded liability' in certain circumstances (FA 2004 Sch 15 para 11(6)). A liability is an excluded liability if the creation of the liability and any transaction by which the person's estate came to include relevant property (or property which derives its value from the relevant property or by which the value of property in his estate came to be derived from the relevant property) were associated operations under IHTA 1984, s 268. This provision is designed to nullify the trust of debt strategy (see **9.11**).

   Relevant property is defined in FA 2004, Sch 15 para 11(9) and is determined by the nature of the property involved and whether the disposal or contribution condition is satisfied.

(b) There is an exemption where the property would be treated as subject to a reservation if it were not an exempt transfer under FA 1986, s 102(5)(d)–(i). This includes gifts to charities, political parties, housing associations, maintenance funds for historic buildings and employee trusts and gifts for national purposes. It does not, however, cover transfers between spouses or civil partners, small gifts and gifts in consideration of marriage.

(c) There is an exemption where the property would be treated as subject to a reservation if it were not a share of an interest in land which the transferor and transferee occupy and where the transferor receives no benefit other than a negligible one under FA 1986, s 102B(4). Where a mother gives her son cash which he uses to buy a house jointly with her in which they both live, sharing expenses equally, there is no reservation of benefit. She is not exempt from an income tax charge because her gift of cash was neither a gift subject to a reservation nor a gift of an individual share in land.

(d) There is an exemption where the property would be treated as subject to a reservation were it not for FA 1986, s 102C(3) and Sch 20 para 6. This covers the situation where a transferor gives a house to a relative, the transferor's circumstances have changed since the original gift and the transferor has become unable to maintain himself for reasons of old age or infirmity.

(e) There is a *de minimis* exemption where the aggregate of the sums chargeable on an individual in respect of pre-owned assets does not exceed £5,000 in a year of assessment. In such a case, no tax will be payable. If the aggregate exceeds £5,000, it will be fully chargeable. The exemption is applied to the aggregate notional annual values before any amounts paid by the former owner are set off in respect of land and chattels. In practice, this is unlikely to exempt many taxpayers from the charge.

Where the charge applies for only part of the year, the de minimis limit is not apportioned.

Example

Madge made a gift of the house in which she lives to her nephew. The appropriate rental value is £7,000. She pays rent to her nephew of £5,000 under a formal agreement which reduces the amount chargeable to £2,000.

The *de minimis* rule will not apply as the appropriate rental value exceeds £5,000.

(f) There is no charge on an individual who is non-resident in the United Kingdom in a year of assessment. This is considered in more detail in **CHAPTER 20 THE OVERSEAS CLIENT**.

In determining whether property falls within (*b*), (*c*) or (*d*) above in a case where the contribution condition in **2.18** (land) or **2.19** (chattels) above is met, the exclusion for gifts of money in FA 1986, Sch 20 para 2(2)(b) is to be disregarded (FA 2004, Sch 15 para 11(8)).

Gifts made under deeds of variation or dispositions which are not treated as transfers of value under IHTA 1984, s 17 are disregarded for the purposes of the pre-owned asset charge (FA 2004 Sch 15 para 16).

Where a person ('A') acts as a guarantor in respect of a loan made to another person ('B') by a third party in connection with the acquisition of any property by B, the guarantee is not regarded as the provision by A of consideration for B's acquisition (FA 2004 Sch 15 para 17).

The Revenue has the power by way of regulation to confer further exemptions from income tax.

Reverter to settlor trusts

[2.23] Revertor to settlor trusts have been used as tax planning vehicles to benefit from the interaction of the gift with reservation rules (FA 1986, s 102) and the pre-owned asset rules (FA 2004, Sch 15). The pre-owned asset charge does not apply if property given away remains comprised in the estate of the transferor for IHT purposes (FA 2004 Sch 15 para 11(1)). Formerly, because of IHTA 1984, s 49(1), an individual entitled to a life interest under a settlement was treated as if he owned the trust property which was charged to IHT on his death. Where, however, on the death of the life tenant the property reverts to the settlor of the trust during the settlor's lifetime, although the life tenant was still treated as owning the trust property, its value was left out of account on his death (IHTA 1984, s 53(3)). Therefore a parent could pass property to his child, who then settled the property on trust for his parent's life, subject to which the property reverted to him. Neither the gift with reservation provisions nor the pre-owned assets charge would apply because of s 49, but on the parent's death the value of the property was left out of account. Since 5 December 2005, the pre-owned assets charge applies where the former owner of an asset (or a person who contributed to its acquisition) enjoys the asset under the terms of a trust which provides that the trust property may revert to the settlor during his lifetime unless he makes an election (see **2.27**) (FA 2004 Sch 15 paras 11 (11)–(13) as inserted by FA 2006, s 80). If an election is made, the pre-owned assets charge will not apply but neither will the revertor to settlor exemption when the interest comes to an end. Of course, (see **Chapters 4** and **5**) s 49 only applies to a limited range of interests in possession and so this planning is only relevant to existing IIPs (see **4.9** below) and transitional serial interests (see **5.4** below). Where this strategy is used it is better for the property to revert to the settlor's spouse (or civil partner) rather than to the settlor so as to preserve the capital gains tax uplift to market value on the death of the life tenant (TCGA 1992 s 73(1)(b)).

Due to a drafting error in FA 2006, s 80, FA 2004 Sch 15 paras 11(11)–(13) have a wider application than was intended. The error is that the amendment made by s 80 applies not only to trusts where the life tenant is another beneficiary but also to those where the life tenant is a settlor himself. Following correspondence between the Chartered Institute of Taxation and HMRC, the Revenue contends that s 80 does not apply provided the life interest of the settlor has subsisted continuously since the creation of the trust. This therefore means that issues arise where the initial trusts were discretionary or conferred interests in possession on other beneficiaries.

The Revenue has said that the effect of s 80 can be avoided by an election being made (see **2.27** below) and so the revertor to settlor provisions do not apply. However the matter may not be as straightforward in certain situations such as where land or chattels are held by a non-resident company and the settlor is non-UK domiciled.

Gifts of cash and gifts of land

[2.24] One of the more common scenarios that an adviser encounters is the situation where a mother either makes a gift of cash to her daughter which is used to buy a property in their joint names or makes a gift of property so the property is held jointly by them. There is a crucial distinction between them which will be illustrated below.

Example

Margaret has sold her house and has agreed to buy a house jointly with her daughter, Gillian. Gillian will live with her mother and they will pay all living expenses equally. The tax consequences are as follows.

If Margaret bought the house in her sole name and then transferred a 50% interest to Gillian so they are joint tenants, there would be a gift of an undivided share of an interest in land. The gift is a PET. Because Margaret receives no benefit other than a negligible one (she contributes equally to the household) the gift with reservation rules do not apply (FA 1986, s 102B(4)). No pre-owned asset charge would arise because the disposal satisfies s 102B(4) above (FA 2004 Sch 15 para 11(5)(c)).

If Margaret made a gift of cash (£400,000) to Gillian which is used to buy a house for £800,000, the gift is a PET. Provided the gift was not conditional on Gillian using the money to buy the house there is no gift with reservation. Because it is a gift of money under FA 1986, Sch 20 para 2(2)(b) the tracing rules do not apply. Under FA 1986, Sch 20 para 6(1) one has to consider the associated operations rules under IHTA 1984, s 268. Read literally it is arguable that s 268 applies but many commentators do not consider that the associated operations rule can be used to re-characterise a gift as being of property rather than of cash. However, the wording in the Revenue's Guidance Notes suggests that HMRC may seek to use the s 268 rules in certain circumstances.

In relation to the pre-owned asset charge such a charge is likely but it is not certain due to the wording in FA 2004, Sch 15 para 11(8) as it appears that it should be assumed that Margaret has given Gillian an undivided share in land. Therefore, as Gillian and Margaret are in joint occupation they satisfy the exemption in FA 1986, s 102B(4) under FA 2004, Sch 15 para 11(5).

Valuation

[2.25] Unless otherwise stated, the value of any property will be the price which the property might reasonably be expected to fetch if sold in the open market at that time. There is no assumption that the price be reduced on the grounds that the whole property is to be placed on the market at one and the same time (FA 2004 Sch 15 para 15).

As stated above the valuation is by reference to the first valuation date and this valuation is used for a period of five tax years. For property within the regime from 6 April 2005 a new market value will be required for 6 April 2010, for the next five tax years (2010/11 onwards). When a property has decreased in value over that time the question arises as to what the position is where a property is sold and the taxpayer moves to a smaller property.

Example

Marion gave £300,000 to her son, Martyn, in April 2000. Martyn used the money to purchase 24 Argyll Road. In April 2002 Marion moves to the property. On 6 April 2005 the house was worth £1m on which her income tax charge will be based for the following five tax years. In 2009 Martyn sold the house and bought a small apartment for £500,000 into which Marion moved.

The Revenue has confirmed that 'relevant land' is the land currently occupied by the chargeable person. A new valuation should be done when the occupation of that property starts, and it is intended that the new valuation should then be used for the remainder of that 5-year cycle. Therefore, Marion should obtain a valuation of the apartment to reduce her income tax charge.

Avoidance of multiple charges

[2.26] It is possible that in any year of assessment there is a pre-owned assets charge on land or a chattel, and also a charge on intangible property which derives its value in whole or part from the same land or chattel. The Revenue uses the example of an individual who occupies land owned by a company in which he is a shareholder.

To avoid multiple charges on the same property FA 2004, Sch 15 para 18 provides that only the higher amount is chargeable and it is that amount which is taken into account for the *de minimis* provisions. FA 2004, Sch 15 para 19 provides that when an income tax charge arises on the same occupation of land or use of any chattel under the pre-owned asset provisions and ITEPA 2003 Pt 3 (benefits from an employer) the income tax charge under ITEPA will take priority with only any excess being subject to a charge under FA 2004, Sch 15.

The Inheritance Tax (Double Charges Relief) Regulations 2005 (SI 2005/3441), gives relief in certain circumstances from a potential double IHT charge which can arise where a taxpayer decides to rearrange his affairs so to avoid a pre-owned asset income tax charge.

Election to opt out

[2.27] Taxpayers who fall within the pre-owned assets provisions may elect to 'opt out' of the charge in relation to a particular asset. Where an election is made in respect of land or chattels, the property is treated for inheritance tax purposes as a gift with reservation which will continue to apply for so long as the taxpayer enjoys a benefit by occupying the relevant land or retaining possession of the chattel and will be subject to inheritance tax on death (FA 2004, Sch 15 para 21). FA 2004, Sch 15 para 22 gives a right of election in respect of intangibles.

The charge to inheritance tax will be incurred unless the occupation or use ceases permanently (and is not recommenced) at least 7 years before their death or (in the case of land or chattels) the chargeable person pays full consideration for use of the relevant property. The Revenue accepts that where the person is already paying full consideration for use of the land or chattels before making an election and then elects there is no deemed PET at that point.

However, if the person ceases to pay full consideration in the 7 years prior to death and is still in occupation of the property, the effect of the election is that they will be subject to an inheritance tax charge on their death.

Any election must be made in the prescribed manner (on form IHT 500) no later than the 31 January in the year of assessment immediately following the initial year (the 'relevant filing date') (FA 2004, Sch 15 para 23) or on such later date, as an officer of HMRC may, in a particular case, allow. HMRC has, since 21 March 2007, been able to accept late elections.

The current guidance states that where a taxpayer can show that an event beyond their control prevented them making the election by the relevant filing date, a late election will be accepted. In the Revenue's Guidance 'Income Tax and Pre-owned Assets', para 3.4, the Revenue gives examples of what it considers to be an event beyond the chargeable person's control which include an election lost or delayed in the post in certain circumstances and serious illness and bereavement. The Revenue has stated that it will accept a late election:

> where the chargeable person can show that they were unaware — and could not reasonably have been aware — that they were liable to an income tax charge under this Schedule, and elected within a reasonable time of becoming so aware.

Unfortunately 'reasonable time' is not defined. The Revenue states that it will only accept a late election provided it is not a result of a chargeable person taking active steps to avoid both a pre-owned assets charge and an inheritance tax charge under the reservation of benefit provisions or a chargeable person wishing to avoid committing to an income tax charge or an election before 31 January in order to have longer to see which will be the most beneficial course of action.

Where there has been a change in the law or HMRC Guidance which results in a charge arising from transactions that did not previously give rise to a charge, a late election will be accepted where the chargeable person can show that they elected as soon as practicable after becoming aware of the change.

There is no right of appeal again the refusal to accept a late election.

In the case of a couple who are married or in a civil partnership who jointly own a property and who are both caught by the provisions of Sch 15, if they both wish to have the property treated as property subject to a reservation, they must both make an election. An election by one cannot affect the other.

An election may be amended or withdrawn, during the life of the chargeable person, at any time before the relevant filing date. Otherwise, an election, once made, cannot be revoked.

There is no provision at present for the transferor to notify the transferee of an election, even though the transferee can be made liable for the inheritance tax due on the transferor's death.

The decision whether to opt out will depend upon a number of factors, including the life expectancy of an individual and the type of assets in the estate. An elderly taxpayer who expects the remaining period of his life to be short may decide to incur an income tax liability rather than have his estate incur a 40% inheritance tax charge.

For more detailed discussion in relation to the application of the pre-owned asset charge on the family home, see **CHAPTER 9 THE FAMILY HOME.**

Capital gains tax

Holdover relief

[2.28] Under TCGA 1992, s 165 and TCGA 1992, s 260, when making a gift it is possible to elect to hold-over certain chargeable gains which would otherwise arise to the transferor. The transferee in effect acquires the gifted property at the transferor's acquisition cost, thus deferring the payment of tax until such time as the transferee disposes of the property in circumstances where it is either not possible to make, or the transferee chooses not to make, a further hold-over election. Hold-over relief is not available on disposals to settlor-interested settlements (or where arrangements subsist under which the settlor may acquire an interest in the settlement) (TCGA 1992, s 169B) nor is it available on a transfer to a trust for the benefit of the settlor's dependent children. A dependent child is defined as a minor who is unmarried or is not a partner in a civil partnership. There is a clawback period during which the held-over gain may be brought back into charge if the settlor later acquires an interest in the settlement or arrangements subsist under which the settlor will or may acquire such an interest. The clawback period begins immediately following the disposal and ends six years after the end of the year of assessment in which the disposal was made (TCGA 1992, s 169C). There are exceptions for heritage maintenance property and certain settlements for disabled dependent persons (TCGA 1992, s 169D).

Gift of business assets

[2.28A] TCGA 1992, s 165 applies to gifts by individuals of the following types of assets.

(a) An asset, or an interest in an asset, used for the purposes of a trade, profession or vocation carried on by
  - (i) the transferor; or
  - (ii) his personal company (as defined in TCGA 1992, s 165(8)(a)); or
  - (iii) a company which is a member of a trading group of companies (as defined in TCGA 1992, s 165A) of which the holding company is the transferor's personal company.

(b) Shares or securities of a trading company (as defined in TCGA 1992, s 165A) or of the holding company of a trading group where
  - (i) the shares or securities are not listed on a recognised stock exchange; or
  - (ii) the trading company or holding company is the transferor's personal company.

  Hold-over relief will not apply to a transfer of shares or securities to a company.

(c) Agricultural property, or an interest in agricultural property, within the meaning of IHTA 1984, Pt V Ch II which is not used for the purposes of a trade carried on as mentioned in (*a*) above.

Gifts of assets attracting an IHT charge

[2.28B] TCGA 1992, s 260 applies to gifts by individuals and trustees to individuals and trustees which are either

(a) chargeable transfers within the meaning of IHTA 1984 (and transfers which would be chargeable transfers but for IHTA 1984, s 19 (the annual exemption)) and which are not potentially exempt transfers; or
(b) exempt transfers within IHTA 1984, s 24 (transfers to political parties), IHTA 1984, s 27 (transfers to maintenance funds for historic buildings) and IHTA 1984, s 30 (transfers of designated property).

In the past, relief under TCGA 1992, s 260 was used mainly in respect of gifts to discretionary trusts, whether or not its value fell within the 'nil rate' band, and on gifts covered by the annual exemption. Since 22 March 2006 relief under s 260 is available for gifts to most types of trust except privileged interest trusts.

The rationale behind the existing statutory rules seems reasonably clear. Where the gift is a potentially exempt transfer and comprises readily realisable assets (eg stock exchange investments) capital gains tax is chargeable on the gift. In the case of most types of illiquid assets (eg land, unquoted shares) either hold-over relief will apply or the tax arising may be paid by equal instalments over 10 years — TCGA 1992, s 281. The instalment option applies to the following assets:

(a) land or an estate or interest in land;
(b) shares or securities giving control of a company;
(c) unquoted shares or securities.

Interest on the unpaid tax will run from the due date and not from the date on which each instalment is due. This detracts from the attraction of the facility.

Where, on the other hand, the gift is subject to inheritance tax or eats into the transferor's 'nil rate' band (which will affect subsequent chargeable transfers), the relief under TCGA 1992, s 260 will be available to avoid any double charge to tax.

In cases where both reliefs might otherwise be applicable, TCGA 1992, s 260 relief takes priority (TCGA 1992, s 165(3)(d)).

Making an Election

[2.28C] A claim for hold-over relief under TCGA 1992 ss 165 or 260 must be made in the prescribed form (Help Sheet HS295) by both the transferor and transferee (except where the transferee is a trustee). For gifts made in 2010/11 a claim must be made within four years. In principle it is necessary to agree the amount of the held-over gain. In practice, however, a computation of the gain and formal valuation is in many cases not required (Statement of Practice SP8/92). Both the transferor and transferee need to make the application, provide full details of the asset transferred and confirm that a gain would occur.

Both reliefs operate to defer any chargeable gain arising on the gift until the transferee sells the donated property or otherwise disposes of it in circumstances where it is not possible to make a further hold-over election. Any chargeable gain which would otherwise arise on the gift (called the 'held-over gain') is reduced to zero whilst the transferee's acquisition cost of the donated property is reduced by a like amount so that in effect the transferee takes over the transferor's acquisition cost (TCGA 1992, s 165(4) and TCGA 1992, s 260(3)).

Where the transferor acquired the asset on or before 31 March 1982, his acquisition cost for the purposes of calculating the held-over gain will be the asset's value on 31 March 1982 (TCGA 1992, s 35(2)) except in the circumstances specified in s 35(3), unless an election is made under s 35(5).

Where the disposal of an asset giving rise to a potential capital gains tax charge also gives rise to an inheritance tax charge (either immediately or as a result of the death of the transferor within 7 years) and a claim for hold-over relief is made under either section, the inheritance tax paid may be deducted from the chargeable gain when calculating the capital gains tax due on a subsequent disposal of the asset by the transferee (TCGA 1992, s 165(10) and TCGA 1992, s 260(7)). Alternatively, IHTA 1984, s 165 allows the capital gains tax arising on the gift, provided it is paid by the transferee, to be deducted when calculating the value transferred for inheritance tax purposes.

Example

A transfers her shares in X Ltd to her son B who is 25 years of age and a higher rate taxpayer. The value of the shareholding is £750,000. It has a base cost of £125,000. A has already used her nil rate band. B sells the shares shortly after the gift. Less than a year after the gift A dies. Should A's executors claim hold-over relief allowing B to deduct the inheritance tax chargeable on the gift on his subsequent disposal of the shares or should they bear the capital gains tax on the gift so that it will be deductible in calculating the inheritance tax on the gift?

Claim for hold-over relief

	£		£
IHT on gift (£750,000 @ 40%)			300,000
CGT on subsequent disposal			
Proceeds	-750,000		
Deduct: Base cost	-125,000		
Deduct: IHT	-300,000		
	325,000		
	325,000	@ 28%	91,000
			£391,000

No claim for hold-over relief			
Proceeds	750,000		
Deduct: Base cost	-125,000		
	625,000		
	625,000	@ 28%	175,000
Value of shares on gift	750,000		
Deduct: CGT	-175,000		
	575,000	@ 40%	230,000
			£405,000

Where an election is made for hold-over relief under TCGA 1992, s 165 or TCGA 1992, s 260 (or has been made prior to 14 March 1989 under FA 1980, s 79), the held-over gain can in certain circumstances be assessed on the transferor (but in the name of, and at the rates applicable to, the transferee) if the transferee becomes neither resident nor ordinarily resident in the UK within 6 years after the end of the year of assessment in which the relevant disposal took place (TCGA 1992, 168(7), (8)).

Methods of protecting the transferor against any contingent liability include:

(a) the retention by him of an amount of the donated property equal to the held-over gain as bare trustee for the transferee for the 6-year period; and

(b) the taking of indemnities from relatives of the transferee who are not likely to go abroad,

although these both may represent 'reserved benefits' thereby possibly tainting the gift for inheritance tax purposes.

Clawback of relief

Trust Becoming Settlor Interested

[2.28D] Hold-over relief may be subject to clawback under provisions in TCGA 1992, s 169C. If, during the clawback period, either of the following two conditions is met, then the relief is withdrawn and the capital gains tax which would have been payable but for the relief will be clawed back:

- during the clawback period, the settlement becomes settlor-interested or an arrangement subsists under which a settlor will or may acquire an interest;
- in computing the chargeable gain which would (assuming that the transfer had not been eligible for holdover relief) accrue to the transferor on the disposal, the allowable expenditure would fall to be reduced as a consequence, either directly or indirectly, of a claim under TCGA 1992, s 165 or s 260 in respect of an earlier disposal made by an individual (whether or not to the transferor) and at any time during

the clawback period the individual has an interest in the settlement or an arrangement subsists under which such interest will or may be acquired by him. The clawback period is the period beginning immediately after the making of the relevant disposal and ending 6 years after the end of the year of assessment in which that disposal was made.

Where the clawback provisions apply, a chargeable gain equal to the amount of the held-over gain on the relevant disposal is treated, for the purposes of tax in respect of chargeable gains, as accruing to the transferor at the time either of the two conditions above is fulfilled.

Example

A transfers her shares in X Ltd to her son B who is 25 years of age. The value of the shareholding is £750,000. The shares have a base cost of £125,000. A year later, the market value of the shares has risen to £850,000. B makes a gift of the shares into a settlement from which he and his wife are excluded from benefit. Once again, an election is made to hold-over the gain. The trust contains a power for the trustees, at the behest of the settlor (B) to add beneficiaries to the settlement. The power cannot be exercised in favour of the settlor, his spouse or civil partner. Five years after making the transfer to the trustees, B enters an agreement with the trustees under which, should B die before his mother, A, the trustees will add A to the settlement as a life tenant of a portion of the trust fund.

A charge will not arise under TCGA 1992, s 169C by reason of the arrangement. B has not acquired an interest in the settlement. Although A has done so, but in the absence of any sort of arrangements between A and B as to the making of the settlement, she is not a settlor of the settlement.

There is an exemption from the clawback provisions in relation to a disposal to the trustees of a settlement which is a heritage maintenance settlement or is a settlement for disabled persons, provided certain criteria in TCGA 1992, s 169D are fulfilled.

Clawback on Death

[2.28E] Where a gain has been held-over into a trust which is or becomes an interest in possession, the held-over gain crystallises on the death of the life tenant (TCGA 1992, s 74(2)).

The inability to claim hold-over relief on gifts to non-residents (TCGA 1992, s 166 and TCGA 1992, s 261) makes gifts of chargeable assets to non-resident trusts unattractive, although there can be circumstances where the immediate capital gains tax charge is an acceptable price to pay for the ability to defer payment of any future capital gains tax on a subsequent disposal of the assets by the trustees, especially where the capital gains tax can be paid by instalments.

Capital gains tax considerations

[2.28F] Capital gains tax is an essential element of lifetime estate planning. Both the nature of assets to be given away and the identity of the transferee need to be carefully considered, as will the funding of any tax charge arising. The following points should be borne in mind when considering any planning strategy.

(1) Where a gift is being made solely to save inheritance tax at 40%, an immediate charge to capital gains tax at either 18% or 28%, depending upon whether the transferor is a higher rate taxpayer, may not be considered to be too high a price to pay for the potential saving. There is an obvious cash flow advantage in deferring any tax charges for as long as possible (ie until death when there will also be the benefit of the capital gains tax free base uplift) although the risk in such a strategy is that the rates of inheritance tax may change for the worse or a less favourable form of taxation may come into force. Another relevant factor is the extent to which the current value of the asset reflects chargeable gain — the charge to capital gains tax is only on the amount of the gain whereas the charge to inheritance tax will be on the asset's full value, including any increase in the value of the asset as time goes on. Where an asset is expected to increase significantly in value, an immediate gift of it (even if subject to an immediate capital gains tax charge) will save inheritance tax both on its present value and on the 'growth' element.

(2) Gifts of non-chargeable assets (eg cash, gilts, qualifying corporate bonds, life policies and chattels under £6,000 in value) do not give rise to any capital gains tax considerations.

(3) Chargeable assets showing the lowest gain should be identified and given away. The rebasing of assets to their 31 March 1982 value may assist here.

(4) The capital gains tax arising on a gift may be reduced if the transferor also realises capital losses (eg by sales or by gifts to the same transferee) in the same tax year. Although one needs to consider the provisions of FA 2007, s 27 which disallow losses arising under arrangements, one of the main purposes of which is to obtain a tax advantage.

(5) Where the gift is a potentially exempt transfer and a chargeable gain arises which cannot be held-over, the tax should be paid by the transferee so that, if the transferor dies within 7 years of the gift, the tax paid will reduce the value transferred by the chargeable transfer (IHTA 1984, s 165). There is a possibility that any agreement between the transferor and the transferee that the transferee will be responsible for the capital gains tax might create a 'gift with reservation' for inheritance tax purposes. On the transferee paying the tax, the benefit would then come to an end and the transferor would be deemed by FA 1986, s 102(4) to have made a further disposition of the property by way of a potentially exempt transfer. This will, in effect, start an additional 7-year period running which the transferor must survive to avoid an inheritance tax charge. The authors however, have never known HMRC Inheritance Tax to raise this argument.

(6) Where possible, advantage should be taken of the option to pay the capital gains tax by instalments.

(7) Gifts of chargeable assets should be made by whichever spouse has an available annual exemption or available capital losses. To allow this to be done, it may be necessary for one spouse to first give the asset to the other. This is, of course, subject to a possible challenge under the provisions of FA 2007, s 27 which disallows losses arising under arrangements, one of the main purposes of which is to obtain a tax advantage.

(8) Because moving assets around a family may create a capital gains tax charge, it is very important that chargeable assets are acquired by the right person (whether an individual or a family trust) at the outset.

Stamp duty and stamp duty land tax

[2.29] Stamp duty is not chargeable on an instrument giving effect to a gift of shares provided that it can be certified in writing as falling within Category L of the Schedule to the Stamp Duty (Exempt Instruments) Regulations 1987 (SI 1987 No 516).

For the transfer of land by way of gift, no stamp duty land tax will be payable provided a self-certificate is completed.

Advice should be sought where the transferee is assuming a liability, for example, a mortgage, as the assumption of any debt will constitute chargeable consideration (FA 2003, Sch 4, para 87).

Which assets to give away?

[2.30] Given that there are a number of ways in which an individual may make immediate gifts without incurring an immediate charge to inheritance tax or capital gains tax, the next aspect to consider is whether in fact he has any assets which he can afford to give away. This can be a very difficult matter. On the one hand, the individual may be concerned about the amount of tax that will be payable on his death, or on the death of his wife, but on the other hand he may be very reluctant to jeopardise his or his wife's present and future standard of living and financial security. He should only be encouraged to give away those assets which are clearly surplus to his present and estimated future living requirements. In theory, the more wealthy a person is, the more surplus assets he will have. In practice, however, it is often the case that the more wealthy a person is, the more he will want to retain to cushion and secure his, usually high, standard of living. The inheritance tax 'gifts with reservation' provisions, as we have seen, can make it extremely difficult for a person to give away an asset whilst retaining the ability to get it back in times of hardship. In addition, the income tax charge being levied on pre-owned assets will act as a deterrent. There are various insurance products currently being marketed which allow individuals to make large capital investments whilst retaining a right to 'income' during their lifetime. These products have been designed to avoid the reservation of benefit rules. For a more detailed consideration see **CHAPTER 7 INSURANCE**. However, most effective estate planning has to be conducted on the basis that once an asset is given away, it is gone for good. Whilst every case is different and must be judged on its own merit, the following are the types of assets which are usually the most suitable subjects of gifts.

Non- or low-income-producing assets

[2.31] Many people tend to live off their income (whether earned or unearned), regarding their capital primarily as a source of income and secondly as a reserve which can be called upon in times of hardship. Any assets which produce little or no income may be suitable for giving away, although it is important not to forget the psychological importance of the mere existence of the reserve.

Unfortunately, in many cases, the major non-income producing asset — indeed the major asset itself — will be the principal residence and the gifts with reservation provisions have rendered ineffective most methods of giving away the entire home whilst retaining the ability to live there. There may be more scope for estate planning with regard to a second home, but again the possible implications of these provisions must be fully explored. These aspects are dealt with in greater detail in **CHAPTER 9 THE FAMILY HOME**.

On the other hand, valuable paintings, books or similar chattels are clearly suitable candidates, provided that both ownership and (to avoid any reservation of benefit) possession are ceded. Woodlands, another non-income-producing asset, is a possible candidate.

Assets likely to grow in value or suffering a temporary reduction in value

[2.32] These types of assets, such as shares in private companies or let property, are obvious candidates because of the advantage in taking the future growth out of the transferor's estate.

In making gifts of assets which are pregnant with gain or in respect of which significant gains are anticipated, it is important to bear in mind that whilst the asset will on the transferor's death escape the charge to inheritance tax, the ability of the transferor's heirs to acquire the asset at its market value at the death of the transferor under TCGA 1992, s 62(1), thereby wiping out any chargeable gain then latent in the value of the asset, will be lost. This may be a significant factor if it is anticipated that the assets will one day be sold by the transferee.

Because the rate of capital gains tax is now either 18% or 28%, depending upon whether the transferor is a higher rate taxpayer, it may be attractive for an individual to make a gift of an asset and pay 18% or 28% (or a combination of both) on any capital gain rather than to hold the asset until death when IHT at 40% would be payable.

Where a transferor has property which is capable of qualifying for inheritance tax business property relief or agricultural property relief and that asset is both pregnant with gain and likely to be sold by the intended transferee it may, for tax purposes, be beneficial to allow the property to pass to the intended transferee on the transferor's death. This would allow advantage to be taken of the capital gains tax-free uplift to base cost. This would be preferable to removing the property from the transferor's estate only to permit the transferee then to suffer an 18% or 28% (or a combination of both) capital gains tax charge on any gain arising on the sale. Obviously, much will depend on how much of the value of the asset reflects a potentially chargeable gain and the level of inheritance tax relief available.

The other factor which now has to be considered is whether, on the gift, any capital gain already latent in the value of the asset can be 'held-over' to the transferee. This will depend upon the nature of the asset and the type of gift — see **2.28** above. In the case of shares in private companies, hold-over relief may be available; but in relation to other assets where the relief is not available, an immediate charge to capital gains tax may be a small price to pay to take the expected increase in value out of the transferor's estate.

Creating surplus assets

[2.33] It is sometimes possible to create surplus assets where none appear to exist. For example, an investment portfolio worth £100,000 and yielding (say) 2%, could be split into two. One half is then invested in higher yielding fixed interest investments to produce (say) a 4% yield and the other half is then free to be given away. This releases assets for a gift whilst maintaining the current income. Two points should, however, be borne in mind. First, the re-investment may create a significant capital gains tax charge. Secondly, the investment in fixed interest securities is likely to destroy the potential for future capital growth.

Encouraging an individual to live off capital itself rather than the income produced by that capital is another way of creating a surplus. For example, an elderly person who expects to live for another ten years and who has an investment portfolio worth £1,000,000 which produces an annual income of £30,000. He could retain £500,000, giving away the balance of £500,000. The individual could then fund a part of their annual expenditure from capital.

Another method which is sometimes suggested for freeing assets, otherwise required to produce income, is for an individual to borrow (usually on the security of his home) in order to buy an annuity, the income of which is intended (after tax) to cover the mortgage payments and provide a suitable level of maintenance. However, the annuity rates are unlikely to be attractive (they are usually below the life office's normal rates) and the net return after the interest payments have been made is often poor. The loss caused if the individual dies prematurely can wipe out the benefit of any saving in inheritance tax as the individual is exposed to the risk of fluctuating property prices and interest rates.

Where it is necessary for the individual to continue to occupy the property, a method of creating a surplus in relation to farmland is for him to grant to a family company or partnership, a lease of the land. This then frees the freehold reversion for a gift. This principle has already been mentioned in connection with reservation of benefit and does not appear to have been nullified by FA

1986, s 102A. Such an arrangement will, however, be subject to an income tax charge on the individual who occupies the property under the pre-owned assets regime. This is examined in more detail in **Chapter 9 The Family Home** and **Chapter 11 The Family Farm.**

The grant of a tenancy can also be used to reduce the value of land to facilitate a gift of the land. The grant of any tenancy which confers statutory security of tenure on the tenant, or which confers a significant term of years on the tenant, will effect an immediate reduction in the value of the property over which the tenancy is granted. In the case of a rack rent agricultural tenancy this can be by as much as 50%. The grant may have inheritance tax, capital gains tax and income tax implications all of which will need to be considered. The main use in estate planning of the granting of a tenancy specifically to reduce value is to enable a subsequent transfer of the freehold reversion to be made to the tenant at a significantly lower value than if the unencumbered freehold had been transferred. Again, this technique is subject to the application of FA 1986, s 102A. It is also considered in more detail in **Chapter 11 The Family Farm.**

Cash gifts

[2.34] Gifts of cash and investments are both equally effective for inheritance tax purposes. There are, however, two points worth considering.

(1) If an individual is contemplating giving his son a cash sum in order for him to buy, say, a car, it is in theory better for the individual to buy the car himself and then give it to his son. The second-hand value of the car is likely to be less than the amount of the cash gift. Clearly, this device will only work in relation to assets which depreciate on resale (unlike land) and, in practice, is only worth doing in respect of assets which are of substantial value and exempt from capital gains tax. Furthermore, the purchase and the gift are so clearly associated operations within IHTA 1984, s 268 that the Revenue may well seek to tax the transferor on the total loss to his estate resulting from the purchase and the gift.

(2) Gifts of investments may give rise to a capital gains tax charge where these are chargeable assets which cannot be 'held over' under either TCGA 1992, s 165 or s 260.

The transferee

[2.35] An individual who has decided that he wants to give assets away and has identified those assets which are surplus to his requirements must also consider the recipient of the gift and the manner in which the gift should be made.

Where the individual is considering a gift to his children, and there are also grandchildren in existence, some thought should be given to skipping the first generation and passing the assets over to the second. This is a course which usually only commends itself to children who consider themselves already adequately provided for, but any property passed to the second generation may, if held in trust, be used to maintain the grandchildren and to meet the cost of their education in an income tax efficient manner (see below). Such an approach can thus indirectly benefit their parents as well.

A gift may be in the form of an outright gift to an individual or may be a gift into trust. It used to be the case that the most common types of trust encountered in estate planning were:

(a) a bare trust for the benefit of a minor;
(b) an accumulation and maintenance trust for children and/or grandchildren;
(c) a discretionary trust;
(d) an interest in possession (life interest) trust.

Since 22 March 2006, gifts to individuals and to a disabled trust and the deemed transfer of value where an immediate post death interest is succeeded by bereaved minors trusts are potentially exempt transfers. Whereas, gifts to discretionary trusts, accumulation and maintenance trusts, and particular interest in possession trusts, are not potentially exempt transfers. Discretionary trusts are most likely to be used as vehicles to receive regular gifts within the inheritance tax annual or 'normal expenditure out of income' exemptions or gifts within a person's nil rate tax band, particularly in view of their flexibility.

Each type of trust has its own uses and limitations and these are dealt with in more detail in **CHAPTER 4 CREATING SETTLEMENTS**. The advantages and disadvantages of a gift to an offshore trust are also briefly discussed in the same chapter. A more detailed analysis is contained in **CHAPTER 6 OFFSHORE TRUSTS**.

An outright gift to a trust for the benefit of a minor child of the transferor does not provide any income tax advantage. Any income arising on the property given away is taxed as part of the transferor's total income under ITTOIA 2005, s 62 whilst the child is a dependent child, subject to the £100 limit for small amounts of income. It used to be the case that gains arising to a trust under which the settlor's dependent children (namely unmarried minors not in a civil partnership) could benefit would be assessable on the settlor. This is no longer the case.

It was the case that up until 23 June 2010 gains were taxed at a flat rate of 18% for both trustees and individuals alike, so there was no tax benefit in making a gift to one rather than to the other. This has changed because for disposals after 22 June 2010 a higher rate of 28% applies for individuals where their total taxable income and gains exceed the basic rate income tax band (currently £37,400). Where an individual's total taxable income and gains do not exceed the limit, gains remain taxable at 18%. For trustees, there is a flat rate of capital gains tax at 28%.

Making a gift

[2.36] A gift of property may be effected in two ways, namely by the appropriate transfer of ownership or by a declaration of trust by the owner. A gift by way of declaration of trust will take effect on the date of the declaration. A gift by transfer of ownership will take effect on the date of the transfer. A gratuitous disposition of heritable subjects in Scotland takes place when it is delivered to the transferee and not when it is recorded in the Register of Sasines (*Marquess of Linlithgow v Revenue & Customs Commissioners* [2010] CSIH 19, [2010] STC 1563).

In the case of gifts to trustees there are further requirements; there must be an effective transfer of property on trusts that are certain and are administratively workable. In reality, there should be little difficulty in establishing that the trust property has been given in a manner complying with the appropriate legal formalities, and some of these rules are set out below. In practice, if difficulties are going to arise it is far more likely that this will be because the gift has not been perfected. As a general rule, if the transferor does not complete all the formalities associated with the gift, then it will fail (*Fry (Re)* [1946] 2 All ER 106); if the transferor (including his agents) has accomplished all that can reasonably be undertaken, but an independent third party delays the legal formalities, the gift is valid (*Rose (Re)* [1952] Ch 499). (See also the decision in *Pennington v Waine* [2002] EWCA Civ 227.)

Transfers of some types of property (eg registered stocks and shares, land, life assurance policies) can only be effected by an instrument of transfer.

If a transfer of chattels is made by deed, except in the case of a marriage settlement, the chattels must be delivered to the transferee and registered under the Bills of Sale Act 1878 if it is not to become void as against the transferor's trustee in bankruptcy and creditors. Where possession remains with the transferor, a complete gift of chattels should be effected by a bill of sale. The registration process is not straightforward and it should be remembered that the register is a public document. For many clients, the lack of confidentiality if there are conditions attached to the gift is particularly off-putting.

Delivery is effected by change of possession. Where the chattel is in the possession of a third party, the transferor must in some way indicate to the third party that he is to look to the transferee as the owner of the chattel. Where the chattel is already in the possession of the transferee, the transfer may be effected simply by words (oral or written) indicating an intention to transfer ownership (*Stoneham (Re)* [1919] 1 Ch 149). Gifts of money in the form of bank notes or an irrevocable banker's draft are made by delivery. Gifts by way of cheque are not effective until the transferee's account is credited (*Owen Dec'd (Re)* [1949] 1 All ER 901). This principle was applied in *Curnock (Personal Representative of Curnock (dec'd)) v CIR* [2003] STC (SCD) 283, (SpC 365)).

Order of gifts

[2.37] When making a number of gifts, care should be taken to ensure that they are made in the most tax efficient order. Where a number of gifts are to be made which are all potentially exempt transfers, the order is important if the transferor survives the gifts by 3 years but dies within 7 years of them. Where the transferor survives the potentially exempt transfer by 7 years, then the order is immaterial. It is also usually immaterial if the transferor dies within 3 years of the gifts because then they will all be chargeable at death rates. There is some merit in all the gifts being made on the same day so that any inheritance tax payable as a result of the gifts (whether immediately payable or payable as a result of the transferor's death within 7 years) is charged on each gift on a pro-rata basis. This is the effect of IHTA 1984, s 266(2) and avoids the later gifts bearing the tax charge due to the earlier gifts using up the nil rate band and any exemptions.

Where, however, the proposed gifts include both a chargeable transfer (a transfer to a discretionary trust) and potentially exempt transfers, the chargeable transfer should be made before the potentially exempt transfers. This is because if the potentially exempt transfer becomes chargeable it will not be necessary to recalculate the tax on the chargeable transfer. In addition any nil rate band would be used by the discretionary trust which would have an impact in reducing future rates of charge on the trust.

The most important point is that, where tax is paid on a lifetime chargeable transfer, it is impossible to obtain a refund of any of the tax paid in the event of the tax recomputed on death producing a lower liability as a result of taper relief (IHTA 1984, s 7(5)). Of course, in the converse position, additional tax would indeed be due. This means that the order of making gifts can be very important where potentially exempt transfers and chargeable transfers together exceed the transferor's nil rate band. The following example, ignoring annual exemptions, illustrates the point.

Example

			Tax £
Day 1:	Potentially exempt transfer of £325,000		Nil
Day 2:	Chargeable transfer of £340,000 Transferee pays tax (340,000 – 325,000) @ 40% × 50%		3,000
Transferor dies 6 years later.			
Further tax due:			
No tax is due on the PET because it falls within the nil rate band of £325,000			Nil
Tax on chargeable transfer:			
340,000 @ 40% × 20%		27,200	
Deduct: Tax previously paid		–3,000	
			24,200
Total tax			£27,200

If, however, the chargeable transfer precedes the potentially exempt transfer

		£
Day 1:	Chargeable transfer of £340,000 Transferee pays tax (340,000 – 325,000) @ 40% × 50%	3,000
Day 2:	Potentially exempt transfer of £325,000	Nil
Transferor dies 6 years later.		

Further tax due:		
Tax on chargeable transfer:		
(340,000 – 325,000) @ 40% × 20%	1,200	
Deduct: Tax paid	–3,000	
		Nil
Tax paid on potentially exempt transfer:		
325,000 @ 40% × 20%		26,000
		£24,200

It is important to bear in mind that for the purposes of the annual exemption and the small gifts exemption the year runs from 6 April to 5 April, whereas the inheritance tax rate bands although subject to indexation on a tax year basis, have in some years been altered as from Budget Day although in recent years it has been from the beginning of the tax year. If a transferor is contemplating a gift early in the year, it can sometimes be advantageous to wait until Budget Day or the start of the next tax year for the rate bands to change. Of course, it has been announced that the nil rate band will remain at £325,000 until 2014/15 and so there is not at present any advantage in waiting.

Who should pay the inheritance tax on lifetime gifts?

[2.38] It is always important for the transferor to decide whether he or the transferee should pay the inheritance tax on a gift.

With immediately chargeable lifetime transfers such as those made to non-privileged trusts the transferor is primarily liable to pay the tax (IHTA 1984, s 199). The gross value of the gift will therefore need to be calculated to reflect the loss to the transferor's estate. Alternatively the transferee, namely the trustees, could pay the tax from the value transferred, therefore avoiding the need to gross up.

For potentially exempt transfers, inheritance tax will only be due if the transferor fails to survive for the necessary 7-year period. If he fails to do so and tax becomes payable, there is no question of grossing-up as the transferor himself has no liability to pay the tax so that the provisions which allow the liabilities to be taken into account in determining the value of a transferor's estate immediately after the transfer do not apply (IHTA 1984, s 5(4)).

The tax liability on a potentially exempt transfer which becomes chargeable falls primarily on the transferee. If, however, the tax is not paid within 12 months after the end of the month in which the transferor died, the transferor's personal representatives also become liable. To avoid any question as between the transferee and the transferor's personal representatives as to who should pay the tax, the matter should be settled at the outset. If the transferee is to pay the tax — and in many cases this is the preferable course especially if the interest-free instalment option is likely to be available — the transferee should enter into a binding commitment to do so. It is difficult to see that such a commitment could amount to a 'reserved benefit' for the transferor as it does no more than reflect where the primary statutory liability for the tax falls. The Revenue is understood to take the same view. If, however, the transferor wishes the tax to be borne by his estate, then a specific provision to this effect should be put in his will. This would amount to a legacy in favour of the transferee for inheritance tax purposes, and if the will includes gifts of residue which in whole or in part qualify for exemption, then the legacy may have to be grossed-up when calculating the inheritance tax payable on the transferor's death (IHTA 1984, s 38).

There are two distinct advantages in ensuring that the burden of the tax falls on the transferee.

(1) In the case of a chargeable transfer, there will be no 'grossing-up' (ie when calculating the inheritance tax payable no account will be taken of the tax itself in determining the reduction in the transferor's estate).

(2) Where the donated property is land, shares or securities in a company which gave the deceased control of that company or certain non-controlling holdings of shares or securities there may, where applicable, be the option of paying any inheritance tax by ten equal annual interest-free instalments. The payment of the tax may then be funded by the transferor by his making further gifts to the transferee within his annual exemption or regular gifts within the 'normal expenditure out of income' exemption. In the case of the inheritance tax payable in respect of a potentially exempt transfer, the interest-free instalment option (if available) may depend on the transferee retaining the donated property until the death of the transferor or until his own death if he predeceases the transferor.

Term assurance

[2.38A] Regardless of whether the inheritance tax is to be borne by the transferee or by the transferor's personal representatives, consideration should be given to term assurance being effected on the life of the transferor. The term should be for 7 years but the policy should ideally have an option to extend the term to cater for any legislative changes. Where the liability to tax is to be borne by the transferee, the policy may be taken out either by the transferee, as he has an insurable interest in the life of the transferor, or by the transferor himself and then assigned to the transferee. Where the liability is to be borne by the transferor's personal representatives, the transferor should take out the policy and ensure that the policy proceeds do not form part of his estate on death by holding the policy on separate trusts, either similar in terms to those in his will concerning his residuary estate or (where appropriate) wide discretionary trusts for the benefit of his family. The premiums on the policy may continue to be paid by the transferor and if met out of income may be exempt from inheritance tax within the 'normal expenditure out of income' exemption. Otherwise, the premiums may be covered by the annual exemption. In the case of a policy taken out by or for the transferee, decreasing term assurance may be appropriate as the tax charge decreases as time elapses. In the case of a policy taken out by the transferor, however, decreasing term assurance may well be inappropriate since although the tax payable on the potentially exempt transfer will decrease, the amount of the potentially exempt transfer will be aggregated with the transferor's estate on death and may therefore operate to increase the overall rate at which his estate is taxed. Indeed, it may be worth considering additional insurance cover to meet this potential increased liability.

Who should pay the capital gains tax?

[2.39] If the gift gives rise to a chargeable gain which cannot be held-over, then the primary liability to the tax falls on the transferor. However, under TCGA 1992, s 282, if the tax is not paid by the transferor within 12 months from the date when it becomes payable, the transferee may be assessed and charged (in the name of the transferor) to the tax.

The advantage of the transferee bearing the burden of the tax is that if the gift is, or becomes (by reason of the death of the transferor), a chargeable transfer for inheritance tax purposes, the amount of capital gains tax borne by the transferee is treated as reducing the value transferred by the chargeable transfer (IHTA 1984, s 165).

It is possible that any agreement between the transferor and the transferee that the transferee should be responsible for the capital gains tax might amount to a 'gift with reservation' for inheritance tax purposes. However, even if this were to be the case, the reservation of benefit should cease on the tax being paid by the transferee, with the result that a second potentially exempt transfer would be made by the transferor at that time (FA 1986, s 102(4)).

The option of paying capital gains tax by instalments conferred in certain circumstances by TCGA 1992, s 281 applies whether the tax is paid by the transferor or the transferee.

Asset conversion

[2.40] The second basic way in which the inheritance tax payable on a person's death may be mitigated is by asset conversion. An estate comprising a portfolio of gilts and securities quoted on the Stock Exchange and a house worth in total (say) £500,000 will (at 2010/11 rates) suffer on death an inheritance tax charge of £70,000. If, however, that estate had solely comprised property which qualified for 50% agricultural property relief, the value of the estate for inheritance tax purposes would reduce to £250,000 and no tax would be chargeable.

This is an extreme example, but it illustrates the basic principle that in inheritance tax terms it is better for a wealthy client with surplus assets which he is not prepared to give away to invest those assets in commercially sound property which qualifies for some form of relief. The types of property most suitable for this exercise include the following.

(a) Agricultural property, tenanted or untenanted.
(b) *Woodlands*. Provided the statutory rules are met, full 100% business property relief should apply. Woodlands also have certain capital gains tax advantages for their owner. For a more detailed analysis, see **CHAPTER 12 WOODLANDS**.

(c) *Lloyd's underwriting assets.* Business property relief is available on a Lloyds' Name's interest in Lloyds. The relief differs depending upon whether the Name is an individual, a member of a SLP or LLP or a shareholder in a NameCo. An individual member at Lloyd's may qualify for business property relief on his Lloyd's deposit, his special reserve fund, his general (or personal) reserve and any assets which secure a guarantee or letter of credit issued by a bank to satisfy the means test up to the amount of the guaranteed sum. The relief will be subject to the overriding constraint that funds eligible for relief cannot be disproportionate to the level of underwriting as a whole. Business property relief is also available on the value of a Name's interest in a Lloyd's SLP or LLP, and the ancillary trust fund assets supporting them, and on the value of shares in a Lloyd's company. Business property relief is not available on an inter-available or third party auxilliary trust fund assets supporting a company. For a more detailed consideration, see **Chapter 16 Planning for Death.** Up to and including 31 December 2006, the Revenue has agreed that Names who have converted to underwriting through a NameCo can, within certain limits, attract business property relief on the value represented by interavailable third party assets put up as Funds at Lloyd's ('FAL'). 'Interavailable funds' are those used to support both the underwriting of a company and that shareholder personally.

(d) *Unquoted shares or securities in a company.*

(e) *Sleeping partner in unincorporated business.* An individual not wishing to take an active role in a business may consider becoming a sleeping partner of an unincorporated business or a member of a limited liability partnership. Business property relief of 100% will be available.

It must be remembered that in order to qualify for business property relief, agricultural property relief or woodlands relief, the deceased must have satisfied various conditions, relating, for example, to the period of ownership of the assets in question.

For the client with a surplus which he prefers not to realise and invest — either because he likes the existing investment or because to do so would give rise to a large chargeable gain — an alternative way of proceeding would be for him to borrow on the security of the non-qualifying assets (thereby reducing their value for inheritance tax purposes) and to invest the borrowings in assets which do qualify for relief. The interest on the borrowings can be a deterrent to this exercise, but in some cases — for example, where the asset purchased is shares in certain close companies or agricultural property which is subsequently let — loan interest may be deducted from his total income for income tax purposes.

One other device for converting assets not qualifying for relief into assets that do, although one which is extremely rare in practice, concerns shareholdings in publicly quoted companies. A controlling shareholding in a quoted company qualifies for 100% business property relief (IHTA 1984, s 105(1)(b)). A non-controlling holding does not qualify for any relief. If two or more individuals own shareholdings which together (but not separately) give control of a public trading company, they could transfer their shares to a newly formed unlisted holding company in return for shares in that company. The shares in the holding company would then qualify for 100% or 50% business property relief depending upon the size of the holding. Section 105(3) provides that business property relief will not apply to shares in companies whose only or main business is, *inter alia*, making or holding investments. However, under s 105(4)(b) the relief will still apply to the holding company of one or more trading subsidiaries.

It will be appreciated that the scope for the 'asset conversion' type of inheritance tax mitigation will be fairly limited. It is also a device to be used with care.

Asset freezing

[2.41] The third way of mitigating inheritance tax is by asset freezing.

Loans

[2.42] The simplest example of an asset freezing measure is a loan. This freezes the value of the monies lent in the lender's estate and, the borrower having invested the monies, allows any capital growth to accrue outside it. To ensure making the loan does not itself give rise to an inheritance tax charge, the loan is usually expressed to be interest free and repayable on demand, so that there is no immediate reduction in the value of the lender's estate.

Where the borrower uses the proceeds of the loan to purchase an asset which is not readily realisable, or which is only immediately realisable for a lower figure than its cost, and has no other liquid assets available to repay the loan and (for whatever reason) is not in a position to borrow funds commercially to do so, then it is conceivable that the Revenue may try to argue that although the loan is expressed to be repayable on demand there may be a possibility that it will not be repaid and therefore there is an immediate reduction in the lender's estate.

It is also possible that the Revenue may attempt to argue that the failure to charge interest represents a waiver of interest and may seek to treat this as a succession of gifts made over the duration of the loan. Such an attempt would be entirely misconceived.

It is sometimes suggested that any income arising from the benefit of the loan in the borrower's hands will form part of the total income of the lender under the income tax settlement rules. This is, however, a difficult argument to sustain because, even if a straightforward loan can be regarded as a 'settlement' for the purposes of ITTOIA 2005, Pt 5 Ch 5, it is necessary first to identify the settled property and then to show that income arises from that property. As the lender is merely exchanging the property lent for a chose in action (namely his rights against the borrower), the settled property can only be either the chose in action, which does not give rise to any income, or the proceeds of the loan in the hands of the borrower in which the lender would seem to have no interest. Nevertheless, the risk of some form of attack from the Revenue clearly exists (as witness the case of *CIR v Levy* [1982] STC 442, 56

TC 68 (Ch D)). The Revenue may attempt to argue that the loan constitutes part of a wider 'arrangement' that the interest would not be paid. In such circumstances, it may seek to argue that any income earned from the capital lent constitutes assessable income in the hands of the lender. In practice it is unlikely that the Revenue will take such an approach.

Another possible problem is the gifts with reservation provisions, but again it is difficult to see how a straightforward loan (even interest-free) could be regarded as a gift for the purposes of FA 1986, s 102. The Revenue's view on this appears to be that the grant of an interest-free loan repayable on demand is not a transfer of value but it is a gift because there is a clear intention to confer bounty; the property disposed of being the interest foregone (see HMRC Inheritance Tax Manual, para 14317). That view is clearly incorrect. The lender cannot be said to have disposed of property which is the interest arising on the loan because that 'property' has never existed. Nor can the lender be said to have disposed of the income arising on the investment of the money lent because that income has never belonged to the lender.

One also has to consider the pre-owned assets charge under FA 2004, Sch 15 where a lender resides in a property purchased by another with money loaned to him by the lender. The Revenue's view is that it does not regard the contribution condition set out in Sch 15, para 3(3) as being met. It is their view that since the outstanding debt will form part of his estate for IHT purposes, it would not be reasonable to consider that the loan falls within the contribution condition and therefore not reasonably attributable to the consideration, even where the loan was interest free. It follows that the 'lender', in such an arrangement, would not be caught by a charge under Sch 15.

The loan may be made either to an individual or to a trust. However, great care is required where a loan is made by a settlor and the trustees invest in income-producing assets. Any repayment of the loan to the lender may give rise to an income tax liability under ITTOIA 2005, s 633. This is broadly to the extent of the amount repaid if the trustees then, or in the future, have any undistributed income.

Where there is a trust with a life tenant and one or more remaindermen, an on-demand loan by the trustees to the remaindermen of assets in the trust fund will effectively freeze the value of those assets in the estate of the life tenant. It may be advisable to charge a modest level of interest on the loan as a means of countering the argument that there has been a partial termination of the life tenant's interest in possession.

A loan is a very effective and much used estate planning device. It is particularly attractive to moderately wealthy parents with some free capital who wish to help out their children but are reluctant to part completely with a part of their estate. The lender can always write off the loan over a period of time using his annual £3,000 exemption and may write it off completely by way of a potentially exempt transfer, if he later finds that he can do without the capital. (Whilst the loan and the subsequent release will undoubtedly amount to associated operations within IHTA 1984, s 268(1), s 268(3) will operate to prevent there being an overall chargeable transfer.)

Where no consideration is given for the release of a loan, the release can only be effected by deed. For a deed to be validly executed, the intention that the instrument is a deed must be made clear in the document. The instrument must either be signed by the person making it in the presence of a witness or be signed at the direction of the person making it in the presence of two witnesses.

Sales of assets

[2.43] A sale is another, but less obvious, type of asset freezing measure. If a father sells his cottage in the country to his son at full market value, any future growth in value will accrue for the benefit of the son. If the father goes on to spend the sale proceeds over a period of time, rather than to retain and invest them, then so much the better as he is reducing his own estate as well. Should the father wish to continue to occupy the property, then the gifts with reservation provisions will not be a problem as the disposal of the cottage will have been by way of a sale rather than by way of a gift. Care will need to be taken to ensure the sale of the property to the son is a transaction such as might be expected to be made at arm's length between unconnected parties if the father is to avoid a charge to income tax under the pre-owned assets regime. The disadvantage of the sale is that it could give rise to a capital gains tax charge for the father and also to a stamp duty land tax liability for the son.

Grants of option to purchase

[2.44] Another example is the grant of an option to purchase property at its market value at the date of the grant. On the exercise of the option any increase in value in the property will flow through to the grantee free of inheritance tax. The grant of the option must be made for full consideration, otherwise the existence of the option will not be fully taken into account when valuing the property in the grantor's estate on his death or on an exercise of the option (IHTA 1984, s 163).

The grant of an option for consideration will be treated as a disposal of a chargeable asset (with a nil base cost) for capital gains tax purposes and may give rise to a chargeable gain (TCGA 1992, s 144(1)). A gain may arise on the exercise by reference to the unencumbered value of the asset where the parties are connected (TCGA 1992, s 18(7)). It should be noted that a stamp duty land tax charge may arise on the grant of the option. It should also be borne in mind that options over land are only valid for a period of 21 years (Perpetuities and Accumulations Act 1964, s 9(2)).

The grant should not be a gift with reservation for inheritance tax purposes because no benefit is received by the transferor from the subject matter of the gift (the option) nor does he receive any collateral benefit referable to the gift.

If an option is allowed to lapse without being exercised, this may result in a transfer of value for inheritance tax purposes (IHTA 1984, s 3(3)) which is not capable of constituting a potentially exempt transfer (IHTA 1984, s 3A(6)).

Other arrangements

[2.45] There are other more sophisticated types of asset freezing arrangement. Those involving companies and partnerships are dealt with in more detail in **CHAPTER 10 THE FAMILY BUSINESS**. One such arrangement for a company (now usually an investment company) involves the creation of two classes of shares, one of which receives the present value of the company on a winding-up, which is retained by the original shareholders, and the other of which carries the excess value, which is given away. There is a similar arrangement involving the issue of deferred shares which is also dealt with in more detail in that chapter.

So far as partnerships are concerned, it is often the case that the entitlement of a retiring or deceased partner will be limited to the balance on his capital account plus his pro rata share of accrued profits. The effect of this is that any underlying growth in value in the partnership assets accrue for the benefit of the continuing partners, who will often be members of the next generation in a family.

Various insurance companies offer products designed to freeze the value of an estate at a given time. These products involve an individual making a capital investment which is treated as a potentially exempt transfer. The capital is invested in a single premium bond which consists of a capital fund and an income fund. The income fund provides an income from an endowment policy which if it is 5% or less will be free from higher rate income tax. For a more detailed explanation see **CHAPTER 7 INSURANCE**.

Conversion of capital assets

[2.46] The fourth basic method by which the inheritance tax payable on death may be mitigated is by the conversion of capital assets into income producing assets.

Where an individual has capital which he no longer requires or needs he may consider purchasing assets which produce income only for a given period of time. For example, income shares of a split capital investment trust which confer rights to receive dividends but not to assets on a winding up. As the predetermined winding-up date approaches the market value of the income share decreases. Thus, the investor receives a stream of large income payments (which he uses for his living expenses) matched by a decrease in the capital value of his investments which reduces the inheritance tax liability on his estate.

This method has a very limited application because of the additional rate of income tax being 50% and inheritance tax and capital gains tax being at the lower rates of 40% and 18% or 28% respectively.

Organisation of an estate

[2.47] The last topic to consider is the best way of organising an estate with a view to facilitating an easy and cost-effective administration after death. This aspect of estate planning should be kept in mind throughout the individual's lifetime and the following is a list of relevant points all of which are further considered in **Chapter 16 Planning for Death.**

(a) *Joint names.* If spouses acquire assets in joint names as joint tenants, the assets will pass to the survivor automatically on the first death without the delay and expense of the personal representatives of the deceased having to transfer them to the survivor. (Where the spouses die in circumstances rendering it uncertain which of them survive the other, they will be deemed to die in order of seniority (Law of Property Act 1925, s 184).) There may, however, be a number of good reasons for vesting assets in the sole name of one of the spouses, for example, where the other is a sole trader or partner in a trading partnership.

(b) *Foreign assets.* It is a costly procedure to register a UK grant, or to take out a fresh grant, in a foreign jurisdiction in order to obtain title to foreign stocks and shares. Small holdings should therefore be liquidated if possible before death. If an individual makes investments abroad, either they should be registered in the name of a UK nominee company, which will avoid the need for a foreign grant, or he should be encouraged to consider indirect investment through a UK unit trust or investment company. The same problems will be encountered with a foreign holiday home and can again be avoided by holding the property in the name of a nominee (which could be a UK incorporated unlimited company specially set up by the client for the purpose). See also **Chapter 18 UK Domiciliaries Investing Abroad** for more on this aspect.

(c) *Life policies.* These should be inspected to see whether the proceeds are payable to the insured's estate or are held in trust. If the former, then unless the insured leaves the proceeds to his spouse and the spouse survives the insured, they will give rise to an inheritance tax charge on his death. Where the proceeds are intended for the spouse and/or children, the benefit of the policy should be put in trust for them during the insured's lifetime. New policies should similarly be settled on trust from the outset. The additional advantage of the trust is that the policy proceeds may be paid out immediately following the death (on production of the death certificate) without the need to wait for a grant. See also **Chapter 7 Insurance** for more on this aspect.

(d) *Pensions.* Where the individual has a right of nomination over a lump sum death benefit payable under a pension scheme, he should be sure to exercise the right to avoid the benefit falling into his estate on death and possibly being charged to inheritance tax. The exercise of the right of nomination could in theory itself give rise to an inheritance tax charge, but provided the client is in good health at the date of the nomination (which will be presumed if he survives for 2 years) and does not subsequently vary that choice, it is understood that the Revenue treats the value transferred as being negligible. Where the benefit is payable under a discretionary trust, then he should make sure that the trustees are aware of his wishes as to their ultimate destination.

These lump sum death benefits can provide useful estate planning opportunities in that by directing the lump sums to his children and leaving his wife to inherit his free estate, an individual may leave all members of his family well provided for on his death without incurring any inheritance tax charge. Reference should also be made to **CHAPTER 8 PENSIONS** for more on this aspect.

(e) *Accident/death in service policies*. Similar considerations apply here. Where the individual has a right of nomination over the proceeds or may express wishes to trustees as to their destination, he should be sure to do so.

(f) *The will*. No client should ever die intestate. Not only is it usually more costly and more time consuming to obtain a grant of letters of administration rather than a grant of probate but also the trusts which can arise under the intestacy rules can be very costly to administer and they are unlikely to reflect the client's true wishes regarding the devolution of his estate.

Chapter 3

Introduction to Trust Law

Introduction

[3.1] In spite of the substantial changes to the taxation of trusts in 2006, trusts are still commonly created as an integral part of estate planning strategies. For those who do not have a legal background (and even sometimes for those more experienced in this area), trust law can prove to be particularly problematic. The aim of this chapter is to outline some of the key concepts involved and highlight potential problem areas. In addition, at the end of the chapter there is a more detailed examination of three areas: powers of maintenance, powers of advancement and protective trusts.

Trustees powers have been substantially widened in several important administrative areas by the Trustee Act 2000. These include the powers of investment, purchasing property, delegating investment management and other decision-making functions, and the power to employ nominees and custodians.

What is a trust?

[3.2] Probably one of the most useful definitions was provided by Sir Arthur Underhill, who described a trust as:

> An equitable obligation binding a person (who is called a trustee) to deal with property over which he has control (which is called trust property) for the benefit of persons (who are called beneficiaries or *cestuis que trust*) of whom he may himself be one and any one of whom may enforce the obligation.

This definition highlights three important areas: first, the duties imposed on trustees are equitable in nature. Secondly, the trustees' ownership of the property does not in itself allow them to benefit from it; they hold it for the benefit of the beneficiaries who own the equitable interest in the property subject to the terms of the trust. The trustees own the legal interest. Thirdly, the equitable rules binding the trustees can be enforced in the courts, primarily by the beneficiaries themselves.

Settlors

[3.3] As a general rule, if a person can give property away, he has sufficient legal capacity to settle the property. If a settlor subsequently becomes incapacitated, that does not invalidate any prior settlement he may have made.

The settlor must understand the nature of his actions in settling the property. *Bhatt v Bhatt* [2009] EWHC 734 (Ch), [2009] STC 1540 is a recent case, founded in the doctrine of mistake, where the court granted rescission of a trust deed entered into on the basis of a fundamental misunderstanding of its effects.

A settlor can establish a trust under which he is the principal beneficiary whilst also being the sole trustee. Legally he is regarded as acting in a number of different capacities. However, if the demarcation lines are not observed, the court may determine that the settlement was a sham and that no settlement was created.

Trustees

[3.4] Trustees are a continuing body of persons who hold the property in a fiduciary capacity on behalf of beneficiaries. Any person can be a trustee provided he or she possesses sufficient legal capacity. There is no requirement for trustees to be individuals and therefore companies can also act as trustees.

Legally, there are few restrictions on the number of persons who may be trustees, although practically there should always be two. This is because there has to be a minimum of two trustees to give a valid receipt for capital received on the sale of land, unless the trustee is a trust corporation. It is rarely sensible for there to be more than four trustees. This is because trustees must act unanimously and if there are too many trustees it may be difficult to achieve unanimity and administratively difficult to obtain the necessary signatures on documents. Four is the conventional maximum because there cannot be more than four trustees holding a legal estate in land (Trustee Act 1925, s 34(2)).

Beneficiaries

[3.5] A beneficiary does not have to be legally competent to benefit under a trust. However, a lack of legal capacity may have other ramifications. For example, where a beneficiary has a deputy appointed by the Court of Protection because he cannot manage his affairs, it does not mean that the trustees cannot exercise their discretion in his favour. It means that they cannot give him the money or property direct, as he is unable to give a valid receipt. Accordingly, the trustees would have to transfer the trust property to his deputy, appointed by the Court, who could then apply the property received for his benefit.

Making a trust

[3.6] In order for a valid trust to be created there must be an effective transfer of property by means of a complete gift on trusts, which are certain and not illegal. It is essential not only that the correct legal procedures are observed but that the donor completes the gift so that the gift is effective. Where the donor is entirely responsible for the delay, the gift will fail. However, as a general rule, if the donor has done all that he can in order to complete the gift but the delay is as a result of the inaction of a third party, the gift will be valid following *Re Rose* [1952] Ch 499, *T Choithram International SA v Pagarani* [2001] 2 All ER 492, 3 ITELR 254 and *Pennington v Waine sub nom Pennington v Crampton* [2002] EWCA Civ 227, [2002] 4 All ER 215.

Whilst no particular form of wording is required to establish a trust, its terms must be certain. In *Knight v Knight* (1840) 3 Beav 148, Lord Longdale identified three certainties that had to be present before a valid trust could exist namely, certainty of words, of subject matter and of the persons or objects intended to benefit under the terms of the deed.

No illegality

[3.7] Over the centuries, case law has evolved indicating that in certain circumstances trusts may be held to be invalid where the object of the trust is clearly illegal, or where recognising their full effect would not be in the public interest.

(a) *Perpetuities.* Under English law, property must vest in a beneficiary within the perpetuity period. The rules relating to perpetuity periods have been reformed by the Perpetuities and Accumulations Act 2009 (the 'New Regime') which came into effect on 6 April 2010. The new legislation is not retrospective and therefore the pre-existing legislation, the Perpetuities and Accumulations Act 1964 (the 'Old Regime') will continue to apply to existing trusts and wills. A will executed prior to 6 April 2010 is subject to the Old Regime, even where the testator's death occurs after 5 April 2010. Under the Old Regime the maximum duration of a trust established after 1964 may be the period of the lifetimes of one or more persons living when the trust is created plus 21 years (the 'Common Law Period') or a fixed period of up to 80 years. The fixed period only applies if specified in the trust. Where an existing will or trust has a Common Law Period and the trustees believe that it is 'difficult or not reasonably practicable for them to ascertain whether the perpetuity period has ended' they may, by deed, irrevocably elect for a perpetuity period of 100 years to apply (Perpetuities and Accumulations Act 2009, s 12). Lifetime trusts made after 5 April 2010 will be subject to the New Regime. Will Trusts will only be subject to the New Regime if the will was executed after 5 April 2010. Under the New Regime the perpetuity period of trusts is 125 years. This period applies irrespective of any period specified in the trust deed (Perpetuities and Accumulations Act 2009, s 5(1)).
Charitable trusts have no perpetuity period limitations.

(b) *Accumulations.* The rule on accumulations of income was introduced to avoid the excessive build-up of wealth in trusts. For settlements created before 6 April 2010 the Perpetuities and Accumulations Act 1964 and Law of Property Act 1925 provides that the permitted accumulation periods are as follows.

(i) The life of the settlor in relation to lifetime settlements where no other period is specified;

(ii) 21 years from the date of death of the settlor or the testator (in the case of will trusts this period will apply where no other period is specified);

(iii) The minority or minorities of any person benefiting under the terms of the trust who was alive at the time the trust is made;

(iv) The minority or minorities of any person who would for the time being, if of full age, be entitled to the income directed to be accumulated;

(v) 21 years from the date of making the disposition;

(vi) The minority or minorities of the persons living or *en ventre sa mere* at the death of the settlor.

Where there was a direction to accumulate for a period in excess of the statutory periods specified above, the entire gift was void if that period was also longer than the perpetuity period. However, where the accumulation period does not exceed the perpetuity period, the direction to accumulate was only invalid as to the excess over the statutory period.

For settlements created after 5 April 2010 the restrictions listed above do not apply. They have been removed by the Perpetuities and Accumulations Act 2009. For settlements created after 5 April 2010 the trustees may retain income within the trust without having to distribute it to the beneficiaries for the entire lifetime of the trust. Trustees of charitable trusts may accumulate income for a period of 21 years only or during the life of the settlor or one of the settlors (Perpetuities and Accumulations Act 2009, s 14).

(c) *Bankruptcy.* Any gift, transaction in consideration of marriage, or sale at an undervalue where the price paid is significantly less than the value of the assets sold in money or moneys' worth will amount to a transaction at an undervalue within the terms of the Insolvency Act 1986. There are four possible situations where the court can set aside such transactions:

(i) Where a petition leading to adjudication in bankruptcy is presented within two years. It is not necessary to prove that the transaction was intended to prejudice creditors or to establish the financial status of the donor at the time of the transaction (IA 1986, s 341).

(ii) Where it pre-dates the presentation of the bankruptcy petition by more than 2 but less than 5 years. The donor must either have been insolvent at the time that the transaction was undertaken or have become insolvent as a result of the transaction. For these purposes a donor is deemed to be insolvent if he cannot pay his debts as they fall due or if the value of his liabilities exceed the value of his assets after taking into account cash flow factors. Where the transaction is with an associate of the donor the burden of proof is on the donor (IA 1986, s 341(2)). The trustee of a family trust will be an associate of the donor where the trust beneficiaries include, or the terms of the trust confer a power that may be exercised for the benefit of, the donor or his associate (IA 1986, s 435(5)).

(iii) Where it can be proved to the court's satisfaction that the transaction at an undervalue was undertaken by the donor in order to put his assets beyond the reach of his existing or future creditors (IA 1986, s 423). In the case of *IRC v Hashmi* [2002] EWCA Civ 981 (CA) the issue arose as to whether it was necessary for an applicant under s 423(3) to show that the statutory purpose had been the dominant purpose behind the transaction, or whether it was sufficient that the statutory purpose was a substantial purpose. The Court of Appeal held that the statutory purpose did not have to be the sole or predominant purpose.

(iv) Where the donor becomes bankrupt as a result of a crime the property can be recovered without any regard to a time limitation.

The result of the transactions being set aside is that they will be void *ab initio* — that is, they will be treated as not having taken place.

Divorce

[3.8] On a divorce a trust will not, by itself, avoid a division of property between the parties (see also **CHAPTER 15 MATRIMONIAL BREAKDOWN**).

First, the court will have jurisdiction under Matrimonial Causes Act 1973, s 24 to make a property adjustment order in relation to the marriage under s 24(1) of the Act. The court has the power to make one or more property adjustment orders as it thinks fit.

Second, it might be tempting for a spouse to give away family wealth so as to exclude the current spouse from benefiting on divorce. Under s 37, a disposition may be set aside if it is made with the intention of preventing financial relief being granted to a party to the marriage. Where an application is made to the court within 3 years of the settlement there is a rebuttable presumption that the settlement was made with the intention to defeat a claim for financial relief (MCA 1973, s 37(5), see *Whittingham v Whittingham* [1978] 3 All ER 805).

The court can also have regard to the availability of other trust funds, not falling within any of the above categories, to be taken into account in dividing the family assets on divorce. In *Browne v Browne* (1988) Times, 25 November, the Court of Appeal held that assets held outside the jurisdiction on discretionary trusts in favour of one spouse were financial resources to be taken into account in considering the other spouse's application in matrimonial proceedings for financial relief. Where a spouse has an interest in a settlement, the Court will ask what the beneficiary may reasonably expect to receive from the settlement, see *J v J* [1989] 1 All ER 1121. More recent cases (*Thomas v Thomas* [1996] 2 FCR 544, [1995] 2 FLR 668 and *Charman v Charman* [2007] EWCA Civ 503, 9 ITELR 913) have reformed the court's approach in undertaking this exercise.

Inheritance laws

[3.9] Unlike most civil law jurisdictions, English law does not impose forced heirship or reserved property rights. For example, a Frenchman is required under the Code Napoleon to leave a very substantial portion of his estate to his surviving lineal descendants where he is survived by his issue.

By way of contrast, under English common law a testator's spouse and children have no legal right to inherit a fixed proportion of his estate. However, when a person dies domiciled in England and Wales, the court has power after death to make provision out of the deceased's net estate for the following.

(i) The deceased's spouse or civil partner.
(ii) A former spouse or civil partner of the deceased who has not remarried or entered into a new civil partnership or any person who, for the whole period of 2 years ending immediately prior to the date of death, was living in the same household as the deceased and as the husband, wife or civil partner of the deceased. This is designed to deal with cohabitees.
(iii) A child of the deceased.
(iv) A person treated by the deceased as a child of the family in relation to any marriage of the deceased.
(v) A dependant of the deceased.

This applies irrespective of whether the deceased left a will or died intestate (Inheritance (Provision for Family and Dependants) Act 1975).

Because the legislation only applies where the deceased is domiciled in England and Wales there have been a number of cases where the domicile of the testator has been challenged in the courts (see *Holliday v Musa* [2010] EWCA Civ 335, [2010] 2 FLR 702, [2010] Fam Law 702).

Applications under the Act must be made within 6 months of the date on which a grant of probate or letters of administration of the deceased's estate were first taken out. The court has an unfettered discretion to extend this time limit in appropriate cases. Where gifts predate the date of death by at least 6 years, they fall outside the ambit of the court's review. It would be unwise to rely on this, however, as it is at least arguable that such a transfer could be challenged under the law concerning fraudulent transfers and bankruptcy.

Trustees' powers and duties

[3.10] A considerable body of case law has evolved over the years clarifying trustees' powers and duties. In addition, relevant legislation includes the Trustee Act 1925, Trustee Investments Act 1961, the Trusts of Land and Appointment of Trustees Act 1996 and the Trustee Act 2000. These are discussed in outline in this chapter. Where lay trustees are involved, the court judges the actions of the trustees by reference to the standard of behaviour that would be expected of an ordinary and sensible businessman. However, a higher standard of care and skill is expected of professional trustees.

When accepting the position of trustee, there are three key areas which require immediate action. First, the trustee should ensure that he understands the trusts involved. In the event of any ambiguity the trustee is under an obligation to clarify matters as soon as possible. It is also essential for the trustee physically to examine the trust instrument. For example, this may reveal a notice of assignment by a beneficiary of a beneficial interest. If the trustee were unaware of this he might distribute trust property to the wrong claimant.

Secondly, all property should be placed in the joint names of the trustees or in proper custodial care. Where a new trustee is appointed to a continuing trust, or where he replaces an existing trustee, certain categories of trust property will automatically vest in the trustees as a result of Trustee Act 1925, s 40 where the appointments are by deed and the relevant declaration is made. The category of assets where automatic vesting occurs is restricted but includes freehold land and bank accounts. It does not extend, for example, to land conveyed by way of mortgage for securing money subject to the trust, certain leases of land, life assurance policies or stocks and shares.

Thirdly, where the trustee appointed succeeds another he may, in the absence of unduly suspicious circumstances, safely assume that the previous trustees have acted properly in discharging their duties. However, where there are suspicious circumstances suggesting earlier previous breaches of trust, he is under a duty to investigate these matters.

Investments

[3.11] Trustees are under a duty to invest trust funds, maintaining an even balance between beneficiaries where they have differing interests in relation to income and capital. Lord Lindley, Master of the Rolls, stated in *Whiteley (Re)* [1910] 1 Ch 600 that the duty of care expected of a trustee is:

> to take such care as an ordinary prudent man would take if he were minded to make an investment for the benefit of other people for whom he felt morally bound to provide.

A leading case on trustees' investment duties is *Cowan v Scargill* [1984] 2 All ER 750. The Vice-Chancellor Sir Robert Megarry's comments summarise the position of trustees as regards investment duties in general:

> [The] trustees [have] to exercise their powers in the best interests of the present and future beneficiaries of the trust, holding the scales impartially between different classes of beneficiaries . . . When the purpose of the trust is to provide financial benefits for the beneficiaries, as is usually the case, the best interests of the beneficiaries are normally their best financial interests. In the case of a power of investment . . . the power must be exercised so as to yield the best return for the beneficiaries, judged in relation to the risks of the investment in question; and the prospects of the yield of income and capital appreciation both have to be considered in judging the return from investment . . . .

Older case law continues to give valuable guidance on the application of general principles to various situations.

The trustees may only invest trust funds in investments authorised by the trust instrument or permitted by legislation.

The powers of trustees of land are governed by the Trusts of Land and Appointment of Trustees Act 1996 (TLATA). 'Trusts of land' are trusts that include land whether or not there are also other assets subject to the trust

(TLATA, s 1(1)(a)). Trustees of land have all the powers of an absolute owner and are given an express power to purchase land for investment (TLATA, s 6). The trustees must exercise these powers according to the statutory duty of care under the Trustee Act 2000 (see below).

With regard to other investments, trustees have a 'general power' of investment. This general power permits a trustee to make any kind of investment he could make if he were absolutely entitled to the assets of the trust (Trustee Act 2000, s 3(1)). This general power does not, however, permit a trustee to make an investment in land other than loans secured on land (Trustee Act 2000, s 3(3)). However, a specific power is given by the Trustee Act 2000, s 8 in relation to land.

In exercising any power of investment, a trustee must have regard to the standard investment criteria which are:

(a) the suitability to the trust of investments of the same kind as any particular investment proposed to be made or retained and of that particular investment as an investment of that kind; and
(b) the need for diversification of investments of the trust in so far as is appropriate to the circumstances of the trust (Trustee Act 2000, s 4).

The trustee is also required to review the investments of the trust from time to time and consider whether, having regard to the standard investment criteria, they should be varied (Trustee Act 2000, s 4(2)).

The general power of investment is in addition to powers otherwise conferred on trustees but is subject to any restriction or exclusion imposed by the trust deed.

'Suitability' includes consideration as to the size and risk of the investment and the need to produce an appropriate balance between income and capital growth to meet the needs of the trust. It also includes any relevant ethical considerations as to the kind of investment which it is appropriate for the trust to make.

Before exercising any power of investment, a trustee must obtain and consider proper advice about the way in which, having regard to the standard investment criteria, the power should be exercised. However, a trustee need not obtain such advice if he reasonably concludes that in all the circumstances it is unnecessary or inappropriate to do so (Trustee Act 2000, s 5(1), (3)).

The Trustee Act 2000, s 8 details the specific powers of trustees in relation to land. A trustee may acquire freehold or leasehold land in the UK for investment, for occupation by a beneficiary or for any other reason. This power is subject to any restriction or exclusion imposed by the trust deed. These provisions apply to all trustees and not just to trustees of land. However, the provisions do not apply to a trust which consists of, or includes, settled land.

The provisions of the Trustee Act 2000 apply to a trust whether or not it was created before, or on or after, 1 February 2001. It has been suggested that it is uncertain whether the Act applies to trusts which are not in writing (such as constructive or resulting trusts). The better view appears to be that it does.

Rather surprisingly, the Act does not widen the definition of investment derived from case law. Many assets popularly regarded as investments, such as life insurance policies and financial futures contracts are not investments within this definition.

Accounts

[3.12] Trustees are under a duty to maintain accounts, and produce them to the beneficiaries on request. Whilst the trustees are not obliged to provide beneficiaries with free copies of the accounts, this has evolved into normal practice. Beneficiaries with interests in the capital of the trust are entitled to see capital accounts, whereas income beneficiaries may see full accounts.

Under Trustee Act 1925, s 22 trustees may arrange for their accounts to be audited once every three years, unless good cause exists to increase the regularity. The audit fees will be payable by the trust. It is unusual for trust deeds to require trusts to be audited. Audit investigations can be instigated by either trustees or beneficiaries, by agreement or by the Public Trustee.

Distributing trust assets

[3.13] Trustees are under a positive duty to distribute trust assets to the correct beneficiaries. Where there is an overpayment of income or capital or payments are payable in instalments, adjustments can usually be made to later payments. The trustees can recover trust property where the payment is made to the wrong person, due to a mistake arising from an issue of fact rather than one of law. An aggrieved beneficiary, as well as having recourse against the trustees, can seek to trace the property given to the wrong person by the beneficiaries. This right extends to the proceeds of sale of the property concerned. However, it does not extend to the property itself where a *bona fide* purchaser for value has acquired it, without notice of the breach of trust.

Where trustees have acted honestly and responsibly, they may claim relief against liability for breach of trust in distributing property incorrectly under Trustee Act 1925, s 61. In any event it is good practice for the trustees to seek an indemnity from beneficiaries upon the trustees presenting their final accounts on termination of a trust. However, the trustees do not have an absolute right to such an indemnity or other discharge.

Duty not to profit

[3.14] Owing to the strict fiduciary nature of trusteeship, there is no entitlement to fees or remuneration other than those authorised in the trust deed itself, by a court or by statute. Trustees must not place themselves in a position of conflict as regards their fiduciary duties. They cannot purchase trust property, or derive any benefit from it, unless expressly permitted to do so by the trust instrument.

Trustee Act 2000, s 29(1) provides that, where no express provision as to trustee remuneration is made in the trust deed, a trustee which is a trust corporation is entitled to reasonable remuneration out of the trust fund except that this does not apply to trustees of charitable trusts. Section 29(2) provides that professional trustees not being a sole trustee (or a trust corporation) may also receive reasonable remuneration in the absence of express provisions in the trust deed, if the other trustees each agree in writing. Again, this does not apply to trustees of charitable trusts. Section 31(1) provides that a trustee is entitled to be reimbursed out of the trust fund for any expenses properly incurred by him when acting on behalf of the trust.

Trustees' decisions

[3.15] Trustees can only exercise powers which are available to them either under the terms of the general law including any statutory provisions, or under the express wording of the trust deed itself. Even where sufficient powers do exist, an effective decision will only be made where the trustees have directed their minds to the issues. Trustees have to consider all the circumstances of the case, and especially the legal consequences of any proposed course of action.

Trustees must make their own decisions, unless they are authorised to delegate them. A failure to make their own decisions will result in a purported disposition of trust property being a nullity (see, for example, *Turner v Turner* [1983] 2 All ER 745).

Delegation

[3.15A] The Trusts of Land and Appointment of Trustees Act 1996, s 9 allows trustees of a trust of land to delegate 'any of their functions as trustees which relate to the land' to a beneficiary of full age who is entitled to an interest in possession in land.

Agents

[3.15B] The Trustee Act 2000, s 11 provides that trustees may authorise any person to exercise any or all of their delegable functions as their agent. A distinction is made between charitable and non-charitable trusts. This chapter will deal only with non-charitable trusts.

The trustees' delegable functions consist of any function other than

(a) any function relating to whether or in what way any assets of the trust should be distributed;
(b) any power to decide whether any fees or other payment due to be made out of the trust funds should be made out of income or capital;
(c) any power to appoint a person to be a trustee of the trust; or
(d) any power conferred by any other enactment or the trust instrument which permits the trustees to delegate any of their functions or to appoint a person to act as a nominee or custodian.

The persons whom the trustees may authorise to exercise functions as their agent include one or more of their number, and a person who is also appointed to act as their nominee or custodian (Trustee Act 2000, s 12). A beneficiary cannot be authorised by the trustees to exercise any function as their agent, even if the beneficiary is also a trustee (Trustee Act 2000, s 12(3)). In addition, two or more persons can only be authorised to exercise the same function if they are to exercise the function jointly.

The statutory duty of care is limited to trustees only. It does not apply to an agent in the performance of his agency, although he will owe a separate duty of care to the trust under the general law of agency. Where a person is authorised under these provisions to exercise a function, whatever the terms of the agency, he is subject to any specific duties or restrictions attached to the function. A person who is authorised to exercise a power subject to a requirement to obtain advice is not subject to that requirement if he is the kind of person from whom it would have been proper for the trustees, in compliance with the requirement, to obtain advice, for example, a reputable independent financial adviser.

Where the trustees have a duty to consult beneficiaries and to give effect to their wishes, the trustees may not authorise a person to exercise any of their functions on terms that prevent them from complying with that duty. The duty is not delegable.

The trustees are able to authorise a person as their agent on such terms as to remuneration and other matters as they may determine (Trustee Act 2000, s 14). The trustees may not authorise a person to exercise functions as their agent on the following terms unless it is reasonably necessary for them to do so.

(i) A term permitting the agent to appoint a substitute.
(ii) A term restricting the liability of the agent or his substitute to the trustees or any beneficiary.
(iii) A term permitting the agent to act in circumstances capable of giving rise to a conflict of interest.

Where asset management functions are delegated by the trustees, a person may not be authorised by the trustees to exercise any of their asset management functions as their agent except by an agreement which is in writing or evidenced in writing (Trustee Act 2000, s 15). In addition, the trustees must first prepare a policy statement which gives guidance as to how the functions should be exercised in the best interests of the trust. This must be in, or evidenced in, writing. The agreement under which the agent is to act must include a term to the effect that the agent will secure compliance with the policy statement or, if the policy statement is revised or replaced, the revised or replacement policy statement.

Such restrictions impose complexity and confusion. The restriction that certain functions cannot be delegated and the restrictions relating to the delegation to beneficiaries only apply to the statutory power of delegation. These restrictions do not apply if the trust confers its own power of delegation (as is the case in the STEP standard form). It is reasonably clear that the same applies to the restriction relating to joint delegation and the matters which can only be delegated if reasonably necessary. It is arguable that the same applies in relation to the restrictions on asset management functions made by the Trustee Act 2000, s 15.

Nominees and custodians

[3.15C] Under the Trustee Act 2000, s 16, trustees may appoint a person to act as their nominee in relation to such of the assets of the trust as they determine (other than settled land), and may take the necessary steps to secure that those assets are vested in a person so appointed. Similarly, trustees may appoint a person to act as a custodian in relation to certain assets of the trust (Trustee Act, s 17). In both cases, the appointment must be in writing or evidenced in writing. These provisions do not apply to any trust having a custodian trustee.

The appointment of a nominee or custodian is subject to certain restrictions. Section 19 provides that a person may not be appointed as a nominee or custodian unless one of the following conditions is satisfied.

(1) The person carries on a business which consists of or includes acting as a nominee or custodian.
(2) The person is a body corporate which is controlled by the trustees.
(3) The person is a body corporate recognised under the Administration of Justice Act 1985.

The trustees may appoint one of their number as a nominee or custodian, if a trust corporation, or two or more of their number, if they are to act as joint nominees or joint custodians. The person appointed as nominee or custodian may also be appointed as custodian or nominee, as the case may be, or be authorised to exercise functions as the trustees' agent.

Generally, the trustees may determine the terms on which a person is appointed to act as a nominee or custodian as they so wish. They may not, however, appoint a person to act as a nominee or custodian on any of the following terms unless it is reasonably necessary for them to do so.

(i) A term permitting the nominee or custodian to appoint a substitute.
(ii) A term restricting the liability of the nominee or custodian or his substitute to the trustees or any beneficiary.
(iii) A term permitting the nominee or custodian to act in circumstances capable of giving rise to a conflict of interest (Trustee Act 2000, s 20).

The Trustee Act 2000 again imposes restrictions on the statutory powers contained in ss 16–20. These can, however, be overridden by suitable wording contained in the trust deed.

There are statutory provisions relating to the review of, and liability for, agents, nominees and custodians. These apply whether they were authorised or appointed under the Trustee Act, or under the trust instrument or by any enactment or any provision of subordinate legislation.

Whilst the agent, nominee or custodian continues to act for the trust:

(a) the trustees must keep under review the arrangements under which the agent, nominee or custodian acts, and how those arrangements are being put into effect;
(b) if circumstances make it appropriate to do so, the trustees must consider whether there is a need to exercise any power of intervention that they have; and
(c) if the trustees consider that there is a need to exercise such a power, they must do so (Trustee Act 2000, s 22).

An agent authorised to exercise asset management functions has a duty of review which includes, in particular:

(i) a duty to consider whether there is any need to revise or replace the policy statement;
(ii) if the trustees consider that there is a need to revise or replace the policy statement, a duty to do so; and
(iii) a duty to assess whether the policy statement (as it has effect for the time being) is being complied with.

A trustee is not liable for any act or default of an agent, nominee or custodian unless he has failed to comply with the duty of care applicable to him either when entering into the arrangements under which the person acts as agent, nominee or custodian or when carrying out his duty of review (Trustee Act 2000, s 23).

Where a trustee has agreed a term under which the agent, nominee or custodian is permitted to appoint a substitute, the trustee is not liable for any act or default of the substitute unless he has failed to comply with the duty of care applicable to him when agreeing that term or when carrying out his duty of review insofar as it relates to the use of the substitute.

There are wider obligations placed upon trustees of land to consult beneficiaries and give effect to their wishes so far as is consistent with the general interest of the trust (Trusts of Land and Appointment of Trustees Act 1996, s 11).

It is important to identify those powers which have to be exercised, and those where an element of discretion is present. The former are known as trust powers and the latter as mere powers. There is also a class of intermediate powers which are somewhere betwixt and between these two categories.

(a) *Trust powers.* These are obligatory, in that there is a direct legal requirement for the trustees to exercise them. This obligation arises from the intention of the settlor, and the courts will enforce the exercise of these powers if the trustees do not exercise them.
(b) *Mere powers.* These impose an obligation on the trustees to consider whether the power should be exercised, but they are under no obligation to exercise it. The trustees need only consider exercising the power where it would be appropriate to do so.

Making a decision

[3.15D] In the case of a trust power, the trustees have to make a decision within a reasonable length of time. However, in the case of a mere power the trustees simply have to consider periodically whether or not to exercise the power, and, if they think it is proper, to exercise it within a reasonable period of time.

The length of time the trustees can delay in taking a decision is unclear. In the case of a mere power, they will lose the ability to exercise it after a reasonable period of time unless there are special circumstances. By way of contrast, a trust power continues to be exercisable albeit only in favour of those beneficiaries who would have been eligible to benefit had the power been exercised promptly. Where the trustees fail to execute a trust power, a court itself will, if necessary, exercise it or procure its execution. In a case of a mere power a court is extremely reluctant to interfere unless it is clear that the trustees are acting improperly, or simply not addressing their minds to the issue at all.

The Hastings-Bass rule

[3.16] The *Hastings-Bass* rule is an exception to the general rule that a court will not interfere in a decision reached following the exercise of a trustee power or discretion. In *Hastings-Bass v IRC* [1975] Ch 25, [1974] 2 All ER 193, [1974] STC 211 the Court of Appeal stated that:

> ' . . . where by the terms of a trust . . . a trustee is given the discretion as to some matter under which he acts in good faith, the Court should not interfere with his action notwithstanding that it does not have the full effect which he intended, unless:
>
> (1) what he has achieved is unauthorised by the power conferred on him; or
>
> (2) it is clear that he would not have acted as he did:
>
> (a) had he not taken into account considerations which he should not have taken into account; or
>
> (b) had he not failed to take into account considerations which he ought to have taken into account.'

This was essentially a negative statement that a disposition would not be set aside merely because the trustees had misunderstood its true effect.

In *Mettoy Pension Trustees Ltd v Evans* [1991] 2 All ER 513, [1990] 1 WLR 1587 (at WLR 1621H) Warner J gave what has become known as the rule in *Hastings-Bass* a positive form as follows:

> ' . . . Where a trustee acts under a discretion given to him under the terms of the trust, the court will interfere with his action if it is clear that he would not have acted as he did had he not failed to take into account considerations which he ought to have taken into account or taken into account considerations which he ought not to have taken into account.'

It is this positive version of the rule that has been applied by courts at first instance in a number of cases (see *Green v Cobham* [2002] STC 820, 4 ITELR 784; *Abacus Trust Company (Isle of Man) Ltd v NSPCC* [2001] STC 1344; *Burrell v Burrell* [2005] EWHC 245 (Ch), [2005] STC 569; and *Sieff v Fox* [2005] EWHC 1312 (Ch), [2005] 1 WLR 3811).

In other cases the courts have said by way of obiter dicta that they would have applied the rule in the alternative to granting some other remedy (see *Amp (UK) plc v Barker* (2000) 3 ITELR 414; and *Gallaher Ltd v Gallaher Pensions Ltd* [2005] EWHC 42 (Ch)).

The most authoritative restatement and refinement of the rule has been provided by Lord Justice Lloyd in *Sieff v Fox* at paragraph 49:

> 'Where a trustee acts under a discretion given to him under the terms of the trust, but the effects of the exercise is different from that which he intended, the court will interfere with his action if it is clear that he would not have acted as he did had he not failed to take into account considerations which he ought to have taken into account, or taken into account considerations which he ought not to have taken into account.'

The formulation was affirmed as a 'comprehensive exposition' of the rule as it currently stands in the recent case of *Futter v Futter* [2010] EWHC 449 (Ch), [2010] STC 982.

The rule is closely linked to the duty of trustees, when exercising their powers, to take account of all relevant factors and to disregard all irrelevant ones. It is implicit in *Edge v Pensions Ombudsman* [2000] Ch 602, [1999] 4 All ER 546 (CA) that the decision of trustees may be invalid for breach of this duty.

The *Hastings-Bass* rule also applies to a power held by a receiver appointed by the Court of Protection under the Mental Health Act 1983 (*Pitt v Holt* [2010] EWHC 45 (Ch), [2010] 2 All ER 774, [2010] 1 WLR 1199). The rule may, therefore, apply to powers held by other classes of fiduciaries other than trustees.

As such the rule forms part of the spectrum of remedies and principles adopted by the courts in order to deal with documentary mistakes of various kinds which include:

(a) declaring a deed void as non est factum;
(b) rectifying a deed which fails to give effect to the true intentions of the parties; and
(c) setting a document aside on the ground of a mistake.

However, the rule in *Hastings-Bass* appears not only to apply in cases where more familiar remedies are not available but also has a threshold which is less onerous than the thresholds for these comparable rules.

This rule has proved useful in a number of cases as a means of avoiding disastrous unforeseen consequences. In *Abacus Trust Company (Isle of Man) Ltd v NSPCC* [2001] STC 1344, for example, a deed of appointment made by the trustees was held to be void ab initio on the grounds that they had failed to take into account the tax consequences of making the appointment on which they had been advised by leading counsel. In *Abacus Trust Co (Isle of Man) Ltd v Barr (re Barr's Settlement Trusts)* [2003] 1 All ER 763 (Ch D), the settlor's wishes were incorrectly communicated to the trustees and an appointment was made on that basis. It was held that although this was not an error by the trustees themselves, the trustees had failed to take adequate measures to ensure that they had received a correct version of the settlor's wishes. It was held that the appointment was voidable. In *Jiggens v Lowe* [2010] EWHC 1566 (Ch), [2010] STC 1899 income was appointed to beneficiaries absolutely. Subsequently the trustees were advised that their appointment was a deemed disposal for capital gains tax purposes giving rise to a significant tax liability. The trustees had not considered whether there was a capital disposal. The tax consequences were considered to be relevant and the deed of appointment was held to be void *ab initio*.

In the case of *Green v Cobham* [2002] STC 820, 4 ITELR 784 the rule was successfully applied. The High Court held that there was no room to doubt that had the then trustees of the will trust under consideration had regard to the possible capital gains tax consequences of an appointment which they had made, they would not have gone ahead with it.

In *Burrell v Burrell* [2005] EWHC 245 (Ch), [2005] STC 569, the trustees made an advance in ignorance of the fact that it would have disastrous inheritance tax consequences. On an application by the trustees, the court set the appointment aside. Similarly, in *Sieff v Fox* [2005] EWHC 1312 (Ch), [2005] 1 WLR 3811 the trustees exercised a discretionary power to make an appointment which had unfavourable inheritance tax and capital gains tax consequences which they had not foreseen. The court applied the *Hastings-Bass* rule to set the appointment aside.

The rule does, however, have its limits. In *Breadner v Granville-Grossman* [2001] Ch 53, Park J refused to treat a power of appointment exercised by trustees one day after the time limit, for its exercise had expired as having been exercised before its expiration. Park J held that to do so would have been an unwarranted extension of the rule transforming a power for the court to regard a transaction as void into a power to substitute a different transaction. Park J said that:

> 'It cannot be right that whenever trustees do something which they later regret and think that they ought not to have done, they can say that they never did it in the first place.'

Whilst the *Hastings-Bass* rule can be helpful in certain circumstances to avoid disastrous consequences resulting from the trustees' exercise of a power, it is clear that there are limitations as to its application and it is to be expected that the courts will take an opportunity in the future to limit the rule. The rule has been the subject of extra judicial criticism by Lord Walker and Lord Neuberger.

Historically, HMRC has declined to be named as a party to proceedings where the *Hastings-Bass* rule has been in issue. In June 2006, however, HMRC announced a change to their policy. Where large amounts of tax are at stake and/or where it is felt that it could make a useful contribution to the elucidation and development of the principle, HMRC will consider intervening. It will be particularly ready to intervene in cases where there would otherwise be no party in whose interest it would be to argue against the application of the principle (Revenue Interpretation 278). HMRC has stated that in the future it is likely that HMRC will take a more active role in resisting the extension of the rule. Interestingly, HMRC first chose to take part in the Guernsey case of *Gresh v RBC Trust Company (Guernsey) Ltd* 2009–10 GLR 216. This was somewhat surprising, particularly as HMRC had written to the Jersey Court in respect of *Re Seaton Trustees Limited* [2009] JRC 050 but were denied locus to intervene. HMRC were refused permission to be joined in the Royal Court at First Instance but that decision was reversed by the Court of Appeal. The Court of Appeal found that HMRC were not indirectly enforcing foreign tax but resolving an issue which may be important to them in enforcing foreign revenue legislation in its own country.

It was in *Futter and Another v Futter and Others* [2010] STC 982, that HMRC was joined as a party for the first time in an English court. An application was made to have capital appointments made to the settlor and his children from an offshore trust set aside because Mr Futter and his advisers were mistaken as to the capital gains tax consequences of these appointments. HMRC put forward various arguments to the court, including first, that where an appointment or distribution achieves its intended legal effect, any more remote consequences should be disregarded. It was held that no distinction should be drawn between effects and consequences for the purpose of the rule. Secondly, HMRC argued that the consequences of the trustee's mistake must be 'objectively significant' and, thirdly, that taking into account relevant considerations actually meant having the relevant issue in mind and then taking reasonable steps to consider the correct answer. These arguments were rejected by the High Court. There was no objective 'significant consequence' threshold test which the court could use to refuse an application of the rule. Where the trustees are obliged to take some fact into account before the power can be exercised, that factor must be the true state of affairs and not merely a reasonable but mistaken belief. The High Court did observe, however, that there is a limitation to the principle; namely that tax consequences may not be factors which the trustee is obliged to take into account if they are subtle or detailed. HMRC have been granted leave to appeal to the Court of Appeal and it is understood that HMRC are keen that the matter be considered by the Supreme Court if necessary.

The question as to whether the effect of the rule in *Hastings-Bass* makes the relevant transaction void or voidable has been described as 'difficult' to answer. A void exercise would have no effect in equity so as to alter the beneficial interests under the trust. A voidable exercise does have such an effect although it can be set aside on application by those interested in the trust. Where a transaction is voidable only the parties have the standing to seek to have it set aside whereas a third party who has been affected (for example, HMRC) would have standing if the transaction were void. In *Futter* the High Court determined that a declaration that a relevant transaction was void was discretionary and it held that the relevant transaction was void *ab initio*.

Unanimity

[3.17] The general rule is that trustees must make collective decisions. There is no 'majority rule' and all decisions must be unanimous. Where a difference of opinion arises, a trustee can quite validly endorse the views of the other trustees where he is relying on their greater experience or simply to avoid deadlock. The general rule will be overridden where the trust deed itself provides for majority decisions. Often in such cases the minority will have the right to record the fact that they dissented. It is unusual for any trusts, other than pension trusts, to include majority voting provisions.

Common powers over income

[3.18] Trustees will usually have powers to apply income in favour of beneficiaries. There are three main areas to consider.

(i) *Fixed entitlements.* Under many trusts, beneficiaries will have a definable and fixed interest in the trust's income. For example, X might be entitled to receive the income from the trust for his life with the remainder going to Y absolutely thereafter. Accordingly, the trustees have no discretion over the beneficiary's current entitlement, although they might have powers under the trust deed which permit them to redirect the flow of income.

(ii) *Powers of appointment.* In cases not within (i) above, principally involving discretionary trusts, trustees will have a power of appointment in respect of income. This will often enable them at their discretion, to allocate trust income amongst a wide class of potential beneficiaries. Usually the balance of any income retained is to be accumulated provided the accumulation period has not expired. Accumulation has the effect of transforming 'income' into trust capital. Where the accumulation period has expired, trustees cannot retain income and it has to be distributed amongst the income beneficiaries. However, trustees will usually retain an element of discretion as to who receives the income within this class.

(iii) *Powers of maintenance.* In the case of infant beneficiaries, it is quite common for express or implied trust powers to enable the trustees to apply income in their favour. The statutory rules introduced by Trustee Act 1925, s 31 enable trustees to maintain infant beneficiaries. The rules can be expressly or impliedly excluded, so great care is required in examining a trust deed in order to establish the trustees' powers. This aspect is considered in more detail below.

Common powers over capital

[3.19] There are four common types of powers that trustees may exercise over capital in favour of beneficiaries.

(i) *Powers of appointment.* These are usually exercisable in favour of a limited class of persons or objects. Limitations created following their exercise are treated as written into the original trust instrument which created them; they do not normally create a new trust. Lord Romer explained in *Muir (Williams) v Muir* [1943] AC 468 it 'is as though the settlor had left a blank in the settlement which [the donee of the special power of appointment] . . . fills up for him if and when the power . . . is exercise'. In some cases a special power of appointment can expressly or by necessary implication authorise trustees to remove assets from the original settlement, by making them subject to the trusts of a separate settlement.

(ii) *Transfers between settlements.* It is common practice to include wide powers of appointment or expressly authorise transfers between settlements. Some older trust deeds contain narrow powers of appointment which will not enable trust assets to be transferred to another settlement.

(iii) *Powers of allocation.* Such powers enable trustees a discretion to allocate assets amongst the various interests of the beneficiaries within the overall framework of the existing trusts without enabling the trustees to establish fresh or overriding trusts.

(iv) *Powers of advancement.* Advances of assets from the settlement, whether under an express power or under statutory rules, are not solely limited to outright payments or transfers to beneficiaries. They can include settled advances, altering or varying the trusts created by the settlement from which it was derived. This aspect is considered in more detail below.

Beneficiaries' rights

[3.20] Beneficiaries do not have an automatic right to interfere with the administration of a trust when its affairs are being properly run. However, where the trust administration is not being carried out correctly, the beneficiary can take steps to ensure proper administration and preserve his interests under the trust. This will almost invariably involve the assistance of the court. When a beneficiary considers that a trust is not being properly administered he can apply to the court either as regards specific issues, or generally. Similarly, a beneficiary can apply to the court where the trustees fail to take steps to preserve the trust assets. The right of application to the court has been considerably widened in respect of beneficiaries with an interest in property subject to a trust of land (Trusts of Land and Appointment of Trustees Act 1996, s 14). A beneficiary also has the right to see 'trust documents' and this is a proprietary right which exists independently of whether a court action has been commenced. Minutes recording the reasons for trustees exercising their discretion are generally private to the trustees (*Re Londonderry Settlement* [1965] Ch 918, [1964] 3 All ER 855).

The courts will not support attempts by the beneficiaries to limit or fetter the exercise of the trustees' discretion. In *Brockbank (Re)* [1948] 1 All ER 287 (Ch D) the beneficiaries were ascertainable and legally competent. Due to a disagreement with the existing trustee they wanted to appoint a new trustee. The court held that the power of appointing a new trustee was exercisable by the existing trustees, and that the beneficiaries could not usurp this discretion. Under the Trusts of Land and Appointment of Trustees Act 1996, s 19, beneficiaries under a trust who are of full age and capacity and together absolutely entitled to the trust property, in the absence of any person nominated to appoint new trustees in the trust deed, may give a written direction that a trustee retire from the trust or that a specified person be appointed as a new trustee. Where all the beneficiaries are known and of full age and capacity, they can bring a trust to an end. In the event that some of the beneficiaries have insufficient legal capacity, or where there is a prospect of as yet unascertained or unknown beneficiaries benefiting under the trust, the necessary consent for terminating or varying the trust will have to be given by the court.

Power of maintenance

[3.21] The Trustee Act 1925, s 31(1) provides trustees with an implied statutory power of maintenance where trust property is held for an infant beneficiary. This enables the trustees to pay trust income to the child's parents or guardian or otherwise apply it for their education, maintenance or benefit. In exercising their discretion the trustees have to consider the availability of any other fund which could be used, together with the legal obligations of any other person to maintain or educate the child. Any income which is not paid or applied in this manner has to be accumulated (s 31(2)). The trustees however, are able to apply such accumulations, or any part of them, as if they were income arising in the current year. This power is particularly interesting as it represents one of the limited number of ways of converting capital into income for tax purposes (*Stevenson v Wishart* [1987] 2 All ER 428, [1987] STC 266 (CA)).

Income at majority

[3.22] Another key feature of the statutory power of maintenance for minors is that Trustee Act 1925, s 31(1)(ii) provides that where a beneficiary has not already attained a vested interest in the trust income by the age of 18, the trustees must immediately pay to him the income of that property and any accumulations until either he attains a vested interest in income, he dies or his interest fails.

Excluding Trustee Act 1925, s 31

[3.23] Trustee Act 1925, s 31 cannot apply in any event where the trust predates 1926. It can be expressly or impliedly excluded by the trust instrument itself (*Turner's Will Trust (Re)* [1937] Ch 15, [1936] 2 All ER 1435) which makes the provision hard to 'pin down' so as to establish with any degree of certainty whether or not it does apply to a particular trust. In *Delamere's Settlement Trusts (Re)* [1984] 1 All ER 584, [1984] 1 WLR 813 (CA), Lord Justice Slade said:

> The present case well illustrates that the existence of section 31 . . . for all its obvious advantages and uses, could in one sense, be said to present a potential trap . . . In many cases the draftsmen may well be advised out of caution either expressly to provide that the section is to apply with or without stated modifications, or expressly to exclude its application altogether.

This power cannot apply where another beneficiary has a prior entitlement to receive the trust income; similarly an express direction to accumulate the whole of the trust's income would have the effect of excluding the statutory power. In addition, the provision has no application where income is distributable amongst a discretionary class of beneficiaries.

Unlike the statutory power of advancement considered below, the statutory power of maintenance will apply irrespective of the type of assets held by the trust. However, like the statutory power of advancement it is quite common for the draftsman to 'tinker' with the terms of the statutory power of maintenance in the instrument itself, usually extending the trustees' discretion so that they can apply income whilst disregarding other sources of income which might be available for these purposes.

The statutory power also has a curious side effect of apparently converting what appear to be vested income interests into contingent interests.

Entitlement to accumulations

[3.24] A beneficiary's entitlement to undistributed income accumulations will be primarily governed by the trust instrument. Where there is no such direction, a beneficiary with a vested income entitlement will become entitled to the undistributed income on attaining 18 or marrying or forming a civil partnership under that age. Similarly, he or she will become entitled to accumulations of income on attaining 18, or marrying or forming a civil partnership under that age, if as a result he or she thereby becomes entitled to the trust's capital.

Power of advancement

[3.25] The implied statutory power of advancement contained in Trustee Act 1925, s 32 represents a valuable planning tool. The power enables trustees to pay or apply trust capital to or for the benefit of those entitled to the trust capital. In this context it does not matter whether the right to participate in trust capital is to some or all of the property or that the interest itself is absolute or simply contingent upon some occurrence. Although the power has a number of important limitations, its great value is its flexibility — particularly in the case of settled advances.

Advancement and benefit have special meanings.

Advancement

[3.26] Viscount Radcliffe in *Pilkington's Will Trust (Re)* [1962] 3 All ER 622, 41 ATC 285 perhaps best summarised the meaning of advancement.

> [the] word "advancement" itself meant in this context the establishment in life of the beneficiary who was the object of the power, or at any rate some step that would contribute to the furtherance of his establishment.

He cited typical instances of such expenditure in the nineteenth century as being 'an apprenticeship or the purchase of a commission in the army or an interest in business. In the case of a girl, there could be an advancement on marriage'. However, the word does also have a slightly restrictive inference. Viscount Radcliffe commented that advancement had to some extent a limited range of meaning since it was thought to convey the idea of some step in life of permanent significance. There was a suggestion in another case that advancement would only really be appropriate where the recipient was starting to make his way in life (*Kershaw's Trust (Re)* 1868 LR 6 Eq 322). In reality, it is not clear how relevant these cases are in the modern context, and in any event the question is largely redundant because of the width given to the meaning of the word 'benefit'.

Benefit

[3.27] The actual scope of the term 'benefit' is immense being 'the widest possible word one could have' (*Moxon's Will Trust (Re)* [1958] 1 All ER 386, [1958] 1 WLR 165). It includes outright applications to the beneficiary direct as well as trustees settling funds on new trusts for a beneficiary (*Pilkington's Will Trust (Re)* [1962] 3 All ER 622, 41 ATC 285) even where the objective is to save tax (*Re Moxon's Will Trust* above). Also, in order to mitigate the charge to tax, an advancement can still be for the benefit of a beneficiary despite his not taking any direct financial interest in the property advanced (*Clore's Settlement Trust (Re)* [1966] 2 All ER 272, [1966] 1 WLR 955). Indeed, 'benefit' need not meet a 'need'. As a result, an advance of funds to establish a new trust for a beneficiary is perfectly proper irrespective of whether the beneficiary actually requires access to those funds.

When does Trustee Act 1925, s 32 apply?

[3.28] The provision of Trustee Act 1925, s 32 can be expressly or impliedly excluded by the provisions of the trust instrument. For example, an express power of advancement contained in the trust deed which does not refer to 'benefit' has been held to exclude the wider statutory provision (*Evan's Settlement (Re)* [1967] 3 All ER 343, [1967] 1 WLR 1294) whilst in *CIR v Bernstein* [1960] 1 All ER 320, 39 TC 391 (CA), a provision for accumulation was held to have the same effect.

The scope of the statutory power is also quite narrow. It only applies to trusts created or effective after the enactment of the Trustee Act 1925. It will not apply to capital money arising under the Settled Land Act 1925. However, it will apply to trusts of land. In a well-drafted trust deed it is quite common for the statutory power to be widened. Usually this relates to the requirement for consent by a beneficiary with a prior interest, and to enable the trustees to advance up to the entire expectant interest concerned. Both of these aspects are considered below.

Statutory limits

[3.29] Trustee Act 1925, s 32 cannot be exercised without the prior written consent of a beneficiary who is of full age and legal capacity and who would be prejudiced by the advancement. Following the case of *Forster's Settlement (Re)* [1942] 1 All ER 180 a power will be improperly exercised where there has been a failure to obtain the consent of a beneficiary who is incapable of being contacted, the court having no jurisdiction to provide the consent required.

The statutory power can only be validly exercised if no more than half of a beneficiary's vested or presumptive share is advanced. The value of the trust fund taken into account is the value at the time of the actual advance itself. As a result, if the value of the fund subsequently increases but a beneficiary has already received his maximum entitlement under the statutory power, no more can be advanced. Similarly, if the value of the trust assets decreases after a beneficiary has received his maximum entitlement — so that retrospectively it appears that he or she has received far too much — the other beneficiaries would not be able to challenge the prior advancement solely on these grounds.

Another limiting factor is the requirement that any advance must be brought into account as part of the share. However, if a beneficiary never becomes absolutely entitled, for example, because his interest ultimately fails, there is no liability to repay the amount advanced or bring it into account.

Settled advances

[3.30] Trustees exercising a power for advancement are normally able to advance funds on new trusts for the benefit of an individual beneficiary. There are, however, two limitations that have to be considered, namely the range of the powers possessed by the new trustees and the perpetuity period.

The trustees must take into account all of the terms of the new trusts, not only those under which the new trustees are likely to act in practice. Viscount Radcliffe outlined the starting point in *Pilkington's Will Trust (Re)* [1962] 3 All ER 622, 41 ATC 285:

> The law is not that trustees cannot delegate: it is that trustees cannot delegate unless they have authority to do so. If the power of advancement which they possess is so read as to allow them to raise money for the purpose of having it settled, then they do have the necessary authority to let the money pass out of the old settlement into the new trusts.

It is therefore necessary to look at the power being used to determine if trust assets can be passed to new trustees who also possess particularly wide dispositive powers.

Protective trusts

[3.31] A protective trust is a particular form of interest in possession trust. Trustees are directed to pay income to the life tenant but if he should sell his right to trust income or becomes insolvent, then his interest ceases and the income becomes held on discretionary trusts for him and his family. The Trustee Act 1925, s 33 provides the statutory mechanism for creating protective trusts. By simply referring to the term 'protective trusts' a draftsman can incorporate the trust provisions set out in s 33. The effect of the Insolvency Act 1986 must, however, be considered.

Protective or spendthrift trusts are particularly useful where a settlor has concerns over the financial stability or maturity of a beneficiary.

The statutory provisions state that where income (including an annuity) is held on protective trusts for the benefit of a person (called 'the principal beneficiary') for a period of his life or a lesser period of time ('the trust period') then the income will be held on the following trusts.

(a) Upon trust for the principal beneficiary during the trust period or until some event occurs whereby that beneficiary would lose the right to receive the income concerned. (This would extend, for example, to situations where the principal beneficiary purports to sell his interest or where he becomes bankrupt.)

(b) If the trust fails or determines during the trust period, then the income is to be held on trust for the remaining period for the maintenance and support of
    (i) the principal beneficiary and his or her immediate family; or

(ii) the principal beneficiary and the persons who would be entitled to the trust property and income if he were dead, provided that the principal beneficiary is not married and has no issue in existence.

The statutory wording can be modified by the trust instrument, and can only apply to trust instruments that post-date the Trustee Act 1925. In practice, a great deal of care has to be taken when dealing with such trusts not to inadvertently trigger the protective discretionary element. For example, in *Dennis's Settlement Trusts (Re)* [1942] 1 All ER 520 the execution by a principal beneficiary of a deed varying the terms of a protective trust caused the protective discretionary trusts to come into play. However, s 33(1)(i) expressly provides that advances under any express or statutory power will not bring the discretionary trusts into operation.

Because of the risk of a discretionary trust arising automatically if a beneficiary tries to dispose of his interest, it may be sensible to provide in the trust deed that the beneficiary's interest is terminable at the trustees' discretion.

Chapter 4

Creating Settlements

Introduction

Devolution by will

[4.1] The simplest way of passing one's wealth to succeeding generations is to leave it by will. Most parents, however, wish to provide for their children during their lifetime. That may be simply from an impulse of generosity or because the circumstances of their children's lives require help immediately rather than later. One's children, for example, may need an income to support them at university or to supplement their earnings in the early years of their career or they may need a house in which to live on leaving home or a more substantial establishment on their marriage. What is more, if one's estate does not pass before one's death its whole value will be brought into charge to inheritance tax. Of course, it is not only parents who wish to help members of a younger generation; grandparents, aunts, uncles, godparents and many others also want to do so.

Outright gifts

[4.2] For these reasons many people make transfers of wealth during their lifetimes. The simplest way of doing that is by way of an outright gift.

Often, however, outright gifts will not be the appropriate way of providing for the next generation. The donee may be too young to have the responsibility of dealing with investment assets or the freedom to spend substantial amounts of cash. A parent, or grandparent, needs to balance his desire to provide for those he loves and to establish their independence against the possibility that the possession of wealth at a young age may undermine their self-reliance and provide a temptation to indolence. The need to provide for a surviving spouse, particularly if that spouse is significantly younger than the other or there has been a previous marriage, may require one to divide rights over property over time. Certain sorts of assets are likely to be difficult to administer if their ownership is divided amongst a group of people wishing to take different approaches to their management. These problems are particularly acute in relation to share holdings in family companies and to farmland and commercial property.

Settlements

[4.3] All of these considerations require one to separate the control of assets from their benefit and to divide interests in assets between individuals either concurrently or over time. It is for these reasons that settlements have always been an important element in estate planning. Their flexibility and adaptability are now valued throughout the world and are, as much as physical inventions, a major achievement of the British genius.

Unfortunately the previous government regarded settlements as mere tax avoidance devices the use of which should be discouraged. From the introduction of capital transfer tax in 1974 until 2006, that tax and its successor, inheritance tax, had dealt with settlements in a conceptually consistent way. Where a person had a right to the income from settled property as it arose (an interest in possession) he was treated as if he were the beneficial owner of the property in which his interest subsisted. Where that was not the case (that is, where the settlement was discretionary) the settlement was treated as an independent entity suffering periodic charges at decennial intervals and a further charge on the settled property ceasing to be held on discretionary trusts. Various particular forms of favoured settlements were then given additional reliefs. The underlying concept was to approximate the taxation of settled property to the taxation of property held absolutely. This rational system of taxation has been replaced by a system designed to penalise the creation of settlements so as to discourage their use.

In this chapter we examine the regime which governs settlements made on or after 22 March 2006. **Chapter 5 Existing Settlements** looks at the rules governing settlements which were made before that date.

What is a settlement? — General principles of tax law

Definitions

[4.4] A settlement is defined for inheritance tax purposes as any disposition of property which is:

(a) held in trust for persons in succession or for any person subject to a contingency; or
(b) held by trustees on trust to accumulate the whole or part of any income of the property. The accumulation of income may be obligatory or subject to the exercise of a power to accumulate income surplus to that paid out by the trustees for the benefit of any persons; or
(c) charged with the payment of an annuity or similar payment for any period.

(IHTA 1984, s 43).

A lease granted for life or lives or for a period ascertainable only by reference to a death will also be treated as a settlement unless full consideration is paid (IHTA 1984, s 43(3)).

Both for capital gains tax and income tax purposes settled property is any property held on trust other than property held as nominee or for any person absolutely entitled as against the trustee or held for any person who would be so entitled but for being a minor or under a disability (or for two or more persons who are or would be jointly so entitled) (ITA 2007, s 466 and TCGA 1992, ss 60, 68). There is no generally applicable definition of a settlement for either income tax or capital gains tax purposes although the anti-avoidance legislation found in ITTOIA 2005 Pt 5, Ch 5 contains a definition of a settlement for the purposes of that legislation only.

Bare trusts

[4.5] It can be seen from the above that property held on bare trusts (ie property held by a trustee as nominee for another or where all the beneficiaries have absolute interests) does not fall within the definition of settled property for either inheritance tax, capital gains tax or income tax purposes.

Preliminary considerations

Duties of trustees and the terms of the settlement

[4.6] By creating a settlement the settlor gives up assets to trustees to be held upon stated terms for the benefit of chosen beneficiaries. Although the donor (or his spouse) may be a trustee of a settlement, thereby retaining a measure of control over the assets given away, their actions must be governed by the terms of the settlement and their powers must be exercised and their duties carried out solely for the benefit of the beneficiaries. The donor must consider the possibility of conflicts arising between his interests and those of the beneficiaries. While a settlement of quoted shares is unlikely to give rise to such problems, settlements of unquoted shares frequently do.

The introduction of new shareholders to a family company may make its management more tiresome, particularly if one or more of the beneficiaries for whom those shares are held (and who may, in due course, become the outright owners of those shares) are not, and have no intention of becoming, active participants in the family business. In these circumstances the settlor, if a trustee, must, unless the settlement otherwise provides, have regard to his duties as a trustee in exercising the powers and discretions conferred by the settlement rather than letting outside considerations (perhaps those which he has as 'founder' of the business) influence his decisions. The trustees cannot merely act upon the settlor's instructions.

If the settlor wishes to retain a power to exclude those beneficiaries who show no interest in the business from benefit and to concentrate the shares of the company into the hands of those who are active participants, it may be advisable for him not to act as a trustee of the settlement. He may then exercise this power, conferred upon him other than in a fiduciary capacity, without regard to any duty to the beneficiaries which he would have as a trustee.

Whilst it may be possible to 'unwind' a settlement which does not achieve the settlor's aims, the terms upon which the trust property is held may make the undoing complex and expensive because of taxation and professional fees. The unscrambling may place property in the hands of the 'wrong' beneficiary. Further, any provision enabling the settlement to be undone in favour of the donor may, as a result of the reservation of benefit rules, negate the intended estate planning benefits. The settlor must, therefore, be sure that the terms of the trust achieve his aims and that they are (within the limits imposed by taxation rules) as flexible as possible in order to enable the trust to be adapted as circumstances require.

Reservation of benefit

[4.7] On the creation of a settlement, one must consider the inheritance tax 'reservation of benefit' rules in FA 1986, s 102. In respect of trusts created after 17 March 1986, the settlor will be treated for inheritance tax purposes on death as beneficially entitled to the trust property unless he is excluded from benefit. If the settlor's spouse is a beneficiary this will not in itself bring the reservation of benefit provisions into effect (FA 1986, s 102(2), (5)). However, property distributed from the trust and used for the benefit of both the settlor and his spouse will not be property enjoyed to the settlor's entire exclusion and will therefore be property subject to a reservation. The value of the gift is not even frozen at the date on which it is made. The current value of the property in which the benefit was reserved will be taken into account in calculating the inheritance tax charge. This charge may arise on death or, if the settlor is subsequently excluded from benefit but dies within 7 years of the exclusion, on a deemed potentially exempt transfer which as a result of his death becomes chargeable (subject to the provisions relating to double charges in such circumstances under the Inheritance Tax (Double Charges Relief) Regulations 1987). The provisions of FA 1986, Sch 20 para 5 ensure that the value of any property representing or deriving from the original property will be taken into account in calculating the charge to inheritance tax in such circumstances.

To ensure that the trust property is enjoyed to the exclusion of any benefit to the settlor the terms of the settlement require careful scrutiny. It should be noted that a settlor as trustee of his settlement may be remunerated for his service without giving rise to a reservation of benefit provided the remuneration is not excessive.

Further, the possibility of a benefit being reserved to the settlor as a result of the nature of the property given away must not be forgotten. For example, a service contract with unusually favourable terms as to remuneration or duration entered into between the settlor and his family company may, in the light of the gift, fail to satisfy the requirement that the property must be enjoyed to the entire exclusion of the donor and of any benefit to him by contract or otherwise. Similarly, land given away which continues to be farmed by a partnership in which the donor is a partner may not be enjoyed to the exclusion of the donor unless a full rent is paid.

Income tax charged on pre-owned assets

[4.8] When considering creating a settlement, one must also consider the income tax charge on pre-owned assets. Intangible property which a UK resident and domiciled settlor transfers into a trust and any land or chattels from which the settlor continues to enjoy a benefit, either immediately following the settlement or at a later date, may give rise to an income tax charge. This is discussed in more detail in **Chapter 2 Lifetime Planning.**

This is particularly important because, once in place, many trust structures may be expensive or difficult to unwind, leaving the settlor with a choice of either doing nothing (and being liable to the income tax charge) or making the election to bring the assets back into his estate (to be treated as though they were subject to a reservation of benefit).

A specific exception provides that where the settlor has a reservation of benefit in the settled property, no income tax charge will arise under the pre-owned assets rules.

Example

In 2003/04, Mr Lawson created a settlement with a life interest for his son, Matthew. Mr and Mrs Lawson were not excluded from benefiting under the trust. Mr Lawson added a Constable painting to this trust. The painting was delivered to Matthew who hung it in his dining room.

As Mr and Mrs Lawson are not excluded from benefiting from the painting, they are treated as having reserved a benefit in it.

In 2010/11, Matthew asks his parents to look after the painting for him while he goes abroad and it is hung in their dining room.

Under the pre-owned assets rules, Mr Lawson enjoys possession of a chattel which he had previously owned and given away. A charge to income tax would arise if it were not for the fact that Mr Lawson has reserved a benefit in the painting.

Categories of settlements

[4.9] Before 22 March 2006, the most useful way of categorising trusts for estate planning purposes was whether an interest in possession in trust income existed. Since 22 March 2006, trusts may be broadly divided between those which are trusts of relevant property governed by IHTA 1984 Pt III, Ch III and those which are not. Trusts which are not relevant property trusts may be divided into five categories:

(a) trusts conferring an interest in possession which has existed since before 22 March 2006. In this book we refer to such interests in possession as 'existing IIPs' and they are dealt with in **Chapter 5 Existing Settlements**;

(b) trusts which either confer or are deemed to confer an interest in possession falling within IHTA 1984, s 49(1A). In this book we refer to such trusts as 'privileged interest trusts' and they are dealt with in this chapter except that one such type of interest, transitional serial interests, is examined in greater detail in **Chapter 5 Existing Settlements**;
(c) young children's trusts being trusts for bereaved minors falling within IHTA 1984, s 71A and age 18–25 trusts falling within IHTA 1984, s 71D which are dealt with in this chapter;
(d) existing accumulation and maintenance trusts qualifying under IHTA 1984, s 71 which are dealt with in **Chapter 5 Existing Settlements**;
(e) specially relieved trusts being various categories of trust receiving a special treatment which are also dealt with in this chapter.

The distinction between trusts conferring an interest in possession and those which do not remains important in relation to privileged interest trusts, existing IIPs and to capital gains tax and income tax.

Interest in possession trusts

[4.10] An 'interest in possession trust' is not defined in the legislation (except in relation to Scotland: see IHTA 1984, s 46) and so in order to determine whether a trust is an interest in possession trust one must turn to case law. The decision in *Pearson v CIR* [1980] STC 318, [1980] 2 All ER 479 (HL) established that only a beneficiary who has an immediate entitlement to income as it arises, net only of proper income-related trust expenses, has an interest in possession. Any dispositive powers of the trustees which may be exercised to withhold income from a beneficiary or direct it to another will prevent the beneficiary from having such an interest. Thus, in *Pearson* the trustees' power to accumulate the income of the beneficiary's share of the trust fund prevented the beneficiary from having an interest in possession for the purposes of capital transfer tax. The beneficiary could not require the income to be paid to him as it arose.

Relevant property trusts

Inheritance tax

Settling assets

[4.11] The settlement of any property will be a settlement of relevant property unless the settlement falls within one of the five categories listed in **4.9** above. Most settlements made after 21 March 2006 will be relevant property trusts. The settlement of relevant property will be a chargeable transfer and cannot be a potentially exempt transfer ('PET'). The settlement will therefore trigger a charge to inheritance tax unless it is covered by an exemption or relief or by the unused portion of the transferor's nil rate band. The exemptions or reliefs which might normally apply are:

(a) the annual exemption;
(b) the exemption for normal expenditure out of income;
(c) the exemption for gifts in consideration of marriage;
(d) the relief for business property;
(e) the relief for agricultural property.

Caution should be exercised when creating a relevant property settlement if other gifts are to be made at or about the same time. A potentially exempt transfer made before a chargeable transfer to a relevant property settlement, which subsequently becomes chargeable, will affect not only the amount of charge on the transfer to the settlement but also the decennial charge, and charges on distributions from that settlement for so long as the settlement continues.

Decennial charges under IHTA 1984, s 64 (see **4.13** below) are calculated in part by reference to the settlor's chargeable transfers in the 7 years before his death. An exit charge under IHTA 1984, s 65 (see **4.14** below) similarly takes into account such chargeable transfers either directly, in the case of occasions of charge before the first decennial of the settlement (s 68), or indirectly because the computation incorporates the computation made on the preceding decennial. If the settlor were to die in the first 7 years after the creation of the settlement, the potentially exempt transfers which he had made in the 7 years before his death would become chargeable. If those chargeable transfers were made before the creation of the settlement they will affect future decennial charges (under IHTA 1984, s 64) and exit charges (under IHTA 1984, s 65). So in deciding whether to make advances from the settlement in the period which ends before the earlier of the settlor's death and 7 years after the settlement is made, the trustees will not know the rate at which tax will be charged under IHTA 1984, s 65. In many cases it will be possible for the trustees to retain sufficient assets as a reserve to guard against this risk or to make some sort of indemnity arrangement but in order to avoid such problems it will usually be prudent to ensure that transfers to such discretionary trusts pre-date any potentially exempt transfers.

The amounts which can be settled without triggering an immediate charge to inheritance tax may be increased significantly if business or agricultural property is used. Business and agricultural property relief may be available at either 50% or 100% depending upon the nature of the property.

Where business or agricultural property would qualify for relief at 100% there is no inheritance tax advantage to be gained from transferring it out of a taxpayer's estate unless it is going to be converted, for example by a sale, into an asset which does not receive the full relief.

So, for example, if one holds shares in a family trading company which one expects to sell within the next 2 or 3 years for cash, one might settle those shares immediately so as to place them in trust with the benefit of the relief. There is, however, a potential trap here. As we shall see (see **4.14** below), on a distribution of property from a relevant property trust prior to the first decennial charge, the exit charge is calculated at a rate derived by reference to the value of property comprised in the settlement immediately after it became so comprised. For the purpose of this hypothetical charge, therefore, the property will not be able to satisfy the minimum ownership periods which are part of the qualifying period for these reliefs. That will not matter if the property continues to qualify for 100% relief but, if it does not, one could be in the position of either suffering an exit charge on advancing the property out of the settlement or suffering a decennial charge (see **4.13** below). What is more, settling such property will have the result that on the settlor's death its base cost for capital gains tax purposes will not be adjusted to its then market value as it would have been had it not been settled.

Of course, there will often be good commercial and other non-fiscal reasons for settling business or agricultural property. Unfortunately, it most circumstances there will be a tax penalty in doing so.

Taxation of the trustees

[4.12] In deciding whether to make a relevant property settlement one obviously needs to consider how the trust will be taxed over its life.

There are two occasions of charge. The settlement will be subject to a decennial charge on each tenth anniversary of its being made and an exit charge applies whenever property, which is relevant property ceases to be so.

Decennial charge

[4.13] At each decennial of a relevant property settlement an inheritance tax charge arises which is calculated as though a transfer of value equal to the value of the property in the settlement, together with the value of property in any related settlement immediately after it commenced, had been made at that date by an individual who had a cumulative total equal to:

(a) the value of chargeable transfers made by the settlor in the 7 years prior to the creation of the settlement; plus
(b) the amounts upon which inheritance tax has been charged on distributions from the settlement made by the trustees in the preceding 10 years.

It is accepted by HMRC that undistributed income retained by the trustees but not as yet accumulated does not fall within the charge (Statement of Practice SP 8/86).

Other settlements made on the same day by the same settlor will be 'related settlements' unless the property is held for charitable purposes only (IHTA 1984, s 62). Whether or not they are relevant property settlements, the property comprised in them immediately after they commence will be taken into account when calculating the decennial charge and the exit charge. Thus, a settlor should not create a relevant property settlement on the same day as any other settlement.

If the settlor's cumulative total was nil immediately before the creation of the settlement and there have been no distributions from the settlement in the 10 years preceding the anniversary in question, no charge will be levied provided the value of property in the settlement does not exceed the current nil rate band of inheritance tax. It is for this reason that a settlor, with property worth less than £325,000 in 2010/11 which will increase substantially in value over the next 10 to 20 years, who has made no previous chargeable transfers and does not anticipate distributions being made from a settlement for some considerable length of time, may be best advised to create several discretionary settlements on separate days. He should divide the assets to be transferred between these settlements in the hope that a charge to inheritance tax may be avoided, at least on the first decennial (and consequently on distributions between the first and second decennial-year anniversaries, see below), because the property comprised in each separate settlement has not, by the time of the first decennial risen to a value greater than the nil rate band after deducting the settlor's cumulative transfers at the time immediately before each settlement is made. The settlor may, thereby, buy himself more time in determining which beneficiaries are to benefit and permit further beneficiaries to be born into the class. The disadvantages of this strategy are the additional administration burdens of doing so and the professional fees and other costs of creating and administering on a continuing basis multiple settlements.

It had been thought that HMRC might claim that multiple settlements made in this way were in fact single composite settlements under what used to be referred to as the *Ramsay* principle (*Ramsay (WT) Ltd v IRC* [1982] AC 300, [1981] 1 All ER 865, [1981] STC 174). It is now recognised that the *Ramsay* line of cases is not a principle at all but merely a number of examples of the general approach to construction that legislation is to be construed in the light of its purpose and applied to a realistic view of the relevant facts (*Barclays Mercantile Business Finance Ltd v Mawson (Inspector of Taxes)* [2004] UKHL 51, [2005] 1 AC 684, [2005] STC 1). It would not appear to be a realistic view of the facts in such an argument, to view seven settlements made on seven separate days as being a single settlement. Even if the differences between settlements are small and, in practice, largely artificial it is likely that the individual integrity of the settlements will be respected by the courts as it was in the case of *CIR v Rysaffe Trustee Co (Channel Islands) Ltd* [2003] STC 536 (CA).

If the trustees have power to retain undistributed income, it should not be necessary to distribute that income prior to a decennial. Any *undistributed* or *income which has not been accumulated* will not suffer a charge to inheritance tax at that time although accumulated income will (Statement of Practice SP 8/86).

Exit charges

[4.14] Distributions from a relevant property settlement are charged at a proportion of the effective rate charged at the previous decennial or, if the distribution is made prior to the first decennial at a rate resulting from a special computational basis (IHTA 1984, s 68). The proportion is 1/40th for each complete quarter from the last decennial (or the creation of the settlement) and the date of distribution (IHTA 1984, s 69).

On any distribution prior to the first decennial under IHTA 1984, s 68, the rate of tax is calculated as though an individual with the cumulative total of the settlor immediately prior to the creation of the settlement had made a transfer of value equal to the total of:

(a) the value of the property in the settlement immediately after it commenced; plus
(b) the value of any added property at the date of the addition; plus
(c) the value of any property in a related settlement (see above) immediately after its commencement.

The effective rate of inheritance tax so determined is applied to any distribution made from the settlement prior to the first decennial.

The rate of charge is multiplied by a fraction of which the numerator is the number of complete successive quarters that has elapsed from the creation of the settlement to the date of the exit charge and the divisor is 40. Thus the earlier the distribution, the lower the rate.

The value of the distribution is calculated by reference to the fall in value of the fund. If the tax is to be paid out of property remaining in the settlement, the reduction in value includes the amount of inheritance tax so payable.

As a result of this method of charging inheritance tax, where the settlor, immediately prior to the creation of a relevant property settlement, has made no chargeable transfers in the previous 7 years and the value of property comprised in the settlement immediately after it commenced, together with the value of later additions, did not exceed the maximum amount that can (at the time of distribution) be transferred without incurring a charge to inheritance tax (£325,000 for 2010/11) distributions from a relevant property settlement may be made free of inheritance tax before the first decennial. This is because the rate of tax for distributions before that date is under these circumstances fixed at nil. However, where the property settled qualifies for agricultural or business property relief, no such relief is taken into account when determining the applicable rate under IHTA 1984, s 65. It is necessary to ensure that the economic value of the property settled falls below the nil rate band unless appointments of property which qualify for 100% agricultural or business property relief are to be made before the first decennial.

Payments received by a beneficiary from trustees of a discretionary settlement which form part of his income do not suffer an inheritance tax charge on distribution to him (IHTA 1984, s 65(5)(b)). This power to convert capital back to income may be valuable if:

(i) the tax paid by the trustees may thereby be recovered; or
(ii) it is used to distribute accumulated income from a discretionary trust prior to a decennial without incurring an inheritance tax charge, thereby reducing the property in the settlement for the purposes of that decennial.

Added property

[4.15] Care must be taken if at any time property is to be added to an existing relevant property settlement. If the settlor has made any chargeable transfers since creating the settlement, his cumulative total prior to the date of any addition, if greater, may be substituted for his pre-settlement cumulative total for the purposes of calculating the rate of inheritance tax on the subsequent decennial (IHTA 1984, s 67). In calculating the settlor's cumulative transfers prior to the date of addition, one ignores transfers which were themselves additions to the settlement. It should be noted, however, that this only applies where a settlor makes an addition to a settlement by way of chargeable transfer; his annual exemption may, for example, be used to top up relevant property settlements without adverse effect as may transfers falling within the normal expenditure out of income rules outlined earlier. Additions may therefore be made before the first decennial without affecting the rate at that time if the settlor's nil rate band (including any uplift since the creation of the settlement) has not been fully utilised.

Creation of several relevant property settlements

[4.16] It should be possible to take advantage of the rules relating to nil rate band trusts (described above) by adopting either a 'cascade' of relevant trusts, or by using the 'added property strategy'.

The 'cascade' strategy

Under this approach a series of pilot relevant property settlements are established at intervals over a period of time by a settlor with no history of chargeable transfers (and ideally no potentially exempt transfers) made within the last 7 years. For example, the establishment of ten successive settlements of £32,500 would have the result that the first settlement of £32,500 would itself have to reach £325,000 in value at its decennial before paying any inheritance tax. However, the 'clock' of each subsequent settlement would take into account the earlier settled gifts, with the scope for future inheritance tax-free growth in the later trusts being reduced accordingly. A practical disadvantage of this approach is that the number of trusts involved may be unwieldy and might be difficult to co-ordinate. For administrative convenience the property in the various trusts could be advanced to one trust. IHTA 1984, s 281 will treat the transferred assets as continuing to be held on separate trusts for inheritance tax purposes but for both income tax and capital gains tax purposes they will be treated as a single trust.

Example

Discretionary Trust No.	*Initial value*	*Available 'margin' for future growth*
	£	£
1	32,500	292,500
2	32,500	260,000
3	32,500	227,500
4	32,500	195,000
5	32,500	162,500
6	32,500	130,000
7	32,500	97,500
8	32,500	65,000

Discretionary Trust No.	***Initial value***	***Available 'margin' for future growth***
	£	***£***
9	32,500	32,500
10	32,500	Nil
	£325,000	£1,462,500

The 'added property strategy'

As outlined earlier, chargeable additions should rarely be made to existing settlements, due to IHTA 1984, s 67. Where such additions have occurred the settlor's prior transfers to be taken into account under IHTA 1984, s 66(5) will be the greater of:

(i) the cumulative total of the settlor's chargeable transfers made during the period of 7 years, ending with the commencement of the settlement, but disregarding transfers made on that day; and
(ii) the aggregate of his chargeable transfers in the 7 years preceding the addition, whilst similarly disregarding transfers made on that day. In addition, no account is to be taken of the value of transfers to the trust to the extent that these have been taken into account under IHTA 1984, ss 65 and 66.

Although complex, these rules can be used to a settlor's advantage.

Example

An individual who has made no inheritance tax transfers establishes five relevant property settlements A, B, C, D and E at 3-monthly intervals, each with initial cash gifts of £5,000. He then makes further cash additions of £60,000 to each trust all on the same day. Ignoring the availability of his annual exemptions, the margin for growth of each trust is as follows.

	A	*B*	*C*	*D*	*E*
Initial value	5,000	5,000	5,000	5,000	5,000
Added property	60,000	60,000	60,000	60,000	60,000
Trusts 'clock'	–	5,000	10,000	15,000	20,000
	65,000	70,000	75,000	80,000	85,000
Margin for growth	260,000	255,000	250,000	245,000	240,000
Nil rate band	£325,000	£325,000	£325,000	£325,000	£325,000

At the decennials of the settlements, the effect of IHTA 1984, s 67(3)(b)(i) is that each trust is looked at in isolation, ignoring the others. These trusts should never be subject to inheritance tax either in respect of an 'exit' charge under s 65 or a decennial charge.

The total scope for future growth taking all of the trusts together is £1,250,000.

Not a single settlement

[4.17] The Revenue had claimed that techniques such as these, in which settlements are created successively, create single settlements by associated operations at the time that the final settlement was made.

In the case of *CIR v Rysaffe Trustee Co (Channel Islands) Ltd* [2003] STC 536 (CA) two brothers each made five discretionary settlements by separate trust instruments. Each settlement was in exactly the same form, except for the date which was inserted by the settlors' solicitors after the execution of the deeds. The trust fund of each settlement was £10 paid by each settlor. When the settlements were made, the settlors intended to issue bonus deferred shares in a private company (of which they were shareholders and directors) and to transfer these to the trustee, one fifth of the total for each settlement. Those transfers subsequently took place, but the issue of the bonus deferred shares was later found to be invalid and some of the existing ordinary shares were therefore re-designated as deferred shares and transferred to the trustee.

A 'settlement' is defined in IHTA 1984, s 43(2) as 'any disposition or dispositions of property' and IHTA 1984, s 272 provides that a 'disposition' includes a disposition effected by associated operations. 'Associated operations' is defined as any two operations of which one was effected with reference to the other, or with a view to enabling the other to be effected or facilitating its being effected, and any further operation having a like relation to any of those two (IHTA 1984, s 268(1)(b)). The Revenue contended that, in respect of each settlor, the creation of the five settlements and the transfer of the shares to the trustee were all associated operations. Therefore, there was a single settlement within the meaning of IHTA 1984, s 43 and, for the purposes of the decennial charge, tax should have been charged under IHTA 1984, s 64 at the rate applicable to the total value in all five settlements. In the alternative they considered that the five settlements were five 'dispositions of property' within the meaning of IHTA 1984, s 43 which resulted in one settlement.

The Special Commissioner rejected the trustee's appeal deciding that the creation of each settlement, and the subsequent transfer of the deferred shares, were indeed associated operations. In the High Court, Park J (as he then was) held that it was not relevant that the five settlements were nearly identical. There were separate documents with separate dates and the settlor had intended to create five different settlements. The five settlements could not be artificially amalgamated merely because their terms were similar. The associated operations rule in IHTA 1984, s 268 was not a 'catch-all' anti-avoidance provision which could be invoked to nullify the tax advantages of any scheme. The section came into effect only insofar as the expression 'associated operations' was of relevance to provisions imposing a charge. The court held that the making of the five settlements were dispositions for IHT purposes and there was therefore no reason to consider the associated operations rule. That rule was designed to identify a disposition made by several transactions and here each disposition was made by means of one act — the entering into each settlement deed. The associated operations provisions did not apply and it was not appropriate to regard the five settlements as created by associated operations. The Court of Appeal confirmed the High Court's decision that the associated operations rule did not apply and that five settlements rather than one were created.

Business and agricultural property relief

[4.18] On any distribution of property from a relevant property settlement prior to the first decennial the rate of charge is calculated by reference to the value of property comprised in the settlement immediately after it became so comprised. No account is taken of the fact that the property (when it became comprised in the settlement) may have been of a type eligible for business or agricultural property relief. This is because one of the steps in calculating the inheritance tax on such a distribution involves calculating the tax that would be due on a hypothetical transfer of property. The value transferred by that hypothetical transfer is the aggregate of three amounts including 'the value, immediately after the settlement commenced, of the property then comprised in it'. That will include the value of agricultural property and business property but the value of that property will not be reduced by business or agricultural property relief because immediately after the settlement commenced the trustees will not have held the property for the minimum ownership period.

Where the assets will not qualify for business property relief on leaving a relevant property settlement because, for example, the property has been replaced by property which does not qualify, the tax charge may be reduced by forward planning.

Example

Mr A intends to settle property qualifying for 100% business property relief on relevant property settlements for non-fiscal reasons. He has made no prior transfers and anticipates that the property will be sold for cash within one year. In five years' time it is likely that the trustees will decide to distribute the trust property to the beneficiaries.

If Mr A makes a single settlement the consequences would be as follows.

There would be no charge on making the settlement because the property would be wholly relieved by business property relief. On the distribution to the beneficiaries the tax charge would be calculated by reference to a deemed transfer when the settlement was created which did not qualify for business property relief as follows:

	£
Amount transferred	600,000
Nil rate band	325,000
Subject to tax	£275,000

Tax charged on hypothetical transfer:

£275,000 × 20% = £55,000

$$\text{Effective rate} = \frac{£55,000}{£600,000} \times 100 = 9.17\%$$

Inheritance tax charged on distribution:

Rate determined under s 68

$$9.17\% \times 30\,\% \times \frac{20}{40}$$

1.37% × £600,000 = £8,220

Instead, Mr A considers two alternative strategies.

Strategy A

Mr A makes two similar relevant property settlements on successive days, settling £1 in each. A few days later he adds business property to each settlement on the same day; being £324,999 to the first settlement ('A') and £324,998 to the second settlement ('B'). The property is subsequently sold for cash and the cash distributed 5 years after the settlement was made. These two settlements are not related settlements because they were not made on the same day even though the additions to the settlements were (IHTA 1984, s 62). Therefore, neither settlement had to take into account the addition made to the other.

There is no inheritance tax charge on the making of the settlements or the additions because the property is wholly relieved by business property relief. The inheritance tax on the distributions is calculated as follows:

	Settlement A	***Settlement B***
	£	**£**
Settlor's cumulative transfers on day before settlement made		1
Value of settled property immediately after settlement commenced	1	1
Value of property added to the settlement	324,999	324,998
Value of property in related settlements	Nil	Nil
	325,000	325,000
Deduct: Nil rate band	325,000	325,000
	Nil	Nil
Tax chargeable on hypothetical transfer	Nil	Nil
Effective rate	$\frac{\text{Nil}}{325,000} \times 100 = \text{Nil}\,\%$	$\frac{\text{Nil}}{325,000} \times 100 = \text{Nil}\,\%$

Strategy B

Mr A makes two relevant property settlements on succeeding days settling business property with a value of £325,000 on each. Again there is no inheritance tax on making the settlements because Mr A's transfers of value are wholly relieved by business property relief. On the distribution from the settlement Mr A's cumulative transfers which are taken into account in calculating the appropriate proportion of the effective rate on the second settlement include his transfer to the first settlement the value of which will have been reduced by business property relief to nil.

	Settlement A	Settlement B
	£	£
Mr A's previous chargeable transfers	Nil	Nil
		(325,000 – 325,000)
Value of property in settlement immediately after it commenced	325,000	325,000
Value of property in related settlements	Nil	Nil
	325,000	325,000
Deduct: Nil rate band	325,000	325,000
	Nil	Nil
Tax chargeable on hypothetical transfer	Nil	Nil
Effective rate	$\frac{\text{Nil}}{325,000} \times 100 = \text{Nil}\ \%$	$\frac{\text{Nil}}{325,000} \times 100 = \text{Nil}\ \%$

Valuation of relevant property

[4.19] One of the interesting consequences of the extension of the decennial and exit charges to most interest in possession trusts is in relation to the valuation of property. If property is held in a trust to which IHTA 1984, s 49 applies it will be valued as if it were owned by the holder of the interest in possession and therefore in conjunction with the property actually owned by that beneficiary. If an interest in possession trust is a relevant property settlement however, the property in the settlement will be valued in isolation. Consider the following example.

Example

The valuations of shareholdings in an investment company, InvCo, reflect the greater control conferred by a majority holding so that the shareholdings have the following values:

An 80% holding = £1,000,000

A 40% holding = £250,000

Mr A owns a 40% holding in InvCo as do the trustees of a trust in which he has an interest in possession. Because the trust was established after 22 March 2006 it is a relevant property trust to which IHTA 1984, s 49 does not apply. Therefore Mr A's shareholding and that of the trust are both valued at £250,000. Had s 49 applied, Mr A would have been treated as owning an 80% shareholding worth £1,000,000 (although a specific valuation rule would have applied had his interest in possession come to an end during his lifetime).

Capital gains tax

The settling of assets

[4.20] The settling of assets will be a disposal of those assets deemed to take place at their market value (TCGA 1992, s 17(1)(a)). Hold-over relief under TCGA 1992, s 260 (gifts on which inheritance tax is chargeable etc) will be available on a transfer to a relevant property trust unless it is non-resident. If the property qualifies as a business asset within TCGA 1992, s 165 hold-over relief for gifts of business assets would be available as an alternative, subject to the same exceptions.

Gains realised by the trustees

[4.21] Trustees of settlements are treated as if they were a single body of persons (distinct from the persons who are trustees of the settlement from time to time) and are therefore subject to capital gains tax on their disposals. The trustees have their own capital gains tax allowance which is normally one half of the personal allowance so that in 2010/11 it is £5,050. However, this exemption is divided by the number of qualifying settlements created after 6 June 1978 by one settlor. Essentially, a qualifying settlement is one which is not either a non-resident settlement, a charity or a retirement benefit scheme. The annual allowance cannot be reduced to less than one fifth of the normal trustee allowance under this provision and so, in 2010/11, cannot be less than £1010.

Gains realised on disposals made after 22 June 2010 by trustees will be chargeable at 28%. For disposals made between 6 April 2010 and 22 June 2010 the rate was 18%.

Gains arising on disposals of assets to beneficiaries by the trustees of a relevant property settlement may also be held over under s 260, regardless of whether the disposal gives rise to an inheritance tax liability. Section 260 will apply only where a chargeable transfer occurs, albeit chargeable at a nil rate of tax. Accordingly, this will exclude a transfer in a quarter beginning either with the date of the settlement or the date of a decennial charge (see *Frankland v CIR* [1997] STC 1450, CA).

Relief for gifts of business assets under TCGA 1992, s 165 may also be available.

Income tax

[4.22] The income taxation of a relevant property trust will depend upon whether the income arising to the trustees is income which is to be accumulated or which is payable at the discretion of any other person and which is not, before being distributed:

(a) the income of any person; or
(b) charitable income; or
(c) income arising, loosely, to a retirement benefit scheme.

Such income is referred to as 'discretionary trust income'. Other income arising to the trustees not falling within the three exceptions given above is referred to as 'IIP income'.

Discretionary trusts

[4.23] Discretionary trust income will be subject to tax at the trust rate of 50% unless it is dividend income in which case it will be taxed at the dividend trust rate of 42.5%. This is subject to the following exceptions.

Where trustees have the power to accumulate, it is advisable that they should also have power to distribute accumulated income as though it were income of the year in which it is so distributed. In this way the ability to utilise the credit for the tax paid by the trustees will not be lost. Accumulated funds may subsequently be distributed as income rather than capital if consideration of the beneficiary's rates of income tax and the rate of inheritance tax charged if a capital payment is made suggest that this would be advantageous.

The first £1,000 of income ('the standard rate band') is chargeable at the basic or dividend ordinary rate depending on the type of income. The dividend ordinary rate which, unsurprisingly, applies to dividend income, is 10%. The basic rate applies to income which is not dividend income and is 20%. Similar provisions to those applying to the capital gains tax annual allowance reduce the standard rate band where a single settlor makes several settlements. The standard rate band cannot be less than £200.

If the trust is a trust for a vulnerable beneficiary (see **4.37** below) and an election has been made the trustees can in effect, be taxed on trust income as if it were income of the vulnerable beneficiary taking into account the beneficiary's personal allowances, starting and basic rate tax bands.

Although it reduces the liability to tax, the tax credit on dividends cannot be repaid. In relation to discretionary trusts, these provisions represent a considerable tax penalty on the use of trusts. An example below, which for simplicity ignores the effect of the standard rate band, illustrates the point.

Example

Trust income

	£	£
Dividend received by trustees		9,000
Tax credit	<1,000>	1,000
Gross income		10,000
Section 479 tax at dividend trust rate of 42.5%	4,250	<4,250>
Tax payable by trustees	3,250	

Trust distribution

	£	£
Net income of trust		5,750
Liability at 50% under ITA 2007, s 496 on gross payment of £9,000 to beneficiary	4,500	
Met from trustees payment (tax credit not repayable)	3,250	
Remaining liability of trustees	1,250	<1,250>
Net distribution to beneficiary		4,500

Beneficiary

	£	£
Net distribution from trust		4,500
Tax credit on distribution under ITA 2007, s 494(3) at 50%	<4,500>	4,500
Gross income		9,000.00
Tax thereon at 50% (satisfied by tax credit on distribution)	4,500	<4,500>
Net income of beneficiary		4,500

The net dividend received by the trustees of £9,000 has therefore borne tax at 50% ((£9,000–4,500) ÷ £9,000) × 100).

Had it been received by the beneficiary directly it would have borne tax at 38.11% calculated as follows.

	£	£
Net dividend		9,000.00
Tax credit	<1,000.00>	1,000.00
Gross dividend		10,000.00

Tax at 42.5%	4,250.00	<3,250.00>
Tax payable	3,250.00	

$$\frac{£3{,}250}{£9{,}000} \times 100 = 36.11\%$$

Interest in possession trusts

[4.24] The trustees of an interest in possession trust do not pay tax at the trust rate except on certain amounts which are capital for trust law purposes but are subject to income tax. They are:

(a) payments made by a company by way of qualifying distribution on the redemption, repayment or purchase of its own shares or on the purchase of a right to acquire its own shares (in this case the dividend rate of 42.5% will apply);
(b) deemed income receipts under the accrued income scheme;
(c) offshore income gains;
(d) chargeable events in relation to employee share ownership trusts;
(e) profits of a property business in relation to lease premiums;
(f) profits on the disposal of deeply discounted securities where the trustees are resident in the UK;
(g) gains on contracts for life assurance;
(h) profits on the disposal of deposit rights;
(i) profits on the disposal of a future or option contract;
(j) proceeds of sale of a foreign dividend coupon;
(k) gains on the disposal of land where the gain is brought within the charge to income tax by the anti-avoidance provisions.

On other income they pay tax at the basic or dividend ordinary rate according to the type of income concerned. Assessable income will not include income mandated to be paid directly to the life tenant. The life tenant will be assessable to income tax on an amount equal to the income arising from the trust in the year in which it arises regardless of whether it has been distributed to him after deduction of trust management expenses deductible from income under general trust principles. He will receive credit for the tax paid on the income by the trustees.

Settlor interested trusts

[4.25] Under ITTOIA 2005, Pt 5 Ch 5, where the settlor or his spouse can benefit under a settlement in any circumstances or where income is paid to, or for the benefit of, an unmarried minor child of the settlor who is not a party to a civil partnership, the income is deemed to be that of the settlor.

Legislation is to be introduced in the Finance (No 2) Act 2010 to provide that, where a settlor receives a tax repayment in relation to trust income that arose after 5 April 2010 (because he is liable to income tax at a lower rate than the trustees) he must pay such repayments to the trustees. Prior to 6 April 2010 a repayment was only required if it was in respect of an 'allowance or relief' which the settlor would not have obtained if the trust income was not deemed to have been his (ITTOIA 2005, s 646).

The Finance Act 2006 contained amendments to ICTA 1988, s 686(2) which were designed to have the effect that income which was deemed to be that of the settlor under ITTOIA 2005, Pt 5 Ch 5 would also be taxable on the trustees with the settlor receiving a credit for the tax which the trustees had suffered. In fact, it is doubtful whether the amended legislation actually imposed the charge on the trustees and it is clear that it does not give a credit to the settlor. HMRC of course, has asserted that the legislation was effective both to impose the charge and to provide the credit. The relevant legislation has now been rewritten under the Rewrite Project in ITA 2007, s 480(3).

Stamp duty and stamp duty land tax

[4.26] Stamp duty is now generally only chargeable under FA 1999, Sch 13 on instruments relating to stock or marketable securities. As a general rule, therefore, stamp duty is payable in relation to stock and marketable securities whereas stamp duty land tax is payable in relation to land.

Stamp duty is not chargeable on an instrument giving effect to a gift of shares provided that it can be certified in writing as falling within Category L of the Schedule to the Stamp Duty (Exempt Instruments) Regulations 1987.

For the transfer of land by way of gift, no stamp duty land tax will be payable provided a self-certificate is completed.

Privileged interests

Inheritance tax

[4.27] An interest in possession will be a privileged interest where the person beneficially entitled to the interest became so entitled after 22 March 2006 and the interest is:

(a) an immediate post-death interest (an 'IPDI'); or
(b) a disabled person's interest (a 'DPI'); or
(c) a transitional serial interest (a 'TSI').

In addition, anti-avoidance provisions introduced in FA 2010 provide that where a UK domiciled individual becomes beneficially entitled to an interest in possession after 8 December 2009 by virtue of a disposition falling within IHTA 1984, s 10 (dispositions not intended to confer a gratuitous benefit) (we refer to such interests in this book as 'section 5(1B) interests') the interest is treated for most purposes in the same way as a privileged interest. A person beneficially entitled to a privileged interest or to a section 5(1B) interest is treated for the purposes of inheritance tax under IHTA 1984, s 49, as beneficially entitled to the property in which his interest subsists. Property which is the subject of a privileged interest is not relevant property and therefore will not be subject to the decennial and exit charges under the Inheritance Tax Act 1984, Ch 3 Pt 3. Property which is subject to a section 5(1B) interest, however, is relevant property and therefore subject to the decennial and exit charges. In effect therefore, such property is subject to a double charge; first in the estate of the IIP beneficiary and secondly under the relevant property provisions.

Immediate post death interests

[4.28] An interest in possession to which a person ('L') is entitled is an IPDI if:

(a) the settlement of the property in which the interest subsists was effected by will or under the law relating to intestacy;
(b) L became beneficially entitled to the interest in possession on the death of the testator or intestate;
(c) the property in which the interest subsists is not held on a trust for bereaved minors ('TBM') within IHTA 1984, s 71A;
(d) the interest is not a disabled person's interest ("DPI") (IHTA 1984, s 49A).

Therefore, most interests in possessions arising on death will be IPDI's and outside the relevant property regime. The ability to create an IPDI is particularly important in situations where the testator is survived both by his spouse and by his children by a former spouse.

Example

Stewart is survived by Lucy and Jane, his daughters by his former spouse from whom he was divorced and by Sarah, his second wife. He is 75 years old, Sarah is 63 years old and Lucy and Jane are 46 and 44 years old respectively.

He wishes to provide for Sarah after his death but for his capital to pass to his children thereafter. He therefore leaves his residuary estate on life interest trusts for Sarah with absolute reversion to Lucy and Jane.

Sarah's life interest is an IPDI. She is therefore treated for inheritance tax purposes as becoming absolutely entitled to the settled property. Because of that, the deemed transfer arising by virtue of Stewart's death will be an inter-spouse transfer and therefore exempt. On Sarah's death her estate will be treated as if it contained the settled property which will therefore bear inheritance tax at the death rate.

If Sarah had renounced her life interest, during her lifetime, she would have made a potentially exempt transfer. That transfer would only have become chargeable if she had died within 7 years of making it.

It is possible, therefore, to use IPDI's for tax planning purposes. Consider the following variation to the facts in the above example.

Example

> Sarah has her own independent wealth and does not need the income arising from the assets in Stewart's estate. In spite of that, Stewart leaves his assets on interest in possession trusts for Sarah but subject to the trustees' power to defeat those interests. That is exempt as a transfer to a spouse. The trustees use their powers to defeat Sarah's interest a year after Stewart's death. That is a potentially exempt transfer. Sarah is in good health and at the time the interest is defeated she has a life expectancy of 15 years and in fact survives for that period. She does not die within 7 years of her PET and therefore the deemed transfer of value arising from the defeat of her interest is not brought into charge to inheritance tax.

It used to be the case that it was possible to create in this way trust interests from which the surviving spouse could benefit. This is no longer the case because the Finance Act 2006 amended the reservation of benefit provisions in FA 1986, with the result that where s 49 applies to treat the holder of an interest in possession as beneficially owning the settled property in which his interest subsists and the interest comes to an end during his lifetime the holder is treated as having made a gift of the property for the purposes of the reservation with benefit provisions.

So, in our example above, if the trustees, after defeating Sarah's interest, continued to have a power to apply capital for her benefit it is arguable that FA 1986, s 102ZA would apply to treat her as having reserved a benefit in the trust property.

Disabled person's interests

[4.29] A DPI is defined in IHTA 1984, s 89B as an interest which falls within (a)–(d) below.

(a) An interest in possession to which a person is treated as being beneficially entitled by virtue of IHTA 1984, s 89(2).
Section 89(2) treats a discretionary trust in which no interest in possession subsists and which secures that not less than half the settled property which is applied during the lifetime of a disabled person is applied for that person's benefit as being subject to an interest in possession in favour of the person.

(b) An interest in possession to which a person is treated as beneficially entitled by s 89A(4).
Section 89A concerns settlements in which no interest in possession subsists which are made by a person, A, and which provide that any of the settled property which is applied to the benefit of a beneficiary is applied for the benefit of A and, in the event that the trusts are brought to an end during A's life, either a person will become absolutely entitled to the settled property or a DPI will subsist in the property.
In addition, A must have satisfied the Commissioners that, when the property was transferred to the settlement, he had a condition that it was at that time reasonable to expect would have such effects on A as to lead to A becoming a disabled person.
Where the conditions of s 89A are satisfied, A is treated as beneficially entitled to an interest in possession in the settled property.

(c) An interest in possession in settled property to which a disabled person becomes beneficially entitled on or after 22 March 2006.

(d) An interest in possession to which a person, A, is beneficially entitled if:
   (i) A is the settlor;
   (ii) A was beneficially entitled to the property immediately before settling it;
   (iii) A satisfies the Commissioners as to the same matters as are summarised in (*b*) above;
   (iv) the settled property was transferred into settlement on or after 22 March 2006; and
   (v) the trusts on which the settled property is held secure that, if any of the settled property is applied during A's life for the benefit of a beneficiary, it is applied for the benefit of A.

Loosely, therefore, (*a*) covers discretionary trusts for a disabled person who was disabled at the time the settlement was made, (*b*) covers discretionary trusts for a person who expects to become disabled, (*c*) covers interests in possession for a person who is disabled, and (*d*) covers interests in possession for a person who is expected to become disabled. (*b*) and (*d*), however, only cover self-settled property. If a person settles property in anticipation of some one else becoming disabled that settlement cannot create a DPI until the beneficiary is actually disabled.

A disabled person is defined in IHTA 1984, s 89(4) as being a person who is:

(a) incapable by reason of mental disorder within the meaning of the Mental Health Act 1983 of administering his property or managing his affairs; or

(b) in receipt of an attendance allowance under the Security Contributions and Benefits Act 1992, s 64 or it's Northern Ireland equivalent; or

(c) would have been in receipt of such an attendance allowance were it not for the provisions denying attendance allowance where a person is undergoing treatment for renal failure in a hospital or is provided with certain accommodation; or

(d) is in receipt of a disability living allowance under the Social Security Contributions and Benefits Act 1992, s 71 or its Northern Ireland equivalent by virtue of entitlement to the care component at the highest or middle rate; or

(e) would have been in receipt of such a disability living allowance were it not for the provisions of those acts which deny the allowance to persons for whom certain accommodation is provided; or

(f) would have been in receipt of the requisite attendance allowance or disability living allowance had he satisfied the relevant residence conditions.

Mental disorder for this purpose uses the definition found in the Mental Health Act 1983, s 1 which is 'any disorder or disability of the mind'. To qualify as a disabled beneficiary under this definition the individual has to be very severely disabled. To be eligible for the requisite attendance allowance or disability living allowance, for example, the individual would have to require prolonged or repeated attendance during the day or night, either in connection with his normal bodily functions or to stop the individual being a danger either to himself or others.

The restrictiveness of this definition has been very much criticised. Many people who will not fall within it would still, in most people's estimation, be incapable of managing their finances. For example, individuals suffering from drug addiction, alcoholism, bipolar disorder or schizophrenia in most cases would not be covered. Before Finance Act 2006 property could have been settled on trusts giving such persons an interest in possession subject to a wide discretionary power of the trustees over capital. The transfer into such a trust would have been treated as a potentially exempt transfer to the life tenant. Now it will be immediately chargeable and the trust itself will be a relevant property trust subject to the decennial and exit charges.

Special rate of charge when settled property affected by potentially exempt transfer

[4.30] Special anti-avoidance provisions exist to limit the inheritance tax planning opportunities of routing property destined for a discretionary trust through an intermediate interest within IHTA 1984, s 49. The point of such planning is that the settling of the trust should be a potentially exempt transfer and the creation of the discretionary settlement should be a chargeable transfer by the holder of the interest in possession who is assumed to have a lower cumulative total than the settlor. To counter such planning IHTA 1984, ss 54A and 54B impose a special charge when the following conditions are satisfied:

(a) an interest in possession comes to an end during the lifetime of the person beneficially entitled to it, or upon his death. Where a person becomes beneficially entitled to the interest on or after 22 March 2006 the provisions apply only if the interest is a DPI or a TSI;
(b) the property in which the interest subsisted became settled property by virtue of a potentially exempt transfer;
(c) the interest in possession ceases and a relevant property settlement arises within 7 years of the potentially exempt transfer having been made;
(d) the settlor is alive at the time the interest in possession comes to an end.

The inheritance tax charge is taken to be the higher of two alternative calculations. The first calculates the tax due in the normal way on the termination of the interest in possession. The rates will either be half rates (where there is an *inter vivos* termination) or full death rates where termination occurs as a result of the life tenant's death.

The second calculation imputes the settlor's cumulative total of transfers at the time the settlement was established to the beneficiary whose interest ceases. In this calculation half rates are used. The rules can be extremely complex in their operation.

There is a further condition found in IHTA 1984, s 54A(2)(d) which must be satisfied before the special rate can apply. The net effect of s 54A(2)(d) is that no charge will arise if within 6 months of the interest in possession ceasing, the trust property becomes either:

(i) held on a trust which is not a relevant property settlement; or
(ii) owned outright by individual beneficiaries.

Transfers between spouses

[4.31] Where, however, a settlor has created an interest in possession for his spouse which is within IHTA 1984, s 49 which is subsequently terminated and the settled property then becomes held on relevant property trusts, ss 54A and 54B will not apply, since the settlor's transfer for the benefit of his spouse was not a potentially exempt transfer but rather an exempt transfer (IHTA 1984, s 18). For that reason, IHTA 1984, s 80 was enacted to treat the date on which the spouse's interest in possession ceases and the settled property becomes held on relevant property trusts as being the date of commencement of a separate settlement. The spouse's cumulative total immediately prior to that time (rather than that of the settlor before the creation of the interest in possession settlement for his spouse or at the time that the property then becomes held on discretionary trusts) will be taken into account for the purposes of calculating the inheritance tax charges on the property held on relevant property trusts. Where the property first became comprised in the settlement on or after 22 March 2006 the provision only applies if the interest in possession is either a TSI or a DPI.

Interests in possession for a spouse

[4.32] The spouse exemption will not take priority over the gift with reservation rules where property is settled on an interest in possession trust for a spouse and, before the death of the settlor, the interest in possession comes to an end (FA 1986, s 102(5A)).

Transitional serial interests ('TSI')

[4.33] A TSI is the final category of privileged interest trusts. It is discussed in CHAPTER 5 EXISTING SETTLEMENTS.

Capital gains tax

On settling assets

[4.34] Because it is established under a will or intestacy the creation of an IPDI will not constitute a disposal for capital gains tax purposes.

Where a DPI is settled during the life of the settlor there will be a disposal of the assets settled by the settlor deemed to take place at market value. If the property settled is business property within s 165 hold-over relief for gifts of business assets will be available on the transfer. Hold-over relief under TCGA 1992, s 260 will not, however, be available, because the transfer into settlement will be a potentially exempt transfer and not an immediately chargeable transfer.

Gains realised by the trustees

[4.35] Gains realised by trustees of settlements in which privileged interests subsist will be subject to capital gains tax in the same way as gains of relevant property settlements as described at **4.21** above except that special provisions apply on the death of the holder of an interest in possession and in relation to trusts for vulnerable beneficiaries.

The uplift on death

[4.36] TCGA 1992, s 71 provides that where a person becomes absolutely entitled to any settled property as against the trustees of a settlement the assets concerned are treated as having been disposed of by the trustees and immediately acquired by them as bare trustees of the person becoming absolutely entitled. Section 17 then operates to deem the trustees' disposal to have been made for a consideration equal to market value. Section 60 treats the trustees' acquisition as bare trustee as an acquisition by the person becoming absolutely entitled to the settled property and, again, s 17 applies to deem that acquisition to be made at market value. The result of this is that in most circumstances where property passes out of a settlement, a chargeable gain or allowable loss will arise.

Section 73 provides that if the occasion on which s 71 applies is the death of a person entitled to an interest in possession in the settled property, no chargeable gain is to accrue on the disposal. Special provisions are also made for property which reverts to the disponer. Thus, the base cost of the asset is uplifted to its market value at the death and yet no gain becomes chargeable. Effectively, any gain accrued up to the date of the death is taken out of charge to capital gains tax.

Where the interest in possession concerned is one to which the deceased became entitled on or after 22 March 2006, s 73 applies only if immediately before the death the relevant interest in possession was a privileged interest or a TBM (see **4.39**) or the deceased beneficiary was under the age of 18 and the trust concerned was an 18–25 trust (see **4.41** below).

TCGA 1992, s 72 deals with the position where an interest in possession terminates on the death of the person entitled to it and the property in which it subsisted continues to be settled property. The section also applies where a person entitled to an interest in possession dies although the interest continues. This might happen where there is an interest in possession for a fixed period or *pur autre vie*.

Where s 72 applies, trustees are deemed to dispose of, and immediately re-acquire, the property in which the deceased's interest subsisted for its market value on the death of the beneficiary concerned. No chargeable gain is to arise on the trustees' disposal. Thus, the base cost of the asset is uplifted to its market value at the death and yet no gain becomes chargeable. Effectively, any gain accrued up to the date of death is taken out of charge to capital gains tax. Again, where the deceased's interest is one to which the deceased became entitled on or after 22 March 2006, s 73 applies only if immediately before the death the relevant interest in possession was a privileged interest or a TBM or the deceased beneficiary was under the age of 18 and the trust concerned was an 18–25 trust (see **4.41** below).

Vulnerable person election

[4.37] A vulnerable person election may be made under FA 2005, s 37 when two conditions are satisfied. First, the person in relation to whom the election is made must be a 'vulnerable person'. Second, the trust in relation to which the election is made must be a qualifying trust. The election must be made both by the trustees and the vulnerable beneficiary.

A 'vulnerable person' for this purpose is a disabled person or a 'relevant minor' (FA 2005, s 23), that is a minor at least one of whose parents is dead. The definition of a disabled person is of like effect to the definition for the purpose of defining a DPI for inheritance tax which is discussed above.

The definition of a 'relevant minor' is the same as the definition of a 'bereaved' minor used in defining TBMs for inheritance tax purposes (see **4.40** below) (FA 2005, s 39).

A 'qualifying trust' in relation to a disabled person is one where, during the lifetime of the disabled person concerned (or on the termination of the trust if that is earlier):

(a) any property applied for the benefit of a beneficiary is applied for the benefit of the disabled person; and
(b) either the disabled person is entitled to all of the income of the trust or such income may not be applied for the benefit of any other person.

Thus not all trusts which qualify as trusts for a vulnerable beneficiary by reference to a disabled person will be DPIs for inheritance tax purposes. That is because, for example, such a trust is a discretionary trust which may cease during the lifetime of the disabled person. Similarly, a trust in which a DPI subsists may not be a qualifying trust for a vulnerable beneficiary because it is a trust settled in anticipation of the settlor becoming disabled within IHTA 1984, s 89A.

Where property is held on trust for the benefit of a minor, the trust is a 'qualifying trust' if it is held on the statutory trusts for a minor arising under an intestacy (under Administration of Estates Act 1925, ss 46, 47(1)). It is also a qualifying trust where the trusts are established under the will of a deceased parent of the minor or under the Criminal Injuries Compensation Scheme and the following conditions are met.

(i) The minor, on or before attaining 18, will become absolutely entitled to the trust property and any accumulated income.
(ii) Until the minor becomes absolutely entitled to the trust property (or dies), any property which is applied for the benefit of a beneficiary is applied for the minor's benefit.
(iii) Until the minor becomes absolutely entitled to the trust property (or dies), either the minor is entitled to the trust income or no income may be applied for the benefit of any other person (FA 2005, s 35).

But a trust will not fail to be a qualifying trust by virtue of the powers conferred by Trustee Act 1925, s 32 (or its Northern Ireland equivalent). It should be noted, however, that in contrast to the Inheritance Tax rules for TBMs (see **4.39** below), if the s 32 power is expressly extended to the whole of the trust fund (as it commonly is) then the trust will not be a qualifying trust (FA 2005, s 34).

A TBM for inheritance tax purposes (see **4.39** below) will be a qualifying trust for a vulnerable beneficiary by reference to a relevant beneficiary unless it contains a power of advancement which is wider than the statutory power under the Trustee Act 1925, s 32.

Where a vulnerable person election is made, the trustees may make a claim for special income tax and capital gains tax treatment. The relief provided under this treatment is complex but in essence it attempts to ensure that the trustees' liability for tax on the income is reduced to the additional liability which would have arisen on the vulnerable beneficiary if the income had arisen to him directly. If the vulnerable person is UK resident gains arising to the trustees are deemed to arise to the vulnerable beneficiary.

If the vulnerable beneficiary is not UK resident, then the calculation of the relief is complex but, in essence, it attempts to ensure that the trustees' liability to tax on capital gains is reduced to the additional liability which would have arisen on the vulnerable beneficiary if the beneficiary had realised the gains.

Income tax

[4.38] The income taxation of the trustees and beneficiaries of a privileged trust will be as set out above in relation to relevant property trusts. That is, it is dependent on whether or not the trust confers an interest in possession and whether ITTOIA 2005, Pt 5 Ch 5 applies because the settlor has retained an interest in the settlement or income is paid to an unmarried minor child of the settlor, who is not a party to a civil partnership. Finally, a vulnerable person election may be made in relation to the settlement as described at **4.37**.

Trusts for bereaved minors ('TBM')

[4.39] As we shall see, the reliefs formerly given to accumulation and maintenance trusts within s 71 have been withdrawn. In their place a much more limited relief is given for trusts for bereaved minors ('TBMs') under IHTA 1984, s 71A and 'age 18 to 25 trusts' ('18–25 trusts') under IHTA 1984, s 71D.

Section 71A applies to settled property if:

(a) it is held on statutory trusts for the benefit of a bereaved minor under the provisions of the Administration of Estates Act 1925 relating to succession on intestacy and statutory trusts in favour of the issue of an intestate; or
(b) it is held on trust for the benefit of a bereaved minor and it is either:
    (i) established under the will of the deceased parent (a parent includes a step-parent (IHTA 1984, s 71H)) of the bereaved minor; or
    (ii) established under the Criminal Injuries Compensation Scheme;
    (iii) established under the Victims of Overseas Terrorism Compensation Scheme (with effect from 8 April 2010)

    and certain conditions are met.

The conditions are that:

(1) On or before attaining the age of 18, the bereaved minor will become absolutely entitled to:
   (a) the settled property;
   (b) any income arising from the settled property; and
   (c) any income that has arisen from the property which has been accumulated.

(2) That, for so long as the bereaved minor is living and under the age of 18, if any of the settled property is applied for the benefit of a beneficiary, it is applied for the benefit of the bereaved minor; and

(3) That, for so long as the bereaved minor is living and under the age of 18, either:
   (a) the bereaved minor is entitled to all of the income (if there is any) arising from any of the settled property; or
   (b) no such income may be applied for the benefit of any other person.

What is meant by 'will become absolutely entitled' in (1)?

[4.40] If one leaves one's estate to one's daughter contingently on her attaining the age of 18 and to one's niece in the event that she does not, is the section satisfied? Can one say that one's daughter will, on attaining the age of 18, become absolutely entitled to the settled property when it is possible that she will not attain that age and will therefore never become entitled to the property?

A similar question arose in relation to the provisions relating to accumulation and maintenance trusts in IHTA 1984, s 71 in the case of *Lord Inglewood v CIR* [1983] STC 133 (CA). In that case, it was held that the trust did not satisfy the provisions of s 71 because the right of the beneficiaries to take the trust property absolutely at a given age was subject to the trustees' power to revoke the trusts and execute new appointments. Counsel for the taxpayer contended that the word 'will' in the predecessor legislation to IHTA 1984, s 71(1) had to be construed as meaning 'will if no event happens to disentitle the beneficiary'.

The trustees contended that if that was not the case one could not accommodate the provisions of what is now s 71 to the facts that:

(a) a beneficiary's interest may be lawfully disposed of by him after he attains the age of 18 and before it vests in possession;
(b) his interest may be taken away from him on bankruptcy;
(c) his interest may be prevented from vesting in him by reason of an order made under Variation of Trusts Act 1958, or under the statutory jurisdiction of the family division on divorce or an order made by the Court of Protection in the event of his incapacity to manage his affairs; or
(d) he may die before attaining a vested interest.

Lord Justice Fox said:

> As to the last of those, it seems to us that the contingency is inherent in the provisions of the paragraph itself. The paragraph applies where a person will, on or before attaining a specified age not exceeding [a stated maximum] become entitled

> to an interest in possession in settled property. The paragraph is dealing with contingent interests. A trust cannot be excluded from the operation of the paragraph because of the possible happening of an event inherent in the contingency which brings the trust within the paragraph in the first place . . .
>
> . . . as to the other matters ((a), (b) and (c)) we think that the answer is this. The paragraph provides that "this paragraph applies to any settlement where . . . ". In our opinion "where" means "whereby". Accordingly we think the paragraph is concerned only with provisions which are contained in the settlement itself. That would include not only the express provisions of the settlement but also any which are incorporated by statutory provision. Some of the matters to which we have referred in (a), (b) and (c) can be so described. Other consequences which cannot be avoided, are the operation of the general law on property interests. They are extraneous to the settlement and are not provisions of the settlement itself . . .
>
> . . . the result in our opinion is this, the word "will" . . . does import a degree of certainty which is not satisfied if the trust can be revoked and the fund reappointed to some other person of an age exceeding [the stated maximum]. But a power of advancement has been for so long such a normal provision in a settlement for a person contingently on attaining a specified age, and since its sole purpose is to enable the trust property to be applied for that person's benefit before he attains a specified age, it would be artificial to regard the trust as not satisfying the provisions of the paragraph. A trust for A if he attains [the stated maximum age] is within the paragraph. It is impossible to see any rational ground why a trust for A if he attains [the stated maximum age] and with a power of advancement should not satisfy it also, and particularly since the exclusion of the power of advancement in such a case must be rare indeed.
>
> Our conclusion regarding the power of advancement is that while the prima facie meaning [of the relevant legislation] is clear it must be interpreted in the context of the practical application of the law of trusts. The statutory power of advancement is so commonly incorporated in trusts that the relevant legislation must be read so as to accommodate that and not so as to withdraw the benefit of the paragraph from a trust containing such a power. We do not regard the much used extension of the statutory power from a moiety to the whole as being in any different position.

It is likely, that the courts would adopt a similar approach to the very similar provisions of s 71A. Guidance published jointly by the Society of Trusts and Estate Practitioners and the Chartered Institute of Taxation on 29 June 2007, which was agreed by HMRC, although not completely on the point, provides an indication that HMRC may accept that this is the case. The final point made in the extract quoted from the judgment in *Lord Inglewood* is given statutory form in IHTA 1984, s 71A(4) which provides that trusts are not to be treated as failing to satisfy these conditions simply by virtue of the trustees having the power conferred by the Trustee Act 1925, s 32 or having such a power freed from the, or subject to a less restrictive, limitation than that imposed by s 32 which allows the power of advancement to be exercised only in relation to one half of the prospective share of the beneficiary concerned.

The Society of Trusts and Estate Practitioners and the Chartered Institute of Taxation published guidance on ss 71A and 71D and accumulation and maintenance trusts in June 2007 which was agreed with HMRC. In that guidance it was stated that:

> Both sections 71A and 71D are drafted by reference to a single beneficiary (in section 71D called 'B' and in section 71A called the 'Bereaved Minor').' However,

> HMRC consider that it is possible to pluralise B or the Bereaved Minor to include all beneficiaries within the relevant class provided that they are alive at the date the section 71A or section 71D trust takes effect and are under the specified age. Accordingly a will trust in the following terms can qualify as a section 71A trust:
>
> 'to such of my children alive at my death as attain the age of 18 years and if more than one in such shares as the trustee shall from time to time by deed or deeds revocable or irrevocable appoint and in default of such appointment in equal shares absolutely at 18 provided that no such appointment shall be made and no such appointment shall be revoked so as to either diminish or to increase the share (or the accumulations of income forming part of the share) of or give a new share (or new accumulations of income) to a child who at the date of such appointment or revocation has reached the age of 18 nor to benefit a child who has been excluded from benefit as a result of the exercise of the power.

This is not an accurate statement of the law and is therefore concessionary. Statements such as these by HMRC containing concessionary treatments disguised as statements of the law pose difficult questions as to how far they may be relied upon by taxpayers.

A bereaved minor is one who:

(a) has not yet attained the age of 18; and
(b) at least one of whose parents has died.

The number of trusts for bereaved minors will be very small and the greater part of them will be trusts arising on intestacy. They can only arise on a death, they can only be made either on an intestacy, or under a will, of a parent of the bereaved minor's (so that, even grandparents cannot set up TBMs under their wills) and the bereaved minor must become absolutely entitled to trust property at the age of 18.

When these changes were first announced the Government was rightly criticised for failing to recognise that it is usually entirely inappropriate to give 18-year olds unfettered control of substantial amounts of money. As we explain below, the Government responded to this criticism by introducing an additional class of privileged trusts, 18–25 trusts.

The effect of a trust qualifying as a trust for a bereaved minor is that it will not be a relevant property trust with the result that the decennial and exit charges will not apply to it. There will be no charge to inheritance tax when a bereaved minor becomes absolutely entitled to the trust assets or upon the death of the bereaved minor or on the property being paid or applied for the advancement or benefit of the bereaved minor.

There is a charge on property ceasing to be subject to a TBM in other circumstances. It is difficult to see what those other circumstances might be. A bereaved minor under the age of 18 can not himself disclaim his interest and once he had reached the age of 18 he would become absolutely entitled to the trust property so that the settlement would have ceased. If trust property is applied in breach of trust the trust would not come to an end. The trustees would have a duty to recover the trust property from those committing the breach including any trustees who were involved in the breach. The most likely circumstance, therefore, in which a charge would arise under s 71B on property ceasing to be subject to a TBM is where the trust is varied by an order of the court.

Age 18–25 trusts

[4.41] The conditions for an age 18–25 trust are to be found in s 71D and are the same as those for a TBM except that the relevant age is 25 years and not 18 years. In addition, s 71D also applies to existing accumulation and maintenance trusts within IHTA 1984, s 71 (see **CHAPTER 5** below) which had altered their provisions before 6 April 2008 so as to fall within the s 71D description.

There is no tax charge on the beneficiary of an age 18–25 trust becoming absolutely entitled to the trust assets on or before the age of 18 or, upon the trust becoming a TBM. Otherwise, when the settled property ceases to be held on age 18–25 trusts there will be a special charge to inheritance tax. Where the charge arises on certain events, it is calculated in a similar way to the normal exit charge, except that the quarters for the purposes of the relevant fraction are calculated from the date at which the beneficiary becomes 18, if that is later than the time at which the property became property within s 71D.

The events are:

(a) the beneficiary becoming absolutely entitled to the trust property on or before the age of 25;
(b) the death of the beneficiary;
(c) the property being paid or applied for the advancement or benefit of the beneficiary.

Where the trust property ceases to be within s 71D on any event other than the three listed above, a different and higher charge applies.

Capital gains tax

[4.42] Unless it is established under the criminal injuries compensation scheme or victims of overseas terrorism compensation scheme a TBM will arise under the will or intestacy of the bereaved minor's parent. Similarly, an age 18–25 settlement which does not arise under the criminal injuries compensation scheme or victims of overseas terrorism compensation scheme will arise under the will of the beneficiary's parent. Normally, the TBM or age 18–25 trust will arise immediately on a death. In those circumstances, the transfer of the asset into settlement will not be a chargeable disposal for capital gains tax purposes.

Such trusts, however, will not always arise immediately on the death of the relevant parent. For example, if A were to leave his property on discretionary trusts for his wife and son to determine on the death of the wife with remainder to the son contingently upon his reaching the age of 18 and the wife were to die during the son's minority the property would be held on a TBM between the wife's death and the son reaching 18. The discretionary trusts would not be a TBM. Once they came to an end, however, the property would be held within a TBM. That is because the son would not be able to give the trustees a good receipt and therefore the trustees would hold the trust property on trust to accumulate the income and with power to make payments out of that income for the son's benefit and would thus fall within IHTA 1984, s 43(2)(b). That settlement would be a TBM because it arose under the will of a deceased parent and provided for the trust capital to be held for the son absolutely and for all income either to be applied for the son's benefit or to be accumulated and passed to the son absolutely on reaching the age of 18.

Because the capital gains tax rules treat a person as being absolutely entitled if he would be so entitled but for being a minor (TCGA 1992, s 62) the TBM will not be a settlement for the purposes of capital gains tax. So when the discretionary trust comes to an end there will be a deemed disposal of the trust property under TCGA 1992, s 71.

If instead of creating a discretionary trust on his death, the father's will had created an interest in possession for his wife, that interest would have been an IPDI. As such, the coming to an end of the spouse's interest in possession on the death of the spouse would have fallen within TCGA 1992, s 73 (a person becoming absolutely entitled to settled property on the death of a person entitled to a privileged interest). The result would have been that the base cost of the assets would have been uplifted to their market value at the time of death of the spouse but no chargeable gain would have accrued.

Where a TBM is a settlement for inheritance tax purposes but not for capital gains tax purposes because the bereaved minor would be absolutely entitled to the trust assets were he not a minor, capital gains tax applies as if the property were vested in the minor and any acts of the trustees were his acts with the result that the minor would be deemed to make any disposals of assets made by the trustees.

Otherwise, both a TBM and an age 18–25 trust will either be an IIP trust or a discretionary trust with the results set out in relation to relevant property trusts (see **4.20** and **4.21** above) and privileged trusts above (see **4.34–4.37** above).

Income tax

[4.43] The income taxation of TBM and age 18–25 trusts will depend on whether or not an interest in possession subsists in the trust property. If it does, the income tax consequences will be as set out in **4.24** above. If it does not, the income taxation consequences will be as set out in **4.23** above. Note that a TBM will also be a qualifying trust for the purposes of the relief for trusts for vulnerable beneficiaries and therefore a vulnerable person election could be made in relation to it with the consequences set out in **4.37** and **4.38** above.

Specially relieved trusts

[4.44] There are various classes of settlement which receive special reliefs under the inheritance tax legislation.

(a) Charitable trusts. These are dealt with in **Chapter 13 Gifts to Charities and Other Non-Profit Organisations.**
(b) Maintenance funds for historic buildings. These are dealt with in **Chapter 14 Gifts for National Purposes.**

(c) Employee trusts. A special relief for trusts for the benefit of employees is conferred by IHTA 1984, s 86.
(d) Newspaper trusts. A special relief for trusts for newspaper publishing companies is conferred by IHTA 1984, s 87.
(e) Protective trusts. Protective trusts are designed to protect a beneficiary from the consequences of his own imprudence and fecklessness. The Trustee Act 1925, s 33 sets out the trusts which are to be treated as applying where any income is directed to be held on 'protective trusts'. These standard provisions can be incorporated simply by the use of the term and may be modified by express provisions. Alternatively, a trust deed may set out expressly trusts of similar or the same effect as those arising under s 33. These are also discussed in **CHAPTER 3 INTRODUCTION TO TRUST LAW**.

IHTA 1984, s 88 provides a special treatment for settled property which is held on trusts to the like effect as those specified in s 33(1) of the Trustee Act 1925.

Under s 33 a life tenant's interest in income will divest if he attempts to charge or assign his interest or is declared bankrupt. On the occurrence of such an event, the income becomes held on discretionary trusts for the benefit of the life tenant, his spouse and his children and remoter issue.

Before 22 March 2006, s 88 applied to treat those discretionary trusts as if they were an interest in possession for the principal beneficiary with the result that s 49 applied both before and after the triggering event which therefore would not give rise to a transfer of value. Section 88 continues on and after 22 March 2006 but, without further provisions, its provisions would provide no advantage on or after that date because most interest in possession trusts are now relevant property trusts. For that reason two special reliefs are given.

First, where settled property became held before 22 March 2006 on protective trusts and the trigger event takes place on or after that date with the result that the principal beneficiary is treated as beneficially entitled to an interest in possession, that interest is treated as if it arose before 22 March 2006. The result of that is that s 49 would apply to the beneficiary's interest who will therefore continue to be treated as beneficially entitled to the trust property. Where a protective trust is established on or after 22 March 2006 and before a triggering event and the interest of the principal beneficiary is a privileged interest that interest is treated as continuing after the triggering event.

Offshore settlements

[4.45] An individual may wish when creating a settlement to do so offshore, ie by establishing a settlement with all of the trustees resident outside the UK.

Tax consequences

[4.46] The creation of an offshore, rather than an onshore, settlement by a UK resident and domiciled settlor does not result in any difference in the inheritance tax treatment of the settlement. Inheritance tax will be chargeable on the settlor's gift to the settlement, during the life of the settlement and on distributions from it in the way described above according to the nature of the settlement. So far as capital gains tax is concerned, hold-over relief cannot be claimed in respect of the transfer of assets direct to the trustees of an offshore settlement (TCGA 1992, ss 166 and 261), so the creation of the settlement may give rise to an immediate capital gains tax charge.

The tax consequences for the settlor and beneficiaries of a non-resident settlement are considered in detail in **CHAPTER 6 OFFSHORE TRUSTS**. As will be seen, the capital gains tax benefits to UK domiciled individuals of creating an offshore settlement are small as any chargeable gains realised by non-resident trustees (calculated as if they were resident in the UK) are attributed to the settlor, if:

(a) the settlor or his spouse or civil partner;
(b) any child of the settlor or his spouse or civil partner;
(c) the spouse or civil partner of any such child;
(d) any grandchild of the settlor or his spouse or civil partner;
(e) the spouse or civil partner of any such grandchild;
(f) any company controlled by any of the persons in *(a)*–*(e)* above; or
(g) any company associated with such a controlled company,

benefit, or are capable of benefiting from, the capital or income of the settlement.

In addition, TCGA 1992, s 87 imposes a capital payments charge on beneficiaries who receive capital payments from a non-resident settlement regardless of whether or not the settlor was domiciled in a country of the United Kingdom. There is also a supplementary capital gains tax charge in addition to the primary charge on beneficiaries who receive capital payments from the settlement.

The result of these provisions is that there are limited advantages during the lifetime of the settlor in creating an offshore settlement where the beneficiaries include the settlor or his immediate family.

The creation of a settlement with non-resident trustees by a person who is domiciled in the UK gives rise to a duty on any person concerned with the making of the settlement in the course of his trade or profession (other than a barrister) to report to the Revenue within 3 months of the making of the settlement the names and addresses of the settlor and the trustees (IHTA 1984, s 218).

Chapter 5

Existing Settlements

Introduction

[5.1] A settlement, like an individual's estate, should be kept under review to determine whether any steps should be taken in relation to the settled property or the terms upon which it is held; the settlement should not be considered in isolation from the beneficiaries and their circumstances.

This overall consideration of the assets of the settlement and the interests and personal circumstances of the beneficiaries may prompt a reorganisation. Often, it will be precipitated by a request from one or more of the beneficiaries for capital or by anticipation of an occasion on which the interests of the beneficiaries will alter, such as the death of a life tenant or the vesting of an interest in possession ('IIP') on a contingency being fulfilled.

This chapter considers steps that may be taken in relation to existing settlements. It considers:

(a) the extent to which the familiar techniques of estate planning may be applied to settlements;
(b) means of dealing with the interests of beneficiaries under settlements and the advantages in leaving some older settlements untouched; and
(c) the export of existing settlements.

Except where otherwise indicated it is assumed that all beneficiaries of the types of settlement considered are resident and domiciled in the UK and that the settlors are all UK resident domiciliaries.

Before dealing with these more general matters, we shall examine the taxation of settlements that were in existence on 22 March 2006. They are settlements in which subsist:

(a) existing IIPs;
(b) transitional serial interests ('TSIs');
(c) accumulation and maintenance trusts.

Each of these categories is examined below.

Existing IIPs

Inheritance tax

[5.2] Section 49 deems a person beneficially entitled to an interest in possession in settled property to be beneficially entitled to the property in which his interest subsists. This rule, is restricted to three types of interests.

First, an interest in possession in settled property to which the holder became beneficially entitled before 22 March 2006 falls within s 49 regardless of its nature except at any time when the property in which the interest subsists is subject to a TBM (see **4.39** and **4.40**). Secondly, s 49 applies to interests in possession arising under privileged interest trusts. Thirdly, it applies to section 5(1B) interests (see **4.19**).

Example

A died on 1 March 2006 leaving property on interest in possession trusts for his son, B, with absolute interest in remainder to his grandson, C. B died in 2040 at which time C was aged 35. All relevant tax law remained unchanged.

When A died, the old rules applied so that B was treated as being beneficially entitled to the trust property immediately on A's death. This treatment continued because B was beneficially entitled to an interest in possession and had become entitled to that interest before 22 March 2006. On B's death, his estate was deemed to include the settled property which was thus brought into charge to inheritance tax. The trust came to an end at that point and C became beneficially entitled to the property and so it formed part of his estate for inheritance tax purposes.

It should be noted that this treatment applies to particular interests in possession and not to settlements. So, if A had settled property before 22 March 2006 on trusts giving a life interest to his son with a succeeding life interest to his daughter and the son had died on say, 31 August 2008, the son's interest would have fallen within s 49 whereas the daughter's would not.

It may be difficult, in some cases, to determine whether an interest in possession is one which has subsisted since before 22 March 2006 or not. Consider the following situations.

Example

Mr A has two sons, B and C. B is 20 years old and C is 10 years old. On 1 March 2006, A settled property on trusts giving B an interest in possession until he was 30 (the 'trigger date'). Contingently on them surviving to the trigger date, B and C were then to take the trust property absolutely in equal shares except that, if either had a child or children living, that one was to take a life interest with absolute interest in remainder to his children. In the event that B or C did not survive to the trigger date and were not survived by issue, the surviving brother was to take the trust property, or an interest in possession in the property if he had children living, to which his brother would have become entitled.

C died 8 years later and, before he was 30, B had become the father of two children. The result of that was that when the trigger date occurred B continued to have an interest in possession in the whole of the trust property.

So at the trigger date B had an interest in possession in the whole of the trust property and he had had an interest in possession in the whole of the trust property since before 22 March 2006 but was it the same interest? His interest from time to time arose under the same settlement but arose under different provisions of that settlement before and after the trigger date. In the authors' view, where, as here, interests in possession exist in the same property under the same settlement and are held by the same person there is a single interest, even though that interest may be governed at different times by different provisions of the trust instrument.

The Society of Trust and Estate Practitioners and the Chartered Institute of Taxation corresponded with HMRC in relation to various examples on which the question in issue was whether an existing IIP continued or a new interest in possession was created. None of the examples exactly matched these circumstances but some were sufficiently close to provide some indication that HMRC will accept that the original interest continues in such a case as this.

The issue becomes more difficult in the following example.

Example

Mr A settled property conferring an interest in possession on his son, B, before 22 March 2006. On 1 April 2011 the trustees exercised a wide power of appointment to advance the trust assets to a new settlement with identical trust provisions except that the trustee is a company resident in the Isle of Man and the governing law is to be that of the Isle of Man. B has an interest in possession in the trust property throughout but is it a single interest or two successive interests? B continues to have an immediate right to the income arising from the property for his life subject to the same powers of the trustees to defeat that interest but his right arises under a different settlement and is governed by a different country's law. It is HMRC's view that there are two interests in possession. The original interest in possession will come to an end when the trustees exercise their power of advancement and a new interest in possession will come into being at that point.

Contracts of life insurance

[5.3] It will be seen from **CHAPTER 7 INSURANCE** that it is common to take out life insurance policies on an individual's life so as to provide a fund with which to pay inheritance tax on his death and alternatively, or additionally, as a convenient means of creating an investment fund for the beneficiaries of one's estate. In either case, it is normal to hold such policies on trust so as to ensure that they fall outside one's estate for inheritance tax purposes.

Smaller policies, which are not expected to attain a value in excess of the nil rate band, are commonly held on standard discretionary trusts. Before 22 March 2006, it was usual to hold larger policies on trusts conferring an interest in possession on the person expected to benefit from the life assured's estate on his death, coupled with a broad discretionary power to defeat those interests and to create new interests in capital or income. Such trusts are commonly referred to as 'flexible life interest trusts'.

Such trusts created before 22 March 2006 where the interests in possession have continued are existing IIPs. There was a problem, however, in that most such policies provided for regular premiums to be paid and it was argued by some that the payment of premiums by the life assured after 21 March 2006 had the result that some part of the property in which the beneficiary had an interest in possession only came into being after 21 March and that therefore, the beneficiary only became beneficially entitled to an interest in possession in that part of the settled property after 21 March 2006. If that had been correct the result would have been that the interest was not an existing IIP and the property in which it subsisted was relevant property. The argument was surely misconceived but in any event it was common for the payment of premiums on such policies to be organised in a different way. The life assured would make regular additions of cash to the settlement and the trustees would in turn pay the premiums. It is clear that in those circumstances a new interest in possession would come into existence on each addition to the settlement. IHTA 1984, s 46A was therefore added to deal with these problems, real and perceived. Section 46B was added to deal with similar problems relating to accumulation and maintenance settlements (see **5.10–5.13** below) and s 46E in relation to TSIs (see **5.4–5.6** below).

Section 46A applies where:

(a) a settlement commenced before 22 March 2006;
(b) a contract of life insurance was entered into before that day;
(c) a premium payable under the contract is paid on or after that day or an allowed variation is made to the contract on or after that day (an allowed variation is a variation which takes place by operation of, or as a result of, the exercise of rights conferred by provisions forming part of the contract immediately before 22 March 2006);
(d) immediately before 22 March 2006 and at all subsequent times up to the time concerned there were rights under the contract that:
    (i) were comprised in the settlement; and
    (ii) formed part of the settled property in which a transitionally protected interest (whether or not the same such interest throughout that period) subsisted.

A transitionally protected interest is an existing IIP or a TSI (see **5.4–5.6** below).

Where s 46A applies, the rights under the contract are treated as if they became comprised in the settlement before 22 March 2006 and the person beneficially entitled to the transitionally protected interest is treated as having become beneficially entitled to that interest before that date. If the payment of the premium is a transfer of value, that transfer of value is a potentially exempt transfer.

This relief is generous and its scope is not restricted to rights arising only in consideration of the payment of premiums by the policy holder which he was contractually bound to make before 22 March 2006. Most single premium policies, for example, permit the policy holder to make further premium payments and the benefits under the policies will normally be determined by reference to a notional investment of those premiums. So if one had a small single premium contract held in a flexible life interest trust one could add very large amounts of money to it and still benefit from treating the interest in possession subsisting in the policy as an existing IIP. It should be noted, however, that the relief does not fully deal with the problem of adding further sums to a settlement to allow the trustees to pay insurance premiums. When the sums are added and before they are paid as premiums they will be relevant property. The addition to the settlement will therefore be a chargeable transfer even though s 46A will relieve the trustees from the decennial and exit charges. Of course, the payment of premiums may be relieved under the normal expenditure out of income exemption or may be covered by the annual exemption but as flexible life interest trusts were mainly used to hold large policies these reliefs will often be insufficient to relieve the addition from inheritance tax.

Transitional serial interests ('TSI')

Inheritance tax

[5.4] There are two forms of TSI and once again there are special rules in relation to insurance contracts.

The two categories of TSI are:

(a) interests to which a person has become entitled during the period 22 March 2006 to 5 October 2008; and
(b) interests to which a person has become entitled on the death of his spouse or civil partner on or after 6 October 2008.

Interests to which a person has become entitled during the period 22 March 2006 to 5 October 2008

[5.5] An interest in possession (the 'current interest') to which a person ('B') is beneficially entitled is a TSI if:

(a) the settlement commenced before 22 March 2006 and immediately before that date the property then in the settlement was property in which an interest in possession ('the prior interest') subsisted;
(b) the prior interest came to an end on or after 22 March 2006 but before 6 October 2008;
(c) B became beneficially entitled to the current interest at that time;
(d) a TBM does not subsist in the property and the interest is not a DPI (IHTA 1984, s 49C).

The following example shows how these rules work.

Example

A settled property on his son, B, for life on 1 March 2006 with succeeding life interests to his daughter, C, and then to his granddaughter, D. B died on 30 June 2006 and C died on 30 June 2007.

B's interest in possession is an existing IIP.

C's succeeding interest in possession is a TSI because:

(i) the settlement commenced before 22 March 2006 and immediately before that date an interest in possession (B's life interest) subsisted in the property;

(ii) B's prior interest came to an end on or after 22 March 2006 but before 6 October 2008;
(iii) C became beneficially entitled to the current interest at the time that B's interest ceased;
(iv) the settlement is not a TBM nor is it a DPI.

D's interest, however, is not a TSI. Although an interest in possession subsisted in the property immediately before 22 March 2006 D did not become beneficially entitled to her interest on that prior interest coming to an end. She became beneficially entitled to her interest when C's interest came to an end and that interest did not exist immediately before 22 March 2006.

Interests to which a person becomes entitled on the death of his spouse or civil partner on or after 6 October 2008

[5.6] Where a person ('E') is beneficially entitled to an interest in possession (the 'successor interest') that interest is a TSI if:

(a) the settlement commenced before 22 March 2006 and immediately before that date the property in the settlement was property in which a person ('F') other than E was beneficially entitled (the 'previous interest');
(b) the previous interest came to an end on or after 6 October 2008 on the death of F;
(c) immediately before F died, F was the spouse or civil partner of E;
(d) E became beneficially entitled to the successor interest on F's death;
(e) the successor interest was not a DPI and the property in which it subsisted was not subject to a TBM (IHTA 1984, s 49D).

Again, an example may help to show how this works.

Example

Before 22 March 2006, A settled property on life interest trusts for his son, B, with a succeeding life interest to his son's wife, C, with absolute interest in remainder to his granddaughter, D. The settlement was subject to an overriding power of appointment exercisable by the trustees.

B died on 31 December 2009. On 31 December 2010 the trustees exercised their power of appointment to defeat C's interest in possession and to advance the trust assets absolutely to D.

B's interest was an existing IIP. His wife's, C's, interest was a TSI. That is because:

(a) the settlement commenced before 22 March 2006 and immediately before that date an interest in possession subsisted in the property which was held by a person, B, other than the person who was to become the holder of the successor interest, that is C;
(b) the previous interest for B came to an end on or after 6 October 2008 on the death of B;
(c) immediately before B died he was the spouse of C;
(d) C became beneficially entitled to her successor interest on the death of her husband, B;
(e) C's interest was not a DPI nor, while it subsisted, was the settlement a TBM.

The result was that s 49 applied to both B and C's interests to treat them, whilst those interests subsisted, as beneficially entitled to the property in which their interest subsisted. Therefore on B's death the settled property was treated as forming part of his estate and as passing to his wife, C, and was therefore exempt as an inter-spouse transfer.

When the trustees exercised their power to defeat C's interest s 49 applied to that interest with the result that she was treated as making a transfer of value in favour of an individual, D, which was a potentially exempt transfer.

Contracts of life insurance

[5.7] Section 49E contains complex provisions to treat interests in possession in rights under a contract of life insurance as a TSI in various circumstances where there is a chain of interest in possessions in the rights each of which came to the end on the death of the person entitled to it.

Capital gains tax

[5.8] One cannot settle further property on an existing IIP. The interest in possession in the added property would not have existed at 22 March 2006 and so it would not qualify as an existing IIP. The further settled property would be relevant property subject to the decennial and exit charges.

The uplift to market value on the death of a person entitled to an interest in possession under TCGA 1992, s 72 or s 73 will apply to an existing IIP (see **4.35** and **4.36**). It may be possible to make a vulnerable person's election in relation to an existing IIP (see **4.37**).

Otherwise the capital gains taxation consequences of an existing IIP will be as set out in **4.20** and **4.21** in relation to interests in possession subsisting in relevant property trusts.

Income tax

[5.9] The income taxation of an existing IIP will be as set out in **4.22** and **4.25** in relation to interests in possession subsisting in relevant property trusts.

Accumulation and maintenance trusts

Inheritance Tax

[5.10] IHTA 1984, s 71 for many years provided generous reliefs to settlements for beneficiaries, loosely, up to the age of 25.

The accumulation and maintenance trust was usually chosen as the best method of settling assets for the maintenance and education of grandchildren. The creation of such a trust was a potentially exempt transfer and so no tax was payable provided the donor survived the settlement of the trust by 7 years.

Although accumulation and maintenance trusts were normally in discretionary form they were not subject to decennial and exit charges under the relevant property regime provided certain conditions contained in s 71 were met. The Finance Act 2006 introduced radical changes to the tax treatment of such trusts. Since 6 April 2008, accumulation and maintenance trusts are subject to the relevant property regime unless s 71 (in its form before amendment by the Finance Act 2006) applied to it immediately before 22 March 2006 and continued to do so until 5 April 2008, and it has satisfied the following conditions since 6 April 2008

(a) one or more beneficiaries will, on or before attaining a specified age not exceeding 18, become beneficially entitled to the trust property;
(b) no interest in possession subsists in the trust property and the income from the trust property which is not applied for the maintenance, education or benefit of a beneficiary is to be accumulated;
(c) either:
    (i) less than 25 years have elapsed since the time at which the trust property became held upon accumulation and maintenance trusts; or
    (ii) all the persons who are or have been beneficiaries are *either* grandchildren of a common grandparent *or* children, widows or widowers of such grandchildren who were themselves beneficiaries but died before the time when, had they survived, they would have become beneficially entitled.

A trust which is a TBM cannot be an accumulation and maintenance trust under s 71 (IHTA 1984, s 71(1B)).

A settlement created primarily for one person's children or grandchildren may continue for longer than those created primarily for children of different families or children from different generations (although step-children may not actually have a common grandparent — for instance, if both parties to a marriage have children by a previous marriage — they count as their parents' children and therefore the test is satisfied (s 71(8)).

Those accumulation and maintenance trusts which did not meet the conditions of s 71 after 5 April 2008, became subject to the relevant property regime on 6 April 2008. The charge accrues from that time because the settlement will then have comprised 'settled property'. The first anniversary charge will be at the first decennial from the date when the settlement was first set up falling after 5 April 2008 but inheritance tax will only be levied by reference to the period when the trust was a relevant property settlement.

Accumulation and maintenance trusts can no longer be settled so that individuals wishing to provide for the education of their grandchildren, for example, will now usually create discretionary trusts which provide flexibility but unfortunately will be subject to the relevant property regime.

What steps may be taken to deal with the settled property?

General principles

[5.11] The basic principles of estate planning are equally applicable when considering whether any steps should be taken in relation to settled property. This is particularly so when considering the interest of a life tenant of an existing IIP or a privileged trust who, whilst not owning the capital of the trust, will be treated as owning that property in which he has an interest in possession (IHTA 1984, s 49) (special considerations apply to section 5(1B) interests (see **4.19**) to which s 49 applies but which are also charged under the relevant property settlement rules). The steps that may be taken to minimise the inheritance tax charge that will arise on the life tenant's death are similar to those that may be taken by an individual in relation to his own estate. He could, for example, surrender his interest in possession in the settled property in a series of tranches over a number of years in order to make use of his annual exemption of £3,000 per annum. Alternatively, the life tenant may assign or surrender his interest in possession by way of a potentially exempt transfer. Provided that, as a result of the transfer, the estate of another individual is increased or property becomes held upon particular types of trust and he survives his deemed transfer of value on the assignment or surrender by 7 years, no inheritance tax will be chargeable.

The principles discussed in **CHAPTER 2 LIFETIME PLANNING** of making gifts in order to reduce exposure to inheritance tax at a later date, and implementing a policy of doing so at an early stage, have less application in relation to relevant property settlements. Provided the settlor has not reserved a benefit in the property settled under FA 1986, s 102, no individual will at any time be treated, for inheritance tax purposes, as being beneficially entitled to the trust property. Unless the settled property is held in a specially relieved trust (see **4.44**) IHTA 1984, Pt III Ch III and thus excluded from the 'relevant property' regime, the settlement may suffer decennial and exit charges. Nevertheless, the approach of a decennial and the rates of inheritance tax applicable to distributions before and after the anniversary may suggest that any distributions proposed should be made sooner rather than later.

Asset conversion

[5.12] Other estate planning steps of a type discussed in **CHAPTER 2 LIFETIME PLANNING** may be advantageously taken by the trustees or beneficiaries of a settlement.

Inheritance tax on property in a settlement may be mitigated if the assets held are converted from ones which do not qualify for any form of inheritance tax relief to those which do, such as agricultural property or relevant business property. This will reduce the value on which inheritance tax will be charged on an advance of trust property, the death of a life tenant or on a decennial depending on the nature of the settlement. However, any sale of property in order to release funds to acquire property qualifying for relief is likely to give rise to a capital gains tax charge for trustees resident in the UK which may outweigh the inheritance tax benefits. For this reason the most obvious occasions for converting assets may arise in relation to settlements with non-resident trustees which are outside the provisions of TCGA 1992, s 86 and Sch 5 (see **Chapter 6 Offshore Trusts**). These settlements will be outside the charge to capital gains tax and any disposal of assets made in order to re-invest the trust fund in other assets will not trigger a capital gains tax charge for the trustees (although beneficiaries resident in the UK will suffer a capital gains tax charge in respect of the gains realised by the trustees if they receive a distribution or other benefit from the settlement). An important exception to this general rule is where such trustees own assets used in connection with a trade, profession or vocation undertaken in the UK through a branch or agency. The fact that trustees are non-resident will not prevent a liability arising on a disposal of the assets or in some cases where the trade etc ceases (TCGA 1992, ss 10, 25).

In the case of a non-resident interest in possession settlement which was created by a settlor domiciled in the UK and which remains liable to inheritance tax even though the life tenant is now domiciled and resident abroad, it may be worth disposing of at least part of the property held and re-investing the proceeds in exempt gilts, subject to the duties that a trustee has in relation to investments. Where certain conditions are met no inheritance tax will be chargeable on the life tenant's death or on a lifetime surrender or assignment by him of his interest in respect of that part of the trust fund invested in exempt gilts (IHTA 1984, s 48(4)). In addition, no capital gains tax will be suffered as a result of the change of investments provided the settlement is outside the provisions of TCGA 1992, s 86 and Sch 5. The conditions are that either the settled property falls within IHTA 1984, s 49 and the holder of the interest in possession is neither resident nor domiciled in a country of the UK or all of the beneficiaries who could benefit from the settlement were neither so resident nor so domiciled.

Similarly, where a settlement with non-resident trustees was created by a settlor domiciled outside the UK for inheritance tax purposes but holds property situated in the UK, that property will not be excluded property within IHTA 1984, s 48 and inheritance tax will be chargeable upon the value of that property. In the case of a settlement within IHTA 1984, s 49, by selling the UK situated property to a company incorporated outside the UK, the property held by the trustees becomes the foreign situated shares in the foreign company and is therefore excluded property and outside the charge to inheritance tax. The rules relating to relevant property settlements are different, as an inheritance tax charge will arise where 'relevant property' ceases to be held. For these purposes excluded property is not relevant property (IHTA 1984, s 58(1)(f)). It would be arguable that, where the trustees dispose of relevant property and acquire excluded property, an exit charge under IHTA 1984, s 65 could arise. There is, therefore, a specific exemption preventing a tax charge arising when relevant property ceases to be situated in the UK, thereby becoming excluded property (IHTA 1984, s 65(7)). Some commentators have suggested that this is a narrow relief and will apply only where the situation of particular property in a settlement changes; for example where a chattel is shipped to another country. Under this view it does not apply where a UK situated asset is replaced with a foreign asset; for example, where UK land is sold and foreign land is bought. The better view is that where s 65(7) refers to 'property comprised in a settlement', it refers to aggregate property just as the reference in subsection 2 to 'relevant property comprised in the settlement' must, in the context, refer to aggregate relevant property so that subsection 7 will have the effect of relieving from charge any fall in the value of relevant property which is due to UK situated property being replaced by property which is not situated in the UK.

Value freezing

[5.13] Techniques of estate planning involving freezing the value of assets held in a settlement are useful in relation to settled property as they are in relation to an individual's free estate. However, legislative provisions and the terms upon which settled property is held may restrict the opportunities available to the trustees to deal with their trust assets more efficiently and their general duty to consider the interests of all beneficiaries and their specific duties in relation to the exercise of investment powers may mean that the steps they are able to take are more limited.

Value shifting exercises may be less appropriate for settlements than for individuals since trustees should not, as a matter of trust law, participate in the reduction or freezing of the value of their trust property. However, such exercises may be valid if the persons benefited by them hold the interests the values of which are frozen. It may, therefore, be appropriate to create a 'parallel' settlement with similar beneficiaries and to arrange for assets with a frozen or gradually depreciating value to remain in one settlement with increasingly valuable assets being held in the 'parallel' settlement.

One possible route is for an existing IIP settlement holding shares in a family company to create a new class of shares in the company with little value at the time of their creation but which will participate in the future growth in value of the company or at a future date become of greater value. The original shares would remain in the settlement in which the interest in possession subsists and, provided that the trustees have power to do so, the new (deferred) shares could be advanced to a new settlement for the benefit only of the remaindermen of the original settlement. Provided the new shares advanced are of little or no value at the time of the advance, no inheritance tax should become chargeable as a result of the advance. On the death of the life tenant it would be hoped that the original shares would have lost a substantial part of their value or, at the very least, would not have increased in value from the date at which the new class was created and that this value or the growth in value since that date would have accrued to the new settlement for the benefit of the remaindermen of the original settlement. (Clearly a sufficiently large holding of shares carrying the necessary degree of control must be held in the first settlement or the other shareholders must agree to the issue for such an arrangement to be implemented.) If the mechanism by which this is achieved is for the deferred shares subsequently to rank equally, or become merged with, shares of another class, in the Revenue's view IHTA 1984, s 98(1)(b) applies because there will be an alteration of rights (Law Society Gazette, 11 September 1991). If the second settlement is a relevant property settlement and the deferred shares rise in value above the nil rate band decennial and exit charges may arise. This problem would not arise if a bare trust were used to hold the deferred shares.

In private trading companies, the necessity of carrying out such value freezing exercises has been reduced because of the availability of 100% business property relief.

Another estate planning opportunity to consider is for the trustees of an existing IIP to make a loan at a low rate of interest, with the life tenant's consent, to a new settlement for the benefit of the remaindermen of the original settlement. The difference between the return obtained (in the form of both income and capital appreciation) by the trustees of the new settlement from the use of the money and the interest being paid to the original settlement would accumulate in the new settlement. The capital value of the loan in the original settlement would have been frozen. Since interest on the loan would be charged it should not be possible for the Revenue to argue that the life tenant's interest in possession had terminated in favour of the beneficiaries of the second settlement; a dubious argument in any case. However, where those beneficiaries are the minor or unmarried children of the life tenant, care should be taken to ensure that the income of the new settlement cannot be taxed as the income of the life tenant under ITTOIA 2005, s 629 since the life tenant's consent to the arrangement would almost undoubtedly make him a 'settlor' within those provisions.

Creation of 'surplus assets'

[5.14] One estate planning measure discussed in **CHAPTER 2 LIFETIME PLANNING** which should also be considered in relation to settlements is that of creating 'surplus assets'.

Surplus assets may be created by investing the trust fund in higher income yielding assets. The principal beneficiary may consider giving away income-producing assets from his free estate in the knowledge that his total income will be undiminished by the arrangement because his income from the settlement has increased. For inheritance tax purposes this gift will be a potentially exempt transfer provided that the relevant conditions are fulfilled. An element of 'value freezing' will also be achieved since high income yielding investments are unlikely also to grow substantially in capital value. The value of the fund will not therefore increase as substantially as it might otherwise have done. Therefore, the potential charge to inheritance tax on the settled property will have been reduced both by this and the inheritance tax on his free estate will have been reduced by his gift.

Where an interest in possession was conferred upon a surviving spouse under the will or intestacy of an individual who died before 13 November 1974, the value of the capital to which the surviving spouse is treated as being beneficially entitled will be left out of account in calculating the inheritance tax payable on his or her death (IHTA 1984, s 273 and Sch 6 para 2). By increasing the amount of income arising to the surviving spouse from such a trust it may be possible to place him or her in a position to give away assets which do not benefit from this exemption during their lifetime by way of potentially exempt transfers, thereby enabling the bulk of his estate to pass free of tax. The capital gains tax implications of restructuring the investment portfolio, as well as that relating to any gift, must always be taken into account.

Dealing with the interests of the beneficiaries

[5.15] The circumstances in which a reorganisation of interests under a settlement or the distribution of capital from a settlement may be appropriate and the most efficient methods of achieving the desired result (together with other means of dealing with settled property to achieve similar ends) are considered later in this chapter. First, it is necessary to consider, briefly, the means by which the interests of beneficiaries may be altered either by the exercise of powers incorporated in a settlement or otherwise and some of the advantages of allowing existing settlements to continue.

How can the interests of beneficiaries be altered?

[5.16] Frequently the terms of older settlements are more rigid than those of more recently drafted settlements. More recent settlements may include wide and flexible powers of appointment exercisable in favour of a wide class of beneficiaries or powers to revoke the existing trusts and declare completely new trusts which may be exercised (by the settlor, the trustees or others) to rearrange the interests of the beneficiaries, whereas older settlements may only incorporate powers to pay over capital to beneficiaries.

It may still be possible to vary older settlements (and will trusts) without such internal powers to alter beneficial interests. Where all of the beneficiaries are of full age and capacity, the rule in *Saunders v Vautier* (1841) 4 Beav 115 allows them to require the trustees to advance the settled property to them absolutely. The beneficiaries, however, can only modify the existing trusts with the consent of the trustees (*Brockbank (Re)* [1948] 1 All ER 287 (Ch D)). In most circumstances, however, this will result in the creation of a new settlement rather than the variation of an existing one. In any event, where there are minor, unborn or unascertained beneficiaries, an application to the court to sanction a variation under the Variation of Trusts Act 1958 will be necessary. Occasionally, an alteration of interests may arise from a compromise following a dispute between beneficiaries as to their rights and interests under a settlement and where minor or unborn beneficiaries are interested the court has power to sanction the compromise on their behalf. However, the court will not exercise its jurisdiction to sanction a compromise where it believes that there is no real dispute or point of uncertainty as to the interests of the beneficiaries (*Chapman v Chapman* [1954] AC 429, [1954] 1 All ER 978). In such circumstances an application under the Variation of Trusts Act 1958 is appropriate; it was as a direct result of the decision in *Chapman v Chapman* that this statute was enacted. A successful application was made in *Ridgeway v Ridgeway* [2007] EWHC 2666 (ChD) for the surviving spouse of the life tenant to be given a life interest on his death and that the trustees power of appointment be exercisable during the life of the life tenant and his spouse.

Although this may have postponed the children's interests, the trustees had a power of appointment to enable potentially exempt transfers to be made which would save inheritance tax. The judge noted that prior to March 2006, one possibility would have been to make advancements on accumulation and maintenance trusts under which the children took at 25.

Alternatively, one beneficiary of an interest in possession settlement may 'sell' his interest to another or he may surrender or assign his interest to another by way of gift. The surrender of an interest by the life tenant, however, will not be sufficient to place capital in the hands of the remaindermen if the interests in remainder are held for a class of beneficiaries living at the death of the life tenant and, therefore, as yet undefined. If the interests of the remaindermen are contingent upon their surviving the life tenant and their interests do not expressly carry the intermediate income, undesirable inheritance tax consequences may follow if as a result of the surrender the income of the trust fund becomes held upon resulting trust for the settlor.

When a beneficiary wishes to sell his interest he must consider the tax implications of doing so. A capital gains tax charge will arise in certain circumstances where a beneficiary of a trust sells his or her interest in it to someone else. Generally, this will affect UK settlements in which the settlor has an interest or where any of the trust property is derived from a trust which was a settlor-interested trust at any time in the previous two tax years (TCGA 1992, s 76A). The effect of the provisions is to treat the underlying assets to which the interest relates as though they are disposed of by the trustees and immediately reacquired by them at market value (TCGA 1992, s 76A and Sch 4A).

The inheritance tax implications for the purchaser also need to be considered where a beneficiary becomes beneficially entitled to an interest in possession after 8 October 2009 as a result of a commercial transaction to which s 10 applies, as his interest will form part of his estate for IHT purposes under IHTA 1984, s 49.

It may be possible to exercise statutory or other powers of advancement to place some or all of the trust fund in the hands of one or more of the beneficiaries, although in some older settlements there may be no express powers to advance capital to a life tenant and the statutory power of advancement (Trustee Act 1925, s 32) may not be extended (as is now common) to include the whole of the beneficiaries' presumptive shares.

Similarly, if property is held on protective trusts, any attempt by the life tenant to assign or surrender his interest will trigger the discretionary trusts which follow the protected life interest. It will be impossible to vary such trusts, whether before or after a forfeiture, without the consent of the court since minor and unborn beneficiaries (and future spouses) will be included in the class of beneficiaries who would or may benefit in the event of the life interest divesting from the protected life tenant. However, under the terms of the statutory protective trusts set out in Trustee Act 1925, s 33, the life tenant may consent to the statutory power of advancement, or an express power of advancement may be exercisable without giving rise to a forfeiture, and similar provisions may have been incorporated in express protective trusts; such powers may therefore be used to achieve some alteration of the interests.

Strict settlements within the Settled Land Act 1925 provide fewer opportunities for variation without the approval of the court since the statutory power of advancement is not applicable and so no rearrangement may be achieved unless specific powers are incorporated in the settlement. However, the life tenant may still assign or surrender his interest (unless it is a protected life interest in which case the planning steps that may be taken without an application to court under the Variation of Trusts Act 1958 will be very limited). There are very few such settlements remaining after the enactment of the Trusts of Land and Appointment of Trustees Act 1996.

Discretionary trusts, being by their nature more flexible, do not, generally, give rise to these problems. The capital and income may be appointed to beneficiaries absolutely or upon new trusts.

Not only may the beneficial trust provisions of older settlements be less flexible than those of their modern counterparts but other dispositive powers, not strictly part of the beneficial trusts, may be more limited. Dispositive powers, incorporated in a settlement, such as that to permit beneficiaries to occupy properties owned by the trust or to lend trust money free of interest to the beneficiaries, may be exercised to confer benefits on individual beneficiaries other than by the outright appointment of capital to them or for their benefit.

When should existing settlements be left alone?

[5.17] Existing settlements are not always burdensome. On the death of the life tenant of an existing IIP there will be an uplift in the base value of all the settled property to its market value at the date of his death free of capital gains tax. If, instead, the settlement had been broken before the life tenant's death and assets passed absolutely to the remaindermen (eg by way of potentially exempt transfer in the hope of avoiding an inheritance tax charge on the trust assets on the death of the life tenant) any unrealised gains which had been held-over into the hands of the remaindermen would still be potentially chargeable to capital gains tax.

If assets incorporating gains have been transferred to an existing IIP or a TSI and a hold-over election under either TCGA 1992, s 165 or s 260 has been made, the death of the life tenant will trigger a claw-back charge on the gains held over if the assets subject to the election are still held in the settlement at the life tenant's death (TCGA 1992, s 74). It may be possible to make a further election for hold-over relief at the life tenant's death to avoid this charge but as noted earlier this will not be possible where a surviving spouse or a UK registered charity have the succeeding interest as the provisions of TCGA 1992, s 260(2)(a) would not be satisfied. In such cases it may be more advantageous to advance the assets to the life tenant absolutely and elect to hold over the gain realised provided the terms of the settlement permit this and the relevant assets still fall within the scope of TCGA 1992, s 165. If the assets fall within his estate at death they will benefit from the tax-free uplift to their market value at the date of the life tenant's death. No claw-back provisions operate in relation to held-over gains crystallising on the death of an outright owner of assets. This technique will operate most successfully where the life tenant is likely to be survived by his UK-domiciled spouse, so that no inheritance tax charge will arise on the beneficiary's death where the spouse inherits the property concerned. An election for hold-over relief on the death of the life tenant will not be possible where the trust is settlor-interested or an arrangement subsists under which the settlor might acquire an interest (TCGA 1992, s 169B).

Accordingly, careful consideration will be required in each case to determine whether the capital gains tax advantages of leaving assets in an existing IIP, a TSI or an IPDI until the death of the life tenant outweigh the inheritance tax and other advantages of breaking or altering the settlement before it has run its course (whether by advance to the life tenant or by some other means). Much will depend on whether the assets are ever likely to be sold. The decision as to whether or not to break the settlement and if so, in whose favour, used to be finely balanced when the maximum rates of capital gains tax and inheritance tax were 40%. Now of course, the rates of capital gains tax are 18% and 28%. Where 100% business property relief is available on the settled assets and no hold-over relief has been claimed in respect of gains arising on the transfer of the assets to the settlement, there may be advantages in leaving the assets settled until the death of the life tenant. This will clearly be the case if a substantial part of the value of the assets represents unrealised gain (potentially chargeable at 28%) which will fall out of charge to capital gains tax on the life tenant's death, whilst the availability of 100% business property relief may relieve the property from all inheritance tax on death provided the settled assets remain unsold.

Some settlements still exist which benefit from the estate duty surviving spouse exemption which, by virtue of IHTA 1984, Sch 6 para 2, continues where the surviving spouse is still living. This exemption provides that property subject to this provision is not taken into account in calculating for inheritance tax purposes the value of the surviving spouse's estate on death, although the property can be taken into account for certain valuation purposes. Such settlements should, ideally, be left untouched to ensure that this protection remains on the death of the surviving spouse. Although the termination of the surviving spouse's interest in possession in such a trust, whether by a lifetime surrender or assignment or on death, would not give rise to a charge to inheritance tax, it is preferable for her not to make a lifetime gift of her interest but to retain the benefit of the complete inheritance tax exemption for the funds in which her interest subsists until her death and to give away by means of potentially exempt transfers other assets which fall within the inheritance tax charge. Unless there is need for income, the assets of such a settlement should ideally be invested for capital growth since the gains will pass free of inheritance tax. An interesting attempt to take advantage of the relief was made in *Davies v HMRC* [2009] UKFTT 138 (TC) but foundered on the inability of the appellants to prove that the surviving spouse had had a life absolute interest in the assets owned.

Discretionary settlements created before 18 March 1986 under which the settlor is included as a beneficiary do not fall within the gifts with reservation provisions since FA 1986, s 102 requires a gift to have been made after 17 March 1986. Such settlements are, therefore, likely to be best left alone. No property should now be added by any interested beneficiary (including the settlor) since the provisions of s 102 would apply to treat the donor beneficiary as beneficially entitled to that property (and property deriving from it) which is held in the settlement at his death. This would necessitate keeping the property separate from the other property in the settlement for identification purposes which from an administrative point of view would be inconvenient. If the settlor at some time during his lifetime is excluded from benefit he would be treated as having made a disposition of the donated property (and property deriving from it) at that time by way of a potentially exempt transfer (FA 1986, s 102(4)). As a result of the income tax settlement rules, the settlor will be assessed on the income received by the trustees. The settlor has a statutory right of recovery against the trustees for any income tax so assessed on him. The settlor may also be subject to an annual income tax charge on any benefit retained under the pre-owned assets charge. This is considered in detail in **CHAPTER 2 LIFETIME PLANNING**.

A reversionary interest which is defined as including any future interest under a settlement whether vested or contingent (IHTA 1984, s 47) is excluded property for inheritance tax purposes with three exceptions (IHTA 1984, s 48). The assignment of a reversionary interest will not usually give rise to a charge to inheritance tax and this is a useful method by which individuals may pass assets to others. Not only does no inheritance tax charge arise immediately on the gift but also there will be no further charge if the donor dies within 7 years of the gift. Further, even if the assignment could not be a potentially exempt transfer (because it was made to a relevant property settlement), no inheritance tax will be payable and the donor's cumulative total will be unaffected. Since a reversionary interest is necessarily a future interest in settled property the donor is less likely to count on receipt of benefits from the interest or to include it in his present assets when considering the resources available to him. He may be more prepared to give away something which he has not yet considered to be his (or at least part of it). For this reason it may be preferable to leave an existing settlement unbroken and for estate planning steps to be taken instead in relation to the reversionary interests existing under it.

There was a strategy which involved using reversionary interests. FA 2010, s 52 was designed to counteract that strategy.

A settlor ('Mr A') settled property on trusts under which, after a period of either discretionary trusts or interest in possession trusts for others, he had an interest in possession ('IIP') for a long fixed period. The retained future IIP was therefore initially a 'reversionary interest' and formed part of his estate. Because the succeeding interest in possession was for a very long period of time there was a very small diminution in the settlor's estate and therefore a very small transfer of value.

When the initial trusts came to an end the falling into possession of the succeeding IIP did not result in a transfer of value because there was no disposition by the settlor at that stage. The interest in possession did not form part of Mr A's estate. Once the interest in possession had arisen, therefore, Mr A could assign it on trust for other beneficiaries without that being an occasion of charge. The settlor had been able to create a relevant property settlement without there being an initial charge.

In order to stop this strategy IHTA 1984, s 81A was introduced in respect of reversionary interests to which a relevant reversioner became beneficially entitled after 8 December 2009.

That section makes two provisions in relation to reversionary interests in relevant property which are owned by persons who either acquired their interests for a consideration in money or money's worth or are owned by the settlor, the settlor's wife or the settlor's civil partner. The first provision is that the falling in of the reversion in circumstances in which the person entitled to it becomes entitled to an interest in possession is treated as a disposition by that person of the reversionary interest. The second is that a transfer of value of such a reversionary interest is not a potentially exempt transfer. The result, in respect of the strategy, is that when the settlor's interest in possession arises he will make a transfer value equal to the value of the reversion and that transfer will be immediately chargeable. It is not altogether clear whether s 81A will have the effect that HMRC intended it to have.

Business and agricultural property relief

[5.18] If business property relief or agricultural property relief would be available on settled assets should a chargeable occasion arise, then care should be taken to ensure that the relief is not lost when the interests of beneficiaries under a settlement are rearranged.

Where an existing IIP or a privileged interest subsists in a settlement the life tenant will be treated as owning the settled property for the purposes of determining whether the period of ownership qualifications are satisfied. If the life tenant's interest terminates (by whatever means) the succeeding 'owners' will have to own the settled assets (whether by being absolutely entitled to them or by holding a privileged interest in the assets for the relevant period before that relief will be available. Careless reorganisations may cause business property relief or agricultural property relief to be unavailable at the crucial moment.

Further, if a life tenant's interest in settled property qualifying for business property relief or agricultural property relief is terminated in favour of others and the termination, because of the nature of the interests, is a potentially exempt transfer, the requirement that the transferees must continue to 'own' that property, or its qualifying replacement, should not be forgotten.

Capital gains tax issues

[5.19] Modern trusts should be sufficiently flexible to permit their internal reorganisation without precipitating a capital gains tax charge especially where hold-over relief would not be available.

When reorganising older, less flexible, settlements, it is often important that the reorganisation does not create a new settlement for capital gains tax purposes. In such an instance there would be a deemed disposal and reacquisition of the property held giving rise to a charge under TCGA 1992, s 71. The fact that the same persons were trustees of the old and the new settlement would not prevent the charge arising.

Such reorganisations can be used to make what are, in effect, gifts to members of a family by enhancing their interests under a settlement, again without incurring any immediate capital gains tax liability.

Key considerations

[5.20] If steps are to be taken to alter the status of a trust, whether for income tax, capital gains tax or inheritance tax mitigation purposes, one needs to identify those situations where a deemed disposal and reacquisition might arise. There are three key considerations to bear in mind:

(a) the nature of the power effecting the reorganisation;
(b) the extent to which that power is being used;
(c) in cases of doubt, the nature of the external evidence that exists indicating that a new settlement has been created.

Under the terms of the trust instrument, the trustees will be subject to a number of binding obligations which regulate the manner in which they hold the settled property on behalf of the beneficiaries and they will also have a range of powers. These powers will divide into those of a purely administrative nature and those of a dispositive nature, the latter enabling the trustees to apply the trust property for the beneficiaries' benefit.

In order to achieve a trust reorganisation, the trustees will rely primarily upon dispositive powers. Such powers come in a variety of forms, each having its own distinct characteristics. Some are more powerful tools than others. Accordingly, the basic approach adopted by the courts has been to identify the type of power the trustees are exercising in order to establish whether a new settlement has arisen. There are four leading cases in this area.

In *Roome v Edwards* (1981) 54 TC 359, [1981] STC 96, [1981] 1 All ER 736 (HL), a settlement was established in 1944. In 1955 further deeds were executed with the net effect of appointing some of the assets to be held primarily for two beneficiaries absolutely, contingent upon their attaining the age of 25 (the appointed fund). After this date the 1944 settlement (the parent trust), and the appointed fund were administered separately, but there continued to be common trustees of both funds. In 1972 non-resident trustees were appointed in respect of the parent trust, whilst the appointed fund continued to have UK resident trustees. The non-resident trustees realised a significant capital gain and the Revenue sought to assess the UK trustees of the appointed fund. It argued that both trusts together constituted one settlement for capital gains tax purposes, with the result that the resident trustees of the appointed fund were liable in respect of the capital gains made by the non-resident trustees. The House of Lords found in favour of the Revenue, and its reasoning is of key importance in determining whether an internal trust reorganisation will trigger a charge under TCGA 1992, s 71.

Lord Wilberforce, delivering the leading speech, said that the existence of separate trusts, separate trustees and separate and defined trust property would not necessarily be decisive. He suggested that a practical and common-sense approach should be adopted, in deciding whether a new trust had been created, after taking into account established legal doctrine. He also sought to distinguish between situations where different types of powers had been exercised by the trustees.

The illustrative comments he made were in the particular context of special powers of appointment (at STC 100e-f), and these should be read in the light of the later gloss added by Vinelott J in *Ewart v Taylor* (post). Taking this into account, where a special power of appointment is exercised it would not be correct to say that 'a separate settlement had been created . . . if it were found that provisions of the original settlement continued to apply to the appointed fund, or that the appointed fund were liable in certain events, to fall back into the rest of the settled property'.

Lord Wilberforce contrasted such an exercise with a power to appoint and appropriate a part or portion of the trust property to beneficiaries and to settle it for their benefit:

> If such a power is exercised, the natural conclusion might be that a separate settlement was created, all the more so if a complete new set of trusts were declared as to the appropriated property, and if it could be said that the trusts of the original settlement ceased to apply to it. There can be many variations on these cases each of which will have to be judged on its facts.

The facts in *Ewart v Taylor* [1983] STC 721 (Ch D) were complex, but a subsidiary issue depended on whether a separate settlement (Angela's fund) had been created for a beneficiary following the exercise by the trustees of a power of appointment. Following Lord Wilberforce's observations in *Roome v Edwards*, the fact that a power of appointment, albeit of a wide nature, had been used suggested that no new settlement had arisen. Against this, the appointment was exhaustive in that it represented a complete severance from the beneficiaries' interest under the main trust, it had its own key management powers and new trustees could be appointed without reference to the original trust provisions.

The intention of the parties in separating Angela's interests from the rest of the original trust and how the trustees' accountants had treated the reorganisation resulted in the court holding that a new trust had been established. The accountants had prepared separate accounts, and the notes to these accounts clearly suggested that they considered that a separate settlement had arisen.

In *Bond v Pickford* [1983] STC 517 (CA), property was transferred to trustees on discretionary trusts for the benefit of a settlor's child and grandchildren in 1961. In 1972, the trustees executed two deeds allocating part of the settled property to the settlor's grandchildren absolutely, contingent upon their attaining 22. The provisions in the 1961 settlement dealing with investments, the execution of trusts and powers, and the appointment and remuneration of trustees still applied to the allocated property and the 1961 settlement trustees continued to act. However, the new trusts exhausted the beneficial interests. The Revenue, relying on this, argued that a new settlement had been created. This, it argued, was supported by the wording of the power of allocation which suggested that the allocated funds were to be governed by their own separate administrative powers. The trustees contended that as the allocated property continued to be held by the same trustees and subject to the same administrative powers as the remainder of the settled property, no separate settlement had arisen. The Court of Appeal found for the trustees.

Lord Justice Slade explained that:

> there is . . . a crucial distinction to be drawn between (*a*) powers to alter the presently operative trusts of a settlement which expressly or by necessary implication authorise the trustees to remove assets altogether from the original settlement (without rendering any person absolutely beneficially entitled to them); and (*b*) powers of this nature which do not confer on the trustees such authority.

He felt that the former represented 'powers in the wider form' and the latter 'powers in the narrower form'.

In *Swires v Renton* [1991] STC 490, 64 TC 315 (Ch D) the trustees of a settlement executed a deed of appointment by which the trust fund was divided into two parts. One part was appointed to Isabelle, the settlor's daughter, absolutely. The second was placed on trust, and the income paid to Isabelle for life. It was agreed that the absolute appointment gave rise to a charge to capital gains tax under TCGA 1992, s 71(1). However, the Revenue argued that a deemed disposal and reacquisition also took place in connection with the second appointment on the basis that a new and separate settlement had been created.

Here a widely drawn special power of appointment was exercised, albeit that the trustees of the original settlement continued to act in connection with the newly appointed settled fund. The new trusts affecting the settled fund were exhaustive in that no part of the original trusts were still subsisting, and there was no possibility of them reviving to govern the future disposition of the trust assets. The administrative powers and provisions, however, continued to govern the trust assets, under the terms of the deed of appointment, which was expressed to be supplemental to the original trust deed.

Despite the fact that the power exercised was found to be in the 'wider form', Hoffmann J found that no new settlement had been created using the approach set down by Lord Wilberforce in *Roome v Edwards* (*above*). Accordingly, the case is a useful authority demonstrating that the exercise of a power of appointment in a wider form will not always create a new settlement. Rather, it is necessary to establish the intent behind the exercise of the power itself. Hoffmann J also observed that where a power in the wider form is exercised which expressly purports to vary the beneficial trusts in some relatively minor way, it would be somewhat artificial for this to be 'construed as the creation of a new settlement to be read with all the provisions of the old one together with the variation' (at 500g).

The position of three commonly encountered powers is discussed below.

Special powers of appointment

[5.21] Special powers are generally exercisable by the trustees under the terms of the trust instrument. They are exercisable in favour of a limited class of persons or objects. The person who exercises the power is seen as fulfilling the original intention of the settlor. Generally, the limitations which arise as a result of such powers being exercised are treated as if they had been written into the original trust instrument which created them. As such they do not usually create a new trust, for example, if a special power of appointment is exercised to alter the vesting age of a beneficiary who has to satisfy some contingency, it is unlikely that any deemed disposal will arise under TCGA 1992, s 71. This is provided that the balance of the trust provisions remains otherwise unaltered.

However, this does not mean that special powers of appointment cannot be exercised either expressly or impliedly to authorise trustees to remove assets from the original settlement, and make them subject to trusts of a new settlement. In such circumstances a chargeable disposal and reacquisition of the trust assets would arise for capital gains tax purposes within TCGA 1992, s 71. For an example of a case where the court held that the exercise of a power of appointment did not operate to resettle an appointed fund and precipitate a capital gains tax disposal, see *Swires v Renton* [1991] STC 490, 64 TC 315 (Ch D).

Powers of advancement

[5.22] Advancement involves expenditure towards establishing a beneficiary in life. Irrespective of whether such advances are made under an express provision in the trust deed or under the statutory power of advancement in Trustee Act 1925, s 32, they need not be limited to straightforward payments or transfers of assets to beneficiaries. They can include settled advances which effectively alter or vary the trusts created by the settlement from which it was derived. As a result, powers of advancement are generally within the wider category of powers capable of removing assets from one settlement and subjecting them to the provisions of another. Not every exercise of a power of advancement, however, will create a new settlement.

Power of allocation

[5.23] A power of allocation is a power to allocate assets to particular interests within a settlement. It does not empower the trustees to create fresh or overriding trusts. This type of power was considered in *Bond v Pickford* [1983] STC 517. Accordingly, such powers fall within the 'narrower form' and no charge under TCGA 1992, s 71 will arise as a result of its exercise. This is the case even if administrative provisions that had previously applied under the original trust instrument cease to be applicable as a result of the exercise of the power of allocation.

Revenue guidelines

[5.24] Following the Court of Appeal's decision in *Bond v Pickford* [1983] STC 517, the Revenue issued a Statement of Practice (SP7/84) which states:

> . . . the Board considers that a deemed disposal will not arise when . . . [powers in the wider form, which may be powers of advancement or certain powers of appointment, are] . . . exercised and trusts are declared in circumstances such that:
>
> (a) the appointment is revocable, or

> (b) the trusts declared of the advanced or appointed funds are not exhaustive so that there exists a possibility at the time when the advancement or appointment is made that the funds covered by it will on the occasion of some event cease to be held upon such trusts and once again come to be held upon the original trusts of the settlement.
>
> Further, when such a power is exercised the Board considers it unlikely that a deemed disposal will arise when trusts are declared if duties in regard to the appointed assets still fall to the trustees of the original settlement in their capacity as trustees of that settlement . . . Finally, the Board accept that a power of appointment or advancement can be exercised over only part of the settled property and that the above consequences would apply to that part.

This statement is quite helpful, as it sets out a 'shopping list' of features that should be taken into account when planning an any internal reorganisation.

Settlements within IHTA 1984, s 49

[5.25] The treatment for inheritance tax, capital gains tax and income tax purposes of privileged interest trusts and section 5(1B) interests which continue to fall within IHTA 1984, s 49 is discussed in detail in **CHAPTER 4 CREATING SETTLEMENTS**. The tax treatment of existing IIP trusts and TSIs are discussed in this Chapter.

Interest in possession for inheritance tax purposes and the consequences of termination

[5.26] For the purposes of the discussion below it has been assumed that the expressions 'life interest' and 'interest in possession' are synonymous, ie that the terms of the settlements considered confer on the life tenant an interest in possession during his life.

For inheritance tax purposes where IHTA 1984, s 49 applies to the settled property, a life tenant is treated as being beneficially entitled to the trust property in which his interest subsists. Any termination of an existing IIP, a privileged interest or a section 5(1B) interest will be treated as though it were a transfer of value made by the life tenant (IHTA 1984, s 52) of a value equal to the value of the property in which the interest subsisted. A disposal of an interest to which s 49 applies is treated as not being itself a transfer of value. Rather the interest which is the subject of the disposal will be treated as coming to an end (IHTA 1984, s 51) with the result that s 52 will apply to treat the beneficiary as if he had made a transfer of value equal to the value of the property in which the interest subsisted.

The fact that the termination of an interest within s 49 is not an actual transfer of value but is merely treated as being such has some important inheritance tax consequences which must be considered on the termination of a life tenant's interest in possession.

(a) *Life tenant becoming absolutely entitled to the settled property.* If, as a result of a deemed transfer of value, the life tenant becomes absolutely entitled to the property in which his interest has terminated, no inheritance tax will be chargeable (IHTA 1984, s 53(2)).

(b) *Potentially exempt transfers.* If, as a result of the termination (in whole or part) of a life tenant's interest in possession, the property in which his interest subsisted becomes:

   (i) comprised in the estate of another; or
   (ii) held upon a DPI within IHTA 1984, s 89, or
   (iii) held on a bereaved minor's trust on the coming to an end of an IPDI,

   the life tenant will be treated as having made a potentially exempt transfer. Provided he survives for a period of 7 years after this, it will not become chargeable (IHTA 1984, ss 3A, 51, 52).

(c) *Other exemptions.* Although IHTA 1984, s 3(4) provides that references in the Act to a transfer of value made by any person include references to events on the happening of which tax is chargeable 'as if' a transfer of value had been made by that person and that 'transferor' is to be construed accordingly. The operation of this sub-section is specifically excluded by IHTA 1984, ss 19–22 which relate to annual exemptions, the small gifts exemptions, the normal expenditure out of income exemption and the gifts in consideration of marriage exemption respectively.

   However, IHTA 1984, s 57 provides that a life tenant may give notice to the trustees that the whole or part of his annual exemption or his exemption for gifts in consideration of marriage is unused. The exemption can then be set against the deemed transfer of value made on the termination of his interest. Even where the deemed transfer of value is not chargeable but is potentially exempt at the time it is made the life tenant should, if appropriate, give notice to the trustees of the availability of these exemptions under s 57. Otherwise, if he dies within 7 years of the deemed transfer of value, the exemptions will not be available to the trustees to set against the potentially exempt transfer which has now become chargeable. A claim must be made within 6 months of the termination in the prescribed form (IHTA 1984, s 57(4)).

(d) *Reliefs for certain dispositions.* Since there is no actual transfer of value on the termination of a life interest, the reliefs relating to dispositions which would be transfers of value (ie dispositions not intended to confer gratuitous benefit (IHTA 1984, s 10), dispositions for family maintenance (IHTA 1984, s 11) and dispositions allowable for income tax (IHTA 1984, s 12)) do not apply. However, IHTA 1984, s 51(2) provides that if the assignment or surrender by the life tenant satisfies the conditions in IHTA 1984, s 11, the assignment or surrender will not be treated as the coming to an end of his interest and, accordingly, no inheritance tax will be chargeable on this occasion.

Value on which inheritance tax is charged

[5.27] There is a further difference between the charge to inheritance tax made when an interest in possession which is an existing IIP, a privileged interest or a section 5(1B) interest is terminated during the life of the life tenant and that which would be made if he were to give away part of his free estate. IHTA 1984, s 52(1) provides that on the termination of an interest in possession by whatever means, the life tenant will be treated as having made a transfer of value equal to the value of the property in which his interest subsisted. This value must be distinguished from the value which he would be treated as having transferred if, instead, he had made a lifetime gift of the same property from his free estate. In that case inheritance tax would be chargeable on the amount by which his estate was diminished as a result of the transfer. This amount might be greater than the value of the property which is the subject of the transfers. For example, where a majority shareholding in a private company is held in an interest in possession settlement, if the life tenant surrenders or assigns his interest in a part of the fund representing a minority shareholding in the company and, after the assignment, has an interest in possession only in a minority shareholding, the charge to inheritance tax will be calculated on the value of the minority holding in which he has released his interest. Had the majority holding of shares been part of his own free estate, the charge to inheritance tax under similar circumstances would have been calculated, not by reference to the value of the minority holding given away, but by reference to the difference between the value of the majority shareholding held before the transfer and the value of the minority shareholding he retained.

This means that the order in which gifts are made may be important.

Example

Mr A owns 46% of the issued share capital of an investment company, Investment Company Limited ('ICL') and has an existing IIP in a trust the only asset of which is a 6% shareholding in ICL. He wishes his two daughters to receive shareholdings of 6% each in ICL. He considers the following alternatives:

(a) Transferring 6% shareholdings to each of his daughters simultaneously.
(b) Transferring a 6% shareholding to one of his daughters and the trustees of the trust then exercising their power of appointment to appoint the trust's shareholding to the other daughter absolutely.
(c) The trustees of the trust using their power of appointment to appoint the trust's shareholding to one daughter absolutely and thereafter Mr A transferring a 6% shareholding to his other daughter.

The value of shareholdings in the company do not vary proportionately to their size but rather reflect the fact that at key points significant degrees of control are acquired; for example a 51% shareholding allows the holder to ensure that an ordinary resolution of the members is passed. The value of the various sizes of shareholdings in the company are as follows:

	£
Value of 52% shareholding	5,200,000

Value of 46% shareholding	2,300,000
Value of 40% shareholding	2,000,000
Value of 6% shareholding	180,000

Because he has an existing IIP in the shares held by the trust, Mr A is treated as the beneficial owner of the shares in which his interest subsists. On the coming to the end of his interest in the trust property the value on which tax would be charged under s 52 would not be the loss to his estate from the termination of his deemed beneficial interest in the property but rather the value of the property in which the interest subsisted. The values on which tax would be charged therefore, under each of the three alternatives are as follows:

(a) The value charged is the fall in value of Mr A's estate resulting from the gift and so his transfer of value is £3,200,000 (£5,200,000 – £2,000,000). Thus the total value charged is £3,200,000.

(b) The value charged on Mr A's gift is the fall in value of his estate resulting from his gift; that is £2,900,000 (£5,200,000 – £2,300,000). By reason of the advance Mr A is treated as making a transfer of value equal to the value of the property in which his interest subsisted; that is £180,000. Thus the total value charged is £3,080,000 (£2,900,000 + £180,000).

(c) By reason of the advance Mr A is treated as making a transfer of value equal to the value of the property in which his interest subsisted; that is £180,000. The value charged on Mr A's gift is the fall in value of his estate resulting from the gift; that is £300,000 (£2,300,000 – £2,000,000).

So the value charged under option (c) is £480,000 compared with £3,080,000 under option (*b*) and £3,200,000 under option (a). The significant difference is that under option (*c*) the combined holding drops from a majority to a minority holding on the appointment by the trustees to which the loss to the donor method of measuring the value transferred does not apply.

Life interest for capital gains tax purposes and the consequences of termination

[5.28] Where settled property within IHTA 1984, s 49 includes assets in respect of which there are held-over gains which will suffer a claw-back charge on the death of the life tenant if they remain settled (TCGA 1992, s 74) it may be advantageous to advance those assets to the life tenant provided the settlement terms allow and s 165 hold-over relief is available. The trustees and the life tenant will have to make an election for hold-over relief. On the life tenant's death, the held-over gains will fall out of the charge to capital gains tax. These considerations will only be relevant if assets which were the subject of a hold-over election when transferred to a settlement have not been, and are not to be, disposed of prior to the life tenant's death since the actual sale of these assets would in any event trigger the capital gains tax charge on held-over gains.

The lifetime termination of a life interest will not give rise to a charge to capital gains tax unless as a result some person becomes absolutely entitled to the settled property. No occasion of charge will arise on the change of interests provided that the property remains settled after the termination of the interest.

The sale of assets by the trustees will be the trigger for a charge to capital gains tax. Where a person does become absolutely entitled to the trust property (either the life tenant who has had the settled property transferred to him or a beneficiary with a succeeding interest who, as a result of the termination of the life tenant's interest, becomes absolutely entitled to the trust property) the trustees will be treated as having disposed of the trust property at market value at the date of termination of the life interest and as having reacquired it at that date as nominees for the individual who has become absolutely entitled (TCGA 1992, s 71). A capital gains tax charge will arise if the market value of the assets at the date of termination is greater than their acquisition cost. Depending upon the nature of the trust assets, it may be possible to hold over the gain under TCGA 1992, s 165 by the trustees and the individual who has become absolutely entitled to the trust property making an election.

In making any decision as to whether to terminate a life interest settlement in favour of the life tenant or the remaindermen or whether to accelerate the interests of the remaindermen or assign the life tenant's interest to others (outright or into some other form of settlement) capital gains tax will be a significant factor. The differing profiles for capital gains of the trustees and the beneficiaries need to be taken into account — for example either the beneficiaries or the trustees may have current year or brought forward losses or may be able to realise losses on assets which have fallen in value.

Motives for breaking a settlement within IHTA 1984, s 49

[5.29] The reasons for breaking a settlement within IHTA 1984, s 49 may be many. It may simply be that the settlement is thought to be too expensive to continue, the administration charges being disproportionately high in comparison to the value of the trust fund. The life tenant or the remaindermen may decide to assign or surrender their interests to each other and thus terminate the settlement or they may partition the fund, each taking part of the capital.

A partition might be proposed for a variety of reasons. For example it would enable a life tenant to invest the capital he receives on the partition in the acquisition of assets expected to increase in capital value rather than to yield a large income. He will also be free to give away that capital as and when and to whom he chooses. Another option is for the life tenant to apply capital received on the partition of the trust property in acquiring an annuity the capital element of which would not suffer income tax in his hands. Since the annuity will have no value at his death, his estate will have been reduced because there will no longer be capital owned by him nor settled property to which he will be treated as being entitled by virtue of his interest in possession.

The property in which the interest in possession subsists will be aggregated with the life tenant's estate for the purposes of calculating the rates of inheritance tax applicable to the settled property on his death. Both the life tenant and the remaindermen may wish to mitigate this potential charge. This can be achieved either by the life tenant surrendering his interest to the remaindermen, by the partition of the trust property between the life tenant and the remaindermen or by the purchase by the remaindermen of the life tenant's interest. One needs to consider, however, the capital gains tax charge that may arise on the trustees under TCGA 1992, Sch 4A. In accordance with the general principle that capital should be passed on down the generations in order to mitigate inheritance tax, the most sensible course for the life tenant to adopt (if he has sufficient other assets available for his needs) would be to surrender his interest in favour of the remaindermen. However, if the remaindermen are not the people whom he wishes to benefit from his estate, a partition of the fund or the sale by the life tenant or the remaindermen of their interests might be appropriate. The life tenant would then secure some free capital with which he would be able to make gifts to those whom he wishes to benefit.

The remaindermen, whose remainder interest confers no immediate benefit, may need capital to start a business or to invest in other ways and may, therefore, prefer to receive capital now rather than to await the death of the life tenant and to suffer an inheritance tax charge on that occasion. They may prefer to take immediate estate planning steps in respect of the capital they receive rather than to risk receiving it when efficient measures may no longer be taken. For this reason they may propose a partition of the trust property, a purchase of the life tenant's interest or a sale to the life tenant of their interests.

Where, on a trust reorganisation, one or more of the beneficiaries becomes absolutely entitled to some of the trust assets, any capital gains arising may be held over if the trust assets are business assets within TCGA 1992, s 165. Even if this relief is not available, it will be possible to pay any capital gains tax due on disposals of land or of certain holdings of shares and securities by ten equal annual instalments (TCGA 1992, s 281). The outstanding balance, however, will bear interest. Whether the charge to capital gains tax outweighs the advantages of the reorganisation will have to be considered in respect of the particular situation and this will entail considering not only the nature of the assets of the trust but also the extent to which their values reflect unrealised gains.

Means of dealing with the interests under a life interest trust within IHTA 1984, s 49

[5.30] The trusts upon which property will be held following a termination of the life tenant's interest may dictate what steps, if any, a life tenant and the remaindermen and/or the trustees may wish to take in relation to the beneficiaries' interests.

There are two basic methods available to a life tenant of dealing with his interest in possession: assignment or surrender of the interest only. In practice, similar results may be achieved by the exercise of powers conferred upon the trustees (such as powers of appointment or revocation). However, the essential difference between an assignment and a surrender is considered here together with other means of dealing with the interests of the beneficiaries in order that further consideration can then be given to particular situations.

Assignment of a life interest

[5.31] An assignment by the life tenant of his interest is effected by a written document of assignment (in order to comply with the requirements of Law of Property Act 1925, s 53(1)(c)). The assignment may be made by the life tenant in favour of others who are beneficiaries of the settlement or to complete strangers to the settlement. In either case the assignee or assignees step into the life tenant's shoes and become entitled to the income arising from the trust property in which his interest subsists during his lifetime. The life tenant may assign his life interest either outright to one or more individuals or to trustees of a new settlement. In the former case the assignee may deal with the income to which he is now entitled as he chooses and in the latter case the trustees must deal with the income which they are entitled to receive in accordance with the provisions of the trusts imposed upon them.

It is possible that a similar result may be achieved by the exercise of powers conferred upon the trustees of the settlement under which the life tenant's interest exists. For example, the trustees may have power to revoke the life interest and to declare that in future the income will be paid to some other beneficiary of the settlement during his life. In this case there will not have been the assignment of an asset; the first life tenant's asset (his life interest) will have ceased to exist and his interest under the settlement will have been replaced by another. That interest may be a TSI or it may be an interest in a relevant property settlement. Where the trustees exercise their powers in this way they may (provided the terms of the settlement permit them to do so) confer a capital interest upon the beneficiary for whose benefit they create the new interest. They may, for example, declare that in future they will pay the income of the trust property to X during his life or until he attains 35 at which time they may specify that they will transfer the capital to him. (Provision will also be made for the eventuality that X dies before attaining 35.)

The life tenant himself will have no power to declare such new interests in the trust property unless the power is expressly reserved to him by the terms of the settlement. So unless the trustees can and are willing to exercise their powers he can only attempt to achieve the same result by assigning or surrendering his interest. It will be necessary for a life tenant to assign his interest in income where the individuals upon whom the life tenant wishes to confer a benefit are not beneficiaries of the settlement. Those to whom he assigns his interest will become entitled to his income interest and can have no greater entitlement to capital than he had. If, under the terms of the settlement the life tenant will become entitled to capital if he attains, for example 35, he may assign this contingent interest to those he wishes to benefit in addition to assigning his income interest. Provided he does not die before his 35th birthday, his assignees will take his share of capital. However, if, under the terms of the settlement, the life tenant is entitled to income only, he can only confer this benefit on others by assignment.

Surrender of a life interest

[5.32] The alternative means by which a life tenant may deal with his interest is to surrender it in favour of those whose interests succeed his. They may either take capital absolutely as a result of his surrender or if their interests are only life interests following that of a life tenant then those interests will be accelerated. The interests under the settlement following the life interest then fall into possession. There may be a temporary gap in the beneficial interests giving rise to a resulting trust for the settlor where there are no interests ready to fall into possession. A surrender by a life tenant may not therefore operate to vest capital in the hands of succeeding beneficiaries and, indeed, their income interests may not even be accelerated. In these circumstances it may be advisable for the life tenant to assign his interest to them rather than to surrender it.

A similar effect to the surrender of the life tenant's interest may be achieved instead by the exercise of express or statutory powers vested in the trustees or others to appoint interests in favour of those whose interests follow the life interest, to extinguish the life interest or to advance assets to remaindermen. Such powers are particularly useful where a surrender by the life tenant will not accelerate the interests of the remaindermen or where the life interest is a protective life interest and an attempted surrender by the life tenant would give rise to a forfeiture. There may be income tax, capital gains tax and inheritance tax advantages if the trustees can exercise powers to achieve an end which, otherwise, the life tenant would achieve by assigning or surrendering his interest. In the case of an assignment or surrender, for example, his minor, unmarried children benefit from the surrender or assignment, for example, then for income tax purposes he would be treated as having made a settlement for the benefit of his children. He would be treated as continuing to be entitled to the income arising to his children unless the income was accumulated for so long as his children remained under 18 and unmarried (ITTOIA 2005, s 629).

Similarly, if the life tenant (or his spouse or civil partner) is capable of benefiting from the interest he assigns (for example, by being a beneficiary of a settlement to which he has assigned his interest), the income may continue to be taxed as his, under the provisions of ITTOIA 2005, s 624 regardless of whether or not he receives it, subject to limited exceptions.

Where an interest in possession, to which s 49 applies, comes to end in the holder's lifetime, the holder is treated as having made a transfer of value equal to the value of the property in which the interest subsisted. This may be a potentially exempt transfer.

If the life tenant continues to enjoy a benefit in some way from the property in which his interest has been lost by the exercise of the trustees' powers, he will be treated as having reserved a benefit and the property in which his interest has ceased will be treated as being part of his estate on death. The pre-owned assets charge contains no equivalent rule.

Assignment by the remaindermen of their interests

[5.33] For inheritance tax purposes an interest in remainder being a future interest under a settlement is a 'reversionary interest'. As reversionary interests are generally excluded property for inheritance tax purposes (IHTA 1984, s 48(1)) interests in remainder may be dealt with by way of gift either to other beneficiaries of the settlement under which it exists or to strangers to the settlement without giving rise to any inheritance tax consequences in certain circumstances.

It is for this reason that assignments of their interests by remaindermen to their children are particularly efficient for inheritance tax purposes.

Normally, the gift will not give rise to any inheritance tax charges and as a result does not require the assignor to survive 7 years; nor can his cumulative total be in any way affected by the gift. Yet when the prior interests terminate, the children will receive the whole benefit of the fund or that part of it in respect of which the reversionary interest was assigned. Although a charge to inheritance tax is likely to arise on the cessation of the prior interests this charge would have arisen even if the assignor had retained his interest. The potential inheritance tax charge avoided is that which might have arisen (either on the death of the assignor or on his making a gift of the assets in which his reversionary interest had previously subsisted) after the reversionary interest had fallen in.

If the remaindermen are all ascertained and of full age and between them will take the entire trust fund on the death of the life tenant, they may assign their interests to the life tenant and he will as a result of the merger of the interests in his hands become entitled to the capital of the trust fund, although as a result a capital gains tax charge under TCGA 1992, s 71 might arise. Although the assignments by the remaindermen of their interests will not have any inheritance tax consequences, it is likely that the life tenant will be older than the remaindermen and it will therefore generally be unwise to place the capital in his hands where it will be chargeable to inheritance tax as part of his estate on his death. Ordinarily, it would be preferable for the life tenant to assign or surrender his interest to the remaindermen thereby passing capital on to future generations.

If the life tenant is not old and intends to deal with the capital to which he becomes entitled, by making gifts of that capital, for example, by way of potentially exempt transfers, the assignment by the remaindermen of their interests to the life tenant may present advantages. However, more frequently, it will be advantageous for inheritance tax purposes for remaindermen to assign their interests, which may be vested (in that they may be kept out of their interests only by the prior entitlement of the life tenant) or contingent (ie dependent upon a particular event happening, for example, their surviving the life tenant), to younger generations.

Where a reversionary interest is given away after 8 December 2009, and the person taking the actual interest either purchased the reversionary interest or is the settlor, spouse or civil partner of the trust, there will be a lifetime chargeable transfer.

Example

Prior to March 2006 Augustus settled £10m on the following trusts:

- on interest in possession trusts for the benefit of his daughters Septima and Posie to provide for their University education;
- on interest in possession for his son Wesley until he reached age 25; and
- on interest in possession trusts for his wife Peggy;

Subject thereto on wide discretionary trusts for his issue.

Septima and Posie completed their studies on 30 September 2009 and Wesley's 25th birthday was on 31 March 2010. Septima's and Posie's interests were existing IIPs but Wesley's interest was in a relevant property trust. Peggy's reversionary interest was a reversionary interest in relevant property and she is the spouse of the settlor. Therefore, when her reversionary interest came to an end on her becoming entitled to an interest in possession, she was treated as having made a disposition of the reversionary interest which was not a potentially exempt transfer. She made a chargeable transfer equal to the value of her reversionary interest immediately before it fell into possession.

Sale of the interests of life tenant or remaindermen

[5.34] Any assignment or surrender by the life tenant or remainderman of their interests may be made by way of sale.

In general trustees do not exercise their powers to alter interests under settlements for consideration (although in certain commercial situations they may do so).

The life tenant or the remaindermen may each be prepared, and have the resources available, to buy the interests of the other to become entitled to the capital of the trust fund. If the sale is an arm's length transaction between unrelated parties it is expected that the cash price paid will relate to the value of the interest to be acquired, assessed by an independent actuary.

If the parties are related and the sale price does not reflect the value of the interest acquired, because it is too high, the inheritance tax consequences may be severe.

Whether undertaken strictly on an arm's length basis or not, the benefits arising from a sale of interests for each party will be that each takes a sum of money or assets absolutely with which they can deal as they please.

If neither remaindermen nor life tenant have sufficient resources to acquire the interests of the other, either may sell his interest to a third party. The life tenant would thereby obtain a capital sum in place of his income interest and the remaindermen would replace their future interests with capital sums in hand.

As will be seen, sales of interests present both inheritance tax and capital gains tax pitfalls.

Partition of the trust fund

[5.35] One of the more usual forms of reorganisation of interests under a settlement is that where a life tenant surrenders his life interest in part of the trust fund to the remaindermen (who following the termination of his interest will become absolutely entitled to the capital of that part of the fund in which the life tenant has surrendered his interest). In return the remaindermen assign their interests in remainder in the balance of the fund to the life tenant. In each part of the fund the interests of the life tenant and remaindermen merge. The life tenant takes the capital of that part of the fund in which he has not surrendered his interest and the remaindermen take the capital of the rest. This arrangement places capital in the hands of each which they may then deal with as they independently determine. Neither has to find a capital sum in order to acquire the interest of the other and this route may, therefore, be preferable to the sale of interests discussed above.

A partition of the trust property as described in the preceding paragraph will frequently be undertaken on an arm's length basis. An actuarial valuation of the life tenant's interest having regard to the prospective lifespan remaining to the life tenant will be obtained. The funds to which each of the life tenant and the remaindermen become absolutely entitled as a result of the partition will be determined according to the values placed upon each of the respective interests.

The transaction is sometimes analysed as one under which each is taking what he is entitled to from the trust fund, assessed according to the value of his interest. The better view is that each of the life tenant and the remaindermen surrenders their interest in part of the fund in order to acquire the other's interest in the remainder so the partition is therefore akin to a sale by each of them of part of their interests.

Such a partition might also be appropriate where one or more of the life tenant and the remaindermen wish to confer a gratuitous benefit on the other or others of them in part of the fund and the amounts of capital to pass to each may be determined by estate planning motives and without regard to the actuarial values of their respective interests.

Exercise of a power of appointment in favour of the life tenant

[5.36] Another means of placing capital in the hands of the life tenant which he can then give to others is the exercise of a power of appointment. It is arguable, however, that trustees should not exercise their power of appointment to confer a capital benefit on a life tenant whom they know intends to use that capital for the benefit of persons who are not beneficiaries under the settlement. This would be the main instance in which consideration may be given to the exercise of a power of appointment to place a life tenant in funds to make potentially exempt transfers. There may be less risk of a claim for breach of trust if the trustees' exercise of their power of appointment is to enable the life tenant to make gifts of capital to the remaindermen.

Taxation consequences

Assignment or surrender by the holder of an interest in possession within IHTA 1984, s 49 by way of gift or sale

Inheritance tax

[5.37] The life tenant's assignment or surrender by way of gift will be a deemed transfer of value which may be potentially exempt if the relevant conditions are fulfilled.

The surrender by a life tenant of his interest may not be sufficient to vest capital outright in the remaindermen if they comprise a class of beneficiaries which has not closed. In this case, the remaindermen then living will become entitled to interests in possession in the settled property. Although this will not enable them to deal with the underlying capital the deemed transfer by the life tenant will still be a chargeable transfer. Until the class closes the settlement will be a relevant property settlement subject to the decennial and exit charges. When the class closes the remaindermen then living would become entitled to the capital of the fund. There would be an exit charge as a result of their becoming so entitled.

In some cases, a surrender by the life tenant may not accelerate the interests of the remaindermen: for example, where their interests are contingent upon their surviving the life tenant. As mentioned in **5.32**, in such a case, the attempted surrender might cause a gap in the beneficial interest if the interest does not carry the intermediate income (Trustee Act 1925, s 31(3)) and a resulting trust of the income to the settlor (or his estate) may arise. This is unlikely to have been the parties' intention and the settlement, unless it qualifies as a TSI, will become a relevant property settlement and a reservation of benefit will arise in the settled property.

If the life tenant sells his interest for a consideration equal to the market value of the interest, to whomsoever, either by assigning it or by surrendering it, inheritance tax will be chargeable as if the value transferred (ie the value of the property in which his interest subsisted) was reduced by the amount of the consideration (IHTA 1984, s 52(2)). It is important to note that because the charge under s 52 is imposed on a hypothetical transfer even if the life tenant were to sell his interest to a complete stranger on a negotiated basis its market value (which would, of course, be less than the value of the underlying capital), the provisions of IHTA 1984, s 10 (dispositions not intended to confer gratuitous benefit) could not apply.

The purchaser of a life tenant's interest may also make a transfer of value of part of the amount of the consideration. This is determined by reference to the actual value of the life interest sold without regard to the fact that the life tenant is treated for inheritance tax purposes as owning the capital of the fund in which his interest subsists (IHTA 1984, s 49(2)). Thus, if a purchaser pays to the life tenant an amount in excess of the capitalised value of the life tenant's interest that excess will be a transfer of value by the purchaser (since his estate will have been reduced by that excess) unless it is a disposition not intended to confer gratuitous benefit under IHTA 1984, s 10. Any transfer of value made by a purchaser of a life interest may, however, be a potentially exempt transfer. If s 10 does apply to the acquisition, the acquired interest will be a section 5(1B) interest (see **4.19**).

Capital gains tax

[5.38] The assignment by the life tenant of his interest (whether to the remaindermen or to strangers to the settlement) or the surrender by him of his interest will only have capital gains tax consequences for the trustees or the life tenant if:

(a) as a result one or more people become absolutely entitled to the trust property. The trustees will be deemed to have disposed of the trust property in which the life tenant's interest ceased (TCGA 1992, s 71) and to have reacquired it at market value as nominees for those who become absolutely entitled. Depending upon the nature of the trust assets, the trustees and the beneficiaries may be able to elect under TCGA 1992, s 165 to hold over some or all of any gain arising and thereby avoid an immediate charge to capital gains tax;

(b) the life tenant acquired his interest for a consideration in money or money's worth or the settlement has been at any time resident outside the UK. A capital gains tax charge will arise to the life tenant on the difference between the market value of his interest at the date of his disposal (assuming no consideration for his assignment or surrender) or the actual sale price (if made to an 'unconnected' person) and his acquisition cost taking into account the wasting asset rules in TCGA 1992, ss 44 and 46; or

(c) the beneficiary sells his interest to another. The underlying assets to which the interest relates are deemed to be disposed of by the trustees and immediately reacquired by them.

Income tax

[5.39] Subject to the points made below, if the life tenant has assigned or surrendered his interest but the property remains settled, the income arising to the assignee or those whose interests are accelerated by the surrender will be chargeable at his or their personal rates of income tax. Where one or more individuals have become entitled to the income, basic rate income tax will be collected by assessment upon the trustees and an assessment will be made on the assignee or remaindermen for any higher rate or additional rate income tax due unless the trustees have authorised the income of the trust assets to be paid direct to the assignee or remaindermen in which case all income tax in respect of that income will be assessed on him or them (TMA 1970, s 76).

Where a life tenant has assigned his interest to a discretionary trust or, following a surrender of his interest, the settled property becomes subject to such trusts, the trustees (of the new settlement in the case of an assignment) will be liable at the trust rate (ITA 2007, s 479). Where the income is applied to or for the benefit of the beneficiaries it will be treated as having been received by them net of the trust rate and the sum of tax which is treated as having been deducted from the distribution received will be treated as income tax paid by the recipient beneficiary (ITA 2007, s 494).

Exceptionally, where the minor and unmarried children of the life tenant are the outright assignees or receive absolute interests following the surrender or if the income or capital is distributed to them from the continuing settlements, the life tenant will suffer income tax on the income which arises to his children (ITTOIA 2005, s 629).

Stamp duty and stamp duty land tax

[5.40] An assignment or surrender by way of sale may suffer either *ad valorem* stamp duty or stamp duty land tax (depending on the type of asset). As a general rule, stamp duty is payable in relation to stock and marketable securities whereas stamp duty land tax is payable in relation to land. Stamp duty is not chargeable on an assignment or surrender by the life tenant of his interest by way of gift, provided that it can be certified in writing as falling within Category L of the Schedule to the Stamp Duty (Exempt Instruments) Regulations 1987. Where the underlying assets are UK land, no stamp duty land tax will be payable provided a self-certificate is completed.

Revocation of the life tenant's interest by the trustees or the exercise of a power of appointment by them to terminate the life tenant's interest and confer benefits on others

[5.41] The taxation consequences of the termination of a life tenant's interest by these means are very similar to those discussed in relation to the assignment or surrender by way of gift by a life tenant of his interest. However, there are some differences. The first of these is the possible avoidance of the charge to income tax under ITTOIA 2005, s 629 where the trustees exercise their powers to terminate the life tenant's interest rather than the life tenant surrendering or assigning his interest to achieve the same result.

The second is the avoidance of the capital gains tax provisions in TCGA 1992, ss 86, 87–98A even if the life tenant can benefit from the settled property or its income following the revocation of his interest or the appointment away from him.

The third is that the termination will not be a disposal for the purposes of the pre-owned-assets charge.

Assignment of interests in remainder by way of gift or sale

Inheritance tax

[5.42] An interest in remainder, being a reversionary interest, is usually excluded property for inheritance tax purposes. The principal exceptions are where the interest was acquired for a consideration in money or money's worth or is one to which the settlor or his spouse or civil partner is (or has been) beneficially entitled. A disposition of excluded property will not be a transfer of value under IHTA 1984, s 3(2).

A sale of a reversionary interest will not give rise to an inheritance tax charge for the assignor and assignee. This is unless a sale is made to the life tenant or between connected persons and is not a bargain at arm's length. If the sale is to the life tenant of the fund in which the reversionary interest subsists the consideration paid by the life tenant will be treated as being a transfer of value since his estate will be reduced by payment of the consideration but will not be increased by the value of the reversionary interest (IHTA 1984, s 55). Moreover, the payment will not qualify as a transaction not intended to confer gratuitous benefit as the operation of IHTA 1984, s 10 is excluded for transactions to which IHTA 1984, s 55(1) applies. In response to the decision in *CIR v Melville* [2001] STC 1271 (CA), IHTA 1984, s 272 was amended to provide that a settlement power is not property for the purposes of inheritance tax. A settlement power for this purpose is ' . . . any power over or exerciseable (whether directly or indirectly) in relation to settled property or a settlement'. The sale of a trust power which is not an interest in a settlement, or which was acquired for consideration, or which subsists in a settlement the trustees of which have been at anytime resident outside the UK, will be a disposal chargeable to capital gains tax.

Because of this change, IHTA 1984, s 55A was inserted to make similar provisions in relation to settlement powers to those applying to reversionary interests under IHTA 1984, s 48. Where a person makes a disposition by which he acquires a settlement power for consideration in money or money's worth:

(a) the exemption for dispositions not intended to confer a gratuitous benefit does not apply;
(b) the person is treated as making a transfer of value;
(c) the value transferred is determined without taking account of any value acquired by the disposition; and
(d) the exemptions for transfers to spouses or civil partners, charities, political parties, housing associations, maintenance funds for historic buildings, etc and for national purposes do not apply to the transfer.

Capital gains tax

[5.43] Where the reversionary interest is sold for actual consideration, the trustees will be treated as having disposed of the underlying trust assets to which the interest relates and as having immediately reacquired them at market value (TCGA 1992, s 76A and Sch 4A). Any gain will not be eligible for hold-over relief under TCGA 1992, s 165 as the deemed disposal is a disposal under a bargain at arm's length (TCGA 1992, Sch 4A, para 9(1)). If the reversionary interest was acquired for a consideration in money or money's worth or if the trustees of the settlement have been at any time resident outside the UK, a charge to capital gains tax will arise on any gain realised on the disposal of the reversionary interest (TCGA 1992, ss 76 and 85). If as a result of the assignment someone becomes absolutely entitled to the settled property, the trustees will be treated, under TCGA 1992, s 71, as disposing of the settled property to which that person has become absolutely entitled and reacquiring it at market value as the nominee of that individual. Depending upon the nature of the trust assets it may be possible for some or all of the gain arising to be held over under TCGA 1992, s 165 by the trustees.

Income tax

[5.44] There will be no income tax consequences as the reversionary interest is a future interest which produces no income. However, if the interest is assigned to the minor children of the remainderman who are unmarried, or to trusts for their benefit, and falls in whilst those children remain unmarried minors, the income arising may be treated as the income of the assignor (ITTOIA 2005, s 629).

Stamp duty and stamp duty land tax

[5.45] No charge to stamp duty or stamp duty land tax will arise on the assignment unless made by way of sale (see **5.43** above).

Partition of a life interest settlement between life tenant and remaindermen

Inheritance tax

[5.46] Under a partition between a life tenant who holds an interest within s 49 and the remaindermen the life tenant who surrenders part of his interest to the remaindermen will be treated as having made a transfer of value under IHTA 1984, s 52 equal to the value of the property in which his interest has ceased. No account is taken of the value of the reversionary interest assigned to him by the remainderman in the part of the fund which the life tenant takes absolutely (IHTA 1984, s 52(2)). This transfer of value should be treated as being potentially exempt if it is a privileged trust. As we have seen, s 55(2) excludes IHTA 1984, s 10 so that the life tenant's surrender will not be prevented from being a transfer of value.

The remainderman will not make a transfer of value by assigning his reversionary interest in that part of the fund to the life tenant since his interest is excluded property (IHTA 1984, s 3(2) and s 48(1)). The transfer of a section 5(1B) interest will, however, be a lifetime chargeable transfer.

If the interest of the life tenant is a section 5(1B) interest there will also be an exit charge under IHTA 1984, s 65.

Capital gains tax

[5.47] Neither life tenant nor remainderman will suffer a charge to capital gains tax as a result of the disposal by each of part of his interest provided that neither acquired their interests for a consideration in money or money's worth (TCGA 1992, s 76(1)) and the trustees have always been resident in the UK or that no actual consideration is given for the disposal of any trust interest.

However, under TCGA 1992, s 71 the trustees will be treated as having disposed of the entire settled property to which the life tenant and the remainderman become absolutely entitled as a result of the partition and as having reacquired it at market value as nominees for the life tenant and the remainderman. They may, therefore, realise a gain although in some cases an election for hold-over relief under TCGA 1992, s 165 may be made.

Income tax

[5.48] The life tenant and each of the remaindermen will become absolutely entitled to part of the trust fund and will subsequently suffer income tax at their own personal rates in respect of future income. It is unlikely in these circumstances that ITTOIA 2005, s 629 will apply to the former, because, unless the partition of the trust fund is undertaken with court approval, a partition will not be possible where the remaindermen are not of full age and capacity. Accordingly, it is unlikely that the remaindermen will be the unmarried minor children of the life tenant, income applied for whose benefit may be treated as being the income of the life tenant under s 629.

Exercise of a power of appointment in favour of life tenant holding an interest within IHTA 1984, s 49

Inheritance tax

[5.49] This will not give rise to an inheritance tax charge by virtue of IHTA 1984, s 53(2).

Capital gains tax

[5.50] The life tenant will become absolutely entitled to the settled property and as a result gains may be chargeable on the trustees under TCGA 1992, s 71 subject to the possible availability of hold-over relief under TCGA 1992, s 165.

Future gains will be taxable in the hands of the life tenant at either 18% or 28%.

Income tax

[5.51] There will be no change in the income tax position.

Stamp duty and stamp duty land tax

[5.52] The instrument effecting the exercise of the power will not be stampable. Any instrument transferring legal title to settled property consisting of shares to the life tenant will be exempt from stamp duty provided it is certified as falling within Category F in the Schedule to the Stamp Duty (Exempt Instruments) Regulations 1987 (but see **5.45** above for the general stamp duty position). Where the underlying assets are UK land, no stamp duty land tax will be payable provided a self-certificate is completed.

Relevant property settlements

[5.53] Since relevant property settlements generally incorporate wide powers which may be exercised to alter the trusts upon which the trust property is held, little needs to be said about the precise mechanics of any changes in the beneficial interests under such settlements. However, the inheritance tax charge that may arise on funds leaving such a settlement or ceasing to be held on relevant property settlements should be considered carefully in the light of the proposed timing of any distribution.

Inheritance tax

[5.54] As the rates of inheritance tax on distributions from post-1974 relevant property settlements are calculated by reference to the value of the trust fund at the preceding decennial or, if a decennial has not passed, at the time of commencement of the settlement, one needs to consider whether the distribution should be made before or after the next decennial.

Example

A relevant property settlement is created by a settlor who had made no previous transfers of value and whose cumulative total at the time of creation of the settlement is, therefore, nil. The property was then worth £100,000 but is now worth £1,000,000. This property can be distributed prior to the first decennial without incurring any charge to inheritance tax. But on the decennial inheritance tax will be charged on the present value of the fund and future charges will be made at rates calculated by reference to the value of the fund at that date.

In two particular circumstances consideration should be given to postponing a distribution from a relevant property settlement beyond a decennial namely:

(a) If the business property or agricultural property relief available is less than 100% in respect of the trust fund or part of it, it may be worth postponing distributions from the settlement until after the first decennial. However, this is only relevant where the settlement is not a nil rate band relevant property settlement, as in such circumstances there would be no inheritance charge on a distribution prior to the first decennial. This is because on any distribution prior to the first decennial the rate of tax applicable will be calculated by reference to the value of the property in the settlement immediately after it commenced. This value is not reduced by business or agricultural property relief as the trustees would not have then owned the property gifted for the requisite period of time. Accordingly, the value of the trust assets, unrelieved by business or agricultural property relief, has to be taken into account in calculating the rate of tax to be applied on any exit charge prior to the first decennial. That does not mean that business property relief or agricultural property relief is to be ignored. Such relief would reduce the value of the trust property (the subject of the exit charge) provided that the trustees had held the assets concerned for the requisite period of time at the time the exit charge arises. By way of contrast, on the first decennial (and subsequent ones) inheritance tax is charged on the trust fund as if there had been a transfer of value of the trust fund at that time. Accordingly, business property relief and agricultural property relief may operate to reduce the value of the trust property and will set the applicable rate of tax for the next decennial until the next decennial charge. As a result, the operation of the rules can make it very difficult to decide whether relieved assets should be appointed from a discretionary trust before, or after, the first decennial. A great deal will depend on the expected growth in value of the property concerned, as well as the level of the nil rate band at the relevant time. Of course, in the case of assets which fully qualify for 100% business property relief or agricultural property relief, these particular considerations are not present and it may well be worthwhile retaining the assets within the trust in any event.

(b) Where a distribution (whether outright or on new trusts) is being considered a few years prior to the occasion of a decennial charge to inheritance tax, it may be worth postponing the distribution beyond that anniversary if, in the intervening time, it is likely that the amount of the nil rate band will increase more substantially than the value of the trust property.

Example

The decennial of a settlement falls in the tax year 2010/11 A distribution of property from the settlement had been under consideration in the tax year 2009/10. The settled property had a value, when the settlement commenced, in excess of the nil rate band at that time and the settlor had made no chargeable transfers in the 7 years prior to the creation of the settlement.

The postponement of the distribution until after the decennial would remove the settled property from charge to inheritance tax on distributions during the 10 years following the decennial if the settled property is at that decennial worth less than the applicable nil rate band.

The rate of tax which applies at any decennial after the first (which in turn determines the rate applicable on subsequent exit charges under s 65) is calculated by reference to a hypothetical transfer by a transferor who has made chargeable transfers in the previous 7 years equal to the transfers made by the settlor in the 7 years before the commencement of the settlement and the amounts on which exit charges under s 65 have been imposed in the last 10 years. Therefore, property which is advanced out of the settlement can continue to affect the inheritance tax charged on the trustees until the second decennial following the advance.

As has been mentioned, discretionary settlements created prior to 18 March 1986 and under which the settlor is a discretionary beneficiary should, if possible, be left alone. The settlor will not be treated as having reserved a benefit in such settlements since FA 1986, s 102 only operates in relation to gifts made after that time. The settlor, therefore, remains able to benefit from such a settlement but the property in it remains entirely outside his estate. Certainly the settlor should not now add any further funds to this type of settlement (other than possibly by will) since to do so would cause the gifts with reservation provisions to apply to the added property.

Generally, the decision whether or not to break a relevant property settlement depends to a large extent on the prevailing rates of inheritance tax applicable to distributions and to the charge on each 10-year anniversary. Where these rates are low (the maximum rate is 6% as it has been for many years), there is every incentive to keep the settlement intact because of the flexibility it offers. The tax charges can often be serviced out of accumulated income. On the other hand, many commentators are predicting increases in the rate of tax applying to decennial and exit charges. Trustees should keep this political factor in mind.

Capital gains tax

[5.55] When a beneficiary becomes absolutely entitled to an asset as against the trustees (on the occasion of a distribution to him) they will be deemed to dispose of the asset and reacquire it at that time as the nominees of the beneficiary. It will usually be possible to hold over under TCGA 1992, s 260 any chargeable gain arising, unless the distribution does not constitute a 'chargeable transfer' for inheritance tax purposes. This will be the case where, for example, a distribution is made within 3 months of the commencement of the settlement or within the 3 months following a decennial of the commencement.

Any other form of reorganisation of the interests under a discretionary settlement will not give rise to any charges to capital gains tax provided that no beneficiary becomes absolutely entitled to any of the trust property as a result.

Income tax

[5.56] If, on a reorganisation of interests under a relevant property settlement, any person becomes entitled to receive the income from a part or the whole of the settled property the trustees will suffer income tax at the basic rate on such income but will cease to suffer the rate applicable to trusts. Instead, the beneficiary entitled to the income will suffer income tax at his marginal rates on the income to which he is entitled but will receive a credit for the tax suffered thereon by the trustees.

Chapter 6

Offshore Trusts

Introduction

[6.1] The aim of this chapter is to examine briefly the main issues arising from the rules relating to non-resident settlements. A comprehensive review of the subject is outside the scope of this book.

This chapter is only concerned with non-UK resident trusts established by UK resident domiciliaries. The position of UK resident but non-UK domiciled settlors is considered in **CHAPTER 19 THE INTERNATIONALLY MOBILE**.

The trustees of a settlement are treated as a single body of persons distinct from the persons who are trustees of the settlement from time to time.

A trust is treated as resident and ordinarily resident in the UK if either:

(a) all the trustees are resident in the UK; or

(b)

- (i) at least one trustee is resident in the UK; and
- (ii) at least one trustee is not resident in the UK; and
- (iii) a settlor of the settlement was resident, ordinarily resident or domiciled in the UK when the settlement was made (that is immediately before the settlor died if the settlement arose on death) (TCGA 1992, s 69).

For this purpose a trustee who is not resident in the UK is treated as if he were resident here at any time when he acts as trustee in the course of a business which he carries on in the UK through a branch, agency or permanent establishment. The inclusion of this rule (the 'professional trustee deemed residence rule') in the Finance Act 2006 has prompted much criticism. 'Permanent establishment' is a phrase of very wide meaning and imprecise scope and the risk that purchasers of ancillary services might inadvertently create a permanent establishment has driven trustees to engage investment management, accountancy, banking and other business services from overseas suppliers which would otherwise have been engaged from UK suppliers. HMRC has issued guidance entitled 'HMRC Trustee Residence Guidance' which sets out their understanding of the principles which govern the application of the professional trustee deemed residence rule and examples of its application.

Background

[6.2] Tax legislation contains a number of measures to discourage individuals who are both resident and domiciled in the UK from seeking to avoid or defer their capital gains tax liabilities through the use of offshore trusts. This is done in four ways. First, there is a capital gains tax charge on the trustees at the time they become non-resident, calculated on the basis that they dispose of all the settled property at the time they change their residence and immediately reacquire it at market value ('the emigration charge') (TCGA 1992, s 80). Secondly, the gains of a non-resident settlement are attributed to its settlor if he is both domiciled and either resident or ordinarily resident in the UK and (broadly) the settlor or his spouse, or any of the settlor's children and grandchildren or of the settlor's spouse or their spouses or any companies controlled by any of them, are capable of benefiting from the income or capital of the settlement ('the offshore settlor charge') (TCGA 1992, s 86 and Sch 5). Thirdly, a charge to capital gains tax is calculated by matching the trustees' gains with capital payments made to, or benefits conferred on, beneficiaries (the capital payments charge) (TCGA 1992, s 87). Fourthly, the amount assessable under the capital payments charge in increased by what is, in effect, an interest charge (the supplementary charge) (TCGA 1992, s 91). A capital gains tax charge will also arise in certain circumstances where trustees make a transfer of value to another person and the transfer is treated as linked with trustee borrowing (TCGA 1992, ss 76A and 76B and Schs 4A and 4B).

In general, during the lifetime of the settlor, offshore trusts will not offer any advantage where the settlor and the beneficiaries are resident and domiciled in the UK. After the settlor's death, however, they continue to offer considerable advantages to beneficiaries, although the sums settled must be large for the taxation savings to outweigh the costs of the structure.

Export charges

Capital gains tax

[6.3] Under TCGA 1992, s 80 where a UK resident trust becomes resident outside the UK, the trustees will be deemed to have disposed of the 'defined' assets and immediately reacquired them at their current market value, and will be assessed to tax on the amount due. 'Defined assets' are all trust assets, other than those which would in any event remain within the UK tax charge because they are used for the purposes of a trade carried on in the UK by the trustees (TCGA 1992, s 80(4)). Anti-avoidance rules apply to UK trusts which fall to be treated as non-resident under the terms of an applicable double taxation agreement (TCGA 1992, s 83). A number of ancillary provisions restrict rollover relief, and prevent a double charge to tax arising by reference to disposals of interests under trusts. Further provisions limit the charge to tax where there is an inadvertent change in residence resulting from the death of a trustee, and the former residence status is resumed within 6 months. Finally, there are provisions governing the liability for tax of past trustees, where a UK trust becomes non-resident and an export charge remains unpaid.

Example

In 1985, Mr Arnold, a UK resident domiciliary settled his 25% stake in Widget Enterprises, a UK trading company, on a UK resident interest in possession trust in his favour. The shares were then valued at £30,000 on a minority basis and had an original base cost on purchase in 1984 of £10,000. The gain was held over. In July 2010, the trust was exported immediately prior to the sale of the shares for £2m as part of a takeover. The trustees would be deemed to realise a chargeable gain of £1,990,000 (£2,000,000 – £10,000) immediately before the change of residence which would be chargeable on them.

The net effect of these provisions in practice normally confines the export of settlements to cases where

(a) either the settlement is holding non-chargeable assets, such as cash, or the gain which will arise on the export of the trust is considered to be a price worth paying for the ability to defer the capital gains tax charge on gains realised by the trustees once non-resident; *and*

(b) either the beneficiaries of the settlement do not include the settlor or members of his immediate family or the settlor is dead; and

(c) there is likely to be a significant gap between the making of the gain and the distribution of the proceeds to the beneficiaries.

[6.4] There are several points to consider where an export of a settlement is proposed.

(a) Whether the settlement is one in which the settlor has an interest (as defined in TCGA 1992, Sch 5 para 2). This broadly is where either the settlor or his spouse, any of their children and their spouses, any grandchild of the settlor or his spouse and the spouse of any grandchild, or any companies controlled by any of them (or any companies associated with any companies so controlled) benefit or are capable of benefiting from the income or capital of the settlement. Where these conditions are satisfied, the settlor will be taxable on any gains realised by the trustees, unless he is:
    (i) domiciled outside the UK in the relevant tax year; or
    (ii) neither resident nor ordinarily resident in the UK during any part of the year; or
    (iii) dead at the end of the relevant tax year.

    This offshore settlor charge arises in the year following the export of the settlement.

    In a family context, therefore, the scope for deferring the payment of capital gains tax by the export of a settlement, the settlor of which is domiciled and either resident or ordinarily resident in the UK, will normally only arise where the beneficiaries of the settlement are the great-grandchildren or remoter issue of the settlor or the unmarried 'cohabitee' of the settlor, unless a specific tax strategy is being followed.

(b) On the trustees of the settlement becoming neither resident nor ordinarily resident in the UK, the trustees will be deemed to have disposed of the settled property and to have immediately reacquired it at its market value. Any chargeable gain arising as a result will be taxable in the hands of the retiring trustees. However, if it is not paid by them within 6 months from the time when it becomes payable, the Revenue can recover the tax from any other person who was a trustee of the settlement within 12 months of the date of export, unless he retired before the end of the 12-month period and can show that when he retired there was no proposal that the settlement be exported.

For some settlements this potential capital gains tax charge may outweigh the advantages of the settlement becoming non-resident. However, there may be cases where the prospect of deferring capital gains tax on anticipated future increase in the value of an asset will outweigh the disadvantage of triggering an immediate charge to capital gains tax.

(c) If the trustees are *at any time* resident in the UK they will be treated as being resident there throughout that tax year. No concession is available to allow the tax year to be split. Therefore, the trustees will not be outside the UK capital gains tax net until the start of the tax year immediately following that in which the settlement is exported. The retiring trustees should also be aware that they will remain liable to capital gains tax in respect of gains realised on disposals of trust assets made by the new non-resident trustees until the end of the tax year in which the new appointment is effected. It is preferable for UK resident trustees to retire towards the end of a tax year in order to minimise their exposure to charges which they will have no assets to meet.

(d) Non-resident trustees will not usually themselves have any capital gains tax liability in respect of gains realised by them, even in the case of settlements within TCGA 1992, s 86 and Sch 5. A further charge ('the capital payments charge') exists, however, to visit those gains upon beneficiaries resident or ordinarily resident in the UK who receive 'capital payments' from the settlement in which those gains were realised. The following is a brief discussion of the position under those rules.

TCGA 1992, s 87 applies where, in any tax year, the trustees of a settlement are throughout the year resident outside the UK, and a beneficiary receives a capital payment from that settlement. A beneficiary will be chargeable if he is resident or ordinarily resident in the UK when the gain is deemed to accrue to him. Gains realised in a year (on actual and deemed disposals) by the non-resident trustees which had the trustees been UK resident would have been chargeable to capital gains tax (the s 2(2) amount for the year) will be apportioned to the beneficiary to the extent that they are matched with his capital payment. Where the gains realised by the non-resident trustees exceed the value of the capital payment received by the beneficiary the excess may be apportioned, to any beneficiary who receives a capital payment in subsequent years. Where a beneficiary receives a capital payment from non-resident trustees in a year before any trust gains have arisen, gains realised by the trustees in subsequent tax years may be apportioned to the beneficiary. The capital payments charge is a significant factor in deciding whether a trust should be exported. The beneficiaries may suffer capital gains tax of between 18% and 44.8% in respect of gains realised by the non-resident trustees (depending upon the length of time that gains have been 'stockpiled') whereas a lower rate (currently 28%) might have been applicable had the settlement not been exported.

The capital payments charge can however, operate in an advantageous manner because, until a capital payment is received by a UK resident and domiciled beneficiary, no capital gains tax will be payable as a result of any disposal by the trustees. If the beneficiaries do not need the proceeds of asset sales, they can be reinvested by the trustees and funds that would have been used to pay capital gains tax can earn profits for the benefit of the beneficiaries. This 'deferral' aspect of s 87 is only partially blocked by the supplementary charge. (This aspect has been touched on above and is considered in greater detail later in this chapter.)

What is a 'capital payment'? This phrase is defined, by TCGA 1992, s 97 as meaning any payment which is not chargeable to income tax on the beneficiary or, if the beneficiary is not resident or ordinarily resident in the UK, any payment received otherwise than as income. The meaning of 'payment' for this purpose is extended to include any transfer of assets or the conferring of any benefit. Where a capital payment is made by way of a loan to a beneficiary the value of the capital payment is taken to be equal to the value of the benefit conferred by the loan (TCGA 1992, s 97(4)).

Most informed opinion considered that capital payments would accrue over time where trustees allowed a life tenant the use of a trust asset on favourable terms, subject to the trustee's right to require the return of the asset at will. An example of this would be where trustees permitted a life tenant to occupy a property without charge but subject to a condition that he must quit the property on being given notice by the trustees. In *Billingham v Cooper; Edwards v Fisher* [2001] STC 1177 (CA), the Court of Appeal held that where the trustees of a non-resident settlement lent trust moneys interest-free and repayable on demand to a life tenant, a capital payment arose.

The capital payments charge applies to any settlement irrespective of the domicile of the settlor.

A non-resident may be deemed to realise capital gains under TCGA 1992, s 87 and yet be outside the charge to capital gains tax by reason of his non-residence. Therefore, an export of a settlement will be particularly advantageous if all beneficiaries are resident outside the UK or if it is anticipated that the beneficiaries who will receive capital payments will become non-resident so that capital payments may be made to beneficiaries who are not within the charge to capital gains tax. Even where some beneficiaries are resident in the UK and it is intended that they will receive capital payments, by careful organisation it may be possible to make payments to non-resident beneficiaries in an earlier tax year than that in which payments are to be made to UK resident beneficiaries. This will ensure that the gains realised by the non-resident trustees are matched first with the payments to the non-resident beneficiaries who will suffer no capital gains tax in respect of them. Care will need to be taken to ensure that the attribution rules which apply where there is a transfer of value to which TCGA 1992, Sch 4B applies (trustee-linked borrowing) are not applicable. This is because payments made to non-chargeable beneficiaries are ignored when calculating the amounts taxable on a UK beneficiary.

The charge on temporary non-residents under TCGA 1992, s 10A provides that gains allocated to non-residents whose period of non-residence is less than 5 years will become chargeable when they resume UK residence.

Where the beneficiary is taxable on the remittance basis under ITA 2007, ss 809B, 809D or 809E (which will only apply to individuals who are not domiciled in a country of the United Kingdom), any gains treated under the capital payments charge as accruing to the individual will be foreign chargeable gains and therefore taxable only if remitted to the UK.

As already mentioned, where a capital payment to a beneficiary precedes the realisation of gains by non-resident trustees, the capital payments charge operates to attribute the trustees' subsequent gains to the beneficiary if they were resident outside the UK when he received his capital payment. A capital payment made to a beneficiary prior to the export of a settlement may also cause gains realised by the trustees once they have become non-resident to be attributed to him. However, TCGA 1992, s 89 gives protection from the capital payments charge if the capital payment received by the beneficiary was not made in anticipation of a disposal made by the trustees in a non-resident period.

(e) Difficulties may also arise where funds held on separate trusts derive from one settlement. TCGA 1992, s 69 provides that trustees are to be treated as a single and continuing body of persons being resident in the UK if there is at least one UK resident trustee. The exportation of one fund of a settlement leaving another with trustees resident in the UK may leave the trustees of the UK fund bearing the capital gains tax liability for gains made by the offshore trustees of the fund exported as happened in *Roome v Edwards* [1981] STC 96, (1981) 54 TC 359, [1981] 1 All ER 736 (HL), and *Bond v Pickford* [1983] STC 517 (CA). It may be difficult to determine on the face of the trust documents whether the funds are separate funds of the same settlement or two different settlements relating to those funds (and by which they were created). However, the Revenue practice set out in Statement of Practice SP 7/84 may be of assistance. In practice, it will be helpful to know whether any charge to capital gains tax was incurred or held over under FA 1980, s 79 (pre-14 March 1989), TCGA 1992, s 165 or s 260 when the two funds separated (as it should have been if separate settlements were created since the trustees of the newly created settlement would then have become absolutely entitled to the settled property over which the power of appointment was exercised) and whether each fund claims its own share of the annual exemption available to trustees. If there is any doubt as to whether or not separate settlements exist, for safety's sake both should be exported.

Inheritance tax

[6.5] The export of an existing settlement by the appointment of non-resident trustees will have no inheritance tax consequences. If, at the time of creating the settlement, the settlor was domiciled in the UK (whether as a matter of general law or under the deemed domicile provisions in IHTA 1984, s 267) the settlement will remain subject to UK inheritance tax even if the trustees become non-UK resident and whether or not the settlor and all beneficiaries are now domiciled and resident outside the UK.

Income tax

[6.6] For income tax purposes, the residence of the trustees of a settlement is determined under ITA 2007, ss 474–476. Trustees resident outside the UK for income tax purposes are not liable to UK income tax except on income arising here.

Income arising in the UK is usually either not charged on non-residents or tax will have been deducted at source and so UK income tax will generally be of little concern to non-resident trustees. Non-resident trustees of settlements under which income may be accumulated or paid out at the discretion of the trustees are liable to income tax at the trust rate under ITA 2007, s 479. As the trustees will be outside the jurisdiction of the UK Courts, the Revenue may have some difficulty collecting this tax from non-resident trustees. It may be able to do so however, should circumstances change. For example, if the trust is repatriated to the UK, the new UK trustees will have to deal with any arrears of tax. Encouragement is given to the trustees to discharge their liability by Revenue Extra-Statutory Concession B18 which is discussed below. In practice, non-resident trustees will not be liable to tax at the trust rate because of ITA 2007, ss 810–814 which limits the UK source income which is chargeable on non-residents.

Income arising under an interest in possession the holder of which is resident and domiciled in the UK whether arising to the non-resident trustees from a UK source or not, will be taxable on the beneficiary in his hands at his personal rates of income tax. Beneficiaries who receive distributions of income from a non-resident discretionary settlement will not be entitled to the tax credits or double tax reliefs to which they would have been entitled had they received the income direct from its original source. Nor will that income be within ITA 2007, s 494 and, therefore, treated as being a net payment from which income tax at the trust rate has been deducted. If income is to be distributed on a regular basis to beneficiaries, it may be advantageous for the non-resident trustees to submit tax returns to the Revenue and pay any tax due on UK source income since under the provisions of Revenue Extra-Statutory Concession B18, the Revenue will then allow the beneficiaries to claim relief for any foreign and UK tax charged on, or withheld from, the trust income.

If the settlor (and his spouse) are not entirely excluded from benefit under the settlement, the settlor may be charged to income tax on income arising to the trustees whilst he remains resident and domiciled in the UK even though he does not actually receive that income (ITTOIA 2005, s 624). Even if he is excluded from benefit but is able to direct how income from the settlement is distributed or has in some other way 'power to enjoy' that income within ITA 2007, Part 13, Chapter 2 (transfer of assets abroad) the income is treated as arising directly to the transferor (normally the settlor) who is charged to income tax on that income (ss 720 and 721). Chapter 2 has effect not only where the settlor has power to enjoy *income* but also where he may receive *capital* from the settlement.

If income is accumulated in an accumulation and maintenance settlement, a trust for a bereaved minor or an 18–25 settlement for the benefit of the settlor's children and no capital sums are paid out to or for their benefit until they attain 18, subsequently each child may suffer a charge to income tax under ITA 2007, s 732 on the income which arose to the trustees (before or after they attained 18) and was accumulated and which could, when it arose, have been (directly or indirectly) used to provide a benefit for them. This charge will arise to the extent that they subsequently do receive a benefit from the trustees if, when they receive that benefit, they are resident and domiciled in the UK. Benefit is widely defined and does not merely include benefits of an income nature.

ITA 2007, s 732 will also operate to impose an income tax liability on a beneficiary (other than the settlor) of a discretionary settlement who receives benefits (from the settlement) to the extent that income has arisen or, in the future arises, to the trustees and has been or is accumulated but which may be used to provide a benefit for him.

It will be seen that provided the settlor and his spouse are excluded from benefit and cannot direct how the income of the settlement should be applied, a measure of income tax deferral may be achieved by the creation of an offshore discretionary settlement since income will only be charged to UK income tax when beneficiaries resident here receive income or benefits from the settlement. For so long as the income is rolled up offshore no charge will arise.

Actual tax cost of export

[6.7] One of the results of the export charge is that many old settlor retained interest trusts will remain UK resident for the indefinite future.

However, there may still be UK resident trusts which were established by settlors who are now dead, or for individuals outside the settlor's immediate family circle which it may be advantageous to 'export' (that is, for the body of trustees to become neither resident nor ordinarily resident in the UK), especially where the value of the property settled is low.

Legal issues

[6.8] Before a trust can be exported, the following legal issues are relevant, in addition to the tax implications of the export.

When may non-resident trustees be appointed?

[6.8A] It had been suggested that it is not possible to exercise the statutory power conferred by the Trustee Act 1925, s 36 to appoint non-resident trustees or, at least, that it is improper to do so. The argument was that as s 36(1) enables new trustees to be appointed where a trustee 'remains out of the UK for more than 12 months' this necessarily implies that a non-resident person cannot be appointed as a trustee.

This argument was rejected by Sir John Pennycuick VC in *Whitehead's Will Trusts (Re)* [1971] 2 All ER 1334, [1971] 1 WLR 833 but *obiter dicta* in that case suggested that in most circumstances such an appointment would be improper.

> On the other hand, apart from exceptional circumstances, it is not proper to make such an appointment, that is to say, the court would not, apart from exceptional circumstances, make such an appointment; nor would it be right for donees of the power to make such an appointment out of court.

The courts have been asked to assent to variations of trust involving the appointment of non-resident trustees under Variation of Trusts Act 1958, s 1. In *Seale's Marriage Settlement (Re)* [1961] Ch 574, [1961] 3 All ER 136 and *Windeatt's Will Trusts (Re)* [1969] 2 All ER 324, [1969] 1 WLR 692 the court approved variations in cases where the beneficiaries were long-term residents of the foreign jurisdiction. In *Weston's Settlements (Re)* [1969] 1 Ch 223, [1968] 1 All ER 720, 3 All ER 388 a variation was refused where a family had taken up residence in Jersey for tax avoidance purposes in circumstances where the court suspected the change of residence might be temporary.

It is therefore argued on the basis of Sir John Pennycuick's *dicta* in *Re Whitehead* and by analogy to the principle applied in *Re Weston* that the appointment of non-resident trustees would normally be 'improper.'

Few now find this argument compelling. In *Richard v Mackay* (1990) 1 OTPR 1 Millett J said:

> . . . I doubt that the language of Sir John Pennycuick is really in tune with the times. In my judgment where the trustees retain their discretion . . . the court should need to be satisfied only that the proposed transaction is not so inappropriate that no reasonable trustee could entertain it.

So the appointment of non-resident trustees under an express or statutory power is unlikely of itself to be 'improper'. It is true that, in *Richard v Mackay*, Millet J commented as *obiter* that the court was unlikely to appoint non-resident trustees 'where the scheme is nothing more than a scheme to avoid tax and has no advantages of any kind'. He drew a distinction, however, between the court's approach when it exercised a discretion of its own from its approach when asked to authorise the trustees' exercise of their own discretion.

> Where the Court is invited to exercise an original discretion of its own . . . the Court will require to be satisfied that the discretion should be exercised in the manner proposed . . . Where, however, the transaction is to be proposed to be carried out by the trustees in exercise of their own discretion, entirely out of court, . . . then in my judgment the question the Court asks itself is quite different. It is

> concerned to ensure that the proposed exercise of the trustees' power is lawful and within the power and that it does not infringe the trustees' duty to act as ordinary, reasonable and prudent trustees might act, but it requires only to be satisfied that the trustees can properly form the view that the proposed transaction is for the benefit of the beneficiaries or the trust estate.

If the appointment is 'improper', however, what is its effect?

It appears from *Re Whitehead* that it is unlikely to mean that the exercise of the power is invalid. If it is invalid then the original trustee will not have been validly discharged from the trusts. If that were the case, the result could be that the settlement concerned will have remained resident in the UK after the purported change of trustees and remained within the charge to capital gains tax.

It is more likely, however, that the retirements and appointments would be valid though improper at the time they were made and therefore the court would be called upon to exercise its jurisdiction to avoid the retirements and appointments on an application of the beneficiaries under, for example, the Trustee Act 1925, s 41. The result of such a decision is that the appointments and retirements would be reversed from the time that the court's judgment was made.

As has been said, in all but the most exceptional circumstances, it is unlikely that the court would interfere with the appointment of non-resident trustees under the statutory, or an express, power of appointment. This must particularly be so where the trust deed expressly authorises the appointment of non-resident trustees.

It is common practice, however, for trustees to protect themselves against whatever residual risk there may be by seeking the agreement of, and an indemnity from, the adult beneficiaries of the settlement.

Other trust points to be watched

[6.8B] There are two particular provisions of the Trustee Act 1925 which must be considered with care when a settlement is to be exported.

(1) Trustee Act 1925, s 37(1)(c) provides that a trustee shall not be discharged from his trust unless there will be either a trust corporation or at least two persons to act as trustees to perform the trust. The exception to this is where a sole trustee was originally appointed and a sole trustee will be able to give a good receipt for all capital money because the settlement only permits the trustees to hold property which is personalty. It is not clear that s 37(1)(c) can be expressly excluded under the terms of the settlement.

If the settlement provides powers for the trustees to buy and sell land, as most will, a sole trustee (other than a trust corporation) should not be appointed even if only one trustee was originally appointed. Since a foreign incorporated company cannot be a trust corporation (Trustee Act 1925, s 68(18) and rules made under Public Trustee Act 1906, s 4(3)) such a company should not be appointed as a sole trustee on the export of a settlement. Where a foreign incorporated company is appointed to be the trustee of a settlement which is to be exported, an additional trustee should be appointed to ensure that the retiring trustee or trustees are discharged from their trusts. If the UK resident retiring trustees are not properly discharged as required by s 37(1)(c) they will remain trustees. The Revenue has been known to argue in particular cases that the result has been that the settlement remained resident in the UK and therefore that the UK resident trustees remained liable to capital gains tax in respect of gains realised on disposals of the settled property.

In the case of *Jasmine Trustees Ltd v Wells & Hind (a firm)* [2007] EWHC 38 (Ch) a husband and wife purported to retire as trustees of the settlement in favour of a single company which was not a trust corporation. Because their retirement was invalid, all subsequent attempted appointments of trustees were held also to be invalid on the grounds that the couple, who, although not aware of that fact, had continued as trustees and had not consented to the appointments.

(2) Trustee Act 1925, s 40 provides that, on the appointment by deed of a new trustee, the settled property will, save in the circumstances mentioned below, vest automatically in the new trustee or trustees whether or not the deed contains an express declaration that it should do so. However, certain types of assets are expressly excluded from vesting automatically (s 40(4)). Therefore, on the appointment of a new trustee or trustees the transfer into the names of the new trustees must be effected by the usual means for transferring such assets. These assets include land conveyed by way of mortgage, land held under a lease and any shares or securities or property which are only transferable in books kept by a company or in a manner directed by Act of Parliament.

If the settlor is either resident, ordinarily resident or domiciled in the UK at the time a settlement is made, an appointment of non-resident trustees will only result in the body of trustees being neither resident nor ordinarily resident in the UK if all of them are resident outside the UK. All assets held in the settlement should be transferred to the new trustees before the beginning of the tax year for which it is desired to ensure that the trustees are non-resident. Care should be taken to ensure that all stock transfer forms have been signed by the retiring trustees and that, so far as possible, all formalities have been completed. Although it should be sufficient if all that remains is for the non-resident trustees to arrange the registration of themselves as shareholders in the various companies.

Doubts have been raised as to whether s 40 is effective to transfer from retiring trustees to new trustees equitable interests (such as reversionary interests) held by trustees or whether, as a result of the provisions of Law of Property Act 1925, s 53(1)(c), these fall within one of the exceptions in s 40(4) as being property the transfer of which must be carried out as prescribed by Act of Parliament. The safest course is to ensure that any equitable interest which is to pass to the new trustees is assigned in writing (this can be incorporated into the deed of appointment of new trustees). Again, this avoids any argument that the administration of the settlement has not been transferred outside the UK.

It used to be the case that the place where a trust was administered was directly relevant to determining the residence of its body of trustees. This is no longer so, but the place where individual trustees carry on their trustee duties may be of relevance to determining their individual residence and therefore, indirectly, be relevant to determining the residence of the body of trustees. This is so particularly where one is dealing with companies carrying on a trust management business. As explained at **6.1** above, there is a special rule that if a trustee of a settlement acts as trustee in the course of business which the trustee carries on in the United Kingdom through a branch, agency or permanent establishment, then in determining the residence of a settlement, that trustee is to be treated as if he were UK resident. The nature of a 'permanent establishment' has been much considered in relation to double tax treaty provisions applying to companies. A very low level activity in a country can be enough for there to be a permanent establishment in that country. The best rule of thumb, therefore, is that all activities in relation to a trust should be carried on outside the United Kingdom. The Government's 'modernisation' of trusts in the Finance Act 2006 achieved the remarkable result of driving trust business away from the country which gave the trust concept to the world.

Since most civil law jurisdictions do not have a trust concept and do not recognise the division of ownership of assets into legal and equitable ownership, it is preferable, when exporting a settlement, to appoint trustees resident in a common law jurisdiction where the courts will enforce the duties and responsibilities of the trustees. Usually, trustees resident in a tax haven are appointed in order to ensure that the jurisdiction in which the new trustees are resident will not impose charges on realised gains similar to the UK capital gains tax they seek to avoid.

Protectors

[6.8C] It is not unusual, before certain trustee powers can be exercised, for the consent to be required of someone upon whom the settlor feels he can rely who is resident outside the UK. That person is often called the 'protector'. The status of 'protectors' in law has yet to be determined. The protector's role is to act as a watchdog over the trust's affairs, sometimes on behalf of the settlor and sometimes in order to protect the interests of all or some of the beneficiaries. Sometimes this function is delegated to an Advisory Committee or Board.

It is not clear whether the powers held by protectors are fiduciary in nature; that is whether the protectors are subject to the same obligations and constraints as those faced by trustees. Whilst this does not seem to be an issue where they simply act as a sounding board, the position is uncertain where they have important powers. Where protectors in effect possess a power of veto over the exercise of certain trustee powers, there may be reasonable grounds for arguing that the powers are not of a fiduciary nature. However, where positive powers are involved (such as the power to replace trustees), there is a higher possibility that those powers are fiduciary.

The risk in this is that protectors possessing fiduciary powers may be held to be a type of trustee, and their residence in the UK may affect the residence of the trust for tax purposes. It is prudent to ensure that where protectors are appointed, they are both resident and ordinarily resident outside the UK. Naturally, it will be important to confirm that there are no local tax difficulties for the person accepting the position. Alternatively, if the settlor insists on the appointment of a UK protector it will be prudent to ensure that the protector only holds powers of veto.

Generally, the role of a protector is to provide an extra comfort for clients who are not entirely comfortable with giving up both the legal ownership and a part of the beneficial ownership of their assets to trustees of whom their knowledge may be small. In practice, the solution to such concerns may be relatively straightforward: it is to identify professional offshore trustees which have been established for a long time and have a reputation for integrity and efficiency.

'Flee clauses'

[6.8D] The possibility of the introduction of expropriatory measures in the country of residence of the trustees needs to be considered. To provide some protection against this, it is usual to include a 'flee clause' in the settlement document which provides that on the occurrence of certain events the trustees will automatically be removed from office and other trustees resident in another jurisdiction appointed. The efficacy of such clauses (which is largely untested) may depend on whether they are triggered before or after the happening of the event the effect of which they are seeking to avoid. If a particular event occurs before the new trustees are automatically appointed it may be impossible to transfer assets out of the names of the old trustees and into those of the new trustees. Even if the automatic appointment of new trustees is triggered before the measures sought to be avoided are introduced there may still be difficulty in transferring assets out of the names of the old trustees. The flee clause may provide that assets will, from the date of the automatic appointment, be held by the old trustees merely as nominees for the new trustees but the success of this provision will depend upon the nature of the measures introduced.

Another solution to this problem would be for the trustees to hold all their investments through an investment company wholly owned by them and incorporated in a different jurisdiction to that in which the trustees are resident. The terms of the settlement — or the governing instrument of the company — would then provide for the automatic vesting of the shares in the company in the new trustees if the flee clause is triggered.

Taxing the settlor

[6.9] Under the offshore settlor charge (TCGA 1992, s 86) gains realised by non-UK resident trustees are attributed to a UK resident and domiciled settlor where a retained interest exists. The settlor is entitled to recover the tax so paid from the trustees. Gains arising during a period of less than five complete fiscal years during which the settlor is non-resident will be assessable either in the settlor's year of departure or return under the charge on gains of temporary non-residents (TCGA 1992, ss 10A and 86A).

This charge applies irrespective of the time the settlement was made. In general terms, a settlor has an interest in a settlement for the purposes of the offshore settlor charge where he or his immediate family can benefit under the settlement, unless the benefit can only arise as a result of certain specified events outside the settlor's control. The charging provisions do not apply if the settlor dies in the relevant year, or if the beneficiary, by virtue of whom the settlor has an interest, dies.

The five linking factors

[6.10] The substantive provisions are contained in TCGA 1992, Sch 5. There have to be five linking factors present before the rules can apply in any year of assessment.

(a) There must be a qualifying settlement.
(b) The trustees must be non-UK resident, or dually resident.
(c) The settlor must be domiciled and resident or ordinarily resident in the UK (subject to TCGA 1992, s 86A).
(d) The settlor must have a retained interest.
(e) Applying the fiction that the trust was UK resident during the year of assessment, there must be a gain arising in respect of a disposal of settled property originating from the settlor.

Qualifying settlements

[6.11] Since 6 April 1999 all settlements have been qualifying settlements. Until that date qualifying settlements were settlements created on or after 19 March 1991 and other settlements which had become 'tainted'. A trust became tainted where, following 19 March 1991, property or income was added to the 'old' trust, or the trust became non-resident, or the settlor or his immediate family benefited for the first time in an unforseeable and unexpected manner. The final category of tainting normally involved a breach of trust.

Non-resident trusts

[6.12] The trusts caught under these provisions are those which are either non-UK resident or non-ordinarily resident for any part of a year of assessment, or become so for any part of a year by operation of a double taxation arrangement.

The settlor

[6.12A] For a settlor to be within these provisions he must be UK domiciled, and resident or ordinarily resident during any part of the year of assessment concerned. A person is treated as a settlor where the settlement concerned contains property treated as originating from him (TCGA 1992, Sch 5 para 7). This will largely be where he provided the property himself or the property in certain circumstances itself represents assets which he originally provided (TCGA 1992, Sch 5 para 8). The rules also catch property added by companies, treating shareholders as settlors (TCGA 1992, Sch 5 para 8(4)). Property added as a result of reciprocal arrangements with others is also caught. Property is to be taken as being added if it is provided directly or indirectly by a person.

In *Coombes v Revenue and Customs Comrs* [2007] EWHC 3160 (Ch), [2008] STC 2984, a beneficiary of an offshore settlement who was not otherwise a settlor gave money to an offshore company owned by the trust. The company used the money to buy land which the trustees later sold at a gain. HMRC assessed the beneficiary on a gain arising under TCGA 1992, s 86 on the basis that he was a settlor of the settlement. It was held that the relevant definition of a settlor was that in TCGA 1992, Sch 5 para 7 and that the beneficiary was not a settlor of the trust within that definition because none of the property of the settlement consisted of, or included, property originating from the beneficiary.

Retained interests caught

[6.13] In broad terms a settlor is treated as having an interest under a settlement if income or property originating from him can or does become available for the benefit of any one or more of the following ('defined') persons, namely

(a) the settlor;
(b) the settlor's spouse;
(c) any child of the settlor or of the settlor's spouse;
(d) the spouse of any such child;
(e) any grandchild of the settlor or of the settlor's spouse;
(f) any spouse of any such grandchild;
(g) a company controlled by any of the above; or
(h) a company associated with a controlled company.

There are a number of limited exclusions which reduce the possibility of a person inadvertently being treated as a settlor as a result of circumstances beyond his control.

A chargeable gain must arise

[6.14] The final condition is that, as a result of the disposal of any settled property originating from the settlor (which has a wide definition), there is an amount on which the trustees would be chargeable to tax if they were UK resident, disregarding the terms of any applicable double taxation treaty.

In quantifying the chargeable gains involved, no account is to be taken of the annual exemption. Full deduction is available for past and current losses made by the trustees in quantifying the amount of gain. In the past the Revenue has taken the view that losses arising at a time before the new rules applied to the settlement could not be set against gains arising at a time when the rules did apply. The Revenue now accepts that the set-off is possible. The trust gains taxable on the settlor can be increased where the trustees hold shares in a non-UK resident company and, had the trust been UK resident, gains would have been apportioned to it under TCGA 1992, s 13. Special provisions apply where a trust holds double taxation treaty protected assets (TCGA 1992, s 86(2)(b) and Sch 5 para 1(4)).

Provided all linking factors are present and apply, an amount of chargeable gains equal to the aggregate gains of the trustees is treated as arising to the settlor in the year of assessment in which the trustees' gains arose. The apportioned gains are treated as forming the highest slice of the settlor's chargeable gains for that year.

Exceptions to charge

[6.15] The charging provisions do not apply where the settlor dies during the year of assessment (TCGA 1992, Sch 5 para 3). Similarly, if the only reason the settlor is caught is because someone other than the settlor has or may benefit under the trust, the settlor's liability will cease when that person dies during that year of assessment (TCGA 1992, Sch 5 para 4). Where the settlor is excluded from benefit, but is caught because two or more persons have or may benefit under the trust, the rules provide that their deaths during the year of assessment will cause his liability to cease (TCGA 1992, Sch 5 para 5).

Link with TCGA 1992, s 87

[6.16] Where a gain is charged on a settlor under the offshore settlor charge, it should be set against and cancel the amount of any trust gains for the purposes of the capital payments charge (TCGA 1992, s 87(4)). However, this will not occur in every situation.

Losses

[6.17] In the past there was a further disadvantage in holding one's assets in an offshore trust because personal losses could not be set against gains allocated to an individual under the capital payments and offshore settlor charges. A settlor can now set personal losses first against personal gains and then against gains attributed under the offshore settlor charge.

Income tax charge on pre-owned assets

[6.18] UK resident domiciliaries must also have regard to the income tax charge on pre-owned assets in relation to their tax planning using offshore structures. This subject is discussed further in **Chapter 2 Lifetime Planning**.

Supplementary charge

[6.19] The supplementary charge applies where beneficiaries receive capital payments which are subject to the capital payments charge. It is important to appreciate that the offshore settlor charge considered earlier and the capital payments and supplementary charges are not mutually exclusive. In some circumstances it is possible for charges to arise under both sets of provisions in respect of the same settlement.

The idea behind the supplementary charge is to discourage the long-term retention of gains within an offshore trust. In essence, the longer trust gains remain undistributed, the greater the potential tax charge when the beneficiary receives a capital payment.

The supplementary charge is calculated by applying a notional rate of interest (currently 10% a year for a maximum of 6 years) to the amount of tax payable under the capital payments charge where the beneficiary receives a capital payment (TCGA 1992, s 97). The amount of the capital payment is allocated to past gains previously made by the trustees, and operates to increase the amount of tax due on the capital payments received by the beneficiary. Hence, if the beneficiary receives a capital payment of, say, £100,000 on which he has to pay capital gains tax of £28,000, he could be faced with an additional tax liability of as much as £16,800 (ie £28,000 × 60%) if the maximum supplementary charge were to apply.

Three additional points are worth noting.

(a) The supplementary charge cannot operate unless a capital payment is made after 5 April 1992. This may still be relevant where a later trust gain is being matched with an earlier capital payment.
(b) The supplementary charge applies regardless of when the trust was established.
(c) The supplementary charge can only apply where the capital payment charge applies.

Operation of the rules

[6.20] A supplementary charge will be imposed where there is at least one tax year between the tax year in which the gain is realised and the tax year in which the capital payment is made. Although the overall effect of these provisions is reasonably straightforward, they are in themselves extremely complicated. Broadly, they operate by matching capital payments made after 5 April 1991 with the gains accruing to the trustees in each tax year. The capital payments are matched with the gains of each year (called 'qualifying amounts') on a 'first in, first out' basis (TCGA 1992, s 92(3)–(6)). Where a number of capital payments are made in the same tax year, they are only matched to the extent that the capital payment results in a trust gain accruing to a beneficiary under TCGA 1992, s 87(4).

Where a capital payment made after 5 April 1992 is matched with a qualifying amount for a particular tax year and there is a gap of at least one tax year between the tax year in which the capital payment is made and the tax year of the qualifying amount, the capital gains tax paid by the beneficiary under s 87 as a result of the capital payment is increased by a deemed interest charge of 10% per annum. This is limited to a 6-year period and therefore the time covered by the charge begins on the later of:

(a) 31 January in the tax year following the year in which the disposal occurred; and
(b) 31 January six years before 31 January in the year of assessment following that in which the capital payment was made

(TCGA 1992, s 91).

This is in fact a very modest charge which will be insignificant if there are several decades between a trust gain being realised and the making of the capital payment with which it is matched.

Where only part of a capital payment is matched with a particular s 2(2) amount, or where a capital payment is matched with more than one s 2(2) amount, then the capital gains tax charge to which the capital payment gives rise has to be apportioned, to enable the interest charge to be calculated on the appropriate proportion of the capital gains tax and by reference to the appropriate number of years (TCGA 1992, ss 87A–87C).

An example may help to show how the provisions work in practice.

Example

Captain Broad, now deceased, had settled property (the 'Captain Broad Settlement') on non-resident trustees. Having made no previous capital gains the trustees made the following capital gains and capital payments in the fiscal years 2010/2011 to the primary beneficiaries of the Captain Broad Settlement, Samantha Duffin and Honoria Tremlett. In all relevant periods Samantha was UK resident and ordinarily resident. Honoria was neither resident nor ordinarily resident in the UK. Neither beneficiary made any other chargeable gains in any of the years concerned.

		Capital payment	
Fiscal year	**Section 2(2) amount**	**Samantha Duffin**	**Honoria Tremlett**
	£'000	**£'000**	**£'000**
2010/2011	500	0	0
2011/2012	0	0	0
2012/2013	250	0	250
2013/2014	500	0	600
2014/2015	0	0	0
2015/2016	0	0	0
2016/2017	0	0	0
2017/2018	0	850	0
Totals	**1250**	**850**	**850**

Tax rates, allowances and rules are assumed to remain unchanged from those ruling in 2010/2011.

TCGA 1992, s 87(4) provides that:

The section 2(2) amount for a settlement for a tax year for which this section applies to the settlement is—

(a) the amount upon which the trustees of the settlement would be chargeable to tax under section 2(2) for that year if they were resident and ordinarily resident in the United Kingdom in that year, or

(b) if section 86 applies to the settlement for that year, the amount mentioned in paragraph (a) minus the total amount of chargeable gains treated under that section as accruing in that year.

Section 87A(2)–(4) provides that:

(2) The following steps are to be taken for the purposes of matching capital payments with section 2(2) amounts.

Step 1

Find the section 2(2) amount for the relevant tax year.

Step 2

Find the total amount of capital payments received by the beneficiaries from the trustees in the relevant tax year.

Step 3

The section 2(2) amount for the relevant tax year is matched with—

(a) if the total amount of capital payments received in the relevant tax year does not exceed the section 2(2) amount for the relevant tax year, each capital payment so received, and

(b) otherwise, the relevant proportion of each of those capital payments.

"The relevant proportion" is the section 2(2) amount for the relevant tax year divided by the total amount of capital payments received in the relevant tax year.

Step 4

If paragraph (a) of Step 3 applies—

(a) reduce the section 2(2) amount for the relevant tax year by the total amount of capital payments referred to there, and

(b) reduce the amount of those capital payments to nil.

If paragraph (b) of that Step applies—

(a) reduce the section 2(2) amount for the relevant tax year to nil, and

(b) reduce the amount of each of the capital payments referred to there by the relevant proportion of that capital payment.

Step 5

Start again at Step 1 (unless subsection (3) applies).

If the section 2(2) amount for the relevant tax year (as reduced under Step 4) is not nil, read references to capital payments received in the relevant tax year as references to capital payments received in the latest tax year which—

(a) is before the last tax year for which Steps 1 to 4 have been undertaken, and

(b) is a tax year in which capital payments (the amounts of which have not been reduced to nil) were received by beneficiaries.

If the section 2(2) amount for the relevant tax year (as so reduced) is nil, read references to the section 2(2) amount for the relevant tax year as the section 2(2) amount for the latest tax year—

(a) which is before the last tax year for which Steps 1 to 4 have been undertaken, and

(b) for which the section 2(2) amount is not nil.

(3) This subsection applies if—

(a) all of the capital payments received by beneficiaries from the trustees in the relevant tax year or any earlier tax year have been reduced to nil, or

(b) the section 2(2) amounts for the relevant tax year and all earlier tax years have been reduced to nil.

(4) The effect of any reduction under Step 4 of subsection (2) is to be taken into account in any subsequent application of this section.

Applying this method to the capital gains and capital payments of the Captain Broad Settlement it is apparent that until the tax year 2012/2013 the s 2(2) amounts are not matched with any capital payments. We shall begin by applying s 87A(2)–(4) to 2012/2013.

2012/2013

Step 1 Section 2(2) amount = £250,000.

Step 2	Capital payments in year = £250,000.
Step 3	Capital payments of 2012/2013 of £250,000 matched with s 2(2) amount of that year under subpara (a).
Step 4	Section 2(2) amount and capital payments of 2012/2013 reduced to nil.
Step 5	Because subsection 3 applies by virtue of sub-subsection 3(a) no further steps can be applied.

Gains equal to the s 2(2) amount for 2012/2013 of £250,000 are deemed to have accrued to Honoria in that year under s 87(2). Because she is neither resident nor ordinarily resident in the UK in the year she is not chargeable to Capital Gains Tax on those gains.

2013/2014

Step 1	The s 2(2) amount is £500,000.
Step 2	Capital payments in year are £600,000.
Step 3	As paragraph (b) applies, the s 2(2) amount for the year is matched with 5/6 of the capital payments for that year.
Step 4	As paragraph (b) of Step 3 applies, the s 2(2) amount for 2013/2014 is reduced to nil and the capital payments for the year are reduced to £100,000 (£600,000 – (£600,000 × 5/6)).
Step 5	Because subsection (3) does not apply, one starts again at Step 1.
Step 1	2010/2011 is the latest previous year in which the s 2(2) amount was not nil. That amount was £500,000.
Step 2	The total amount of the capital payments for 2013/2014 reduced under Step 4 above is £100,000.
Step 3	As paragraph (a) applies £100,000 of the 2010/2011 s 2(2) amount is matched with the capital payment to Honoria made in 2012/2013.
Step 4	As paragraph (a) of Step 3 applies, the s 2(2) amount for 2010/2011 is reduced by £100,000 to £400,000.
Step 5	Because subsection (3) applies by virtue of subsubsection (3)(a), no further steps are applied.

Total gains of £350,000 (£250,000 + £100,000) are deemed to accrue to Honoria in 2013/2014. Because she is neither resident nor ordinarily resident in the UK in the year, she is not chargeable to Capital Gains Tax on these gains.

2017/2018

Step 1	The s 2(2) amount for 2017/2018 is 0.
Step 2	The total amount of capital payments in 2017/2018 is £850,000.
Step 3	As subparagraph (b) applies, the capital payment made in the year is reduced by the relevant proportion. The relevant proportion is 0 (£0 / £850,000).
Step 4	As paragraph (b) of Step 3 applies, the s 2(2) amount for 2017/2018 is nil and the capital payments for the year are £850,000 (£850,000 – (£850,000 × 0/850,000)).
Step 5	As subsection 3 does not apply, start again at Step 1.

Step 1	2010/2011 is the latest previous year in which the s 2(2) amount is not nil. After reduction by the capital payments made in 2013/2014 that amount had become £400,000.
Step 2	The total amounts of capital payments in the year were £850,000.
Step 3	As paragraph (b) applies the s 2(2) amount for 2010/2011 is matched with the capital payment to Samantha.
Step 4	As paragraph (b) of Step 3 applies the s 2(2) amount for 2010/2011 is reduced to nil and the capital payment made to Samantha in 2017/2018 is reduced to £450,000 (£850,000 – £400,000).
Step 5	Because subsection (3) applies by virtue of subsubsection (b), no further steps are applied.

Gains of £400,000 are deemed to accrue to Samantha. She is assessable in the following way.

	£	£
Gains charged under s 87	400,000	
Less annual exemption	<10,100>	
	389,900	
CGT thereon at 28%		109,172
Supplementary charge under s 91:		
Chargeable period: 1 December 2013 – 30 November 2019 (6 years)		
£109,172 × (6 × 10%) =		65,503
Capital Gains Tax chargeable		174,675

There are unmatched capital payments in respect of 2017/2018 of £450,000. These may be matched with gains accruing to the trustees in the future.

Notice that the trustees have distributed £1,700,000 (£850,000 + £850,000) and have realised gains of £1,250,000 but only £400,000 of gains have been brought into charge which have suffered tax of £174,675.

In the light of the provisions of TCGA 1992, ss 87 and 97 it is prudent to assume that, where all involved are resident and domiciled in the UK, gains realised by the trustees will eventually give rise to capital gains tax charges equal to (or possibly greater than) those that would have been suffered had a UK trust been established. Thus, if it is anticipated that on the disposal of an asset incorporating large gains the proceeds will be distributed almost immediately to UK resident and domiciled beneficiaries, the appointment of non-resident trustees will not achieve any postponement of the capital gains tax liability and the costs of the exercise will be wasted.

Even where the interval between the realisation of the gain and any distribution from the settlement is likely to be less than 6 years (the maximum period over which the interest charge may be calculated), the appointment of non-resident trustees will only be advantageous if the funds which would otherwise have been paid over to the Revenue in capital gains tax can earn profits for the beneficiaries in excess of 10% per annum. Where, however, the gap between the disposal and the distribution is likely to exceed 6 years, then there is still likely to be merit in appointing offshore trustees.

Minimising the charge to tax

[6.21] As the supplementary charge is based upon the amount of capital gains tax levied on a capital payment, reducing the tax on a capital payment under s 87 will also reduce the supplementary charge under s 91. There are a number of techniques which, if properly implemented, should avoid or minimise the capital gains tax charge which would otherwise arise on providing a benefit to the beneficiaries. These include:

(a) the offshore trustees providing free use of assets to a beneficiary rather than providing him or her with the funds to acquire the property concerned; and
(b) the offshore trustees investing for income rather than capital gains in cases outside ITA 2007, ss 720–730 and the income tax rules relating to settlor retained interest settlements. The supplementary charge will only apply in respect of capital gains and not income 'gains', although it will be important to consider the position under ITA 2007, ss 716–735.

Chapter 7

Insurance

Introduction

[7.1] Insurance is used widely by private clients and the businesses they own and operate. From a simple way of protecting from catastrophe to a sophisticated cross border savings medium, its uses are varied and diverse.

The insurance industry has been tarnished with a reputation for high costs and clever marketing but it is necessary to understand the cost structure of the various types of policy which can deliver significant tax deferral benefits once sales commissions are removed or reduced.

The introduction of an 18% capital gains tax rate in 2008 reduced the attraction of insurance as a long term savings vehicle although its attractiveness was partially restored by the increase of the rate to 28% from 23 June 2010. If, however, the underlying investments held in the policy would not be subject to CGT if held directly, then tax deferral advantages still remain. One might contrast, for example, insurance policies with non-distributor offshore funds the gains of which are subject to UK income tax on disposal.

Regulatory background

[7.2] The regulation of insurance business is governed by the Financial Services and Markets Act 2000 (FSMA 2000). The Financial Services Compensation Scheme (FSCS) was established by this Act. For long-term insurance which includes savings related insurance products, the compensation limits are 100% of the first £2,000 and up to 90% of the balance. The cost of the FSCS is funded by a levy on authorised firms.

For insurance companies looking to transact business within the European Economic Area, legislation is contained in the European Union Consolidated Life Directive. Under this directive, an EEA insurance company can transact business in the UK without direct authorisation under the FSMA 2000.

Professional advisers should also be aware of the provisions of the Financial Services and Markets Act 2000 in relation to the giving of investment advice which can constitute investment business. Under s 19 of that Act, it is a criminal offence to carry on investment business without appropriate authorisation. Any contravention is actionable at the suit of a person who suffers loss.

Nature of insurance

[7.3] Before considering in detail the uses that can be made of insurance in the context of estate planning, it is important to understand in general terms the nature and types of insurance available and also the bases on which insurance policies may be held.

The basic contract

[7.4] In general terms, insurance involves a contract (evidenced by the policy) by virtue of which an insurance company (the insurer) undertakes in return for the agreed consideration (the premium) to pay to another person (the insured) a sum of money on the occurrence of a particular and specified event, the happening of which is uncertain. In life assurance, this uncertain event will be the death of a named person (the life insured).

Insurable interest

[7.5] Life Assurance Act 1774, s 1 requires that a person taking out life insurance must have an insurable interest in the life insured and any policy effected in contravention of this provision is void. The insurable interest must exist when the insurance policy is taken out (*Dalby v London Life Assurance Co* (1854) 15 CB 365), but it is not required at the time of loss (for example, on the death of the life assured).

Thus, it is necessary to establish exactly what constitutes an insurable interest in a life. Section 3 of the Act provides that, when an insured has an insurable interest, he may recover under the policy in question no more than the amount of the value of his interest. On this basis, the person taking out the policy must have a pecuniary interest in the life of the life assured and case law has established that this will be measured by the amount or value of the pecuniary loss which the person for whose benefit the insurance is effected is likely to sustain by reason of the death of the life assured.

An individual may take out a policy on his own life, or on the life of his spouse for his own benefit and is presumed to have an insurable interest of an unlimited extent in the policy regardless of the amount insured. In all other circumstances there must be a pecuniary interest which means that the insured must show that he would suffer financially by the loss of a legal right on the death of the life insured. Apart from the case of a spouse (and the special case of industrial life assurance), an insurable interest cannot be presumed merely from a family relationship. In the family context, therefore, a relative must have a claim for support enforceable by law, or some other pecuniary interest enforceable by law. Thus, generally speaking, parents will not have an insurable interest in the lives of their children. On the other hand, a child who is a minor would probably have an insurable interest in the lives of his parents who will usually have a legally enforceable duty to support the child who would suffer financially by the loss of that right on their death. On the other hand, it might be argued that a liability of support only crystallises when a maintenance order is made by the court. Certainly, an adult child would be unlikely to have an insurable interest in his parent.

In practice, insurance companies are often prepared to take a relaxed view as to the presence or not of an insurable interest. To do otherwise in respect of a policy on which premiums have been duly paid and received would create bad publicity. Strictly, however, if a policy is void, any premiums paid to the insurance company should be returned to the payer or to his or her personal representatives and, thus, are capable of falling back into the estate of that person.

The requirement for an insurable interest does not exist in many offshore jurisdictions. It is therefore possible to insure multiple lives, for example, parents and children.

Uses of insurance

Protection

[7.6] Life assurance was originally designed and developed to provide protection and financial stability for dependants from adverse financial consequences in the event of a person's premature death. This function has continued and grown in importance. In many cases, protection is the main reason for effecting appropriate cover. Life assurance is also important in business. 'Keyman' life policies, for example, are specifically designed to protect businesses against the losses arising from the death or extended incapacity of key executives and to provide appropriate financial compensation. In the context of partnerships, it is common for each partner in a firm to effect a policy on his own life, written in trust for the benefit of his surviving partners, or to effect policies on a life of another basis on the other partners, and include where appropriate 'cross-option' agreements.

Home ownership

[7.7] Life assurance is also important in the area of home ownership. Although it is becoming less common, lending institutions may well insist on life assurance to ensure that a repayment mortgage is discharged on the premature death of the borrower. This will be a form of term assurance and will either secure a decreasing capital sum, designed to match the capital liability under a repayment mortgage, or a fixed capital sum, designed to match the capital liability under an interest only mortgage. Endowment mortgages which were once very common are also insurance based. The proceeds of a related endowment policy (which is charged to the lender as additional security) are used to repay the loan, with the policy maturing at the end of the mortgage term or earlier on the death of the life assured. Some insurance companies now attach critical illness cover to endowment policies so that the mortgage is paid off on diagnosis of one of a number of pre-defined diseases.

Funding tax liabilities

[7.8] Life assurance is important in funding tax liabilities arising on the death of an individual. Seven year gift 'inter vivos' term assurance on the life of a donor is common to cover the potential inheritance tax liability should the donor die within 7 years of making such a transfer. The lump sum payable is reduced in line with the potential inheritance tax liability tapering over 7 years. Also, appropriate insurance (if written in trust) can provide the family and dependants of the life insured with funds shortly after death to settle any inheritance tax due, without the need to wait for the administration of his estate to be completed. To this end, insurance companies will provide model trust-wordings. Independent advice should be taken to ensure the applicability of the model wordings to an individual's circumstances. The impact of FA 2006 and specifically of writing policies under trust needs to be considered.

Investment

[7.9] Lump sum insurance policies (known as single premium bonds) have been an important tax deferral wrapper in which to hold investments. Tax liability is deferred until the occurrence of a 'chargeable event' and in this way the investor benefits from a tax deferral which over a long period of time can deliver a significant benefit. Investments that can be held in single premium bonds are now mainly restricted to collectives.

Such policies carry a tax disadvantage as gains on an equity based fund which would be taxable at 28% if held directly are converted into taxable income suffering income tax at 50% for a top rate taxpayer if they are held in a single premium bond.

Regular premium policies (mainly endowments) have become less popular as a savings medium in recent years.

Life policy taxation

[7.10] For income tax purposes policies are divided between qualifying and non-qualifying policies.

The proceeds of qualifying policies are not normally subject to income tax in the hands of the policyholder unless the policy is surrendered or otherwise realised prematurely, whereas on the surrender of a non-qualifying policy any gain will be subject to income tax. Although it is not appropriate to set out in detail here the precise basis on which policies are classified, a general understanding of the rules and their taxation consequences is important.

Generally speaking, most policies issued by UK companies apart from single premium policies will be qualifying policies.

The following is a summary of the more important conditions applying to the main types of assurance policy described above if they are to be qualifying policies. The legislation is contained in ICTA 1988, Sch 15.

(a) Where *term assurance* is taken out for 10 years or less, the policy must secure a capital sum on death and the surrender value (if any) must not exceed the total premiums paid. A term assurance policy for less than 1 year, however, cannot be a qualifying policy.

(b) The premiums payable in respect of *whole life assurance* must be payable at yearly or shorter intervals until the death of the life assured or for a minimum period of 10 years. The sum of the premiums payable in one year must not exceed more than twice the total premiums payable in any other year. The sum assured on death must not be less than 75% of the total premiums that would have been paid if death occurred at the age of 75. Where, however, two lives are insured by means of a single policy, for the purposes of calculating the minimum sum assured, the relevant age is assumed to be that of the older life if the sum assured is payable on the first death or that of the younger life if the sum assured is payable on the second death.

(c) The term of an *endowment assurance* policy must not be less than 10 years and premiums must be payable at yearly or shorter intervals for a minimum of 10 years. The sum assured on death must not be less than 75% of the total premiums payable, if the age of the policyholder when the policy is taken out is under 55. If, however, the age of the policyholder when the policy is taken out exceeds 55, the 75% figure is reduced by 2% for each year of the excess over 55. Where an endowment policy is for more than 10 years, premiums must be payable at yearly or shorter intervals until the death of the life assured or for a minimum period of 10 years or three-quarters of the policy term (whichever is the shorter period).

One important result of these conditions is that a *single premium* whole life or endowment policy cannot be a qualifying policy.

Consequences

[7.11] There are two main consequences of a policy being qualifying rather than non-qualifying.

(1) Premiums paid on a qualifying policy of life assurance effected before 14 March 1984 are eligible for life assurance premium relief (ICTA 1988, s 266). Such relief is not, however, available in respect of premiums paid on policies effected after 13 March 1984. There are also rules which result in the withdrawal of tax relief if the terms of pre-14 March 1984 policies are varied, either making them non-qualifying or extending the term or increasing the benefits thereby capable of being provided.
In most cases the relief available is given at source. That is to say, the policyholder pays the premiums to the insurance company net of the available relief at 12.5%. The insurance company then reclaims the difference between the gross and net premiums from the Revenue.

(2) A policy must be a qualifying policy if its proceeds are to be received free of further tax in the hands of the policyholder (ITTOIA 2005, s 485). Generally speaking, if a policy has been maintained for a minimum period before realisation, the proceeds on realisation will be

free of income tax although the investments within the insurance companies' funds will already have suffered tax at approximately 20%. The minimum periods in question are 10 years from the making of the policy or, if sooner, three-quarters of the term of the policy. A realisation in the context of a life assurance policy is likely to be either its total or partial surrender in return for a capital sum or its maturity (ie when it reaches the date on which it is set to mature) or the death of the life assured.

If a qualifying policy is surrendered (and sometimes when there is a partial surrender, such as a withdrawal of capital) or assigned for value before the expiry of 10 years from the making of the policy or, if sooner, three-quarters of the term of the policy, a higher rate income tax charge will be made on any gain arising on such a chargeable event. A charge may also arise on any gain arising on a surrender, on an assignment for value, on the death of the insured or on the maturity of a policy if the policy has been converted into a paid-up policy within the same period (ITTOIA 2005, ss 484, 485). (A policy is made 'paid up' when the policyholder agrees with the life office to stop paying premiums under the policy but not to surrender the policy, so that it still continues in being. In such a case the life office may reduce the sum assured payable under the policy.) Thus, neither the death of the insured nor the maturity of a qualifying policy will give rise to an income tax charge unless the policy has been paid up within the specified period.

The amount to be treated as the gain in respect of a policy depends on the chargeable event in question. If the event is an assignment for value, the amount will be the excess of the amount of the consideration received over the total premiums previously paid under the policy. If the event is the maturity of the policy, the surrender of rights under it or the death of the insured, the amount is the excess of the value of the sums then payable over the total premiums previously paid under the policy and any chargeable event gains which have previously arisen in respect of the policy (ITTOIA 2005, ss 491–497).

Such a gain will be treated as part of the total income of the individual policyholder for the year of assessment in which the event occurs if he is UK resident in that year, but the tax charged will be the excess of the higher rate of income tax over the basic rate. Where immediately before the chargeable event giving rise to the charge to income tax, the policy in question is held on trusts created by an individual or is held as security for a debt owed by him, the tax liability in respect of the gain will fall on that individual and any chargeable event gains previously charged in respect of the policy (ITTOIA 2005, s 465).

An individual who is chargeable to tax in respect of amounts being included in his total income for a year of assessment may claim a form of 'top slicing' relief (ITTOIA 2005, ss 535–537). The effect is that the whole gain will (subject to certain rules) be effectively charged to income tax at the rate which would be applicable if only an 'appropriate fraction' (broadly, the gain divided by the number of years for which the policy ran) was included in his total income.

There will be no capital gains tax liability on the disposal or surrender of a life policy unless it has been acquired at any time for consideration other than the payment of premiums under the policy. Where a policy has been acquired in the second-hand market, the price paid for the policy and future premiums paid are set against the proceeds of disposal to determine the gain. There is a thriving market in 'second-hand' endowment policies. Policies traded in this way are known as Traded Endowment Policies ('TEPs'). Where a person acquires an existing policy for consideration, a chargeable event gain may arise on its subsequent disposal. In the case of non-qualifying policies, a chargeable event gain arises if the maturity value and benefits paid exceed the premiums paid over the entire life of the contract. The gain is charged to income tax. Any chargeable capital gains arising on the maturity of the policy will be computed subject to TCGA 1992, ss 37 and 39 which provide relief for amounts charged to income tax (see *Drummond v Revenue and Customs Comrs* [2009] EWCA Civ 608, [2009] All ER (D) 292 (Jun)).

Non-qualifying policies

Disadvantages

[7.12] The main disadvantage of a non-qualifying policy is that income tax will be due on the occurrence of a chargeable event. (But see below regarding partial surrenders).

A chargeable event will occur on (ITTOIA 2005, s 484):

- a surrender of the policy;
- an assignment for money or money's worth;
- the death of the last life assured;
- the maturity of the policy;
- a loan being made under the policy.

If the policy is owned beneficially by an individual, the gain will normally be deemed to form part of his total income in the year of assessment in which the chargeable event in question occurs (ITTOIA 2005, s 465). If, however, the policy has been transferred into trust and the individual who assigned the policy is still alive or his death gave rise to the gain, or if the policy is held as security for a debt owed by an individual, it will be deemed to form part of that individual's total income for the year of assessment in which the chargeable event in question occurred (also ITTOIA 2005, s 465). Again, top slicing relief may be available to the individual on making a claim to the Revenue (ITTOIA 2005, ss 535–537).

Where a non-qualifying life assurance policy is held on a bare trust for a minor, HMRC will assess any gains on the minor with effect from 2007/2008 (HMRC Brief 51/08). Prior to this change of practice, such gains were assessed on the settlor. Where, however, either of the child's parents is the settlor of the bare trust they will still be assessable under ITTOIA 2005, s 629. The Revenue states that this is because income for this purpose includes amounts deemed to be income for tax purposes such as chargeable event gains. However, this view is subject to challenge on the grounds that ITTOIA 2005, s 629 catches 'income arising' under a settlement and, while imposing an income tax charge, the chargeable events legislation does not deem the relevant gains to be income.

Partial surrenders

[7.13] A partial surrender of a non-qualifying policy of an amount not exceeding 5% of the premiums paid may be made each year without giving rise to a tax liability at that time (ITTOIA 2005, s 507(5)). Any unused part of the 5% may be carried forward to subsequent years. Thus, such surrenders can be used to provide the policyholder with a regular (annual) supply of money (often marketed as 'income') which can be utilised as the policyholder thinks fit. Indeed, regular 5% annual withdrawals can be made for up to 20 years without a tax charge. However, when the policy is finally surrendered or matures, the gain subjected to higher rate income tax at that stage is the surrender or maturity value together with the amount or value of any previous partial surrenders, less the original premiums paid (ITTOIA 2005, s 491).

Onshore and offshore policies

[7.14] Life policies may be issued onshore (ie by companies resident in the UK) or offshore (ie by companies not so resident).

Offshore policies cannot be qualifying policies unless issued by either:

(a) a company resident outside the UK which is lawfully carrying on life assurance business in the UK through a branch and the policy premiums are payable to that branch and form part of the company's business receipts arising from that branch, or
(b) a company resident outside the UK if a portion of the company's life fund income is subject to corporation tax.

Offshore single premium bonds allow for gross roll-up of investment income and capital gains subject to withholding tax and imputed tax deducted in the country of origin. Over time this tax deferral can present the investor with a substantial benefit. Furthermore, a UK or overseas based portfolio can be held within an offshore insurance bond and still provide gross roll-up of income and exemption from capital gains tax on any sales made within the bond.

The law which governs a policy issued by a non-UK insurance company may not contain a requirement for there to be an insurable interest. For this reason, by including lives assured on the policy who are far younger than the owner (eg children or even grandchildren) the death of the last life assured and hence the chargeable event can be delayed for many years.

On the occurrence of a chargeable event on an offshore policy, tax will be due on any gain at the investor's marginal income tax rate, probably 50%. For an onshore policy the chargeable event gain will be taxed at 30% reflecting the fact that tax has been suffered at source in the insurance company's internal life fund. As the chargeable event on an onshore policy is on the gain net of tax already deducted (ie it is not grossed up) the effective overall tax rate may only be 44%, not 50%.

In computing a gain in respect of an offshore policy, a reduction may be made to take account of periods of residence which the policyholder may have spent outside the UK (ITTOIA 2005, s 528). Generally, though, no reduction will be made if the policy is or was held by trustees resident outside the UK (ITTOIA 2005, s 529).

Capital redemption bonds — definition

[7.15] Capital redemption bonds (CRBs) are not defined in the legislation but ICTA 1988, s 431(2ZF) states:

> In this chapter 'capital redemption business' means any business of a company carrying on insurance business in so far as it consists of the effecting on the basis of actuarial calculations, and the carrying out, of contracts under which, in return for one or more fixed payments, a sum or series of sums of a specified amount become payable at a future time or over a period.

CRBs are very similar in nature to offshore single premium bonds but with no life assured. For this reason CRBs can continue for many years without a chargeable event arising for income tax purposes. In the case of offshore single premium bonds similar long-term income tax deferral can be achieved by having multiple lives assured.

The relevant legislation for taxing the emerging benefits from a capital redemption bond is contained in Part IV Ch 9 of ITTOIA 2005.

Personalised portfolio bonds

[7.16] The legislation relating to personal portfolio bonds (PPBs) is contained in ITTOIA 2005, ss 515–546.

Where a bond is of a highly personalised nature, the Revenue has in the past applied ITA 2007, s 721 (previously ICTA 1988, s 739) to assess all investment income on the policyholder, but s 721 does not apply to capital gains tax. In the case of *CIR v Willoughby* [1997] STC 995, [1997] 4 All ER 65 (HL) the House of Lords held that whether the benefits arising on insurance bonds were linked to the issuer's funds or to an individual portfolio was of no significance in determining whether ICTA 1988, s 739 applied.

In response to this decision, legislation now found in ITTOIA 2005, s 526 was enacted to confer a wide power on the Treasury to make regulations to tax personal portfolio bonds (PPBs). In March 1999, the Revenue laid regulations relating to PPBs before Parliament. A PPB is defined as a policy which allows the policyholder, or anyone connected to the policyholder or acting on his/her behalf to choose the property held in the policy. The regulations are very wide ranging and designed to catch policies in respect of quoted and unquoted shares, family company shares and exotic assets such as fine wines, vintage cars, paintings and racehorses.

There is however, an exemption under ITTOIA 2005, s 517(2) for property detailed in s 520 which includes:

- internal life funds offered by the insurance company;
- units in authorised unit trusts, shares in investment trusts and OEICs;
- cash (excluding cash acquired for speculative purposes);
- interests in collective investment schemes constituted by non-UK resident including offshore units trusts and any other arrangements which create rights in the nature of co-ownership under the law of a country outside the UK.

In addition to falling within s 520, the property held in the bond must also meet one or both of:

(a) the general selection criteria of ITTOIA 2005, s 521(2) — this is satisfied if the property is available for selection by all policy holders of the insurance company;
(b) the class selection condition of s 521(3) which is satisfied if the opportunity to select the property falls to a particular class of policyholders not limited to connected persons.

For bonds that are personalised, a taxable gain is deemed to arise in each policy year. This is calculated as 15% of the sum of the total amount of premiums paid under the bond and the aggregate total of similarly calculated 15% amounts for earlier years since the bond was first taken out. Tax is charged at the individual's marginal rate on the gains each year.

PPBs taken out before 17 March 1998 can also continue to hold stocks, shares, warrants and options listed on a recognised stock exchange, AIM and the Unlisted Securities Market. Pre-17 March 1998 PPBs must, however, not be enhanced.

Income tax and policies held on trust

[7.17] ITTOIA 2005, ss 467 and 468 charge tax on trustees and beneficiaries where the settlor has died.

Gains arising on bonds held within a trust can be taxed on the settlor of the trust, the trustees or even the beneficiaries. Furthermore, bonds can be assigned out of the trust without creating an immediate tax charge, hence transferring the liability to the recipients of the bonds.

These rules, therefore, provide much scope for tax planning with a variety of different tax rates to select from. For example, if a bond is surrendered within a trust while the settlor of the trust is still alive, then the tax charge will fall on the settlor at his marginal rate. If the bond is surrendered after the settlor's death, then the trustees will be liable to tax at 50% with an allowance for basic rate tax in the case of a UK policy. If the trustees assign the bond to beneficiaries who then surrender it, the beneficiaries will pay tax at their marginal rates. If they are non-UK resident, they may escape tax altogether.

Estate planning with insurance

[7.18] The use of insurance for estate planning falls into two categories.

(1) Funding for an IHT liability by using a term or whole of life policy;
(2) Mitigating exposure to IHT by using a lump sum invested into a single premium bond.

Funding for an IHT liability

Term policies

[7.19] These provide for a capital sum to be paid in the event of death within a specified period or before a specified age. No payment will be made, however, if the insured survives to the end of the period or attains the specified age, hence these are one of the cheapest forms of life assurance available.

Basic term policies lack flexibility. Due to this most life offices market a convertible term assurance where, at the end of the term, there is a right to convert the policy (usually without further medical evidence) to an endowment or whole life policy (or, sometimes, to renew the existing policy for another term). The value of this right is that it preserves insurability in cases where the policyholder in question has otherwise become uninsurable or insurable only at a higher than normal premium, because, for example, a health problem has arisen.

Term policies are not investment vehicles as they do not usually acquire a surrender value. Their main use in estate planning, apart from preserving insurability, has been as a comparatively inexpensive way of providing 'disaster' cover. For example, a young newly-married man may have few resources to maintain his young family if he dies. He might therefore take out life cover by term assurance as a temporary measure for which the premium per annum would be less than for whole life cover of a similar amount. (Whole life cover is dealt with in **7.20** below.)

The insurance industry has responded to the increased market for term policies. Some insurance companies offer policies which enable cover to be increased or decreased if circumstances change or if the period of cover needs to be extended.

When the purpose of taking out the policy is to fund an IHT liability which will arise on the death of the life assured, the policy can be taken out by the person on whose death the liability will arise (the 'donor') and then assigned to, or into trust for the benefit of, the person who will bear the economic burden of the liability (whom we shall call the 'donee'). Alternatively, the donee could take out the policy for his own benefit but on the life of the donor, since he will have a sufficient insurable interest in the donor's life. In either case, the donor may require the donee to enter into a legally binding commitment with the donor to be responsible for the inheritance tax liability in exoneration of the donor's personal representatives (who have a secondary liability to pay the tax if the donee fails to pay within 12 months of the end of the month in which the donor died (IHTA 1984, s 199(2) and IHTA 1984, s 204(8)).

Although the inheritance tax liability if the donor dies within the 7-year period will be determined by using the death rates prevailing at the time of the death where they have altered for the better (IHTA 1984, Sch 2 para 1A), the level of cover will usually be fixed by reference to the rates in force at the time of the gift. Decreasing term assurance may also be appropriate because the rate at which inheritance tax is charged will be tapered where the donor dies more than 3 years after making the gift. However, to provide adequate protection for the donee, it will be necessary to insure the full amount of inheritance tax potentially payable for the first 3 years after the gift was made by the donor.

In assessing the likely tax liability (and therefore in effecting the appropriate level of term cover), other factors may need to be taken into account. For example, where a potentially exempt transfer may prove to be a chargeable transfer, and thus become subject to inheritance tax, and business property or agricultural property relief may then be in point, additional requirements relating to the donee must be satisfied. That is to say, in the case of relevant business property (for example), if such relief is to be available in full, the donated property must have been retained in the ownership of the donee from the date of the gift until the death of the donor or the earlier death of the donee or the conditions relating to replacement property must be satisfied (see IHTA 1984, ss 113A, 113B). Any term assurance effected should therefore take account of the possibility that the relief in question may not be available. In other words, when planning for inheritance tax one may wish to consider the 'worst possible case' to prevent an unwelcome shortfall in the insurance cover which is to meet the tax liability.

Term cover may also be considered where a donor makes an actual chargeable transfer as death within the 7-year period following the transfer will result in the death rates (subject to tapering relief) rather than the lifetime rates of inheritance tax being applicable. The position may be further worsened where the chargeable transfer is made after a potentially exempt transfer. The death of a donor, who has made both potentially exempt transfers and subsequent chargeable transfers in the 7 years before his death, will necessitate the re-calculation of the inheritance tax payable on the chargeable transfers. The inheritance tax on the chargeable transfers will originally have been calculated on the basis that the potentially exempt transfers were exempt. This will have to be corrected since the potentially exempt transfers will come into cumulation as prior chargeable transfers if made within the previous 7 years. The personal representatives will also need to calculate the liability to inheritance tax in respect of the potentially exempt transfers themselves and the amount of tax will also be determined by reference to the cumulative total of chargeable transfers (if any) in the previous 7 years prior to the date of the potentially exempt transfers in question.

The existence of chargeable transfers in the 7 years prior to the donor's death (whether original chargeable transfers or potentially exempt transfers which have been brought into charge by reason of the death) may also affect the amount of tax payable on the donor's estate because the earlier transfers will be brought into cumulation. Therefore, consideration should be given to taking out 7-year *level* term assurance to cover the increased amount of tax payable by the personal representatives and putting the policy in trust for the donor's residuary beneficiaries under his will who can then use the proceeds to help fund the tax. As there is currently a single rate of inheritance tax above the nil rate, the increase is effectively limited to 40% of the value of the nil rate band (currently £325,000).

Another use for term policies is as a means of providing the funds to pay inheritance tax where an individual emigrates from the UK. Under IHTA 1984, s 267 a person cannot shed his UK domicile for inheritance tax purposes until he has ceased to be resident in the UK for at least 3 complete tax years. For inheritance tax purposes, an individual is deemed to be domiciled in the UK if he has been resident in the UK for 17 out of the last 20 years. The risk of the emigrant dying within this period and incurring an inheritance tax charge in respect of his world-wide estate can be insured against, with the policy proceeds being settled outside his estate.

Term assurance, when used in inheritance tax planning, is normally limited to 7 years. However, longer terms, extending well beyond the likely date of the life assured's death, might be used as a way of funding for an eventual liability, similar to a whole of life contract.

Whole life policies

[7.20] Whole life policies provide for a capital sum to be paid on the death of the insured, whenever it occurs, or on earlier surrender.

All whole life policies are now either unit-linked or guaranteed although this used not to be the case. Unit-linked policies rely on a certain level of investment return to sustain the level of cover at the amount set at outset. If the required return is not achieved then the level of cover may be reduced or the premiums increased generally after a review once the policy has been in place for 10 years and thereafter at more regular intervals.

Guaranteed policies provide a set level of cover but have no investment content and therefore are not subject to review. As there is no investment content guaranteed policies do not have a surrender value.

Most unit-linked policies are established on one of the following bases.

- Maximum cover. These policies provide for maximum insurance and minimum investment. Therefore, they are generally the cheapest form of whole life cover available, but are unlikely to have much of a value if surrendered early. Furthermore, in the past, in calculating the premiums necessary to maintain the original level of cover and premiums throughout the policy's life, many life offices assumed that underlying investment growth on premiums would be in the region of 6–7% pa net of charges. In practice, returns in recent years have been negative and consequently many policies are now being reviewed and premiums increased and/or cover reduced.
- Balanced cover. These policies provide a balance between investment and insurance. Therefore, premiums are normally higher than maximum cover policies.

Whole life policies are often employed to fund the likely inheritance tax payable on death, in respect of an individual's estate, regardless of when the death occurs.

Where one is advising a married couple, the basic question to be decided is which of the two lives should be insured:

(a) the first to die (whether husband or wife); or
(b) the survivor.

The answer will depend on when the main (or only) inheritance tax charge will fall. Whole life policies can be applicable in either situation. The appropriate policy under (b) is a joint life last survivor policy.

Whole life cover is the best way of establishing a fund which will grow over the years and will be available to fund the anticipated inheritance tax charge on death, but the provision of such cover (particularly full cover) is usually expensive, except for young individuals. Also, whilst the level of cover is likely to be fixed by reference to the inheritance tax payable should the life assured die immediately after the policy is taken out, regard should be had to the likely increases in the assured's estate through income accumulation, capital growth and inflation and augmentation by gifts or legacies. A level of cover which seemed appropriate originally may, after a number of years, become inadequate (even with the addition of bonuses). The amount of cover should always be kept under review.

Term and whole of life policies held in trust

[7.21] When used for estate planning purposes policies will generally be written in trust so as to ensure that the sum assured falls outside the life assured's estate. An appropriate trust can allow the person taking out the policy a greater degree of control over the destination of the proceeds than an outright assignment of the policy so that he can ensure the proceeds are applied for the purpose he intends.

The form of trust most often used to hold a life policy is a flexible power of appointment trust (a type of life interest trust). Prior to FA 2006 for IHT purposes there were no initial, decennial or exit charges on such a trust. For policies issued on or after 22 March 2006, it is necessary to consider whether or not the value of the policy is in excess of the nil rate band. If it is, then an immediate charge to IHT will arise at 20% of the excess over the IHT nil rate band.

At the decennial or when there is a distribution of assets, whether or not a policy is held on interest in possession or discretionary trusts, it is necessary to calculate whether a decennial or exit charge arises. In some cases, where the life assured dies soon after a 10-year charge HMRC might claim that the policy had a higher value than the aggregate premiums paid at the 10-year point, reflecting the poor health of the life assured.

The impact of FA 2006 is only felt on policies either issued on or after 22 March 2006 or placed in trust on or after that date unless the terms of an existing trust are altered.

Mechanism

[7.22] Procedures for creating an effective trust from the outset vary from life office to life office, but the usual way of doing so is for the individual concerned (as proposer) to complete a trust form declaring that the policy is to be held under trust and requesting that the office issue it to him as sole trustee. This ensures that the trust is completely constituted and thus enforceable from the moment the life office goes on risk. Most life offices will have standard forms available to effect such a trust which can be completed by the individual before payment of the first premium. The policy itself will be effective once the proposal has been accepted by the life office which will usually go on risk once the first premium has been paid.

The sole trustee should always appoint additional trustees of the policy to act jointly with him, so that on his death when the policy proceeds become payable (assuming of course that the proposer is also the life assured, which will often be the case) they can be paid immediately to the continuing trustees on production of the deceased's death certificate without any need to obtain a grant of representation to the deceased's estate.

The creation of such a trust should only have inheritance tax consequences for the individual in relation to the payment of the first premium which will prima facie be a transfer of value but may fall within the individual's annual exemption or normal expenditure out of income exemption. Subsequent premium payments may also have inheritance tax implications. Assuming that the declaration of trust is effective, beneficial ownership of the policy will have vested immediately in the named beneficiaries.

The main taxation benefit of the overall arrangement is that the policy (and thus its proceeds) will fall outside the estate of the individual for the purposes of inheritance tax on his or her death.

Married Women's Property Act 1882 policies

[7.23] It will not, however, be necessary to create an express trust where a policy falls within the ambit of the Married Women's Property Act 1882. The effect of s 11 of that Act is to create in the appropriate circumstances, a trust of a life policy where no express declaration of trust is made. When a policy is effected by a man on his own life and expressed to be for the benefit of his wife and/or children or, alternatively, effected by a woman on her life and expressed to be for the benefit of her husband and/or children, s 11 will then create a trust in favour of the beneficiaries named in the policy. There is no need to use words expressly declaring a trust or even to refer to the Act in the policy (although it is preferable to do the latter so as to ensure there is no doubt that the policy is intended to create a trust under the Act).

The Act only applies where policies are effected for the benefit of a spouse or of children. An express trust remains necessary where a policy is effected for the benefit of remoter issue (such as grandchildren) or other relatives. The Act applies to all forms of life policies but only to those with a single life assured. It does not extend to policies on joint lives. A joint life policy for the benefit of a spouse or of children therefore needs to be written in trust expressly.

A trustee (or trustees) of the policy can be appointed by the assured in the policy itself or by any memorandum under his hand and legal title to the policy will vest in the trustees so appointed without there being an express assignment of the policy into their names. If he makes no appointment (or until he does so), he himself will be the sole trustee and, if he dies, his personal representatives will become the trustees.

Notwithstanding the ease with which the Act enables a trust of an appropriate policy to arise, it is wiser to specify the precise terms of the trust expressly so as to tailor the trust to the circumstances of the beneficiaries. Under Married Women's Property Act 1882, s 11 a policy for the benefit of a named spouse or child will give that person a vested interest in the whole policy. So far as children are concerned, it may be desirable to make their interests contingent perhaps on reaching a specified age or on surviving the life assured.

Existing policies

[7.24] Where a policy is already in existence, its removal from the beneficial ownership of the insured will normally involve the insured assigning the policy either outright to another person or to trustees (who may include the insured) to be held by them for specified beneficiaries. If such an assignment is effective, the policy (and its proceeds) should no longer form part of the assignor's estate for inheritance tax purposes. It is therefore important to ensure that the assignment is effective.

Assignments

[7.25] An assignment of a life policy must comply with the Policies of Assurance Act 1867. The Act provides for the legal assignment of life policies, giving an assignee the right to sue an insurer in his own name, if three conditions are satisfied.

(a) There must be an effective equitable assignment of the policy, indicating that its object is to transfer the benefit of the policy to the transferee (s 1). The assignment must be sufficient to transfer the property in the policy itself (ie beneficial ownership).

(b) The assignment must be in writing, either by endorsement on the policy itself or by a separate instrument, in the words or to the effect set out in the Act. For assignments made after 30 November 2003, stamp duty is generally not payable on assignments of policies.

(c) Written notice of the date and purport of the assignment must be given to the insurers before the assignee can sue on the policy.

Initial transfer

[7.26] The assignment itself may or may not lead to an immediate inheritance tax charge. If the policy is transferred by way of outright gift to an individual or into a bare trust for one or more persons, absolutely entitled, it will constitute a potentially exempt transfer for the purposes of inheritance tax. It will therefore occasion no immediate charge to tax, and no charge at all provided the transferor survives the required 7-year risk period. A transfer into a relevant property settlement will trigger an immediate charge to IHT on any value above the nil rate band. The donor must not be capable of benefiting under the trust or the gift will be rendered ineffective by the gifts with reservation provisions of the Finance Act 1986 the application of which is examined in greater detail below.

The value transferred will be the price that the policy might reasonably be expected to fetch if sold on the open market at the time of transfer, subject (except in the case of most forms of term policy) to a minimum value equal to the total cost incurred in providing the policy (ie the premiums or other consideration paid) at that time less any sum which has been paid under the policy or contract in question (IHTA 1984, s 167).

A transferor in these circumstances, however, should be able to take advantage of his nil rate band and any other relevant exemptions (such as the annual exemption) to restrict his liability to inheritance tax on the initial transfer into settlement. The tax liability (if any) will also be affected by the type of policy to be transferred. Most types of life policy will have a low initial surrender value if they have one at all. For example, a term assurance policy will, on the basis mentioned above, have little if any value, having no surrender value in any circumstances, and its transfer into settlement should not therefore occasion a transfer of value.

The assignment into trust will not give rise to any charge to capital gains tax (TCGA 1992, s 210).

Receiving trust

[7.27] As to which form of trust should be used, much will depend again on the circumstances of the case (in particular, the type of policy involved) and on the basic tax treatment afforded the trust in question. As mentioned above, the transfer of the policy itself to the trust should occasion only a minimal charge to inheritance tax. Provided that the initial value of the policy when first settled and when aggregated with any chargeable transfers made by the settlor in the 7 years preceding the creation of the trust do not exceed the inheritance tax nil rate band, there should be no exit charge (IHTA 1984, s 65) provided the proceeds are distributed before the first 10-year anniversary of the creation of the trust. It would, however, be necessary to check the settlor's history of chargeable transfers of value at the time the settlement is to be created before transferring the policy. Also, account would have to be taken at that time of any property likely to be added to the settlement by chargeable transfer as this will affect the computation of any exit charge.

It may also be unwise for the settlor to pay further premiums in respect of the policy after it has been settled if such payments would be chargeable transfers, as the Revenue would then have an alternative 7-year history of the settlor's chargeable transfers (ie those within 7 years of the payment of the premium in question) for determining the rate of an exit charge (IHTA 1984, s 67). The settlor should always, however, consider whether any of the inheritance tax exemptions would be applicable, as these could enable premiums to be paid without being chargeable transfers. In particular, the annual exemption and the exemption for normal expenditure out of income could be applicable.

Types of policy

[7.28] The most appropriate type of trust under which to hold the policy will depend upon the purpose for which the policy was made.

If, for example, a whole life policy taken out to fund inheritance tax on death is to be held on trust, in most cases the trust should mirror the interests of the residuary beneficiaries under the insured's will, who can then use the proceeds to fund the tax.

It is of course always possible that the beneficiaries under the will may be changed. It may therefore be necessary to ensure that the trust employed is sufficiently flexible to cater for this and that some form of discretionary (or power of appointment) trust would be appropriate.

If a 7-year term assurance is taken out to cover a potential liability to inheritance tax and the policy is effected by the donor, it should be held on trust for, or assigned to, the donee of the gift in question so as not to be payable to the donor's estate on his death and be available to the donee to pay the tax.

Where some form of insurance-based savings scheme is entered into to provide a lump sum (when the policy matures) during the lifetime of the person taking out the policy, the capital sum in question can be accumulated outside the estate of that person by ensuring the policy is held on trust. For example, an individual could take out an endowment policy on his own life, but held on trust for the benefit of his children (say under an accumulation and maintenance settlement). When the policy matures, the proceeds will pass to the trust and then to his children free of any inheritance tax liability falling on him. If, however, the individual himself wishes to benefit from the policy, then a trust will be inappropriate.

Payment of premiums

[7.29] Once the basic estate planning structure has been established and the policy in question has become held on trust, the question of who then should continue to pay the premiums under the policy must be decided. The settlor will probably have paid the first premium to ensure the life office assumes risk. If the settlor is to continue to pay them, they are capable of being transfers of value for inheritance tax purposes. However, if the policy in question is beneficially owned by an individual or held in a privileged interest trust or an existing IIP, there is no reason why the payment of premiums by an individual should not be structured so as to constitute potentially exempt transfers. The individual could make gifts of cash to the individual donee or trustees in question who could then use the cash to fund payment of the premiums. However, there are two occasions where it may be more appropriate for the settlor to pay the premium direct to the life office. These are where:

(a) the settlor wants to continue to obtain life assurance premium relief; or
(b) the policy was issued before 18 March 1986 and is held on trusts under which the settlor is capable of benefiting — in which case the inheritance tax gifts with reservation provisions will only not apply to the premium payments if they are paid by the settlor 'under the terms of' the policy and arguably this means direct to the life office.

If, however, the settlor does pay the premiums direct to the life office, the payments will only constitute potentially exempt transfers if the policy is beneficially owned by another individual or is held in an existing IIP or a privileged interest trust and only then to the extent that an individual's estate is increased in value (IHTA 1984, s 3A(2)(b)). Thus, to the extent that the amount of the premium is not reflected in the increased value of the policy (which would usually *not* be the case), the payment will not be potentially exempt.

If the payment of premiums can only be made as transfers of value, there are certain inheritance tax exemptions which may be applicable, such as the annual exemption and, if the premiums are funded from income, the normal expenditure out of income exemption. To qualify under this latter exemption, however, there is a need for regularity in the payments made for them to qualify as part of the normal expenditure of the person making the payments (IHTA 1984, s 21(1)).

Where a life policy is held on a trust established on or after 22 March 2006 any initial value on transfer or premiums paid, will constitute chargeable lifetime transfers.

Lump sum plans

[7.30] When considering any of the lump sum IHT plans, careful analysis is required to make sure that any IHT saving is not negated by additional fees and a charge to income tax arising generally after the settlor's death. This is especially important now that the top rate of income tax is higher than the rate of IHT.

In many cases, the investor might be better advised to invest in low yielding assets potentially chargeable to capital gains tax, where any capital gain is eradicated on death, leaving an IHT charge at 40% rather than a non-qualifying insurance policy held in some form of trust where the beneficiaries may escape IHT at 40% but instead face income tax at 50%.

The sections below consider some of the lump sum plans currently being offered in the UK by leading international insurance companies.

Discounted gift trusts

[7.31] A discounted gift trust generally consists of either a single premium investment into a single premium bond, capital redemption bond, or into a series of non-surrenderable maturing endowment policies subject to either a discretionary trust or an absolute trust.

Under a discounted gift trust, an individual (or more than one acting jointly) writes a trust and retains an absolute interest to a series of fixed withdrawals from the underlying fund or maturing policies during his lifetime or until the trust fund is exhausted. It is argued that the retained rights are sufficiently well defined to preclude the gift being a gift with reservation. The value of these withdrawals is determined following an assessment of the life assured's life expectancy using normal underwriting and actuarial principles.

The balance of the fund is held for the beneficiaries of the trust, and the settlor creating the trust is excluded from benefiting from this part of the fund. For joint settlements, the relevant value of each of the funds is independently determined.

An investment into a discounted gift trust constitutes a transfer of value for inheritance tax (IHT) purposes. The value of the transfer is determined on the loss to the estate principle under IHTA 1984, s 3(1) and represents the difference between the amount invested and the value of the retained rights.

Discounted gift trusts can be seen to fall into two basic types:

(a) A 'trust level carve-out' – this is a scheme whereby regular, normally, annual sums (the 'regular payment rights') are paid to the settlor by the trustees. The trustees are responsible for making the pre-determined regular payments as defined in the trust instrument and must make provision to do this. Under these types of schemes it is normally possible to change the underlying investment and for the trustees to satisfy any appropriate periodic and exit charges by making encashments from the underlying investment vehicle. It should be noted, however, that this could, have tax implications for both trustees and/or the settlor if he is alive.

(b) A 'policy level carve out' – under these schemes the regular payment rights are paid directly from the underlying policy, eg the investment bond inside the trust. Such schemes do not depend on the trustees to make an accurate payment of the pre-determined regular payments and will automatically make the payments at the pre-determined date. This releases the trustees from having to make or account for the payments to the settlor.

Calculating the discount

[7.32] HMRC issued a Technical Note in May 2007 setting out its practice in arriving at the calculation of the discount. HMRC attaches an open market value (OMV) to the rights retained by the settler, ie the amount that the settlor would obtain for the rights if they were sold in the market. This OMV is determined by a number of factors including the settlor's sex, age and health at the time the gift is made. These factor's determine the insurability of the settlor. HMRC's view is that if the retained rights were sold in the market any purchaser would expect to insure the rights against the early death of the seller otherwise the purchaser is at risk of losing virtually their entire investment. Therefore if the settlor is uninsurable, the OMV of the retained rights is minimal. For this reason HMRC believes that an individual over the age of 90 effecting a discounted gift trust would not merit a discount as it would be very difficult to insure such an individual. In *Revenue and Customs Comrs v Bower (executors of Bower (decd))* [2008] EWHC 3105 (Ch), [2009] STC 510, 79 TC 544 the value of a reserved annuity in respect of a 90-year old woman was considered and the High Court broadly accepted the Revenue's view of the issue.

In the case of joint settlors, HMRC takes the view that the rights should be valued in their entirety and then apportioned to each settlor by reference to the OMV of each settlor's retained rights.

How the transfer is treated for IHT depends on which trust is selected, a discretionary trust or an absolute trust.

Trust choices

Discretionary trust

[7.33] A gift into a discounted gift scheme that is subject to a discretionary trust will be treated for IHT purposes as a chargeable lifetime transfer (CLT), which, if it exceeds the nil rate band (£325,000 in 2010/11) when added to any other CLTs made in the previous 7 years, will be subject to IHT on the excess amount at the lifetime rate. It is the discounted value of the gift that is relevant in calculating the chargeable lifetime transfer.

It should be noted that whilst the lifetime rate is 20% this assumes the trustees pay the tax from the settled capital in the trust. During the lifetime of the settlor it is not normally possible for capital to be applied for this purpose and so, normally, the settlor will pay the IHT at the grossed up rate of 25% (20% (100% ÷ 80%)). Also, if at each 10-year anniversary, the settlor is still alive, he/she will usually pay the periodic charge as the trustees will normally be unable to access capital for this purpose. However this does depend upon the nature of the discounted gift scheme. See below.

Provided the settlor lives for more than 7 years, the CLT will fall out of account for IHT purposes.

Absolute trust

[7.34] The transfer will be treated as a potentially exempt transfer (PET) which, provided the settlor lives for more than 7 years, will fall out of account for IHT purposes.

The absolute trust creates 'bare trusts' of both the fund deemed to be owned by the donor and the remaining fund at outset for the named beneficiaries. The beneficiaries are absolutely entitled to their share of the trust fund and this interest is included in the beneficiaries' estates for inheritance tax. Following death, provided a beneficiary is *sui juris*, he can request the trustees pay him his benefits. A person is *sui juris* when they are aged at least 18, are mentally capable and are not an undischarged bankrupt.

It should be noted that under both absolute and discretionary trusts the value of any investment growth is immediately outside the client's estate for IHT purposes.

Options after death

[7.35] The trustees normally have the following options after death.

A chargeable event will be created at the point of death of the last life assured. If the policy has been set up with multiple lives assured then the chargeable event can be avoided at this point assuming at least one life assured is still alive at the settlor's death. (In any case this will not be a problem with a capital redemption bond as there are no lives assured in respect of such policies).

It may be possible to consider an assignment of the single premium bond out of the trust at this point as this would not trigger a chargeable event if it is not for money or money's worth (ITTOIA 2005, s 484). The beneficiaries can then surrender their segments of the bond and will be taxed with regard to their own tax rates.

If a policy utilising maturing endowments has been selected then these policies will generally be structured so that they have no surrender value immediately before death.

Additionally, if the bond is maintained, the selected investment funds can continue to be changed as the need arises.

Tax on 'income' during the lifetime of the settlor/donor — single premium investment bond

[7.36] The tax treatment of the regular payment is the same for both the absolute trust and the discretionary trust. For each investment made, UK tax residents are currently entitled to withdraw up to 5% of the original investment each policy year for 20 years and defer any income tax payable. Where the full 5% entitlement is not taken in any policy year, the unused amount is carried forward for use in future years. If the withdrawals in any year exceed 5% of the purchase price, the excess will give rise to a chargeable event gain and there may be a liability to income tax. UK resident investors must include details of any chargeable event gain arising in their UK tax return. Also any withdrawals in excess of the 5% entitlement may affect the availability of any age-related allowance(s).

Gifts with reservation

[7.37] There are two gift with reservation provisions that might catch discounted gift trusts.

Finance Act 1986, s 102 might apply as the settlor would appear to retain certain benefits from the gift made. However, what the settlor actually does is to make a gift of part of the capital and to retain the balance which then funds his income/capital withdrawals. HMRC appears to take the view that there is no gift with reservation apparently on the basis that the retained part is sufficiently well defined. Indeed in a Technical Note issued in May 2007, HMRC stated that 'essentially a DGS (discounted gift scheme) involves a gift of a bond from which a set of rights are retained, typically withdrawals or a set of successively maturing reversions. The retained rights are sufficiently well defined to preclude the gift being regarded as a gift with reservation for IHT purposes.' Whether that view is correct is, at the least, unclear.

Finance Act 1986, Sch 20 para 7 contains certain provisions, deeming arrangements to be gifts with reservation. The Finance Act 1986 states:

> Where arrangements are entered into under which there is disposal by way of gift which consists of or includes, or is made in connection with, a policy of insurance on the life of the donor or his spouse, or on their joint lives, and the benefits which will or may accrue to the donee as a result of the gift vary by reference to benefits accruing to the donor or his spouse/civil partner (or both of them) under that policy . . . the property comprised in the gift shall be treated [as being a gift with reservation].

However in practice discounted gift trusts are designed so that either:

- the policyholder is expressly excluded from benefiting from any of the rights that make up the gifted fund and those benefits will not vary by reference to the benefits which will accrue to the policyholder. The beneficiaries will only benefit on the death of the policyholder; or
- the policyholder is not a life assured; or
- para 7 cannot apply as the policy is not a 'policy of insurance' because the policy concerned is capital redemption bond.

Pre-owned assets and discounted gift trusts

[7.38] In March 2005, the Revenue published a technical guide to pre-owned assets containing comment on the treatment of life policies.

(a) *Discounted gift schemes*. The Revenue provided an example where a settlor effects a discounted gift scheme and retains certain rights, represented by a series of single premium policies that revert to the settlor providing he is alive on the relevant maturity date. The Revenue states that where the right to the reversion is held on bare trusts for the settlor, FA 2004, Sch 15 para 8 does not apply because a bare trust is not a settlement for inheritance tax purposes.
Furthermore, where the settlor's rights are held on an actual trust, HMRC say that it would normally be treated as a separate trust of those benefits in which the settlor had an interest in possession and no pre-owned assets tax charge would arise by virtue of FA 2004, Sch 15 para 11(1).
Finally, in any event, where the conditions in FA 2004, Sch 15 para 11 do not provide an exemption from the pre-owned assets charge, the actual charge would be based on the value of rights held on trust for the settlor, not the value of the underlying life policy.

(b) *Loan schemes*. The Revenue states that the pre-owned assets charge will not apply to these schemes as there is no reservation of benefit, the settlor is not a beneficiary of the trust receiving the loan and the making of the loan does not constitute a settlement.

Loan trusts

[7.39] A loan trust could be suitable to anyone whose estate will be liable to IHT on their death, but who is unable, or unwilling, to make outright gifts because they may require continuing access to their original capital — either on a regular basis to supplement income, or perhaps as a one-off lump sum.

They must, of course, have a lump sum available for investment.

There are many variations of this type of arrangement on offer from life companies. Loan trusts can be established by individuals, married couples or civil partners. Typically the investor (settlor) should be relatively young — perhaps someone who is just retired or coming up to retirement and who wishes to take action to mitigate IHT but does not want or is not able to give up access to their capital.

How does a typical loan trust work?

[7.40] The settlor creates a trust and makes an interest-free loan, which is repayable on demand, to the trustees of the loan trust. The money is invested by the trustees, typically into a single premium investment bond. The scheme allows the settlor to take regular repayments of the debt replacing the income which would have arisen on the capital sum had it not been invested in the scheme.

Any growth in the value of the investments belongs to the trust, not the settlor, and is outside the settlor's estate for IHT purposes and goes to the beneficiaries of the trust. Critically, the settlor has access to the original amount of the loan which remains part of the estate for IHT purposes. By taking an 'income', (typically 5% per annum of the original value of the loan), the value of the outstanding loan will reduce over time and the IHT benefit will increase. It is, of course, vital that the settlor spends these loans repayments in order to remove their value from his estate.

Setting up a loan trust

[7.41] In most instances the settlor uses a trust deed to establish a discretionary trust. To be effective for IHT the settlor cannot be a beneficiary. It may be possible to use an absolute trust to establish the loan trust. In that case, however, the interests of the beneficiaries cannot be changed.

Lending the trust money

[7.42] Using the loan agreement, the settlor lends the trust a sum of money which is expressed as being interest-free and repayable to the settlor on demand. It is possible to require any amounts to be paid back at any time — up to the value of the original loan.

It is also worth noting that where the settlor requests a repayment of the loan, particularly if the request is made early in the lifetime of the scheme, it is possible that the full value may not be payable due to the performance of the underlying investment.

The tax position of the settlor

[7.43] As the settlor makes an interest-free loan (which is repayable on demand) to the trustees, there is no financial loss to his or her estate. No immediate IHT liability should therefore arise at inception, regardless of the size of the loan.

When the settlor dies, the amount of any outstanding loan will be a debt due to his or her estate and so will form part of the estate for IHT purposes.

Trust replacement plan

[7.44] One life office markets a scheme that attempts to replicate the benefits of existing interest in possession trusts (see Chapter 5). This was introduced in response to the inheritance tax changes introduced by the Finance Act 2006.

An investor invests an amount into an offshore single premium bond with general conditions written in a standard format. A special provision is written into the policy schedule providing that:

(a) the full surrender option is removed for a period of x years and
(b) there is a similar suppression of the 5% withdrawal facility for the same term

The investor then assigns the policy by way of outright gift to, or to bare trustees for, a child, grandchild or other relative etc.

When the policyholder takes out the policy he makes a transfer of value as value is removed from his estate in return for an insurance policy. This transfer of value is not a PET as it is not made to an individual or trust. It is doubtful that the transfer is potentially exempt under IHTA 1984, s 10,

Section 10 provides that a disposition is not a transfer of value if it is shown that it was not intended and was not made in a transaction intended, to confer any gratuitous benefit and either that it was made in a transaction at arm's length . . . or that it was such as might be expected to be made in a transaction at arm's length . . .

Viewed as a composite transaction it is difficult to see how the disposition consisting of making the policy can satisfy the condition that it was ' . . . not made in a transaction intended to confer any gratuitous benefit on any person . . . '

Special care should therefore be taken when entering into this type of contract so as to ensure that there is not an immediate charge to IHT based on a transfer of value in excess of the nil rate band.

The assignment of the policy on bare trusts is a potentially exempt transfer as it is:

(a) made by an individual on or after 22 March 2006
(b) would otherwise be a chargeable transfer and
(c) constitutes a gift to an individual

Discounted valuation arrangement

[7.45] One life office markets a scheme which relies on a discounted value being attached to the policy on death.

The policyholder invests in a policy, with general conditions and written in a standard format. The policy is written with several lives assured so as to reduce the likelihood of a chargeable event. The policyholder is named as the first life assured. The other lives assured are likely to be much younger than the policyholder.

A special provision is written into the policy schedule to provide that:

(a) the surrender option is removed, and also that
(b) cumulative partial surrenders and regular withdrawals are limited to:
    (i) 10% pa (of the original premium) while the policyholder is living, then

(ii) 1% / 2% / 3% pa beginning in the first calendar year after the policyholder's death.

The policyholder has access to a flexible income, but there is no compulsion to take it.

On the policyholder's death the life assurance bond continues because other lives assured survive him. The executors to the deceased's will assent or assign the policy to the beneficiary or beneficiaries entitled.

Access is limited under (b)(ii) above.

The idea is to provide HMRC with actuarial evidence that the value of the policy at death is considerably less than the value of the underlying assets. A leading firm of actuaries has indicated the likely extent of any discount(s) and will also provide a expert valuation for probate purposes.

When the individual enters into the policy this will probably lead to depreciation in the value of their estate due to the policy's restricted conditions. To prevent this depreciation in the value of the estate being viewed by HMRC as a transfer of value, IHTA 1984, s 10 is relied on. This provides that the transfer will not create a transfer of value providing it was not intended to confer a gratuitous benefit upon any person and it was made at arm's length. That argument is doubtful.

IHTA 1984, s 167 substitutes total premiums paid on a policy (less any withdrawals) for the policy value where the policy value is less than the total premiums. This might appear to create a problem for this scheme but s 167(2)(a) provides an exemption for a transfer of value made on death and in the case of this scheme, the policyholder owns the policy on death forming part of his estate immediately before that time.

At some point in the future the new legal owner(s) of the policy may ask the insurance company to consider a non-contractual request for policy surrender, or to access policy benefits via higher withdrawals. The insurance company will consider each request on its merits, subject to such reasonable terms and conditions that it may wish to apply. No consideration will be given to requests made either before probate, or within a reasonable period of time thereafter.

The scheme is marketed as a flexible alternative to discounted gift trust planning. Higher capital access is coupled with flexibility of income, and there is no reliance on medical underwriting, ie the discount is a feature of limited access post-death of policyholder.

Annuities — back-to-back schemes

[7.46] An elderly taxpayer may wish to increase his net spendable income through a back-to-back insurance and annuity arrangement. First, he would purchase an annuity for the duration of his life. After having done so, in order to replace the capital he has used to purchase the annuity, he may then consider effecting a whole life policy on his own life, which he will write in trust for his heirs, providing that the original capital sum (plus bonuses) will be payable on his death. He has thereby provided himself with a source of income and also effectively removed the capital cost of the annuity from his estate.

Regard must be had to IHTA 1984, s 263 in relation to this type of arrangement. The section applies where the taking out of two policies are associated operations (as defined in IHTA 1984, s 268(1)(b)) and the taxpayer is deemed to have made a transfer of value at the time the life policy became held in trust equal to the lower of the total consideration paid for the annuity and the life policy and the value of the greatest benefit capable of being conferred by the life policy. It seems, however, that in practice policies and annuities taken out in such circumstances will not be regarded by the Revenue as associated operations (and thus s 263 will not be applied) provided the life policy was issued on full medical evidence of the assured's health and would have been issued on the same terms if the annuity had not been purchased at the same time (see Revenue Statement of Practice SP E4).

It is also necessary to consider which IHT exemption is being relied on for the payments of the whole of life premiums. If it is the exemption for gifts out of income then it should be remembered that a major part of the annuity will be treated as a return of capital and cannot therefore qualify for this exemption.

Non-domiciled individuals and offshore single premium bonds

[7.47] If the policyholder is resident but not domiciled in the UK, an offshore policy (or any policy issued under seal and held abroad) might be attractive as it would fall outside the ambit of inheritance tax (if any) payable on his death, being property situated outside the UK and thus excluded property for inheritance tax purposes (IHTA 1984, s 6(1)). However, chargeable event gains do not benefit from the remittance basis for income tax and therefore care should be taken in adding sufficient lives assured or in using a capital redemption bond so that any chargeable event can be deferred until the non-domiciled individual has left the UK.

Chapter 8

Pensions

Introduction

[8.1] On 6 April 2006 ('A Day') the entire pension landscape in the UK changed. A Day represented a radical overhaul of UK pension tax legislation with an attempt to both simplify existing tax rules and limit the tax relief available to the highest earners (especially those who were effectively uncapped).

Prior to A Day, tax relief on UK pension contributions was controlled by either:

(a) placing a cap on the maximum pension that could be funded; or
(b) stipulating a maximum percentage of earnings that would attract tax relief.

Post-A Day, an annual allowance limits the maximum tax relievable contributions in any tax year and a lifetime limit controls the maximum pension fund that can be accumulated without attracting a tax charge when pension benefits are drawn. A system of 'grandfathering' applies to individuals with pension benefits in excess of, or close to, the lifetime limit at A Day. This rational and straightforward system was not free from tinkering for very long. Ever since its introduction, the integrity of the system has been undermined.

The Finance Act 2009 introduced restrictions on tax relief on pension contributions for individuals earning more than £150,000 pa (see below). In the emergency budget on 22 June 2010, the government announced that the whole subject of higher rate tax relief on pension contributions was once more under review. Furthermore, the Finance (No 2) Act 2010 introduced a temporary two year extension to the date at which it becomes necessary to annuitise or draw a secured income, from 75 to 77.

In most cases the established pre-A Day pension scheme legal structures continue; ie Defined Benefit and Defined Contribution Occupational Schemes, Personal Pension Plans ('PPPs'), Self-Invested Personal Pension Plans ('SIPPS'), Small Self-Administered Schemes ('SSAS'), Retirement Annuity Plans ('RAPs'). The way in which the tax relievable contributions to these schemes are calculated, however, changed at A Day.

State pension

[8.2] The state provides two elements of state pension — basic and earnings related.

Basic state pension

[8.3] The maximum basic pension is achieved by making full national insurance contributions for at least 30 years. This changed with effect from 6 April 2010. Previously a maximum pension was achieved by making full national insurance contributions for at least 90% of a working life. The retirement age for men is set at 65. The retirement age for women is 60 for those born before 6 April 1950, rising gradually to 65 for those born on or after 6 April 1955. Between 2024 and 2046 the basic state pension age will increase to 68.

The basic state pension for 2010/11 is £97.65 per week for a single person and £156.15 per week for a married couple.

Earnings related state pension

[8.4] The State Earnings Related Pension Scheme ('SERPS') commenced in 1978 and was only relevant for employed individuals (not self-employed). It was replaced in 2002 with the State Second Pension ('S2P').

SERPs provided an earnings related element to the state pension, originally intended to deliver up to 25% of average best year's earnings which was subsequently trimmed to 20% of average lifetime earnings and eventually replaced in April 2002.

Many individuals 'contracted out' of SERPs as a result of their employer's pension schemes taking the decision to contract out. Additionally many individuals chose to 'contract out' of SERPs in return for a national insurance rebate being paid to a personal pension of their own choice. There has been much debate in recent years about whether or not individuals should contract back into the State Second Pension.

The replacement in April 2002 of SERP's by the State Second Pension ('S2P') was aimed at delivering more pension than SERPs would deliver for those on low or moderate income.

Annual allowance (FA 2004, s 228)

[8.5] The maximum contribution that can be made to a UK pension plan is now set by the annual allowance. In the current tax year (2010/11) the annual allowance is £255,000. The annual allowance will be reviewed by the Treasury and cannot decrease (FA 2004, s 228(2)).

The annual allowance measures the total pension inputs in a pension input period ending in the tax year. This means that contributions made during a pension input period beginning but not ending during a tax year will not count towards the annual allowance of that pension input period (FA 2004, s 238(2)(a)). This may provide scope to make tax relievable pension contributions in excess of the annual allowance in any one tax year. The annual allowance applies to contributions made by or on behalf of an individual and therefore it is now possible to be a member of an occupational scheme and also make significant contributions to a PPP, RAP or SIPP.

The annual allowance is overridden by the level of annual relevant earnings as mainly defined in ITEPA 2003, s 7(2) and ITTOIA 2005, Pt 2. (It is thought that this definition may include gains on the exercise of share options and share related schemes.) Therefore it is not possible for an individual with relevant earnings of say £50,000 pa to obtain tax relief on a contribution of higher amount. An individual contribution in excess of relevant earnings, or the annual allowance, is possible but such a contribution will not attract tax relief. Any employer contributions in excess of the annual allowance will be taxable on the employee at up to 50% via self-assessment under FA 2004, s 227.

In most cases it will be easy to measure the pension input. Where a cash contribution is made by an employee or employer then the pension input is simply the value of the cash contribution. However where benefits accrue in a defined benefit pension scheme then the pension input is equal to the increase in capital value of the individual's pension rights in the pension input period multiplied by a factor of 10.

The annual allowance does not apply in the tax year in which the individual becomes entitled to all of the benefits from that arrangement. This presents the possibility of a significant top up in excess of the annual allowance in the tax year in which all benefits are drawn from the relevant scheme.

It is no longer possible to carry forward unused relief from previous tax years or to carry back a contribution to a previous tax year.

Contributions — occupational schemes

[8.6] All individual contributions will normally be made via payroll and tax relief at up to 50% will, therefore, be delivered automatically. Employer contributions will largely be made in the same way. If the employer contributions are made via a salary bonus or sacrifice arrangement then there will also be a saving of employer and employee NIC on the amount that would otherwise have been paid as remuneration.

Contributions — PPPs and RAPs

[8.7] For contributions to personal pension plans (including SIPPS) contributions by employed and self-employed individuals are made net of basic rate tax relief. The additional higher rate relief is claimed by way of the annual tax return. Additionally an employer can still contribute to an individual's PPP.

For RAPs, contributions can still be made gross. It was originally anticipated that RAPs would switch to a net of tax relief basis post-A Day, but there were difficulties for RAP providers in adapting long established systems.

Lifetime limit (FA 2004, ss 214–216)

[8.8] The lifetime limit is the maximum that an individual can hold in pension plans without facing a punitive tax charge when they come to take pension benefits. The lifetime limit for 2010/11 is £1.80m. The lifetime limit will be increased by treasury order and, as with the annual allowance, cannot be reduced (FA 2004, s 218(3)).

Some individuals may be entitled to an enhanced lifetime limit if they have had a period of residence overseas and have contributions to a pension on which UK tax relief was not available (see **8.25** below), or in some circumstances if a pension splitting order following divorce is in place (see **8.26** below). Individuals who have elected for either enhanced or primary protection may also have an enhanced lifetime limit (see **8.11**).

An individual's pension or pensions are tested against the lifetime limit on the occurrence of a Benefit Crystallization Event (BCE) (FA 2004, s 216, Sch 32). There are several BCEs when a test must be made and these are:

- BCE 1: where funds are designated to provide a pension member with unsecured pension income (USI);
- BCE 2: where a member becomes entitled to a scheme pension;
- BCE 3: where a scheme pension already in payment is increased beyond a permitted margin;
- BCE 4: where a member becomes entitled to a lifetime annuity under a money purchase arrangement;
- BCE 5: where a member reaches age 75 and still has uncrystallised benefits under a defined benefit scheme;
- BCE 5A: where a member reaches age 75 and is still in USI;
- BCE 6: where a member becomes entitled to a lump sum;
- BCE 7: where a relevant lump sum is paid on the death of the member
- BCE 8: where a members pension benefits are transferred to a qualifying recognised overseas pension scheme.

In the simplest case where an individual has only one pension arrangement and takes all of the benefits at the same time then the BCE is calculated by looking at the value of those pension benefits and deducting the lifetime limits. If the benefits are part of money purchase arrangement then it is the cash value of the benefits at the time of the BCE that will determine whether or not there is a lifetime limit charge. Any charge is provided for under FA 2004, s 214.

Example

On the 31 September 2008, Andy who is aged 60 has a SIPP valued at £2m and takes 25% tax free cash and purchases an annuity with the balance. His BCE is calculated as £2m less the prevailing lifetime limit of £1.65m, giving an excess of £350,000.

However, in many cases the calculation will not be so simple. For individuals with a number of different pension arrangements and where these arrangements are vested at different times, it may be necessary to test against the lifetime limit more than once. If for example Andy above had two SIPPs both valued at £800,000 each and only one of these vested in September 2008, this would use 48% of his lifetime limit. If he then vested the other in September 2010 he would have 52% of the then lifetime limit (£1.8m × 52%) left for this second BCE.

For individuals with defined benefit arrangements or with pensions in payment at A Day the pension is capitalised in order to create a monetary cash value that can be tested against the lifetime limit on the occurrence of a BCE. A factor of 20:1 should be applied for defined benefit arrangements and a factor of 25:1 for pensions in payment at A Day.

Investment growth

[8.9] Although investment growth does not affect the annual allowance in any way, it can affect the lifetime limit. An individual with total pension values below the lifetime limit at A Day could still face a lifetime limit charge if their pension fund investment performance exceeds the increase in the lifetime limit.

Lifetime limit charge (FA 2004, s 214)

[8.10] The charge is levied on a BCE where the benefits exceed the available lifetime limit. The charge is at 55% for any amounts that are drawn as cash and 25% for any amounts that remain within the scheme or are used to purchase an annuity (although of course the income from the annuity will then be taxed at marginal rates).

Example

Andy above has a SIPP valued at £1.4m at A Day. This is below the lifetime limit. By September 2010 Andy's SIPP has increased in value to £2m and he then takes full benefits leading to a BCE. In September 2010 the lifetime limit is £1.8m and therefore Andy has excess benefits over the lifetime limit of £200,000. He can draw this as cash and face a one off tax charge at 55% on £200,000 or apply it to an income (either an annuity or USI) and pay a one off charge of 25% on £200,000.

Protection

[8.11] See FA 2004, Sch 36 and Registered Pensions Schemes Manual, section 3.

Enhanced protection

[8.12] Individuals with pensions in excess of the lifetime limit at A Day (or with pensions below the lifetime limit but who expected their pension benefits to exceed the lifetime limit when they were drawn) could elect to protect the fund from the lifetime allowance charge. In return the individual undertook to make no further contributions to any pension schemes post-A Day including contributions made to a pension scheme to acquire life assurance (eg, pension term assurance). This election had to be made by the 5 April 2009.

Once protected in this manner, on a BCE the pension fund is not referenced against the lifetime limit and there can be no lifetime limit charge. For defined benefit schemes there is a complex calculation which allows for some increase in final pension entitlement.

Death benefits are not similarly protected because they are contingent benefits to which the individual does not have an absolute entitlement. However, death benefits may be paid within the protected limits for pension benefits.

Primary protection

[8.13] Unlike enhanced protection, primary protection only applies where the total pension benefits to which an individual is entitled exceed £1.5m at A Day. Again the election had to be made by 5 April 2009.

If an election has been made, the individual's pension rights are protected from the lifetime limit charge up to the percentage increase in the lifetime limit between A Day and the relevant BCE.

Example

George has a SIPP which was valued at £2.25m at A Day. This was equivalent to the lifetime limit at that time multiplied by a factor of 1.5. George elected for primary protection. Seven years later when George's SIPP is valued at £2.9m (and the lifetime limit is, say, £2m) he takes all of his pension benefits. The lifetime limit is enhanced by 1.5 and therefore increased to £3m. George's SIPP is below £3m and therefore there is no lifetime limit charge.

At first glance there might appear to be little point in electing for the limited protection afforded by primary protection when enhanced protection protects the entire fund irrespective of any increase in value. However, primary protection permits further contributions to be made in the future if for example a pension fund falls in value due to poor investment performance.

UK pensions and high earners (FA 2009, Sch 35)

[8.13A] It should be noted that in the emergency budget on 22 June 2010, the government announced that the high income excess relief charge (see below) due to be introduced from 6 April 2011 will not go ahead. Indeed the Finance (No 2) Act 2010, s 5 contains a provision allowing for a repeal of this charge and the government is consulting on methods 'reforming' the pensions relief rules so as to raise additional tax revenue equivalent to the additional revenue which would have been raised if the high income excess relief charge had been allowed to proceed. The government's favourite solution is significantly to reduce the Annual Allowance to somewhere between £30,000 and £45,000. The law, however, is currently as follows.

The Finance Act 2009 introduced a special annual allowance charge which restricts tax relief for contributions made by 'high earners' to pension schemes, known as the high income excess relief charge. Unless the power under the Finance (No 2) Act 2010, s 5 is exercised, from 6 April 2011 tax relief will be restricted to 20% only for individuals earning more than £150,000 pa. This will create a situation where for 'high earners' pension tax relief will be restricted to 20% yet pension income, when drawn, will be taxable at up to 50%.

The restrictions will also apply to 'high earners' who benefit from employer pension contributions. From April 2011 there will be an additional tax charge on such employees to reclaim tax relief given at source which may represent relief at up to 50%. This will take the form of a benefit in kind charge levied after the end of the tax year.

Many 'high earners' may decide to leave their employer schemes to escape these punitive tax charges, instead receiving a cash replacement payment that is paid into another, less restrictive savings vehicle.

Anti-forestalling

[8.13B] In order to prevent individuals obtaining tax relief at up to 50% by funding their pensions heavily in advance of April 2011, some complex anti-forestalling provisions have been introduced. These block higher rate tax relief on any pension contributions that were not in place and were not being made on a regular basis on budget day (22 April 2009). To qualify as regular the payments must have been being made on at least a quarterly basis. Such established regular payments are known as 'protected pension input amounts'.

There is an exemption of £20,000 pa (the 'Special Allowance') from the anti-forestalling rules until April 2011 but this is reduced by protected pension input amounts and is therefore not particularly generous. Such a deduction in the allowance can reduce it to nil but cannot, of itself, create a charge. The Special Allowance is increased if the average yearly money purchase contributions not qualifying as protected pension input amounts exceed £20,000. The increase is the lower of that excess and £10,000.

Taking benefits

[8.14] The whole area of taking benefits from a pension scheme is once more under consultation with the relevant consultation document 'Reviewing the requirement to annuitise by age 75' issued in July 2010. The consultation period will end in September 2010 with legislation expected in April 2011. In the meantime the Finance (No 2) Act 2010 increases the maximum age at which an annuity or a secured income must be taken, to 77 from 75 in relation to individuals who were aged 75 or over on or after 22 June 2010.

The key proposals contained in the consultation document are:

(1) Currently there is an effective requirement to annuitise by age 77. This is due to the fact that Alternatively Secured Pension (ASP) (see below) is unattractive to most pension holders. The consultation document proposes that Unsecured Pension Income (USP) (see below) will be able to continue for the whole of a pension holder's life.

(2) There will be two component parts of the new USP:
Capped drawdown – this is likely to be similar to the current USP limits or possibly lower.

Flexible drawdown – this will allow additional unlimited withdrawals from a pension fund providing the individual pension holder can prove that they have a minimum income which is sufficient to support them through the remainder of their life. This will be known as the 'Minimum Income Requirement.'

(3) It will be possible to take a tax free lump sum post-age 75.

(4) Any pension fund remaining on death and not required to pay a pension to a dependant, will be paid to the beneficiaries of the pension holder less a tax recovery charge which is likely to be at 55% where pension benefits have begun to be paid. This will apply to both pre-and-post age 75. A tax recovery charge of 55% is therefore an improvement on the current position applying post-age 75/77 under ASP and worse than pre-age 77 where a 35% charge currently applies.

There are now an increased number of ways in which pension benefits may be taken on retirement, or before retirement as it is not necessary to retire in order to take pension benefits. The option of taking an annuity still exists along with the familiar methods of taking a scheme pension under an occupational defined benefit scheme or compulsory purchase annuity under an occupational defined contribution scheme.

Under FA 2004, s 165(1) and s 279(1), the normal minimum pension age is 55 and in most cases the lower retirement ages for specialist occupations such as sportspeople will disappear from 2010.

Unsecured Pension Income ('USP') (FA 2004, s 165 and Sch 28)

[8.15] To a great extent USP replaces income drawdown which was introduced in 1995 to give greater flexibility to the way in which a pension income is drawn.

USP provides for a pension income to be delivered either direct from the pension fund or via a short-term annuity.

The maximum limit is 120% of a basis amount that is calculated using government actuary department (GAD) tables and the yields on 15-year GILTS. It is broadly similar to 120% of the maximum single life annuity rate that could be achieved at that age assuming no escalation and no spouse's pension.

The selected income withdrawal amount must be reviewed every five years although it is possible to move between the minimum and maximum limits.

The minimum limit for USP taken from the pension fund is zero and hence this opens up the possibility of taking maximum tax free cash, drawing no income and hence leaving the fund free to grow in a tax free environment (ignoring dividend tax credits which have not been repayable since July 1997).

However, it should be noted that both using a USP fund to purchase an annuity or switching from USP into Alternatively Secured Pension constitute a further BCE. This means that a pension fund below the lifetime limit on entry into USP could be above the limit (and hence subject to a lifetime limit charge) when this second BCE occurs. For this reason consideration should be given to drawing maximum income approaching a further BCE which is taxable at a maximum of 50% rather than face a lifetime limit charge at 55% if the cash option is take.

If USP is taken via a short-term annuity then this must be payable by an insurance company, cannot be payable for a term of more than 5 years and must cease before the member reaches the age of 75.

On death during USP the remaining fund is available for:

(a) a lump sum which is subject to tax at 35%;
(b) dependant's pensions or annuities;
(c) dependant's USP with the fund on the death of the dependant also being available as lump sum, again subject to 35% tax charge; or
(d) ASP if the dependant is over 75.

The term 'dependant' is defined in under FA 2004, Sch 28 Part 2 as:

(i) A person who was married to the member at the date of the member's death.
(ii) A child of the member aged under 23 dependent on the member due to physical or mental disability.
(iii) A person who was financially dependent on the member under a relationship of financial mutual dependence, or dependent on the member due to physical or mental disability.

Alternatively Secured Pension (ASP) (FA 2004, s 165 and Sch 28 para 20(2) and (3), FA 2007, Sch 19)

[8.16] The Alternatively Secured Pension ('ASP') was introduced in order to allow schemes to comply with the Sharia. ASP makes it possible for a pension holder to continue drawing an income from their pension post-age 75 but without taking an annuity.

Under ASP the income levels can be set at a minimum of zero (as with USP) but the maximum is set at 70% of the GAD rate to prevent the pension fund being depleted. Reviews must take place annually instead of every 5 years (as under USP).

On the death of the pension holder there are a number of choices. If there are surviving dependants of the pension member then the remaining ASP fund must be used to provide an annuity or USP (if the dependant is aged under 75) or a continuing ASP (if the dependant is aged over 75). Where there was no dependant on the death of the member then prior to the Pre-Budget Report 2006, two further choices arise:

(a) charity lump sum death benefit which would be exempt from IHT (Sch 29 para 18); or
(b) transfer lump sum death benefit (FA 2004, Sch 29 para 19).

An unauthorised payment charge is imposed where a pension holder in ASP dies without dependants; and opts to have his pension paid as a Transfer Lump Sum Death Benefit to enhance the pension of another member of the same pension scheme. This unauthorised payment charge can be up to 70%.

FA 2007, Sch 19 amends IHTA 1984 so that:

- ASP funds are to be treated as the top layer of someone's estate on death; and
- the ASP fund taken into account on death is reduced by any income tax arising from the unauthorised payment charge.

The combination of income tax and IHT amount to a total tax charge of up to 82% (70% + ((100% – 70%) × 40%)).

Interaction of USP and ASP

[8.17] It is possible that two tax charges could arise following the death of a pension scheme member or of their dependant. The member in ASP must of course be aged over 75. If their dependant is aged under 75, selects USP, decides to leave any remaining fund as a lump sum to a beneficiary and dies under 75, the remaining pension fund will be taxed at 35% under USP rules and then the balance related back to the estate of the original member and subject to IHT at 40%. This could represent a tax rate of 61% and is a heavy penalty to pay for extracting funds from a pension in fund in cash form.

Death benefits from uncrystallised funds (FA 2004, s 167, Sch 28 Pt 2)

[8.18] Complex rules used to apply to death benefits pre-vesting, ie before any pension had been drawn.

The rules are now simplified and provide that the following benefits can be paid from an uncrystallised money purchase pension on the death of a pension scheme member.

(a) An unsecured pension where the dependant is under 75.
(b) An alternatively secured pension where the dependant is 75 or over.
(c) A dependant's annuity.
(d) A lump sum death benefit.

In the case of a defined benefit pension the following may be provided:

(i) A dependant's scheme pension.
(ii) A defined benefits lump sum death benefit.

Lump sum death benefits must be distributed within 2 years of the member's death if IHT is to be avoided. The payment of a lump sum death benefit represents a benefit crystallisation event and the amount will count towards the lifetime limit. If the value of uncrystallised pension rights and lump sum death benefits exceeds the lifetime limit then a lifetime limit charge at 55% will arise. This can be avoided by using the excess to provide dependant's pensions.

Following A Day there was a growth in popularity of pension life cover. Premiums for life cover paid under pension's rules attracted tax relief at 40% for a higher rate taxpayer. Prior to A Day tax relief was also due where premiums for life cover were paid under pensions rules but the limits were far less attractive. However, FA 2007, Sch 18 denies tax relief on pension premiums paid on or after 6 April 2007 unless the insurer received the application for the policy before 29 March 2007 and the policy was taken out as part of the pension scheme before 1 August 2007.

Lump sum death benefits and inheritance tax

[8.18A] The Finance Act 2006, Sch 22 contains the legislation which formalised HMRC's practice dating back to 1992 (Inland Revenue Tax Bulletin 2 February 1992).

An IHT charge can arise under IHTA 1984, s 3(3) if a member does not exercise their right to take pension benefits. The charge applies at the latest time when the right could be exercised; that is, immediately before death. Therefore if a pension holder does not take their pension benefits at their normal retirement date (NRD) as indicated in their pension contract, and subsequently dies, an IHT charge can arise.

Finance Act 2006 legislated so that no IHT charge can arise where the beneficiary of the pension fund is a spouse, civil partner or financial dependent or where the individual omitting to exercise the right was in good health at the time and did not subsequently die within the following two years (Finance Act 2006, Sch 22 (2)(c)).

The case of *Fryer (personal representatives of Arnold (deceased)) v Revenue and Customs Comrs* [2010] UKFTT 87 (TC), [2010] SFTD 632 has attracted considerable publicity due to the fact that HMRC successfully pursued a claim to IHT on the pension fund of an individual who died within two years of their normal retirement date, having failed to take pension benefits. The facts were as follows:

On 6 November 1955 Mrs Patricia Arnold transferred her existing pension rights into an NPI personal pension scheme and declared a trust of the lump sum death benefits of which her children were beneficiaries

The normal retirement date on the NPI policy was 8 September 2002 when Mrs Arnold would be 60 although the plan actually allowed for retirement between ages 50 and 75 as is fairly standard for pension plans.

In April 2002 Mrs Arnold was diagnosed with advanced cancer and she died in July 2003. NPI had written to her in May 2002 asking if she wished to take her retirement benefits and she did not respond to the letter.

Following her death the pension fund was paid into the discretionary trust. HMRC considered that Mrs Arnold had made a transfer of value of part of her estate for the purposes of IHTA 1984, s 3(3). They charged IHT on the grounds that the deceased's omission to exercise a right had diminished her estate.

The decision in the case has been strongly criticised.

It may be sensible now to leave the normal retirement date on pension contracts to as late as possible, reducing the chance of a challenge.

On 1 July 2010 HMRC stated in the document 'Pensions – Treatment of Persons at age 75'

> 'The changes still leave the prospect of a charge to inheritance tax under S 3 (3) IHTA where the member of a registered pension scheme has reached age 75 and dies having deliberately omitted to take his retirement benefits so that the death benefits can pass to his chosen beneficiaries.'

Qualifying investments

Residential property and exotic assets

[8.19] The original pensions simplification consultation document issued in December 2002 included proposals to permit residential property as a qualifying investment in UK pension plans. During the following 3 years numerous articles appeared in the press regarding the possibility of including 'buy to let' homes, second properties and holiday homes in SIPPs. Many individuals made plans to acquire such properties with their pension plans and even in some cases to make 'in specie' transfers of existing properties into their pensions.

Perhaps fearing the possibility of a further UK property boom fuelled by demand from UK pensions holders and the loss of considerable tax revenue, the government decided to amend its new system for pensions before it had even come into effect. A press release following the pre-Budget speech statement in December 2005, announced that investment in residential property and certain 'exotic' assets including fine wines, works of art, antiques and stamps, would be subject to punitive tax charges. This was followed by legislation contained in FA 2006, Sch 21 inserting a new Sch 29A into FA 2004.

As a result of this new legislation various punitive tax charges will result where investment regulated pension schemes invest in taxable property. FA 2004, Sch 29A Pt 1 defines investment regulated pension schemes as a registered pension scheme where the member or a person related to the member can directly or indirectly influence or advise on the investments. This includes RAPs, SIPPS and SSASs.

Taxable property is defined by FA 2004, Sch 29A Pt 2 as:

(a) residential property, which includes buildings used as or suitable to be used as a dwelling and the gardens or grounds. It also includes hotels, similar accommodation and beach huts. For these purposes, residential property excludes homes or institutions providing accommodation for children or the elderly. It also excludes property occupied by an employee who is required to occupy it as a condition of their employment or property used in connection with a business premises e.g. a flat above a shop. However, in both cases the individual occupying the flat must not be a member of the pension scheme or connected to a member of the pension scheme. Connected person is as defined in ICTA 1988, s 839; or

(b) tangible moveable property.

Where the taxable property is held then a number of tax charges may apply. These include:

(i) an unauthorised payments income tax charge at 40% of the value of the taxable property levied on the recipient of the payment;
(ii) an unauthorised payments surcharge where the unauthorised payment represents 25% or more of the pension fund value. This is an additional 15% income tax charge, again levied on the recipient of the payment;
(iii) denial of tax exemption for the pension fund on any income or gains from the property;
(iv) a scheme sanction income tax charge at 40% levied on the scheme administrator (although offset by any unauthorised payment charge);
(v) a possible deregistration charge at 40% if the value of the taxable property exceeds 25% of the fund value.

Member connected investments

[8.20] The old rules relating to member connected investments have now mostly disappeared provided any transactions take place on an arm's length basis. If not then the benefit in kind rules will apply. For these purposes assets are valued in accordance with TCGA 1992, s 272 at the price that those assets would reasonably be expected to produce on the open market. Furthermore, there are value shifting rules in FA 2004 to prevent value being extracted from pension schemes and placed in the hands of a member or employer.

Loans to employers

[8.21] Any loans to employers must meet the following conditions:

(a) be at an interest rate of 1% above the average base rate rounded up to the nearest 0.25%;
(b) be secured as a first charge on assets;
(c) last for less than 5 years;
(d) be repaid by equal annual instalments;
(e) not exceed 50% of the value of the pension scheme's assets.

Scheme borrowing

[8.22] Total borrowing is limited to 50% of scheme assets which is considerably less flexible than the pre-A Day position.

Investment in sponsoring employer

[8.23] Pension schemes are now restricted to investing under 5% of pension scheme assets in any one sponsoring employer and under 20% of the value where the shareholdings relate to more than one sponsoring employer. Where the scheme is not sponsored by the employer (eg a SIPP) then higher levels of shareholdings may be possible).

Trustee responsibility

[8.24] HMRC Registered Pension Manual para 7101010 reminds trustees that:

> general trust law requires the trustees to act prudently, conscientiously and honestly when making decisions in respect of the scheme. Trustees should at all times act in the best interests of scheme members in their capacity as trustees and not as employees, shareholders etc.

Although pension schemes are able to invest quite widely in, for example unquoted shares, in practice, professional pension trustee companies are reluctant to hold assets that might be in breach of their trustee responsibilities. Furthermore many unquoted shares now qualify for generous tax reliefs in their own right (including IHT business property relief and possibly Enterprise Investment Scheme relief) so it is often advantageous to hold such assets outside a pension scheme.

The international element

[8.25] Under FA 2004, ss 221–226, an individual who has been a member of a recognised overseas pension scheme or has been a member of a UK scheme whilst resident abroad may be able to apply to HMRC to have their standard lifetime allowance enhanced.

Where there is a transfer from a recognised overseas pension plan the key point is that the funds in the pension are not UK tax relieved, hence the reason for the enhancement to the lifetime limit. However, there may be an impact on the annual allowance where the transfer is into an occupational scheme.

For a scheme to be a recognised overseas pension scheme it has to meet certain criteria. It must be established in:

(a) a member state of the European Economic Area;
(b) a country or territory with which the UK has a double tax agreement providing for exchange of information; or
(c) any other country or territory if at the time of the transfer the rules are broadly equivalent to UK pension scheme rules.

Where the member is a relevant overseas individual then contributions made to a UK pension plan whilst overseas may not have been relieved for UK taxation purposes, hence the reason for permitting an enhancement to the lifetime limit.

It is also possible for a UK individual moving abroad to arrange for a transfer from their UK scheme to a qualifying recognised overseas pension scheme (QROPS). A QROPS has to notify HMRC that it is a recognised overseas pension together with providing other information to HMRC regarding its recognised status. It must also confirm its country of establishment.

Divorce

[8.26] The legislation enabling pension splitting came into effect on 1 December 2000. Pension splitting is the court's preferred option for dealing with pensions on divorce as it allows a clean break with the fund of the pension member simply split according to the divorce agreement. Pension earmarking is still available but this does not provide a clean break as the recipient of the earmarking order has to wait until the pensions scheme member takes their pension.

A pension splitting order may have an impact on the lifetime limit of both the recipient former spouse and the pension scheme member.

If the pension splitting order is post-A Day, then the credit amount will count against the recipient former spouse's lifetime limit, not the pension member's. This means that the pension member may be able to rebuild their pension fund post divorce.

Where the pension came into payment post-A Day, the recipient former spouse can claim an enhancement to their lifetime limit to reflect the fact that the pension will already have been tested against the member's lifetime limit.

Where the pension sharing order was in place pre-A Day, the recipient of the pension credit can claim an enhancement to their lifetime limit. The pension member's lifetime limit excludes any amount paid away as pension credit to a former spouse.

The calculation of the enhancement factor is provided by FA 2004, Sch 36 Pt 2.

Unapproved arrangements

[8.27] The attraction of unapproved pension arrangements (principally Funded Unapproved Pension Schemes ('FURBS') and Unfunded Unapproved Pension Schemes ('UURBS')) was much eroded prior to A Day with the imposition of capital gains and income tax at 40% following trust taxation reform. The schemes have now been renamed as Employer Financed Retirement Benefit Schemes ('EFRBS').

There is no tax or NIC charged on the employee or employer when contributions are made but neither does the employer receive a tax deduction. Once benefits come into payment they are subject to income tax. NIC is also due unless at least 75% of the benefits are drawn as a pension income and the employee has left the employment. This is the point at which the employer receives a tax deduction.

Post-A Day FURBS continue to deliver a worthwhile IHT shelter for funds contributed prior to A Day providing there are no further contributions post-A Day. If further contributions are made then the pre-A Day fund is protected from IHT together with an element of indexation reflecting the level of the retail price index to the September before the payment.

Unless FURBs or UURBs are transferred into a registered scheme then they do not count towards the lifetime limit.

Chapter 9

The Family Home

Introduction

[9.1] The family home is the principal asset of many people who seek estate planning advice, and as it is often their only significant asset, it merits separate treatment in this book. As long as 40 years ago, Lord Diplock observed in *Pettitt v Pettitt* [1970] AC 777 that we have witnessed 'the emergence of a property owning, particularly a real property mortgaged to a building society owning, democracy'.

Although the opportunities for mitigating the charge to inheritance tax on the family home are limited, they are nonetheless the ones frequently of most concern to clients.

This chapter is not exclusively concerned with the position of married couples and, where appropriate, will highlight estate planning considerations that are relevant to unmarried couples and others who buy a home jointly, or in their sole name. Except where a planning suggestion depends on creating different interests in land, no distinction will be made between freehold and leasehold ownership. References to a spouse are to be taken to include references to a civil partner.

Ownership of property

[9.2] In order to set estate planning considerations in context, it is first necessary to outline the two forms of joint ownership recognised by English land law.

English law draws a distinction between legal and beneficial ownership of land. Where legal ownership is held by two or more individuals they will hold it as joint tenants. The legal joint tenants will hold the land on trust for the beneficial owners (who may be, and usually are, themselves) and on the death of one joint owner the legal title vests in the survivor or survivors.

The law recognises two forms of beneficial ownership, namely:

(a) joint tenancy; and
(b) tenancy in common.

While in both cases, each beneficial co-owner is as much entitled to possession of any part of the land as the other so that no one joint owner can claim this or that piece of the land as his own, there are two essential differences, which are of fundamental importance for estate planning. First, in the case of a beneficial joint tenancy, each co-owner can only have an equal interest in the land, or in its net proceeds of sale if it is sold, whereas in the case of a tenancy in common, it is possible for one owner to have a greater or lesser share than the other co-owner(s). For this reason, when people contribute to the purchase price of land in unequal shares, they should insist on the beneficial ownership being in the form of a tenancy in common, unless they are content to accept the equality of interest created by a joint tenancy (which in itself will result in a gift by one of the co-owners to the other with possible inheritance tax consequences). Secondly, and more importantly, in the case of a beneficial joint tenancy, when a co-owner dies, his interest passes automatically (and irrespective of any will which he may leave) to the surviving co-owner; whereas, in the case of a tenancy in common, the share of a joint owner passes on death in accordance with his will or, if he leaves no will, the rules of intestacy. For these reasons, of the two forms of beneficial joint ownership, a tenancy in common is usually to be recommended as being the more useful and flexible form of joint ownership for estate planning purposes.

In the case of unmarried couples, if a property is held on a tenancy in common, each co-owner should make a will dealing with the property on their death. This will avoid the property devolving under the intestacy rules in a manner contrary to the deceased's wishes.

Married couples, however, are still frequently recommended to purchase property as beneficial joint tenants on the ground that this is the most convenient and cost effective method of holding property should one of them die. It is true that, in the event of death, no probate or other formalities are required beyond the simple one of placing a certified copy of the death certificate with the title deeds or, in the case of registered land, by submitting an application to the land registrar together with evidence of the death which would normally be a death certificate. Such advice, however, overlooks the risk of marital breakdown and the lesser risk of both spouses dying at the same time, for example, in a road accident.

In the event of a break-up of the marriage, each party will normally be advised by their respective lawyers to terminate the beneficial joint tenancy in order to ensure that, in the event of premature death before the financial settlement on divorce has been completed, their respective interests do not go to their spouse. Similarly, the risk of both dying at the same time should not be overlooked. The Law of Property Act 1925, s 184 provides that where two people die in circumstances where it is not possible to say which of them died first, the elder will be deemed to have died first. This rule is modified in the case of spouses where the elder dies intestate so that each spouse will be deemed to have pre-deceased the other (Administration of Estates Act 1925, s 46(3)). However, this modification to the terms of s 184 does not apply to beneficial joint tenancies, so that, irrespective of whether or not the elder spouse left a will, his or her interest will pass automatically to the other spouse and then in accordance with that spouse's will, or intestacy. This could result in unintended consequences, with the property, in the case of a young couple without children, passing to one set of parents to the exclusion of the other. In the case of a tenancy in common, each spouse's interest in the property will pass on intestacy as if the other had predeceased and this may result in a fairer division of the property between each spouse's immediate family.

Whichever form of co-ownership is used, the legal ownership must operate through a trust of land (Law of Property Act 1925, ss 34–36) so that the legal owners hold the property on trust for the beneficial owners who will usually be themselves. Under the Trusts of Land and Appointment of Trustees Act 1996 ('TLATA 1996') trustees are not under a duty to sell the property. Neither party can sell the property without the consent of the co-owner unless an application is made to the court.

Where co-owners cannot agree on a sale, either may apply to the court for an order of sale (TLATA 1996, s 14). In considering whether or not to order a sale, the court, which has complete discretion in the matter, will take into account the intentions of the person who created the trust, the purpose for which the property subject to the trust is held and the welfare of any minor who occupies or might reasonably be expected to occupy any land subject to the trust as his home (TLATA 1996, ss 14, 15).

The legal joint tenants are under a statutory duty to consult beneficiaries and give effect to their wishes insofar as these are consistent with the general interests of the trust (TLATA 1996, ss 5 and 11). Naturally, that is usually only of importance where the legal interests are held by different persons or in different proportions to the beneficial interests.

For the estate planner, the principal advantage of a tenancy in common is that it permits each co-owner to deal with his or her interest during life, or on death, according to their wishes. When compared to this flexibility, the advantages of a beneficial joint tenancy are small in most circumstances. A joint tenancy may be severed at any time by a notice in writing to the other joint tenant (Law of Property Act 1925, s 36(2)). The property will then be held as tenants in common. In the case of *Grindal v Hooper* (2000) Times, 8 February the High Court held that for a severance to be effective, notice had to be served. In that case, the conveyance to the parties specified that any notice of severance should be annexed to the conveyance. This notice whilst served was not attached to the conveyance until after the death of one of the owners. The court held that annexation was not essential to the validity of the notice.

A beneficial joint tenancy has an appeal for married couples for whom there is peace of mind in the knowledge that when one of them dies the other automatically becomes entitled to the entire family home, without the need to go to the trouble and expense of obtaining probate. The surviving spouse will take the interest of the first to die subject to any subsisting mortgage debt unless the will provides that another part of the estate will have this burden (Administration of Estates Act 1925, s 35). Repayment of the mortgage debt can be provided for by means of a mortgage protection policy or a low cost insurance policy. Apart from this, the surviving spouse is free to sell or mortgage the property without further formality, as the trust terminates on death and the survivor can give a good receipt for the sale proceeds. Where property is held as tenants in common, the trust of land survives the death of the first co-owner (unless the survivor inherits the share of the deceased co-owner) and the survivor must appoint a co-trustee in order to sell or otherwise deal with the property.

For both inheritance tax and capital gains tax purposes, no distinction is drawn between a beneficial joint tenancy and a beneficial tenancy in common in equal shares. In either case each tenant will be treated as the absolute beneficial owner of his share in the property. In the case of the death of a beneficial joint tenant, this result comes about for inheritance tax purposes because the tax is calculated by reference to the value of the deceased's estate immediately before his death which will include his beneficial interest in the property. An act of severance will not give rise to either an inheritance tax or a capital gains tax charge; nor to any stamp duty or SDLT liability.

When drafting a will purporting to dispose of a share in jointly owned property, the adviser is under a duty to ensure that the joint tenancy has been or is later severed (*Keckskemeti v Rubens Rabin & Co* (1992) Times, 31 December).

Purchasing the family home

[9.3] The first concern of most married couples is to ensure that, in the event of one of them dying, there will be a secure roof over the head of the survivor. Therefore, it is usual for the family home to be purchased in joint names so that, whoever provides the purchase price or pays the mortgage instalments, each spouse has a beneficial interest in the family home. Although a tenancy in common is generally to be preferred, if the total wealth of the couple does not, and is not likely in the foreseeable future, to exceed the inheritance tax nil rate band (£325,000 in 2010/11), the convenience and cost effectiveness of a beneficial joint tenancy may well outweigh the advantages of a tenancy in common.

If the family home is purchased by a couple as tenants in common, then it is important that the spouses either make or review their wills at the same time as completing the purchase. This is of paramount importance if there are children, because in that event the surviving spouse may find that in the absence of a will her entitlement on intestacy may not be sufficient to give her the other half share in the family home.

The entitlement of a surviving spouse or civil partner on intestacy is set out in the following table (in which references to a spouse include a civil partner) (Administration of Estates Act 1925, s 46, as amended):

Surviving next of kin of the deceased	*Spouse's entitlement*
Spouse alone (ie no children, no parents, no siblings or their issue)	Whole of the estate absolutely
Spouse and other relatives (ie parents, brothers and sisters and their issue) but no children	(*a*) Personal chattels (*b*) Statutory legacy of £450,000 (*c*) Half interest in residue absolutely
Spouse and children	(*a*) Personal chattels (*b*)Statutory legacy of £250,000

Surviving next of kin of the deceased	*Spouse's entitlement*
	(*c*)Life interest in half of the residue

The surviving spouse can elect to take the family home in whole or partial satisfaction of any absolute interest in the deceased's estate, including the capital value of any life interest (Intestates' Estates Act 1952, s 5, Sch 2). If, as is often the case, the family home consists of the larger part of the value of the estate, the spouse could find herself in a position where part of the family home is held in trust for the children. Moreover, the home is appropriated at its value when the spouse makes her election and not at its probate value, so that increasing property values can have the effect of reducing the value of the statutory legacy, unless an election is made promptly.

Although the rules of intestacy are intended to reflect the wishes of the average person, they should not be relied upon as a substitute for a will. The intestacy rules will not necessarily result in the most appropriate devolution of one's estate; indeed, they may have effects which are entirely out of accord with the deceased's wishes.

In the case of unmarried couples, security and provision for what is to happen on death is even more important than for married couples. Under the intestacy rules an unmarried partner has no right to any share of the deceased partner's estate. The Inheritance (Provision for Family and Dependants) Act 1975 provides a partial remedy in that if the survivor was immediately before the death of the other partner being maintained either wholly or partly by him, the survivor can apply to the court for reasonable maintenance out of the deceased partner's estate. This will provide the unmarried partner with provision in the nature of income. Although the court has power to capitalise the sum awarded, it has no power to make capital provision. It is therefore imperative that both partners make wills giving their respective interests in the property to their partner. The Civil Partnership Act 2004, Sch 4 para 7 grants a surviving civil partner the same rights on intestacy as a surviving spouse.

There will of course always be circumstances where the couple wish the house to be bought only in the name of one of them. For example, where one spouse is a partner in a business or a sole trader, it may be appropriate that the property is bought in the sole name of the other spouse in the hope of providing some protection against the results of the first spouse becoming bankrupt.

Where property is occupied by an unmarried couple but has been purchased in the sole name of one of the parties, the entire value of the property will normally be subject to inheritance tax on the death of that party. The Revenue has argued that even where the surviving cohabitee has made contributions to the cost of the property, this does not reduce the value of property on the death of the deceased cohabitee. The Revenue takes the view that the beneficial rights of the surviving cohabitee do not exist unless and until a court order is obtained. Whether this view is correct is doubtful as such arrangements create a beneficial tenancy in common either under a constructive trust or by proprietary estoppel which is then enforced by the court after litigation. Therefore, prior to the death of the deceased cohabitee, the surviving cohabitee is already a joint owner in equity of the property (Taxation, 22 May 1997). It is also arguable that the value of the deceased cohabitee's share should be discounted on the basis that a notional purchaser in the open market would have to share possession with the surviving cohabitee. This argument was followed by the Special Commissioners in *Arkwright (Williams' Personal Representatives) v CIR* [2004] STC (SCD) 89 which involved a husband and wife and the related property rules in IHTA 1984, s 161. On appeal to the High Court ([2004] STC 1323), the issue of whether a notional purchaser of the deceased's half share might take the surviving wife's right of occupation into account and, if so, how that would affect the value were considered. It was held that these were matters for the Lands Tribunal to determine on proper evidence.

The Revenue argued before the Special Commissioner that the related property rules in IHTA 1984, s 161(4) applied so that the deceased's share of jointly held property was a straightforward mathematical one half of the vacant possession value. Section 161(4) provides that the aggregate value is to be apportioned in accordance with the proportion that its value on its own bears to the sum of the separate values. It was held that whilst s 161(4) could apply to property which had a distinct individual existence as a unit, such as unit trusts or a set of furniture (for example twelve dining chairs), it did not apply to fractions of units.

Although this issue was not considered further when the Revenue's appeal against the decision was heard by the High Court, the Revenue said that it had received legal advice that s 161(4) may apply to fractional shares of units. The Revenue issued Brief 71/2007 stating that in relation to cases where an account is received after 28 November 2007, it will apply the apportionment method in s 161(4) when valuing shares of land as related property. It has also said that it will consider litigation in appropriate cases.

Making provision in a will

[9.4] There are various ways in which a tenant in common can deal with his beneficial interest in a property by will. When provision for the surviving spouse is of overriding concern, the will of each spouse should contain an absolute gift of their respective interests in the home to the other. The terms of the gift should not be limited to any particular property they may own at the time, but should be phrased to apply to whatever property is owned at the date of death. This will avoid the need to amend the wills every time the couple move home.

It is also advisable to include in the gift the benefit of any mortgage protection or insurance policy in order to prevent any argument that the surviving spouse must account for the part of the policy which is used to repay the survivor's share of the mortgage debt. It is even more important to cover this point where the house and mortgage are in joint names but the policy is taken out on the life of the principal salary-earner alone. A specific gift of the policy will also mean that any surplus from the policy in excess of the sum needed to repay the loan will pass to the same legatee and will not pass under the gift of residue. If this is not desired, then the will should provide accordingly.

At the same time provision should be made for what should happen in the event that both spouses die at the same time; for example, in a road accident. While the gift to the surviving spouse will be free of inheritance tax, the gift in default may not be, and consideration should be given to whether or not the tax should be borne by the beneficiary who receives the interest in the family home or by the residuary estate. In the absence of express provision, the tax will be treated as a general testamentary expense and paid out of residue (IHTA 1984, s 211). An unmarried couple also need to consider who should bear the tax.

Before the introduction of the transferable nil rate band (see **16.3**) where the family home was the principal family asset, care was needed to ensure that the opportunity to pass part of the family wealth equal to the nil rate band was not missed. One method was to leave a share of the property equal in value to the deceased's unused part of the nil rate band to the next generation either outright, or on discretionary trusts. The surviving spouse (who might also be a trustee) and their children (and remoter issue) would then be included in the class of beneficial objects of the trust. The will trust would contain a power to enable the trustees to allow the surviving spouse to occupy the property. A problem with this is that if the surviving spouse is given an exclusive or joint right of residence, the Revenue may argue that an interest in possession has been created (see Revenue Statement of Practice SP10/79). Statement of Practice 10/79 states that where trustees exercise their powers 'with the intention of providing a particular beneficiary with a permanent home the Revenue will normally regard the exercise of the power as creating an interest in possession'. In *IRC v Lloyds Private Banking Ltd* [1998] STC 559 (Ch D), [1998] 2 FCR 41 the Court of Appeal held that a life interest was created where a will provided that a surviving tenant in common was to have the right of exclusive occupation of the property concerned for life. Similar decisions were reached in *Woodhall (Woodhall's Personal Representative) v IRC* [2000] STC (SCD) 558, (SpC 261) and *Faulkner (trustee of Adams, dec'd) v IRC* [2001] STC (SCD) 112, (Sp C 278). These decisions provide some support for the Revenue's views expressed in SP 10/79 but it should be noted that the cases did not concern the occupation of property at notice by a discretionary beneficiary. The case of *Judge v Revenue and Customs Corms* [2005] SpC 500 supports the opposing view. The Special Commissioner found that an interest in possession did not exist where a will provided that the trustees were to permit a widow the use and enjoyment of the property 'for such period or periods as they shall in their absolute discretion think fit'. The widow did in fact occupy the property but the will provided that any income from the property was to be held upon the trusts of residue.

The use of the word 'normally' in the Statement is unhelpful. The STEP and the CIOT wrote to the Revenue for clarification of a number of points in respect of this statement. The Revenue said in reply that the circumstances in which it would not regard the exercise of the power by trustees to give an exclusive right of occupation as creating an interest in possession, would be rare. Instances where HMRC said that there might not be an interest in possession were where there was no evidence of an intention by the trustees to provide a particular beneficiary with a permanent home or where significant doubt about the trustees' intentions existed. The Revenue also said that where there is evidence that trustees have knowingly exercised their powers so as to give a beneficiary exclusive occupation then an interest in possession will have been created and that the trustees themselves could reasonably form a view on this point if the relevant facts justified that conclusion.

The Debt Strategy, as it was known, was devised to avoid any difficulties where an estate did not have sufficient assets to satisfy a nil rate band legacy apart from the family home. In such a case the nil rate band legacy was satisfied by a debt from the surviving spouse or civil partner where the residuary estate has passed directly to them or was held on trust for them. To avoid the risk of a surviving spouse or civil partner having an interest in possession the debt was expressed to be repayable on demand. The strategy can be rendered ineffective where the estate of the first spouse to die contains assets derived from the surviving spouse. In *Phizackerley (Personal Representatives of Phizackerley deceased) v Revenue & Customs Comrs* [2007] SpC 591 the debt strategy failed because the debt was held not to be deductible under FA 1986, s 103 as the deceased's share in the family home had derived from her surviving husband. Where the surviving spouse has funded the purchase price of a property alone, the deceased's share in the property subject to the debt should be held on trust for a class of beneficial objects which include the surviving spouse. In that case, FA 1986, s 103 should not apply because the debt will not be incurred by the surviving spouse but by the trustees.

As mentioned above, because an unused nil rate band on the first death can be utilised by the surviving spouse on their death, it may seem that nil rate band discretionary trusts no longer need to be used. The freezing of the nil rate band until 2014/2015 has tilted the balance of advantage back towards utilising it on the first death. It will often still be appropriate to include in a will a provision to allow the deceased's interest in the family home to be utilised to ensure the nil rate band is fully used on the first death.

Another approach to the problem was to use a discretionary trust of which the surviving spouse was not a beneficial object. He or she would then rely on the right given to him or her by virtue of being a co-owner under a tenancy in common in respect of the remainder of the property in order to occupy the property. Even so, the efficacy of this route is doubtful in light of the decision in *CIR v Eversden (executors of Greenstock (dec'd))* [2003] STC 822 (CA), for, as Lightman J pointed out, since the enactment of TLATA 1996 a tenant in common no longer has an automatic right of occupation unless the conditions of s 12 of that Act are fulfilled. Furthermore, this strategy can bring other problems. First, it is considered that the capital gains tax relief for principal private residences will not be available in respect of the proportion of the property held in the discretionary trust (although, in practice, any liability on disposal may be small due to the uplift to market value that will have occurred on death). It is understood, however, that HMRC does not consider that s 12 prevents relief where trustees have the power to allow occupation under the terms of the trust. Secondly, there is the question as to whether the trustees are properly exercising their fiduciary obligations by retaining a proportion of a property which is not producing income and which is occupied by a non-beneficiary. For that reason, there is risk for the surviving spouse unless occupation of the property was secured by some form of tenancy agreement. The trustees may be under a duty to seek to force a sale of the property in order to realise the trust's interest in it by an application to the court under the Trusts of Land and Appointment of Trustees Act 1996, s 14 (see **9.2** above).

Often the deceased will prefer to leave his share of the family home directly to the next generation or in trust. It may be felt that the decision as to whether the property should be jointly owned is best left to the surviving spouse as the person directly involved and best placed to judge matters following the death.

The surviving spouse may decide to vary the dispositions of property devolving under the will or passing by survivorship within 2 years of death (IHTA 1984, s 142). The surviving spouse may decide to give a share of the property equal in value to the deceased's unused part of the nil rate band to the next generation either outright or in trust by means of a deed of variation. Provided the instrument effecting the variation contains a statement that IHTA 1984, s 142 is to apply to it, the gift will be treated as if effected by the deceased. Even if the widow continues to occupy the property, there is no scope for the gift with reservation provisions contained in FA 1986, s 102 and Sch 20 to apply since, if a variation is made, the widow will be treated as not having made a gift within s 102(1). Neither is there scope for a charge to arise under the provisions applying to pre-owned assets because by virtue of IHTA 1984, s 17, the disposition is not treated for the purposes of inheritance tax as a transfer of value by the chargeable person (FA 2004, Sch 15 para 16). If the share is placed by the variation into trust, however, the same issues arise as to whether an interest in possession is created as are discussed above.

For unmarried couples, similar considerations apply to will drafting, but special care is needed when considering the payment of inheritance tax. As a spouse exemption is not available to unmarried couples, they must pay particular care as to how inheritance tax can be paid by the surviving partner. If cash or other assets are not available, life insurance is generally the cheapest solution. However, it is important that the policy proceeds are written in trust for the survivor so that they do not form part of the deceased's estate thereby increasing the inheritance tax payable.

There is also a trap for the unwary if the property is mortgaged and there is an endowment or mortgage protection policy. If such a policy is not written in trust the proceeds will form part of the deceased partner's estate for inheritance tax purposes. This may have two unexpected consequences. First more tax than would otherwise be the case may be payable so that the property may have to be sold in order to pay the tax. Secondly, the policy proceeds may fall into residue and pass to the wrong beneficiary either under the will or on intestacy.

Lifetime planning

[9.5] Lifetime planning for the family home has always been an area of estate planning fraught with difficulties. On the one hand, an individual wishes to give away all or part of the wealth represented by his home at a low or nil tax cost, and on the other he wishes to continue living in the property. Whilst potentially exempt transfers encourage lifetime planning as no immediate charge to tax arises, at the same time the gift with reservation provisions (FA 1986, s 102 and Sch 20) and the provisions which impose an income tax charge on pre-owned assets (FA 2004, Sch 15) make it difficult for an individual to continue to live in the property and to give away some of the wealth represented by his home.

Any gift by an individual, including a gift of his home or an interest in it, is capable of constituting a potentially exempt transfer. No inheritance tax will be chargeable on a potentially exempt transfer unless the donor dies within 7 years of making the gift. In the event of a transfer between 3 and 7 years before death taper relief is available.

In practice, nearly all lifetime planning for the family home tends to concern a gift to another individual, and only in exceptional circumstances will an individual wish to make a settlement of the family home.

Gifts with reservation

[9.6] Before considering the planning opportunities available, it is necessary to consider the gifts with reservation provisions in order to understand the restrictions they place on planning in this area. This is discussed in more detail in **CHAPTER 2 LIFETIME PLANNING**.

Under FA 1986, s 102, where an individual makes a gift of property and either:

(a) possession and enjoyment of the property is not bona fide assumed by the donee within 7 years of the donor's death; or
(b) at any time within the 7-year period the property is not enjoyed to the entire exclusion, or virtually to the entire exclusion, of the donor or of any benefit to the donor by contract or otherwise,

the property is said to be subject to a reservation, with the consequence that the property (or its traceable proceeds) will be brought into charge to tax when the donor dies as if he were still beneficially entitled to it at that time.

There are a number of exemptions to the application of this provision set out in s 102(5) but they are of limited relevance to an individual wishing to benefit anyone other than his spouse.

If the property ceases to be subject to a reservation, the donor is treated as making a potentially exempt transfer at the time of the cessation (FA 1986, s 102(4)).

FA 1986, Sch 20, and in particular para 6, provides two further exemptions of importance in the case of gifts of interests in land. First, the donor may retain or assume actual occupation of land or actual possession of a chattel in return for full consideration in money or money's worth. This is a valuable concession which will be considered later. Secondly, an exemption may apply where the donor has made a gift of a property to a relative, or to a relative of his spouse or civil partner, in circumstances which did not give rise to a reservation of benefit, but subsequently comes to re-occupy it as a result of an unforeseen and unplanned change in the circumstances of the donor. Provided that at the time concerned the donor has become unable to maintain himself through old age, infirmity or any other reason and his occupation represents reasonable provision by the donee for his care and maintenance, his re-occupation will be disregarded in determining whether the property is subject to a reservation. For example, a father, on retiring to the country, gave a house in London to his son. He subsequently became infirm through ill-health, which resulted in him no longer being able to look after himself. If he had moved back into the house and lived with his son, provided his re-occupation represented reasonable provision by the son for the care of his father, no gift with reservation would have arisen. Following the introduction of the income tax charge on pre-owned assets in FA 2004, Sch 15, such an arrangement will now be caught even though the donor's re-occupation of the house in London was unforeseen and notwithstanding that it represented reasonable provision by the son for the care of his father. If the father does nothing, he will be assessed to income tax on an amount equal to the market rent of the property. There are, however, steps the father can take to mitigate this income tax liability. These are considered in more detail in **9.7** below.

The gifts with reservation provisions make it very difficult for a person to remove property from his taxable estate whilst continuing to occupy it whether his occupation is long-term under some form of tenancy or other binding arrangement entered into by the donee or merely intermittent under a gratuitous licence of the donee. Clearly, the use of the word 'virtually' in FA 1986, s 102(1)(b) is designed to prevent merely occasional visits by a donor to the donee from tainting the original gift (see Revenue Inheritance Tax Manual, para 14333). The Revenue's view on how the word 'virtually' is to be interpreted is discussed in detail in **CHAPTER 2 LIFETIME PLANNING** under **2.15**.

Four strategies emerged which were of practical relevance to an individual whose wealth was tied up in his home. They attempted to enable him to unlock some of this wealth whilst continuing to live in the home.

The four strategies were:

(a) co-ownership;
(b) use of the 'full consideration' exemption;
(c) 'shearing'; and
(d) the trust of debt.

Before discussing each of the strategies, the application of the income tax charge on pre-owned assets must be considered.

Income tax charge on pre-owned assets

[9.7] FA 2004, Sch 15 introduced a new charge to income tax on pre-owned assets which took effect from 6 April 2005. This income tax charge is discussed in detail in **CHAPTER 2 LIFETIME PLANNING**, but in relation to tax planning for the family home, there are some specific points which should be made. First, the income tax charge will not arise in circumstances in which a reservation of benefit has arisen. If it were not for this provision, arrangements might create an annual income tax charge on the family home as well as an inheritance tax charge on the value of the property following the death of the donor. In order to prevent this double charge, the pre-owned assets provisions provide an exemption for property which is subject to a reservation (FA 2004, Sch 15 para 11(5)(a)). As is illustrated in **9.6** above, there will be situations in which a gift may have been validly made in the past under which no reservation of benefit has arisen, but which may now (or at some point in the future) be caught by the income tax charge on pre-owned assets.

Broadly, the income tax charge will arise in a situation where an individual (the chargeable person) occupies any land (referred to as the 'relevant land'), whether alone or together with other persons, and either the 'disposal condition' or the 'contribution condition' is met in respect of the relevant land.

The 'disposal condition' is met in circumstances in which, at any time after 17 March 1986, the chargeable person

- owned an interest in the relevant land (or in other property the proceeds of which were directly or indirectly applied by another person towards the acquisition of an interest in the relevant land), and
- disposed of all, or part of, his interest in the relevant land or the other property, otherwise than by an excluded transaction.

The 'contribution condition' is met in circumstances in which, at any time after 17 March 1986, the chargeable person has (directly or indirectly) provided, otherwise than by an excluded transaction, any of the consideration given by another person for the acquisition of

- an interest in the relevant land, or
- an interest in any other property, the proceeds of the disposal of which were (directly or indirectly) applied by another person towards the acquisition of an interest in the relevant land.

In the example given in **9.6** above, the father, having made a gift to his son which is not subject to a reservation of benefit, will, on moving back into the house in London to live with his son, fulfil the disposal condition in relation to that house.

In the same example, if, instead of giving the house directly to his son, the donor had sold the house and given the proceeds of sale to his son then the situation would be slightly different. If the son had subsequently used the proceeds from the London house and aggregated them with a further sum of his own money to purchase a new property, on the father moving in with his son due to illness, the contribution condition would have been met in relation to the new property and an income tax charge would have arisen on the father. Since the father had given his son an outright gift of cash, the charge would only arise if the father had moved in with his son within 7 years of the date of the gift. Provided that the earliest date on which the father occupied the house was more than 7 years after the gift, the disposal would be an excluded transaction for the purposes of the charge.

Advisers need to consider the pre-owned assets provisions in relation, not just to new tax planning strategies which their clients may wish to undertake, but also in relation to tax planning which their clients have undertaken in the past and which has been in place for many years. In the above example, if we suppose that the father made the gift to his son in 1988, and moved in with his son in the year 2000 without suffering any adverse tax consequences, there is a danger that the father would not realise that he would now be liable to income tax. An adviser should therefore carry out a detailed fact-find going back at least to 17 March 1986 and earlier if possible. Undoubtedly there will be many people who are now subject to an income tax liability in relation to gifts they have made in the past, without any tax avoidance motivation, without their being aware of that fact.

The income tax charge is based on the appropriate rental value of the relevant land less any payments which, in pursuance of any legal obligation, are made by the chargeable person to the owner of the relevant land in respect of the occupation of the land by the chargeable person. It is important to note that it is only payments under a legal obligation which are deductible from the rental value. This means that any payments made informally will not count. A chargeable person may mitigate his liability to the income tax charge by paying a full market rent for the period of occupation under a legal obligation. By so doing, the amount on which the income tax charge is assessed would be reduced to zero.

Example

In the example in **9.6** above, the father was 44 at the time he made the gift in 1988 and so he was 61 on 6 April 2005, and, notwithstanding his illness, is expected to live to the age of 75. He intends to live with his son for the rest of his life.

If we assume that the house will be worth £1,600,000 at the time of his death and that his available nil rate band is used up by legacies under his will, then, at current rates, the gift of the house to his son will save him £400,000 in inheritance tax. If the annual rental value of the property is £80,000 and the father is a higher rate taxpayer (but not an additional rate taxpayer), he will pay £32,000 (£80,000 at 40%) annually in income tax from 6 April 2005. As he is expected to live 14 years after the imposition of the pre-owned assets charge, he will have paid (assuming that the current rental value does not increase) £448,000 in income tax in order to save £400,000 of inheritance tax.

If, instead of being 61, the father had been 81 years of age on 6 April 2005, and he had been expected to live to 86, then the income tax he would have paid over the period to his death would have been (£32,000 × 5 = £160,000) in order to save £400,000 of inheritance tax.

If the father could afford to pay a full market rent to his son then, provided there is a formal tenancy agreement between them, the father would have no income tax liability in respect of his occupation of the property, although of course, the son would be charged to income tax on the rent. This may be an effective way of passing further value out of the father's estate by reducing it by the amount of the rent paid.

If the chargeable person can neither afford to pay the income tax nor a full market rent, then he may consider making an election under FA 2004, Sch 15 para 21. A chargeable person may make an election which will have the result that the pre-owned assets provisions will not apply to him but, in return, for as long as the chargeable person continues to occupy the relevant land, he will be treated as having a reservation of benefit in that property. Any such election must be made in the prescribed manner determined by regulations (on Form IHT 500) by 31 January in the year of assessment that immediately follows the initial year of assessment. The 'initial year' is any year of assessment in which, but for the election, a person would be chargeable by reference to his enjoyment of the relevant property, provided that he has not been chargeable under the relevant provision in respect of that property (or any other property for which it has been substituted) in any previous year of assessment. This means that for people who find themselves subject to the pre-owned assets charge for the first time in 2010/11, the relevant filing date is 31 January 2012. Where an election is made, the result will be that the relevant land will be deemed to be subject to a reservation of benefit (irrespective of whether or not a reservation of benefit would otherwise arise) and the value of the asset will be brought back within the donor's estate for inheritance tax purposes. However, for capital gains tax purposes and income tax purposes, the relevant land will be treated as belonging to the donee. Once made, an election cannot be withdrawn and the deemed reservation of benefit will continue for so long as the chargeable person continues to enjoy the land.

Clients who now find themselves caught by an income tax charge which they cannot or do not wish to pay, may take steps to 'undo' the tax planning undertaken. In many circumstances, this will simply not be possible or, where it is possible, it is likely to be costly.

Another possibility for those clients wishing to avoid the charge is to move out of the property. Finally, the client may attempt to go back to square one.

Example

> In the circumstances outlined in 9.6 above, the son may consider transferring the land back to the father. In addition to the inevitable costs, the son will have made a potentially exempt transfer for the purposes of inheritance tax and, should he die within 7 years of making the transfer, the value of the property would form part of his estate for inheritance tax purposes. The son could take out a policy of life assurance to cover this risk.

Co-ownership

[9.8] This involves the donor making a gift of an undivided share in land so that, after the gift, the donor and the donee share ownership and occupation of the property. A common application of this is where a parent who solely owns their own property transfers an interest in the property to a child or close relative who either takes up occupation or continues occupying the property. FA 1986, s 102B(2) provides that all gifts by an individual of an undivided share of an interest in land are gifts with reservation, subject to two exceptions.

One of these exceptions is found in FA 1986, s 102B(4) which provides that there is no gift with reservation of benefit where the donor and donee occupy the land and the donor does not receive any benefit other than a negligible one which is provided by or at the expense of the donee for some reason connected with the gift. Where there is some collateral arrangement (ie an agreement that the donee should pay more than a proportionate share of the running costs), this will amount to a benefit to the donor 'by contract or otherwise'.

Where the donor and donee occupy the land within the exception found in FA 1986, s 102B(4), there is no reservation of benefit and the pre-owned assets provisions must be considered. Under FA 2004, Sch 15 para 11(3)(a), there will be a complete exemption from the charge.

Beneficial interests may be conferred by the original owner entering into a declaration of trust specifying in what proportions the beneficial interests are to be shared; and in the case of a sole owner (eg a surviving spouse) one or more other members of the family, or a professional adviser, should be appointed as co-trustee of the legal title to ensure there are at least two (Law of Property Act 1925, s 27(2)) but not more than four trustees of land (Trustee Act 1925, s 34(1)). A gift of the beneficial interest will constitute a 'potentially exempt transfer' for inheritance tax purposes.

The question often arises as to what percentage should be given away. Although it is possible to give away 99% because the remaining 1% will still entitle the donor to occupy the property, it may not be advisable to do so. The Revenue may regard anything in excess of 75% as aggressive tax planning. Unfortunately, although there would appear to be no authority in law for this view, it would be imprudent to adopt the largest possible percentage. For the reasons explained in **Chapter 1**, the adviser must now be cautious of arousing the irrational hostility of HMRC.

The donor must bear at least his proportionate share of the maintenance and running costs of the property. A distinction should be drawn between capital expenditure and running costs. Capital expenditure should be borne in proportion to ownership whereas running costs should be borne in proportion to occupation. Where a donor and donee have equal shares, the donor should bear at least 50% of his costs so that the donor does not receive a benefit from the donee arising out of the gift.

A problem will arise if and when any one or more of the donees decides to move out of the property. If the donor continues to occupy the entire property the gifts to the donees who move out will become gifts with reservation and this will largely defeat their original purpose. Where the gifts become subject to a reservation in this way, the donor's occupation of the property will be completely exempt for the purposes of the pre-owned asset provisions.

FA 2004, Sch 15 para 11(5)(c) provides that if property would fall to be treated as property which is subject to a reservation but for FA 1986, s 102B(4), the pre-owned assets charge will not apply. Therefore the pre-owned asset charge will not apply to co-ownership arrangements exempted from the inheritance tax reservation of benefit rules by s 102B(4).

Use of the 'full consideration' exemption

[9.9] The second exception is found in FA 1986, s 102B(3) which provides that in the event that one of the joint owners does not occupy the property, there will not be a gift with reservation if the donor pays full consideration for his occupation.

An individual might give away his home entirely and enter into an arrangement with the donee which allows him to continue living there. The arrangement might take the form of either a lease or a licence depending on the circumstances. What is important is that the occupation is for full consideration in money or money's worth (FA 1986, Sch 20 para 6(1)(a)). The Revenue accepts that if the terms are the result of a bargain negotiated at arm's length with the parties being independently advised and follow the normal commercial criteria in force at the time they are negotiated, the condition of FA 1986, Sch 20 para 6(1)(a) will be satisfied (Revenue Inheritance Tax Manual, para 14341). The provisions of FA 1986, s 102A explained in **9.10** below contain similar provisions to para 6(1)(a) allowing a donor to occupy property for full consideration (FA 1986, s 102A(3)).

The terms of the agreement and the amount of any rent or licence fee would also be an important commercial consideration. 'Full consideration' implies, in the case of a tenancy, an open market rent. As full consideration is required throughout the period the rent paid must be periodically reviewed. The Revenue does, however, recognise that there is no single value at which consideration can be fixed as 'full' (Revenue Interpretation RI55).

For the purposes of the income tax charge on pre-owned assets, the payment of full consideration (ie the full market rent) is likely to reduce the chargeable amount to nil under FA 2004, Sch 15 para 4(1), provided that the payments are made in pursuance of a legal obligation. It would therefore be advisable to draw up a tenancy agreement so as to ensure that the amounts paid are deductible.

An alternative to charging an open market rent would be to grant a lease, for example a long lease with a term of at least 21 years at a peppercorn rent but at a market premium. As the lease would normally be for less than 50 years, a part of the premium would attract an income tax charge at a rate of up to 50% depending on the donee's marginal rate of income tax. The lease would be within the terms of the Local Government and Housing Act 1989, Sch 10 which would give the donor, or if he had died in the meantime, his successor, the right to continue in occupation after the lease expired. In addition, the Leasehold Reform Act 1967 might give the donor the right to buy back the freehold on favourable terms.

The clear disadvantages of this type of arrangement from the donor's point of view are, first, the payment (out of net income or capital) of the rent or any premium and, secondly, that the lease itself may be a valuable asset in the donor's estate. Whether this is an acceptable price to pay for the ability to divest his estate of a capital asset free of inheritance tax will depend on individual circumstances.

There is a further disadvantage under the pre-owned assets provisions for an arrangement involving the payment of a premium. The gift of the freehold interest would meet the disposal condition in FA 2004, Sch 15 para 3(2) for so long as the donor continued to occupy under the terms of the lease and the donor would, accordingly, be subject to income tax on the rental value of the property, notwithstanding the payment of the premium. This is because, for each year of assessment in which the pre-owned assets provisions applied in respect of a property, the only payments which are permitted deductions against the charge to income tax are those made pursuant to a legal obligation in that year of assessment (FA 2004, Sch 15 para 4(1)). Accordingly, in the year the premium is paid, it can be deducted from the appropriate rental value for that period but, in the following periods, no deduction will be permitted.

'Shearing'

[9.10] Apart from the addition of the words ' . . . or virtually to the entire exclusion' in FA 1986, s 102(1)(b), the gifts with reservation provisions are in identical terms to those which applied under the estate duty regime. Both the Revenue and commentators accept that the case law on the estate duty provisions and the principles that these cases establish are still relevant although comments by Lightman J in the case of *Melville v CIR* [2006] STC 627 (Ch D) throw doubt on the extent to which a court will have regard to estate duty principles in relation to inheritance tax. Although the Court of Appeal confirmed the High Court's decision in that case ([2001] EWCA Civ 1247 (SpC)) it did not specifically consider this issue.

The case of *Munro v Comr of Stamp Duties of New South Wales* [1934] AC 61 (PC) established the principle that there was no reservation of benefit where the donor retained a benefit referable to a prior right rather than to the property which is the subject of the gift. This led to a strategy being developed under which an individual owning the freehold of his home would grant a lease to a nominee for himself, thereby creating a leasehold interest and a freehold reversion. He then gave away the reversion and continued to occupy the property by virtue of his leasehold interest without, it was hoped, falling foul of the gifts with reservation provisions. The scheme was considered by the House of Lords in *Ingram v CIR* [1999] STC 37 (HL). The following discussion sets out the theory of the scheme in detail and then discusses the *Ingram* decision and the insertion of FA 1986, ss 102A–102C which followed that decision.

The *Ingram* Scheme

[9.10A] The scheme involved a two-stage operation. First, the prospective donor granted a lease for a term equal to his life expectancy plus a margin of 5 or 10 years, as appropriate, to a nominee without reserving any rent. As the donor had to create the lease first, he had absolute control over the terms of the lease and there was no necessity to use open market terms. However, to avoid a Revenue claim that the lessor's covenants created a reserved benefit the covenants were not onerous, because when the reversion was given away, the donee took the benefit of those covenants.

Secondly, the donor gave the freehold reversion to the donee by way of a potentially exempt transfer.

If the lease still had some time to run at the donor's death, its remaining value would be subject to inheritance tax.

If the lease expired before the donor died, then the donor would have to either move out of the property or pay a rack rent to avoid being in receipt of a 'reserved benefit'.

If the donor did not own the freehold, it was possible to achieve the same result with a leasehold interest by creating a sub-lease, provided it was permitted by the head lease. Many modern leases do not. The House of Lords found this scheme effective in *Ingram*. Legislation was introduced to stop the strategy in the form of FA 1986, ss 102A–102C.

Section 102A applies when an individual disposes of an interest in any land by way of gift after 8 March 1999. If the donor or his spouse enjoy a significant right or interest, or is a party to a significant arrangement in relation to the land, the interest disposed of will be property subject to a reservation. A right, interest or arrangement is 'significant' for these purposes if it entitles or enables a donor to occupy all or part of the land (or enjoy some other right), otherwise than for full consideration in money or money's worth. The right, etc is not significant if it:

(a) cannot prevent another person or persons enjoying the land virtually or entirely to the exclusion of the donor;
(b) does not enable the donor to occupy the land immediately after the disposal but would have done so were it not for the disposal; or
(c) was granted or acquired more than seven years before the gift.

Similar provisions also apply to gifts of undivided shares in land under s 102B.

For the purpose of these provisions, no account is taken of occupation in circumstances where it would be ignored under FA 1986, Sch 20 para 6(1)(b). This is, broadly, where the donor falls on hard times and the donee makes provision for the donor out of the gift.

The *Ingram* scheme clearly falls within these provisions. As is unfortunately becoming common where anti-avoidance provisions are sponsored by the Revenue, so too will many other arrangements which are not the provisions' ostensible target. For example, the provisions apply in relation to some family farming partnerships.

Under the pre-owned assets provisions, any *Ingram* scheme already in existence will be subject to an income tax charge where the donor continues to occupy the property. The gift of the freehold interest will satisfy the disposal condition and an income tax charge will arise on the donor. The different options available to the donor for mitigating the income tax charge are discussed in **9.6** above. Which is the most suitable option will depend on the age and financial circumstances of the donor.

The Deferred Lease Strategy

[9.10B] There was always, however, an alternative method of achieving the same economic effect whilst avoiding the difficulties of the lease carve out which, in many circumstances, will not be caught by ss 102A–102C. Instead of making a gift of the freehold subject to an immediate lease in the donor's favour, the donor could make a gift of a long lease the rights of which are deferred for a period. For example, one might grant a 999 year lease which is not to commence for 20 years. A lease may defer the right of possession which it confers for up to 21 years after its execution (Law of Property Act 1925, s 149(3)). As the deferred lease is of small value, the value of the potentially exempt transfer is only small. However, the longer the individual survives, the lower the value of the freehold as the period to the beginning of the lease shortens. In effect, the value of the property is transferred to the deferred lease which is outside the estate for inheritance tax purposes. The freehold on the death of the donor will therefore have a much reduced value. The Revenue has always indicated that in its view the associated operations provisions apply to this scheme. That seemed entirely misconceived as, unless one regards death itself as an operation, the scheme consists of only one operation; the grant of the lease. The deferred lease version of the shearing scheme circumvents s 102A if the freehold concerned was originally acquired by the donor more than 7 years before the transfer. HMRC claimed that the grant of the deferred lease would be a 'significant arrangement' within FA 1986, s 102A(2) even if the grantor acquired the freehold of the land more than 7 years before the grant. Now it was clearly true that the grant of the deferred lease is an 'arrangement' to which the donor is a party. The question was whether it is a significant arrangement. The provisions of s 102A(4) are dense but clearly prevent such a grant from being a 'significant arrangement'. HMRC has acknowledged that reversionary interest lease schemes made before 9 March 1999 were effective but had indicated its view that the strategy was ineffective in relation to reversionary leases executed on or after 9 March 1999. That view was at odds with the clear wording of the legislation.

On 29 January 2007, HMRC published a statement to say that they now considered 'that where the freehold interest was acquired more than 7 years before the gift, the continued occupation by the donor would not be a significant right, and contrary to [their] previously held view, a gift with reservation of benefit claim will not arise'. The paragraph went on to say, however, that the donor's continued occupation of the land would give rise to a pre-owned assets charge.

This strategy has a number of disadvantages; namely the base cost of the property concerned for capital gains tax purposes will be very low because, at the time of acquisition, the deferred lease is not very valuable. In addition, the holder of the deferred lease will not receive the principal private residence exemption (see above) and there will be only a small uplift on death. This strategy is only likely to be appropriate where the property is held until death and it is a family property which is not intended to be sold.

There is a further disadvantage under the pre-owned assets provisions as the disposal of the deferred lease will satisfy the disposal condition and an income tax charge will arise on the donor.

Sale at full value

[9.11] It may be possible for parents to sell their home for its full value to their children, thus ensuring that any future capital appreciation accrues to the children. The money may be raised by way of a qualifying loan to reduce the purchase price, with the parents paying full rent against which the children's interest liability could be set. This should avoid the gift with reservation of benefit problems because there would be no disposal by way of gift. It should also avoid the income tax charge on pre-owned assets provided that the terms of the sale are such that might be expected to be made at arm's length between persons not connected with each other. If this proviso is met, the disposal will be an excluded transaction for the purposes of the pre-owned assets provisions and no income tax charge will arise (FA 2004, Sch 15 para 10(1)(a)). However, there are problems with security of tenure and there will be stamp duty land tax on the sale by the parents to the children. In addition, the principal private residence exemption is unlikely to be available on the ultimate sale by the children.

There is, however, a difficulty when there is a part disposal of an interest to a connected person which took place after 6 March 2005. For example, a son buying a 25% interest in his father's property, This is because such a transaction is not an excluded transaction under FA 2004, Sch 15 para 10. In such circumstances there is a charge on the 'benefit' obtained by the father from his continued occupation being a proportion of the market value rent.

Equity Release Schemes

[9.11A] There are two main types of equity release scheme, namely lifetime mortgages and home reversion schemes. With the former, a loan is granted to an individual and the interest accrues until the property is sold or the individual dies. This is a more popular type of scheme. The home reversion scheme involves an individual selling a share or the whole of their property to a provider and a lease for life being granted back to the individual at a nil rent. This type of scheme is only available to people who are 65 or older.

When the pre-owned asset legislation was introduced there was a concern that Equity Release Schemes involving a part disposal would not be excluded transactions under FA 2004, Sch 15 para 10. The Charge to Income Tax by Reference to Enjoyment of Property Previously Owned Regulations 2005, SI 2005/724, reg 5(1)(a) provides that no pre-owned asset charge will arise in relation to a disposal of part of an interest in any property if the disposal was by a transaction made at arm's length with a person not connected with him. In addition, a charge will not arise in relation to a disposal of part of an interest in any property if the disposal was by a transaction such as might be expected to be made at arm's length between persons not connected with each other and:

(a) the disposal was for a consideration not in money or in the form of readily convertible assets; or
(b) the disposal was made before 7 March 2005 (SI 2005/724, reg 5(1)(b)).

Evidence will be, as is often the case, crucial in the matter.

Trust of debt strategy

[9.12] A fourth strategy for reducing inheritance tax on the family home which was much used before the introduction of the pre-owned assets charge is the trust of debt strategy. Under this strategy, the owner of the home settled a small sum on trusts (the 'residence trust') of which he was the life tenant. He then sold his home to the trustees of the residence trust for an amount which was to be payable upon his death and which was to bear interest which was to be rolled up. He now had a debt due to him which he settled on trusts (the 'debt trust') for those he wished to benefit. He had reserved a benefit in the property which he transferred to the trustees but as he was treated by IHTA 1984, s 49(1) as the beneficial owner of that property, the fact that the property was subject to a reservation did not lead to an increased inheritance tax charge (FA 1986, s 102(3)).

The donor had not reserved a benefit in the debt. Although the debt was not repayable until after his death, the property settled was the contractual debt itself including all of its terms. The net effect was that the donor had taken the current value of the debt (which was normally roughly equal to the market value of the property) out of his estate for inheritance tax purposes.

There was no capital gains tax charge on the donor on the assumption that the house had been his principal private residence throughout the time that he owned it. There was, however, a stamp duty land tax charge on the sale of the home to the residence trust.

It is strongly arguable that the trust of debt strategy does not give rise to an income tax charge on the donor under the pre-owned assets rules. It is also strongly arguable that, if a charge does arise, an election to treat the property concerned as property subject to a reservation may be made under FA 2004, Sch 15 para 21 without thereby increasing the taxable total of the donor's estate. This is because the value which is brought back into the chargeable estate is the value of the house at the date of death subject to the loan note. A detailed discussion of these arguments is beyond the scope of a general book on estate planning such as this. The description given above is generic and it is advisable that the precise transactions and their implementation are considered very carefully.

The pre-owned assets rules were clearly intended to catch the trust of debt strategy but they appear to have missed their target.

If the strategy were now implemented the residence trust would be a relevant property settlement subject to decennial and exit charges. That could become significant if the value of the property were to become very much greater than the value of the liability to pay the debt for its purchase price. In schemes implemented before 22 March 2006, however, the interest in possession in the residence trust will be an existing IIP and therefore not a relevant property settlement. If the gift of the debt is made on trusts other than on bare trusts the gift will be an immediately chargeable transfer.

'Eversden Schemes'

[9.13] The case of *CIR v Eversden (executors of Greenstock dec'd)* [2003] STC 822 (CA) was also widely seen as permitting a tax planning strategy. In that case a settlor settled her home ('Beechwood') as to 5% for herself absolutely and as to 95% on trusts giving her husband a life interest subject to a wide power of appointment in favour of a class of beneficiaries which included the settlor. The settlor and her husband occupied Beechwood together until the husband's death. Thereafter, the trustees sold Beechwood and brought another house ('Maitland') again as to 5% for the settlor absolutely and as to 95% subject to what was now a discretionary trust. The settlor continued to occupy Beechwood and then, after its purchase, Maitland until her death. The question for decision was whether the 95% interest held on discretionary trusts was property subject to a reservation in relation to the settlor.

The court held that, by virtue of the settlor's occupation of the house, the trust fund was not enjoyed to the entire, or virtually to the entire, exclusion of benefit to the settlor. The settled property was not property subject to a reservation, however, because the settlement of the property was an exempt inter-spouse transfer under IHTA 1984, s 18. FA 1986, s 102(5) disapplies the gifts with reservation provisions where the gift is exempt under various provisions which include s 18.

The decision led to the marketing of tax planning strategies branded as '*Eversden* Schemes'. HMRC's riposte was to amend FA 1986, s 102 to provide that the fact that a transfer receives the spouse exemption will not prevent it from being a gift with reservation where the following conditions apply; property is settled creating an interest in possession for the donor's spouse, at some time after the disposal but before the donor's death the spouse's interest in possession comes to an end and on that occasion the spouse does not become entitled absolutely to, or to a further interest in possession in, the settled property.

Most *Eversden* Schemes which are already in place will now be subject to an income tax charge on the donor under the pre-owned assets provisions. Although the initial gift into trust for the donor's spouse is an excluded transaction under FA 2004, Sch 15 para 10(1)(c), where the spouse is entitled to an interest in possession, if that interest has come to an end otherwise than on the death of the spouse, the original disposal into trust ceases to be an excluded transaction (FA 2004, Sch 15 para 10(3)).

Long-term planning

[9.14] It seems that the most effective form of planning, for both the reservation of benefit and the pre-owned asset provisions, will be gifts of cash. Provided that the cash is applied to purchase a property which the donor does not occupy until at least 7 years after the gift, there will be no income tax charge.

Example

> In April 2009, a father gave £250,000 cash to his son. The son used the cash to purchase a house in London. In 2010, the father moved in with his son in the London house and paid no rent. There was no charge to income tax.

If the donor wishes to make a gift of cash to enable another person to buy a property, careful consideration should be given to structuring the gift.

Example

A father gives his daughter £10,000 towards the purchase of a flat worth £170,000. The remainder of the purchase price is met by way of a mortgage. The daughter spends £10,000 on furnishing the flat.

If the father moves into the flat within 7 years of making the gift, a charge to income tax will arise.

If, however, the gift were applied in a different way, the result would be different.

Example

The daughter purchases the flat using her savings and raising the balance of the purchase price by way of mortgage. Following the purchase, the father gives his daughter £10,000 to spend on furnishing the flat. After 6 years, the father moves into the property. No income tax charge will arise.

In the second example, the gift of cash is not used as any part of the consideration for the purchase of an interest in land. Provided there was no prior arrangement in place that the gift would be made, the gift could not be an indirect contribution towards the consideration for the acquisition of an interest in land.

Other considerations

[9.15] Before embarking on any tax planning affecting the family home, the beneficial ownership of the property should be clarified together with the existence of an outstanding mortgage. A transfer of the ownership of the property subject to a mortgage will require the consent of the mortgagee. The transfer of the equity can also trigger a charge to stamp duty land tax to the extent of the mortgaged debt.

Capital gains tax

[9.16] The capital gains tax consequences of any gift of land (or of an interest in land) have to be carefully considered. In relation to the donor's only or main residence there is unlikely to be a problem because any gain arising on the gift is likely to be exempt under TCGA 1992, s 222 as a gain arising on a disposal of a main residence. Where, however, the gift relates to a home where the main residence exemption is not, or is not wholly, applicable, a chargeable gain will arise which can only be held over if the gift constitutes a chargeable transfer for inheritance tax purposes (TCGA 1992, s 260). Generally, this will only be where the gift is a gift to a relevant property settlement (even if its value falls within the nil rate band).

If a charge to capital gains tax which cannot be held over does arise, then the tax may be paid by ten equal annual instalments (TCGA 1992, s 281), although interest on the tax will run from the date the tax is payable under TCGA 1992, s 7.

In relation to a second home, it may be possible to mitigate the capital gains tax charge by electing, under TCGA 1992, s 222(5)(a), for the second home to be treated as the donor's main residence for the 2 years immediately preceding the gift, although this may result in there being a charge on any later sale or gift of the donor's other property.

Summary and other points

[9.17] In addition to the arrangements discussed above, the following, rather more obvious but no less effective, options should always be considered.

(a) *Move to a smaller home.* Perhaps the most efficient step that can be taken is to sell the property, move to somewhere smaller and thereby realise some of the accumulated capital value. This creates two assets — the new home and a capital gains tax free cash sum that can be given away. This option is likely to be viable only where the children have reached adulthood and have left home.

(b) *Reduce the value of the home by mortgage.* If a couple are reluctant to move, but still wish to give away during their lifetime some of the accumulated value of their home, they may be able to do so by borrowing against its value and giving away the proceeds. This is only feasible if there are sufficient funds available from other sources to service the borrowing and it should be borne in mind that the interest payments will not be deductible in computing the borrower's assessable income. On death the outstanding mortgage debt will be deductible for inheritance tax purposes, although, of course, the debt itself will still have to be met by the estate.

(c) *Equity release scheme.* This is a variation on the theme above and is discussed above. This option is usually expensive. Care should be taken to ensure that the pre-owned asset legislation does not apply.

Where the donors are prepared to give away a property, for example, a second home, without wishing to occupy it again, then the inheritance tax position is, by comparison, straightforward; but as we have seen the capital gains tax position may be more complicated.

As in all lifetime planning, but especially in the case of the family home, the primary concern will be for the security of the owner or owners — tax saving should always take second place to that. For this reason, lifetime estate planning for the family home is often very limited in scope.

Chapter 10

The Family Business

Introductions

[10.1] This chapter deals with estate planning for the person who carries on business either as a sole proprietor, as a partner in a family partnership, as a member of a limited liability partnership ('LLP') or as a shareholder in a family company. Planning for such persons is normally dealt with together under some general heading like 'business property' because of the connection between the financial affairs of the individuals and those of their businesses, stemming from the fact that interests in a business and shares in a trading company may be capable of qualifying for inheritance tax business property relief. Although this chapter follows this practice, it should be borne in mind that the ideas presented here can apply to all types of 'business property' even if not technically capable of qualifying for the relief. Whilst the tax treatment of companies and partnerships can give rise to considerable complexities and, because of their legal nature, can require rather more sophisticated planning techniques, the basic estate planning principles set out in **CHAPTER 1 WHAT IS ESTATE PLANNING?** and **CHAPTER 2 LIFETIME PLANNING** apply to shares and business interests in exactly the same way as they do to any other item of property.

Inheritance tax

Business property relief

[10.2] Business property relief is a particularly valuable relief which, depending on the type of property, reduces the amount of the value of the business property transferred by either 100% or 50% (IHTA 1984, s 104). The value transferred must be attributable to the net value of the 'relevant business property'. There is no requirement that there must be a transfer of a business, a transfer of business assets will also be eligible for relief (*Revenue and Customs Comrs v Trustees of the Nelson Dance Family* [2009] EWHC 71 (Ch), [2009] STC 802).

Relevant business property is:

(a) Property consisting of a business or an interest in a business.
(b) Securities of an unquoted company which, either by themselves or together with other such securities owned by the transferor gave the transferor control of the company. 'Control' for these purposes means voting control on all matters affecting the company as a whole, other

than questions as to the winding up of the company or the varying of class rights (IHTA 1984, s 269(1), (4)). The votes attaching to any shares owned by the transferor's spouse or civil partner, or by a charity (IHTA 1984, s 269(2)), or by a trust in which the transferor has a beneficial interest in possession (IHTA 1984, s 269(3)), will be taken into account in determining whether the transferor has control. No account is taken of the capacity of the shareholder, or of any of the other shareholders, to exercise their votes (*Walding v IRC* [1996] STC 13).

(c) Any unquoted shares (but not securities) in a company.

(d) Quoted shares which confer control.

(e) Land, building, machinery or plant used wholly or mainly for the purposes of a business carried on by a company controlled by the transferor or by a partnership of which he is a partner.

(f) Land, building, machinery or plant which is settled property in which the transferor has an interest in possession and which is used wholly or mainly for the purposes of a business carried on by him.

For the purposes of business property relief, shares or securities are 'quoted' if they are listed on a recognised stock exchange (IHTA 1984, s 105(1ZA)). Unquoted shares are those shares which are not listed. Shares dealt in on the Alternative Investment Market are regarded as unquoted because they are not included in the official UK list maintained by the FSA (HMRC Guidance Note: 29 March 2007).

It is provided that property to which an LLP is entitled, occupies or uses is treated as property to which its members are entitled or which they occupy or use as partners. (IHTA 1984, s 267A).

The value of a business or an interest in a business is taken to be its net value (IHTA 1984, s 110). The net value is the value of the assets used in the business reduced by the aggregate amount of any liabilities incurred for the purpose of the business. It is the Revenue's view that money loaned to an LLP by a member of an LLP is not eligible for relief. One also has to identify the assets used in the business. In the case of *Ninth Marquess of Hertford (executors of Eighth Marquess of Hertford (dec'd) v CIR* [2005] STCD 177 (SpC 444) the question arose as to whether the whole of the freehold of Ragley Hall or only part was eligible for relief. Ragley Hall was open to the public. The exterior of the Hall was accessible for viewing by the public but only 78% of the interior was open. The Eighth Marquess gave the business to his son within 7 years of death. The same parts of the Hall remained in private occupation after the transfer, part of which was let to the Eighth Marquess. It was held that the nature of the business and the part played in it by the physical structure of the Hall meant that the Hall was plainly important as the single structure and the whole building was a vital backdrop to the whole business carried on. The whole interest qualified for relief.

Business or interest in a business

[10.2A] A 'business' is not defined apart from that a 'business' includes 'a business carried on in the exercise of a profession or vocation, but does not include a business carried on otherwise than for gain' (IHTA 1984, s 103(3)).

The first question which needs to be determined is whether an activity is a business. It is accepted that the six indicators identified by Gibson J in the VAT case of *C&E Comrs v Lord Fisher* [1981] STC 238 are appropriate when deciding such a question. The Revenue considers that they 'are equally applicable as a test for IHT purposes' (HMRC Inheritance Tax Manual, para 25152).

A business or an interest in a business which consists wholly or mainly of one or more of the following activities cannot be relevant business property, namely making or holding investments or dealing in securities, stocks, shares, land or buildings (other than as a market maker or a discount house); nor can shares and securities in a company whose business wholly or mainly consists of one or more of those activities unless the company is wholly or mainly the holding company of one or more trading companies whose businesses do not consist of one or more of those activities (IHTA 1984, s 105(3),(4)). The HMRC Inheritance Tax Manual states that one should look at 'the main activities of the business, and to its assets and sources of income or gains, over a reasonable period preceding the transfer' (para 25263). In *Phillips (executors of Phillips (dec'd)) v HMRC* [2006] SWTI 2094 (SpC 333) a company had a business of lending money to related companies although it did not start its life as such. It was held that a loan made to a related investment company was not an investment. The fact that the company to whom the loan was made was controlled by the deceased and family did not make any difference. Nor did the fact that the loans were not made on commercial terms.

Example

Katie has a property investment company, Invco, holding a property worth £1m. The shares do not qualify for business property relief because Invco's business consists of making or holding investments. She also has money on deposit of £1m. Neither asset qualifies for business property relief.

If Katie were to set up Newco, subscribe for £1m of shares and Newco were then to lend the money to Invco, business property relief would be available on her shareholding in Newco because its business would not consist wholly or mainly of holding investments. Invco would have net assets of £1m (£1m of properties plus £1m of cash less a liability of £1m) so she would have halved her taxable estate by obtaining business property relief of £1m.

This is on the assumption that Newco's activities amount to a business. If all it has done is to make a single loan to one person, interest free and repayable on demand and to leave that loan outstanding, it is doubtful that its activities amount to a business.

Because the test is whether the business consists 'wholly and mainly' of the prohibited activities, a taxpayer may conduct, within a single business, two activities one of which is an investment business, yet the business property can still be relevant business property in its entirety. In determining of what a business consists one has to look at the whole question in the round, paying attention to the overall context of the business, the capital employed, the time spent by the proprietors and employees as well as at the turnover and profits

(*Weston (Weston's Executor) v CIR* [2000] STC 1064 (Ch D)). In the case of *Clark v HMRC* SpC (2005, unreported) although the investment activity was greater in terms of turnover and profit it was smaller in terms of the time estimated to have been spent and so the company was held to have been carrying on a business mainly of holding investments.

In *HMRC v Brander (Personal Representatives of the Fourth Earl of Balfour)* [2010] UKUT 300 (TCC), [2010] All ER (D) 94 (Aug) the Earl had the life rent (a right to income of the estate and the power to manage the estate within certain limits). The estate consisted of farms (managed and leased), woodland, shooting and leased cottages. In 2002 the trust was wound up and the Earl became absolutely entitled. The estate was put into a farming partnership that he set up with his nephew jointly. The Earl died in 2003. The executors claimed relief on his partnership share relying on the replacement property provisions in s 107. HMRC argued that the business was an investment business. The Tribunal considered that a preponderance of the business activity had to be established. Relevant factors such as turnover, profit, expenditure and time spent by everyone in carrying on the various business activities had to be looked at. In most cases there would not be sufficiently detailed records available for a precise assessment to be made and so ultimately the matter would have to be judged in a more general manner. That involved reviewing the activities being carried on 'in the round', an approach emphasised in *George* (see below). The Upper Tribunal upheld this decision as one of fact. The Upper Tribunal also stated that the fact that the Earl 'as liferenter did not have a direct interest in the capital realisations of timber from the woodlands' did not prevent the woodlands from being business property qualifying for relief. This case is seen as particularly helpful and an endorsement on being able to claim business property relief on non-qualifying activities integrated into a main business. Some may consider integrating non-qualifying business activities within a qualifying business in order to claim relief on the whole. Care does need to be taken to ensure that such integration does not have the adverse effect of no relief being available. It should be remembered that in this case it was held that the Earl appeared to manage the estate and control its running.

In *Brown's Executors v CIR* [1996] STC (SCD) 277 (SpC 83) a company held the sale proceeds of an asset in a deposit account until suitable business premises were found but the shareholder died without new premises having been acquired. The Revenue asserted that the company's business had become one of holding investments. It was found that the business continued to consist of the original trading activity and relief was still available. The business of letting furnished flats on assured shorthold tenancies is considered to be a business of making and holding investments and not eligible for relief (see *Burkinyoung (Burkinyoung's Executor) v CIR* [1995] STC (SCD) 29 (SpC 3)).

Traditionally, the Revenue has required a minimum number of holiday cottages to be within the business for relief to be available on furnished holiday lets. This particular requirement seemed to have been removed. It is now stated (at HMRC Inheritance Tax Manual para 25278) in relation both to caravan parks and holiday lettings that:

> 'In the past we have thought that business property relief would normally be available where:
>
> - the lettings were short term, and
> - the owner, either himself or through an agent such as a relative, was substantially involved with the holidaymakers in terms of their activities on and from the premises.
>
> Recent advice from Solicitor's Office has caused us to reconsider our approach and it may well be that some cases that might have previously qualified should not have done so. In particular we will be looking more closely at the level and type of services, rather than who provided them.
>
> Until further notice any case involving a claim for business property relief on a holiday let should be referred to the Technical Team (Litigation) for consideration at an early stage.'

A number of cases have examined the boundary between business activities consisting of holding investments and those which do not in relation to caravan parks (see, in particular, *Farmer (Farmer's executors) v CIR* [1999] STC (SCD) 321 (Sp C 216); *Weston (Weston's Executors) v CIR* [2000] STC 1064 (Ch D) and *CIR v George and Loochin (Stedman's Executors)* [2004] STC 147 (CA)).

A business consisting mainly of the trade of building and developing can qualify for relief and housing stocks held as stock in trade are not excepted assets. In *Executors of Piercy (dec'd) v Revenue and Customs Comrs* [2008] STC (SCD) 858 it was held that a development company's shares qualified for relief notwithstanding the receipt of rent from certain properties. The Special Commissioner held that it was possible for the company to have retained unsold stock and appropriated it as an investment, whilst still conducting a development trade.

In the case of *McCall (Personal Representatives of McLean (dec'd)) v Revenue and Customs Comrs* [2008] STC (SCD) 752, [2008] SWTI 1256 the question arose as to whether a particular type of agricultural land arrangement in Northern Ireland qualified for business property relief. The Special Commissioner held that it did not because whilst the activity was a business, it was one of making investments. There were no substantial services being offered apart from making the land available for grazing.

Ownership requirement

[10.2B] To qualify as relevant business property, property must have been owned by the transferor throughout the 2 years immediately preceding the relevant transfer (IHTA 1984, s 106). The incorporation of a business will not affect the 2-year ownership period (IHTA 1984, s 107(3)). It is not a requirement that the property must have been relevant business property throughout that period. The ownership requirement is modified where the property has been acquired to replace other relevant business property or has been acquired by a person on the death of his or her spouse or civil partner (IHTA 1984, ss 107, 108).

Changes due to the formation, alteration or dissolution of a partnership are disregarded (IHTA 1984, s 107(3)). In *HMRC v Brander (Personal Representatives of the Fourth Earl of Balfour)* [2010] UKUT 300 (TCC), [2010] All ER (D) 94 (Aug) (see **10.2A** above) the Earl had a life rent and was treated as beneficially entitled to the whole estate. The assets of the estate were used in the business, which was exactly the same before the limited partnership as after, and relief was available. A reorganisation of unquoted share capital will not result in a break in the ownership period provided certain conditions are satisfied (IHTA 1984, s 107(4)). There must however, based on the evidence, be a reorganisation. In *Vinton (Executors of Dugan-Chapman (dec'd)) v Revenue and Customs Comrs* [2008] STC (SCD) 592, [2008] SWTI 370 the Special Commissioner held that there was a rights issue and not a reorganisation.

In certain situations the successive transfer relief in s 108 can be helpful in mitigating inheritance tax.

Example

Augustus owns a family trading company which qualifies for 100% relief. His wife, who owns a half share in their house and share portfolio is seriously ill and is unlikely to survive for more than a few months. Augustus transferred some of his family company shares to his wife; there were no IHT or CGT implications as they were inter-spouse transfers. On his wife's death under the terms of her will the shares were passed to a discretionary trust for the benefit of Augustus and his family. Business property relief at 100% was available because Augustus' period of ownership was treated as that of his wife. The shares benefited from the CGT uplift on death. Augustus could benefit from the trust without the reservation of benefit rules applying. Further, he could now buy back some of the family company shares from the trustees so as to have another bite of the cherry.

The principle of aggregation does not apply to inter vivos transfers. Assets given by one spouse or civil partner to the other by way of a lifetime transfer must be retained by the donee for at least 2 years before the assets will qualify for business property relief.

The rule for replacement property provides that where the original property has been sold and replaced by other relevant business property the two-year ownership period is taken to be satisfied provided the original property and the replacement property were owned for a total of at least two years within the preceding five-year period. The question arises as to whether all of the sale proceeds of the original assets must be invested into the replacement business assets. The Inheritance Tax Manual is silent on the matter. The clawback provisions relating to transfers within the seven-year period before death found in s 113A requires the whole of the consideration to be applied in acquiring other property (IHTA 1984, s 113B). Section 107 does not contain such a provision and so it would seem that a partial replacement would qualify.

Excepted assets

[10.2C] Where part of the value of any relevant business property is attributable to an asset which is not used for the purposes of the business or is not required for future use in the business, the value of that asset will not be taken into account when determining the value of the relevant business property (IHTA 1984, s 112). An example of this would be where a company, shares in which qualify for business property relief, owns a house or a yacht which is used solely for the personal benefit of one of the shareholders. HMRC will argue that a large cash balance will be an excepted asset. It is understood that the Revenue typically raises this argument where the cash balance exceeds 25% of turnover. Where there is cash in a deposit bank account which has not been used for a long period it may be excluded from relief because it cannot be said to be 'required' for future use if it was not in fact used for a long period (*Barclays Bank Trust Co Ltd v CIR* [1998] STC (SCD) 125 (SpC 158)). In that case however, it does not appear that the taxpayer argued that the cash deposit was itself a business activity. In order to demonstrate that a cash balance is required for future business use it is essential that contemporaneous board or partnership minutes etc are maintained. In some circumstances the receipt of interest can amount to a business activity (*IRC v Dale Steamship Co Ltd* (1924) 12 TC 712), although it will not do so in normal circumstances (*Jowett (Inspector of Taxes v O'Neill and Brennan Construction Ltd* [1998] STC 482, 70 TC 566). In order to apply the excepted assets test one looks at the whole business including activities which, if the business consisted wholly or mainly of those activities, would cause shares or an interest in a business not to be relevant business property by virtue of IHTA 1984, s 105(3).

Where a company has substantial cash balances, the company may consider funding an employee benefit trust for the benefit of all employees of the company. It should be noted that care is required where a close company is funding such a trust.

The relief

[10.2D] The relief operates to reduce the value of any relevant business property transferred by an actual or deemed transfer of value by 100% in the case of property falling within paragraphs (*a*), (*b*) and (*c*) at **10.2** above. In all other cases, the reduction in value is 50%.

Example

> Carrie has a small company 'Jamboree Ltd' which makes luxurious jams and jellies and is worth £500,000. She owns the freehold premises, worth £2m, from which the business is carried on. The shares in the company will qualify for 100% relief but relief is only available on the premises at 50%. If the company had owned the premises relief at 100% would still have been available on the shares, the value of which would have been increased by the company's ownership of the premises.

The relief applies both to lifetime transfers of value and to the deemed transfer of value arising immediately before a person's death under IHTA 1984, s 4. The relief can also apply to a potentially exempt transfer which becomes chargeable, and to a lifetime chargeable transfer which becomes chargeable to additional inheritance tax, by reason of the transferor's death within seven years of the transfer. However, in the latter cases, for the relief to apply, certain additional conditions have to be met. Broadly speaking, the transferee must continue to own the property until the transferor's death, or until his own death if earlier, and on the assumption that a transfer of value of the property concerned were to take place on the transferor's death, or on the transferee's death if earlier, the property would then satisfy all the conditions necessary for the relief to apply other than the minimum period of ownership requirement. That is, the property must continue to qualify as 'relevant business property' as defined in IHTA 1984, s 105 (IHTA 1984, s 113A). The transferee may dispose of the original property given to him provided, broadly, that he reinvests the proceeds in other 'relevant business property' within three years or such longer period as the Revenue allows. (IHTA 1984, s 113B).

As much business property is wholly relieved from inheritance tax by business property relief it might be thought that the impact of inheritance tax on business property can safely be ignored. It is, however, important to remember that, even if 100% business property relief is prima facie available in respect of a gift, that relief will be lost if the transferor dies within seven years of making the gift unless the necessary conditions are still satisfied at the time of the transferor's death.

The transferee should therefore be warned, for instance, of the consequences of a sale of the business property within the seven-year period. Less obvious perhaps is the effect of shares which have previously been the subject of a transfer of value becoming quoted on a recognised stock exchange within seven years of the transfer. For instance, where shares were previously unquoted, or dealt in on the Alternative Investment Market and the transferor, prior to the gift, did not have control of the company concerned, a listing of shares on a recognised stock exchange would result in the complete loss of business property relief on the transfer which would otherwise have been available at 100%.

Business property relief may apply to property owned both by individuals and by the trustees of a settlement whether the settlement is one with an interest in possession or not. Where the settlement is one with an interest in possession within IHTA 1984, s 49 the beneficiary with that interest will be the 'transferor' for the purposes of the relief and he will also, by reason of his interest, be treated as the 'owner' of the property comprised in the settlement.

Subject to a binding contract for sale

[10.2E] Any property which is subject to a binding contract for sale at the date of the transfer cannot be relevant business property, except where the property is either an unincorporated business, or an interest in one, and the sale is to a company which will carry on that business in exchange for shares or securities of the company, or the sale relates to a reconstruction or amalgamation of shares or securities in a company (IHTA 1984, s 113). Section 113 can sometimes apply in unexpected situations. The Revenue states that there is a binding contract for sale where partners or shareholder directors of companies enter into an agreement under which, in the event of the death of one of them, the personal representatives of the partner or director are obliged to sell, and the survivors are obliged to purchase, the interest of the deceased in the business or company. A binding contract similarly arises where such an agreement relates to retirement. See Revenue Statement of Practice SP 12/80. These are commonly known as 'Buy and Sell Agreements'.

There are a number of common arrangements for partnerships in relation to retirement or death, one of which is known as the 'accruer arrangement'. This typically provides that the partnership continues with the share of the former partner accruing to the continuing partners and with the estate entitled to a payment based either on a valuation or on a formula. In such a situation, a deceased's interest does not pass to his personal representatives but it accrues to the surviving partners. At first, when the Revenue was asked to confirm whether business property relief would be available in these circumstances, it gave a cautious response, stating that 'the existence of an accruer arrangement does not necessarily prevent business relief from being available'. Since then, the Revenue has stated that business property relief will be available where there are such arrangements. This treatment is confirmed in the HMRC Inheritance Tax Manual, para 25292 which states that 'agreements under which the deceased's interest passes to the surviving partners, who are required to pay the personal representatives a particular price . . . do not constitute contracts for sale'.

Section 113 will also not deny relief where there is a provision which confers an option on the continuing partners to buy the share (or indeed cross options which can be exercised to compel such a sale).

Interest-free instalment option

[10.3] In addition to business property relief, certain types of business property may qualify for the option to pay inheritance tax by ten equal annual instalments. The relevant statutory provisions are to be found in IHTA 1984, ss 227–229 and 234. This option applies to the following types of property.

(a) Land of any kind.
(b) Property which consists of a business or an interest in a business.
(c) Quoted or unquoted shares or securities which confer control (as defined by IHTA 1984, s 269).
(d) Unquoted shares and securities where the charge arises on death and not less than 20% of the total tax charged at that time is attributable to the value of those shares or securities or to other property which qualifies for the instalment option.
(e) Unquoted shares or securities if the Revenue is satisfied that the tax attributable to them cannot be paid in one sum without undue hardship. In considering whether undue hardship exists, the Revenue looks primarily to whether it is reasonable to expect the tax to be paid immediately in the light of available resources (Hansard Official Report, 22 June 1972, Standing Committee, Cols 1358–1359).
(f) Unquoted shares (but not securities) if the value transferred exceeds £20,000 and either the nominal value of the shares is not less than 10% of the nominal value of all shares of the company at the time of the

transfer or the shares are ordinary shares and their nominal value is not less than 10% of the nominal value of all ordinary shares of the company at that time.

If the property concerned is land (except land qualifying for agricultural property relief) or shares in a company the business of which consists wholly or mainly of dealing in securities, stocks or shares, land or buildings or making or holding investments, of being a holding company of such a company or being a market maker or discount house, interest will be chargeable on the normal date calculated by reference to the transfer of value. So, in effect, interest will be charged on the outstanding balance. Where the instalment option applies in other circumstances interest is charged from the date at which the instalment is due (IHTA 1984, ss 233 and 234).

The instalment option is also available on woodland under IHTA 1984, s 229.

For the purposes of ss 227 and 228 'unquoted' in relation to any shares or securities means not listed on a recognised stock exchange.

The instalment option applies to chargeable transfers on death but only to lifetime chargeable transfers if the transferee bears the burden of the tax and to charges on trustees of relevant property settlements where the property concerned continues to be comprised in the settlement. The option only applies to the tax chargeable on a potentially exempt transfer which becomes chargeable, or to the additional tax payable on a lifetime chargeable transfer, because of the death of the transferor within seven years. There is an additional condition in the case of unquoted shares or securities that they must remain unquoted until the death of the transferor or the earlier death of the transferee.

If the property qualifying for the instalment option, or part of it, is sold, then the option ceases to apply to the unpaid tax or, in the case of a sale of part, the relevant proportion of the unpaid tax. For these purposes the payment under a partnership agreement of a sum in satisfaction of the whole or part of a partnership interest will be treated as a sale of that interest.

The impact of the 100% rate of business property relief is significant when considering estate planning for sole traders, partners, members and shareholders.

Because business property relief is such a valuable relief it is important that regular reviews are undertaken to ensure that the relief is still available. It is the authors' experience that often, large cash balances are held within incorporated and unincorporated businesses and it is therefore necessary to consider both whether the cash is an excepted asset within IHTA 1984, s 112 and whether the business of the company consists wholly or mainly of one of the activities listed in IHTA 1984, s 105(3). Where a large sum of cash is being held for a particular purpose, for example, the purchase of an expensive piece of machinery or land, the purpose should be documented.

It is the authors' experience that although the binding contract for sale rule is well known there remains a substantial number of old partnership agreements which contain a right for continuing partners to acquire the interest of a deceased or retiring partner. This will prevent relief being available. This can be avoided by restructuring the rights as options.

In the past, HMRC has been reluctant to determine the availability of relief unless there is inheritance tax at stake. HMRC will now however, give business owners and their advisers its view of the application of the tax consequences of significant commercial issues where there is uncertainty regardless of when the relevant legislation was enacted. The facility will also apply to transfers of value that involve a change of ownership of a business where the transfer, leaving aside the application of business property relief, would result in an immediate inheritance tax charge. Applicants must demonstrate the commercial significance of the transaction which is subject to genuine uncertainty and identify which aspects of the law or HMRC practice they consider to be uncertain. HMRC will not accept an application where it considers that the arrangements concerned are primarily to gain a tax advantage.

Individuals and trustees may be able to obtain HMRC's view of the construction of tax law which concerns legislation passed under the last four Finance Acts under procedures set out in its Code of Practice (COP) 10.

Where neither of these procedures are available, one might consider establishing a nil rate band discretionary trust and transferring to it property the status of which one wishes to determine, with the transfer conditional on the gift qualifying for business property relief.

Capital gains tax

[10.4] Capital gains tax is chargeable at either 18% or 28% on any chargeable gains arising on the disposal of chargeable assets. There are however, various reliefs which maybe available. These are discussed below.

Entrepreneurs' Relief

Outline

[10.5] Entrepreneurs' Relief provides relief from capital gains tax arising on 'qualifying business disposals' (TCGA 1992, s 169H). This relief introduced in the Finance Act 2008 is loosely based on the old Retirement Relief which was phased out between 1998 and 2003.

Entrepreneurs' Relief is available to individuals involved in the running of a business on gains made:

- on the disposal of all or part of a business; or
- on the disposal of assets following the cessation of a business.

Relief is available on qualifying disposals made after 5 April 2008. The first £2m of gains made on disposals made between 6 April 2010 and 22 June 2010 which qualify for relief will be subject to capital gains tax at an effective rate of 10%. This is achieved by substituting a deemed amount of gains which is $^5/_9$ths of the relevant gains qualifying for relief for those relevant gains. Any gains made in that period in excess of £2m will be charged at 18%. The relief can be claimed on more than one occasion up to the relevant lifetime total. For disposals made after 22 June 2010 the first £5m of gains will be subject to capital gains tax at 10%. Gains in excess of £5m will be chargeable at either 18% or 28%. The method of computation is now more straightforward.

Qualifying disposals

[10.6] Relief is available on gains made by individuals arising on qualifying business disposals. These consist of:

- all or part of a sole trader's business;
- all or part of an interest in a partnership;
- shares or securities in an individual's personal company;
- certain disposals of business assets used in a business before cessation; and
- associated disposals.

A disposal for Entrepreneurs' Relief can therefore either be of sale, a gift or a transfer at an undervalue, a capital sum derived from an asset, or a capital distribution received in respect of shares held in a company.

The disposal of certain business assets, shares and securities by trustees may also qualify for relief provided that a qualifying beneficiary has a qualifying interest in the relevant company. However, it should be noted that the limit on gains eligible for relief applies to the trustees and the qualifying beneficiary jointly.

Sole traders and partnerships

[10.7] The relief is available for gains arising on the disposal by an individual of the whole or part of a qualifying business. A business means anything which is a trade, profession or vocation within the meaning of the Income Tax Acts and is conducted on a commercial basis with the view to the realisation of profits (TCGA 1992, s 169S(1)). For the purposes of Entrepreneurs' Relief, a trade also includes the commercial letting of furnished holiday accommodation as defined in ITTOIA 2005, Pt 3 Ch 6. It should be noted that there is currently a consultation in respect of the minimum periods over which a property is available for letting and actually let. This could result in a change in the definitions with effect from 2011/12.

The disposal of a business will qualify for relief if the following conditions are met on the date of disposal:

(a) the business must have been owned by the individual or the individual is a member of a partnership that owned the business for at least 12 months; and
(b) the disposal includes at least one relevant business asset.

There is no requirement that the business has to be disposed of as a going concern and indeed all the assets do not have to be sold to one purchaser. Care does need to be taken regarding timing where assets are to be disposed of to a number of purchasers. Where some assets are sold before the substantial part of the business and a trade continues, gains made on those smaller assets are unlikely to qualify for relief. This is because they will not qualify as part of a business or as disposals made after a cessation. Difficulties can arise where an asset is disposed of under an unconditional contract. TCGA 1992, s 28 provides that the disposal is deemed to take place at the time the contract is made and not at the time the asset is transferred. The trade may not have ceased at that time. It is understood that HMRC will grant the relief if there is a genuine business disposal linked to a general business cessation.

Relief is also available on the disposal of part of a business. However, relief is not available on a disposal of one or more business assets unless the business in which they were used has ceased. In practice, distinguishing between the two may cause difficulties. Under retirement relief a number of cases were heard on this point including *McGregor (Inspector of Taxes) v Adcock* [1977] 3 All ER 65, [1977] 1 WLR 864. The Revenue acknowledges that the existing case law will not always provide certainty for the taxpayer (CG Manual para 64015).

The disposal by a partnership of the whole or part of its business attracts relief on the basis of the whole partnership being one sole trader. Special rules apply to ensure certain disposals made by an individual partner attract relief as if he had been a sole trader. These rules apply where:

- an individual transfers assets to a partnership, on the occasion of him joining that partnership and the partnership takes over his business;
- a partner disposes the whole or part of his interest in the assets of the partnership;
- any partner disposes of a business asset and they are treated as if they had owned the whole of the partnership business (TCGA 1992, s 169I(8)).

Where a qualifying business is not disposed of but simply ceases, relief will be available on gains on assets in use in the business at the time it ceased where the assets are disposed of within three years of the date of cessation.

It should be noted that gains on disposals by sole traders and partners of shares or securities or on assets held as investments will not qualify for relief. But there are circumstances in which relief will be available on the disposal of shares and securities in a trading company and on 'associated disposals'.

Disposal of shares or securities

[10.8] Relief is available on the disposal of shares or securities provided that all of the following conditions are met throughout the one-year period ending with the disposal:

- The company must be the individual's 'personal company'. A personal company is defined as one where an individual holds at least 5% of the ordinary shares of the company and the individual controls at least 5% of the voting rights of the company which are associated with those ordinary shares. In calculating whether a shareholding meets this threshold, shares held by associates or held in another capacity are not included. In the situation where shares are held in the joint names of a husband and wife or civil partners, they are each deemed to have a 50% beneficial interest in the whole shareholding. There is no requirement that the shares disposed of must be ordinary shares in order for relief to be available.

- The shareholder must be an employee or an officer of the company or of a company within the same group. Shadow directors are not considered to be officers whereas non-executive directors are (TCGA 1992, s 169S and ITEPA 2003, s 5(3)). An employment is defined in TCGA 1992, s 169S(5) and ITEPA 2003, s 4, for the purposes of the relief. The employment does not need to be full-time or indeed for a minimum number of hours.
- The company must be a trading company or a holding company of a trading group.

A trading company, trading group and holding company of a trading group are defined in TCGA 1992, ss 165A and 169S which is in the same terms as the definition which applied for taper relief. Therefore, Revenue guidance in respect of taper relief may also apply for Entrepreneurs' Relief.

HMRC have confirmed that relief will in certain circumstances be available where the 12 month ownership period includes the holding period of the original shares where there has been a share for share exchange.

Trading company

[10.9] A trading company means a company carrying on 'trading activities' whose activities do not include to a substantial extent activities other than trading activities (TCGA 1992, ss 169S and 165A). 'Activities' is interpreted by the Revenue as meaning 'what a company does'. Trading activities are those carried on by a company in the course of, or for the purposes of, a trade that it is carrying on or is preparing to carry on. The Revenue provides guidance at Capital Gains Tax Manual para 64060 as to whether the generation of investment income constitutes a trading or investment activity.

Provided that non-trading activities are not carried on to a substantial extent those activities will not prevent a company from being a trading company. It is the Revenue's view that 'substantial extent' in this context means no more than 20% (Capital Gains Tax Manual para 64090). There are a number of factors that the Revenue considers when ascertaining a company's trading status. However, the Manual provides that a HMRC Officer must weigh up the relevance of each factor in the context of the individual's case and judge the matters 'in the round'. Where a company lets property surplus to its current requirements certain activities do not necessarily indicate a non-trading activity (Capital Gains Tax Manual para 64085).

Post-cessation disposals

[10.10] The disposal of certain business assets within 3 years after the business ceased may be eligible for relief provided certain conditions are satisfied (TCGA 1992, s 169I(4)). An individual does not have to dispose of his business to a third party for a related disposal of assets to qualify for relief. The date at when a business ceases is usually a question of fact (Capital Gains Tax Manual para 64105).

In order for the disposal to qualify for relief the asset must be a relevant business asset of the business, in use at the time that the business ceased and the owner of the asset must have owned the business for at least 12 months ending with the date of cessation.

A relevant business asset includes any assets including goodwill used for the purposes of a business carried on by the sole trader or partnership. It does not include excepted assets which are shares and securities and other assets held as investments (TCGA 1992, s 169L). Therefore any shares or securities held by a sole trader or a partnership will not be eligible for relief even when there is a business reason for holding them.

The asset does not have to be used for any particular length of time before the business ceases, it just needs to be in use at the time that the business ceased. Assets which have both a mixed business and non-business use also qualify as relevant business assets. The legislation does not impose a requirement that between the date the business ceased and the disposal of that asset, the asset has to be put to a particular use. The owner may let the asset for a commercial rent for that period and still be able to claim relief on its disposal and the period can be as long as 3 years.

When an individual receives a capital distribution on the liquidation or winding up of a company, he is treated as having disposed of his interest in the shares at that time (TCGA 1992, s 122). Entrepreneurs' Relief may be available if the following conditions are satisfied:

- the company has been the individual's personal company;
- the shareholder has been an employee or officer of the company or of a company in the same group;
- the company has been a trading company or a holding company of a trading group.

These conditions must have applied for a 12-month period ending with either the date that the company ceased to trade or the date that the company left a trading group without becoming a trading company. The date must also not be more than three years before the date the shares are treated as disposed of.

Associated disposals

[10.11] Where an individual qualifies for relief on a material disposal of shares or securities or of a partnership interest, relief may be available on disposals of assets owned by that individual used in the business of a partnership of which he was a member or in his personal company. The relief cannot apply in respect of a sole trader, any such disposal would be within the post cessation rules discussed above.

Certain conditions must be satisfied. These are:

- the disposal must be made as part of the shareholder's withdrawal from participation in the business carried on by the partnership or by the company;
- the asset must have been used for the purpose of the business for at least one year to the date of disposal of the shares or partnership interest, or the date of cessation of the business.

There is no definition given of 'withdrawal from participation'. The Revenue state, however, that it is not necessary for the individual to actually reduce the amount of work they may do for the business for the condition to be satisfied (Capital Gains Tax Manual para 63995). It is the view of some commentators that the gift of only one share might be sufficient to constitute a material disposal.

There is no time limit given in the legislation during which the associated disposal must be made. The Capital Gains Tax Manual at para 63995 states that both the disposal of the shares or partnership interest and the associated disposal of the asset must be caused by the same event and there should be no significant time interval between the disposals. The legislation states that the asset disposal must be connected with the withdrawal from business; however, the Revenue implies in its manual that the event causing the disposal should be the withdrawal from participation in the business.

It is often the case that there will be a delay between the disposal of shares or of a partnership interest and the disposal of assets.

There are restrictions in certain situations on the amount of gain which is eligible for relief. If the following apply, the gain is reduced on a just and reasonable basis:

- the asset has only been used by the business for part of the period of the individual's ownership — the gain will reflect the period of business use;
- only part of the asset has been used for the purposes of the business — the gain will reflect the proportion of the asset used for business;
- the individual has only been involved in the business as a partner or officer or employee for part of the time during which the asset was used in the business;
- any payment of rent was made for the use of the asset by the personal company or partnership for a period after 5 April 2008.

Qualifying corporate bonds

[10.12] Individuals selling their personal companies often receive qualifying corporate bonds (QCBs) in exchange for their shares. The gains arising on the shares are deferred until the disposal of the QCBs which is often when they are redeemed for cash on maturity. Special rules relating to the relief have been introduced both for QCBs exchanged before 6 April 2008 and for those exchanged after that date (see TCGA 1992, s 169R). The rules are beyond the scope of this book. It should be noted that a taxpayer will now have the option of not treating the gain as deferred and therefore be able to claim the relief in respect of disposals after 22 June 2010. This will result therefore in an immediate charge to Capital Gains Tax where there are no funds available. It will therefore be essential for advisers to advise their clients of this difficulty and arrange (if necessary) for the redemption of sufficient loan notes at the relevant time to meet the liability.

Calculation of the relief

[10.13] For disposals made before 23 June 2010 the relief reduced the capital gain on a qualifying disposal by 4/9ths leaving a residue of 5/9ths which could be reduced further by the annual exemption, losses and other CGT reliefs. For disposals made after 22 June 2010 the calculation is more straightforward. Capital gains tax at 10% is charged on the gain.

Example

Cory and Luke jointly owned the entire share capital of 'Boys R Us' which they founded in 2001. They had each invested £100 in the company. In October 2009, they sold the company for £1m. Their gain were as follows:

	£
Proceeds	500,000
Acquisition cost	100
Gain	499,900
Entrepreneurs' Relief (4/9 x 499,900)	(222,178)
Taxable gain	277,722
Tax at 18%	49,990

The effective rate of tax on the gain is 10%.

If the disposal had taken place in October 2010 the gain would be calculated as follows:

	£
Proceeds	500,000
Acquisition cost	100
Gain	499,900
Tax at 10%	49,990

Claim for relief

[10.14] The relief must be claimed by the individual. Where gains have been made by the trustees, both the trustees and the qualifying beneficiary must make the claim (TCGA 1992, s 169M). The claim must be made by the 31 January following the tax year in which the gain arose. A claim may be withdrawn within the same period.

Interaction with other reliefs

[10.15] HMRC's view is that hold-over relief under TCGA 1992, ss 165 and 260, roll-over relief on business assets (TCGA 1992, s 152), enterprise investment scheme deferral relief (TCGA 1992, s 169) and incorporation relief

(TCGA 1992, s 162) all take priority over Entrepreneurs' Relief. The better view is that Entrepreneurs' Relief takes priority over hold-over relief and incorporation relief.

Hold-over relief

[10.16] The implications of the hold-over relief provisions in TCGA 1992, s 165 and TCGA 1992, s 260 have been considered in **CHAPTER 2 LIFETIME PLANNING** at **2.28** and reference should be made to that coverage for a more detailed discussion of these provisions.

The hold-over relief conferred by TCGA 1992, s 165 will apply to most forms of 'business asset' dealt with in this chapter. The relief is capable of applying to disposals made by both individuals and the trustees of settlements. Hold-over relief is not, however, available on disposals to settlor-interested trusts or trusts for which there subsists an arrangement under which the settlor will acquire an interest in the trust. A settlor interested trust will include any trust from which the settlor's dependent child enjoys a benefit (TCGA 1992, s 169B). A dependent child is an unmarried minor or a minor not in a civil partnership (TCGA 1992, s 169F(4)). There is a clawback period during which the held-over gain will become chargeable where the settlor has an interest in the trust or an arrangement subsists for him to acquire such interest. This is dealt with in **CHAPTER 2 LIFETIME PLANNING.**

In the case of trustees owning assets used for the purposes of a trade, profession or vocation, the trade, etc may be carried on either by the trustees or by a beneficiary with an interest in possession in the settled property (TCGA 1992, Sch 7 para 2(2)(a)). Where trustees own shares or securities of a trading company or of the holding company of a trading group, the shares or securities must either be not listed on a recognised stock exchange (and for these purposes shares dealt in on the Alternative Investment Market are not listed on a recognised stock exchange) or the trustees must hold at least 25% of the voting rights exercisable by the company's shareholders (TCGA 1992, Sch 7 para 2(2)(b)).

It is interesting to note that s 165 refers to assets 'used for the purposes of a trade, profession or vocation' but not to 'a business or an interest in a business'. At first sight this might seem to preclude any application of the relief to a gift of the whole or part of a business or an interest in a partnership; but since a business is made up of a collection of separate assets used for the purposes of the business (eg stocks, plant and equipment, goodwill, etc), there appears to be nothing preventing s 165 applying to each separate asset and thus in effect to the whole business. Indeed, the Revenue accepts that s 165 applies to a transfer of an entire business to a company (Capital Gains Tax Manual para 66973).

Since s 165 applies both to business assets and to 'an interest in' business assets, the same argument should admit the application of s 165 to gifts of interests in a partnership. The business in question must, of course, be a trade, profession or vocation.

If the asset has not been used by the transferor for the purposes of the trade, etc throughout its period of ownership, the amount of the held-over gain will be correspondingly reduced (TCGA 1992, Sch 7 paras 5, 6). On the disposal of shares, if the assets of the relevant company, or where that company is a holding company, any of its subsidiaries, include chargeable assets which are *not* used in the company's trade, profession or vocation, then the held-over gain is reduced to reflect the proportion which the chargeable business assets bear to all the chargeable assets of the company or group (TCGA 1992, Sch 7 para 7).

When considering estate planning for the businessman, it is essential to bear in mind that for capital gains tax purposes all assets owned by a deceased person immediately prior to his death are deemed to be acquired by his personal representatives at their current market value (TCGA 1992, s 62). This provides a tax-free uplift on death. However, this will not arise where the asset has been given away during his lifetime so that any inheritance tax savings which may be achieved by lifetime planning must be considered in the light of the loss of this capital gains tax-free uplift.

Hold-over relief is not available on disposals of shares or securities to a company (TCGA 1992, s 165(3)(ba)).

Where 100% business property relief may be available for inheritance tax purposes even where the businessman still owns the business property on his death, consideration of the capital gains tax implications of estate planning is extremely important and may be a significant deterrent to making lifetime gifts. However, other factors may still prevail and it should always be remembered that business property relief may be changed or abolished in the future, so that there may be considerable merit in taking advantage of the generous rates of relief whilst they remain.

Incorporation

[10.17] Before considering in detail estate planning in relation to each of the businesses of a sole proprietor, a partnership, a limited liability partnership ('LLP') and a company, a few general points will be made about the advantages and disadvantages of incorporating a business.

A business may be either incorporated or unincorporated. The decision whether or not to start a new business through a company or a LLP or to roll an existing business into a company or LLP will be governed by a number of factors, including the need for limited liability and the taxation consequences. Some of these factors are pertinent to estate planning although with 100% business property relief applying to small minority shareholdings in private trading companies, the major tax advantage once associated with a partnership as opposed to a company or LLP (ie the availability of 100% relief of any partnership interest irrespective of its size) no longer applies.

There are, of course, far more formalities involved in setting up and running a company or LLP than a partnership. There are accounts to be made up and filed, annual returns to be made, annual meetings to be held. In a family context, this extra degree of administration may be an important consideration. On the other hand, shares in a company are, subject to any restrictions or rights of pre-emption contained in the Articles of Association, generally more easily transferable around a family than interests in a partnership or an LLP. Whilst a partnership interest can be assigned without the assignee becoming a partner (Partnership Act 1890, s 31), more usually partnership interests are transferred by inviting the intended donee to join the partnership. It is easier in practice to be a passive shareholder in a company or a passive member of a LLP than a passive partner in a partnership.

A further important tax consideration in comparing a partnership or LLP with a company arises if the vehicle is holding, or is likely to hold, chargeable assets on which a significant capital gain is likely to be realised. A common example is land. On any sale of such an asset by a partnership or LLP, the disposal is treated as made by the partners or the members and is charged to capital gains tax at either 18% or 28% on the chargeable gain. The proceeds are then freely distributable to the partners or members without further tax cost. On the other hand, the same sale by a company would result in a corporation tax charge for the company at 28% (21% if the small companies rate applies) of the chargeable gain and a further capital gains tax charge of either 18% or 28% for the shareholders if the company is ever liquidated or the shares are sold. It will rarely be appropriate to liquidate a company simply in order to extract the proceeds of a capital disposal by the company. In that case, the capital proceeds could be extracted by way of a dividend which would be taxable on a higher rate taxpayer at 42.5%. Thus, increases in the value of company assets are potentially subject to a double charge.

Example (at 2010/11 rates of tax)

> A company sells some land with a base cost of £20,000 for £120,000 so that a chargeable gain of £100,000 arises.
>
> There will be a corporation tax liability (assuming the full rate applies to the whole gain) of £28,000. If a dividend of £72,000 is paid out of the sale proceeds, it will be accompanied by a non-repayable tax credit of £8,000. If the shareholders pay additional tax, they will have an additional liability of £26,000, giving rise to a charge at an overall rate of 38.33% of the gross gain arising to the company.
>
> Had the asset been sold by a partnership or LLP then (ignoring the availability of any annual or other exemptions a capital gains tax charge of £28,000 (at 28%) would have arisen.

From the point of view of flexibility and simplicity there is much to commend the unincorporated business though, for many businesses, the limited liability conferred by incorporation will often be the deciding factor. LLPs offer the advantage of conferring limited liability on the members whilst the income and gains of the LLP are taxed as if they arose to the members directly.

A sole proprietor, partners in a partnership or members of a LLP wishing to transfer their business to a limited company in exchange for shares in that company can do so without any inheritance tax or capital gains tax arising. For inheritance tax purposes, there will be no transfer of value (IHTA 1984, s 10) and for capital gains tax purposes either TCGA 1992, s 162 or s 165 will apply to 'roll-over' or hold-over any gain which would otherwise accrue on the disposal of the business into the shares issued in exchange. 100% business property relief is available on small minority holdings in private trading companies. In addition, the replacement property provisions (IHTA 1984, s 107) ensure that minority holdings received on incorporation will qualify for relief immediately.

It used to be the case that incorporating a business by making gifts within TCGA 1992, s 165 had the added advantage that only nominal stamp duty was payable. Unfortunately, in most incorporations a gift of land to a company will now be treated as a transfer on sale for a consideration equal to the market value of the property. A gift of UK land to a company is subject to stamp duty land tax at rates of up to 4%. Where there are other assets involved such as goodwill, such assets will not attract any stamp duty.

Incorporation may also have income tax consequences (for example, there will be a cessation of the business) which will need to be carefully considered.

Sole proprietor

[10.18] The sole proprietor of a business will usually depend on that business for his livelihood. He is therefore likely to retain it either until his death, when it will be brought into charge to inheritance tax (although 100% business property relief will be available provided the necessary conditions are satisfied) or at least until he retires, when the business may either be sold or passed on to other members of his family who are interested in taking it over. At this stage he may wish to give the business to, for example, his children and again it is possible that 100% business property relief will be available for inheritance tax purposes. Even if it is not because, for example, he does not satisfy the two-year ownership rule, the gift may constitute a potentially exempt transfer (IHTA 1984, s 3A) which will escape the inheritance tax net completely provided he survives for a period of seven years after the gift. Any chargeable gains arising on a gift, provided it is a material disposal within TCGA 1992, s 169I, may be relieved by Entrepreneurs' Relief. If relief is not available, any gains may be held-over under TCGA 1992, s 165. Holdover relief is not available on disposals made to settlor-interested trusts or trusts for which there subsists an arrangement under which the settlor will acquire an interest in the trust. A settlor-interested trust includes any trust from which the settlor's dependent child enjoys a benefit (TCGA 1992, s 169B). A dependent child is a minor who is neither married nor a party to a civil partnership (TCGA 1992, s 169F(4A)). There is a clawback period during which the held-over gain will become chargeable where the settlor has an interest in the trust or an arrangement subsists for him to acquire such interest. This is dealt with in **CHAPTER 2 LIFETIME PLANNING**.

A gift of a business may involve the donee agreeing to indemnify the donor against his liabilities to unpaid creditors. Whilst the commercial reality behind such an agreement is clear and in effect simply means that the donee takes over the net assets of the business, the true legal analysis of the gift is that it involves the sale of the business for a consideration equal to the outstanding liabilities, which will have certain tax consequences. First, stamp duty land tax where land is involved will be payable on the consideration if it is in excess of

£150,000 (if it is a non-residential property). Secondly, the ability to hold-over any chargeable gains which would otherwise accrue to the donor on the gift under TCGA 1992, s 165 may be restricted if the consideration exceeds the donor's acquisition cost (TCGA 1992, s 165(6)). Thirdly, there may arguably be a gift with reservation for inheritance tax purposes under FA 1986, s 102. The argument for the contrary view is that, even assuming that a sale at an under-value can be a gift within s 102, as to which there must be some doubt, those provisions can only apply to the gift element of the transaction and provided no benefit is reserved to the donor which is referable to the gift element, there can be no reserved benefit. The indemnity from the donee does not, the argument goes on, relate to the gift element. To amount to a gift with reservation there must be a benefit additional to the indemnity.

The sole proprietor of the business may, however, wish to share the running of the business, and its profits, prior to his retirement with other members of his family. In practice, it is most likely that he will do this by bringing them into either a partnership or a LLP with him. For example, he may bring his wife into a partnership or LLP in order to share with her some of the profits of the business which may reduce their overall income tax burden. Provided that his wife takes an active role in the partnership or LLP and her share of the profit is commensurate with this there may be a resulting income tax saving. The Revenue, attempted unsuccessfully in *Jones v Garnett (Inspector of Taxes)* [2007] UKHL 35, [2007] 4 All ER 857, [2007] STC 1536 to apply the income tax settlement provisions to situations where it considered that a company was being used as a vehicle for diverting income from one spouse to another. The previous government announced their intention to introduce legislation to prevent this but it did not materialise. The Coalition government have not indicated any intention to do so.

Before turning to consider the creation of a partnership, however, two further points should be made. The first is in relation to borrowings. This general point is relevant to any property which is capable of qualifying as relevant business property for inheritance tax purposes. If the sole proprietor proposes to provide additional funds for his business by borrowing, he should ensure as far as possible that the borrowings are charged on assets owned by him which do not form part of the business. In this way the charge will be an incumbrance under IHTA 1984, s 162(4) and should, in principle, reduce the value of that property which will not qualify for any relief on his death rather than reducing the value of property which would in any event qualify for 100% business property relief. It should be noted, however, that the Revenue may seek to argue that the value of the business for the purposes of the relief must still be calculated after deducting the liability. This is on the basis that IHTA 1984, s 110 provides that the value of a business for the purposes of the relief is its net value and that the net value is after deducting liabilities 'incurred for the purposes of the business'. It is not clear whether s 110 overrides s 162(4) or vice versa although HMRC consider that such liabilities 'should be deducted firstly against any business property' (HMRC Inheritance Tax Manual, para 28393).

It is important to remember that in the context of a sole proprietor, inheritance tax business property relief only applies where the value transferred is attributable to the value of the whole of a business or to a share in that business and not where it is attributable to the value of an asset used in the business. In *Revenue and Customs Comrs v Trustees of the Nelson Dance Family* [2009] EWHC 71 (Ch), [2009] STC 802, it was held that all that is required is that the value transferred should be attributable to the value of relevant business property and, where an asset is transferred which has been part of the assets of a business, this condition is satisfied because the value of the business is reduced by the transfer. It is possible, therefore, to receive 100% relief on the transfer of an asset used in a business but only if that business is a business owned by the transferor,

Finally, one of the kinds of sole business proprietor frequently met in practice is the Lloyd's Underwriter or 'Name'. However, the nature of his business is such that there is no scope for lifetime estate planning in relation to the Name's underwriting interests other than making sure his will is properly drawn up and for this reason Lloyd's underwriting interests are dealt with in **CHAPTER 16 PLANNING FOR DEATH** at **16.46**.

Partnerships

General

[10.19] Partnerships are extremely flexible vehicles but are subject to considerable complexities and uncertainties in their tax treatment. In particular, it is very difficult to apply the capital gains tax legislation to them largely because of the legal distinction which exists between (on the one hand) the notion of partnership property and (on the other) the share or interest of a partner in a partnership. The latter is a chose in action comprising a bundle of contractual rights which one partner has against the other partners and does not necessarily represent a specific quantifiable interest in the underlying partnership assets, although each partner has an interest in those assets and they are jointly owned by the partners. For capital gains tax purposes, the chose in action is largely irrelevant and each partner is treated as owning a specific proportion (whatever that may be) of the underlying assets (see TCGA 1992, s 59) Where the partnership is carrying on a trade, any dealings with the assets of the partnership are treated as dealings by the partners individually.

As a result of the uncertainty which the complex legal nature of partnership rights creates, reliance is placed upon Statements of Practice SP D12, SP1/79, SP1/89 and HMRC Brief 3/2008.

When creating a partnership many factors have to be considered, but foremost from an estate planning point of view are the following.

(a) The amount of cash or other property to be contributed to the partnership by each partner and the extent to which this is to be reflected in his or her capital account.
(b) The rights of each partner (or his personal representatives) to extract from the partnership his share of the partnership assets on his death or retirement.

(c) The proportions in which the partners are to share both the trading profits of the partnership and on a dissolution any surplus assets remaining after all creditors and all capital contributions of the partners have been repaid. (Surplus assets will be shared by the partners in the same proportions as they share in the trading profits, unless the partnership agreement states otherwise.)

An asset surplus on a dissolution will only usually arise as a result of an increase in value in the partnership assets above their original book values (ie ignoring any depreciation and any replacement of assets). Unless there is a revaluation of the partnership assets, with a corresponding increase or decrease in the partners' capital accounts, the original book value of the partnership assets will correspond to the amounts of capital contributed by the partners. Any increase in value therefore will represent a capital profit of the partnership which may be realised or unrealised by the time of dissolution. On a dissolution, the surplus will be distributed between the partners either in stated proportions or, if the partnership agreement is silent on the matter, in the proportions in which the trading profits of the partnership are shared. The partnership agreement may, on the other hand, state that all the capital profits (whether realised or unrealised) arising in respect of a particular asset shall belong to one or more particular partners, and the result of this is that on the dissolution the division of surplus assets will be modified accordingly.

For capital gains tax purposes, the disposal of a partnership asset is taxed in the hands of the partners in the proportions in which they share the surplus assets of the partnership at the time of the disposal (Statement of Practice D12 para 2). Where an automatic accruer or option provision applies on the death of a partner (see below), he may still be treated for capital gains tax purposes as owning a share in the assets of the partnership during his lifetime and taxed accordingly.

The possible permutations on all the factors mentioned above are enormous and the following are examples of some of the more common types of partnership arrangement.

(1) A, B, and C agree to introduce capital equally and to share trading profits and any surplus assets on dissolution equally. On the death or retirement of any one of them, he (or his personal representatives) is entitled to take from the partnership the full value of his partnership interest, subject to the continuing partners having the option to buy it for its full market value. Alternatively, if A, B and C contribute capital in unequal shares, they may decide to share the trading profits and surplus assets in the same proportions rather than equally.

(2) As in (1), except that on the death or retirement of any partner, he (or his personal representatives) is entitled only to take the balance on his capital account and his share of accrued trading profits, with the rest of his partnership interest accruing automatically without payment to the continuing partners.

(3) A, B and C agree to introduce capital equally and to share trading profits equally, but agree that any surplus assets on a dissolution shall belong only to B and C equally. On the death or retirement of A, he (or his personal representatives) is entitled only to take the balance on his

capital account and his share of accrued trading profits (with the rest of his share accruing automatically without payment to B and C); but on the death or retirement of B or C, they (or their respective personal representatives) are entitled to receive the full value of their partnership interests subject only to an option for the continuing partners to buy it at its full market value.

Each arrangement will have differing inheritance tax and capital gains tax consequences for the partners which are discussed in what follows.

Family limited partnerships

[10.19A] In recent years limited partnerships have generated a great deal of interest. Because of the changes made to the taxation of trusts in FA 2006, people are now considering such partnerships as an alternative to trusts. A family limited partnership (FLP) is a limited partnership which holds assets on behalf of a family in accordance with the terms of the partnership agreement. The Limited Partnerships Act 1907 authorised the formation of such partnerships among partners to have their liability limited. The attraction of a limited partnership is the ability to separate the economic benefits (held by the limited partners) from control (which is held by the general partner). The partnership should be operated as a business with a view to profit but it can hold a range of investments provided they are actively managed. For tax purposes a limited partnership is transparent in the same way as a general partnership. In some jurisdictions a limited partnership is treated as a separate legal entity. An FLP can provide asset protection on a divorce because the courts do not usually have the power to vary a partnership agreement.

As you would expect there are some drawbacks to an FLP. First, in the UK, FLPs operate as collective investment schemes and are therefore subject to regulation by the Financial Services Authority ('FSA'). It is therefore necessary to appoint an FSA authorised investment manager which will increase costs. This can be avoided if the FLP is located in another jurisdiction, for example, Jersey. Secondly, problems can arise in relation to the transfer of partnership interests. Although the partnership agreement can be drafted to restrict limited partners from selling their shares, the validity of such provisions have yet to be tested in the courts. Thirdly, there are complications where there are minors. There is a risk that on reaching the age of 18 a person will repudiate the partnership agreement thereby dissolving the FLP. Nevertheless, FLPs are useful entities in the appropriate situation. Where the value of assets are below the nil rate band or business or agricultural property relief is available, a trust may be more appropriate.

Formation of a partnership

Inheritance tax

[10.20] In the case of the sole proprietor of a business who wishes to bring his son into partnership, it is probable that 100% business property relief will be available so that no actual inheritance tax liability will arise. It is, however, useful to consider how the transaction will be analysed for inheritance tax purposes as there may be occasions where the relief is not fully available, or is subsequently lost because the proprietor dies within seven years of the gift and the necessary conditions are not met at that time (IHTA 1984, s 113A).

The proprietor and his son are connected persons under IHTA 1984, s 270. There will be no transfer of value on the formation of the partnership if the father did not intend to confer any gratuitous benefit on his son (or indeed on any other person) and that the terms of the son's entry into the partnership were such as might be expected to be made in a similar arrangement at arm's length between unconnected persons (IHTA 1984, s 10). In general, for this condition to be satisfied it will be necessary for the son to provide such consideration as would have been required had the transaction been a normal commercial one, but in the context of a family partnership, it is often difficult to identify precisely what would amount to normal commercial terms. Some of the relevant factors are considered below.

Where the formation of the partnership cannot be brought within IHTA 1984, s 10, there will be no transfer of value provided there is no reduction in the value of the father's estate as a result of the formation of the partnership. For example, if the father has the business valued and then introduces it to the partnership with his capital account being credited with the full value of the business then, even if he and his son share the trading profits of the partnership equally, there should be no inheritance tax consequences for the father. This is particularly so if he is able to determine the partnership and recover his capital contribution on demand or within a reasonably short period (say 3 months).

If the full value of the existing business is not credited to the father's capital account and, for example, the father and son share profits equally, then on the partnership being wound up and the business sold, unless otherwise agreed, the son will share the proceeds of sale equally with his father after the balances on capital account have been repaid. This is the effect of Partnership Act 1890, s 44, which provides that, in the absence of any express agreement, any surplus assets left after the payment of all debts, advances and capital contributions are shared between the partners in the proportions in which they shared the profits. Partners do not share surplus assets in proportion to their capital contributions unless this is expressly agreed. As a result, the father, on taking his son into partnership on such terms, will clearly have made a gift to him of part of the business unless the partnership agreement was such as might have been made between unconnected persons dealing at arm's length and the father had no gratuitous intent towards either his son or any other person.

One would generally expect that in a normal commercial arrangement the son would have to buy into the partnership and effectively purchase a share of the business from his father. Arguably, a capital contribution by the son which is credited to his own capital account would not be sufficient. There would have to be some consideration passing to the father — either outside the partnership or perhaps by way of credit to the father's capital account. The case of *A-G v Boden* [1912] 1 KB 539 is often cited as authority for the proposition that consideration may be non-monetary. In that case, it was held that two sons had given full consideration (in the form of an agreement to devote as much time and attention to the business as it required as compared with their father being only required to devote as much time and attention to the business as he thought fit) for a provision that their father's share in the goodwill of the business would automatically accrue to them without payment on his death. It is, however, dangerous to rely on the principles of this case applying to circumstances other than ones very similar to its facts. It may be appropriate to regard a covenant to work full-time in a business as adequate consideration for the deferred acquisition of goodwill on the death of a partner — goodwill being an asset which depends to a great extent on the amount of time and energy put into a business — but it is quite another thing to regard such a covenant as adequate consideration for the acquisition of an immediate interest in a partnership and an interest extending beyond the goodwill to the other assets of the partnership. Undoubtedly, each case will turn on its own facts and there may be circumstances where a similar covenant could make up the difference between partial and full consideration.

Even if 100% business property relief is not fully available, any element of gift inherent in the formation of the partnership may constitute a potentially exempt transfer by the father to his son and will escape inheritance tax provided the father survives for the necessary seven-year period. One can insure against the risk of his death in this period.

Reservation of benefit

[10.21] Will the formation of a partnership amount to a gift with reservation for inheritance tax purposes? The provisions of FA 1986, s 102 can apply to a gift where either possession and enjoyment of the property concerned is not *bona fide* assumed by the donee or the property is not enjoyed to the entire exclusion of the donor and of any benefit to him by contract or otherwise. In the context of a partnership, it is often quite difficult to decide whether or not the provisions have any application. Clearly, if the formation of the partnership is on full commercial terms, there is no gift and therefore no question of the provisions applying. Where, however, there is an element of gift, it is essential to first identify the subject matter of the gift. On the formation of the partnership, the subject matter of the gift will not be an interest in the partnership because prior to the gift the partnership will not have existed. Instead, it is the granting of certain contractual rights against the donor in respect of the property which is to become the property of the partnership (the business) coupled with the acquisition of the legal title to and/or a beneficial interest in that property. In almost all cases, possession and enjoyment of the subject matter of the gift will be *bona fide* assumed by the donee; so it is important to establish whether or not the donor is excluded from any benefit from the property given away. It is also necessary to consider the anti-shearing provisions of FA 1986, ss 102A–102C (see **CHAPTER 9 THE FAMILY HOME** at **9.10**). It should also be borne in mind that the income tax charge on pre-owned assets may apply where the donor continues to derive benefit from assets he has given away in circumstances in which the reservation of benefit rules do not apply. The charge will only apply in relation to land, chattels or intangible property contained in a settlement in circumstances in which the donor derives a benefit (see **CHAPTER 2 LIFETIME PLANNING**). The Revenue has confirmed that there would be no income tax charge in the situation where a father admits his son into a partnership in return for the son's agreement to take on most of the day-to-day running of the partnership, provided that the transaction is one that might be expected to be made at arms' length. This supposes that there is a disposal of the underlying assets (land or chattels) rather than a disposal of the partnership interest. The Revenue has stated that 'they do not regard the partnership interest as transparent and the disposal of a share is unlikely to give rise to a Schedule 15 charge in any circumstances" (Appendix to Guidance Notes).

A father who is already in partnership with one of his sons, may give his partnership share to another son and retire from the partnership but remain as a consultant or employee. Provided the employment is on commercial terms and the remuneration is not excessive, this would not be regarded as a gift with reservation. What is reasonable is to be tested by reference to what might reasonably be expected under an arm's length arrangement between unconnected parties.

If the father were to give his son an interest in a specific percentage of the capital assets of the partnership (eg by way of crediting his capital account), together with an interest in a corresponding percentage of the trading profits, it is unlikely that there will be a problem. However, there may be a problem where the son is given an interest in a particular share of the assets of the partnership but a lesser share of the profits so that the father takes a share of the profits greater than his retained share of the capital assets. This is because the father could be said to have reserved a benefit out of the property given to his son by reason of his receiving a share of the profits in excess of the capital retained by him. The Revenue has given the following example of where the reservation of benefit rules will not apply.

Revenue example

> Father and son have been in partnership together since 1980 sharing profits equally. The land is owned by the father and occupied by the partnership rent free without any formal tenancy agreement. In 1989 the father gives the land to the son but the partnership continues to occupy it on the same basis. At the same time the profit sharing ratio is adjusted in favour of the son.
>
> Provided the increase in the son's share of profits represented full consideration in money or money's worth for occupation of the land FA 1986 Sch 20 para 6(1)(a) will apply and this will not be a gift with reservation.
>
> The father is in effect occupying the land through the partnership and this *prima facie* constitutes a reservation. However, we accept that the let-out in para 6(1)(a) may be satisfied by an appropriate upward adjustment (in lieu of rent) reflected in the donee's share of the partnership profits. The circumstances of the case must determine what is 'appropriate' having regard to what might be agreed under an arm's length deal between unconnected persons (HMRC Inheritance Tax Manual, para 14341).

If, therefore, the father wishes the son to take a greater share of the assets of the partnership but a lesser share of the profits, it is probably safer from the gifts with reservation viewpoint to defer the son's right to share in the assets by means of an option provision to take effect on the father's death or retirement rather than by giving him an immediate interest (see below). However, as we shall see, the introduction of an automatic accruer or option provision gives rise to other inheritance tax problems.

A similar reservation of benefit problem could arise where the father reserves a right to receive the first slice of any profits of the partnership up to a specific amount.

Capital gains tax

[10.22] If the business introduced by the father into the partnership includes any chargeable assets (eg goodwill, land or tangible movables worth more than £6,000 each), then there may be a 'disposal' of these assets for capital gains tax purposes giving rise to a capital gains tax charge. As the assets of a partnership are, for capital gains tax purposes, treated as belonging to the partners in the proportions in which they share surplus assets (which in turn will be the proportions in which they share the profits of the partnership unless stated otherwise), for capital gains tax purposes there will be a disposal to the extent of the interest taken by the son. For example, if the father and son simply agree to share profits equally, then there will be a disposal of 50% of the chargeable assets.

It was accepted practice that any assets transferred to a partnership on its formation by way of capital contribution were treated as being contributed by the partners on a no gain/no loss basis. There would therefore be no capital gain arising. So there would be no disposal where under the terms of the partnership, all capital profits in relation to the business are expressed to belong to the father. The Revenue issued HMRC Brief 03/2008 changing this practice. It now considers that where an asset is transferred to a partnership by means of a capital contribution, the partner in question should be treated as having made a part disposal of the asset concerned equal to the fractional share that passes to the other partners. Although this is a similar approach to that adopted for changes in partnership sharing ratios, different rules apply when establishing the disposal consideration. The consideration for such a disposal is a proportion (based on the fractional share of the asset passing to the other partners) of either:

(a) the total consideration given by the partnership for the asset; or
(b) the market value of the asset if the transaction is between connected persons, or not on arm's length terms.

If the partnership agreement is subsequently altered so that the son becomes entitled to a proportion of those profits, this alteration will be treated by the Revenue as a part disposal for capital gains tax purposes of the father's partnership interest (see Statement of Practice SP D12 para 7) but hold-over relief (under TCGA 1992, s 165) should then be available as no consideration would have been given for the disposal. Where there is a change in the ratios in which surpluses on assets are shared between *unconnected* partners, the Revenue treats the disposal as taking place at book value (ie on a no gain/no loss basis), unless there is a direct payment of consideration outside the partnership or there is or has been a revaluation of the partnership assets and a corresponding increase in the partners' capital account (Statement of Practice SP D12 paragraph 4).

A similar capital gains tax problem arises if the father has first taken his wife into partnership with him. At that stage he may well not have had his business valued because of the availability of the spouse exemption (IHTA 1984, s 18) preventing any inheritance tax consequences. However, if their son is taken into partnership having first valued the business and having that value credited to their capital accounts, then on the son receiving a share in the assets of the partnership, the Revenue would treat his parents as making a part disposal of the partnership assets (Statement of Practice SP D12).

Options and accruers

[10.23] The terms of the partnership deed should also provide for what is to happen on the death or retirement of one of the partners. It is quite common for an agreement to contain a provision which allows the retiring partner or the personal representatives of the deceased partner to extract his capital contributions and his share of accrued trading profits with the remainder of his partnership interest accruing automatically to the surviving partners or, alternatively, granting the continuing partners an option to acquire the interest for a nominal consideration. Although the Revenue does not consider that automatic accruer clauses are contracts for sale, it is advisable for a partnership deed to provide for an option to purchase the share rather than an accruer clause. In such a case, when valuing the interest of the deceased or retiring partner in the partnership, its value should be restricted to the sums due under the partnership agreement and no account should be taken of the then value of the underlying assets of the partnership business. Although the case of *Burdett-Coutts v CIR* [1960] 3 All ER 153, [1960] 1 WLR 1027 is sometimes cited as authority for the proposition that the value of the partnership interest of a deceased partner should be by reference to the underlying assets of the partnership, that case was in fact dealing with the position where the death caused the partnership to dissolve. That is not comparable to a situation which a partnership continues notwithstanding the death of one partner.

In the opinion of the Revenue such an automatic accruer or option provision amounts to an exclusion or restriction on the right of the deceased or retiring partner to dispose of his share (HMRC Inheritance Tax Manual, para 25120) and it should only therefore be taken into account when valuing his interest to the extent that consideration was given for it (IHTA 1984, s 163). Whilst the Revenue's argument may have some force if the automatic accruer or option provision is added as a term of a partnership *after* its formation, it is more difficult to sustain where the provision is a term of the partnership from the outset. This is because, on introducing any property to the partnership, the partner concerned will exchange his interest in that property for the 'chose in action', comprising his bundle of partnership rights in which the restriction on what he may extract from the partnership on his death or retirement is inherent from the outset. There is no question of the partnership agreement itself placing an exclusion or restriction on his right to dispose of any property which pre-existed the agreement.

If, however, the Revenue's argument is correct — and, in practice, it is advisable to order one's affairs on the assumption that it is correct, unless one is prepared to go to considerable time and expense in arguing to the contrary

— then on the death of the outgoing partner the existence of the automatic accruer or option provision will only be taken into account in valuing the interest if the continuing partners gave full consideration. This will be a question of fact in each case and will depend on all the circumstances surrounding either the formation of the partnership or, if later, the time when the provision was introduced as a term. In determining this the precise scope of the accruer or option will have to be taken into account: whether it relates to the entire partnership share, or just to the outgoing partner's interest in surplus assets, or to his share of the goodwill of the partnership. Other factors include the respective amounts of capital contributions; the profit-sharing ratios and the surplus asset-sharing ratios; the time each partner is required to devote to partnership matters; the respective ages of the partners; the duration of the partnership; and the terms on which distributions will be made on the death or retirement of any of the partners. It is understood that if all the partners are of commensurate age, and each partner's share is subject to the same automatic accruer or option provision, then each gives full consideration for its existence because none of them knows which of them is likely to die first. However, the same argument cannot be applied where there is a considerable divergence in the ages and therefore is of little help in a family partnership which includes members of different generations. Possibly, on the strength of *A-G v Boden* [1912] 1 KB 539, a covenant to work full-time in the partnership business by members of the younger generation could count as (or towards) full consideration, if no similar covenant is required of the older generation. In addition, an agreement by the younger partners to provide an annuity to any retiring partner or to the widow of a deceased partner in return for the partnership share could be taken into account as full or partial consideration, although in the Revenue's view (see the ICAEW Memorandum of 19 September 1984 reproduced in Tolley's Yellow Tax Handbook 2010/11) an automatic accruer on death in return for a widow's annuity will result in a loss of business property relief.

Since then, the Revenue has stated that business property relief would be available where there are such arrangements. This treatment is confirmed in the HMRC Inheritance Tax Manual, para 25292 which states that 'agreements under which the deceased's interest passes to the surviving partners who are required to pay the personal representatives a particular price . . . do not constitute contracts for sale.' Although the instalment option ceases on sale and the balance of tax falls due at once if the surviving partners pay the purchase price in stages, each part-payment is treated as a part sale of the business (IHTA 1984, s 227(6) and HMRC Inheritance Tax Manual, para 25122).

Unless an automatic accruer or option provision has been incorporated for full consideration, it is unlikely to prevent an inheritance tax charge arising on the death of a partner in respect of the whole of his partnership share subject, of course, to the availability of business property relief. Subject to this, when bringing one or more children into partnership, the father should aim to give to them as large an interest in the partnership as he feels comfortable about giving away in the hope that he will survive the gift by seven years. Due to the impact of the gifts with reservation provisions, the share of trading profits retained by the father should not exceed his interest in the assets of the partnership. An automatic accruer or option provision could also be inserted in an attempt to limit the taxable part of the father's partnership interest to (say) just the balance on his capital account plus his share of any accrued trading profits, but as we have seen this may not be successful.

Alternatively, the partnership agreement could provide that any capital profits, whether realised or unrealised, of the partnership should belong to the next generation. As the passing of the growth element is immediate rather than deferred until death or retirement, IHTA 1984, s 163 should not apply. However, if there is any element of gift in the creation of the partnership the reservation of benefit rules may apply. Another problem with this type of provision is that to insert it in the partnership *ab initio* may well result in a disposal for capital gains tax purposes by the father of the entire business (to the extent it includes any chargeable assets) and (as we have seen) TCGA 1992, s 165 may not be available to hold-over the gains. However, such a provision could subsequently be inserted in a pre-existing partnership and in such circumstances the relief should be available.

Existing partnerships

[10.24] Returning to the earlier example, let us assume that the father has now brought his son into partnership with him. The full value of the father's business has been credited to his capital account. The son has introduced a sum of £10,000 into the business which has been credited to his capital account. They share profits equally; but on the death or retirement of either, he, or his personal representatives, are only entitled to extract from the partnership the sum credited to his capital account and his share of accrued trading profits. The balance of the share in the partnership automatically accrues to the survivor without payment. The son has also covenanted to devote his full time to the business but there is no corresponding obligation on the father.

As we have seen, this type of arrangement is designed to freeze the value of the father's partnership interest so that any growth in value of the partnership assets will accrue automatically to the son. What further estate planning steps are now available to the father?

In considering the following paragraphs it should be remembered that, in most instances, 100% business property relief will be available whether further steps are taken during the father's lifetime (subject to potential loss of relief if he dies within seven years of the gift) or whether the son inherits under his father's will. In addition, there will be a capital gains tax-free uplift if the father still owns his share at the time of his death.

Transfer of capital

[10.25] The father may over a period of time make gifts to his son of his partnership capital, simply by debiting his capital account and crediting his son's. This process can use up the father's annual inheritance tax exemption of £3,000; alternatively, larger sums may be passed over as potentially exempt transfers. The Revenue appears to accept that a partner's capital account amounts to an interest in a business, rather than just an asset used in the partnership business (HMRC Inheritance Tax Manual, para 25060). Therefore, if the father were to die within seven years of making a potentially exempt transfer, 100% business property relief will be available (assuming all the other conditions are satisfied) to reduce the value of the gift to nil.

Where sums are left on capital account after a partner's retirement from the partnership, they will not represent an interest in a business and will not, therefore, receive business property relief (*Beckman v CIR* [2000] STC (SCD) 59 (SpC 226)).

Is a gift of part of the capital account a gift with reservation for inheritance tax purposes? As the sum still remains part of the capital of the partnership, it is clearly arguable that the donor continues to benefit from it whilst he remains a partner. However, it will also depend upon whether the proportion given away is also reflected in a reduction in the capital and profit sharing ratios. Where a certain proportion of capital is given away, and there is a corresponding reduction in the profit and capital sharing ratios, it is arguable that there is no reservation of benefit. The Revenue gives the following example.

Revenue example

> A farmer, on taking his son into partnership, makes a gift to him of a share of all the partnership assets including the land. They then share the profits and losses in the same proportion as they own the partnership assets at commencement. The farmer dies ten years later.
>
> This is not a GWR. The son has taken possession and enjoyment of the partnership share gifted to him in the form of his share of profits. The father's share of profits is referable to his own partnership share, not the share gifted.

The analysis is based on there being no reservation initially rather than on the basis that full consideration was paid to prevent the reservation of benefit rules applying.

(HMRC Inheritance Tax Manual, para 14332.)

Introduction of accruers or options

[10.26] Where an existing partnership deed does not contain any automatic accruer or option provision, it would be possible to incorporate one by a supplemental agreement. If this gives rise to an immediate reduction in the value of the father's estate but the son gives full consideration the exemption conferred by IHTA 1984, s 10 should apply. What will amount to full consideration will depend on the precise circumstances and, in particular, the scope of the automatic accruer or option provision itself. If the son does give full consideration, then on the death or retirement of his father full account will be taken of the automatic accruer or option provision and IHTA 1984, s 163 will not be applicable. If, on the other hand, the son does not give full consideration, then any transfer of value by the father will be a potentially exempt transfer for inheritance tax purposes. However, IHTA 1984, s 163 may apply on the subsequent death or retirement of the father to bring the full value of the father's partnership interest into the charge to inheritance tax, subject to the availability of business property relief. Although the Revenue accept that an automatic accruer clause is not a contract for sale, it is advisable for an option clause to be included rather than an accruer clause. It is unlikely there would be a gift with reservation for inheritance tax purposes, since the property given is a right to all or a part of the donor's partnership interest only on his death or retirement and there is therefore no question of the donor ever benefiting from the subject matter of the gift, unless, possibly, the donor becomes entitled to, or receives, an annuity on retirement.

If such a variation in the terms of the partnership is made as part of a bargain of such a kind as would have been reached between parties dealing at arm's length, it is the practice of the Revenue not to impose a charge to capital gains tax (see Statement of Practice D12 para 7). Otherwise, the hold-over relief provisions of TCGA 1992, s 165 should be applicable.

Gift of capital profits

[10.27] Instead of incorporating an automatic accruer or option provision the father could make an immediate gift of any future growth in the capital assets of the partnership by inserting the type of provision which confers the benefit of any capital profits on his son. Provided this does not involve any immediate reduction in the value of the father's estate, there will be no immediate inheritance tax consequences although it could amount to a gift with reservation unless it can be argued either that there is no disposition of any property within FA 1986, s 102 or that if there is, the father's right to benefit from the property given away (by reason of his continuing to draw the same level of profits) is not referable to the subject matter of the gift but to his pre-existing contractual rights under the partnership. The capital gains tax position is the same as above. The pre-owned assets legislation should be considered to determine whether an income tax charge would arise.

Gift of partnership interest

[10.28] Alternatively, the father may simply decide to increase his son's share in the capital assets of the partnership with immediate effect by transferring capital between their capital accounts and by altering their respective surplus asset sharing ratios. This may be done without reducing his share of the trading profits at the same time. The advantage of this over the former course is that it avoids completely any question of the application of IHTA 1984, s 163 on the death or retirement of the father. If full consideration is not given by the son, then the variation will constitute a potentially exempt transfer for inheritance tax purposes. For the same reasons as given above in relation to gifts between capital accounts, it is considered that a gift by way of increase in the son's share in the assets of the partnership, without a corresponding increase in his profit share, will not amount to a gift with reservation, although the Revenue may well not share this view. The pre-owned assets legislation should be considered to determine whether an income tax charge would arise.

So far as capital gains tax is concerned, either the disposal is treated as taking place on a 'no gain/no loss' basis (Statement of Practice SP D12) or hold-over relief under TCGA 1992, s 165 should be available.

Trustee partners

[10.29] Where there are minor children involved, it would be possible to bring into an existing partnership (or into a new partnership) the trustees of a settlement established for their benefit. The trustees will of course have to have the necessary powers in the trust instrument to enable them to become partners and to contribute capital. As the trustees pay tax at 50% on their share of the profits of the partnership, there will be no income tax saving, but the arrangement will enable the settlor to pass on some benefit to his children for inheritance tax purposes. The trustees should ideally pay full consideration for their partnership interest (eg by contributing the appropriate amount of capital, etc), to avoid any argument that the partnership agreement itself amounts to a 'settlement' within ITTOIA 2005, Pt 5 Ch 5 and that the settlor is taxable on the trustees' share of the trading profits. Further, the trustees should withdraw their share of the profits each year, to avoid any argument that they have made a loan to the settlor or his spouse (by leaving their share in the partnership) and thus fall within ITTOIA 2005, s 633. Section 633 applies where trustees of a settlement make a loan to the settlor and allows the Revenue to tax the settlor on any undistributed income of the settlement.

Retirement

[10.30] If on the retirement of a partner, his share automatically accrues to the continuing partners or is subject to an option to acquire at nominal value, this should not result in any chargeable transfer if his share has been subject to this provision at all times. This is because the reduction in the value of his share by reason of his retirement will always have been inherent in it and consequently any reduction in the value at the date of his retirement should be minimal. However, the Revenue may not accept this view. The position would undoubtedly be different if the provisions had been introduced as a result of a later agreement (as in the case, for example, of *A-G v Ralli* (1936) 15 ATC 523 (KB)) since IHTA 1984, s 163 will be applicable and the automatic accruer or option provision will only be taken into account if it was granted for full consideration. This may or may not have been the case. If not, then any reduction in value on retirement should amount to a potentially exempt transfer for inheritance tax purposes, and in any event 100% business property relief is likely to be available provided all the relevant conditions are fulfilled.

The capital gains tax position is more complicated. Either para 4 of the Statement of Practice SP D12 will apply to deem the disposal to take place on a 'no gain/no loss' basis or hold-over relief under TCGA 1992, s 165 may be available.

If, on retirement, the continuing partners are obliged to pay to the outgoing partner an annuity, the payments by them will not give rise to any inheritance tax charge if the annuities form part of an arm's length transaction between them. Otherwise, the payment of the annuities should fall within the normal expenditure out of income exemption.

Death

[10.31] The position on death is similar to retirement, except for the fact that no capital gains tax will be payable; and any chargeable transfer arising by reason of the death cannot constitute a potentially exempt transfer and will therefore give rise to an immediate tax charge, subject to the availability of 100% business property relief and the interest-free instalment option (if necessary). There will be no question of any subsequent loss of the business property relief.

Insurance

[10.32] The death or retirement of a partner is likely to necessitate the continuing partners (if the partnership continues) finding the cash either to repay to the partner (or his personal representatives) the sums due on his capital account or to purchase his interest in the partnership. To provide for this eventuality, and in particular where the partnership includes members from different generations, the elder partners should take out whole life policies on their lives and hold them on trust for the other partners subject to an overriding power of appointment exercisable in favour of a class consisting of the life assured's spouse or civil partner and his issue and his parents. Ideally, there should also be power to add other persons (other than the settlor) to the members of this class. Many life offices have standard 'flexible trust' wordings along these lines. Property held on such trusts will be 'relevant' property and subject to the settlement charges under IHTA 1984, Pt III, Ch III.

On the death of the life assured, the policy will provide the continuing partners with cash which they can use to fund any payments due to the deceased's personal representatives. In the event that the life assured retires from the partnership the policy may be surrendered and the proceeds similarly used. If the partnership is dissolved the policy can be appointed away from the continuing partners to members of the life assured's family.

If new partners enter the partnership, they may be included in the class of objects of the overriding power and this power may then be exercised in their favour so as to allow them to benefit from the policy along with the existing partners.

The settlor is usually excluded from the trusts to ensure that the inheritance tax gifts with reservation provisions cannot apply. However, the provisions may still apply where all the partners make similar reciprocal arrangements since the settlor, by reason of his being a beneficiary under the other trusts, could be said to have reserved a benefit by associated operations (FA 1986, s 102(1)(b) and FA 1986, Sch 20 para 6(1)(c)). Where such reciprocal arrangements are entered into as part of a commercial agreement between the partners, they may lack the element of bounty necessary to bring s 102 into play at all; but the Revenue is known to take the view that if beneficiaries other than just the other partners are capable of benefiting under the trusts then the arrangements will not be regarded as 'commercial'.

In relation to the income tax charge arising under the pre-owned asset regime, the Revenue has confirmed that, provided a partner is not a potential beneficiary of his own policy, then an income tax charge will not arise. Where, however, the partner retains the benefit for himself, for example, where they can cash in the policy during their lifetime for their own benefit, then, even if the arrangement is on commercial terms so that it is not a gift with reservation, the trust is a settlement for inheritance tax purposes and a charge to tax under para 8 will arise [Guidance notes Income Tax and Pre-Owned Assets Guidance 5].

Assets held outside the partnership

[10.33] It is necessary to consider carefully whether assets should be held within or outside the partnership. Assets, such as the premises from which the business is run, held within the partnership as part of the partnership assets qualify for 100% business property relief, whilst those held outside but used for the partnership business qualify for 50% relief only.

From a taxation viewpoint therefore there is considerable merit in transferring the asset, whether by way of gift or sale, into the partnership, subject to any stamp duty land tax charge. However, other factors must be taken into consideration, and the tax consequences of the transfer into the partnership must not be forgotten. The simplest transaction would involve the creation of a new class of partnership capital to which the transferor is entitled. Any transfer which benefits other members of the partnership will need careful consideration where the partners are other than an individual and his spouse or civil partner.

Liabilities

[10.34] One other important factor to consider is the nature of the assets upon which any debt is secured.

If an asset is eligible for 100% business property relief, securing a debt upon it has the effect that the debt reduces the value of an asset which would, in any event, be wholly exempt from inheritance tax. The benefit of deducting the liability would, therefore, be wasted.

Accordingly, care should be taken to secure the debt against assets which are not otherwise eligible for relief. A partner should therefore borrow against personal assets in order to contribute additional partnership capital. Such borrowings should be a loan rather than an overdraft. ITA 2007, s 384 provides that no income tax relief is available for interest paid on an overdraft. The borrowings should not be secured on any partnership asset or on the partner's interest in the partnership. It will not therefore be an incumbrance on his interest or a partnership asset and will not be deducted from the value of his interest under IHTA 1984, s 162(4).

Such a transaction should not prejudice relief against income tax which will be available under ITA 2007, ss 383 and 398 subject to ss 384A and 385. Section 384A provides that tax relief will not be available on a loan which is entered into to provide capital to a partnership where the loan is made as part of arrangements which 'appear very likely to produce a post-tax advantage and the arrangements seem to have been designed to reduce any income tax or capital gains tax to which the individual would be liable apart from the arrangements'.

Limited liability partnerships

[10.35] The Limited Liability Partnership Act 2000 ('LLPA 2000') permits the creation of partnerships where members may participate in the management of the business of the LLP whilst having limited liability.

For tax purposes, an LLP is generally transparent, that is to say that the tax is levied on its members rather than on the corporate body itself. Apart from tax, there are other factors which affect the choice of an LLP as an appropriate business structure, the chief one being the protection of limited liability which is offered to its members. This advantage is also afforded by incorporation as a company, but that may also produce for its members liability to pay-as-you-earn tax and Class 1 and 1A National Insurance contributions.

LLPA 2000, s 1(2) provides that such a partnership is a body corporate with a legal personality separate from that of its members.

An LLP is formed by being incorporated under LLPA 2000. Its members are those persons who subscribe their names to the incorporation document and any other persons becoming members by and in accordance with an agreement with the existing members. A person may cease to be a member by death or by dissolution of the LLP, by agreement with the other members or by giving reasonable notice to the other members. The mutual rights and duties of members are governed by agreement between the members or between the LLP and its members.

ITTOIA 2005, s 863 provides that where an LLP carries on a trade, profession or other business with a view to profit, all its activities are treated as carried on in the LLP by its members and not by the LLP itself. Anything done by, to, or in relation to the LLP for the purposes of, or in connection with, any of its activities is treated as done by, to, or in relation to the members as partners. The property of the LLP is treated as held by the members as partnership property.

An LLP carrying on a trade, profession or other business with a view to profit is treated as a partnership for the purposes of capital gains tax (TCGA 1992, s 59A). The partnership assets are treated as belonging to the members who are directly taxable on their share of any chargeable gains arising on disposal of those assets. If there is a temporary cessation of trade, the tax status of the partnership continues. This is also the case in a winding up, provided that the process is not unnecessarily prolonged and that the purpose of the winding up is not the avoidance of tax.

On the liquidation of an LLP, however, the LLP ceases to be treated as such from the earlier of the appointment of a liquidator or a court order for winding up. The normal capital gains rules then cease to apply and the LLP is taxed through the liquidator as a company on any chargeable gains arising on disposals of its assets. The only asset then held by the members is their capital interest in the partnership; there will be a disposal of the whole or part when capital distributions are made by the liquidator. The acquisition dates and costs of these capital interests will depend on their actual acquisition by the member concerned.

The commencement and cessation of a partnership's status as an LLP does not of itself give rise to a charge to capital gains tax on its members. TCGA 1992, s 169A, however, provides that any gain held over under TCGA 1992, s 165 when the LLP status no longer applies does not fall out of charge. Where a member holds an asset acquired from a disposal to him, any gain which has been held over under TCGA 1992, s 165 or s 260, immediately becomes chargeable.

As an LLP will have the same tax transparency as a normal partnership, similar considerations in relation to estate planning will apply, as discussed above.

Family company

Gifts of shares

[10.36] The majority shareholder in a company may find himself in something of a dilemma. His shareholding, by virtue of its ability to control the company, will carry most of the company's value. Under present legislation, business property relief at 100% is available provided various conditions are fulfilled (see **10.2** above).

There may be some merit in his giving away some or all of his shares now to take advantage of this relief, which may not still be available at the time of his death. On the other hand, a lifetime gift will mean the loss of the tax free uplift on death for capital gains tax purposes under TCGA 1992, s 62 since hold-over relief under TCGA 1992, s 165 merely postpones the liability to tax. In addition, there may be claw-back of the business property relief if the donor dies within seven years (see above).

In addition, for the donor to reduce his holding below 50% may deprive him of control over a business on which his livelihood depends, and a gift of all his shares would have an even more dramatic effect.

Before making any gift of shares, the prospective donor and his advisers should consider the following questions.

(a) Does the donor rely on his director's fees or other emoluments for his livelihood? If so, should any steps be taken to secure these prior to the gift?

(b) Does the donor rely on any dividend income from the shares? Again, can any steps be taken to compensate him for this loss if he gives away his shares?

(c) Is there likely to be a sale or a stock exchange quotation of the shares of the company in the foreseeable future? If so, this may have an impact on any decision whether or not, and if so, to whom, the shares should be given.

(d) Are there any pension arrangements in place for the donor and his wife which may be prejudiced by the gift?

(e) Are there any surplus profits in the company which the donor would like to extract prior to the gift (although any distribution of these by way of dividend will result in an income tax charge)?

(f) Will the intended donees of the shares be involved in running the company or merely passive shareholders? Is there likely to be any friction between them if more than one person is involved?

In many cases where 100% relief is available lifetime gifts may now be positively disadvantageous because the capital gains tax uplift on death will be lost. However, there are a number of circumstances where lifetime gifts may still be worthwhile or necessary. In particular:

(i) where it is likely that the company will be sold prior to the death of the shareholder but probably not in the next 7 years;
(ii) where 'excepted assets' within IHTA 1984, s 112 are held in the company and business property relief will therefore be severely restricted; and
(iii) where family circumstances require the next generation, who may be heavily involved in the company, to be given an interest.

In these circumstances it may be sensible for the majority shareholder to consider reducing his holding to the minimum 51% by making regular use of his annual inheritance tax exemption or by making a potentially exempt transfer and insuring against the risk of his death within the seven-year period.

Where 100% business property relief is not available it is sensible for any shareholder who wishes to divest himself of control simply to make the gift (which will be a potentially exempt transfer) and insure his life.

What can be done to protect the shareholder from his loss of control? Any attempt by him to entrench his right to remuneration as, for example, an executive director, by giving himself a long-term service contract, or even a contract for any length which allows him remuneration beyond that commensurate with his duties, may be treated as a gift with reservation within FA 1986, s 102, as would any attempt to secure favourable pre-emption rights over the shares given away. On the other hand, there should be no difficulty in his continuing to draw a reasonable commercial remuneration under a pre-existing service contract or renewing that contract on similar terms (provided they are still appropriate and reasonable) when it expires. Similarly, it is considered that he may still benefit from any pre-emption rights contained in the Articles of Association of the company prior to the gift.

One way of providing a degree of control for the donor would be for him to give the shares to a discretionary trust of which he is the first named trustee. Because this will be a chargeable transfer for inheritance tax purposes, an inheritance tax charge is likely to arise unless the value of the shares are within the nil rate band or are fully relieved business property. The case of *Comr of Stamp Duties of New South Wales v Way* [1952] AC 95, [1952] 1 All ER 198 (PC) provides authority for the proposition that powers exercisable by a person in a fiduciary capacity do not amount to a reservation of benefit for estate duty purposes and the Revenue accepts that this is the case for inheritance tax purposes (HMRC Inheritance Tax Manual, para 14394). In addition, the donor's spouse or civil partner can be a trustee. However, the settlor as a trustee, must exercise his votes in the best interests of the beneficiaries under the trust and not in his own interests. Failure to do so may make him susceptible to an action for breach of trust by an aggrieved beneficiary; it may also allow the Revenue to claim that there has in fact been a gift with reservation. The settlor should also bear in mind that although as first named shareholder he is the one who is able, so far as the company is concerned, to exercise the votes (the company having no notice of the trust), he should only exercise them as all the trustees agree, as trustees have to be unanimous in exercising their powers unless the settlement itself says otherwise. Any provision in the settlement attempting to give the settlor sole control over the votes must cast doubt on his exercising them in a fiduciary capacity and hence the gift with reservation provisions may apply.

Where the settlor-trustee is also a director of the company, if the settlement contains any provisions relieving him of his duty to account to the trust for any profits made through using, or failing to use, the trust votes to secure his position, the gift may amount to a gift with reservation. The Revenue, however, has indicated that such relieving provisions will not in its view prejudice a gift where they permit the retention of reasonable commercial remuneration (HMRC Inheritance Tax Manual, para 14395).

When structuring the capital of a company, it is important to consider the precise wording of the definition of 'relevant business property'. For example, if a shareholder has sufficient shares to give him control of the company and also owns non-voting securities, the shares will be relevant business property but the securities will not. This is because the securities do not give the shareholder control of the company together with the unquoted shares. The shares give control in their own right. It should be remembered that for inheritance tax purposes there is a distinction between shares and securities.

Minority holdings

[10.37] All sizes of minority shareholdings in unquoted trading companies may be eligible for business property relief at 100%. As for controlling holdings, it may be sensible to retain the shares until death and obtain the capital gains tax uplift. However, it may be, for the same reasons as are set out above in respect of controlling holdings, that lifetime gifts are appropriate.

The minority shareholder may, however, have fewer non-tax-related problems in deciding whether to make a lifetime gift. If he considers his interest in the company purely as an investment and does not rely on it to help secure a remunerated office, his only loss in giving away the shares will be any dividend income (which in the case of many unquoted companies may be negligible if not non-existent) and any loss in capital appreciation.

To enable shareholders to reduce their taxable estate, but at the same time to retain their dividend rights, the company's Articles of Association could be altered to allow any shareholder to convert each of his shares into two separate shares. One share would carry the right to any dividends declared by the company, the right only to repayment at par on a winding-up of a company but no voting rights; the other share would carry the right to vote and the right to the remaining equity of the company on a winding-up, but no dividend rights. The former share would then be retained and the latter given away. It is not considered that a gift of the voting shares would amount to a gift with reservation for inheritance tax purposes, since no benefit accrues to the donor which is referable to the gift. Although, on the conversion, value will pass out of the original shares, this will not result in a capital gains tax charge under the value shifting provisions contained in TCGA 1992, s 29. For s 29 to apply it is a requirement that the party or parties making the deemed disposal could have obtained consideration for the disposal and, since the new shares are issued to the same shareholder, it is impossible to see how any consideration could have been obtained.

A similar device involves the issue of fixed dividend preference shares by way of bonus to existing shareholders. The preference shares are non-voting and on the winding-up of the company carry the right only to repayment at par. The idea is that the bonus issue frees the ordinary shares (which, depending on the income and net asset value of the company, may well carry the bulk of the value of the company), for gifts, whilst allowing the donor to retain the benefit of the income from the preference shares. This type of scheme may be attractive both to minority shareholders who rely on regular dividends to secure their standard of living and to controlling shareholders nearing the age of retirement who wish to pass control of the family company on to the next generation but at the same time need the security of an income flow to support them in their retirement.

Quoted shares

[10.38] If shares become quoted, ie listed on a recognised Stock Exchange they will cease to qualify for any inheritance tax business property relief unless they are part of a controlling holding owned by the transferor (IHTA 1984, s 105(1)(b)). The loss of relief can be a significant disadvantage especially where there are a number of elderly shareholders. Where minority shareholdings are concerned, the effect may be to move the holding from a non-tax paying position (because 100% business property relief was available whilst unquoted) to a position where it is fully taxable at 40%. Additionally, its value may considerably increase.

If a flotation is considered necessary in order to give the company access to the public as a new source of funds, rather than simply to unlock the value inherent in the shares, a solution would be for the company to create and issue a new class of shares for the purposes of the public sale leaving the existing shareholders with their original shares which would continue to be unquoted and therefore capable of qualifying for business property relief. The new class of shares issued should rank *pari passu* with the existing shares in all material respects. To enable the existing shareholders to realise their shares, they could be made convertible into the quoted class at the option of the holder.

A similar problem exists where unquoted shares have been the subject matter of a potentially exempt transfer but have become quoted before the seven-year period has expired. In such a case, the shares would not attract business property relief if the transferor dies within the period (IHTA 1984, s 113A(3)). Again, a new class of shares could be created specially for the purposes of the flotation.

Where there are two or more shareholders who between them control a quoted company, by transferring their shares to a newly formed 'holding' company which they own jointly they can in effect convert shares which will not qualify for business property relief (ie the quoted shares) into shares which do (ie the unquoted shares in the holding company). Although the only business of the new company is the holding of investments, this does not prevent the shares of the company from being relevant business property (IHTA 1984, s 105(4)(b)).

Once shares or securities have become quoted they also cease to be assets capable of qualifying for hold-over relief under TCGA 1992, s 165 unless in the case of an individual the company concerned is the transferor's personal company (as defined in TCGA 1992, s 165(8) or in the case of trustees, they are able to exercise 25% of the voting rights exercisable by the company's shareholders in general meeting (TCGA 1992, Sch 7 para 2). However, in the appropriate circumstances, hold-over relief under TCGA 1992, s 260 may still be available.

Other devices

[10.39] Two other strategies involving companies must be mentioned: the 'deferred share' proposal and the 'value freezing' proposal. Both are designed to pass the value inherent in a company to other members of a family, the first by creating a new class of shares to which deferred rights are attached but which automatically convert into ordinary shares after a specified period of time; the second by creating a new class of shares which from the outset carry any increase in the value of the company over its value at the date of issue. Although strategies of this nature are of less relevance because of the availability of 100% business property relief it is still worthwhile including them in this chapter as they are of relevance where 100% business relief is not available.

Deferred share strategy

[10.40] A bonus issue of deferred shares is made to the existing ordinary shareholder or shareholders of the company. For a fixed period these deferred shares carry minimal (or no) voting rights, dividend rights or rights to receive distributions on a winding-up. At the end of the period the deferred shares automatically rank *pari passu* with the existing ordinary shares, or assume all the rights previously attached to the ordinary shares, with the ordinary shares correspondingly losing their rights (and becoming valueless).

The idea is to create a new class of shares which are initially of low value (and an important factor in determining this value is the length of the fixed period) and can therefore be given at little or no inheritance tax cost, but which then grow in value over a period of time and at the end of the period assume virtually the full value of the company if at that time the rights attaching to the ordinary shares cease.

It is debatable whether the expiry of the fixed period will result in a disposition by the ordinary shareholders in the company (assuming of course that the company is 'close' for tax purposes) under IHTA 1984, s 98. However, it is understood that the Revenue is of the view that an alteration of rights within the meaning of IHTA 1984, s 98(1)(b) occurs when deferred shares come to rank equally with another class of shares (Shares and Assets Valuation

Manual, para 108280). Even if this is the case it is difficult to see how an inheritance tax charge can arise because the reduction in value (if any) of the shareholders' estates due to the disposition is minimal. This is because the value of the ordinary shares will discount the coming to an end of the fixed period when the deferred shares will rank *pari passu* in all respects with the other shares, and will therefore gradually decrease in value over the years as the value of the deferred shares increases, so that immediately before the disposition the ordinary shares are likely to have virtually the same value as after the disposition.

To counter the argument that prior to the end of the fixed period the failure of the ordinary shareholders to cancel the deferred shares or to liquidate the company results in a transfer of value under IHTA 1984, s 3(3), it is important that the rights of the deferred shareholders are entrenched by giving them the ability to block any resolution to alter the rights attaching to their shares or to wind up the company or to create any new share capital. For the same reason it is also important that the ordinary shareholders ensure that as much of the profits of the company as are not required commercially for its operations are paid out by way of dividend. This is to ensure that value is not left in the company which the ordinary shareholders fail to extract. This 'enforced' payment of dividends may make the scheme unattractive to some shareholders.

To allow as much time as possible for the relevant period to expire (and therefore for the ordinary shares to lose their value) before an event which gives rise to an inheritance tax charge occurs, the ordinary shareholders should leave their ordinary shares to their respective spouses on their deaths.

So far as capital gains tax is concerned, the value shifting provisions contained in TCGA 1992, ss 29 and 30 should not be in point. Section 29 does not apply because the deferred shares are initially issued to the ordinary shareholders and consequently there is no transaction for which any consideration could have been obtained. Section 30 also does not apply because although the gift of the deferred shares would be a disposal for the purposes of the section, there has been no scheme or arrangement whereby the value of the deferred shares has been materially reduced.

As gifts of unlimited amounts may be made without inheritance tax implications, provided the donor survives for the necessary seven-year period, and with business property relief at 100% being available, the use of the deferred share scheme has diminished. A straightforward gift of shares must be far less provocative to the Revenue than what is undeniably a very artificial arrangement involving a number of complicated — and potentially contentious — tax points. The scheme also involves the creation of a complex share structure for the company which of necessity must last for a number of years. Having said that, however, the scheme still has its place in estate planning. An owner of a company who expects to retire in 10 years in favour of his sons, may find it attractive to enter into a scheme now which can secure the passing of control on his retirement without the need to make an immediate outright gift of his shares and without the worry as to whether the present favourable inheritance tax regime will still remain in a decade's time.

The deferred share strategy is less apposite for investment companies. This is because shares in investment companies tend to be valued on a net asset basis and in this regard the most crucial right attaching to the shares is the ability to wind up the company. As mentioned above, the deferred shares must carry the same voting rights on a winding up as the ordinary shares and although for the duration of the fixed period the ordinary shares carry the right to the bulk of the distributions on a winding up, the ordinary shares will not carry the ability to wind up the company. This may therefore limit the discount attaching to the value of the deferred shares over the ordinary shares (to take account of the other deferred rights).

Value freezing strategy

[10.41] Alternatively, investment companies, for reasons which will be discussed, are more suitable vehicles for the value freezing strategy. This proposal involves a new class of shares being issued to the existing shareholders, again by way of a bonus issue, which carry the right to participate in the winding up of the company only insofar as the net asset value of the company then exceeds its value at the date of issue of the new shares. In this event, the new shares carry the right to participate in all the excess. The new shares may carry dividend and voting rights ranking *pari passu* with the ordinary shares. It is important, for the same reasons as was the case with the deferred share strategy, that the new shares are able to block any resolution to wind up the company or to alter the rights attaching to the shares. These additional voting rights will not prevent the ordinary shares from qualifying for business property relief (assuming it to be otherwise available, which in the case of an investment company will often not be the case), provided they give control on all other matters (IHTA 1984, s 269).

The ordinary shares are retained and the new shares, which will initially be of little value, are given away. It should be remembered that shares in an investment company are not capable of qualifying for hold-over relief under TCGA 1992, s 165, although relief under TCGA 1992, s 260 may be available.

This strategy is best confined to investment companies because the basis of calculating value in respect of their shares is more certain — the net value of the company's assets is taken and then discounted by a percentage depending upon the size of the holding. The valuation of shares in a trading company is usually calculated on an earnings basis whereby an appropriate multiplier is applied to the earnings per share. This method of valuation is more difficult to apply and determining the initial value of the company is more problematic. This in turn will make it difficult to 'freeze' the value of the company.

As with the deferred share strategy, the existence of the potentially exempt transfer has lessened the importance of this type of arrangement in estate planning. However, its advantages over a straightforward gift of shares is that it enables the donor to retain an interest in both the capital and income of the company, and also in its management (by reason of the votes attaching to the shares) whilst at the same time enabling the future benefit of the company to flow through to the next generation. Clearly, a value freezing exercise such as this is long-term in its operation and effects.

It is considered that under both strategies the gifts of the new shares will not contravene the gifts with reservation provisions because the donor does not benefit in any way from the property which is the subject matter of the gift, nor does he receive any collateral benefit referable to the gift. Any benefits he continues to receive are from the company and flow from pre-existing property retained in his estate, namely the original shares.

Dividend waivers

[10.42] A shareholder paying higher or additional rate income tax might consider waiving his rights to dividends in order to divert the income to taxpayers paying lesser rates of tax, eg a basic rate taxpayer. With the top rate of income tax on dividends now at 42.5%, the saving has increased. Basic rate taxpayers are liable to pay tax at 10% on their dividend income with a tax credit of one ninth of the dividend so that the tax credit will entirely cover the income tax liability. Trusts currently pay 50% on their general income and 42.5% on dividend income also with a tax credit of one ninth of the dividend.

Provided the waiver is made within 12 months before any right to the dividend accrues, it will not be a transfer of value for inheritance tax purposes (IHTA 1984, s 15).

Subject to the articles of association of the company, in the case of an interim dividend, the right accrues from the date of payment; and in the case of a final dividend, it accrues from the date it is declared unless the dividend is expressed to be payable at a future date, when the right accrues at that date (see *Potel v CIR* [1971] 2 All ER 504 at 511, 512).

A dividend waiver should be by deed. For the purposes of ITTOIA 2005, Pt 5 Ch 5 the Revenue treats most dividend waivers as 'settlements'. However, not all dividend waivers will be treated as such (see Revenue Trusts Manual, para 4225). Any waiver which results in a greater dividend being paid to minor unmarried children, a spouse or civil partner of the settlor will result in the dividends continuing to be taxed as part of the total income of the settlor. Although this will clearly destroy any income tax benefit of the waiver, the inheritance tax advantage of reducing the settlor's estate by the after-tax amount of the dividend still remains.

Assets held outside the company

[10.43] As with partnerships, there is a significant inheritance tax disadvantage in holding assets outside a company. This is because such assets can only qualify for 50% business property relief where the owner of the asset is the controlling shareholder of the company. Where he is only a minority shareholder there will be no relief at all, even though the asset may be used exclusively for the company's purposes.

For instance, if two or more individuals (not being husband and wife) own an unquoted company equally, their shareholdings in the company will qualify for business property relief at 100%. On the other hand, a property also owned by them equally and let to the company for the purposes of its trade will not qualify for business property relief.

The solution as with a partnership (see above) is to transfer the asset such as land into the company with the owner(s) either giving the asset to the company or selling it for its capital gains tax base cost. In either case to avoid an actual capital gains tax liability a hold-over election under TCGA 1992, s 165 would be required.

A gift to a company is not a potentially exempt transfer for inheritance tax purposes (IHTA 1984, s 3A) so care needs to be taken where the company is owned other than by the individual transferor or that individual and his spouse. Even where the property and the shares in the company are owned in the same proportions, there may be an element of loss to the transferor's estate because of the discount applied to minority holdings and a careful valuation will have to be carried out.

It may be possible to issue shares to the transferor(s) in exchange for the asset so as to avoid any element of gift for inheritance tax purposes. As this will prevent an election for hold-over relief for capital gains tax purposes under TCGA 1992, s 165, any unrealised gain on the asset will be brought into charge. In addition, where land is being transferred to a connected company a stamp duty land tax charge based on market value will arise.

The capital gains tax liabilities on the ultimate disposal of an asset should also be considered. If the asset is held by the individual, capital gains tax at either 18% or 28% will be payable. If the asset is held by a company, corporation tax at either 21% or 28% will be payable.

Each case will need to be carefully considered depending on all the circumstances.

Liabilities

[10.44] As discussed more fully in the coverage on partnerships at **10.34** above, it is important to ensure that debts are secured on assets which do not qualify for business property relief. In the case of holdings in companies, therefore, it is important to ensure that borrowings are secured on the shareholder's other assets rather than on the shares themselves.

Death

[10.45] Historically, unquoted shares have always caused problems on death. These problems, however, are much alleviated by the availability of business property relief at 100%. The main problem, namely of an inheritance tax charge arising on an asset which is not readily realisable, will now only apply:

(a) where there are 'excepted assets';
(b) where the company is not a trading company; or
(c) where the shares are ineligible for relief for some other reason.

Where an actual liability to tax is likely to arise, whole of life insurance should always be considered as a means of funding the tax. This can either be on a single life basis, if a charge is likely to arise on the death of the shareholder, or on a joint life last survivor basis if the shareholder proposes to leave the shares to the surviving spouse or civil partner, when the inheritance tax charge will arise on the second death. However, particularly where business property relief is available at 100%, leaving shares to the surviving spouse or civil partner should be avoided unless done for purely practical reasons. It is preferable to leave assets qualifying for 100% business property relief to children or grandchildren (or in trust for them) compensating the spouse or civil partner with other assets not qualifying for relief.

Another way of funding the inheritance tax on the death of a shareholder is for the company, assuming it has power to do so in its articles of association, to buy some or all of the deceased's shares. The payment made by the company will not amount to a distribution of income for corporation tax purposes provided the company is an unquoted trading company or the unquoted holding company of a trading group and the whole or substantially the whole of the payment is used (apart from paying any capital gains tax) to discharge an inheritance tax liability within two years of the death (ICTA 1988, s 219). This relieving provision does not apply where the tax could be paid in some other way without under hardship.

Where the company has surplus funds sufficient to discharge the inheritance tax liability on the death of a controlling shareholder, the Revenue takes the view that there is no hardship since the liability can be met by dividend payments (Hansard 17-3-88).

Enterprise Investment Scheme (EIS)

[10.46] EIS relief is a multi-faceted relief which essentially comprises a capital gains tax deferral, an income tax relief and a capital gains tax exemption. A detailed analysis of the rules surrounding the relief is outside the scope of this book but the following describes the relief in broad terms and goes on to consider how the relief might usefully be employed in an estate planning context.

Capital gains tax deferral

[10.47] The relief allows the deferral of capital gains tax arising on the disposal of any assets if the gain is reinvested in newly issued ordinary shares of a qualifying unquoted trading company within certain time limits. The effect is to defer the tax liability until the EIS shares are sold and even then the charge may be further deferred by reinvesting the gain in different qualifying EIS shares.

The asset disposed of can be virtually any asset except that, on the disposal of shares or securities, the investment cannot be in the same company or group of companies (TCGA 1992, Sch 5B para 10).

For this element of the relief there is no connected persons rule beyond substitution of market value in certain cases. It is possible for an individual to invest in a company which he already owns or controls.

The qualifying investment must be made within a period commencing one year before and ending 3 years after the disposal of the original asset (TCGA 1992, Sch 5B para 1(3)(a)). This period can be extended at the Revenue's discretion. (TCGA 1992, Sch 5B para 1(3)(b)).

A qualifying investment is an acquisition for cash of newly issued eligible shares in a qualifying company. Eligible shares are defined as fully paid up ordinary shares which for a period of three years, do not carry present or future preferential rights to dividends or assets or any present or future right to be redeemed (TCGA 1992, Sch 5B para 19). Most trades are qualifying trades but amongst those which do not qualify are dealing in land, commodities, futures, shares, other financial instruments, leasing, providing legal or accountancy services, property development, farming, woodlands or market gardening, operating hotels, nursing homes, shipbuilding, producing coal or steel, or residential care homes. The total amount of relevant investments made in the company in the previous year must not exceed £2m.

The gross assets of the investee company must not exceed £7m immediately before the investment or £8m immediately after. For shares issued after 18 July 2007, there is an additional requirement that the company should not have 50 or more full time employees at that time (ITA 2007, s 186A).

The investment must be made by subscribing in cash for 'eligible shares'. The amount of EIS relief is limited to the amount claimed by the taxpayer, which allows him to first make use of capital losses, annual exemptions and hold-over relief. There is no minimum holding period for the shares in which the gain is reinvested. However, relief will be clawed back if there is a disposal of the shares otherwise than to a spouse or if the conditions on which the relief was granted cease to be fully met at any time within 3 years after the investment.

Relief can also be denied or clawed back under complex anti-avoidance provisions. These counteract any return of value within three years after reinvestment. This concept is widely defined, catching, for example, instances where there are advance arrangements for a return of value at any time (eg guaranteed exit route).

Any clawback charge can itself be deferred by further investment, subject to satisfying the normal conditions.

Income tax relief and capital gains tax exemption

[10.48] To obtain income tax relief of up to 20% on qualifying investments of up to £500,000 in any fiscal year the following additional conditions must be satisfied:

(a) the taxpayer must be liable to UK tax;
(b) the taxpayer must make a minimum investment of £500;
(c) the taxpayer must not be connected with the company at any time during the period beginning 2 years before the issue of the shares and three years after the share issue in question;
(d) the taxpayer must not receive value from the company (or have breached any of the other anti-avoidance provisions) during the defined period.

The taxpayer will be connected with the company where he, and his associates, own (as widely defined) more than 30% of the company.

Provided that the EIS shares are held for at least three years and EIS income tax relief has not been withdrawn, any capital gains arising on the disposal of the shares (excluding the held-over gains) will be exempt from capital gains tax.

Relief in estate planning context

[10.49] Whilst the relief affords considerable scope for deferring capital gains tax, there are significant commercial risks involved in making any qualifying investment. This point is reinforced by the fact that specific anti-avoidance legislation ensures that relief is denied where there is a guaranteed exit route at the outset. The financial services industry is becoming more successful at developing products which minimise the risks whilst still qualifying for the relief but EIS investments are not low risk investments. The main role of the relief in an estate planning context is in the sphere of the private company proprietor. He will understand the risks involved and, in the case of many disposals, will have a ready made vehicle in which he may invest.

If the investor and his associates own more than 30% of the investee company they will receive capital gains tax deferral relief but not income tax relief or capital gains tax exemption on a later sale of the shares.

Take, for example, a private company proprietor, Mr A, who makes a substantial gain on a disposal of quoted investments when aged 55. The gain will be charged to capital gains tax at either 18% or 28%. To defer this liability he might, however, subscribe for new shares in his existing private company. Providing he subscribes for 'eligible shares' and the company is a 'qualifying company', EIS capital gains tax deferral relief will, in principle, be available. It will be necessary for the company to retain its qualifying status for the next three years but there is no reason why this should not be achieved providing the cash is wholly employed for permissible purposes. Care must be taken to ensure that there is no return of value (as widely defined) which would result in a clawback of relief but this does not preclude the payment of reasonable remuneration and dividends.

If instead of being a company proprietor, Mr A was in business as a sole trader or in partnership with his wife, he might still be able to take advantage of EIS relief. For example, he could form a company and give to it the assets of the existing business, any gain arising being held-over under TCGA 1992, s 165 (although it is likely that a stamp duty land tax charge would arise on the transfer of any land to the company). He could then subscribe for capital in the newly-formed company to the extent of the gain made on his investment disposal. EIS relief should be available provided the necessary criteria are met as regards the new company. It would, of course, be necessary to consider all the other tax and non-tax implications of incorporation if this route were to be pursued.

Venture capital trusts (VCT)

[10.50] As with EIS investments, investments in VCTs used to qualify for a special form of capital gains tax deferral. It is still possible to claim income tax relief of 30% on investments in VCTs of up to £200,000 in a fiscal year. VCTs are quoted investment trusts which invest in certain qualifying unquoted trading companies. Restrictive rules govern the types of investment which may be acquired, the activities of the investee companies and the size and diversity of the VCTs investments.

It should be remembered that an investment in a VCT will not qualify for business property relief because its shares are quoted.

Chapter 11

The Family Farm

Introduction

[11.1] The farmer has very particular, and probably unique, problems in relation to estate planning as he owns a valuable capital asset which is absolutely vital to his business. In the past, the death of a landowner has often imposed a massive capital taxation burden on those heirs who wished to continue to farm the land for whom the capital value of the land is irrelevant. Under inheritance tax, agricultural property relief, which is at a rate of 100% on untenanted land and on let land where the tenancy began after 31 August 1995, this problem has been greatly alleviated. However, it is still necessary to ensure that the criteria for qualification are met and that the best possible use is made of the relief. Inheritance tax is still payable on tenanted land let prior to 1 September 1995 as only 50% relief is available.

Over the years, farmers have seen many fundamental changes. Farming structures have changed as more farmers are engaging farming contractors to farm their land. There have also been changes in relation to farming subsidies. Farming subsidies are essentially no longer related to production but are based on area and historical entitlement through the single farm payment. Planning is often also complicated by the fact that the farmer may want one of several children to succeed to the farming business.

As the farmer is primarily a man of business much of **CHAPTER 10 THE FAMILY BUSINESS** will also be relevant to the family farm and reference should be made to it. There will be a number of matters in this chapter which will repeat topics covered there and accordingly they will not be dealt with in such detail here.

The farmer may be the sole proprietor of the farming business; or there may be a partnership or a family company, each of which will be complicated by the existence of the farmland itself. In the case of a partnership or a family company, the land may either be owned by the partnership or the company, or it may be owned by one of the partners or one of the shareholders of the company. In the latter case, the partnership or company may have an agricultural tenancy of the land or it may simply occupy it under a gratuitous licence. Each one of these possibilities has different estate planning ramifications and they will be considered below. First, however, the inheritance tax and capital gains tax provisions having most impact on farmers will be considered.

Inheritance tax

[11.2] Fortunately, the regime for inheritance tax recognises the difficulty, often encountered by his heirs, in funding the tax payable on the death of a farmer in respect of his farm when there are no other easily realisable assets in the estate out of which the tax may be funded. As a result, the legislation first applies a discount to the value of farmland of either 50% or 100% to reduce the burden of the tax or eliminate it completely. Secondly, where tax is payable there is the option of paying it by ten equal annual interest-free instalments.

Agricultural property relief

[11.3] The relief for agricultural property is given by IHTA 1984, ss 115–124B, which reduces the 'agricultural value' of any 'agricultural property' by a stated percentage.

The 'agricultural value' is the value of the property on the assumption that it is subject to a perpetual covenant prohibiting its use otherwise than as agricultural property (IHTA 1984, s 115(3)). Any development or hope value or value attributable to minerals, therefore, is not relieved.

The relief only applies to agricultural property in the UK, the Channel Islands, the Isle of Man or a state which is an EEA state (IHTA 1984, s 115(5)). Where a UK domiciled individual owns farmland outside the EEA, no agricultural property relief will be available. However, there is no such territorial limit in respect of business property relief and so business property relief may be available on the farmland. Business property relief may not be available on the farmhouse.

Agricultural property

[11.3A] The definition of 'agricultural property' has three limbs:

(1) agricultural land or pasture;
(2) woodland and any building used in connection with the intensive rearing of livestock or fish if the woodland or building is occupied with agricultural land or pasture and the occupation is ancillary to that of the agricultural land or pasture;
(3) such cottages, farm buildings and farmhouses, together with the land occupied with them, as are of a character appropriate to the property (IHTA 1984, s 115(2)).

The meaning of 'agriculture'

'Agriculture' is not defined for the purposes of inheritance tax. The definition found in the Agricultural Tenancies Act 1995, s 38(1) may give some indication as to how it should be construed. This definition includes ' . . . horticulture, fruit growing, seed growing, dairy farming and livestock breeding and keeping, the use of land as grazing land, meadow land, osier land, market gardens and nursery grounds.'

Under a farm business tenancy, it is the activities of the tenant that are relevant to determining occupation. It is therefore essential that the tenant covenants that the land will only be occupied for agricultural purposes.

Property used for the breeding and rearing of horses on a stud farm and the grazing of horses in connection with those activities qualifies (IHTA 1984, s 115(4)). There is no definition in the legislation as to what constitutes a stud farm. It is the Revenue's view that relief will only be available where the normal requirements for commerciality apply. It does not consider that relief will be available for a hobby which is not carried on for gain. The Revenue considers a number of factors when determining whether there is a stud farm and these are listed in HMRC Inheritance Tax Manual, para 24068. A field which was let for the grazing of horses used for leisure was held not to be 'occupied for the purposes of agriculture' (*Wheatley's Executors v IRC* [1998] STC (SCD) 60 (SpC 149)). The decision focused on the nature of the animals grazing rather than on the main purpose of the occupation of the land. This decision highlights the difficulty where landowners or their tenants diversify into horse and paddock activities.

The relief also applies to farmland dedicated to wildlife habitats (IHTA 1984, s 124C).

In the case of *Dixon v IRC* [2002] STC (SCD) 53 (SpC 297) it was held that although fruit growing and the use of land as grazing land could be agriculture, whether or not these activities were agriculture was a matter of fact and degree to be determined in the light of the purposes of the Act.

In its Inheritance Tax Manual, the Revenue gives illustrations of what land it accepts as being for agricultural purposes (see para 24061).

Agricultural land or pasture (Limb 1)

[11.3B] Limb 1 of the above definition is restricted to bare land and pasture used for agriculture and does not include buildings (*Starke (Brown Executors) v CIR* [1995] STC 689 (CA)) (HMRC Inheritance Tax Manual, para 24031).

Where a farmer gives away the bulk of his farm, which was the situation in *Starke*, whilst retaining only the farmhouse and a small amount of land, such retained property will rarely qualify for relief. This problem may be avoided if the farmer continues to be a partner with perhaps a relatively small partnership share.

Occupation (Limb 2)

[11.3C] In *Williams v Revenue and Customs Comrs* [2005] STC (SCD) 782 (SpC 500), the issue arose as to the nature of the link required, for example, whether occupation or ownership between a property (in this case broiler houses) and the agricultural land or pasture to which the occupation of that property must be ancillary. It was held that the broiler houses would qualify only if they were occupied as an 'add on' to or as a subsidiary part of the purposes of a larger agricultural enterprise carried out on other land with which they were occupied.

Farmhouses (Limb 3)

[11.4] A farmhouse will only qualify as 'agricultural property' under IHTA 1984, s 115(2) if it is 'of a character appropriate' to the bare land or pasture owned and occupied by the householder. There is essentially a dual purpose test. First, the property must be a farmhouse and, secondly, it must be of a character appropriate to the property.

A farmhouse

[11.4A] There is no statutory definition of a farmhouse in the inheritance tax legislation. It is therefore not surprising that over the years there have been a number of cases dealing with farmhouses. In *Lindsay v CIR* (1953) 34 TC 289 it was described as 'a building used by the person running the farm'. In the later case of *CIR v John M Whiteford & Sons* (1962) 40 TC 379 the Court of Session accepted the Revenue's contention that *Lindsay* defined a farmhouse as a building used by the person running the farm. In *Korner v CIR* (1969) 45 TC 287 (HL) Lord UpJohn stated *obiter* that the question should be judged in accordance with 'ordinary ideas of what is appropriate in size, content and layout, taken in conjunction with the farm buildings and the particular area of farmland being farmed and not part of a rich man's considerable residence'. Since the case of *Starke* in 1995 there have been a number of cases relating to farmhouses which are discussed below. We have only included a very brief summary of the facts of the cases discussed.

In *Higginsons Executors v IRC* there was little evidence of any agricultural use having been made of the house, the Lodge, the status of which was at issue in the case. It was held that the Lodge was not a farmhouse but an attractive residential property surrounded by an estate.

In *Antrobus No 2*, the Lands Tribunal adopted a narrow construction of what may constitute a farmhouse. It said that 'a farmhouse . . . is the house of the person who lives in it in order to farm the land comprised in the farm and who farms the land on a day to day basis'. Although the Lands Tribunal's function is to value land rather than to determine taxation concepts, so that it is arguable that it exceeded its competence in this case, the Lands Tribunal's definition was adopted by the Special Commissioner in *Arnander (executors of McKenna, dec'd) v Revenue and Customs Comrs* [2006] STC (SCD) 800, [2007] RVR 208. The Special Commissioner made a useful review of the legal principles to be gleaned from the preceding line of cases on which she based her decision that the house was not a farmhouse within the meaning of s 115(2).

On the basis of decided cases it can be said that the property must be agricultural land or pasture land owned by the person who owns the cottages, farm buildings and farmhouses on which relief is claimed. The building must be used in conjunction with the agricultural land and pasture.

In the Revenue's revised guidance on the matter published in 2009 it is stated that:

> 'the occupant of a "farmhouse" must be a "farmer". In other words, the person farming the land on a day to day basis. Whether a person is actually a "farmer" of the land will depend on all the facts of a particular case. So a person with overall

control of an agricultural business is not necessarily a "farmer". The key factor is to identify if the occupant of the house has a significant role in the management, or actual operations, of the farming activity being carried out on the land involved. Conversely, it is not necessarily the case that a "farmer" of land is a person whose principal occupation consists of farming the land.

The test is therefore essentially a functional one. As the Special Commissioner in *Arnander (Executors of McKenna (dec'd)) v Revenue and Customs Comrs* [2006] STC (SCD) 800 pointed out, "the proper criterion is the purpose of the occupation". Since in that case the day to day farming was undertaken solely by contractors and a land agent was responsible for the management of the land, the deceased's residence was not a "farmhouse".

So you will need to investigate in detail exactly what the occupier of the residence was doing in the way of agricultural activity in the relevant period prior to the deceased's death to be able to determine whether their residence could properly be called a "farmhouse". You should be particularly careful in cases where the farmer had retired and let their land on grazing agreements'.

(Inheritance Tax Manual para 24036)

Where the executors claim agricultural property relief, the revised IHT Form 400 requires a considerable amount of information in respect of the day to day farming activities carried out on the farmland and of its use by the deceased.

What is clear from the above is that claims for relief made on the basis that management is conducted from the farmhouse, will be subject to close examination. It would be useful, therefore, to record all meetings, activities and decisions that are made at the farmhouse so that they can be used as evidence of the operations if required.

Character appropriate test

[11.4B] To fall within the definition of 'agricultural property', farmhouses, cottages and outbuildings must be 'of a character appropriate to the property'. 'The property' to which reference is made is not expressly stated in the legislation. The use of the definite article indicates that it should be property to which reference has been made previously in the subsection but the only previous use of the word 'property' is in the phrase 'agricultural property', which is the subject of the definition and which cannot therefore be the property referred to. On the basis of decided cases it can be said that the property must be agricultural land or pasture land owned by the person who owns the cottages, farm buildings and farmhouses on which relief is claimed. The building must be used in conjunction with the agricultural land and pasture. The property to which the farmhouse must be appropriate is the farmland and will not, for example, include land subject to fishing rights, industrial units or a farm shop selling bought-in produce (*Starke (Brown's Executors) v CIR* [1995] STC 689). There must be some connection or nexus between 'such cottages, farm buildings and farmhouses, together with the land occupied with them' and the property to which they must be of a character appropriate. The argument that the nexus must be derived from common ownership rather than common occupation was accepted by the Special Commissioner in *Rosser v IRC* [2003] STC (SCD) 311 (HMRC Inheritance Tax Manual, para 24051).

The question of whether a farmhouse is of a character appropriate to the agricultural land is one of fact and degree and any factor could be relevant. There has been a number of Special Commissioner's decisions which have applied various principles to determine whether a farmhouse is of an appropriate character. Whilst an extensive analysis of these cases is beyond the scope of this book, a brief narrative of the relevant cases follows.

The case of *Dixon v CIR* [2002] STC (SCD) 53 (SpC 297) concerned a cottage standing in 0.6 acres of ground comprised of a garden and an orchard. The case turned primarily on the question of whether the orchard and garden were agricultural land or pasture. The Commissioner found on the facts that it was not but went on to consider the question of whether '[i]f the land was agricultural the cottage was of a character appropriate to it'. The Commissioner quoted with approval the ninth supplement of McCutcheon on Inheritance Tax, para 14.72 as follows:

> The present position is that the "character test" is considered against three main tests:
>
> (1) the elephant test:
> although you cannot describe a farmhouse which satisfies the character test you will know it when you see it!
> This can hardly be said to be a principle at all-rather it is just a power of arbitrary decision.
>
> (2) man on the (rural) Clapham Omnibus:
> would the educated rural layman regard the property as a house with land or a farm?
> Again this can hardly be said to be a principle at all.
>
> (3) Historical dimension:
> how long has the house in question been associated with the agricultural property and is there a history of agricultural production?

In *Lloyds TSB (Personal representatives of Rosemary Antrobus dec'd) v CIR* [2002] STC (SCD) 468, Miss Antrobus had occupied and farmed Cookhill Priory for 59 years as a tenant and grazing licensee. The farmhouse was in a very poor state of repair. The land and buildings were agreed to be agricultural property with the exception of the Priory and two let properties. The Revenue argued that the Priory was not 'of a character appropriate' to the land owned by Miss Antrobus. In finding for the taxpayer, the Special Commissioners summarised the relevant principles for deciding the s 115(2) test as follows:

- Is the house appropriate, by reference to its size, content and layout, to the farm buildings and the particular area of farmland being farmed? In applying this principle two factors were relevant, namely the history of the property and comparison with other properties in the area.
- Is the house proportionate in size and nature to the requirements of the farming activities conducted on the agricultural land or pasture in question?

The relevant facts were the history of Miss Antrobus' personal involvement in the business (although it was not financially successful in her later years), together with the evidence that most farmers were making less profit than previously and financial information in respect of comparable farms.

- Although one cannot describe a farmhouse which satisfies the 'character appropriate' test, one knows one when one sees it.
- Would an educated rural layman regard the property as a house with land or as a farm?
- How long has the house in question been associated with the agricultural property? Was there a history of agricultural production?

In *Rosser v IRC* [2003] STC (SCD) 311, there was a farming partnership between the deceased and her husband, the assets of which included 41 acres of land, a house and a barn. In 1989, they gave 39 acres to their daughter, Mrs Rosser, who farmed the land. In 1990 she also farmed the 2 acres retained by the farming partnership. The partnership was dissolved in 1996 and the agricultural activities carried out in the house were the provision of refreshments to the farm workers and the storage of pesticides and tools. The barn was used for agricultural purposes in respect of the 2 acres. The Revenue argued that neither the house nor the barn were 'of a character appropriate' to the agricultural land. It was held that relief was available in respect of the barn but not the house. The house was not considered to be a farmhouse but rather a retirement home for the deceased and her husband.

The case of *Arnander (Executors of McKenna, dec'd) v Revenue and Customs Comrs* [2006] STC (SCD) 800, [2007] RVR 208, involved a Cornish estate consisting of a house with 6 acres of garden and domestic outbuildings ('the house') and land of 187 acres, the majority of which was farmland. It was purchased in 1945. The house was not associated with the farming activities from 1908 to 1984 when a tenant farmer surrendered his tenancy. At that time, Mr and Mrs McKenna entered into arrangements for an arable farming contract. A land agent was responsible for managing the land and dealings with the contractors. Meetings were held with Mr McKenna who prepared and maintained detailed records of the arrangements. After a period of ill health Mr and Mrs McKenna died within a short period of each other. The Special Commissioner said that the principles derived from the authorities were that a farmhouse was a dwelling for the farmer by whom the farm was managed. The farmer was the person who farmed it on a day-to-day basis and not the person who had overall control of the agricultural business. The purpose of the occupation of the property had to be considered. It was held that the house was not the main dwelling from which the agricultural operations over the land were conducted and managed. Although it was held that the house was not a farmhouse, the Special Commissioner did address the character appropriate issue on the hypothesis that the house was indeed a farmhouse. The Commissioner stated:

> In my view it is not appropriate to compile an exclusive list of relevant factors which are to be considered in deciding whether a farmhouse is of a character appropriate to the agricultural land. The question is one of fact and degree and any factor could be relevant. No one factor is determinative but relevant factors in this appeal are: the historical associations; the size, content and layout of the house; the farm outbuildings; the area being farmed and whether the house is proportionate to the value of the land being farmed; the view of the educated rural layman; and the relationship between the value of the house and the profitability of the land.

It would seem that the class of relevant factors is not closed and only some may be material in particular cases. It is of interest that the Special Commissioner accepted that profitability and the value of the house are both relevant. Of more concern was the fact that the Special Commissioner concluded that even if the house had been a farmhouse and of a character appropriate to the agricultural land or pasture, because the deceased was unable to engage in farming matters in the two years before death because of ill health it could not have been a farmhouse immediately before the deceased's death.

The Revenue state that a temporary cessation of activity due to ill health will not in itself prevent a residence being a farmhouse provided it 'can properly be considered as functionally remaining attached to the farm'. It is difficult to ascribe any clear meaning to this.

In *Atkinson v Revenue and Customs Comrs* [2010] UKFTT 108 (TC), [2010] SWTI 2123, Mr Atkinson's estate included farmland let on an agricultural tenancy to a family farming partnership of which Mr Atkinson was a partner. The farmland included a bungalow in which Mr Atkinson lived until he became ill in 2002 when, after a spell in hospital, he went into a care home. The other partners, his grandson and daughter-in-law attended the bungalow two to three days a week to collect post and deal with frost and to access the water supply. Mr Atkinson continued to be a partner until his death, took part in partnership discussions concerning the farm and returned to the bungalow occasionally which continued to house his possessions.

HMRC unsuccessfully contended that the building was not occupied by the deceased for the purposes of agriculture for the two years ending with Mr Atkinson's death as is required by IHTA 1984, s 117(a).

The Revenue's view

[11.4C] The Revenue has produced, in HMRC Inheritance Tax Manual, para 24051, a list of the main factors which in its view should be considered when determining whether a farmhouse is of a 'character appropriate'. These are:

'• Is the farmhouse appropriate when judged by ordinary ideas of what is appropriate in size, layout, content, and style and quality of construction in relation to the associated land and buildings?
- Is the farmhouse proportionate in size and nature to the requirements of the agricultural activities conducted on the agricultural land? You should bear in mind that different types of agricultural operation require different amounts of land. This is an aspect on which the VOA will be able to give advice.
- Within the agricultural land does the land predominate so that the farmhouse is ancillary to the land?
- Would a reasonable and informed person regard the property simply as a house with land or as a farmhouse?
- Applying the "elephant test", would you recognise this as a farmhouse if you saw it? Although this test involves some subjectivity it can be useful in ruling out extremes at either end of the scale.
- How long has the farmhouse and agricultural property been associated and is there a history of agricultural production? The matter has to be decided

on the facts that existed as at the date of death or transfer but evidence of the farmhouse having previously been occupied with a larger area of land may be relevant evidence.

- Considering the relationship between the value of the house and the profitability of the land, would the house attract demand from a commercial farmer who has to earn a living from the land, or is its value significantly out of proportion to the profitability of the land? If business accounts have been supplied, copies should be forwarded to the VOA. Business accounts can give a useful indication of the extent of the agricultural activity being carried on, although a loss making enterprise is not on its own considered to be a determinative factor.
- Considering all other relevant factors, including whether any land is let out and on what terms, is the scale of the agricultural operations in context?
- There must be some connection or nexus between "such cottages, farm buildings and farmhouses, together with the land occupied with them" and the property to which they must be of a character appropriate. The argument that the nexus must be derived from common ownership rather than common occupation was accepted by the Special Commissioner in *Rosser v Inland Revenue Commissioners* [2003] STC (SCD) 311.'

The manual goes on to say:

'For the purposes of Section 115(2) IHTA 1984 you should in particular note that property can include

- the deceased's/transferor's interest in an agricultural tenancy or farm business tenancy, even though the tenancy may be treated as of negligible value as an asset in the deceased's estate, and
- agricultural land or pasture owned by a company controlled by the deceased/transferor, or owned by a partnership of which the deceased/transferor was a partner.

You should be aware that for character appropriate (IHTM 24050) purposes land leased by the deceased may increase the likelihood of any farmhouse being within IHTA 1984 Section 115(2). But, it may work in the opposite direction regarding the occupation of the farmhouse for the purposes of agriculture (IHTM 24060) if the farming operations and management were being conducted by others from elsewhere.'

As can be seen from the above, it will be necessary to take care when advising clients on the availability of relief.

Contract farmers

[11.4D] Many landowners made use of share/contract farming agreements. The Revenue, relying on the decision in *Arnander*, take the view that the farmhouse must be occupied by a working farmer with the result that they will attempt to deny relief in respect of a house owned by a landowner who has entered into a contract farming agreement. The distinction between a person conducting the day to day operations of the farm and one who merely has overall control of the farm is not always an easy one to draw. It is important for individuals with such arrangements to keep contemporaneous records of meetings, telephone conversations and decisions to provide evidence to support a relief claim.

Farm cottages

[11.4E] A farm cottage is eligible for relief if it satisfies the following conditions:

(i) it is occupied for the purposes of agriculture; and
(ii) it is of a character appropriate to the agricultural land.

HMRC accept that relief is available on cottages occupied by persons employed solely for agricultural purposes in connection with the agricultural property concerned (HMRC Inheritance Tax Manual, para 24034).

Cottages occupied by retired farm workers (who have worked on the agricultural property concerned) or their widowed spouses or surviving civil partners are often also eligible for relief (Extra-Statutory Concession F16) provided certain conditions are satisfied. In HMRC Inheritance Tax Manual, para 24034, the Revenue state that the term 'retired' means someone who has ceased full-time work and is in receipt of a pension. It does not include a person who has simply quit one job to work elsewhere.

Relief at 100% is available for farm cottages where:

(a) The agricultural worker's occupation of the cottage was protected and the benefit of the 'transitional provisions' contained in IHTA 1984, s 116(2)(b) and s 116(3) are available to the transferor;
(b) The agricultural worker occupied the cottage under an unprotected service tenancy or assured shorthold tenancy;
(c) The worker's occupation arose under a tenancy which began after 31 August 1995.

In all other cases, the Revenue takes the view that the rate of relief will only be 50% (Revenue Inheritance Tax Manual, para 24034). This view is based upon the fact that under the Rent (Agriculture) Act 1976, the farmer does not have the right to actual unimpeded physical enjoyment of the farm worker's cottage.

Ownership and occupation

[11.4F] No relief is given unless either the agricultural property was:

(a) occupied by the transferor for the purposes of agriculture throughout the period of 2 years ending with the date of the transfer; or
(b) owned by the transferor throughout the period of 7 years ending with that date and was throughout that period occupied (by him or another) for the purposes of agriculture (IHTA 1984, s 117).

Agricultural property relief will also be available on agricultural property owned by trustees, whether or not an interest in possession subsists in the settled property. Where an interest in possession subsists in the settled property and is a privileged interest, the holder of the interest will be regarded as the 'transferor' of the property and also as the 'owner' of the property and if the trustee's interests carries the right of vacant possession, as having that right. In the case of a trust without a qualifying interest in possession, the trustees are the 'transferor' and the 'owner' of the property.

Occupation by a company which is controlled by the transferor is treated as occupation by the transferor; and occupation of any property by a Scottish partnership is treated as occupation of it by the partners (IHTA 1984, s 119).

'Control' of a company is defined by IHTA 1984, s 269 and means control of powers of voting on all questions affecting the company as a whole which, if exercised, would yield a majority of the votes capable of being exercised on them. When determining if a person has control, the votes attaching to any shares or securities which are 'related property' within the meaning of IHTA 1984, s 161 (broadly, property comprised in the estate of the transferor's spouse or civil partner or which is or has been owned by a charity or charitable trust because of a transfer made by the transferor's spouse or civil partner) are taken into account. The votes attaching to any shares or securities owned by the trustees of a settlement in which the transferor has a beneficial interest in possession will also be taken into account (IHTA 1984, s 269(2), (3)).

For the purposes of agricultural property relief it is possible for a person to inherit the periods of occupation or ownership of a deceased spouse or civil partner. If, for example, farmland passes to a farmer's widow, she can add to her period of occupation or ownership that of her husband's (IHTA 1984, s 120(1)(b)). In addition, where farmland is sold and replaced by other farmland, the successive periods of occupation or ownership of the two areas of land may, in certain circumstances, be treated as one to ascertain whether the minimum periods of occupation or ownership are satisfied (IHTA 1984, s 118).

Where there are two successive transfers of agricultural property, and the first transfer was eligible for the relief, or would have been so eligible if the relief had been available at the time, then the relief will be available in respect of the second transfer even if the transferor has not at the time satisfied the minimum ownership or occupation requirements provided:

(i) the transferor in relation to the second transfer (or his spouse or civil partner) acquired the property as a result of the first transfer;
(ii) at the time of the second transfer the property is occupied for the purposes of agriculture either by the second transferor (or his spouse or civil partner) or by the personal representatives of the transferor in relation to the earlier transfer; and
(iii) either the first transfer or the second transfer was made on the death of the transferor (IHTA 1984, s 121).

It should be remembered that the property must be occupied for agricultural purposes. The test of occupation is factual. HMRC has listed the situations in which it considers a property is occupied (HMRC Inheritance Tax Manual, para 24072). As we have seen, this can lead to difficulties where a farmer has fallen ill and has either left the property or somebody is running the business in his absence. It would seem that the Revenue accepts that relief may still be available in such circumstances but that such cases may be 'contentious and difficult to decide'. The Revenue will look at the facts of each cases including the 'desire on the part of the transferor to return' and how insurance and the community charge are dealt with (HMRC Inheritance Tax Manual, para 24083). It is therefore essential for complete records to be kept to support such a claim.

One asset or many?

[11.4G] When dealing with land, an issue which often arises is whether there is one asset or many. In the business property relief case of *Ninth Marquess of Hertford (Executors of Eighth Marquess of Hertford Deceased) v CIR* (see **10.2**), it was held that the land concerned was a single asset. It is understood that the Revenue considers that 'land can only be regarded as a single asset if it was acquired in one transaction and if acquired as one asset given the normal meaning of the word 'asset'. In particular, this has meant that a rural estate that is contiguous and acquired in one transaction will normally be regarded as a single asset. However, if the estate has been lotted for sale or divided into natural units for valuation purposes on death, then each lotted part will normally be regarded as a separate asset.

Unquoted shares

[11.4H] In addition to agricultural property, relief is also given in respect of shares of a company the assets of which include agricultural property where the value of the company's shares can be attributed to the agricultural value of that property (IHTA 1984, s 122(1)). However, the relief only applies if the transferor has control of the company immediately before the relevant transfer (IHTA 1984, s 122(2)). In order for the shares to qualify for the relief, the company must also fulfil the same ownership and occupation requirements of the land as an individual and, in addition, the transferor must have owned the shares for whichever of the 2 or 7-year minimum periods is appropriate (IHTA 1984, s 123(1)).

Rates of relief

[11.4I] Agricultural property relief operates to reduce the whole or part of the value transferred by a transfer of value which is attributable to the agricultural value of agricultural property. The reduction is either 100% or 50%. Relief at 100% is available where:

(a) The interest of the transferor in the property immediately before the transfer carried the right to vacant possession or the right to obtain it within the next 12 months. Extra statutory concession F17 extends the relief where the transferor's interest in the property immediately before the transfer either carried the right to vacant possession within 24 months of the date of the transfer because an unchallenged notice to quit had been served prior to the date of transfer. Relief is also available by concession where the transferor and the tenant are so closely connected that in practice the open market value of the property is broadly equivalent to its vacant possession value.

(b) The interest does not carry such a right to vacant possession because the property is let on a tenancy which began after 31 August 1995. Where a transfer of value occurs following the death of a tenant after 31 August 1995 but before a new tenancy has been formally granted to a successor who takes under a statutory provision, relief will be available. In addition, where a tenant has, prior to the transferor's death, given notice of his intention to retire in favour of a new tenant and the actual retirement takes place after the death but within 30 months after the notice was given, relief will also be available.

In all other cases the rate of relief is 50%.

As relief at 50% will only be available for pre-1 September 1995 tenancies one might consider creating a new tenancy through the doctrine of implied surrender and re-grant of the tenancy whilst protecting the tenant's security (see HMRC Inheritance Tax Manual, para 24143). However, one must consider the CGT and SDLT implications of such a transaction.

Where land is owned by one or more joint tenants or tenants in common, if the interests of all of them together carry that right each interest is taken to carry a right to vacant possession (IHTA 1984, s 116(6)). Accordingly, where land is owned by a farming partnership, the relief will apply to the value transferred by any transfer of a partnership interest so far as its value is attributable to the agricultural property. Where land is owned outside the farming partnership but occupied by the partnership on licence but with no partnership agreement or other documentation detailing the terms of occupation, it is understood that HMRC Inheritance Tax takes the view that 100% relief may not be available to the landowner. As such a partnership can usually only be terminated on the next accounting date following notice being given, this may take in excess of the 12-month period. HMRC Inheritance Tax argues that, until the partnership can be determined, the landowner does not have vacant possession. A counter argument to this is that, subject to any agreement to the contrary among the parties, under the Partnership Act 1890, s 26 retirement can be effected simply by notice. The partnership will be dissolved as soon as the notice is communicated to all the parties or, if later, on the date specified in the notice. In such cases, therefore, a document should be entered into confirming that the partnership can be dissolved and the landowner can recover his land within a period of less than 12 months. It is advisable in any event that the partnership agreement contains a clause entitling the owner partner to vacant possession within the 12-month period.

Where a farmer owns a farmhouse and, in partnership with his children, farms the land occupied with the farmhouse, the amount of land which will be taken into account for the purposes of the character appropriate test in IHTA 1984, s 115(2) will depend on the provisions in the partnership deed. If the farmer is only entitled to 20% of income and capital profits, it is understood that HMRC Inheritance Tax's view is that the farmer will only be entitled to agricultural property relief on 20% of the land occupied with the farmhouse, ie the amount of land which is commensurate with the farmer's partnership share. This point has to date been untested and does need clarification.

Where the relief is to be applied to the value of shares in a farming company which owns agricultural property, then the rate of relief will depend on the interest of the company itself (IHTA 1984, s 122(3)).

Working farmer's relief

[11.4J] There is one further case where the 100% relief is available. This is where the transferor has been beneficially entitled to his interest since before 10 March 1981 and:

(1) if the transferor had disposed of his interest by a transfer of value immediately before that date and had duly made a claim under the earlier agricultural property relief provisions contained in FA 1975, Sch

8, the value transferred would have been relieved in accordance with those provisions and would not have been limited by the restrictions then applying on transfers exceeding £250,000 in value or 1,000 acres; and

(2) the transferor's interest did not at any time during the period beginning with 10 March 1981 and ending with the date of the transfer carry a right to vacant possession or the right to obtain it within the next 12 months and it did not fail to carry this right by reason of any act or deliberate omission of the transferor during that period (IHTA 1984, s 116(2)(b), (3)).

Broadly, the old 'working farmer' relief applied where the transferor was in at least 5 of the 7 tax years preceding the year of the transfer wholly or mainly engaged in the UK in farming (either as a sole trader, a partner, an employee, a director of a farming company or a person undergoing full-time education) and the property was occupied by him for agricultural purposes and was so occupied throughout the 2 years immediately preceding the transfer (FA 1975, Sch 8 para 3).

The effect of these provisions, known historically as the 'transitional relief' or the 'double discount', enables tenanted farmland where the transferor would have qualified for the old relief in respect of a transfer made immediately before 10 March 1981, to qualify for 100% relief. Strangely, the transitional relief is not lost if the transfer would not have qualified for the old relief at any time after 9 March 1981. If, for example, an individual subsequently ceased to be a director of the family farming company the crucial time is the position immediately before 10 March 1981 and later events (apart from the requirement that the land remains tenanted) are irrelevant.

There are three important points to make about the continuing availability of transitional relief. The first is that it is vital to ensure that any tenancies in existence at 10 March 1981 are continued, to ensure that there is no question of the transferor's interest ever carrying the right to vacant possession, or the right to obtain it within 12 months. Secondly, apart from the case where the land passes on death to a surviving spouse or civil partner when the survivor may step into the deceased's shoes and preserve the relief (IHTA 1984, s 120(2)), the transitional relief will apply only to the first transfer of the relevant land after 9 March 1981. It is important, therefore, not to waste the relief by, for example, an inter vivos transfer of the land to a spouse or civil partner, when the transfer would be exempt in any event. Thirdly, the relief no longer applies once the cumulative transfers of agricultural property qualifying for the old relief, or in relation to post-9 March 1981 transfers qualifying for the transitional relief, exceed £250,000 in value or 1,000 acres.

Binding contract for sale

[11.4K] Agricultural property relief will be lost if the transferor has entered into a binding contract for sale prior to the transfer unless the sale is made for the purposes of reconstruction or amalgamation (IHTA 1984, s 124).

Business property relief

[11.5] In cases where both agricultural property relief and business property relief might be available, agricultural property relief takes precedence over business property relief (IHTA 1984, s 114(1)). Thus, for example, where there is a transfer of an interest in a partnership which owns agricultural property, the value of that partnership interest which is attributable to agricultural property will qualify for 100% agricultural property relief assuming the relevant conditions are met. The remaining value of the partnership interest will qualify for business property relief.

In a farming context, there will be some cases where business property relief is available where agricultural property relief is not. For example, where the agricultural land is situated outside the UK, the Channel Islands, the Isle of Man or a state which is an EEA state; or where the value of agricultural property exceeds its 'agricultural value' because it has some development or hope value. In such cases, business property relief will be capable of applying to the excess value. Business property relief may also be available in relation to assets of a farming business apart from the land, for example, farm machinery and stock. In *Farmer (Farmer's Executors) v CIR* [1999] STC (SCD) 321 (SpC 216) a farming partnership had carved out of its farming operations some buildings and land which had been let. In deciding whether or not business property relief was available the Special Commissioners decided that the matter must be looked at in the round. Regard must be had not just to the issue of profitability but also the turnover of the respective sides of the business, the market values of the underlying assets used in the trading and investment sides of the business, and the time spent on each side of the business. It was held that there was a single business and the let property was not excluded from relief.

It may be advantageous, therefore, to keep a single set of accounts for the whole business, including the farm, and to exercise unified management over the whole business.

However, where the rental income vastly outweighs the farming income, consideration should be given to restructuring the occupation of the buildings by using a limited liability partnership. An LLP for a fixed term where the owner of the buildings allow the partners to use them in return for a fixed profit share may in certain cases provide a result similar to the traditional excluded 1954 Act letting. The income will be income derived from a trade or business and business property relief will be available on the buildings.

As discussed in **CHAPTER 10 THE FAMILY BUSINESS**, business property relief is not available if the business is wholly or mainly one of dealing in land or buildings or making or holding investments. In *McCall and another (Personal representative of McClean, dec'd) v HMRC* [2009] NICA 12, [2009] STC 990, land was let under both conacre and agistment agreements. A letting in conacre is a temporary easement creating a licence to use the land. Agistment by contrast is a letting of land for grazing. The Northern Ireland Court of Appeal held that the business was one which consisted wholly or mainly of making investments. The activities carried on on behalf of the deceased, such as inspecting and repairing fences, weed control and finding tenants were all activities related to making the land available and related to the business of holding an investment. Care needs to be taken when advising on grazing agreements. Where possible, one should provide that some of the agricultural operations are carried out on the farm by the owner. In the case of grassland it may be sensible to have grazed livestock on the land before the agreement commences or for the owner to graze some of his own stock on the land in addition to the grazier's stock.

The conditions governing the availability of business property relief are considered in detail in **CHAPTER 10 THE FAMILY BUSINESS** at **10.2**.

Instalment option

[11.6] Where an inheritance tax liability payable by the donee, on death or in respect of a lifetime transfer, is attributable to property which qualifies for agricultural property relief, the tax can be paid by ten annual equal interest-free instalments (IHTA 1984, s 227 and IHTA 1984, s 234). The interest-free instalment option also applies to controlling shareholdings in a family farming company and in certain circumstances (considered in **CHAPTER 10 THE FAMILY BUSINESS** at **10.3**) to specific minority shareholdings in unquoted companies.

Lifetime exemptions

[11.7] A potentially exempt transfer is a transfer of any amount or value either to an individual or to certain types of settlement. It should be noted that different rules apply to gifts made before 22 March 2006. A transfer will escape inheritance tax completely provided the donor survives the gift by a period of 7 years (IHTA 1984, s 3A). If the transferor of a potentially exempt transfer dies within the 7-year period, inheritance tax may be payable. Where the tax is attributable to the value of agricultural property, agricultural property relief may be available to reduce the value transferred, provided certain conditions are met. These are:

(a) that the agricultural property is owned by the transferee throughout the period beginning with the date of the potentially exempt transfer and ending with the death of the transferor (or if earlier the death of the transferee). The property must not at the date of death be subject to a binding contract for sale;
(b) that the property has been occupied (by the transferee or another) for the purposes of agriculture throughout this period; and
(c) where the agricultural property consists of shares in or securities of a company, throughout the relevant period the land was owned by the company and occupied (by the company or another) for the purposes of agriculture (IHTA 1984, s 124A).

There are provisions extending the availability of the relief, subject to certain conditions, where the original agricultural property is transferred by the transferee to a company in return for an issue of shares in that company (IHTA 1984, s 124A(6)(b)), although there is some doubt as to whether s 124A(6)(b) is effective to achieve its purpose. Where the transferee sells the property and replaces it with other agricultural property which is occupied for agricultural purposes throughout the relevant period (IHTA 1984, s 124B) the relief will be extended. It appears, however, that the replacement property provisions contained in s 124B will only operate where the transferee sells land and buys more land (HMRC Inheritance Tax Manual, para 24181). They will not apply where the transferee either sells land and instead buys shares in a land-owning company; or sells shares in a land-owning company and buys land; or sells shares in a land-owning company and buys further shares (IHTA 1984, s 124A(6)).

An even more extraordinary quirk of ss 124A and 124B is apparent where a transferor transfers farmland into a discretionary trust under which his son will become entitled to the settled property absolutely. If the transferor dies within seven years of the transfer and his son has not acquired an absolute interest, then (assuming all the conditions are met) agricultural property relief can apply to relieve the value transferred providing all the conditions are met. If, however, the son has acquired an absolute interest, then s 124A cannot apply in any circumstances because, on the son acquiring an absolute interest, the trustees of the settlement (who will be the 'transferees' for the purposes of the section) will cease to 'own' the original property and therefore the condition contained in (*a*) above cannot be satisfied. This should be borne in mind when considering the amount of any insurance cover on the life of the donor.

Gifts with reservation

[11.8] The gifts with reservation provisions contained in FA 1986, ss 102–102C and FA 1986, Sch 20 operate where either the donee does not *bona fide* assume the possession and enjoyment of the property given more than seven years before the donor's death or at any time within the seven years preceding the donor's death the property is not enjoyed to the entire exclusion, or virtually to the entire exclusion, of the donor and of any benefit to him by contract or otherwise. They are designed to nullify the inheritance tax effects of a gift of property where the donor continues to enjoy or benefit from the donated property or receives any other form of collateral benefit which is in some way referable to the original gift. For example, the provisions would nullify the effect of a gift by a farmer of his farm to his son if the donor continues to occupy the property or enjoy any benefits from it. In addition, an income tax charge may arise on the donor of a gift of property where he has retained a right to use or enjoy the asset given away and which is not subject to the gifts with reservation rules. The income tax charge will affect past arrangements as well as those made after 6 April 2005. These provisions are considered further in **Chapter 2 Lifetime Planning**. The provisions also have a considerable impact in relation to farming partnerships and this is considered in some detail in **Chapter 10 The Family Business** at **10.21**.

Currently, occupation by the donor of land which he has given away is disregarded for the purposes of the reservation of benefit provisions if he provides full consideration in money or money's worth (for example, if he pays a rack rent under a tenancy (FA 1986, Sch 20 para 6(1)(a)). This exemption also applies where a donor gives away an undivided share in land which is then occupied jointly by the donor, provided the donor does not receive any benefit, other than a negligible one, which is provided by or at the expense of the donee for some reason connected with the gift (FA 1986, s 102B(4)). Such arrangements should be reviewed in the light of the income tax charge on pre-owned assets. Provided that, in the above example, the donor of the land pays a full market rent for the property, in accordance with the provisions set out in Finance Act 2004, Sch 15 para 4, there should be no benefit on which the income tax charge will arise.

Agricultural property relief at 100% will often protect against the effects of the gifts with reservation provisions as is illustrated by the example given in HMRC Inheritance Tax Manual, para 24205.

Example

> In 1980 A purchases a farm and occupies it. In May 1990 he gives it to his son B. But A continues in occupation rent-free until his death in December 1992 (without infringing B's right to vacant possession).
>
> This is a GWR. The farm qualifies for relief at the date of gift. Although B has neither owned the property for seven years nor occupied it for agricultural purposes for two years ending with the date of the notional transfer by B on A's death, relief is available at the higher rate (100%) because B can count A's occupation as his own.

A farmer can now make the ultimate reservation of benefit (ie retaining the property until death rather than giving it away) and still have the property wholly exempt from tax. Nevertheless, the provisions must still be considered in planning for tenanted land let pre-1 September 1995 and other situations where a gift should be made for reasons which are not concerned with taxation.

Grant of tenancies of agricultural property

[11.9] The grant of a tenancy of agricultural property in the UK, the Channel Islands or the Isle of Man for agricultural purposes is not a transfer of value for inheritance tax purposes by the grantor if he makes the grant for full consideration in money or money's worth (IHTA 1984, s 16). This provision is, however, applied strictly.

To ensure in a family context that any grant of an agricultural tenancy is for full consideration in money or money's worth, the initial rent for the tenancy should be that which would be obtainable on a grant of the tenancy in the open market. To ensure that such a value is achieved between the parties, independent valuers should act both for the grantor and the grantee.

In determining whether there is full consideration, one needs to take account of all the surrounding circumstances, such as the terms of the tenancy and the personal circumstances of the tenant. It is assumed that full consideration requires the rent payable under the tenancy to be the 'open market rent', ie the rent which would be expected to be achieved on the grant by a willing grantor to a willing grantee of the tenancy in the open market (on its particular terms) of the land in question. In determining the open market rent, one would place greater weight on evidence of 'tender rents' in the area (ie the rent which would be expected to be achieved by an owner inviting tenders for the grant of a new tenancy) rather than local 'arbitration rents' (ie the new rent determined on a three-yearly rent review of an existing tenancy).

Capital gains tax

[11.10] Where a farm has been in a family for generations and is likely to remain the only or main source of livelihood for succeeding generations, capital gains tax is likely to have minimal impact because the land is unlikely to be sold.

A gift of farmland or a farming business will be subject to capital gains tax at 18% on any chargeable gains arising. The gain arising on a gift to a family member may be held over under TCGA 1992, s 165 or 260. Hold-over relief will defer the chargeable gain until a subsequent disposal by the donee.

Hold-over relief is not available on disposals to settlor-interested trusts or trusts for which there subsists an arrangement under which the settlor will acquire an interest in the trust. There is a clawback period during which the held-over gain will become chargeable if the settlor acquires an interest in the trust or a later arrangement subsists for him to acquire such interest. This is dealt with in **CHAPTER 2 LIFETIME PLANNING**.

The farmer who wishes to raise funds by making some small sales from his holding can elect that the transfer should not be treated as a disposal for capital gains tax purposes (TCGA 1992, s 242). TCGA 1992, s 242 provides that an election can be made where there is a disposal of land forming part only of a holding, and the consideration for the sale does not exceed the lower of £20,000 and one-fifth of the market value of the holding prior to the sale. The consideration received will be taken into account on a subsequent disposal of the holding.

Where land has been purchased and subsequently part is resold, the gain arising on the disposal cannot be rolled over into the acquisition cost of the property still retained by the taxpayer (*Watton (Insp of Taxes) v Tippett* [1997] STC 893 (CA)).

In considering possible lifetime gifts of farmland where there is a likelihood that the land will one day be sold (eg following the death of the present owner/occupier), the loss of the capital gains tax free base uplift available on death (TCGA 1992, s 62) should not be overlooked and should be weighed against the potential inheritance tax saving on the death. This is of even greater importance if agricultural property relief is available. Where the land will qualify for 100% inheritance tax agricultural property relief on the death, any liability to capital gains tax will amount to an additional charge to tax as the property could have been retained until death at no inheritance tax cost and the capital gains tax free base uplift obtained. The impact and interaction of these provisions is considered in more detail in **CHAPTER 2 LIFETIME PLANNING** at **2.30**.

Reference should also be made to **CHAPTER 2 LIFETIME PLANNING** at **2.28** and **CHAPTER 10 THE FAMILY BUSINESS** at **10.4** for a more detailed discussion of the workings of TCGA 1992, s 165.

Structure of the business

[11.11] The comparative advantages and disadvantages of an incorporated and an unincorporated business have been considered in **CHAPTER 10 THE FAMILY BUSINESS**. In the context of a farming business, the corporate advantage of limited liability is less likely to be a significant consideration and, in any event, may now be obtained through a limited liability partnership. One must, however, consider the rate of corporation tax payable by a company and the rate of income tax payable by an individual, either as a sole trader or through a partnership. In the average farming family, the ability to spread the farming assets around the family by transfers of small blocks of shares is probably of more theoretical than practical benefit. The principal disadvantage of a company, however, namely the potential double liability to a capital gains charge, will not be a significant consideration if the land a company owns is unlikely ever to be sold. As always, it is important when structuring a business to aim for as flexible a structure as possible, which will enable both lifetime gifts to be made, but which will also minimise the tax payable on death.

In relation to companies and partnerships, the most difficult question to resolve is exactly what to do about the land. Should it be owned by the partnership or the company; or should it be retained outside the farming vehicles? If so, should it be tenanted or not? With the sole proprietor of an unincorporated business, these questions do not arise.

Tenanted or untenanted?

[11.12] Agricultural property relief is available at 100% in respect of vacant possession land, land let on a tenancy commencing after 31 August 1995 and certain succession tenancies providing all the normal criteria are met. This effectively removes inheritance tax from the decision making process where new structures are being contemplated.

However, a tenancy has other implications which can be disadvantageous. One (which is alleviated to some degree by the Agricultural Tenancies Act 1995) is its lack of flexibility, but the principal one is the fact that it will give rise to rental payments. The payment of a rack rent may cause cash flow problems for the company or partnership paying it. The payment of rent under a tenancy will convert earned income into unearned income.

Rental income can always be waived by a deed before its due date for payment. However, to avoid the application of the associated operations rules in IHTA 1984, s 268, the waiver should not be made within three years of the grant of the tenancy. Such waivers can themselves constitute transfers of value, but if done on a regular basis, it is possible to argue that the normal expenditure out of income exemption applies to avoid any liability to inheritance tax. This is equivalent to the provisions in IHTA 1984, s 15 which provide that waivers of dividends do not by reason of the waiver constitute a transfer of value.

It should be remembered that an agricultural tenancy may have a capital value which is important in valuing an interest in a partnership, or shares in a company, which owns a tenancy. To date, the question has been debated in relation to tenancies protected under the Agricultural Holdings Act 1986 and the following discussion relates specifically to such tenancies. With regard to farm business tenancies under the Agricultural Tenancies Act 1995, the position will depend on the degree of security of tenure given to the tenant under the terms of the lease and its length although it seems likely that, in practice, it will be difficult to ascribe any significant capital value to most tenancies dealt with under the 1995 Act.

At one end of the spectrum it has been suggested that an agricultural tenancy has no value and at the other that a tenancy may have a value somewhere in the region of one half of the difference between the vacant possession value and the tenanted value of the land (on the basis that this is what a landlord might be prepared to pay to obtain vacant possession of his farm). The truth probably lies somewhere between these two extremes. Even if an agricultural tenancy may be expressly non-assignable, this does not prevent a hypothetical sale of the tenancy being assumed for valuation purposes, although in valuing the tenancy account must be taken of the fact that the hypothetical purchaser would be in the same position as the hypothetical vendor and accordingly unable to assign the tenancy (*CIR v Crossman* [1939] AC 26). This factor may mean that the tenancy in question has a very low value because no tenant is likely to pay much in the way of a capital sum for an asset which he himself cannot realise and which commits him to paying a rack rent.

Two general approaches have developed to the valuation of these tenancies. *Baird's Executors v CIR* (1990) SVC 188 (Lands Tribunal) puts the emphasis on the vacant possession premium. If land subject to a tenancy is worth less than if it were vacant, that difference in value could be unlocked by the merging of the two interests. The valuation of this purchase would be based on the division of the vacant possession premium reflecting the balance between the two parties which is often assumed to be equal. The Baird approach would apply where it is shown that there is a special purchaser for the tenancy.

In the case of *Walton (Walton's Executor) v CIR* [1996] STC 68 (CA) it was held that a tenancy will not automatically be valued on the basis of a percentage of the freehold value on the assumption that the freeholder will always be a special purchaser. The sale has to take place 'in the real world' and the actual persons in addition to the actual property need to be taken into consideration. This reflects the value of the tenancy compared with other tenancies of its kind. It is based on an appraisal of profit rent which compares the current rent, the rent potentially due at the next review and a rent where the land is newly let. The case of *Greenbank v Pickles* [2002] All ER D 1479 appears to confirm the *Walton* basis in the absence of a special purchaser of the tenancy.

It is therefore essential to determine whether there are or were any special purchasers at the date of valuation. This will usually be the landlord.

Where the current rental under the tenancy is less than the open market rent and the next review date is in a couple of years, this may give some value to the tenancy. Another factor to be taken into account is the event which requires the value of the tenancy to be calculated. Under the 'hypothetical sale' procedure, the hypothetical purchaser is placed in exactly the same position as that occupied by the vendor. If the time of valuation is the death of the vendor, the hypothetical purchaser would pay nothing for the tenancy on the basis that the landlord would be in a position to serve an incontestable notice to quit on the deceased tenant's personal representatives (Agricultural Holdings Act 1986, Sch 3 Pt I Case G). On the other hand, where the tenancy is not vested solely in the deceased, for example, where it is owned by a partnership, the tenancy could have a value as it could continue until the death of the last of the joint owners.

Farming business carried on by a company

[11.13] If the farmland is owned by a company, then its shares will qualify for 100% agricultural property relief to the extent that their value is attributable to the farmland, provided the transferor of the shares controls the company. The remaining value of the shares should qualify for business property relief if the farmland is not let. A minority holding will qualify for 100% business property relief but not agricultural property relief because the transferor will not control the company. On the valuation of a minority holding a significant discount will, of course, be achievable on the net asset value of the company.

If farmland is let to a company under a tenancy, then the freehold reversion will qualify for 50% agricultural property relief if the tenancy was entered into before 1 September 1995 and 100% relief if entered into or succeeded to after 31 August 1995. Where the company is wholly owned by the landowner, or is at least controlled by him, the Revenue argues that the 100% or controlling shareholding together with the freehold reversion to the land will have an aggregate value approaching the land's vacant possession value. An open market purchaser would be prepared to pay such a sum, so the argument goes, because of his ability either to liquidate the company and merge the tenancy with the reversion (this assumes a 100% holding), or to compel the company to surrender the tenancy, thereby securing vacant possession.

The argument has some force, but whether an open market purchaser would be prepared to pay anything like the vacant possession value must be doubtful and will depend upon the particular facts in each case. So if, in arriving at a value, one assumes that the land owner will exercise his control of the company to procure a surrender of the tenancy before the sale and the purchaser would pay a price recognising that he could do so after the sale, one would also have take into account the tax charge which might arise on the hypothetical surrender which is likely to be a distribution. Where the shareholding is less than 100%, one would take into account the fact that, to avoid prejudicing the minority interests, the landlord would have to purchase the tenancy from the company at its full surrender value with all the taxation and other costs that that would entail.

Even if the Revenue's argument is correct, where the land was let prior to 1 September 1995 the land will nevertheless only qualify for the 50% relief because of the existence of the tenancy.

In the case of a company owning a tenancy of agricultural property which it farms, the shares will qualify for business property relief at 100%. As we have seen, the tenancy itself may have some value within the company, and probably the shares themselves, if a majority holding, will have an even greater value than that reflected by the value of the tenancy alone, since the company has perpetual existence and since the tenancy, even if non-assignable, becomes *de facto* assignable through a transfer of the shares which are not so restricted.

It can be seen that the letting of farmland to a company with the owner retaining the freehold reversion will give rise to an unnecessary exposure to inheritance tax where the land is let on a tenancy which commenced prior to 1 September 1995 and where no succession has occurred since that date. The question arises as to whether such tenancies should be terminated with a new agreement being entered into which will enable the let land to benefit from the 100% relief.

The creation of a new farming company is likely to be an unattractive structure unless there are commercial reasons for creating a company. There are two situations where a company structure may be sensible. The first is where there is a large unrealised gain on a possible disposal of development land. The whole business, including the land, could be transferred to a company in consideration of shares. Under TCGA 1992, s 162 the gain would be rolled over into the shares of the company. Therefore, the company would acquire the assets at market value at the date of the transfer. The company could then sell the land soon after, thus realising an insignificant gain. Like everything, there are disadvantages. The first being that the gain rolled over crystallises when the shares are sold although, if the shares are held until death, there will be the free capital gains tax uplift on death. In addition, an SDLT charge would arise on the transfer of the land to a connected company at a rate of up to 4%.

A company may also be used to take advantage of the larger tax deduction for contributions made to an approved company pension scheme for directors and employees.

Farming business carried on by partnership

[11.14] As in the case of a company, a partnership or limited liability partnership carrying on the farming business may either own the land on which that business is carried on or occupy it either under an agricultural tenancy or under a gratuitous licence.

Where the partnership owns the land, the partners' interests in the partnership, to the extent that their value is attributable to the value of the land, will qualify for 100% agricultural property relief, with the balance of the value qualifying for 100% business property relief.

Where the partnership occupies the farmland under a tenancy, 50% agricultural property relief will be available if the tenancy was entered into before 1 September 1995 and 100% relief will be available if entered into or succeeded to after 31 August 1995. Business property relief at 100% will be available in respect of the partnership interests of the partners and depending upon the terms of the partnership the value (if any) of the tenancy may be taken into account.

Where the land is let to a partnership and the freeholder is himself a major partner, the freehold reversion and partnership share is treated as a single unit of property for the purposes of valuation (see *Fox's (Lady) Executors v CIR*

[1994] STC 360 (CA)). The effect is to remove the majority of the discount normally applicable to tenanted land. In *Walton (Walton's Executor) v CIR* [1996] STC 68 (CA) no allowance or discount was made in calculating the deceased partner's interest. This basis appears to have been confirmed in *Greenbank v Pickles* [2000] All ER D 1479.

Where a farmer owns a farmhouse and, in partnership with his children, farms the land occupied with the farmhouse, the amount of land which will be taken into account for the purposes of the character appropriate test in IHTA 1984, s 115(2) will depend on the provisions in the partnership deed. If the farmer is only entitled to 30% of income and capital profits, HMRC's view is that the farmer will only be entitled to agricultural property relief on 30% of the land occupied with the farmhouse, ie the amount of land which is commensurate with the farmer's partnership share. This point has yet to be tested.

Where an Agricultural Holdings Act 1986 protected tenancy is already in existence see the comments above in relation to a farming business carried on by a company with regard to the possibilities of terminating the existing arrangements and entering into new ones.

Milk quotas

[11.15] A milk quota is the specific quantity of milk which a farmer can produce without creating a liability to pay a levy for over-production. The quota can be a very valuable asset to the farmer.

Capital gains tax

[11.16] The quota is treated as a separate asset (*Cottle v Coldicott* [1995] STD (SCD) 239 (SpC 40)). On the sale of quota a capital gains tax liability will arise. It was argued unsuccessfully in the case of *Foxton v Revenue and Customs Comrs* [2005] STC (SCD) 661 (SpC 485) that a milk quota fell within the definition of land in the Interpretation Act 1978 and therefore the disposal of the quota was a part disposal. Where quota is acquired by allocation there will be a nil base cost. No deduction will be given for any part of the historic cost or March 1982 value of the land. Where quota is acquired by purchase, an allowable acquisition cost will be available to reduce any capital gains.

Where a farming business is carried on in partnership, milk quota may be registered in the name of the partnership firm and treated as a partnership asset. Any gain arising on the disposal of quota will therefore be allocated amongst the partners in the usual manner.

As mentioned above the disposal proceeds in some cases may represent the capital gain arising and a significant tax liability could arise.

Compensation payments for permanent cuts in milk quotas are capital sums derived from an asset which give rise to a deemed disposal under TCGA 1992, s 22(1)(a), (2). This is taxable in the year of receipt.

Inheritance tax

[11.17] In general, milk quota should be treated as an asset distinct from the land. However, where an owner uses his land for a dairy farm, the Revenue states that the quota should be valued as part of the land and agricultural property relief will be available on the 'full combined value if the land itself qualifies for relief' (HMRC Inheritance Tax Manual, para 24250). Of course, business property relief is likely to be available in the alternative providing the relevant conditions are satisfied (HMRC Inheritance Tax Manual, para 24250).

Single farm payments

[11.18] The Single Payment Scheme was introduced to replace a number of direct aid schemes. Direct payments to farmers are no longer linked to production but relate to area and historical entitlement of the land. It now means that a farmer can cease to produce agricultural products together and still receive financial support. In order to receive the full single payment, landowners must comply with a series of standards. Failure to comply can result in penalties being imposed. Landowners have had to establish entitlement which will allow them to receive payment on an annual basis provided certain conditions are satisfied. The payment entitlement ('PE') can be traded in the same way that milk quotas can be traded.

Capital gains tax

[11.19] A PE is a chargeable asset for capital gain tax purposes (Revenue Tax Bulletin June 2005). Any gains arising from transactions in PEs will be chargeable to capital gains tax following the normal capital gains tax rules. A PE is not linked to a particular parcel of land and therefore does not form part of the land for capital gains tax purposes. As it is a separate asset that was not derived from any pre-existing asset, its base cost is nil in relation to an originating statutory claimant. The Revenue view is that in relation to an originating statutory claimant, PE came into existence on 1 January 2005. It has said that a PE is not a wasting asset within TCGA 1992. Whether a PE is a business asset for capital gains tax purposes will depend on the facts of each case. Broadly, if the income from a PE is charged to income tax as the profits of a trade under ITTOIA 2005, s 9 or s 10 then a PE is likely to be a business asset for capital gains tax purposes.

Inheritance tax

[11.20] Transfers of a PE are liable to inheritance tax like the transfer of any other asset.

As a PE is an asset separate from the land in relation to which it is granted, it cannot qualify for agricultural property relief. It may however, qualify for business property relief provided it is an asset of a trading business which satisfies the normal conditions for the relief. Revenue Tax Bulletin June 2005 states that "the transfer of PE by someone who is not carrying on a trading business will not qualify for business property relief". Similarly, the transfer of a PE as an individual asset, rather than the transfer of a business or an interest in the business one of the assets of which is a PE, will not qualify for business property relief. For the Revenue's view of the tax treatment of single farm payments see www.hmrc.gov.uk/bulletins/tb-se-june05.pdf.

A claim for a single farm payment can only be made by a person with a PE who owns a farm business registered with the Department of Agricultural and Rural Development so it is important that one does not bequeath the PE to a person who will not be the owner of a registered farm business.

Example

> Giles has two children, Sam and Katie. Sam helps his father with the day-to-day running of the farm whilst Katie is a civil servant. Under the terms of his will Giles leaves the farm to Sam and the residue to Katie. Sam will receive the farm and the PE will pass to Katie as part of the residue but she will be unable to claim it as she has no registered farm business.
>
> Giles should therefore change his will to ensure the PE passes with the land to Sam.

Strategies for the farmer

[11.21] We examine below a selection of estate planning strategies for the farmer and his family. No single strategy is necessarily the best one. Each case must be considered separately taking into account the circumstances of the family, the nature of the farming business and the personalities involved.

Doing nothing

[11.22] Doing nothing is a strategy that has appealed to many farmers over the years because they are often by nature conservative. Due to agricultural property relief being available at 100% for untenanted land and for land let on tenancies commencing after 31 August 1995, the vast majority of working farmers can now retain their land until death and obtain complete exemption from inheritance tax on its value. Any unrealised capital gain inherent in the value of the land will also be washed out on death, thus achieving the optimum result in respect of both taxes.

Whilst a policy of doing nothing will now be the most effective policy for most farmers, that will not be the case for all. For example, practical circumstances may require the property to be passed down to the next generation prior to death or there may be a pre-1 September 1995 tenancy which does not qualify for 100% relief.

Where action is required by a working farmer, this breaks down into two categories, action on retirement and action before retirement.

Action before retirement

[11.23] Where a farmer has one or more children who wish to come into the business, then he should consider bringing them into partnership. Farmers have in the past brought their wives into partnership or made them shareholders of a family company in order to transfer taxable income to their wives. The Revenue tried unsuccessfully to apply the settlement provisions to husband and wife partnerships and company arrangements in circumstances in which it considered that the assets transferred were being used as a vehicle for diverting income from one spouse to the other (see *Jones v Garnett*). If the provisions had applied, they would have deemed the partnership concerned to be a settlement and the settlement income to be that of the 'settlor'; the settlor for these purposes being the spouse (normally the husband) who was the original farmer of the land.

It will usually be best to keep land outside a family farming partnership. For the taxation consequences of so doing, see the previous discussion under **11.14** above. If one does wish to bring the land into the partnership one would normally do so by transferring it into the joint names of the partners. The farmer may decide to credit his capital account in the partnership with the full value of the land brought in by him, and in this case he may also wish to perform a 'value freezing' exercise by incorporating automatic accruer provisions in the partnership, under which any surplus value in the land will pass to his children on his death or retirement from the partnership, or by providing that any realised or unrealised capital profits attributable to the land shall belong only to them. Alternatively, he may decide to share the land immediately with his children either by crediting both his and their capital accounts equally with the full value of the land or by specifying in the partnership deed how the land is to be beneficially owned. The gifts with reservation rules will not apply if the profits are shared in the proportions in which the partners own the partnership assets at commencement (HMRC Inheritance Tax Manual para 14332). It is often the case that older family partners transfer assets into a partnership on the understanding that the younger partners will devote more time to the business. It is argued that such transfers are not intended to confer a gratuitous benefit and are such as might be expected to be made in a transaction at arm's length between persons not connected with each other and are therefore not a transfer of value by virtue of IHTA 1984, s 10. It would seem that, if a transfer satisfies the second arm of the s 10 test, the income tax settlement provisions will also not apply. However, if the donor receives profits from the partnership in excess of his share of the land, the gift with reservation rules will apply. No income tax charge on pre-owned assets will arise in this situation because of the application of the gift with reservation rules.

Even if the untenanted land is brought back into the estate of the donor, it may still qualify for 100% relief on death. However, it is dangerous to rely on this as it is necessary for certain criteria to be met at that stage. To avoid a gift with reservation, the children might enter into the partnership on full commercial terms in order to ensure that there is no element of gift — although, in a family context this is often impractical.

As is considered in more detail in **Chapter 10 The Family Business** under **10.22**, the introduction of land into a partnership may give rise to a capital gains tax charge which cannot be held-over under TCGA 1992, s 165 to the extent that the landowner receives a credit for the land in his capital account.

Borrowings

[11.24] Any borrowings of a farming business secured on land qualifying for inheritance tax agricultural property relief should be restructured and secured on property which does not qualify for any form of relief. This is because the existence of the borrowings will be taken into account when valuing the relevant property *before* the application of the relief. Thus, the deduction of the borrowing will be wasted because it would reduce a value which would otherwise be reduced by agricultural property relief. In addition, it is essential that the donee does not assume any liability or give any indemnities to the donor as otherwise a reservation of benefit issue may arise. Therefore, the opportunity should be taken to restructure any borrowings before the death of the landowner.

The problem with outstanding debts which reduce the value of property qualifying for agricultural property relief is well illustrated by the case of a tenant farmer buying the freehold reversion from his landlord. If the tenant dies between the date of the contract of sale and its completion, the outstanding purchase price will constitute a lien on the property purchased and accordingly reduce its value before agricultural property relief is applied.

Action on retirement

[11.25] On his retirement, the retiring farmer may be prepared to give away his farming business, including the land, to those of his children who wish to continue the business. They may, in fact, already be farming in partnership with their father and the land may either be an asset of the partnership or may still be owned by the father, with the partnership occupying under a tenancy or a gratuitous licence. Such a gift of the farming business and the land should be structured as a potentially exempt transfer, with the father's life being insured for the seven year period to the extent that the gift does not qualify for 100% relief.

Entrepreneurs' Relief may be available to reduce the capital gains tax payable on any gift provided certain conditions are satisfied (see **10.5**). In addition, an election may be made under TCGA 1992, s 165 to hold-over the balance of chargeable gains arising on the gift. Where a substantial gain will arise, the gift should be considered very carefully as retention by the donor until death will result in the gain being washed out as described above.

A gift 'on retirement' should ideally be made just before retirement to ensure that the farmer will have occupied the property for the purposes of agriculture for the two years prior to the gift. Otherwise, agricultural property relief may be lost unless the seven year ownership test can be satisfied.

Whilst the retiring farmer may be prepared to give up the farmland and his share of the business to the next generation, he may be reluctant to move out of the farmhouse in which he may well have lived for almost all his life. If the farmhouse remains in the ownership of the farmer, then on his death the Revenue is likely to refuse agricultural property relief on it, on the grounds that it was no longer occupied for agricultural purposes (*Starke (Brown's Executors) v CIR* [1995] STC 689, [1996] 1 All ER 622).

HMRC Inheritance Tax has indicated that, in the situation where a farmer falls ill and is unable to continue to farm, IHTA 1984, s 117 may be satisfied but the stated intentions of the owner need to be tested against the evidence (HMRC Inheritance Tax Manual, para 24083).

Where the retiring farmer wishes to exercise sporting rights over the land he should ensure that he pays a full commercial rent for doing so, so as to bring himself within the exemption provided by FA 1986, Sch 20 para 6(1)(a).

The 'two sons' problem

[11.26] It is a common problem that, although a farmer wishes all of his children to benefit equally from his estate, only one or some of them may wish to be involved in farming the family farm. For example, consider a farmer who has two sons, one of whom wishes to take over the business (and the land) and the other of whom does not, as he wishes to pursue his own career. To carry on the business, however, the farming son may require all of the land. In many cases this will mean that the bulk of the inheritance will have to pass to the farming son. How may the other son be compensated?

Sadly, there is no general solution to the problem. Possibly, the two sons could inherit the freehold of the land, with the farming son taking a rack rent tenancy. This would enable the non-farming son to derive an income from the land and would at the same time give him a share in the capital asset. The payment of rent, however, may place an intolerable burden on the business of the farming son.

Alternatively, the two sons could inherit the land jointly and farm it together in partnership. The non-farming son could be a sleeping or limited partner with a small profit share, to give him an income from the property. This may be a more satisfactory solution than a tenancy, but does make the farming son vulnerable to an attempt by the non-farming son to use his rights as co-owner to force a sale of the land and, in effect, put an end to the farming business. Under the Trusts of Land and Appointment of Trustees Act 1996, s 12, a tenant in common does not have an automatic right to enforce a sale but he can apply to the court which has a discretionary power to do so.

Another possibility would be for the parents to leave the non-farming son a legacy charged on the farmland which is to be paid only on the death of the other son or on a sale of the land, if earlier. In practice, such a legacy may be of limited value to the non-farming son because of its deferred payment, although it does enable him to benefit from the land if it is ever sold.

Perhaps, ultimately, farming parents who find themselves in this position should grasp the nettle and ensure that the farming son alone inherits the farming business and the land (including the entitlement to the single farm payment (see **11.20** above)). At the same time, they should endeavour to compensate the non-farming son on their deaths out of their other property and concentrate on building up funds for the benefit of the non-farming son during their lifetimes. These funds could either be left to him on their death or made over to him from time to time during their lifetimes by the appropriate use of the lifetime exemptions. The taking out of a regular premium with profits or unit-linked whole life policy settled in trust for the non-farming son would be one way of achieving this objective.

Death

[11.27] Where a farmer dies leaving to his widow his farming business or land which is occupied at his death by either a farming partnership (which may include his widow and one or more of his children) or by a company (the shareholders of which may include his widow and children), the widow has a number of options. She may:

(a) retain the land and business in her estate with a view to it passing on her death to the next generation — in many circumstances agricultural property relief at 100% will be available on her death;

(b) decide to redirect the property to one or more of her children by way of a deed of variation effected within 2 years of the death — in this case the property would again pass reduced by agricultural property relief normally at 100%; or

(c) where relief at 100% is not available, decide to give the property to one or more of her children by way of a potentially exempt transfer in the hope that she will survive the 7-year period so that the gift will escape tax completely.

The right option will depend on the precise family circumstances in each case, and, of course, the availability of agricultural property relief.

Where an inheritance tax liability is anticipated on the death of the farmer or his widow, consideration should always be given to funding the tax by a whole life insurance policy written either on a single life or a joint life last survivor basis held in trust for the next generation.

Chapter 12

Woodlands

Income tax

[12.1] Income derived from the occupation of commercially managed woodlands in the UK is outside the scope of income tax (ITTOIA 2005, s 11). The occupation of commercial woodlands does not give rise to a trading profit or loss.

Since trees on commercially managed woodland are outside the scope of capital gains tax (TCGA 1992, s 250(1)), any profit arising from the sale of such trees is completely outside the scope of any charge to tax. As a corollary, the expenses of planting and managing such trees cannot create a deduction for income tax purposes.

However, income from the grant of an easement of, for example, shooting rights, may be assessable as profits of a property business. In addition, the profits of a separate trade carried on in conjunction with the occupation of the woodlands (for example, the production of finished timber goods) which goes beyond such basic activities as felling and sawing which are necessary to render raw timber marketable may be assessable as trading profits (*Christie v Davies* [1945] 1 All ER 370, (1945) 26 TC 398).

Short rotation coppice is treated for tax purposes as farming rather than forestry, so that land under such cultivation is farm or agricultural land and not woodlands (ITA 2007, s 996(3)) and is therefore assessable to income tax. Short rotation coppice is a perennial crop of tree species planted at high density, the stems of which are harvested above ground level at intervals of less than ten years. In *Jaggers (t/a Shide Trees) v Ellis* [1997] STC 1417 (ChD), 71 TC 164 it was held that the income from land planted with coniferous trees, intended to be sold as Christmas trees, were not within the exemption provided by ITTOIA 2005, s 11 since the land was not woodland as it was covered by trees resembling bushes rather than timber trees.

Capital gains tax

[12.2] TCGA 1992, s 250(1) provides that in the case of woodlands managed by the occupier on a commercial basis and with a view to the realisation of profits, the consideration for the disposal of trees from the woodlands is excluded from the capital gains tax computation on the disposal by the occupier. This exemption applies whether the trees are standing, felled or cut. Similarly, sums derived from an insurance policy effected in respect of the destruction of, or damage or injury to, the trees are also excluded. Section

250(3) provides that in this respect the provisions of s 22(1) dealing with disposals arising on the receipt of a capital sum are overridden. Section 250(4) and (5) stipulates that in computing the cost and the gain on the disposal of woodland, the cost or consideration, as the case may be, which is attributable to trees (which by virtue of s 250(6) includes saleable underwood) growing on the land is to be left out of account (Revenue Capital Gains Tax Manual CG73210).

If the woodland has been commercially managed then any consideration for the disposal of the trees alone (whether felled or standing) is excluded in computing any gain on the disposal provided the person making the disposal is the occupier. In any other case, each felled tree is treated as a single chattel and a chargeable gain will only arise if each tree has a value in excess of £6,000 (TCGA 1992, s 262). The provisions of TCGA 1992, s 262(4) regarding 'sets' do not apply to trees (Revenue Capital Gains Tax Manual CG73220).

Trees growing on woodland may be disposed of by the owner granting to another person the right to enter the woodland and fell the trees. If the trees are growing on commercial woodland, the exemption in TCGA 1992, s 250(1) will apply. If the trees are not growing on a commercial woodland, HMRC take the view that the capital gains tax consequences will depend on the precise nature of the right which is granted. If the person to whom the right is granted is not entitled to benefit from the future growth of the trees, that is if he must fell the trees within a short time, the owner of the woodlands is treated as disposing of the trees as individual chattels. If the person to whom the right is granted is entitled to benefit from the future growth of the trees, that is if he is granted the right to fell trees over a long period, then the owner is treated as having made a part disposal of his land (Revenue Capital Gains Tax Manual CG73221).

Woodland managed on a commercial basis is an asset used for the purposes of a trade within TCGA 1992, s 165 and therefore a gift of woodlands is capable of qualifying for hold-over relief under that section and for roll-over relief under TCGA 1992, s 158(1)(b).

Inheritance tax

[12.3] Woodlands managed on a commercial basis are eligible for business property relief at 100%. However, where the woodlands do not represent a business or an interest in a business in the hands of the transferor or do not qualify for another reason (eg they have been held for less than two years) the treatment for inheritance tax purposes will vary depending on whether the woodlands form part of an estate on death or are the subject matter of a lifetime gift. A useful decision flowchart can be found in the HMRC Inheritance Tax Manual, para 4372.

Relief on death

[12.4] Where part of the value of a person's estate immediately before his death is attributable to the value of land in the UK or another state which is an EEA state on which trees or underwood (which do not represent agricultural property) are growing, an election can be made to have the value of such trees or underwood excluded in determining the value of the estate on death for inheritance tax purposes (IHTA 1984, s 125). Prior to the 2009 Budget announcement, relief was only available in respect of land situated in the UK. The change followed a formal request by the European Commission to the UK to amend its legislation because the previous law was considered discriminatory. Short rotation coppice is treated as being agricultural property, however, so woodlands relief cannot be claimed in respect of the land on which the trees or underwood stand.

The election is made by the deceased's personal representatives or any other person who would otherwise be liable to pay the inheritance tax on the deceased's estate. The election must be made within two years of the death or such longer period as the Revenue may allow. Where the woodlands can be divided into clearly distinct geographical areas, the Revenue accepts that elections may be made in relation to one or more of the areas (HMRC Inheritance Tax Manual, para 4375).

To prevent exploitation of the relief by death-bed purchasers of woodlands, there is a condition that the deceased must either have been beneficially entitled to the land throughout the five years immediately preceding his death or have become beneficially entitled to the land otherwise than for a consideration in money or money's worth (ie by gift or devise).

The effect of a claim under IHTA 1984, s 125 is to reduce the overall inheritance tax bill on the estate. However, the election acts only to give a deferral of the tax that would otherwise have been charged rather than a total exemption.

The deferred inheritance tax will become chargeable on the first disposal of the trees or underwood in respect of which relief has been claimed (excepting a disposal to the transferor's spouse (IHTA 1984, s 126)), provided the disposal occurs before the land on which the trees or underwood stood again passes on someone's death. Thus, if the recipient of woodlands on another's death makes a gift of the trees or underwood or sells it during his lifetime, the inheritance tax charge deferred from the deceased's death will become chargeable. If, however, the recipient dies with the trees or underwood still forming part of his estate the inheritance tax charge deferred from the first deceased owner's death will fall out of charge, although the trees or underwood will form part of the second deceased owner's estate. Relief may again be claimed under s 125 in relation to the inheritance tax chargeable on his estate.

The inheritance tax charge which arises on the subsequent disposal depends on whether the disposal is a sale for full consideration in money or money's worth. If it is, the amount on which tax is calculated is the net proceeds of sale whether the disposal is of the trees and underwood or of an interest therein. If the disposal is not such a sale, the amount on which tax is calculated is the net value at the time of disposal of the trees or underwood (IHTA 1984, s 126). The amount on which tax is charged is then added to the deceased's cumulative total, which for these purposes includes all the property in respect of which inheritance tax was chargeable on his death, and tax is charged at the highest marginal rate. Where there has been a subsequent reduction in the rates (ie a raising of the thresholds for each rate band or a change in the rates themselves) the tax chargeable on the disposal is calculated on the rates in force at the date of disposal (IHTA 1984, Sch 2 para 4).

The inheritance tax charged as a result of the subsequent disposal is payable by the person entitled to the sale proceeds or who would be so entitled if the disposal were a sale (IHTA 1984, s 208). The tax is due six months after the end of the month in which the disposal took place (IHTA 1984, s 226(4)).

This last provision could produce some strange results. Suppose, for example, that the deceased has made a specific devise of the woodlands to a beneficiary and, because of a direction in the will, the tax in respect of this devise is to be borne out of residue. The deceased's personal representative (who is 'the person liable for the whole or part of the tax') elects for relief under s 125. The value of the trees and underwood on the woodlands is then left out of the calculation of the tax due on death (to the benefit of the residuary beneficiary). However, if the timber is sold a few years later it is the specific legatee of the woodlands who has to pay the inheritance tax charge arising. Not only is the amount of tax on the timber (almost certainly) more than it would have been had the election not been made, but also the specific legatee is liable to pay that tax despite the direction that the tax should be borne by residue. It is unclear whether the specific legatee could claim to be indemnified by the residuary legatee and/or the personal representative as the Inheritance Tax Act 1984 does not provide him with a specific right of recovery. Equally unclear is whether the specific legatee could apply, as one of the persons liable for the tax on the timber (under IHTA 1984, s 200), to have the personal representative's election under s 125 disallowed. Where a request is made more than two years after death for the election to be withdrawn, and there are special circumstances, the HMRC Inheritance Tax Manual, para 4375 states that 'the case should be given sympathetic consideration but enquiry should be made whether the timber has been or is about to be sold'.

If the woodland is agricultural property, relief is not available under s 125 although agricultural property relief will be available if the woodlands are occupied and the occupation is ancillary to that of the agricultural land or pasture.

Where the woodland constitutes 'relevant business property' for the purposes of business property relief, business property relief is still available to relieve the land on which the trees or underwood stand where a s 125 election is made and will also be available when the deferred inheritance tax charge becomes chargeable on the subsequent disposal of the timber provided that business property relief would have been available on the previous owner's death if a s 125 election had not been made (IHTA 1984, s 127(2)). This is only of academic interest in most cases as 100% relief will be available rendering an election under s 125 unnecessary.

For land on which the timber stands, there is no relief for the tax chargeable in respect of its value, apart from business property relief. The tax can , however, be paid in ten equal annual instalments provided a written election is made (IHTA 1984, s 227). The balance outstanding will become payable if the land is subsequently sold and interest at normal rates will run on the balance outstanding after the date when the first instalment is due (ie six months after the end of the month in which death occurred). Where the land itself qualifies for business property relief then the instalments are only subject to interest if they are not paid on the due date.

Relief for lifetime gifts

[12.5] There is generally no specific relief for a lifetime gift (chargeable transfer or potentially exempt transfer) of woodlands unless business property relief is available.

There is an exception where the lifetime gift is a disposal which revives an inheritance tax charge deferred from the previous owner's death in which case two forms of relief are available. The first is that the amount of tax charged on the transferor by reference to the deceased previous owner's estate and cumulative total can be deducted from the value transferred by him on his subsequent gift (IHTA 1984, s 129). (This is a relief of tax against taxable amount, not tax against tax). The second is that the tax charged in respect of the subsequent gift can be paid by ten equal annual, interest-free, instalments if an election is made. It is available regardless of whether the donee or the donor is paying the tax. The first instalment is due when the tax as a whole would have been due but for the election to pay by instalments.

For land on which timber stands there is no relief for the tax chargeable in respect of its value, unless business property relief is available. The instalment option will, however, be available.

Making sensible use of the tax treatment of woodlands

The person who does not own woodlands

[12.6] Clearly, the financial returns to the investor in woodlands must be scrutinised as closely as the tax benefits. Investing in woodlands will require substantial expenditure on the purchase of land and planting of trees. Depending on the rate of growth of the trees chosen, there will be no income generated by the investment for several years (ten or more). In addition, the investment will be difficult to realise and the return uncertain (unless the price of timber can be accurately predicted many years hence).

The incentive to invest in woodlands has over the years been reduced. Apart from the favourable inheritance tax treatment of 100% business property relief available to woodlands managed on a commercial basis, their tax treatment is akin to more conventional forms of investment, with no tax deduction on investment but the advantage of a tax-free profit. It will be a considerable length of time, however, before any profit accrues. A gift of immature woodlands into trust has the attraction that it is a gift of an asset producing no income but considerable capital growth in the longer term.

If an individual considers woodlands attractive as a long-term investment for the benefit of his minor children, he might, for example, buy the woodlands, plant them with trees predicted to mature in 15 to 20 years time. After two years the woodlands could be settled on discretionary trusts for his children. Provided 100% business property relief was available the gift would be free of inheritance tax. Hold-over relief under s 165 would not be available on any gift to a settlor-interested trust. When the timber matures and is sold, any profits arising can be passed to the children free of tax.

The person who already owns woodlands

[12.7] If a person inherits the woodland, he should consider whether or not an election under IHTA 1984, s 125 should be made in the two years following the deceased's death. Where business property relief is available at 100%, there will be no reason to make the election. In fact, because of an apparent quirk in the drafting of IHTA 1984, s 127(2), it would seem positively disadvantageous to do so as relief would then only be available at 50%.

Where 100% business property relief is not available, the decision as to whether or not the s 125 election should be made is not always an easy one. There is a definite cashflow advantage in making the election. In addition, the rate of tax charged on a subsequent disposal of the timber will be reduced if there has been a reduction in the rates since the date of death. However, this must be set against the fact that the tax is charged on the net disposal proceeds or market value of the timber at the date of disposal and not the value at the date of the deceased's death. Also, consideration should be given to who will bear the tax if an election is not made.

If the present owner has a life expectancy of less than seven years, he is unlikely to obtain much of a benefit by making a lifetime gift of the woodlands. If a s 125 election is made in respect of the timber and in relation to the deceased previous owner's death, then if he dies with the woodlands still forming part of his estate the deferred inheritance tax charge relating to the previous owner's death will never be revived. In such a situation it may be worthwhile for him to make the election, subject to the comments made earlier.

Subject to the above comments, the wisdom of making an election will probably depend on the maturity of the trees. If they are very young and the present owner intends to hold the woodlands as part of his estate for some time, it will probably make sense not to make the election. Alternatively, if he intends to give away the timber or the woodlands quite soon, he might consider making the election (particularly if he would be bearing the tax if no election were to be made) if only because the amount of tax charged as a result of the disposal in relation to the deceased previous owner's death can be deducted from the value transferred by his subsequent lifetime transfer. However, if the subsequent lifetime transfer is to be made at a time when the woodlands have become eligible for 100% business property relief, this deduction will be of no relevance. Where he wishes to transfer the woodland within two years of the previous owner's death, he would be well advised to consider making the transfer by means of a variation and election under IHTA 1984, s 142.

Chapter 13

Gifts to Charities and Other Non-Profit Organisations

Introduction

[13.1] No book on estate planning would be complete without some mention of charities and how best to structure gifts to them. Individuals considering making an absolute bequest or devise to a charity should be warned that some charities have become increasingly aggressive in their pursuit of bequests and devises. The Royal Society for the Prevention of Cruelty to Animals (the 'RSPCA') was criticised by the judge in the case of *Royal Society for the Prevention of Cruelty to Animals v Sharpe* [2010] EWHC 268 (Ch), [2010] STC 975 (see **16.3**). It is also suggested to advise a client who is considering making a large gift to a charity under their will to inform close family members and explain their reasons. This will give the testator the opportunity to inform his family of his intentions and avoid unnecessary legal action (see *Gill and Woodall*).

A 'charity' means any body of persons or trust established for charitable purposes only (IHTA 1984, s 272 and ITA 2007, s 519). A charity is defined by the Charities Act 2006 ('CHA 2006') as 'an institution which is established for charitable purposes only'. A charitable purpose is a purpose which falls within the purposes listed below and is for the public benefit (CHA 2006, s 2). Charitable purposes include:

- the prevention or relief of poverty;
- the advancement of education;
- the advancement of religion;
- the advancement of health or the saving of lives;
- the advancement of citizenship or community development;
- the advancement of the arts, culture, heritage or science;
- the advancement of amateur sport;
- the advancement of human rights, conflict resolution or reconciliation or the promotion of religious or racial harmony or equality and diversity;
- the advancement of environmental protection or improvement;
- the relief of those in need by reason of youth, age, ill-health, disability, financial hardship or other disadvantage;
- the advancement of animal welfare;
- the promotion of the efficiency of the armed forces of the Crown police, fire and rescue services or ambulance services; and
- a 'sweep up' category for charitable purposes not listed in the other categories, plus any purposes analogous to recognised charitable purposes.

Under CHA 2006, s 3 a charity will have to demonstrate that its activities are for the public benefit. The Act removes the presumption of public benefit but it does preserve the definition that has developed through case law. The Charity Commission has produced its own guidance on what the public benefit requirement means. This can be found at www.charitycommission.gov.uk.

To qualify as a charity, a charity must be subject to the jurisdiction of the courts of the UK (*Dreyfus (Camille and Henry) Foundation Inc v CIR* [1956] AC 39, [1955] 3 All ER 97 (HL) and *Gaudiya Mission v Brahmachary* [1998] Ch 341, [1997] 4 All ER 957). Therefore, a lifetime gift or legacy to a foreign charity would not qualify for an inheritance tax exemption. However, in the recent case of *Persche v Finanzamt Ludenscheid: C-318/07* [2009] All ER (EC) 673, [2009] 2 CMLR 819 the European Court of Justice has held that German legislation which stated that a tax deduction for expenditure incurred for charitable purposes was only available where the charity was established in Germany, was in contravention of the EC Treaty.

As a result of that case, legislation was introduced in FA 2010 to extend various tax reliefs to certain organisations and Community Amateur Sports Clubs in the EU, Norway and Iceland. At the same time legislation was introduced to align the definition of charity for all charitable reliefs and exemptions. FA 2010, Sch 6 introduces a new definition of a charity with effect from 6 April 2010 in respect of Gift Aid and at some later date to be appointed by statutory instrument in respect of all other matters (later in 2010/11 according to the Budget press release 24 March 2010).

Under FA 2010, Sch 6 a charity means a body of persons or trust that:

(a) is established for charitable purposes only. The definition is the same as that found in CHA 2006, s 2 for charities in England and Wales (see above) which is extended to cover charities wherever established;
(b) meets the Jurisdiction Condition;
(c) meets the Registration Condition; and
(d) meets the Management Condition (FA 2010, Sch 6 para 1).

The Jurisdiction Condition will be satisfied where the body of persons or trust is within the authority of the High Court, Court of Session, High Court in Northern Ireland or any other court of a corresponding jurisdiction under the law of another EU Member State or Territory to be specified in regulations (FA 2010, Sch 6 para 2). As from 20 August 2010, Iceland and Norway will be relevant territories.

The Registration Condition is satisfied where a body of persons or a trust is a charity within the meaning of the Charities Act 1993 has complied with any requirement to be registered in the Register of Charities kept under s 3 of that Act or where a body of persons or trust has complied with the law of a territory outside of England and Wales to be registered in a similar register (FA 2010, Sch 6 para 3).

The Management Condition is satisfied by a body of persons or trust if its managers are 'fit and proper persons to be managers of the body or trust' (FA 2010, Sch 6 para 4). Managers are the persons having the general control and management of the administration of the body or trust. The condition will be satisfied if HMRC consider that any failure to meet it has not prejudiced the charitable purposes of the charity or it is just and reasonable to do so (FA 2010, Sch 6 para 5). There is no statutory definition of a 'fit and proper person' although needless to say guidance has been issued by HMRC which can be found at www.hmrc.gov.uk/charities. According to this guidance, which of co urse does not have the force of law, the 'fit and proper persons' test is concerned with 'ensuring that charities are not managed or controlled by individuals who present a risk to the charity's tax position.'

The guidance identifies some factors that 'may lead to HMRC deciding that a manager is not a fit and proper person [and] include, but are not limited to, individuals:

- with a history of tax fraud
- with a history of other fraudulent behaviour including misrepresentation and/or identity theft
- for whom HMRC have knowledge of involvement in attacks against or abuse of tax repayment systems
- barred from acting as a charity trustee by a charity regulator or Court, or being disqualified from acting as a company director.'

Capital gifts

Inheritance tax

[13.2] A charitable donation made by an individual is a transfer of value which is generally exempt from inheritance tax (IHTA 1984, s 23) to the extent that the value transferred by it is attributable to the donated property. Where the value transferred exceeds the value of the gift in the hands of a charity, the Revenue takes the view that the exemption extends to the value transferred (Statement of Practice SP E13).

Example

A holds 60% of the shares in a company. The shareholding is worth £200,000. A 30% shareholding is worth only £50,000, since it is only a minority shareholding. A gives half of his 60% shareholding to a charitable trust. The loss to his estate (because the property in the trust is 'related property' under IHTA 1984, s 161(2)(b)(i)) is £100,000 ($^1/_2$ × £200,000). The value of the gift in the hands of the charity is £50,000.

In the above example, the value transferred by the transfer of value is £100,000, but is it wholly or only partly 'attributable to property' given to the charitable trust? The Revenue has stated that in such a case the transfer would be wholly exempt (Statement of Practice SP E13). (The phrase 'attributable to property' is also used in IHTA 1984, s 3A in the definition of potentially exempt transfer. It is understood that the Revenue applies the same interpretation.)

Section 23(1) refers to 'property which is given to charities'. The terms 'give', 'given', 'gift' are rarely to be found in the inheritance tax legislation, and nowhere are the words 'give' and 'gift' actually defined. However, s 23(6) provides that ' . . . property is given to charities if it becomes the property of charities or is held on trust for charitable purposes only . . . '. Therefore, to qualify for exemption a gift (*inter vivos* or by will) need not be to a recognised charitable body provided it is applicable only for charitable purposes. This is an important planning point, for it enables the testator of a will to leave a legacy, or a share of residue, for charitable purposes and at the same time express a wish that the money be applied by his executors to particular named charities or to charities of a certain type or class.

A charity must acquire an interest on the death of a testator. In the case of *Bailhache Labesse Trustees Ltd v Revenue and Customs Comrs* [2008] STC (SCD) 869, [2008] SWTI 1680, it was held that appointments made by trustees within 12 months of death to charities were transfers of value and not exempt transfers under IHTA 1984, s 23 with effect from the date of death.

Anti-avoidance provisions

[13.3] IHTA 1984, s 23 contains provisions (in subsections (2) to (5)) to prevent the avoidance of tax by use of the general exemption for property given to charities in subsection (1).

Since it is only individuals who can make chargeable transfers, there are no charging provisions dealing with the situation where a charitable company or the trustees of a charitable trust make a transfer of value. It might be thought that by giving a limited interest to a charity a transfer could be made by an individual which would be entirely free from inheritance tax.

Example

> A wishes to create a discretionary trust. If he transfers property to trustees on discretionary trusts there would be an immediate charge to inheritance tax on A. However, if A were to make the transfer to a trust in which a charity had an initial interest in possession (say for one year) with the remainder on discretionary trusts, he might hope that the transfer would be exempt and that there would be no charge on the termination of the charity's interest in possession.

Quite apart from the vulnerability to an attack under the associated operations rules (IHTA 1984, s 268) and the tendency of the courts to depart from the literal construction of legislation where transactions are undertaken for the purposes of tax planning, s 23(3)(b) provides that there is no exemption available where the property transferred to the charity is given to it for a limited period.

If, instead of creating an interest for a limited period, it is decided to create a defeasible interest (ie one liable to be terminated on the happening of a specified event), the exemption will also not be available by virtue of s 23(2)(c). For these purposes any disposition which has not been defeated within

12 months of the transfer and is not defeasible after that time is treated as not being defeasible (whether or not it was capable of being defeated before that time).

Similarly, where the property transferred consists of an interest in other property, then if the transferee charity's interest is less than the transferor's interest, no exemption will be available (IHTA 1984, s 23(3)(a)). Thus, where the holder of a freehold estate in land grants a lease of that land to a charity (with the probable aim of transferring the freehold estate in reversion at a greatly reduced value) no exemption will be available.

If a postponed interest, or an interest subject to a condition precedent which is not satisfied within the following 12 months, is created, no exemption will be available (IHTA 1984, s 23(2)(a) and (b)).

Section 23(4) contains special 'reservation of benefit' provisions applying to gifts to charities. FA 1986, s 102(5)(d) disapplies the general reservation of benefit provisions in s 102 to transfers where the s 23 exemption is available. Subsection (4)(a) disallows the exemption where the transferor transfers land or a building to a charity subject to the right for him, his spouse, civil partner or a connected person to possess or occupy the property transferred rent-free or other than on arm's length terms. Subsection (4)(b) applies where the property transferred is not land or a building. The exemption is disallowed where there is an interest reserved to or created by the transferor other than one for full consideration or which does not substantially affect the enjoyment of the property by the transferee charity.

Finally, subsection (5) provides that where the whole or any part of the property given may be applied for purposes other than charitable purposes no exemption will be available in respect of any part of the gift.

As a result of these anti-avoidance provisions there is no economic advantage to an individual in making a gift to charity. While such gifts may be exempt from inheritance tax and other taxes, an individual cannot usually bestow a greater benefit on himself or someone else (a non-charity) by making a gift of property to charity than if he retained the property or gave it to that other person.

Capital gains tax

[13.4] TCGA 1992, s 257 provides that gifts to charities are to be treated as disposals for a consideration producing neither a gain nor a loss.

Strategy for capital gifts

[13.5] The would-be benefactor of charities should consider making a Gift Aid donation to charity or charitable trust within ITA 2007, ss 414 and 521, so as to obtain income tax relief on his gift as well as inheritance tax relief.

Lifetime gifts v transfers on death

[13.6] The timing of a would-be benefactor making a gift to a charity is important and depends to a large extent on his personal circumstances and the assets to be given. Since outright gifts to charity are exempt from inheritance tax, it is usually sensible for an individual to make lifetime gifts to his family (since these are not exempt *ab initio* although they may be potentially exempt) and to make any gifts which he wishes to make to charity in his will (given that he will probably need to retain some capital in his estate during his lifetime).

Example

> A widow has an estate of £500,000. Her children have already been well provided for. She decides that she would like £100,000 of her estate to go to charity and £400,000 to her children. She calculates that she can afford to give away £100,000 now. If she makes a potentially exempt transfer of £100,000 in favour of her children and survives for the following seven years, no tax would be payable on the potentially exempt transfer and she would leave a chargeable estate (assuming no change) of £300,000 on which no inheritance tax would be payable. If, on the other hand, she makes a lifetime gift of £100,000 to charity and leaves the whole of her estate to her children, she will leave a chargeable estate (assuming no change) of £400,000 on which inheritance tax at 2010/11 rates amounts to £30,000.

If an individual decides to make a lifetime capital gift to charity, he should consider making a direct gift of assets with large unrealised capital gains rather than a gift of cash, since the disposal of the assets will not result in any charge to capital gains tax (TCGA 1992, s 257) and will not reduce his cash resources. The charity, if it requires cash, can immediately sell the assets and realise a gain free of tax provided the proceeds are applicable and applied for charitable purposes (TCGA 1992, s 256). This is an important planning point, because small charities may sometimes be reluctant to receive donations in any form other than cash. If the would-be benefactor informs the charity that he can give them more in non-cash assets than he could if they would only take cash and reminds them that they can sell the assets free of capital gains tax the charity may be willing to receive a donation in a non-cash form.

If an individual wishes to make a gift of cash to a charity or a charitable trust he should consider making a Gift Aid donation within ITA 2007, ss 414 and 521 to obtain both income tax relief and inheritance tax relief. Of course, this is dependent on the individual paying sufficient income tax or capital gains tax.

This can be achieved by executing an appropriately drafted will. Although this can be done in a number of ways, one such way is described below.

Under his will, the testator makes a pecuniary legacy to a beneficiary who has sufficient income (which exceeds the amount of the legacy or which at least exceeds one half of the legacy). The beneficiary should not benefit directly from any increase in the value of the residuary estate. In his will the testator expresses a non-binding wish that the beneficiary should give the legacy to a specific charity. Once the beneficiary receives the legacy from the estate he gives it to the charity in accordance with the testator's wishes within two years of the death. The tax effects are that the testator's estate will qualify for Inheritance Tax relief on the legacy under IHTA 1984 s 143 because the gift is treated for inheritance tax purposes as made by the testator. The gift will qualify for gift aid so that the charity is able to reclaim the basic rate tax on the gift and the beneficiary will enjoy the higher rate tax relief on his gift because for income tax purposes the gift is treated as made by the beneficiary.

Nothing is perfect, and there are certain disadvantages to this suggestion. First, from the testator's point of view there is a risk that a beneficiary will not carry out his wishes. Secondly, the beneficiary can only benefit from the arrangement if he makes a gift to charity and claims Income Tax relief. It is therefore essential that the amount of the legacy exceeds the beneficiary's annual income. Thirdly, there is always the risk that anti-avoidance legislation will be introduced between the date of the will and the date of death but that is a risk with all forms of tax planning.

An income tax deduction is also available on gifts by persons carrying on a trade, profession or vocation of assets which are manufactured or sold in the course of the activity or which are machinery or plant used in that activity (ITTOIA 2005, s108).

An income tax deduction is also available on gifts to a charity of qualifying investments or qualifying interests in land. (ITA 2007, s 431). Qualifying investments for this purpose are shares or securities listed on a recognised stock exchange or dealt in on any designated UK market, units in an authorised unit trust, shares in an open-ended investment company, interests in offshore funds and a qualifying interest in land (ITA 2007, s 432). A qualifying interest in land is defined as a freehold interest in land or a leasehold interest in land which is a term of years absolute where the land in question is in the UK (ITA 2007, s 433). Agreements to acquire a freehold interest and agreements for lease are not qualifying interests in land. Relief is calculated by way of a formula which uses the net benefit to the charity thus preventing an income tax advantage being secured on an amount in excess of the benefit received by the charity.

Restrictions are imposed on transactions between a charity and a 'substantial donor' as defined by ITA 2007, s 549. A substantial donor is defined by ITA 2007, s 549 as an individual who gives 'relievable gifts to a charity of at least £25,000 . . . in a period of 12 months . . . or at least £150,000 . . . in a period of six years in which the tax year wholly or partly falls'. A 'relievable gift' is simply a gift for which the donor has received tax relief. In such situations the charity's tax relief will be restricted. Such a donor will be treated as a substantial donor for at least the subsequent 5 years. The rules will not apply where either ITA 2007, s 431, ICTA 1988, s 587B or TCGA 1992, s 287 applies.

At the time of writing an informal consultation is being undertaken in relation to proposals to replace the substantial donor rules. In the meantime, care must therefore be taken when advising a client on charitable gifts to ensure that the gift does not fall within these provisions resulting in a restriction of relief available to the charity.

Gifts from inherited capital

[13.7] An individual may want to make a capital gift to charity because of a change in his personal circumstances. If he has inherited capital (by will or on intestacy) he should consider executing a deed of variation to give capital to the charity and making a statement under IHTA 1984, s 142 to have the disposition treated as if it had been made by the testator (provided the 2-year period has not yet expired).

Example

> Catherine dies leaving the whole of her estate of £412,000 to her son Ben (an only child). Inheritance tax on the estate at 2010/11 rates amounts to £34,800. Of the £377,200 which Ben receives he decides he would like to make a gift to charity of £25,000. If he makes a simple gift of £25,000 the gift will be exempt from inheritance tax and he will be left with £352,200. If, on the other hand, he executes a deed of variation of Catherine's will and makes a statement under s 142 to have the disposition treated as if it had been made by Catherine, he will transfer £25,000 to the charity but will be able to claim a repayment from the Revenue of £10,000 (£25,000 at 40%) by way of overpaid inheritance tax, leaving himself with £362,200 (£377,200 - £25,000 + £10,000). No income tax relief under ITA 2007, s 414 would be available on the grounds that a benefit under ss 416(7) and 418 had been received in that the amount of inheritance tax payable on the estate had been reduced (*St Dunstan's v Major (Insp of Taxes)* [1997] STC (SCD) 212). In that case, it was held that, because under Gift Aid rules a donor should not receive a benefit in excess of 2.5% of the gift (this has now been changed), relief was not available. However, if it can be arranged for the inheritance tax saving to accrue to a third party or be added to the gift, it may be arguable that income tax relief will be due. It is understood that a case challenging the *St Dunstan's* case has been heard by the first-tier Tax Tribunal but no decision has yet been released.

Where a gift of either quoted shares or an interest in land is made to a charity, there is a different rule relating to benefits to the donor. The rules operate in a different way and there is no mention of a defined percentage instead the amount of the gift on which tax relief is claimed is reduced by the value of any benefit received by the donor. It may therefore be sensible to have a deed of variation relating to the shares or land. In the above example, if a gift of quoted shares equal to £25,000 was made, the inheritance tax saving would be £10,000. As a higher rate taxpayer he could claim income tax relief under ITA 2007, s 413 on £15,000 (£25,000 – £10,000) giving an income tax saving of £6,000. If he were an additional rate taxpayer the income tax saving would be higher, namely £7,500.

Gifts out of income

Gift Aid

[13.8] Having been introduced in 1990 Gift Aid is the successor to deeds of covenant. Relief is given for payments which are qualifying donations to charity within ITA 2007, s 414 ('Gift Aid'). To be a qualifying donation, the payment must take the form of a cash payment.

There is no minimum limit for gifts, instead the relief applies to any gift made by a donor who has sufficient income charged to UK tax. If a gift qualifies for relief the donor is treated as having deducted income tax at the basic rate from his gift. The tax deemed to have been deducted by the donor can be recovered by the charity. There is additional transitional relief available to the charity for gifts made up to 5 April 2011. If a taxpayer pays less income tax or capital gains tax than the amount recovered by the charity then the taxpayer will be assessed to tax on an amount equal to the difference. Care should be taken to ensure that a taxpayer has sufficient tax to pay to avoid a nasty surprise.

A simple form of certification is required under which the donor merely gives to the charity an appropriate declaration. This declaration can be given in writing, orally or by means of electronic communication and must contain the following:

(a) his or her name and home address;
(b) the name of the charity;
(c) a description of the gift which may be a single gift or a series of gifts;
(d) a statement that the gift or gifts to which the declaration relates are to be treated as qualifying donations for ITA 2007, s 414; and
(e) where the declaration is given in writing, a statement explaining the effect of ITA 2007, s 414.

A declaration may cover gifts since 6 April 2000 and all future gifts.

Where an oral declaration is made (ie a gift aid donation is made by telephone) special rules apply. The charity must send a written record to the donor who will then have 30 days to change his mind. (Donations to Charity by Individuals (Appropriate Declarations) Regulations 2000 (SI 2000 No 2074)).

A donor may elect that qualifying donations be treated as if they were made in the previous year of assessment (ITA 2007, s 426). Such an election must be made in writing within certain statutory time limits. Care needs to be taken to ensure that the claim for gift aid relief is made in the claimant's original return (ITA 2007, s 426(6)). In *Cameron v Revenue and Customs Comrs* [2010] UKFTT 104 (TC), [2010] SFTD 664) Mr Cameron made an election to carry back gift aid relief in an amended tax return. The Revenue refused the claim saying that it should only be made in the original return; it was too late to make it in an amended return. The Tribunal examined the relevant legislation but could not find anything that supported the taxpayer's claim that the return could be an amended return, nor did it matter that the amended return had been submitted before the 31 January deadline. The relief was not allowable.

It is also possible for a taxpayer who is due to receive a repayment in respect of overpaid tax to direct that the whole or part of the repayment is made to a specified charity. The gift will be treated as being a qualifying gift for gift aid.

Gifts of shares and securities

[13.9] As mentioned above, Gift Aid payments must be in cash. If a potential donor has shares pregnant with capital gains, it may be better to give the shares to the chosen charity which will be treated as a no gain no loss transfer, rather than sell the shares, pay capital gains tax and give the net proceeds. This is especially so because income tax relief is available on the value of shares and securities which are listed on a recognised stock exchange or dealt in on any designated market in the UK, units in authorised unit trusts, shares in open-ended investment companies and interests in offshore funds given to charities (ITA 2007, s 431).

Gifts of real property

[13.10] There is a relief from income tax, similar to that given in relation to gifts of shares and securities, where a qualifying interest in land is given to a charity (ITA 2007, s 431). Therefore, where a potential donor has a qualifying interest in land on which there is an unrealised gain, it may be more tax efficient to give the property to the chosen charity rather than sell the property and give the proceeds to the charity.

In order to claim the relief the taxpayer must have received a certificate from the charity which contains a description of the qualifying interest in land, the date of the disposal and a statement that the charity has acquired the qualifying interest in land.

There will be a clawback of relief on the happening of a disqualifying event within the defined relevant period. A disqualifying event occurs if the donor or a person connected with him becomes entitled to an interest or right in relation to all or part of the land to which the disposal relates or becomes party to an arrangement under which he enjoys some right in relation to all or part of that land otherwise than for full consideration in money or moneys worth. There is no disqualifying event if a person becomes entitled to a right or interest as a result of a disposition of property on death. The relevant period is the period beginning with the date of disposal and ending with the fifth anniversary of 31 January following the end of the year of assessment in which the disposal was made (ITA 2007, s 444).

Example

Cheryl has just received a significant dividend on her family company shares and has some development land on which she has recently obtained planning permission for residential properties. This land has a significant unrealised capital gain on which she will have to pay capital gains tax. She has decided that she has assets which she can afford to give away and so decides to make a gift of the land to a local charity. There will be no capital gains tax on the disposal nor will any stamp duty land tax be payable (FA 2003, Sch 8). Income tax relief will be available on the gift so her income will be reduced by the value of the land transferred.

Gifts made by a person carrying on a trade

[13.11] A person carrying on a trade is able to donate any items manufactured or of a class or description sold by the donor in the course of the trade to a charity, a registered club or certain designated bodies or a designated educational establishment without bringing its market value into account for tax purposes (ITTOIA 2005, s 108).

Payroll deduction scheme

[13.12] The payroll deduction scheme provides that an employee wishing to make a gift to charity can authorise his employer to withhold any amount from his wages. The deductions must be made pursuant to a scheme which is approved by the Revenue or is of a kind approved by the Revenue. The employer must pay the sums withheld to a Revenue approved agent under the Charitable Deductions (Approved Schemes) Regulations 1986 (SI 1986 No 2211). The agency must distribute the donations within 60 days of their receipt from the employer. The donor will then obtain tax relief as if the deductions were allowable expenses of his employment.

Charities Aid Foundation

[13.13] In many cases people would like to be able to earmark some of their salary for charity before the end of each tax year, but postpone payment until such time as they find charities they want to benefit and then divide the sums earmarked amongst whatever charities and in whatever amounts they care to choose. All these demands can be satisfied by the person involved making a Gift Aid payment to the Charities Aid Foundation ('CAF'). The Foundation receives the sums paid and reclaims the basic rate tax withheld at source by the payer. The sums paid (subject to a small deduction for administration) and the tax reclaimed are then held by the Foundation to be distributed to charities as the original payer directs. Donations can be made via the internet, using the charity cheque book or the charity card. It is not an inapt analogy to think of the Foundation as a charitable bank with whom the donor has an account, sums only being capable of being withdrawn from the account for payment to a charity. More details of the scheme can be obtained from www.cafonline.org.

Payments from discretionary trusts

[13.14] A further tax-efficient way to support a charity is for income to be paid from a discretionary trust assuming that the trustees have the power to make such a payment. The charity will be able to reclaim the relevant amount of income tax paid by the trustees on the sum given. This is because ITA 2007, s 497 enables the charity to reclaim a tax credit equal to the rate applicable to trusts (50% for 2010/11) applied to the payment grossed up by the tax credit. If a capital payment is made by the trustees, IHTA 1984, s 76 should ensure that there will be no inheritance tax charge on the property leaving the trust.

General rules for charitable gifts

[13.15] The greatest tax saving from making charitable donations is generally achieved by the payments being made direct from the source from which the donor would derive the money with which to make the donation.

Example

> As outlined above the recipient of property by will, or on intestacy, might seek to make a capital donation by means of a deed of variation and a statement under IHTA 1984, s 142 to have the disposition treated as if it had been made by the testator.
>
> Similarly, a director and controlling shareholder of a company might authorise the company (assuming that it has power to do so under its memorandum and articles of association) to make charitable donations rather than give some of his own income to charity or make contributions under the payroll deduction scheme.

Within a family, the income and inheritance tax savings can be maximised by the family member who pays the highest rate of tax making the donations.

Creating your own charitable trust

[13.16] A wealthy individual may wish to create his own charitable trust. If he is anticipating doing this by will, he should be careful to ensure that the trust will be a valid charitable trust, since if it fails it will be too late to take any remedial action once the testator has died. The gift would probably lapse as a result. However, it might be effective to create a valid non-charitable trust if the trust is not invalid for uncertainty of objects. Alternatively, he could set up a charitable trust with a small sum during his lifetime which is registered with the Revenue in order to obtain the tax benefits. He could then, following the advice given above, make lifetime gifts to non-exempt beneficiaries and in his will make a substantial donation to that trust.

Drafting gifts to charity

[13.17] Care needs to be taken in drafting deeds of gift and wills containing charitable gifts as was illustrated in the case of *Gibbs v Harding* [2007] EWHC 3 (Ch).

First, and most importantly of all, the charity's correct name and address should be ascertained. It should be checked that the body or trust in question is in fact a charity. Some bodies which have members, such as the Prayer Book Society, are charities (or, as in the particular case of the National Trust, may be a specifically exempt body under IHTA 1984, s 25 and IHTA 1984, Sch 3); however, many are not.

Second, when drafting a will it is advisable to include a 'mergers' clause, specifying that if the charity has been taken over, wound up or simply re-named, the gift shall be construed as a gift to the body which has taken over the charity or received the surpluses applicable for charitable purposes on the winding-up or the newly named body. Charities Act 1993, s 75C contains provisions allowing any merger of charities to be noted on a register of mergers with the result that any future legacies to the merged charities will automatically be passed on to the successor charity. Where no such clause is included, it may be possible to continue the charitable gift through an application to the Charity Commission for a scheme for the property to be applied cy-pres, ie to some other charitable purpose as nearly as possible resembling the original trusts.

Third, when drafting a will it is helpful to include a receipt clause specifying that the receipt of the treasurer, or other proper officer for the time being of the charity, shall be a good discharge to the testator's executors who need be under no further obligation to see to the application of the monies or assets given.

Temporary charitable trusts

[13.18] Mention should be made of funds which are held on charitable trusts for a specified period, following which the funds are held for non-charitable beneficiaries. This situation may occur unexpectedly, for instance, if a site given for a school or village hall is no longer required and reverts to the descendants of the original donor.

Inheritance tax

[13.19] During the 'charitable period', there is an exemption from the decennial charge and the charge on distributions. Instead, a charge arises when the property ceases to be held on the charitable trusts and the rates of tax applicable are set out in IHTA 1984, s 70(6). The longer the charitable period, the greater the charge when that period ends but subject to a maximum rate chargeable of 30% after 50 years.

Capital gains tax

[13.20] Under TCGA 1992, s 256, when property ceases to be held on charitable trusts, the trustees are deemed to have disposed of, and immediately reacquired, the property at its market value. Any gain not accruing to the trustees is liable to capital gains tax, subject to a claim for hold-over relief under s 260 of that Act. In addition, to the extent that the property at that time represents, directly or indirectly, the consideration for the disposal of assets by the trustees, any gain accruing on that earlier disposal (and previously exempt) is treated as not having accrued to the charity and capital gains tax is applied as if the exemption had never applied. A cumulative liability may, therefore, arise. An assessment may be made within 3 years of the end of the year of assessment in which the property ceases to be held for charitable purposes. Such an assessment seems to be able to be made even where the gain arising on the earlier disposal is outside the normal time limit for assessment.

Community Amateur Sports Clubs

[13.21] There are a variety of tax reliefs available to Community Amateur Sports Clubs ('CASCs') (CTA 2010, ss 662–665). A sports club can apply to the Revenue for a status as a CASC provided certain criteria are met (CTA 2010, s 658).

Gift Aid is available on individual donations only. Whilst inheritance tax relief is available and gifts of assets are on a no gain/no loss basis for capital gains tax, no income tax relief is available on gifts of shares to a CASC.

Gifts for national purposes

[13.22] IHTA 1984, s 25 extends the s 23 exemption for gifts to charities to gifts to bodies named in Sch 3 to the Act. These bodies include UK national museums, local authorities, government departments and universities or colleges. The anti-avoidance provisions in IHTA 1984, s 23 (see **13.3** above) also apply to gifts for national purposes. Gifts to these bodies are also treated for capital gains tax purposes as disposals for a consideration producing neither a gain nor a loss (TCGA 1992, s 257).

Gifts to political parties

[13.23] A gift of any amount made either during a person's lifetime or on his death to a qualifying political party is exempt from inheritance tax (IHTA 1984, s 24).

A qualifying political party is defined in s 24(2) as one in respect of which, at the last general election preceding the transfer of value, two members of the party were elected to the House of Commons or one member was so elected and the party received not less than 150,000 votes overall.

Gifts to non-qualifying political parties do not qualify for any exemption or relief.

The anti-avoidance provisions in IHTA 1984, s 23 (see **13.3** above) also apply to gifts to political parties.

Chapter 14

Gifts for National Purposes

Introduction

[14.1] Encouraging the preservation of our national heritage through the giving of tax privileges is not a new concept. The Finance Act 1896 first gave the Treasury discretion to waive estate duty in respect of settled chattels considered to be of national, scientific or historical interest, such as paintings, books and other works of art.

The current reliefs, encompassing inheritance tax, capital gains tax, income tax, stamp duty and stamp duty land tax aim to help in the preservation of our national heritage property. Generally, these reliefs tend to encourage continued private ownership of heritage property including land and buildings of outstanding interest as well as land essential for the protection of the character and amenities of an outstanding building and objects historically associated with such a building. This is illustrated by the availability of relief for 'maintenance funds' which are tax-efficient vehicles for providing funds for the upkeep of heritage property kept in private ownership. However, there are also specific reliefs which facilitate tax-free gifts or sales of heritage property to certain national bodies.

The legislation continues to refer to the 'Treasury' but FA 1985, s 95 provided that the functions of the Treasury in respect of these provisions were to be transferred to the Commissioners of Inland Revenue and their functions have, of course, in turn been transferred to HMRC.

Inheritance tax

[14.2] The reliefs available can broadly be split into those which enable the property to be placed in some form of public ownership and those which do not. The two sets of reliefs interact.

Gifts for national purposes

[14.3] Transfers of property to various national and local bodies are exempt from inheritance tax (IHTA 1984, s 25). The bodies to which such gifts may be made are listed in IHTA 1984, Sch 3 and include the National Gallery, the British Museum and other national museums, the National Trust, any museum or art gallery maintained by a local authority or university, any university library, and any local authority or government department. A list of the qualifying bodies can be found in the HMRC Inheritance Tax Manual, para 11224.

Conditional exemption for heritage property

[14.4] The provisions allowing heritage property to be retained in private ownership are found in IHTA 1984, ss 30–35A which provide that a transfer of value of heritage property is exempt from inheritance tax provided certain conditions are met (the 'conditional exemption').

Prior to 31 July 1998, conditional exemption was generally available for chattels where property had been designated under IHTA 1984, s 31 as being of national, scientific, historic or artistic interest, ie of museum quality. In addition, undertakings had to be given that certain agreed steps would be taken to maintain and preserve the property, to provide reasonable access to the public and to keep movable property in the UK (unless the Treasury, or later, the Revenue, agreed to a temporary absence for a specified purpose, for example, an exhibition).

For claims made after 30 July 1998, objects (other than those historically associated with a qualifying building) qualify only if they are pre-eminent for their national, scientific, historic or artistic interest. For undertakings given after that date, the facility allowing owners to opt for public access by prior appointment only is not available.

When does it apply?

[14.4A] Conditional exemption applies to transfers of value occurring on death and to certain chargeable lifetime transfers. For lifetime transfers, either the transferor must have acquired the property by a transfer on death which was itself a conditionally exempt transfer or the transferor (or spouse or civil partner) must have been beneficially entitled to the property for the 6 years immediately preceding the transfer (IHTA 1984, s 30(3)). Property held on trust may also qualify for conditional exemption in certain circumstances which are discussed separately below.

Transfers of value which are already exempt from inheritance tax because they are either gifts to charities or inter-spouse or civil partner transfers cannot also be conditionally exempt transfers (IHTA 1984, s 30(4)).

Similarly, potentially exempt transfers cannot also be conditionally exempt transfers unless the transfer subsequently becomes chargeable due to the transferor dying within seven years. Conditional exemption can only be claimed after the transferor's death if the property has not been disposed of in the interim unless the disposal is to a body within IHTA 1984, Sch 3 or is in satisfaction of tax under IHTA 1984, s 230 and, in either case, the property has been or could be designated as heritage property under IHTA 1984, s 31 (IHTA 1984, s 26A).

Conditional exemption may also be claimed if the property has been disposed of by the donee provided the disposal was by way of gift and the new owner, is prepared to give the necessary undertakings.

Where relief is given, the transfer is a conditionally exempt transfer (IHTA 1984, s 30(2)). Provided the undertakings are observed the inheritance tax liability can be postponed.

Chargeable events

[14.4B] The deferred charge will become payable if a 'chargeable event' occurs (IHTA 1984, s 32). There are three occasions on which such an event can arise, namely:

(a) the death of the beneficial owner of the property (with certain exceptions);

(b) the disposal, whether by sale or gift, of the property (with certain exceptions); and

(c) the failure of the relevant person to observe, in any material respect, an undertaking given to the Treasury or Commissioners for HM Revenue and Customs.

The exceptions to *(a)* and *(b)* above are, broadly, if the transfer of value on death or disposal by gift is itself a conditionally exempt transfer, the sale or disposal is to a body within IHTA 1984, Sch 3 or is in satisfaction of a tax liability under IHTA 1984, s 230 or the requisite undertakings under IHTA 1984, s 31 are given by such persons as the Revenue considers appropriate in the particular circumstances. It is no longer acceptable for such replacement undertakings to simply correspond with the old undertakings.

The Revenue do not regard an appropriation or allotment of conditionally exempt property in satisfaction of a legatee's entitlement, as a chargeable event provided the legatee does not pay an equivalent amount in money (para 7.1 of the Capital Taxation and the National Heritage Memorandum).

Calculating tax

[14.4C] The inheritance tax charge is calculated according to the rules contained in IHTA 1984, s 33 which depend upon what triggers the charge and the market value of the relevant property at the time of the chargeable event. The value of the property will be taxed by reference to the transferor's rates of inheritance tax. Where an individual is still alive, his cumulative total of chargeable transfers is adjusted upwards by the amount of the value of the property on which tax is paid (IHTA 1984, s 34). Where this person is dead his estate will be similarly increased and this can affect the rate of tax applicable on the event of a second and subsequent chargeable event. The legislation provides that where property has been sold (with no intention to confer a gratuitous benefit on anyone), the value is taken to be the proceeds of sale (IHTA 1984, s 33(3)). Where the chargeable event is not a sale, the computation is more complex because two transfers could occur, on the gift and on the triggering of the deferred charge. Where the gift is a chargeable event (not including PETs), the tax payable on the gift is credited against the triggered deferred charge. Where the gift is a chargeable transfer but not a chargeable event and so no charge arises the credit will be available to be offset against future chargeable events affecting that property.

There are special rules which apply in respect of the interaction between the transferable nil rate band and the tax payable on a chargeable event under s 32 (see IHTA 1984, s 8C).

The rate of tax depends upon the relevant transferor.

It is the responsibility of the owner of heritage property to notify HMRC Inheritance Tax of the ending of the conditional exemption. This should be done on Form IHT100 and IHT100F within six months from the end of the month in which the event occurs.

The rules applicable to maintenance funds are dealt with separately below.

Meaning of 'disposal'

[14.5] There has been much debate about what constitutes a 'disposal' for the purposes of IHTA 1984, s 32. At one time there was concern that mortgaging the property as security for a loan would be treated as a disposal. Mortgaging a property to raise finance to restore it would not be treated as a disposal. (Capital Taxation and the National Heritage Memorandum para 7.2). Indeed, HMRC's view is that mortgaging a property is not a disposal of it for these purposes and nor is the grant of a lease. However, an adviser should ensure that any lease granted 'does not undermine the integrity of the lessor's undertakings as to amount to a failure to observe them in a material respect'.

If in doubt, the Heritage Team of HMRC should be consulted before any plans are made to grant leases or raise capital from the property by way of mortgage.

Interaction with agricultural property relief and business property relief

[14.6] In the case of landed estates qualifying as heritage property, much of the land will also qualify for agricultural property relief at either 50% or 100%. The relief is given as a reduction in the value transferred by a transfer of value. In addition, there may be situations where property qualifies not only as heritage property but also for business property relief.

A chargeable event occurs if conditional exemption is forfeited on one of the three occasions mentioned above. A charge under IHTA 1984, s 32 will arise as explained above and also under the associated property provisions of IHTA 1984, s 32A. Under ss 32 and 33, tax is charged on 'an amount equal to the value of the property at the time of the chargeable event' (IHTA 1984, s 33(1)). There is no transfer of value (deemed or otherwise) and therefore any agricultural property relief or business property relief is not available. It is usually better, therefore, to make a chargeable transfer subject to business or agricultural property relief rather than to claim conditional exemption.

Making a claim for conditional exemption

[14.7] Conditional exemption from inheritance tax relies upon the property being 'designated' by the Commissioners for HM Revenue and Customs and 'appropriate undertakings' being given by the relevant person. Furthermore, if capital gains tax relief is to apply under TCGA 1992, s 258(2) the appropriate undertakings must have been given and if relief is to apply under TCGA 1992, s 258(3) (see below), the property must have been, or must be capable of being, designated for inheritance tax purposes and the appropriate undertakings must be given.

Designation

[14.8] There is no definition of 'heritage property' in the legislation. However, IHTA 1984, s 31 states that the Treasury may designate:

(a) a relevant object which is pre-eminent for its national, scientific, historic or artistic interest or a collection or group of relevant objects which, taken as a whole, is pre-eminent for its national, scientific or artistic interest. A relevant object is defined as a picture, print, book, manuscript, work of art or scientific object. The test of pre-eminence, which replaced the old test of 'museum quality', requires a higher standard to be reached;
(b) land of outstanding scenic, historic or scientific interest;
(c) buildings of outstanding historic or architectural interest;
(d) land essential for the protection of the character and amenities of a building falling within (*c*) above; and
(e) objects historically associated with a building falling within (*c*) above.

In the past, IR 67 'Capital Taxation and the National Heritage' provided useful guidance as to what the Revenue considered to be appropriate property. This was withdrawn and the Revenue have been consulting with stakeholders in preparing revised guidance. It was announced in June 2010 that this work has almost been completed and copies of the revised guidance found in the Capital Taxation and the National Heritage Memorandum can be obtained from HMRC. This guidance in the Capital Taxation and the National Heritage Memorandum has been incorporated into this chapter of the book. There are some areas still to be finalised and it is recommended that, in the meantime, an adviser contacts the Heritage Team with any queries.

When determining if an object or collection is pre-eminent, regard should be had to any significant association of the object or collection with a particular place.

The Commissioners for HMRC are, of course, unable to determine themselves what objects, buildings and land should be designated as national heritage property. HMRC Heritage Team (the 'Heritage Team'), which is responsible for designating property, takes expert advice before deciding whether to designate a property.

As regards land and buildings, the Heritage Team mainly receives advice from bodies such as Natural England, English Heritage, Historic Scotland, Cadw Welsh Historic Monuments and other more specialist advisers such as the Royal Botanic Gardens (for rare trees), etc.

If a building is listed in England and Wales as Grade I or II or Grade A in Northern Ireland and Scotland or is a scheduled monument that is a *prima facie* indication that it will be accepted as outstanding. Land essential for the protection of the character and amenities of an outstanding building is also eligible for exemption. The factors to be taken into account here include 'the need to protect the views from an outstanding building (eg to landscaped parkland); the views of and approaches to it and the need to prevent undesirable development close to it'. The Revenue state that 'the "essential" in "essential amenity land" must be viewed initially from the perspective of the claimant. That an expert might regard a larger area than that in claim as "essential" amenity land cannot in itself preclude conditional exemption for the smaller area' (para 6.2 of the Capital Taxation and the National Heritage Memorandum). The conditional exemption for amenity land will include the trees and underwood on the land provided they do not detract from the qualifying interest. There is no requirement that the land has to adjoin an outstanding building (para 6.3 of the Capital Taxation and the National Heritage Memorandum). Buildings on essential amenity land qualify for exemption in their own right if they are of outstanding historic or architectural interest. When they are not eligible for exemption in their own right, the exemption granted to such essential amenity land will nonetheless extend to buildings on it providing that they do not compromise the protection of the character and amenities of the outstanding buildings (para 6.4 of the Capital Taxation and the National Heritage Memorandum).

For 'objects' within categories (a) and (e), HMRC take advice from the Council for Museums, Libraries and Archives. On 26 July 2010 the government announced its intention to abolish the Council. HMRC will be working with the Department for Culture, Media and Sport to 'ensure that relevant input currently provided by [the Council] continues to be available to HMRC.' An object is considered to be 'pre-eminent' if it falls within one of the following:

- Does the object have an especially close association with our history and national life?
- Is the object of especial artistic or art-historical interest?
- Is the object of especial importance for the study of some particular form of art, learning or history?
- Does the object have an especially close association with a particular historic setting? (para 11.12 of the Capital Taxation and the National Heritage Memorandum)

Foreign objects as well as British works may fall within the definition.

Undertakings

[14.9] As mentioned above, undertakings will have to be given which will depend upon the particular nature of the property and facts of the case. The undertakings must be given 'by such person as the [Revenue] think appropriate in the circumstances of the case' (IHTA 1984, s 30(1)(b)). Such a person can include a company. The undertakings may include matters such as the maintenance, repair and preservation of the assets, the management of any land, the conservation plans for buildings and their contents and the proposed public access and how it is to be provided and publicised. Although the legislation does not specifically refer to a Heritage Management Plan, it is a common requirement by HMRC that one is prepared which is incorporated into the undertakings. Such a plan is described by Natural England as 'a policy and priorities statement under which the day to day management will operate and a frame of reference against which detailed working decisions will be taken by those managing the property.' The preparation of such a plan is a time consuming and very costly exercise. The Revenue has stated that a heritage management plan should be agreed prior to the designation of the property. Therefore, conditional exemption will not be given until an agreed Heritage Management Plan is in place unless based on the facts it would be plainly unreasonable.

Monitoring undertakings and the provision of public access

[14.10] Not surprisingly, these are two of the main areas of controversy regarding heritage property.

Because of the concerns that heritage property was not readily available for public viewing as was originally intended and that many owners were not fulfilling their undertaking to provide public access, the Finance Act 1998 provisions were introduced. It was claimed that they were designed to give the public improved access to tax exempt assets while maintaining the protection of heritage property. The facility for owners to opt for public access by prior appointment only was withdrawn.

Variations on undertakings

[14.10A] Both existing and future undertakings may be varied by the Revenue, including undertakings given after 6 April 1976 and before 31 July 1998. At any time the Revenue may propose a variation of the original undertaking to the owner for agreement. A judge sitting in the first-tier Tribunal (Tax) may direct that the proposed undertaking is to have effect from a specified date, which is not to be less than 60 days after his direction, if he is satisfied that:

(a) the Board has made a proposal for the variation of such an undertaking to the person bound by the undertaking;
(b) that person has failed to agree to the proposed variation within 6 months after the date on which the proposal was made; and
(c) it is just and reasonable, in all the circumstances, to require the proposed variation to be made (IHTA 1984, s 35A).

In the case of *Re Applications to vary the undertakings of A and B* [2005] STC (SCD) 103 the Revenue's application was dismissed on the basis that the accumulated burdens placed on the owners as a result of the proposals would so outweigh the benefits to the public that it would not be just and reasonable to direct that they took effect. It was considered that the increased risks of theft and damage to the owners' possessions would go beyond what Parliament had in mind when empowering the inclusion of extended access requirements and publication requirements. The Special Commissioner listed seven principles in 'no particular order of importance' to be considered when determining whether proposed variations are reasonable.

The Revenue is not able to seek adjustments to terms attaching to estate duty exemptions.

Compliance

[14.10B] The legislation imposes a tax charge if the undertakings are not observed in a material respect (IHTA 1984, s 32(2)). There is little guidance as to what the phrase 'in a material respect' means in practice in the Capital Taxation and the National Heritage Memorandum. The Memorandum does state that one opportunity to remedy matters within a reasonable time frame will be offered in certain circumstances (para 7.2).

Under the monitoring procedures it is understood that owners of outstanding land or buildings will generally be required to make annual reports to the Revenue about the maintenance of the assets and the provision of public access. Exempt land and buildings will be inspected usually every five years (para 5.2 of the Capital Taxation and the National Heritage Memorandum).

Public access

[14.10C] 'Public access' above means that all owners of exempt assets will have to provide a measure of 'open' access to those assets in accordance with the terms of an undertaking agreed with the Revenue. 'Public access' must be reasonable and this will depend upon the nature of asset.This will vary from property to property depending on factors such as features of interest, size, location, content and other individual circumstances. There is, therefore, 'no hard and fast rule' (para 6.2 of the Capital Taxation & the National Heritage Memorandum).

In the case of exempt buildings and their amenity land, the Revenue states that:

> 'as a general guide, we seek access to the interior of a smaller building on at least one day a week plus public holidays during the Spring and Summer months amounting to 28 days (or 25 if appropriate in Northern Ireland, Scotland and Wales) each year but:
>
> '• for some buildings, it might be appropriate to seek fewer days' access (or none at all) to the interior. Such buildings might include those of specialised interest, or whose structure, contents or decoration would suffer from excessive internal access. They might also include those whose historic interiors had been removed or destroyed or were of no intrinsic interest. The decision to allow more limited access is dependent solely on the nature of the building while
>
> • for larger buildings likely to attract, and be capable of handling larger numbers of visitors, anything up to 120 days' internal access might be appropriate' (para 6.14 of the Capital Taxation and the National Heritage Memorandum).

It is understood that the maximum number of days will be changed to 156.

In the case of land, the access will, in general be 'to afford public access for walking and, if appropriate, riding on existing rights of way and permissive paths, supplemented where necessary by new access of either type.' It is recognised that for some land of scientific interest, it may be appropriate to impose restrictions with agreed closure periods for sporting activities, land management, nature conservation, etc. In most circumstances it will be open to the individual to charge a fee to view the exempt building but this must be reasonable from the point of view of the public at large. The Revenue did consider that such charges should be 'along the lines of those made by locally comparable sources, eg the National Trust' (HMRC IHT & Trusts Newsletter — December 2007).

For chattels exempt in their own right, 'open access' may be provided by displaying the objects at:

(a) the residence of the individual or at the place the object is kept (and unless the building itself is tax exempt, access may be limited to the area of the building where the chattels are displayed);
(b) a museum or gallery to which the public have access;
(c) any other building open to the public, eg a local Record Office;
(d) the appropriate European Heritage Open Days event free of charge (ie Heritage Open Days (England), Doors Open Days (Scotland), London Open House, and European Open Days (Wales and Northern Ireland); and
(e) local, regional or touring exhibitions.

Objects may be loaned for display in public collections for special exhibitions and this period counts as 'open'. An owner must give an undertaking that an object will be kept permanently in the United Kingdom and will not leave the country temporarily except for an approved purpose and period, eg a temporary public exhibition abroad. An application must be sent to HMRC before applying for an export licence (in the case of objects more than 50 years old). Loans to public collections may be covered by the Government Indemnity Scheme to relieve the borrower of the need to take out commercial insurance.

Access should be given for a suitable period and time each year, and without the need for a prior appointment. The Revenue states that it would not expect this annual period to be less than a month or so (or, where it suited an owner and an institutional borrower, a corresponding triennial arrangement). It is considered that only in very exceptional circumstances would gaps of 3 or more years be reasonable.

Historically-associated objects will normally be displayed in the building with which they have an historical association.

Publicising access and undertakings is a requirement of conditional exemption for heritage assets. The Revenue will expect the individual to make any undertaking available to any member of the public who asks to view it. The undertaking in relation to the building or exempt chattel may be displayed at the premises and will be displayed on the Revenue's website database (www.hmrc.gov.uk/heritage). The information required for the website is:

- a description of each object, group or collection;
- the county (though not the full address) in which it can normally be seen;
- viewing details including the dates the public can see it and, if applicable, the museum, gallery or other venue for its display;
- a contact point for information, for by appointment access and for loans for special exhibitions.

Owners of buildings open to the public will have their own publicity. The publicity for the attraction, together with the Revenue's web-site publicity, will be sufficient. For items displayed in houses not normally open to the public, further publicity will be necessary — in the local press or at a local tourist information centre and in a national publication or guide.

It is important that these details are renewed and updated annually to avoid an inadvertent loss of the exemption. Appendix 1A of the Capital Taxation and the National Heritage Memorandum contains the Revenue's views of what it considers is acceptable or not and common problems encountered.

Making a claim

[14.11] A written claim for relief from inheritance tax under IHTA 1984, s 30 must be made to HMRC within two years after the date of death or date of transfer. The Revenue has the discretion to extend this period and has indicated that an oversight or mistake on an individual's part or his adviser's part, or the making of a post-death variation will not normally by itself be an acceptable reason to allow a late claim. In the case of both lifetime chargeable transfers and transfers on death (including potentially exempt transfers which became chargeable as a result of death), a claim cannot be made until after the event. With lifetime chargeable transfers this was, perhaps, not such a problem but where the relevant transfer was as a result of death the procedural delays can cause significant problems for the executors as regards administration of the deceased's estate.

Unfortunately, there is no formal advance clearance procedure. However, Natural England will usually give an informal indication of the likelihood of land qualifying for relief on the basis of it being of outstanding scenic interest. Where a claim is likely to be made, perhaps because of the poor health of the current owner, it is worthwhile seeking in advance informal advice from Natural England. This will, at least, allow alternative planning steps to be considered if the property is unlikely to meet the required standards.

One situation where a claim for designation will be considered in advance is the intended lifetime creation of a maintenance fund in support of an outstanding building, outstanding or amenity land and historically associated chattels (IHTA 1984, Sch 4 para 1(2)).

Another situation where a claim will be considered in advance is in connection with the decennial charge arising under IHTA 1984, s 64. It is essential to ensure that a claim is accepted and the property designated under IHTA 1984, ss 31 and 79 as heritage property *before* the charge actually arises. It is not sufficient merely to have made the claim before the date on which the charge arises. HMRC has no discretion to backdate a designation to cover an earlier decennial charge even though the conditions would have been met had a claim been received. Hence, the claim for relief should be submitted in good time, considering that it can take as long as two years to process a claim.

Capital gains tax

[14.12] The heritage property provisions tend to be regarded largely as an inheritance tax relief. However, there are equally generous capital gains tax reliefs which interact with the inheritance tax reliefs. This is most obvious in that the capital gains tax legislation only gives relief in respect of property falling within the relevant inheritance tax provisions (TCGA 1992, s 258).

Transfers to certain heritage bodies

[14.12A] Disposals to certain national bodies within IHTA 1984, Sch 3 (IHTA 1984, s 25) qualify for capital gains tax relief under TCGA 1992, s 258. Relief is given by exempting the gain in full. As indicated above, neither of these inheritance tax provisions are strictly in respect of heritage property only.

Disposals of conditionally exempt property

[14.12B] Section 258 also gives capital gains tax relief for the gift of any asset which either has been or could be designated heritage property under IHTA 1984, s 31. This relief includes gifts to a settlement and disposals by trustees of property vesting absolutely. If no inheritance tax designation has actually taken place (for example, because the relevant asset was the subject of a potentially exempt transfer and the gift has not therefore created an immediate inheritance tax liability) then the equivalent undertakings required under IHTA 1984, s 31 must be given in order to claim the capital gains tax relief.

As regards heritage property falling within IHTA 1984, s 31, capital gains tax relief is given by deeming the relevant disposal to be a no gain, no loss disposal. Any relief given can subsequently be clawed back by deeming there to have been a disposal at market value upon one of three occasions.

(a) Where the property is sold and an inheritance tax charge arises under IHTA 1984, s 32.
(b) Where an undertaking has not been observed in a material respect.
(c) Where there is a disposal other than by way of sale and no new undertaking is given. This could apply, for example, where the new owner of the property subsequently dies and no new undertaking is given by the transferee. In this instance, the owner of the asset is treated as having immediately reacquired it at market value.

These broadly correspond to the occasions on which a chargeable event occurs for inheritance tax (see **14.4** above).

Therefore, where there is a clawback and the property has increased significantly in value, there will be a gain arising of not only the clawed back gain but also the gain accruing since the no gain, no loss disposal.

Where a capital gains tax charge arises due to the clawback of relief and inheritance tax is also chargeable, the capital gains tax payable is allowed as a deduction in determining the value of the asset for inheritance tax purposes (TCGA 1992, s 258(8)).

Maintenance funds

[14.13] The beneficial tax treatment afforded by the heritage property provisions outlined above may not alone be sufficient to enable a private individual or family to retain and maintain a substantial heritage property. By their very nature, many heritage properties are not income-producing or are unlikely to create sufficient income to be self-maintaining. Generally, other means of support are required.

Legislation designed to alleviate the problems facing the owners of heritage properties exists to exempt funds set aside to maintain the properties from capital taxes. Maintenance funds are now a useful tool in the preservation of heritage properties. They are not, however, always the best solution.

Statutory conditions

[14.14] A qualifying maintenance fund is one which falls within IHTA 1984, Sch 4 Pt I. Such funds are tax favoured as they attract inheritance tax reliefs, and to some extent, capital gains tax and income tax reliefs.

To qualify for relief, a fund should be for the benefit of land and/or buildings (and/or historically associated objects) which qualify, or could qualify, for conditional exemption and the fund must be held on the terms of a trust. In the first 6 years the trust fund must not be capable of being applied for a use other than for the maintenance, repair and preservation of, or making provision for public access to, heritage property, except that income not so applied and not accumulated can be paid to a qualifying charity or to a body included in IHTA 1984, Sch 3 (IHTA 1984, Sch 4 para 3). The property comprising the trust fund must be of an appropriate character and amount 'and regard will be had to other sources of upkeep available to the owner'. In practice, this means it must produce sufficient income to maintain the relevant heritage property. The trustees of the settlement must be approved by the Revenue. The trustees or a majority of them should be UK resident and must include either a trust corporation, a solicitor or an accountant or a member of such other professional body (IHTA 1984, Sch 4 para 2).

Although the provisions are reasonably stringent, there is some scope for flexibility. In particular, funds can be withdrawn from the settlement after the initial 6-year period (subject to an inheritance tax charge) if it becomes apparent that they are required for other purposes or are excess to requirements. It is also possible to add further funds at a later date, for example, on the death of the settlor if this is found to be necessary.

Inheritance tax

[14.15] The maintenance fund is, in effect, a discretionary trust. Without any reliefs there would be an inheritance tax charge on transferring funds into the trust, a decennial charge and an exit charge in the event of trust capital being used to maintain or otherwise benefit the heritage property itself. However, there are inheritance tax reliefs which exempt such transfers of value from inheritance tax (IHTA 1984, s 27 and Sch 4).

A maintenance fund can be established not only for national heritage property which has already been subject to a claim for conditional exemption, but also prior to a claim for conditional exemption. The Revenue can designate the relevant heritage property (ie confirm they believe it to be of sufficient national importance to qualify) and accept undertakings given by the current owner as if it had been the subject of a chargeable transfer. This allows the maintenance fund to be formed prior to, say, the death of the owner. This course of action is a means of testing whether heritage property is of an acceptable standard to be designated prior to claiming conditional exemption.

Additional property can be added to an existing maintenance fund, free of inheritance tax, by an individual. Under IHTA 1984, Sch 4 para 16, property held by a discretionary trust can be appointed to a maintenance fund without an exit charge arising under IHTA 1984, s 65. The property may pass either straight to the maintenance fund or via a beneficiary of the discretionary trust provided the beneficiary transfers the property to the maintenance fund within 30 days. The trustees of the maintenance fund must not have acquired an interest in the discretionary trust for money or money's worth or, where the property passes via an individual, that individual must not have acquired the property for money or money's worth.

On the death of a life tenant, property already in an interest in possession settlement can be transferred to a maintenance fund free of inheritance tax (IHTA 1984, s 57A). Where a person became entitled to an interest in possession after 21 March 2006, relief will not be available unless the interest was immediately before the person's death in one of the privileged trusts, namely an immediate post-death interest, a disabled person's trust, a transitional serial interest or a section 5(1B) interest in possession.

The transfer must be made within two years after the death of the life tenant or within three years if a court order is required to change the terms of the settlement.

A claim for inheritance tax relief must be made within two years after the date of the transfer concerned or within such longer period as the Revenue may allow.

If property leaves a maintenance trust for a purpose other than to repair, preserve or maintain the property and is not given to a qualifying charity or to a body falling within IHTA 1984, Sch 3, an exit charge arises (IHTA 1984, Sch 4 Pt II). Although property can be reclaimed from the maintenance fund after six years, there is a penalty for doing so. One notable exception to this charge is where the property is transferred to another qualifying maintenance fund (IHTA 1984, Sch 4 para 9) which again gives some flexibility to the arrangement.

Income tax

[14.16] The income of a heritage maintenance settlement is taxed under the normal income tax provisions applicable to settlements, subject to the provisions contained in ITA 2007, ss 507–517. Where the settlor has retained an interest in the trust fund, even an indirect interest by virtue of his owning the heritage property which the trust is established to benefit, the income arising is treated as that of the settler (ITTOIA 2005, ss 624–629). However, ITA 2007, s 508 enables the trustees to elect that the trust income, which would otherwise be taxable as the settlor's income, be taxable as if it were the trustees' own income. The election must be made on or before the first anniversary of the self-assessment filing date for the tax year to which it relates. If the election is made, the trust's income will be taxable at 50%. If the settlor does not pay additional rate tax it will be better for the trust income to be taxed as if it were the settlor's. Should the settlor be a Lloyd's underwriter, the possibility that losses may become available may make it preferable for the income to be taxed on the settlor.

Where property of the maintenance fund (either capital or income in nature) is applied for a non-qualifying use, or the fund ceases to qualify and the Revenue's direction is withdrawn, any income which has arisen since the establishment of the settlement and which has not been applied in the upkeep of the heritage property is, with certain exceptions, subject to an additional tax charge under ITA 2007, ss 512–513. This additional tax charge is at a rate equivalent to the difference between the additional rate of income tax and the trust rate. Due to the trust rate being 50%, the rate of the additional charge will be 0%.

Care needs to be taken to avoid a situation where an election is made to treat the income as the trustees' own income taxable at 50%, while the settlor is not paying tax at all.

Capital gains tax

[14.17] Specific hold-over relief for transfers into maintenance funds is provided by TCGA 1992, s 260(2)(b)(iii). The relief is available on the establishment of the maintenance fund, on the addition of further funds at a later date and on transferring funds from an existing maintenance fund to a new maintenance fund.

The provisions in TCGA 1992, ss 169B and 169C, which prevent hold-over relief being available on transfers into a settlor-interested trust and which provide for clawback of the tax in certain circumstances, do not apply to a disposal to the trustees of a settlement which is a maintenance fund for historic buildings (TCGA 1992, s 169D(1)) where an income tax election under ITA 2007, s 508 has been made. Gains made by the trustees will be subject to capital gains tax in the usual way.

Settled heritage property

[14.18] Historically, owners of heritage property have used trusts to ensure continuity of ownership and management and also to protect the property from improvident heirs.

Broadly speaking, property can be subject to the settled heritage property provisions in three circumstances.

(a) Where the property is the subject of a chargeable transfer into trust.
(b) Where an individual dies with a life interest in settled heritage property.
(c) Where property is held on discretionary trusts and is therefore subject to the relevant property regime.

These three situations are dealt with in turn below, followed by a brief review of problem areas encountered in practice.

Transfer of property into trust

[14.19] Since 22 March 2006, the lifetime transfer of property to either an interest in possession (or to a trust which would previously have been an accumulation and maintenance trust within IHTA 1984, s 71) is not a potentially exempt transfer but a lifetime chargeable transfer unless a relieving provision makes it exempt. Therefore the conditional exemption will be of importance not only in relation to transfers to discretionary trusts but also to transfers to interest in possession trusts. A claim is made in the normal way and, if conditional exemption is granted, the trustees will have to give the required undertakings.

Therefore, a lifetime transfer of heritage property to a trust other than a privileged trust, where conditional exemption is relied upon to mitigate the potential inheritance tax liability, can be an expensive strategy if conditional exemption is not, subsequently, granted.

Termination of life interest on death

[14.20] The termination of a life interest on death may be a chargeable transfer by the holder of the interest if the interest either existed before 22 March 2006 or was a privileged interest. If that is not the case, it may be an occasion of charge on property ceasing to be relevant property under IHTA 1984, s 65 because, for example, an individual becomes absolutely entitled to the trust property. In either circumstance, the charge may be avoided if the property is designated as heritage property in relation to that occasion.

Property held on trust

[14.21] A trust can be exempt from inheritance tax in respect of heritage property for the purposes of the decennial charge (IHTA 1984, s 79) and also when heritage property leaves the trust subject to certain ownership conditions (IHTA 1984, s 78).

Generally, the trust is exempt from the decennial charge if either the trust property has previously been the subject of a conditionally exempt transfer (and has therefore already been designated) or there has been an exempt disposal for capital gains tax purposes (also requiring designation). Alternatively, the trust property may be specifically designated as heritage property prior to the decennial charge to avoid tax on that event. As explained above, this is the only occasion the statute provides for advance designation of a property, and the property *must* actually be designated before the decennial.

Gifts with reservation

[14.22] Where heritage property is settled on trust and the original owner is included as one of the initial beneficiaries, the gifts with reservation provisions need to be considered regardless of whether the settlor actually receives any benefit. FA 1986, s 102(5) provides an exemption from the provisions for exempt transfers of property to maintenance funds but not for transfers of the heritage property itself. Presumably this is because the heritage property is conditionally exempt and should continue to be exempt provided the undertakings are not broken and, therefore, the gift with reservation provisions should not cause any difficulty.

Pre-owned assets

[14.23] A charge to income tax will arise on donors who continue to enjoy a benefit from property of which they have previously disposed. Where the arrangements put in place reserve a benefit to the original owner, there will be an exemption from the pre-owned assets charge. If, however, the original owner is excluded from the class of beneficiaries under the trust but later derives some benefit from the property, an income tax charge will arise. There is an exemption from the charge for transfers of property to maintenance funds for historic buildings although there is no exemption for transfers of the heritage property itself.

Acceptance in Lieu of Tax

[14.24] The Revenue has a discretion to accept particular heritage property in satisfaction of the payment of inheritance tax, estate duty or interest (IHTA 1984, s 230).

Land can be accepted where it has been agreed between HMRC and the person liable to pay the tax. Objects can be accepted provided they are, or have been, kept in any building if:

(a) the building is being or has been accepted in lieu of tax or estate duty;
(b) the building or interest in the building belongs to the Crown, the Duchy of Lancaster, the Duchy of Cornwall, a Government Department or held for the purposes of a Government Department;
(c) the building is under the guardianship of the Secretary of State under the Ancient Monuments and Archaelogical Areas Act 1979;
(d) the building belongs to any body listed in IHTA 1984, Sch 3

and it appears to the Secretary of State desirable for the objects to remain associated with the building (IHTA 1984, s 230(3)).

Pictures, prints, books, manuscripts, works of art, scientific objects, other things or collections thereof which are considered pre-eminent can also be accepted.

There is a financial incentive in using an arrangement known as 'the douceur'. No tax is payable on the accepted property. The amount of tax is satisfied by agreeing a special price. A special price is usually the net value of the property (market value less the notional tax liability) plus a percentage of the value of the tax. An offer must be made to HMRC detailing certain information (para 11.5 of the Capital Taxation and the National Heritage Memorandum).

Example

Honoria inherited her uncle's residuary estate which included a pre-eminent painting for which she did not care. It was worth £500,000.

Agreed open market value	500,000
Less: notional inheritance tax (40% @ 500,000)	200,000
	300,000
Plus: 25% douceur of the inheritance tax	50,000
	350,000

Strategy

[14.25] When considering the strategy for a particular set of circumstances, there are three main questions to be answered.

(a) Does the family wish to, and indeed is it able to, retain and finance the upkeep of the heritage property in future years?
If the answer is 'yes', then it is necessary to consider whether, and how best, to utilise the various heritage property reliefs. In some circumstances where one qualifies for conditional exemption it may be beneficial not to claim it.

(b) Is a lifetime gift appropriate or should conditional exemption be claimed on death?
To some extent, lifetime gifts are encouraged by the inheritance tax legislation and heritage property is no exception. A gift on trusts under which neither an existing IIP nor a privileged interest subsists would be a chargeable lifetime transfer and conditional exemption may therefore be claimed. Other gifts will generally be potentially exempt transfers and may, therefore, escape the impact of inheritance tax altogether or, if the donor dies within seven years, conditional exemption may be claimed on death. Furthermore, a lifetime transfer is deemed to be a no gain, no loss disposal for capital gains tax purposes where the property is either designated or could be designated as heritage property.
One potentially significant disadvantage of a lifetime gift is the loss of the tax-free capital gains tax uplift on death. This may be relatively unimportant where the property is to be retained by the family and can continue to be designated as heritage property or where the property is unlikely to appreciate significantly prior to the death of the transferor.

However, if the property is ever sold, or conditional exemption lost for other reasons, the cost of losing the capital gains tax uplift on death may be substantial.

A lifetime gift on flexible trusts may be considered as it enables the choice of eventual heir to be left open and the transferor can oversee such matters as the provision of public access to the newly designated heritage property. However, there are problems as explained above with this strategy.

Waiting until the death of the current owner of potential heritage property before claiming conditional exemption may have its advantages. This enables the capital gains tax uplift on death to be utilised. However, it also means that the deceased's executors and family will have to make an application for conditional exemption.

(c) Should 'supporting property' (ie property to provide funds for the upkeep of the heritage property itself) be placed in a maintenance fund or not?

Maintenance funds do have advantages and they are flexible vehicles. In particular, a lifetime gift of property to a maintenance fund has the advantage that it requires the relevant heritage property to be designated even where no chargeable transfer of the actual heritage property has been made. The establishment of a maintenance fund can therefore be used to test whether the relevant property is of sufficiently high standard to be designated as heritage property. However, the use of property held in a maintenance fund is severely restricted for the first six years. This restriction will need to be weighed against the tax advantages of using a maintenance fund.

An alternative to a maintenance fund is to advance supporting property direct to the transferor's heir. Such a gift, during lifetime, would be a potentially exempt transfer and no inheritance tax would be payable if the transferor survives for seven years. However, this is risky as, if it fails, it is not then possible to obtain relief retrospectively by transferring the property to a maintenance fund and asking for the now chargeable potentially exempt transfer to be ignored. It is understood that the Revenue is aware that this can cause a problem but does not consider the existing rules to be unfair. The income tax and capital gains tax advantages of maintenance funds are not huge and the motivation for using a maintenance fund will be almost purely inheritance tax driven.

The final decision as to whether to use a maintenance fund may well be determined on practical grounds, such as whether the family is comfortable with the supporting property being almost entirely alienated from their control for six years. The attractiveness of a maintenance fund from an inheritance tax perspective should not, however, be overlooked.

Chapter 15

Matrimonial Breakdown

Divorce/dissolution

Note. The non-fiscal laws, practices and procedures referred to in this chapter relate to England and Wales only and not to Scotland.

Establishing dates

[15.1] When a marriage irretrievably breaks down, it is necessary to determine the date when the parties permanently separated. This date will normally be fixed by mutual agreement and may be recorded in a deed of separation or court order. The date of separation is important for capital gains tax. In the limited circumstances where the husband is still entitled to a married couple's allowance (see **15.2** below), his entitlement will cease from the following tax year even if he voluntarily maintains his wife. By way of contrast, it is the date a divorce becomes final that is important for inheritance tax purposes, as will be seen later in this chapter. It may be in the interests of both spouses to defer the date of formal separation until the former matrimonial property has been transferred between them. Consideration should also be given as to whether separation can be deferred until after 5 April in any given year to mitigate any capital gains tax that might otherwise arise as part of the separation process.

Both parties to the marriage should notify the Revenue that they have separated. The Revenue will write to each party to determine the date of permanent separation. If the spouses give differing separation dates, the Inspector of Taxes will write to each party to try to agree a date. However, in some circumstances the Revenue may allow different dates for each spouse in order to bring matters to a close. Where the separated spouses are still living in the same house, the Inspector will usually seek nothing more than a formal assurance that the separation is indeed permanent.

Personal allowances

[15.2] The married couple's allowance was abolished with effect from 6 April 2000 except where one of the spouses or civil partners was born before 6 April 1935. Where, in the limited circumstances in which the married couple's allowance is still available, the couple separate, in the year of separation the husband and wife or civil partners will continue to receive the married couple's allowance that they were entitled to at the date of separation. For 2010/11, the maximum amount of married couple's allowance is £6,965 and the minimum is £2,670. If the marriage occurred before 5 December 2005 and at least one spouse was born before 6 April 1935, the husband can claim the allowance. If the marriage occurred on or after 5 December 2005 or there is a civil partnership and at least one spouse or partner was born before 6 April 1935, the person with the higher income can claim the allowance. The tax bill is reduced by 10% of the applicable allowance and the allowance is determined by reference to the husband's or claimant's income (as appropriate). If the income concerned is over £22,900 the allowance is reduced progressively from £6,965 down to the minimum of £2,670. The allowance is reduced by £1 for every £2 of income above the limit. The personal allowance can be reduced below the basic personal allowance where the income is above £100,000. If the couple have elected, prior to the start of the tax year in which the separation takes place, to split the married couple's allowance, this cannot be altered after the date of separation and remains in force until the end of the tax year. No married couple's allowance is due to either party for subsequent years although transitional rules apply where a married couple separated before 6 April 1990. In such a case, provided they are not divorced and the husband continues to maintain his wife by *voluntary* payments, full transitional married couple's allowance can be claimed by the husband for years subsequent to the year of separation.

In years of assessment following the year of separation, the single personal allowance is due.

Procedure

[15.3] Upon the irretrievable breakdown of a marriage proceedings can be issued to bring about a divorce. If the divorce is undefended, the divorce process has three stages, commencing with the petitioner filing a petition at court; upon the respondent acknowledging receipt of the petition and acceding to it the petitioner applies for the first decree of divorce, the decree nisi. Decree nisi is pronounced in open court, but the parties need not attend unless directed to do so. It is at this stage that a consent order concerning the division of finances can be filed for the court's approval; before the decree nisi the court is unable to seal any consent order agreed. Six weeks and one day after a decree nisi is pronounced the petitioner can apply for a decree absolute; only after a further three months can the respondent apply if the petitioner has not done so.

The court can dissolve a civil partnership in much the same way as a marriage, save that adultery by the respondent is not one of the grounds for dissolution.

Decree absolute is the final decree and marks the conclusion of the marriage. Until the parties are divorced (or their civil partnership is dissolved), property will still pass on their deaths under the terms of any will and commonly, one spouse will have bequeathed a substantial part of his or her estate to the other. Even where no will has been made, the rules on intestacy will apply and a large part of the intestate's estate will go to the spouse. A separated spouse may therefore inherit most of the deceased's assets unless action is taken at the time of separation to reverse the position by executing a new will or a codicil to the existing one.

Under the Law Reform Succession Act 1995, which applies to all deaths after 1 January 1995, a divorced spouse will be treated as if he or she predeceased the deceased person on the date of the divorce for all purposes. A gift in a will to a former spouse will therefore lapse on divorce. This may possibly disinherit the children of the former marriage. Similarly, the appointment of the former spouse as executor and trustee will be void unless the will provides otherwise. If there is a wish to leave property to a former spouse, it should be borne in mind that the spouse exemption does not apply to divorced spouses and such a gift may be liable to inheritance tax.

Following the divorce, either or both former spouses may marry a new partner. Marriage revokes a will unless the will was made in contemplation of the new marriage. Similarly, the children of a new partner will have no rights under intestacy. However, if the children of a new partner are adopted, they will then rank equally with the children of the former marriage. This may well be in accordance with the wishes of those immediately concerned, but if other people, such as grandparents, have left property to 'the children of X' this will equally also include the adopted children.

Nullity

[15.4] Nullity proceedings declare that the marriage was either void from the beginning or is voidable, meaning that the marriage is valid and subsisting until a decree of nullity is obtained. Where it has been held that the marriage is void or voidable then the parties to the suit for nullity are entitled to apply for all the financial orders which are available on divorce or dissolution. A voidable marriage will revoke a will made prior to it (again save where the will has been in contemplation of marriage). However, where it is held that the marriage was void it has no impact on a will. Irrespective of whether the decree of nullity is granted on the basis of the marriage or civil partnership being void or voidable it will have the same consequences for a then existing will as a decree of divorce. Such a decree also means that neither spouse will be able to claim in the event of the other party's intestacy. Nullity cases are comparatively rare and require a hearing. It is therefore often more efficient to pursue a divorce.

Judicial separation

[15.5] Judicial separation does not dissolve the marriage or civil partnership but can be used in cases where for example religious beliefs prevent divorce. As a judicial separation does not dissolve the marriage or civil partnership it only releases the parties from a duty to live together and therefore does not affect existing wills. It is therefore important to advise clients to review their wills in light of any judicial separation. The same menu of financial orders is available on judicial separation as in divorce or dissolution proceedings.

Ancillary relief

Overview

[15.6] In deciding how to approach the division of a couple's assets on divorce the court will rely on s 25 of the Matrimonial Causes Act 1973 ('MCA 1973'). Section 25(1) states:

> It shall be the duty of the court in deciding whether to exercise its powers under sections 23, 24 . . . above and, if so, in what manner, to have regard to all the circumstances of the case, first consideration being given to the welfare while a minor of any child of the family who has not attained the age of eighteen.

The Act then provides in s 25(2) a list of eight relevant factors:

(a) The income, earning capacity, property and other financial resources which each of the parties to the marriage has or is likely to have in the foreseeable future, including in the case of earning capacity any increase in that capacity which it would in the opinion of the court be reasonable to expect a party to the marriage to take steps to acquire;
(b) The financial needs, obligations and responsibilities which each of the parties to the marriage has or is likely to have in the foreseeable future;
(c) The standard of living enjoyed by the family before the breakdown of the marriage;
(d) The age of each party to the marriage and the duration of the marriage;
(e) Any physical or mental disability of either of the parties to the marriage;
(f) The contributions which each of the parties has made or is likely in the foreseeable future to make to the welfare of the family, including any contribution by looking after the home or caring for the family;
(g) The conduct of each of the parties, whatever the nature of the conduct and whether it occurred during the marriage or after the separation of the parties or (as the case may be) dissolution or annulment of the marriage, if that conduct is such that it would in the opinion of the court be inequitable to disregard it;
(h) In the case of proceedings for divorce or nullity of marriage, the value to each of the parties to the marriage of any benefit (for example, a pension) which, by reason of the dissolution or annulment of the marriage, that party will lose the chance of acquiring.

Guidelines for practitioners on how to interpret these factors, including the relative weight to be attributed to each factor, are established by case law (see **15.17** below). There is no set formula for the division of assets. Case law has given a wide construction to the words of the statute, such that the advice of a matrimonial lawyer will be needed to assess the likely value of a matrimonial claim.

The court is also to give regard, when exercising its powers, to whether 'it would be appropriate to exercise those powers so that the financial obligations of each party towards the other will be terminated as soon after the grant of the decree as the court considers just and reasonable.' A clean break may be imposed in relation to capital claims, income claims or both, but a court will not permit a clean break in relation to maintenance for a child.

The Family Proceedings Rules 1991 establish the procedure for the issuing of a financial claim for ancillary relief. The overriding objective is to enable the court to deal with cases justly. The main steps in the standard ancillary relief process are as follows:

(1) Issuing the appropriate form;
(2) Preparing financial disclosure;
(3) First Appointment hearing at court;
(4) Financial Dispute Resolution hearing at court ('FDR');
(5) Final hearing at court.

Settlement may be achieved at any time during this process and the timetable can be compressed. For example, it is possible for the First Appointment to be converted into an FDR.

Issuing the appropriate form

[15.7] A notice of intention to proceed with an application for ancillary relief which has been made in a divorce petition or answer, or an application for ancillary relief, must be made by notice in a Form A. When the court receives a Form A it will fix a First Appointment not less than 12 weeks and not more than 16 weeks after the date of the filing of the notice.

Preparing financial disclosure

[15.8] Prior to the First Appointment, which is usually listed for 30 minutes of court time, both parties must simultaneously exchange their financial disclosure in a Form E, to which the parties will attach prescribed financial documents. At least 14 days before the hearing of the First Appointment each party must then file with the court:

- a concise statement of issues between the parties;
- chronology of important dates during the marriage and litigation;
- a questionnaire setting out by reference to the concise statement of issues any further information or documentation requested from the other party;
- a notice in Form G stating whether that party will be in a position at the First Appointment to proceed on that occasion to a FDR appointment;
- confirmation that all relevant parties, including mortgagees and pension providers, have been served with the Form A.

First Appointment

[15.9] The Family Proceedings Rules explain that the First Appointment must be conducted with the objective of defining the issues and saving costs. The judge will consider whether directions are required to value assets, to obtain further disclosure and to seek expert evidence. The majority of cases will then be set down for an FDR hearing.

FDR Hearing

[15.10] The Family Proceedings Rules provide that the FDR appointment must be treated as a meeting held for the purposes of discussion and negotiation. At least 7 days before the FDR appointment, the applicant will have filed all offers and proposals and the judge at the appointment will give an indication to the parties as to how he or she would deal with the case at final hearing. This will often precipitate agreement, as the parties are able to hear a judicial opinion on the merits of their respective cases. If an agreement is reached at the FDR then the judge will consider that agreement and if appropriate, will make a court order in the terms agreed.

Final hearing

[15.11] If the FDR does not result in settlement the judge who conducted the appointment will have no further involvement with the case. A final hearing will be listed, usually for at least 1 day of court time. Directions may be given for further evidence, such as statements required to prepare the case for final trial. At a final hearing a judge will hear appropriate evidence from both parties and submissions by their representatives and will hand down judgment.

Interim applications

[15.12] At any time during the ancillary relief process, the parties can make interim applications, for example:

- to deal with interim maintenance provision, which is called maintenance pending suit (see **15.14** below);
- to freeze vulnerable assets and prevent them being spent or transferred offshore, which is called a s 37 application;
- to seek the court's assistance in the disclosure process, for example, if a party is refusing to disclose documents.

Costs

[15.13] At each court appointment the parties must provide the court with details of the costs they have incurred during the litigation. Offers can be made throughout the proceedings on an open or a without prejudice basis. Only open offers will be considered at the final hearing for the purposes of determining whether the other party should pay costs. Generally the court will decide that there should be no order for costs, save where there is relevant conduct that should be taken into account. See for example *A v A* [2007] EWHC 1810 in which Munby J ordered the wife to pay a substantial portion of the husband's costs 'as a consequence of the misplaced zeal with which she chose to conduct a case built on exiguous foundations'. In *F v F* [2008] Fam Law 182 Baron J found the husband's conduct in presenting a false claim to be so serious as to qualify as conduct under s 25(2)(g) (see **15.6** above), warranting an increase in the award to the wife. Furthermore, in *M v M* [2009] EWHC 1941 (Fam), King J ordered that the wife pay 20% of the husband's costs as her application was misconceived. Interestingly, King J did not require a detailed assessment and instead applied CPR rules 44.3(7) and 44.3(6)(b), thereby awarding a lump sum payment towards the costs. In *J v J* [2009] EWHC 2654 (Fam) (see **15.17** below) helpful guidance was set out for where the court is minded to make a costs order. For the costs treatment of third parties, see *Ben Hashem v Ali Shayif and Radfan Ltd* [2009] EWHC 864; *Baker v Rowe* [2009] EWCA Civ 1162 and *KSO v MJO and Another* [2009] 1 LFR 1036.

Powers of the court

Menu of Orders and their tax implications

[15.14] On the granting of a divorce, decree of nullity or judicial separation or on the dissolution of a civil partnership the court has wide statutory powers under MCA 1973 to redistribute the assets of the parties.

Maintenance pending suit

[15.14A] The court may make an order for maintenance pending suit under MCA 1973, s 22. The payments will be made periodically (weekly, monthly etc) for a term beginning with the date of presentation of the petition and ending on the grant of the decree absolute. This form of maintenance is available to a spouse to provide for immediate rather than capital or long-term needs and may include provision for legal costs, while the question of long-term financial provision is being determined (see *A v A (Maintenance Pending Suit: Provision for Legal Fees)* [2001] 1 FLR 377, followed by *G v G (Maintenance Pending Suit: Costs)* [2003] 2 FLR 71 and *Moses-Taiga v Taiga* [2005] EWCA Civ 1013, [2006] 1 FLR 1074, CA). In *Currey v Currey* [2006] EWCA Civ 1338 the Court of Appeal considered the factors relevant to an application for a costs allowance within a s 22 application. It was a necessary condition that the applicant could not reasonably procure legal advice by any other means. The ability to obtain provision for legal costs in a maintenance pending suit order is especially significant following the amendment to the Family Proceedings Rules, abolishing *Calderbank* offers and introducing a general rule that the court will not make costs orders in ancillary relief cases.

If a divorce eventually proceeds in a foreign jurisdiction, the court has no power to order the refund of maintenance pending suit already paid, see *M v M* [2009] EWCA Civ 1427, [2010] 1 FLR 1413, [2010] Fam Law 335.

Periodical payments

[15.14B] This type of order, under MCA 1973, s 23(1)(a), is the one most commonly recognised as a 'maintenance' order. Either party can be ordered to make payments to the other for such term as may be specified. A periodical payments order can be made once the decree nisi has been pronounced and will take effect on decree absolute. The order may continue until the death of the recipient or the payer or, if earlier, the remarriage of the recipient (MCA 1973, s 28(1)(b)). The periodical payments may be ordered for an extendable term of years or alternatively for a term which, pursuant to MCA 1973, s 28(1A), may not be extended.

The order can be varied by further application to the court under MCA 1973, s 31, whereupon the court has jurisdiction to make lump sum, property adjustment and pension-sharing orders in discharge of the maintenance order (see *Pearce v Pearce* [2003] 2 FLR 1144). Furthermore, in cases where maintenance has been awarded on the basis of a compensation argument, the court can order for periodical payments to be varied upwards (see *McFarlane v McFarlane* [2009] EWHC 891 (Fam) and *Hvorostovsky v Hvorostovsky* [2009] EWCA Civ 791). The effect of subsequent cohabitation with another party by the payee was considered in *Grey v Grey* [2009] EWCA 1424, approving *Fleming v Fleming* [2004] 1FLR 667. Notwithstanding social changes, cohabitation is not to be equated with marriage. In assessing the impact of cohabitation the court should have regard to the overall circumstances, including its financial consequences and duration.

Secured periodical payments

[15.14C] Under MCA 1973, s 23(1)(b), the court can order the payer of the periodical payments under **15.14B** above to set aside a fund from which such payments are to be made, or to earmark assets to secure payment thereof. The court can specify the term of the periodical payments, but if they are to the former spouse this will not extend beyond the remarriage or the death of the recipient (MCA 1973, s 28(1)(b)). Essentially, this represents an order for the transfer of income-producing assets to trustees with the income to be used to pay maintenance to the other spouse. Once the obligation to pay maintenance ceases, the trust ends and the property reverts back to the transferor.

The advantage of such an order is that it continues for the duration of the payee's life and will not cease on the death of the payer. Also, the order secures the source of the payments where the payer's other assets diminish or, in an extreme case, where the payer becomes insolvent (although in the latter case it is always necessary to consider the full implications of the Insolvency Act 1986).

Tax implications of paying and receiving maintenance

[15.14D] As far as income tax is concerned, the payment of maintenance under a court order or an agreement does not confer any benefit on the taxpayer and the receipt of the maintenance does not create any tax liability in the recipient's hands. The income remains throughout that of the payer and is taxed at the payer's highest marginal rate.

For inheritance tax purposes, the date of the decree absolute rather than the date of separation is relevant. Up until that date, transfers between spouses are covered by the spouse exemption provided that the recipient spouse is UK-domiciled for inheritance tax purposes (or both spouses are non UK-domiciled for those purposes). This also includes maintenance payments.

Where maintenance is paid to a spouse under a court order, the exemption for transfers which are not gratuitous should apply (IHTA 1984, s 10). In 1975, the Senior Registrar of the Family Division issued a statement with the agreement of the Revenue.

Alternatively, it can be argued that the exemption for dispositions for family maintenance under IHTA 1984, s 11 applies. This exemption covers transfers of value by one spouse to another, or to a former spouse. It will also cover transfers to children of either spouse where the transfer is for the maintenance of the recipient or the maintenance, education or training of the child who must be either under 18 or, if older, in full-time education or training.

Maintenance payments will not be within the scope of inheritance tax where either of the above exemptions or the exemption for normal payments out of income applies. Otherwise they will be potentially exempt transfers which will become chargeable if the payer dies within 7 years, subject to the £3,000 annual exemption.

Maintenance payments on a voluntary basis to a former spouse or to a child after the decree absolute will be potentially exempt transfers unless they fall within the exemption for dispositions for family maintenance, the exemption for normal expenditure out of income, or the £3,000 annual exemption.

Lump sums

[15.14E] Under MCA 1973, s 23(1)(c) and (f) the court can order a party to pay to the other, or to a child of the family, a lump sum or sums. A lump sum order may specify payment by instalments. A lump sum order cannot be varied by the court, but the court can vary, suspend or even discharge the instalments of a lump sum. A lump sum order is frequently made in conjunction with an order dealing with the matrimonial home.

A spouse is entitled to apply for one lump sum order only (although as mentioned above, the court does have power on an application to vary a periodical payments order to make a second lump sum order). Lump sum orders are also available for children, although they are rare. They may, for example, be relevant in the case of a child who is disabled.

Property Adjustment Orders

[15.14F] Under MCA 1973, s 24 the court can order one party to transfer property to the other party or to a child. A property adjustment order is final, only one such order can be made and it is not possible to vary these orders (save as referred to above, the court has power to make a further property adjustment order on a variation of a periodical payments order).

The most common options open to the courts in respect of the family home have been as set out below. The Finance Act 2006 had an impact on the popularity of *Mesher* and *Martin* orders. Such orders made on or after 22 March 2006 will normally create relevant property settlements. Although they may not constitute chargeable transfers (being within IHTA 1984, s 10 or s 11) such settlements may be subject to decennial and exit charges.

(i) *Outright transfer*. It is unusual for a court to order an outright transfer of the family home if it is the only family asset.

(ii) *Mesher orders*. A court can order that the parties retain shares in the former home, but defer the sale of the house until the earlier of any number of negotiated terminating events, such as the youngest child reaching 18 or the wife co-habiting for more than 6 months, remarrying or dying. This is called a *Mesher* order. It can leave the spouse who remains in the property very vulnerable if the house must be sold once the youngest child attains 18. These orders consequently became unpopular but they have been coming back into fashion following *White v White* (see **15.17** below).

(iii) *Martin orders*. A *Martin* order is often considered by the court to be fairer than a *Mesher* order. The conditions are generally the same with the important distinction that there is no requirement to move once the youngest child attains 18. The order takes the form of a settlement.

(iv) *Charge back*. A variation on *Mesher* and *Martin* orders involves the outright transfer of the house to the occupying spouse, but the house is charged with a payment in favour of the other spouse, the charge not to be realised until a specified event. This charge-back can be on the basis of:

- a charge of a fixed percentage of the market value on sale;
- a charge of a percentage of the net market value at the time of the order plus interest accrued at an appropriate rate; or
- a charge of a percentage of the net market value at the time of the order, index-linked to a property-based index.

There are potential drawbacks to the first two of these bases. The first basis provides no incentive for the occupying spouse to improve the property and, in fact, the occupying spouse could allow the property to deteriorate (unless safeguards are added to the order). The second basis is arbitrary and takes no account of fluctuations in the property market. The third basis appears the fairest.

(v) *Order for sale*. This is most commonly encountered where the former matrimonial home is large or more luxurious than is justified by the needs of the occupying spouse or the non-occupying spouse has greater need of the capital represented by the house. The order may contain consequential and supplementary provisions directing, for example who is to have conduct of the sale and how the price is to be fixed. In the rare circumstances where there is no realistic chance that either party would be able to obtain an outright transfer or a deferred sale in the ancillary relief, the court can make an interim order for sale under the Trusts of Land and Appointment of Trustees Act 1996 (see *Miller-Smith v Miller-Smith* [2009] EWCA Civ 1297).

Tax implications of transfers between spouses: While a husband and wife are living together, and before the decree absolute, transfers between them are deemed to be made for a consideration which gives rise to neither a gain, nor a loss (TCGA 1992, s 58). The transferee spouse takes over the base value. In effect, the transferee spouse steps into the shoes of the transferor spouse in relation to the asset for capital gains tax purposes. The no gain, no loss rule cannot be disapplied. Any actual consideration for the transfer is ignored. This relief applies for the years up to and including the tax year of separation but does not apply in subsequent years. While the spouses are separated but not divorced, they will be connected persons for capital gains tax. This means that transfers between them will be deemed to be at full market value. Once the couple divorce, they will normally cease to be connected and transfers will be for actual consideration, if any.

The matrimonial home will be exempt from capital gains tax provided it was the only or main residence of the transferring spouse throughout the period of ownership. The last 3 years of ownership always count as a period of residence, even if a new qualifying residence has been acquired (TCGA 1992, s 223(1)). In certain circumstances (for example, where job-related accommodation is provided) other periods of absence are also ignored. In some cases, the house may be transferred after a period considerably in excess of 3 years after the transferring spouse leaves it, in which case a time-apportioned part of the gain will be assessable. Even then, the gain may be covered by the annual exemption which for 2010/11 is £10,100. If a house is jointly owned, both spouses must have resided in it throughout the period of ownership for the exemption to apply.

TCGA 1992, s 225B provides that the home may be regarded as continuing to be the only or main residence of the transferring spouse from the date that spouse ceased to occupy the house until the date of transfer. However, certain conditions need to be satisfied:

- the house must be transferred to the former spouse as part of the agreement made in contemplation of, or in connection with the dissolution or annulment of the marriage or civil partnership or a judicial separation;
- it must have remained the only or main residence of the former spouse; and
- the transferring spouse must not have elected in the meantime for some other house to be treated as his or her only or main residence.

It may in fact be more advantageous not to claim this relief. If the transferring spouse has another property eligible for relief it may be better to make the transfer of the former home to the other spouse within three years of leaving the former matrimonial home. Otherwise, a proportion of the relief on the new house may be lost.

The transferring spouse may retain an interest in the matrimonial home being transferred. This may arise from a mutual agreement or an order of the court (see above). If the transferring spouse is to receive a specified sum (not exceeding his or her current entitlement), but postponed until the earliest of certain events, no capital gains tax liability arises when the sum is paid because of the principal private residence exemption which was due when the interest in the home was transferred to the remaining spouse. This would apply, for example, where the former matrimonial home is transferred to the remaining spouse in return for a cash sum paid from the proceeds of its eventual sale. However, if the non-occupying spouse holds a charge for a percentage of the equity on a future sale, a capital gains tax liability could arise when paid. Arguably, the deferred charge is a new chargeable asset for capital gains tax purposes (following the decision in *Marren v Ingles* [1980] STC 500, [1980] 3 All ER 95 (HL)) and the realisation of the charge will constitute a disposal. However, there is a contrary argument that such a secured charge is in reality a debt and, as such, no capital gains tax charge arises on its realisation. However, the issues are by no means clear cut and each case will turn on its own circumstances.

With regard to a *Mesher* order, the Revenue considers that such an order creates a settlement for capital gains tax purposes (see Capital Gains Tax Manual para CG65365). At the date of the order the spouses are treated as disposing of the property to trustees at market value. Any gain would be exempt provided that no more than three years had passed since the non-occupying spouse left the family home permanently. When the *Mesher* order lapses there will be a deemed disposal and reacquisition under TCGA 1992, s 71 on termination of the settlement. However, an exemption may be available as the beneficiary will have occupied the property throughout the period of ownership by the trustees (TCGA 1992, s 225).

For inheritance tax purposes the transfer of the matrimonial home between separated, but not divorced, spouses falls within the spouse exemption. After the decree absolute has been made, transfers will be potentially exempt transfers unless it can be shown, as is generally the case, that either the exemption for transfers which are not gratuitous (IHTA 1984, s 10) or the exemption covering dispositions for family maintenance (IHTA 1984, s 11) applies. These exemptions are considered above.

It would be prudent to ensure that all property transfers are effected prior to the decree absolute to take advantage of the spouse exemption.

(vi) As noted above, a *Mesher* order may be regarded as a settlement for capital gains tax purposes. It is likely that the Revenue may also regard a *Mesher* order as a settlement for inheritance tax purposes which could have inheritance tax consequences for the trustees. The settlement of any property will be a settlement of relevant property unless the settlement falls within one of the categories listed in **4.9**. The settlement will be a chargeable transfer unless the s 10 or s 11 exemptions are available to avoid a 20% charge to inheritance tax. Decennial and exit charges will still arise and therefore the funding of these charges will need to be agreed.

Surviving spouses or civil partners will be able to claim the proportion of available nil rate band (£325,000 for 2010/11) unused by the first spouse or civil partner on their death provided they were married or in a civil partnership at the time of the first death. If 100% of the nil rate band of the first to die is available, the nil rate band available to the survivor is effectively doubled. It is not possible to exceed this level of allowance, even in the case of a widow or widower remarrying. Separated couples are able to benefit from a transfer of the unused nil rate band. However, divorce will extinguish the ability for any unused nil rate band to be transferred to the survivor. This is discussed in more detail in **Chapter 16 Planning for Death**.

Overseas aspects – capital gains tax and inheritance tax implications: in a tax year subsequent to the year of separation, a spouse who is not resident and not ordinarily resident in the UK who transfers property to his or her former spouse will generally not be liable to capital gains tax. Being not resident and not ordinarily resident in the UK does provide scope for tax planning which is considered elsewhere in this book.

Where the inheritance tax spouse exemption is in point, it is necessary to bear in mind that a transfer to a non-UK domiciled spouse by a UK-domiciled individual is only exempt up to a limit of £55,000.

In some cases, one or both spouses may be beneficiaries of an offshore trust. It should be remembered that, depending on their personal circumstances, income tax or capital gains tax may be payable in respect of any payments to them from the trust as part of the divorce agreement.

Stamp duty land tax and stamp duty: stamp duty is only chargeable under FA 1999, Sch 13 on instruments relating to stock or marketable securities. Stamp duty land tax is payable in relation to land.

There are exemptions from both stamp duty and stamp duty land tax on the conveyance or transfer from one party to a marriage to the other in certain circumstances (Stamp Duty (Exempt Instruments) Regulations 1987 (SI 1987/516) and FA 2003, Sch 3 para 3). There may however, be some circumstances where it is not clear if a transfer is for consideration or not and so care needs to be taken.

Council tax: where the original council tax demand has been issued in joint names, the departing spouse may be able to negotiate a cessation of joint liability with the local authority at the time he or she leaves the property on a permanent basis. Otherwise joint liability will cease on grant of the decree absolute.

Where a separation has taken place and the remaining spouse can prove himself or herself to be the sole adult occupant, a discount of 25% is available.

Transfers of other property

[15.14G] The court can order property other than the matrimonial home or cash sums to be transferred between the spouses. Alternatively, this may be done by mutual agreement. In either event, the capital gains tax and inheritance tax implications will broadly be the same as those considered above except for the absence of principal private residence relief.

A transfer of assets between spouses on separation will be a disposal which, because spouses are connected persons, will be deemed not to be a bargain at arm's length (TCGA 1992, s 18(2)). The disposal will therefore be deemed to take place at market value. If the recipient spouse gives no actual consideration for the acquisition of the asset (or gives consideration not exceeding the base cost of the asset), full hold-over relief under TCGA 1992, s 165 may be available (relief under TCGA 1992, s 260 will not be available) but only if the asset is a business asset. However, it may not be in the interests of the recipient spouse to join in a hold-over election because he or she will receive the assets at the transferor's original low base cost. The question arises as to whether consideration is given by the parties. The disposal of an asset from one spouse or civil partner to the other is, where there is no recourse to the courts, usually made in exchange for a surrender by the donee of rights which they would otherwise be able to exercise to obtain alternative financial provision. The

Revenue take the view 'that the value of the rights surrendered represents actual consideration of an amount which would reduce the gain potentially eligible for hold-over relief to nil.' (Revenue Capital Gains Manual para CG67192). Unless the parties are able to demonstrate that there was a substantial gratuitous element in the transfer so that no consideration passed in the form of surrendered rights, hold-over relief will not be available. It is the Revenue's view that where assets are transferred between divorcing partners or civil partners of a dissolved civil partnership by reason of a Court Order the relief should not be restricted because actual consideration has been given by the transferee.

The capital gains tax liability is deferred and passed to the recipient which may be payable on a future disposal.

This only applies to business assets. It does not, therefore, relate to any other assets such as residential property or works of art. A business asset is defined as an asset used for the purposes of a trade, profession or vocation carried on by an individual or in partnership or by a company in which an individual claiming relief holds at least 5% of the voting rights. Hold-over relief is also available on shares in a listed company where the individual owns more than 5% of the voting rights or agricultural property for the purposes of inheritance tax.

There must be a court order, which includes a consent order formally ratifying an agreement reached by the parties.

Where a court makes an order for ancillary relief under MCA 1973, including transfer of rights under a life assurance policy from one spouse to another, or formally approves an agreement reached by divorcing parties that includes a transfer of assets including a life assurance policy, then the transferee of the life assurance policy does not give consideration in money or money's worth for the transfer and, as a result, no chargeable event gain can arise on the transfer (see Revenue Insurance Policyholder Manual para 7370).

Pension sharing orders

[15.14H] Pension sharing orders can be made by the courts under the Welfare Reform and Pension Act 1999 ('WRPA 1999'), s 85 where a petition for divorce on nullity is filed. They are not available in judicial separation proceedings. Pension sharing orders are a revolutionary concept and override all previous Revenue restrictions on the ability of a third party to have the benefit of another person's pension scheme.

The powers of the court extend to making 'one or more' pension sharing orders in relation to the marriage. Section 21A defines a pension sharing order as:

> an order which:
>
> (a) provides that one party's—
>
> (i) shareable rights under a specified pension arrangement, or
>
> (ii) shareable State scheme rights,
>
> be subject to pension sharing for the benefit of the other party, and
>
> (b) specifies the percentage value to be transferred.

Advisers have to consider:

(i) the value of all those rights — the cash equivalent transfer value (CETV) and a percentage of that being transferred from one spouse to the other (WRPA 1999, s 29(2));
(ii) what rights the recipient spouse can derive from the percentage transferred; and
(iii) what rights will be left with the other spouse.

CETV is the sole method of valuation under WRPA 1999; in the case of a pension in payment the valuation is called the cash equivalent of benefits (CEB) (Pensions on Divorce (Provision of Information) Regulations 2000, reg 3). Only benefits at the 'valuation date' can be taken into account by the court. The rules for calculating CETV assume employees' service terminates on the valuation date and does not take into account projected increases to the pension fund for possible future service. The pension administrators will implement the pension share within 4 months of the decree absolute or court order, whichever is the later.

Pension sharing orders can be made over:

- personal pension plans;
- retirement annuity contracts;
- employer's pension schemes (whether money purchase or final salary schemes);
- small self-administered schemes;
- services pension schemes;
- pension plans which are the product of a pension sharing order from a previous marriage;
- pension schemes without Revenue approval (eg employers funded arrangements);
- pension in payment; and
- an annuity or insurance policy which provides pension benefits but not widows/dependants pension in payment.

The order will provide for a percentage of the pension to be shared.

The court does not have power to make a pension sharing order over a pension scheme which is:

(i) subject to a pensions attachment order from a previous marriage; or
(ii) subject to a pensions attachment order from the current marriage.

A pension provided by a pension sharing order has the same tax treatment as any other pension scheme. The recipient spouse will be entitled to a tax free lump sum on drawing benefits and will be taxed on the pension payable as income. Death in service benefits will pass outside the estate for tax purposes provided the right of nomination has been properly used or they are written in trust.

Generally speaking a pension sharing order made under an approved pension scheme will not be at risk of falling into the hands of the trustee in bankruptcy. Even if it is determined that a former spouse has made excessive contributions to a pension prior to the presentation of the bankruptcy petition then they are deemed to have been made from the bankrupt member's portion of the shared pension and should be recovered from that portion, although if the bankrupt member's rights are exhausted, then the trustee could then proceed against the spouse.

Pension attachment. The court will still have the power to make immediate or deferred lump sum orders and/or periodical payments orders taking effect against any of the following benefits under a pension scheme.

- Members retirement pension.
- Lump sum commutation.
- Death in service lump sum.
- Guaranteed lump sum on death in retirement (MCA 1973, ss 25B–25D).

These are known as pension attachment orders (previously known as earmarking) and are less favoured by applicants than pension sharing orders. Unlike pension sharing orders, pension attachment orders are available in judicial separation proceedings. Orders made under MCA 1973, ss 25B–25D do not effect a true pension split — they merely attach the member's own benefits. The pension continues to be taxed as the member's income while the earmarked maintenance is tax free in the hands of the recipient. An earmarking order is one kind of financial provision order and, as in the case of maintenance, it lasts only during the joint lives of the parties or until the remarriage of the receiving party.

Orders relating to children

[15.15] There are two regimes covering financial provision for children. The first is the Child Support Agency (CSA) and the Child Maintenance and Enforcement Commission (CMEC). CMEC was introduced in November 2008 and currently operates alongside the CSA; in 2013/2014 a single system of child maintenance will be in place which now has almost exclusive jurisdiction to deal with child maintenance. The second is the court which retains jurisdiction to deal with those cases where the CSA/CMEC has no jurisdiction; the court continues to make orders where the parents have reached agreement on the level of provision to be made (but such an order is binding for one year only and thereafter either parent can apply to the CSA/CMEC); in respect of step-children who are children of the family; if the child or one of the parents is not habitually resident in the UK; in respect of school fees; in respect of children with special needs; where the child is in post-secondary education and where the paying parent's net income exceeds the CSA's maximum currently £104,000 per annum, the CMEC maximum is £156,000.

Under MCA 1973, where the court has jurisdiction it can order that provision be made for children in one of three ways.

(a) Payments can be ordered to be made by one spouse to the other for the maintenance of the child.
(b) The court can order that a trust be set up for an infant unmarried child.
(c) Payments can be ordered to be made either directly to a child or to a third party (eg a school) on behalf of the child.

The Child Support Act 1991 ('CSA 1991'), s 1(1) provides that 'each parent of a qualifying child is responsible for maintaining him'. The absent parent meets his or her responsibility by paying child support maintenance according to an assessment made by the child support officer. A 'qualifying child' is a child, one or both of whose parents are absent from him (CSA 1991, s 3(1)). 'Parent' is defined as the natural mother and father and adoptive parents, but *not* step-parents (unless they are, in broad terms, looking after the child).

The Child Support, Pensions and Social Security Act 2000 is in the process of being phased out by the Child Maintenance and Other Payments Act 2008, which came into effect on 1 November 2008. The CSA basic scheme is that a payer will pay 15% of his/her net weekly income (up to a maximum of £2,000 per week) for one child, 20% for two, and 25% for three or more. The Child Support (Maintenance Calculations and Special Cases) Regulations 2000 detail how net weekly income should be calculated. Basically, it is net of tax and national insurance, with pension contributions being deducted in full. Income from savings, investments and benefits are excluded but overtime, bonuses and commissions are included.

There are provisions for shared care leading to deductions from the maintenance payable by the non-resident parent (NRP). If the child stays overnight with the NRP for 52 to 103 nights per annum, there will be a reduction in child support of 1/7th; for 104 to 155 nights of 2/7ths; for 156 to 174 nights of 3/7ths and for 175 nights or more of one half.

From 2011, a gross income statutory maintenance scheme will be introduced, taking into account the latest available tax year information from HMRC. If a taxpayer earns between £200–£800 gross per week, he or she will pay 12% for one child, 16% for two children and 19% for three or more children. If his or her income is between £800–£3,000 gross per week, he or she will pay 9% for one child, 12% for two and 15% for three or more children. In both cases, where the payer has other children, the gross weekly income will be treated as reduced by 12% where there is one child, 16% where there are two children and 19% where there are three or more children. Furthermore, the definition of child has been changed to increase the maximum upper age limit from 19 to 20. New methods of enforcement against parents who do not pay have recently been introduced by CMEC. This includes (in addition to their previous powers) the ability to order a regular deduction order or a lump sum deduction order on the payer's bank account irrespective of whether it is joint or not to collect maintenance or record arrears, the imposition of a curfew and the ability to apply through a magistrates court to disqualify an individual from holding or obtaining a passport or driving licence.

School and university fees

[15.16] School and university fees can be an important element in any financial settlement and the court has power to make an order for payment of the school fees of a child. At first sight, it may appear sufficient to calculate a global figure for the maintenance of a child. However, the provision for fees can be more complex. For example, the level of fees will increase over time and the frequency of payments should be co-ordinated with the school's terms. An added complication can arise where a maintenance assessment has been made under the Child Support Act 1991, but whether this remains the case once the Child Maintenance and Other Payments Act 2008 is fully operational remains to be seen.

There is no jurisdiction for the court to order maintenance for children during a 'gap' year.

There is now no tax advantage in having a school fees order.

Factors taken into account by the court

Case law

[15.17] In his leading speech in the House of Lords' decision in the seminal case of *White v White* [2001] 1 AC 596 (HL), Lord Nicholls said (para 2):

> The Matrimonial Causes Act 1973 confers wide discretionary powers on the courts over all the property of the husband and the wife. This appeal raises questions about how the courts should exercise these powers in so-called "big money" cases, where the assets available exceed the parties' financial needs for housing and income.

The judgment reasserts that the objective of the Matrimonial Causes Act 1973 is to achieve a fair outcome and to achieve this objective there must be no discrimination between a husband and wife on divorce. He found that if a judgment does provide for an unequal distribution then the judge needs to check the decision against a yardstick of equality of division and provide articulated, good reasons for the departure, to try to avoid discrimination between the parties. However, the court shied away from a legal presumption of equal division of assets. It ended the reign of the test of reasonable requirements, which had effectively put an upper limit on the capital award payable, usually to the wife, once her reasonable requirements had been met. The court robustly addressed the question: 'where the assets exceed the financial needs of both parties, why should the surplus belong solely to the husband?' (para 35)

Over the next five years, the judiciary, practitioners and academics wrestled with the 'yardstick of equality' in interpreting the *White v White* judgment. Then in May 2006, less than 6 years after *White*, the House of Lords heard the cases of *Miller v Miller; McFarlane v McFarlane* [2006] UKHL 24 from which the principles of needs, compensation and sharing have been distilled and are now applicable to ancillary relief cases. Many cases fall at the needs hurdle, when parties do not have the luxury of surplus funds to which the concepts of compensation and sharing should be applied. However, if there is a surplus, then courts will look to compensation to redress economic disparity or 'relationship generated disadvantage' (para 140) and to a sharing of the 'fruits of the matrimonial partnership' (para 141).

Uncertainty abounds until these concepts have been interpreted through practical application by the courts. As regards inheritance, which in *White* included 'property acquired during the marriage by one spouse by gift or succession or as a beneficiary under a trust' (para 41), this is likely to be labelled as 'non-matrimonial property' as opposed to 'matrimonial property' or 'matrimonial acquest'. The general view is that an inheritance will have to be included in the pot of available assets if needs require this, but otherwise, the fate of that asset, and the applicability of the sharing concept, depends on a whole raft of factors, including the length of marriage.

Further guidance is found in the Court of Appeal judgment in *Charman v Charman* [2007] EWCA Civ 503 which held that consideration of the equal sharing principle need no longer take place at the end of the statutory exercise, but is instead the presumption from the start. To 'the extent that their property is non-matrimonial, there is likely to be better reason for departure from equality.' (para 66) This case also quantifies a tariff reduction to be applied within the sharing principle in cases involving a special contribution.

Since *Miller* and *McFarlane* the courts have sought to apply the reasoning in those cases. In *H v H* [2007] EWHC 459 (Fam), Charles J addressed the distinction between matrimonial and non-matrimonial property in a case involving substantial bonuses. The judge concluded that matrimonial property should be assessed at the date when the 'mutual support' of a marriage is at an end and found in this case that a bonus was no longer matrimonial property. The judgment includes a detailed analysis of the law on this issue. In *Murphy v Murphy* [2010] EWCA Civ 1258 the judge found that a modest departure from equality was justified to reflect the husband's greater earning capacity. Another illustration is provided by the decision in *L v L (Ancillary Relief)* [2008] Fam Law 12 where the sharing principle was applied but the judge found there was good reason to depart from equality based on the assets the husband had brought into the relationship and an inheritance he had received. See also *R v R* [2009] EWHC, although a reserved judgment from the Court of Appeal is awaited and *J v J* [2010] EWHC 2654.

Due to the current recession, there have been a number of applications seeking to set aside an order on the basis of a change in the value of assets and/or circumstances since the order was made under *Barder v Barder (Caluori Intervening)* [1988] AC 20. To date, the impact of the recession on the value of assets whether shares or real property has not been considered to be a *Barder* event sufficient to revisit the original order. In *Myerson v Myerson* [2009] EWCA Civ 282, [2009] 2 FCR 1 the Court of Appeal held that the fact that his company shares had plummeted in value from £2.99 to 27.5p per share did not constitute a *Barder* event. See also *Judge v Judge* [2008] EWCA Civ 1458, [2009] 2 FCR 158, and *Walkden v Walkden* [2009] EWCA Civ 627, [2010] 1 FLR 174.

Trust assets

[15.17A] *Charman* also provided the post *White* Court of Appeal's view on how to deal with trust assets on divorce. The facts in that case enabled the court to hold that it was acceptable for trust assets to be considered as Mr Charman's personal assets. Provided those trust assets could be drawn on in times of need, the court reasoned that their inclusion in the pot was justified on the basis that the assets were needed to meet the husband's legal obligations, ie a pay out to his wife (para 53). Sir Mark Potter stated that it would have been an emasculation of the court's duty to be fair if the trust assets in that case had not been attributed to Mr Charman and he encouraged the judiciary to carry out a balancing exercise to achieve an outcome that reflects the reality of the situation:

> 'Prior to the decision in *White*, the elaborate enquiry in the present case as to the attributability of the assets in a trust to a party as part of his or her resources would probably have been unnecessary. But, whenever it is necessary to conduct such an enquiry, it is essential for the court to bring to it a judicious mixture of worldly realism and of respect for the legal effects of trusts, the legal duties of trustees and, in the case of offshore trusts, the jurisdictions of off-shore courts.'
>
> (para 57)

The House of Lords refused Mr Charman's appeal from the Court of Appeal decision.

The courts will continue to have regard to the case of *Thomas v Thomas* [1995] 2 FLR 668 at 677G, particularly where the trust assets are not pseudo-personal assets. In that case, Glidewell LJ provided the following three-pronged test:

(a) Where a husband can only raise further capital, or additional income, as the result of a decision made at the discretion of trustees, the court should not put improper pressure on the trustees to exercise that discretion for the benefit of the wife.

(b) The court should not, however, be "misled by appearances"; it should "look at the reality of the situation".

(c) If on the balance of probability the evidence shows that, if trustees exercised their discretion to release more capital or income to a husband, the interests of the trust or of other beneficiaries would not be appreciably damaged, the court can assume that a genuine request for the exercise of such discretion would probably be met by a favourable response. In that situation if the court decides that it would be reasonable for a husband to seek to persuade trustees to release more capital or income to him to enable him to make proper financial provision for his children and his former wife, the court would not in so deciding be putting improper pressure on the trustees.

In *C v C* [2009] EWHC 1491 (Fam), the court considered whether a husband's reversionary interest in a trust fund was a 'financial resource' that could be included in a settlement. The trust fund was valued at between £4m and £6.2m. On the husband's mother's death, he would receive one quarter of the trust fund. However, during her lifetime, the trustees had no power to benefit the husband without the consent of his mother, who had an unfettered discretion to grant or withhold her consent. Munby J decided 'without much enthusiasm' that the fund was a resource, although 'very close to the outer extremity of what can properly be considered a financial resource'. It was emphasised that while the judge at the final hearing should have regard to the husband's interest under the trust, he could exercise his discretion not to make any order at all.

The High Court case of *A v A* [2007] EWHC 99 (Fam) enabled Munby J to find that the sham trust is a rare breed as '[t]he only way, as it seems to me, in which a properly constituted trust which is not, ab initio, a sham could conceivably become a sham subsequently would be if all the beneficiaries were, with the requisite intention, to join together for that purpose with the trustees.' (para 44)

In matrimonial cases involving trusts, and particularly discretionary trusts, there will be a conflict between the courts desire to agree a fair division of the assets of a marriage and the fiduciary duty of the trustees to act in the best interests of beneficiaries as a group. Cases such as *TL v ML* [2005] EWHC 2860 (Fam), [2006] 1 FLR 1263 and *Re C* [2007] EWHC 1911 (Fam) have discussed the extent to which the court should make awards where there is a probability that, with or without judicial encouragement, the family trusts would in all likelihood 'come to the rescue' of the beneficiary when faced with a court order against them. Under the Family Proceedings Rules 19.2(2), the court can add a party to the proceedings if it believes the joinder will enable the court to resolve the matters in dispute. In some cases the trustees may wish to join the proceedings voluntarily to ensure their views are represented, but trustees should consider such a move very carefully before taking it (particularly if they are resident in another jurisdiction). There may also be issues over whether or not the trustees will provide financial/other information relating to the trust (particularly an offshore trust). Offshore cases such as *Re H Trust* [2006] 9 ITELR 133, [2006] JRC 57 and *In the matter of the Truro Trust and the PF Life Interest Trust* [2007] JRC 189 and *C Trust Company Ltd* [2009] have indicated that some foreign courts are willing to encourage trustees to provide full financial information to an English Court and the spouses (even if the trustees are not joined) in order that an English Court has a full understanding of the overall financial position.

A court order or agreement may require the establishment or variation, of one or more trusts. Where a trust is ante or post-nuptial the court has power to vary the trust provisions under the Matrimonial Causes Act 1973, s 24(1)(c). In order to qualify as a nuptial trust, the trust must have been made with reference to the marriage. The issue of whether a trust may or may not fall within this category is regularly debated in the courts and surrounding negotiations.

The Court of Appeal confirmed in the case of *Charalambous v Charalambous* [2004] EWCA Civ 1030 that, according to the English court at least, the English court has jurisdiction to vary even foreign trusts under the powers of the Matrimonial Causes Act 1973, s 24(1)(c). There are however questions over whether an English court's decision is capable of enforcement in offshore jurisdictions (often depending on the jurisdiction concerned). Cases such as *Minwalla v Minwalla* [2005] 1 FLR 771 where the Jersey trustees refused to submit to the English jurisdiction, *Re B Trust*, *Re H Trust* and *In the matter of the Truro Trust and the PF Life Interest Trust* highlight the evolving case law on the position of trusts in matrimonial proceedings. In *Re IMK Family Trust* [2008] JRC 136, the Royal Court in Jersey made it clear that foreign court orders will not be directly enforced in Jersey (even where the trustees have submitted to the jurisdiction of the English court) but that where the order attempts to vary rather than alter a Jersey law trust, it will consider whether to give effect to that order.

In the matter of *C Trust Company Ltd* [2009] JRC 048 the court considered whether it was appropriate for the trustees to take steps to safeguard assets for the benefit of certain beneficiaries where two Jersey trusts were involved in ancillary relief proceedings in the English court. The judgment endorsed the decision in *Re H Trust* that there are occasions when it is important that the English court has full information about the financial affairs of the trust.

Much may also of course depend on the *situs* of the trust assets and indeed the specific provisions of the relevant offshore jurisdiction's trust and private international law.

Use of trusts

[15.18] A trust was often the most tax efficient means of providing for a spouse or children of a former marriage. They were used for the:

(a) settlement of assets on trust for the benefit of the children of the former marriage;
(b) settlement of the former matrimonial home on trust to enable the former spouse to remain in occupation until some specified event (for example, remarriage); and
(c) settlement of high-income-yielding assets to provide a fund for maintenance payments, effectively giving the transferor relief for maintenance by taking the income stream out of his or her hands.

Now, however, most new lifetime trusts will be subject to the relevant property regime. Although the establishment of a trust pursuant to a court order should qualify for the inheritance tax exemption applicable to transfers which are not gratuitous (IHTA 1984, s 10), a trust within the relevant property regime will nevertheless be subject to decennial and exit charges. Therefore, although trusts will continue to be a useful mechanism when making financial provision on separation or divorce, it will be more important than ever to give careful prior consideration to the tax implications of using a trust in these circumstances before taking any action. The different types of trust and their tax treatment are considered in **Chapter 4 Creating Settlements** and **Chapter 5 Existing Settlements**.

Inheritance (Provision for Family and Dependants) Act 1975

[15.19] Where a former spouse has not remarried, she may have a claim under the Inheritance (Provision for Family and Dependants) Act 1975 ('IPFD 1975'). Therefore the husband, for example, may consider leaving a written statement accompanying his will as to the reasons for excluding such a former spouse from benefiting under the will. He might record, for example, that he made adequate provision for her on the marriage breakdown. It is noteworthy that for inheritance tax, IHTA 1984, s 146 provides that where an order is made under IPFD 1975 the property is treated as having devolved on death and is therefore subject to a 'reading back' provision similar to IHTA 1984, ss 142 and 144 but without the 2-year deadline.

The Law Commission is currently considering the operation of the IPFD 1975 generally and a report is expected in late 2011.

Financial Relief after an overseas divorce

The English courts have the power to make orders where no or inadequate financial orders are made after a foreign divorce provided there is a substantial connection with England and Wales (Matrimonial and Family Proceedings Act 1984 Part III). Jurisdiction can be established either by one of the parties':

(a) being domiciled in England and Wales on the date of the application for leave or was so domiciled on the date on which the divorce, annulment or legal separation obtained took effect in that country;

(b) being habitually resident in England and Wales, for one year prior to the application or the date of the foreign divorce, annulment or separation;

(c) having at the date of the application a beneficial interest in possession in a house in England or Wales which was the matrimonial home at some time during the marriage (Matrimonial and Family Proceedings Act 1984, s 15)

Leave of the court to bring the application must be obtained before an application is made (s 13). The Supreme Court, in *Agbaje v Akinnoye- Agbaje* [2010] UKSC13, has considered for the first time, Part III and given guidance on the proper application of the statute. It is thought that more applications for leave will be issued as a result of *Agbaje*.

Cohabitation

[15.20] In May 2006, the Law Commission published a consultation paper concerning the financial hardship suffered by cohabitants or their children on the termination of the relationship by separation or death. The final report to Parliament was published on 31 July 2007. It concluded that reform was necessary having found that the existing law as it relates to cohabitants is uncertain and may give rise to unjust results. At present, cohabitants cannot make a claim for periodical payments and are limited, if there is a jointly owned property, to making an application under the Trusts of Land and Appointment of Trustees Act 1996 for an order declaring the nature or extent of their interest in the property. Where there is a child, an application under the Children Act 1989, Sch 1 can be made for a periodical or secured periodical payments order, a lump sum order or for the settlement or transfer of property. Under the Law Commission's proposals financial relief would not be available to all cohabitants, but only to those who had had a child together or who had lived together for a minimum duration (between two and five years is suggested) and who had not agreed to disapply the scheme. It would also be necessary for an applicant to show that the respondent retained a benefit or that the applicant had a continuing economic disadvantage as a result of contributions made to the relationship. However, cohabitation reform is not on the current parliamentary agenda following the change of government.

Insolvency

[15.21] Bankruptcy has been of increasing significance in the recession. The bankruptcy of a spouse creates difficult problems for matrimonial practitioners and leads to a situation where the other spouse and the creditors have to compete for the matrimonial assets. Historically, the creditors have prevailed as a result of powers under the Insolvency Act 1986 to set aside 'transactions at an undervalue'. In the case of *Haines v Hill* [2007] EWCA Civ 1284, the Court of Appeal redressed the balance and concluded that a property adjustment order made in the course of ancillary relief proceedings cannot be attacked as a transaction at an undervalue, finding that the right to apply under MCA 1973 was not only a right recognised by law but also had value.

Efforts must be made to check whether the bankruptcy is genuine. See *Paulin v Paulin* [2009] EWCA Civ 221, [2009] 3 All ER 88n, (2009) 2 FLR 354.

Pre and post-nuptial settlements

[15.22] Pre-nuptial settlements are formal written agreements entered into by some couples prior to getting married. Such agreements usually set out who will own what when they are married and what will happen if they divorce.

In many countries, pre-nuptial agreements are treated as binding and enforceable by the courts. In England and Wales, such agreements have been considered to be against public policy and therefore void. Whilst they cannot oust the jurisdiction of the court to make orders on the division of assets on a divorce, they can however, be taken into account in doing so (provided that the agreement has been properly negotiated in good time before the marriage, with equally competent legal advice for both parties, full disclosure having been made and proper consideration being given to the arrival of children). However, pre-nuptial agreements have gained recognition in a number of recent cases, including *Radmacher (formerly Granatino) v Granatino* [2009] EWCA Civ 649, [2009] 2 FCR 645 in which the Court of Appeal allowed an appeal by a wife against a High Court decision to set aside a German pre-nuptial agreement. The couple had agreed that neither party would gain financially in the event of divorce. However, the High Court had awarded the husband a lump sum of £5.56m and the wife appealed.

The appeal was allowed and the husband's lump sum reduced to approximately £1m together with a fund of £2.5m to purchase a house which is to be returned to the wife when the youngest child of the marriage reaches the age of 22. Thorpe LJ recommended that judges should give due weight to pre-nuptial agreements entered into by parties freely and knowingly. This, however, contradicts the Privy Council's view in *MacLeod v MacLeod* (see below) that 'it was not open to them to reverse the long standing rule that ante-nuptial agreements are contrary to public policy and thus not valid or binding in the contractual sense' and that the 'difficult issue of the validity and effect of ante-nuptial agreements is more appropriate to legislative rather judicial development'. It is therefore unclear whether the enforceability of such agreements has really changed on a practical level. In *Radmacher*, the husband has filed an appeal to the Supreme Court and, at the time of writing, judgment is awaited. In addition, the Law Commission is expected to report on the circumstances in which the courts should uphold pre-nuptial agreements by 2012. In the meantime, the case of *F v F* [2010] Fam Law 128 has provided further guidance on how to approach pre-nuptial agreements. The court disregarded a separation of property contract signed in France on the basis that it was an administrative inconvenience imposed by the state. It was very different to the agreement in *Radmacher* which had been imposed by the wife's family as a condition of marriage.

Post-nuptial agreements are similar to pre-nuptial agreements but are entered into by some couples once married. Such an agreement was considered in the case of *MacLeod v MacLeod* [2008] UKPC 64, [2009] 1 All ER 851. Prior to this case, such agreements were considered to be against public policy and therefore void. However, in *MacLeod*, the post-nuptial agreement was held to be valid and enforceable. It remained subject to the court's powers of variation but although the agreement provided the wife with less than she could have expected without it, the Privy Council decided there was no basis to interfere. The couple had also entered into a pre-nuptial settlement, hence the comments made by the Privy Council about such agreements (referred to above) but the importance of this case is in recognising the enforceability of post-nuptial agreements.

The Law Commission report on pre-nuptial settlements will be eagerly awaited but until such time as the enforceability of pre-nuptial agreements is more certain, it is likely that post-nuptial agreements will be increasingly used. In the meantime, some couples might wish to confirm a pre-existing pre-nuptial agreement in a post-nuptial contract.

Chapter 16

Planning for Death

Wills

[16.1] A crucial element of estate planning for an individual is the preparation of a will, correctly drawn to ensure that the property remaining at his death is distributed among his family and dependants and other beneficiaries in a tax-efficient manner. It is essential to this strategy to ensure that the testator's spouse or civil partner (and other dependants) are adequately provided for at the minimum tax cost in each case.

There is no certain formula for determining what will amount to adequate provision for dependants. It used to be suggested that a capital sum equal to ten times the husband's annual salary was required to provide adequately for his widow and family. Certainly, in smaller estates of less than £1,000,000 there may be little scope for anything but provision for the surviving spouse unless she has means of her own.

The importance of having a will, correctly drawn and regularly reviewed, is three-fold. First, it ensures that the deceased's estate devolves exactly as he desires and in as tax-efficient a manner as possible. If there is no will, then the statutory intestacy provisions will apply which may achieve a devolution in the deceased's estate in a manner which does not fulfil his wishes. These provisions are discussed in more detail below. Secondly, it simplifies the administration of the estate thereby saving time and the expense to which an intestacy invariably gives rise. Finally, it enables the testator to choose suitable, competent executors to administer his estate, which is preferable to relying on the statutory order in the case of an intestacy.

Use of exemptions and reliefs

Spouse exemption

[16.2] IHTA 1984, s 18 provides that gifts by a donor to his spouse or civil partner are exempt from inheritance tax.

Example

(a) Tony makes an absolute gift of £500,000 to his wife June during his lifetime.
(b) Under the terms of his will Tony leaves £2m to his wife June absolutely.
(c) Under the terms of his will Tony leaves to June an immediate interest in possession in his residuary estate.

There is a limitation of £55,000 to the spouse exemption where the transferor spouse or civil partner is domiciled in the UK but the transferee spouse is domiciled outside the UK (IHTA 1984, s 18(2)).

Where the limit applies, gifts are set against it first and never fall out of account, even after seven years. This is in contrast to the potentially exempt transfer regime. Where the £55,000 limit has been utilised the nil rate band may be available.

Example

> Tessa transferred £300,000 in 2000 to her husband, Tristram who is non-UK domiciled. The first £55,000 is exempt and the remaining £245,000 is a potentially exempt transfer. Under the terms of Tessa's will, she leaves all her property to Tristram. Tessa dies in 2010 when Tristram is still non-UK domiciled.
>
> Although Tessa made a gift more than seven years ago, the £55,000 exemption has been used and is therefore not available. Her nil rate band of £325,000 is available however, as seven years have passed since the gift in 2000.

In *Holland (Holland's Executor) v CIR* [2003] STC (SCD) 43 (SpC 350) it was held that the spouse exemption applied only to persons legally married and did not apply to a person who had lived with another person as husband and wife.

The spouse exemption is not available for lifetime gifts into a trust of which the settlor's spouse or civil partner is the life tenant.

Example

> On 12 April 2006, Tony made a gift to an interest in possession trust for the benefit of June. The gift was a lifetime chargeable transfer and the spouse exemption was not available.
>
> If the gift had been made two months earlier, the gift would have been a potentially exempt transfer on which the spouse exemption would have been available.

The restriction on the spouse exemption being available on lifetime transfers to an interest in possession trust may cause some difficulties.

Before 22 March 2006, it did not matter whether a gift to a surviving spouse was of an interest in possession or an absolute interest because IHTA 1984, s 49 treated the person with an interest in possession as owning the assets in which that life interest subsisted. This is still the case for individuals becoming beneficially entitled after 21 March 2006 provided that the interest in possession for the benefit of the surviving spouse or civil partner is an immediate post-death interest as defined in IHTA 1984, s 49A. There should be scope for the surviving spouse to make potentially exempt transfers if he or she finds that the benefits conferred are in excess of requirements. The surviving spouse could surrender her interest in whole or in part. Termination of the life tenant's immediate post-death interest will be treated as a potentially exempt transfer if the trust property is vested in an individual absolutely or if there is a gift into a disabled person's trust or if the initial trust was established under the will of a parent and the immediate post-death interest is terminated and replaced by a bereaved minor's trust. In all other circumstances, the termination will be a lifetime chargeable transfer creating a potential inheritance charge (IHTA 1984, s 3A).

The decision as to whether a gift by will should be absolute or limited not only involves inheritance tax considerations but often involves other considerations such as:

(a) the testator's confidence as to whether his spouse or civil partner will pass that property on to their children either by lifetime gifts or by his will;
(b) the testator's concern that his spouse or civil partner may remarry and leave property to the new spouse or the new spouse's or civil partner's family; or
(c) the testator's wish to protect a spendthrift spouse or civil partner from himself.

For further consideration of the spouse exemption, see under **16.12** below.

Transferable nil rate band

[16.3] It has long been the case that an essential element of estate planning was the utilisation of an individual's inheritance tax nil rate band. Many wills of a husband and wife were drafted so that they each left everything to each other which meant that on the first death the nil rate band was unused. It is now possible to for a nil rate band unused on a person's death to be transferred to the estate of their spouse or civil partner.

A formal claim must be made to transfer any unused nil rate band from the estate of the deceased spouse (IHTA 1984, s 8B).

The legislation is found in IHTA 1984, ss 8A–8C. In addition, HMRC has published 'guidance' in relation to these three new sections which can be found in the HMRC Inheritance Tax Manual, para 43000.

For spouses, the first death can have occurred at any time; indeed, the first death could have occurred under Estate Duty Rules. It should be borne in mind that there was no general spouse exemption under the estate duty provisions until 1972 when a £15,000 exemption was introduced with a complete exemption from 1974. As a result, nil rate bands were frequently utilised. The interaction of the transferable nil rate band legislation with some of the rules which apply to deaths which occurred under estate duty provisions has caused some confusion. For example, in relation to deaths of persons killed or missing in action before 12 March 1952 (see IHT Newsletter April 2009). For civil partners, however, the first death must have occurred after 4 December 2005 which was the date that the Civil Partnership Act 2004 became law. The parties to a legal relationship equivalent to civil partnership entered into before that date under the law of another jurisdiction are treated as having formed a civil partnership on 5 December 2005. Where there is a divorce or a dissolution of a civil partnership any unused nil rate band is not available to be transferred to the surviving former spouse or civil partner.

Where a marriage ceremony has taken place abroad it must meet the legal requirements of that country 'if the parties to the marriage are to be regarded as "spouses" for the purposes of transferring the unused nil rate band'. The transferable nil rate band will be available in relation to the Scottish Marriage of Cohabitation and repute if, on the first death, the spouse exemption was granted. (HMRC Inheritance Tax Manual, para 43003).

Before the introduction of the transferable nil rate band, wills were drafted to ensure that both spouses' nil rate bands were utilised. This was usually done by creating nil rate band discretionary trusts (see **16.4**). This was sometimes done by defining the amount to be settled on trust as being 'the maximum sum that I can leave without inheritance tax being payable'. This wording can now result in a maximum of £650,000 being settled on discretionary trusts. Whereas if the will stated that 'a sum equal to the upper limit of the nil percent rate band in the table of rates of tax (applicable on my death) in Schedule 1 of the Inheritance Tax Act 1984' is settled on trusts then an amount equal to a single nil rate band will be settled. This is an important issue to discuss with clients to determine their wishes. The wording has become of significance particularly in relation to situations where the residue of an estate is left to a charity. Charities have become increasingly aggressive in the pursuit of bequests and devises under wills, both in pressurising executors to administer estates quickly and in construing wills in ways which are most favourable to the charity with scant regard to the likely wishes of the testator. The case of the *Royal Society for the Prevention of Cruelty to Animals v Sharpe* [2010] EWHC 268 (Ch), [2010] STC 975 was a particular example of this. The RSPCA was a residuary legatee of a will subject to specific legacies to the brother and lifelong friends of the deceased. The legacies were framed by reference to the maximum amount which the testator could bequeath without inheritance tax being payable. Mr Justice Smith said:

> 'It is a matter of regret in my view that this action was ever brought. It clearly caused great distress to the defendant and I cannot believe the deceased would have been happy to see arguments by the RSPCA designed to erode the largess in favour of his friends and relative to their benefit in this way . . . I know it is said that trustees of charitable organisations are required to maximise the return for their charity but I really wonder whether the discharge of that duty required this action to be brought. In my view the RSPCA whatever the view as to the will ought really to have considered that the residuary legacy that I have determined it is entitled to was generous and ample provision out of this estate. The impact of the arguments on the size of the bequest to the deceased's brother was quite stark. This action has plainly caused distress to the defendants and in my view ought not to have been brought.'

In making wills, testators should now hesitate before making outright bequests or devises to charities and should consider, instead, leaving assets on discretionary trusts, guiding the trustees, by means of a letter of wishes, to consider making appropriate advances to the testator's chosen charities.

Unused nil rate band

[16.3A] The first issue to determine is whether there is an unused nil rate band. IHTA 1984, s 8A contains a formula to determine the question. A person has an unused nil rate band if:

$$M > VT$$

Where:

M is the maximum amount that could be transferred on the first death at 0%. This is therefore the nil rate band on the first death less the chargeable value of any lifetime transfers that use up the nil rate band first.

VT is the chargeable value of the transfer on death. This includes all non-exempt or relievable legacies passing under the will or intestacy, assets passing by survivorship, gifts with reservation chargeable at death and any settled property.

Where M is greater than VT, that amount is expressed as a percentage of the nil rate band available on the first death and is the amount by which the nil rate band on the second death is increased. That percentage is:

$$\frac{E}{NRBMD} \times 100$$

Where:

E is the amount by which M is greater than VT; and

NRBMD is a nil-rate band maximum at the first death.

Example

Malcolm died on 1 November 2002, leaving an estate as follows:

Net estate	£300,000
Chargeable legacies	£100,000
Residue to Edna (his spouse)	£200,000

Malcolm had made no lifetime chargeable transfers. The nil rate band was £250,000 and so M was £250,000. The chargeable value (VT) was £100,000.

E is therefore £150,000 (£250,000 less £100,000). The percentage of nil rate band available to transfer is:

$$\frac{£150,000}{£250,000} \times 100 = 60\%$$

Edna died on the 16 September 2009 when the nil rate band was £325,000. On her death her nil rate band would be calculated as follows:

£325,000 + (60% of £325,000) = £520,000

Where the deceased dies with a cumulative total of lifetime transfers, the nil rate band is first set against those transfers.

Married more than once

[16.3B] Special rules apply to limit the amount of the available nil rate band where a spouse or civil partner has been a party to more than one marriage or civil partnership.

Example

> Sophie was married to Edward who died in 1988 leaving an estate of £200,000. Under his will he left £50,000 to their daughter and the remainder to his wife. At that time the nil rate band was £110,000. No tax was payable. In 1998, Sophie married Clive who died in 2005 leaving an estate of £300,000. Under his will he left £100,000 to a nephew and the remainder to Sophie. The nil rate band was £275,000.
>
> Sophie died in June 2009.
>
> On the death of Edward, 54.5% of his nil rate band was unused calculated as follows:
>
> (110,000 > 50,000 therefore the unused nil rate band was 60,000/110,000) = 54.5%
>
> On the death of Clive, 63.6% of his nil rate band was unused calculated as follows:
>
> (275,000 > 100,000 therefore the unused nil rate band = 175,000/275,000) = 63.6%
>
> On the death of Sophie the unused nil rate band is calculated as follows:
>
> Although the amount of the unused nil rate band is £383,825 ((54.5% of 325,000 = 177,125) + (63.6% of 325,000 = 206,700)) = 383,825). The amount of the unused nil rate band is limited to £325,000. Sophie will have a nil rate band available on her death of £650,000 (IHTA 1984, s 8A(5)).

To avoid the restriction on the amount of nil rate band available a discretionary trust can be used (see **16.4** below).

Simultaneous deaths

[16.3C] Special rules apply where there are simultaneous deaths. The rules are different in England and Wales than to those which apply in Scotland and Northern Ireland. In England and Wales, where spouses and civil partners die leaving wills in circumstances rendering it uncertain which of them survived the other, there is a presumption that the elder person died first (the 'Commorientes Rule'). IHTA 1984, s 4(2) provides that where it cannot be ascertained which of two people survived the other then it is assumed for inheritance tax purposes that both deaths occurred at the same time. This means that the property of the elder falls outside the charge to inheritance tax on the younger's death. HMRC's Guidance states that 'the younger's estate could benefit from a double nil rate band and the assets accruing to their estate from the elder are excluded' (HMRC Inheritance Tax Manual, para 43040).

In Scotland and Northern Ireland, both spouses or civil partners are treated as dying at the same moment, so neither can inherit from the other. Each person's estate will pass to their heirs whether by will or under an intestacy. In the event that one spouse or civil partner had any unused nil rate band it is available to be transferred to the estate of the other, if required.

Example

Sebastian is 65 and Susan is 45. They both have estates worth £500,000. Under their wills each leaves his or her estate to the other survivor and, subject to that, thereafter to their son Augustus.

Unfortunately they are both involved in an accident and it is not possible to determine who died first.

If their wills did not contain survivorship clauses Susan is deemed to have survived Sebastian and so inherits his assets.

For IHT purposes Sebastian and Susan are assumed to have died at the same time. The spouse exemption will be available on Susan's inheritance from Sebastian. Because Sebastian's assets cannot have formed part of Susan's estate immediately before her death there is no inheritance tax payable on Sebastian's assets as a result of Susan's death.

Susan's estate is valued at the moment immediately before her death at £500,000. At that time she had not inherited Sebastian's assets and so his assets will not form part of her estate. As Sebastian had not utilised his nil rate band, Susan has a nil rate band of £650,000 to utilise. Augustus therefore inherits his parents' estates free of inheritance tax.

If Susan and Sebastian's wills had contained a 30-day survivorship clause their assets would have passed directly to Augustus. The inheritance tax payable on each estate would be as follows:

(500,000 – 325,000) x 40% = 70,000.

A total of £140,000 of inheritance tax would have been payable.

The above example illustrates that where both estates are in excess of the nil rate band a survivorship clause where the Commorientes Rule produces an unnecessary tax charge.

Care should therefore be taken when considering a survivorship clause and its effects should be explained to the client.

Making a claim

[16.3D] The transfer of an unused nil rate band must be claimed (IHTA 1984, s 8B) within the permitted period. This period is defined as 2 years from the end of the month in which the survivor dies or if it ends later, 3 months from when the personal representatives act as such or such longer period as an HMRC Officer may allow. The phrase 'first acted as such' is not defined in the legislation and so follows the general law concerning acts done by the executors. The Revenue gives examples in its guidance as to when a late claim may be permitted (Inheritance Tax Manual para 43009).

When a claim is made various records should accompany it. These are listed in the Inheritance Tax Manual at para 43006.

It is important that taxpayers retain records from the first death to support a future claim. Obviously for some individuals records will not have been retained. The first death may have happened a considerable time ago. HMRC's Guidance states that 'provided the documents show the claim is valid and any tax due has been paid, you can release form IHT421/C1. You should then consider the risk to tax in deciding whether or not to accept the claim as offered. Where records don't exist, personal representatives are entitled to complete their claim to the best of their ability and based on the information available. Provided there is no evidence that any other assets were chargeable, you can accept the claim.' (HMRC Inheritance Tax Manual, para 43011). It would seem that there is not the same discretion where the first death happens on or after the pre-Budget announcement.

Once a claim has been submitted it can only be withdrawn within one month of its submission.

Nil rate band discretionary trusts

[16.4] There has been much written about whether the ability to transfer the unused nil rate band has made nil rate band discretionary trusts redundant.

Under a will an individual will leave a legacy equal to the nil rate band in force at his death (or equal to the unused amount of the band taking into account transfers within seven years of death) on discretionary trusts with the surviving spouse or civil partner as one of the objects of the discretion. It is important that attention is paid to the wording of the nil rate band legacy. It was often the case that the wording used was a cash sum of 'an amount equal to the largest amount that can pass without payment of inheritance tax'. This has the potential to pass double the amount of the full inheritance tax nil rate band. The trustees (given the appropriate guidance in a letter of wishes) can then exercise their discretion over the income of the fund (and where appropriate, capital) each year in favour of the surviving spouse or civil partner. If there are minor children of the testator included in the class of beneficiaries, then the discretion over income could instead be exercised in their favour to utilise their income tax personal allowances in each year. The income so appropriated may be paid to the spouse or civil partner as guardian of the children to be used for their maintenance, education or benefit, thereby relieving the surviving spouse's or civil partner's own income from this burden.

This route enables a surviving spouse or civil partner to benefit from the income of the testator's property whilst at the same time keeping it outside his or her estate. If the testator's widow or civil partner dies before the tenth anniversary of the death, then the capital of the trust may in most cases be distributed to the children without incurring any inheritance tax charge regardless of the then value of the fund. This is because inheritance tax on a capital distribution before the first decennial is calculated by reference to the initial value of the trust fund plus any chargeable transfers made by the settlor in the seven years before making the settlement. If that total does not exceed the nil rate band, no tax is payable. However, it will be important to ensure that no 'related settlements' are created by the will as the value of property in any related settlement is taken into account in calculating the tax on a distribution. Before 22 March 2006, where a will established a nil rate band discretionary trust and an interest in possession for a spouse in the remainder of the estate, the interest in possession trust was not related property and therefore ignored when considering the situation of the nil rate band discretionary trust. This will still be the case where a spouse or civil partner has an immediate post-death interest or a disabled person's interest after 21 March 2006. Where the value of the property transferred to the trust fund only fell within the nil rate band by virtue of the availability of business property relief or agricultural property relief. In calculating the inheritance tax on a capital distribution before the first decennial the initial value of the trust fund in these circumstances is the unrelieved value and a charge may therefore arise. If the widow is likely to survive the decennial, then a decision will have to be made as to whether it is better to break the trust before the anniversary or to pay the ten-year charge.

The nil rate band discretionary trust still has a large part to play in estate planning.

The nil-rate band discretionary trust allows the taxpayer to 'hedge his bets'. Taking advantage of a claim under IHTA 1984, s 8A capital can be appointed out to a surviving spouse or civil partner within two years of death. Alternatively, the chargeable transfer can simply be left in being with or without absolute appointments to beneficiaries.

Where an individual has children from their first marriage it may be preferable to set up a nil rate band discretionary trust under the will of the first spouse to die rather than relying on transferring the unused nil rate band on the death of the second spouse.

Example

> Robert has two children from his first marriage to Liz. He has recently married Elspeth and is concerned to ensure that his children benefit under his will whilst utilising his nil rate band. By including a nil rate band discretionary trust he will achieve his aim.

As discussed above there are restrictions on the amount of the unused nil rate band that can be transferred where there have been multiple marriages. Because there are no such restrictions on the number of discretionary trusts that can be created the discretionary trust may be a useful tool in avoiding the restriction.

Example

> Winnie married Felix in 1984. He died in 1988 leaving his estate of £400,000 to Winnie. The nil rate band was £110,000. In 1993 Winnie married Augustus. He died in 2005 leaving his estate of £1m to Winnie. The nil rate band was £275,000.
>
> Winnie died in May 2010.
>
> On the deaths of both Felix and Augustus, 100% of their nil rate bands was unused. However, on Winnie's death the increase in her nil rate band is limited to 100% thus increasing her nil rate band by £325,000.
>
> If both Felix and Augustus had created nil rate band discretionary trusts for the benefit of Winnie and their children their nil rate bands would have been utilised on their deaths. Therefore £110,000 would have been transferred to a discretionary trust on Felix's death and £275,000 would have been transferred to a nil rate band on Augustus's death making a total of £385,000. If Winnie had needed funds during her lifetime the trustees could have advanced funds to her. On her death these trusts would not have formed part of her estate on death and therefore would not be subject to inheritance tax.

The use of nil rate band discretionary trusts can allow a husband and wife to reduce the impact of the relevant property regime.

Example

> Bonnie and Clyde are husband and wife both owning assets worth £325,000 each. Bonnie dies first leaving her assets to Clyde and so no tax is payable. When Clyde dies he leaves his assets on discretionary trusts to his children. Clyde uses his own and Bonnie's nil rate band which exactly matches the value of his estate of £650,000. Whilst no inheritance tax was payable on his death, future decennial charges on the discretionary trust will be based on the total value of the trust property (currently being £650,000) plus any capital growth. If Bonnie and Clyde had made separate nil rate band discretionary trusts and there would either have been no charge or only a very small one.

The nil rate band discretionary trust is also of benefit where there are assets with the prospect of high growth in their capital values. It can also be used as a means of losing the marriage value of various assets.

A benefit or not

The provisions allowing the transfer of the nil rate band are undoubtedly useful in that they allow the nil rate bands of both spouses to be utilised but the above example illustrates that the nil rate band discretionary trust is still of significance in many situations. The wording of any nil rate band discretionary trusts in an existing will needs to be reviewed to ensure that it still accords with the testator's wishes (see **16.3**).

There are situations where the availability of a transferable nil rate band causes difficulties which would not have occurred previously.

Example

Bob was married to Bunty and had two children. They divorced in 1998 and he married Brenda. Brenda had also been married before and had one child. Brenda dies in 2010 before Bob. Under her will, Brenda has left the residue of her estate on a life interest trust for Bob with remainder to her children. She did not use her nil rate band. In 2011 Bob makes a gift of £650,000 to his two children. He dies later that year. To ensure that Brenda's nil rate band is utilised, Bob's executors make a claim. Assuming that the nil rate band has remained at £325,000, Bob will have a nil rate band of £650,000. This is first set against the PET to Bob's children which has now become chargeable and so the entire £650,000 is utilised. The termination of Bob's IPDI under Brenda's will is chargeable at 40%. This has therefore resulted in the benefit of Brenda's unused nil rate band being fully utilised by Bob's children and not by her own. Before the introduction of the transferable nil rate band this issue would not have arisen because Brenda would have had to have used her nil rate band on death to ensure that it was not lost.

Agricultural and business property

[16.5] Property which qualifies for agricultural or business property relief should, where possible, be given to non-exempt beneficiaries since the relief will be lost if given to a surviving spouse or civil partner who fails to satisfy the necessary conditions to obtain the relief on his or her death. It is important that the property qualifying for relief should be the subject of a specific gift. If it is not, than the relief must be apportioned over the whole estate, including that part which is spouse exempt. The expression 'specific gift' is defined, somewhat inadequately, in IHTA 1984, s 42(1). The following points should be noted. An appropriation of business property in satisfaction of a pecuniary legacy does not count as a specific gift. A direction to pay a pecuniary legacy out of business property is likewise not a specific gift of that property (IHTA 1984, s 39A(6)). If necessary, a formula can be used to leave business property equal in value to the nil rate band after relief at 50% (where applicable). Leaving a specific gift to non-exempt beneficiaries means that a proportionately larger gift can be made for the same inheritance tax cost.

Example

A gift in the testator's will of a property which is valued at £650,000 on death and which is used by a company he controls is entitled to 50% business property relief. If given to his children or other non-exempt beneficiaries no inheritance tax will be suffered on the testator's death (provided he has made no chargeable transfers or potentially exempt transfers within 7 years of his death).

Alternatively, it may be possible to obtain either business or agricultural property relief twice where one spouse leaves the property qualifying for relief to a discretionary trust in favour of his family including the other spouse. On the first spouse's death, agricultural or business property relief would be available. Under the terms of his will, the first spouse would leave his investment assets to the other so no inheritance tax would arise on those assets. The surviving spouse could then purchase the agricultural or business assets at arm's length from the trustees of the discretionary trust. Provided she survives for two years after the purchase, the assets should also be eligible for agricultural or business property relief. In addition, the capital gains tax uplift on death will be available on both the agricultural and business property and the investment assets.

Agricultural property relief

[16.6] Agricultural property is defined in IHTA 1984, s 115(2) as agricultural land or pasture and includes both woodland and any buildings used in connection with intensive rearing of livestock or fish if occupied with agricultural land and the occupation is ancillary to that of the agricultural land. It also includes farmhouses, farm buildings and cottages, and the land occupied with them, which are 'of a character appropriate to the property'. Section 115(4) extends the definition to include stud farms. The relief also extends to controlling shareholdings in agricultural companies (IHTA 1984, s 122).

The relief is given on the agricultural value of agricultural property only, and not in respect of any value attributable to non-agricultural use. Relief of 100% is available if vacant possession of the land is available at the time of, or can be obtained within 12 months of, the transfer. By a current concession, HMRC Inheritance Tax extend this period to 24 months (see Extra-Statutory Concession F17 and HMRC Inheritance Tax Manual, para 24144). Land let on tenancies commencing after 31 August 1995 will receive 100% relief as will agricultural tenancies acquired as a result of the death of the previous tenant after 31 August 1995. In the latter case, the tenancy will be treated as commencing on the date of death. Otherwise relief is at the rate of 50%. Relief is available for controlling shareholdings on the agricultural value element inherent in the value of the shares at either 100% or 50% as if the company's occupation was occupation by the transferor of the shares. To the extent that agricultural relief is not available, business property relief at either 100% or 50% may apply.

There are minimum ownership requirements contained in IHTA 1984, ss 117 and 123. The property must either be:

(a) occupied by the transferor (or the company) for the purposes of agriculture throughout the period of 2 years prior to the transfer (ie in the case of a gift by will, 2 years prior to the death); or
(b) owned by the transferor (or company) throughout the period of 7 years (ending with the death) and throughout that period occupied (by him or another) for the purposes of agriculture.

Where a company is involved, the shares must have been owned by the transferor throughout the 2 or 7-year period, whichever is applicable. There are also provisions which modify the ownership requirements in the case of agricultural property which has replaced other agricultural property (IHTA 1984, s 118).

Agricultural property relief is considered in more detail in **Chapter 11 The Family Farm**.

Business property relief

[16.7] The relief for 'relevant business property' is contained in IHTA 1984, ss 103–114. Relevant business property is defined as:

	Property	Rate
(a)	property consisting of a business or interest in a business;	100%
(b)	securities of a company which are unquoted and which (either by themselves or together with other such securities owned by the transferor and any unquoted shares so owned) gave the transferor control (as defined by IHTA 1984, s 269) of the company immediately before the transfer;	100%
(c)	any unquoted shares in a company;	100%
(d)	shares in or securities of a company which are quoted and which (either by themselves or together with other such shares or securities owned by the transferor) gave the transferor control of the company immediately before the transfer;	50%
(e)	any land or building, machinery or plant which, immediately before the transfer, was used wholly or mainly for the purposes of a business carried on by a company of which the transferor then had control or by a partnership of which he then was a partner; and	50%
(f)	any land or building, machinery or plant which, immediately before the transfer, was used wholly or mainly for the purposes of a business carried on by the transferor and was settled property in which he was then beneficially entitled to an interest in possession.	50%

Business property relief may be available on shares in unquoted family companies and other shareholdings or securities which fulfil the voting criteria specified in the Act. It also includes, in category (*a*), partnership interests and a business of which the deceased was sole proprietor, which includes the underwriting interests of a member of Lloyd's. Categories (*b*) and (*c*) include shares dealt in on the Alternative Investment Market (AIM). Relief is not available in respect of a business or an interest in a business, or shares or securities of a company carrying on a business, where the business consists wholly or mainly of dealing in securities, stocks or shares, land or buildings or making or holding investments (excluding market makers and discount houses and companies which are the holding companies of a trading group, none of the businesses of which are prescribed under the above criteria) (IHTA 1984, s 105(3)).

There is a two-year minimum period of ownership in order to qualify for relief but relief can be given on business property which has replaced other business property, provided the necessary conditions are met (IHTA 1984, s 107).

No business property relief will be available if the property is subject to a binding contract for sale (IHTA 1984, s 113). The Revenue considers there is a binding contract of sale where partners or shareholder directors of a company enter into an agreement whereby on the death of a partner/director the surviving partners/shareholders are obliged to purchase the deceased's business interest or shares and the deceased's personal representatives are obliged to sell. Statement of Practice SP 12/80 sets out the Revenue's view that s 113 applies where there is an obligation to buy and sell but not merely an option to do so.

A gift in a will of any relevant business property may lapse if the testator retires from the business or sells the property in his lifetime. Such a step should be an occasion for the testator to review the will.

Business property relief is considered in more detail in **Chapter 10 The Family Business.**

Attribution of values

[16.8] IHTA 1984, s 39A contains rules relating to the attribution of values to gifts in a will when part of the residuary estate is given to an exempt beneficiary and part of the residuary estate also qualifies for agricultural or business property relief. Any agricultural or business property relief is, in effect, apportioned between any specific gifts and the property in the residuary estate. Specific gifts of agricultural or business property are treated as gifts of the value of that property reduced by the relevant relief and if expressed to be free of tax the gifts will be grossed-up (see **16.23** below).

Charitable and other gifts for public benefit

[16.9] Gifts by will to charities are exempt from inheritance tax (IHTA 1984, s 23). However, relief will be precluded where the gift to charity only takes effect on the termination of any other interest, or depends on a condition which is not satisfied within 12 months of the death, or is for a limited period, is defeasible (s 23(2), (3)).

An exemption is also available for gifts to:

(a) political parties (IHTA 1984, s 24);
(b) certain bodies of national importance specified in IHTA 1984, Sch 3 (IHTA 1984, s 25);
(c) maintenance funds for historic buildings (IHTA 1984, s 27);
(d) Community Amateur Sports Clubs (FA 2002, Sch 18 para 9(2)); and
(e) housing associations.

For further details, see **Chapter 13 Gifts to Charities and Other Non-Profit Organisations**

Limitations on reliefs available on death

[16.10] Certain reliefs available in respect of lifetime gifts are not available on death (in some cases, for fairly obvious reasons). These are:

(a) the annual exemption, currently £3,000;
(b) the small gifts exemption, currently £250 per person;
(c) the normal expenditure out of income exemption;
(d) the exemption for gifts in consideration of marriage; and
(e) the exemption for certain dispositions for the maintenance of a family.

One relief available only on death is limited to a person who is not domiciled and neither resident nor ordinarily resident in the UK at his death. IHTA 1984, s 157 provides that the balance on any qualifying foreign currency account of such a person, or of the trustees of settled property in which he is beneficially entitled to an interest in possession, is to be left out of account in determining the value of the estate.

Dividing the estate between the family

Intestacy rules

[16.11] In the absence of a will the estate will pass on death under the intestacy rules which may, but much more likely will not, bring about the desired result in the distribution of the estate. Where a spouse and issue survive the intestate, the intestacy rules provide for a statutory legacy (currently £250,000), together with the personal chattels, to go to the surviving spouse, together with a life interest in one-half of the residue of the estate. The other one-half of residue is given to the issue absolutely if they are over 18 or when they marry or form a civil partnership, and on the statutory trusts if they are unmarried (and are not parties to a civil partnership) and under the age of 18. Such statutory trusts will be bereaved minors' trusts provided the conditions in IHTA 1984, s 71A are satisfied (see **CHAPTER 4 CREATING SETTLEMENTS**). On the death of the first spouse, the only charge to inheritance tax on the estate that may arise is in respect of the one-half of the residue passing to the issue. On the death of the second spouse, however, a charge to inheritance tax will arise on his or her estate (reflecting the benefit of the deceased's personal assets and the statutory legacy to the extent it is not spent in that spouse's lifetime) including, for inheritance tax purposes, the one-half share of residue of the deceased's estate which passes to the children.

The Civil Partnership Act 2004 grants a surviving civil partner the same rights on intestacy as a surviving spouse.

Gifts to a spouse or civil partner

Equalisation of estates

[16.12] In the past, it has been important that some measure of equalisation with regard to the values of the spouses' or civil partners' respective estates should be considered to ensure that both nil rate bands can be utilised regardless of the order in which a husband and wife or civil partner die. Although this may seem to be of less significance now because unused nil rate bands can be transferred between the estates of husbands and wives and civil partners, it is still an essential element of estate planning. Equalisation will allow both spouses or civil partners to make potentially exempt transfers and gifts within the annual exemption. Such gifts between spouses or civil partners will generally not give rise to any inheritance tax, capital gains tax, stamp duty or stamp duty land tax liabilities. This equalisation of estates will also help to ensure that the survivor is provided for adequately.

The possible impact, however, of the related property provisions contained in IHTA 1984, s 161 should not be overlooked. Section 161 provides that where the value of any property forming part of the estates of both spouses or civil partners taken together is greater than the value of the spouses' or civil partners' respective shares or interests in the property when valued individually, then the value to be adopted is the appropriate proportion of the value of the property as a whole. In *Arkwright v CIR* [2004] STC (SCD) 89 (SpC 392) it was successfully argued before the Special Commissioners that s 161(4) was intended to apply to the splitting of related property where the property had a distinct individual existence as a unit, such as unit trusts or a set of furniture but it did not apply to fractions of units such as freehold property held as tenants in common.

Although this issue was not considered further when the Revenue's appeal against the decision was heard by the High Court, the Revenue claimed to have received legal advice that s 161(4) may apply to fractional shares of units. The Revenue has issued Brief 71/07 stating that it will apply the apportionment method in s 161(4) when valuing shares of land as related property. The related provisions do not nullify the purpose of the equalisation procedure.

Where gifts are being made between spouses or civil partners, it is advisable that a deed of gift is used to record the gift so as to provide evidence that the donor intends beneficial ownership to pass to the donee.

Absolute gifts v life interests

[16.13] The question as to whether a surviving spouse or civil partner should be given property absolutely by the will, or be given a life interest only in the whole or part of the estate, has been mentioned briefly above at **16.2**. The inheritance tax consequences on the death of a surviving spouse or civil partner will be the same provided the interest in possession is an immediate post-death interest (IHTA 1984, s 49A). The spouse or civil partner who has a life interest will be treated as if he or she owns the underlying assets and tax is charged accordingly on his or her death (IHTA 1984, s 49(1A)). Therefore, the property given absolutely or in trust for life (which is an immediate post-death interest) by a husband to his wife or between civil partners will be exempt from tax on the first death but on the second death will be taxed in some form or another. The decision may be made for personal rather than fiscal reasons. A testator who has confidence in his or her spouse or civil partner can give capital instead of a life interest. Where a testator is concerned that the surviving spouse or civil partner will fritter away or mismanage the estate so that there is nothing left for any children, then clearly the testator should consider only giving the spouse or civil partner a life interest, with the capital passing automatically on the spouse's or civil partner's death to the children. The survivor's life interest could also expressly be made to come to an end on any subsequent marriage or registration of a civil partnership.

A combination of a life interest, coupled with a power for the trustees (who may or may not, depending on the circumstances in which the gift is made, include the testator's spouse or civil partner) to release capital to the life tenant will produce a more flexible provision for the surviving spouse or civil partner whilst preserving part of the capital for future generations at no extra inheritance tax cost. The release of capital to the spouse or civil partner, who already has an interest in possession and is consequently treated for inheritance tax purposes as owning the assets provided the interest is an immediate post-death interest, will not give rise to a charge to tax (IHTA 1984, s 53(2)). However, depending upon the nature and value of the assets released, there may be a charge to capital gains tax on the release.

Providing the surviving spouse or civil partner with a life interest will not preclude the capital of the trust passing from the spouse or civil partner to the next generation by way of potentially exempt transfers.

Gifts to children and remoter issue

[16.14] A gift may be either vested, that is the right to the gift is certain, or contingent, that is dependent upon an uncertain future event. A vested gift may be either vested in possession, that is of immediate effect, or vested in interest, that is coming into effect on a certain future event such as the expiry of a period of time.

Vested gifts

[16.15] Where a gift is vested in possession, no particular tax problems are usually encountered. If the vested gift is to a legatee who is a minor, the executors will on the completion of the administration hold as bare trustees until the minor attains 18 and can give them a valid receipt. The income and any capital gains will be taxed as those of the minor. In the absence of any contrary intention in the will the Trustee Act 1925, ss 31 and 32 will apply and the trustees will be able to release the income for the minor's maintenance, education and benefit and up to one half of the capital for his advancement or benefit (though it is usual to extend s 32 to enable the whole of the capital to be released).

Contingent gifts and gifts vested in interest

[16.16] The tax consequences of contingent gifts are more complex. In the absence of an express direction in the will, the general rule is that the gift will not carry the intermediate income unless it is a gift of residue or is a specific gift (Law of Property Act 1925, s 175). Therefore, the income of a contingent gift which does not carry the intermediate income (such as a general pecuniary legacy to a child of the testator upon attaining an age exceeding the age of majority) will be payable to the residuary beneficiaries until the contingency is attained. On the occurrence of that event the residuary beneficiaries' interests in possession in the contingent fund will be terminated. Whether or not a termination is a potentially exempt transfer will depend upon its nature (see **CHAPTER 4 CREATING SETTLEMENTS** and **CHAPTER 5 EXISTING SETTLEMENTS**).

On the occurrence of the contingency there may be a disposal by the trustees for capital gains tax if the gift is of chargeable assets. However, depending upon the nature of the assets a hold-over election under TCGA 1992, s 165 may be available. Where the gift does carry the intermediate income it may qualify as an accumulation and maintenance trust under IHTA 1984, s 71 or a trust for a bereaved minor or an 18–25 trust. In such circumstances hold-over relief under TCGA 1992, s 260 might be available, whatever the nature of the asset, provided the satisfaction of the contingency results in capital and income vesting contemporaneously.

For income tax purposes income which is accumulated or over which the trustees have a discretion will be subject to income tax at the trust rate (currently 40% or 32.5% on dividend income) unless the minor has a vested interest in the income in which case it will be taxed as his or her income.

One other financial burden of a contingent gift will be the costs of administration of the continuing trust including preparation of accounts and tax returns each year and of tax advice to the trustees.

Generation skipping

[16.17] If the testator's children are sufficiently well provided for, then consideration should be given to skipping a generation in the will to provide for grandchildren, present and future. Even if the testator's children are not particularly wealthy, the advantages of enabling them to use the grandchildren's income tax personal allowances each year, which might otherwise be lost, may be a significant benefit to a child of the testator by relieving his own income from the burden of maintaining or educating his children.

Skipping a generation will ensure that property reaching the grandchildren will avoid at least one charge to inheritance tax which would otherwise have arisen on the death of the parent. Before 22 March 2006, such trusts would have been in the form of a gift to an accumulation and maintenance trust because of its flexibility and inheritance tax benefits. Such trusts no longer enjoy a favoured tax status. Although there is nothing preventing such trusts being created they will now be taxed in accordance with the relevant property regime. A gift under a will to grandchildren could be in the form of an interest in possession trust or a discretionary trust. An interest in possession trust for the benefit of grandchildren may be an immediate post-death interest ('IPDI') if it falls within IHTA 1984, s 49A. The trust will not be subject to decennial charges nor exit charges. Instead, on the death of the life tenant, the underlying assets will form part of the deceased's estate under IHTA 1984, s 49.

Where the trust is not an IPDI or other form of privileged trust, then the trust will be subject to the relevant property regime. Of course, a discretionary trust offers more flexibility and in many cases will be preferable.

The family home

[16.18] Very often a testator will ask for advice on giving away his matrimonial home or, where this is owned by both spouses or civil partners, for advice on giving away his share of it. A gift of a share of the home can only be made by will if the property is beneficially owned as tenants in common. In the case of a joint tenancy, the share of the property will automatically pass by survivorship. A joint tenancy should be severed *inter vivos* by notice in writing.

If the property is owned jointly as tenants in common, the property will be held by them in trust. They each have an interest in the proceeds of sale of the property and a right to reside there while it remains unsold. These rights will pass to a legatee if a share of the property is given by the will.

A discretionary will trust (see **16.20** below) often permits the surviving spouse or civil partner to continue to occupy the family home. It is understood that the Revenue's view is that the trustees should act like trustees and enter into commercial arrangements concerning rent on the property.

Where the testator is proposing a gift in his will of his interest in the property, other than to his wife, he will usually be concerned to preserve the ability for his wife to reside in the property. The Revenue's view is that any right given to the wife for her to continue to reside there will create an interest in possession in favour of the wife in the testator's half of the property (*CIR v Lloyds Private Banking Ltd* [1998] STC 559 (Ch D); *Woodhall (Woodhall's Personal Representative) v CIR* [2000] STC (SCD) 558 (SpC 261) and *Faulkner (Trustee of Adams, dec'd) v CIR* [2001] STC (SCD) 112 (SpC 278)). In *Judge v HMRC* [2005] SpC 506 the husband had owned the whole house and under a discretionary will trust had provided that the trustees should permit the use and enjoyment of the property 'for such periods as they shall in their absolute discretion think fit'. It was held that the wife did not have the right as against the trustees to occupy the property because the trustees had an absolute discretion as to whether or not they would permit her to exercise that right. Accordingly, she did not have an interest in possession. SP10/79 was not considered in the case. A termination of an interest will occur on the subsequent death of the wife or possibly on an earlier sale.

Where under the terms of a will, a property is left on discretionary trusts and the trustees permit the beneficiary to occupy the property, on HMRC's view of the matter there will be an interest in possession but the trust will be a relevant property settlement and not an IPDI. In correspondence between CIOT/STEP and HMRC, HMRC has said that where a discretionary trust is created and funded by a share in a property which the trustees permit a surviving spouse to occupy on an exclusive basis at their discretion on similar terms to those in *Judge*, the trust will not automatically be an IPDI but it will depend upon the terms on which the spouse occupies. Where the trust arises on a death and the spouse's occupation commences within two years of the death it is clear that if a spouse's occupation amounts to an interest in possession it will be an IPDI (IHTA 1984, s 144).

Similar considerations apply where the matrimonial home is in the sole name of one spouse. Should it be left to the surviving spouse alone, to the surviving spouse and children jointly or to the children alone? The testator's primary concern will often be the security of the surviving spouse but he may have to balance that security against the fact that if the home is left solely to the children and they allow their surviving parent to occupy it for the rest of his or her life, the gifts with reservation provisions will not apply. Of course, if the house is likely to be sold on the first death, different considerations will apply.

Where the joint owners are an unmarried couple living together, consideration should be given to the surviving cohabitee's position after the death of the first to die. Where a property is purchased by only one of the cohabitees, the purchaser may wish to make provision for the surviving cohabitee on his death. The tax consequences are discussed in detail in **CHAPTER 9 THE FAMILY HOME**.

Survivorship clauses

[16.19] It is common practice to make gifts to individuals in wills contingent on them surviving the testator for a given period, usually three months. Such a survivorship clause can serve various purposes.

(a) It can prevent a double charge to tax where the legatee dies shortly after the testator.
(b) In the case of a gift to a spouse or civil partner it can prevent a greater charge to inheritance tax arising than would otherwise have arisen on the death of the spouse or civil partner by preventing the deceased's property from passing to the surviving spouse or civil partner and being aggregated with his or her own estate.
(c) It ensures that property will devolve, in the event of the second death occurring within the survivorship period, to a substituted legatee of the first testator's choosing and will not pass under the will of the second to die.
(d) It avoids the same property having to be administered twice over in two different estates within a relatively short space of time.

IHTA 1984, s 92 provides that a survivorship clause for a period not exceeding six months is back-dated to the date of death for inheritance tax purposes and tax will be charged on the death depending on whether the legatee survives for the period or dies before the period expires.

In some instances it may be desirable that if a married couple die simultaneously, for example, in a car accident, that the survivorship period should not apply. In the situation where spouses die together and it is not certain who died first, the elder spouse is deemed to die first (Law of Property Act 1925, s 184). Therefore, if the survivorship period does not apply, the elder spouse's estate will pass to the younger. IHTA 1984, s 4(2) provides that where it cannot be ascertained which of two people survived the other then it is assumed that both deaths occurred at the same instant. This means that the property of the elder falls outside the charge to inheritance tax on the younger's death. Therefore, from the point of view of inheritance tax, a survivorship clause need not operate in the event of a common accident.

As illustrated in **16.3C** above, the inclusion of a survivorship clause in a 'commorientes' case can have a disastrous effect on the transferable nil rate band. Because of this, it is becoming accepted practice for a survivorship clause not to be included in wills for spouses or civil partners.

Survivorship clauses can cause severe cash flow problems (and worry) for a dependent spouse. For this reason the will should contain a power for the executors to use either the capital or the income to maintain the spouse during the survivorship period. Alternatively, it should be coupled with a joint bank account or other similar arrangements so that the dependent spouse is not deprived of funds for a lengthy period.

Discretionary wills

[16.20] Often, an individual wishing to make a will is, at the time, precluded by financial or family circumstances from making a decision as to how his property should be distributed on his death. When drafting his will a testator cannot be certain what resources he and his survivors will have at his death or indeed who will survive him. After his death it will be much clearer to the executors and the family to how assets should be divided between those whom he wishes to benefit and also whether there is scope to skip a generation. In these circumstances the appropriate solution may be to give his estate, or some part of it, to his executors to be held on discretionary trusts. The trustees would be given a wide power of appointment exercisable in favour of a specified class of beneficiaries, leaving them to distribute it or declare trusts of it following his death. If the executors exercise the power within two years of the death, and no-one has obtained an interest in possession within that time, then tax will be chargeable as if the gifts or trusts were made by the testator on his death, and the appointment will not be subject to the usual inheritance tax regime for discretionary trusts (IHTA 1984, s 144). It is not essential that the power of appointment be vested in the executors. It could instead be vested in, for example, the testator's spouse (although consideration would then have to be given to the possibility of the spouse predeceasing the testator).

The essential elements are as follows.

(a) The power of appointment must be exercised within two years of the death. To ensure that this is achieved it may be advisable that the will should provide that the trust will automatically terminate at the end of the two-year period and contain a gift in default of the exercise of the power.
(b) The power must be exercised before an interest in possession subsists in the property, namely before an IPDI or a DPI exists in the property for deaths after 21 March 2006.
(c) The will must give adequate power to the appointor to enable trusts, discretionary or otherwise, to be declared over the property, and to enable the appointor to confer whatever powers are needed or are appropriate, within the confines of the testator's overall requirements.

The 'back-dating' operation of s 144 only applies where, on a distribution from the trust, tax would otherwise have been charged. As a result, if the discretion is exercised within three months of the death, s 144 will not apply because tax would not otherwise have been chargeable. See *Frankland v CIR* [1997] STC 1450 (CA) and *Harding (Loveday's Executors) v CIR* [1997] STC (SCD) 321 (SpC 140). This can be a dangerous trap for the unwary.

Example

> Tan Harvey died, survived by his wife, Pippa. Under his will an amount equal to the nil rate band was to be held on discretionary trusts of which Pippa was a beneficiary, with the residue passing to Pippa absolutely. Two months after his death, the trustees advanced the trust assets to Pippa absolutely. Six months later Pippa died leaving her estate of £1m to her children absolutely.
>
> Because the trustees' advance was made within 3 months of Tan's death it would not have given rise to a charge, even disregarding s 144 (IHTA 1984, s 64(4)). Therefore, s 144 did not apply to treat the advances as taking place under Tan's will. The legacy on discretionary trusts was therefore charged on Tan's death but covered by his nil rate band. On Pippa's death, the assets advanced to her from the settlement formed part of her estate on death. Because Tan's nil rate band was used on his death, there was no unused nil rate band to be 'transferred' to Pippa to be used on her death, in spite of the fact that the assets chargeable on Tan's death were charged again on Pippa's death. Tan's nil rate band had, therefore, been wasted.
>
> If the advance had been made a month later, it would have been read back into Tan's will with the result that it would have been exempted by the spouse exemption (IHTA 1984, s 18) so that Tan's nil rate band would have been unused and available to be 'transferred' to Pippa under ss 8A–8C. Alternatively, if the trusts had created an interest in possession in Pippa's favour instead of advancing the assets to her absolutely, s 144(4) would have deemed Pippa's interest in possession to have been created by Tan's will. In that case it would have been an IPDI and exempt under the spouse exemption. Again, the result would have been that Tan's nil rate band would have been unused on his death so that it could have been 'transferred' to Pippa.

To avoid an accidental advancement within the three-month period, the will should provide that advancements within three months of death are invalid. The disadvantages of a discretionary will should not be overlooked:

(1) The circumstances which led the testator to delegate his testamentary responsibility to his executors may still exist at his death or at the end of the period of two years from his death — nonetheless, even if the uncertainties are not fully resolved, the executors/trustees will at least know the latest situation.

(2) The executors may be at a disadvantage insofar as they are not as familiar with the circumstances of the family as the testator himself — but the executors will normally be either family members or long-established family advisers.

(3) The testator must appreciate that he will have to rely on others to make decisions and judgements about his family over which he will have no control — he can guide his executors, however, by means of a letter of wishes and provide 'long stop' provisions within the will in the event that the executors cannot agree amongst themselves.

Despite these supposed disadvantages, it is still preferable to have a discretionary will rather than to rely on a possible variation of the will by the beneficiaries, following the death. The scope for a variation may be limited unless all beneficiaries are *sui juris* and willing to agree. In addition, where a parent beneficiary confers a benefit on his relevant children (unless they are vulnerable beneficiaries) by a variation he will fall within the provisions of ITTOIA 2005, s 629 in relation to the income of the property. An appointment under a discretionary will is outside the provisions of that section. It has been argued, surely erroneously, that where the power is vested in the deceased's executors a surviving spouse, who is the sole executor (or even one of the executors) may be regarded as a settlor for the purposes of s 629 in exercising, or concurring in the exercise, of this power.

Financial consequences

[16.21] There are other financial consequences to be considered in relation to a discretionary will.

Payment of inheritance tax

Inheritance tax will be payable on the application for a grant of probate on the value of the property subject to the discretionary power unless the power is exercised before the application is made. This is assuming that the property does not qualify for the instalment relief in which case only those instalments which have fallen due at that date will be payable. In such cases, executors often have to fund this tax by bank borrowing which can be expensive. If the property is subsequently appointed to an exempt legatee such as a spouse or civil partner, the inheritance tax would be repayable.

Capital gains tax difficulties

Capital gains tax complications may arise. TCGA 1992, s 62, which applies to variations within two years of death, does not apply to discretionary wills. An absolute appointment made under the trust is treated as a disposal under TCGA 1992, s 71. Hold-over relief under TCGA 1992, s 260 will not be available because any disposition of the trust assets within the two-year period will not be an occasion of charge to inheritance tax as IHTA 1984, s 144 prevents a charge arising. Hold-over relief under TCGA 1992, s 165 may, however, be available. If relief is not available, whether or not a chargeable gain results will depend on whether there has been any increase in value of the property appointed since the date of death.

If the appointment is not absolute but on continuing trusts it will be necessary to consider whether a new settlement has thereby been created or whether the trusts are a continuation of those established by the will, in accordance with the principles laid down in *Roome v Edwards* [1981] STC 96, 54 TC 359, [1981] 1 All ER 736; *Ewart v Taylor* [1983] STC 721, and *Bond v Pickford* [1983] STC 517. Where property was already settled under the will or intestacy and then becomes comprised in another trust as a result of the variation, the deceased person is treated as the settlor for capital gains tax purposes. The position is, however, less clear where a variation only amends or varies a will trust rather than transferring the property to a new settlement or where the person making the variation simply varies their own interest under the settlement. If a new settlement is created a disposal to the new trustees will have taken place (although hold-over relief may be available). If the trusts are merely a continuation, there will be no disposal. However, other difficulties may arise where a number of different trusts are established under an exercise of the power in that each of the trusts established will be treated for capital gains tax purposes as one fund with the result that only one annual exemption, apportioned between the separate funds, will be available.

Chose in action

A further complication will arise where an absolute appointment is made before the estate is fully administered, unless the assets which are the subject of the appointment have first been appropriated by the deceased's personal representatives to the trustees.

There is an argument that the subject matter of the appointment will be a chose in action in accordance with *Marshall v Kerr* [1994] STC 638, [1994] 2 All ER 106 (HL) which will have a nil base cost and therefore a significant chargeable gain could arise. However, the Revenue takes the view that where the trustees exercise their powers of appointment before the assets have vested in them, the assets are still held by the personal representatives at that time. When the assets vest, they will be treated as passing directly to the appointee (Revenue Capital Gains Manual CG31432).

There is a disposal of the assets in question by the personal representatives to the person who benefits under the appointment.

The Revenue view is that the exercise of the power of appointment is, however, read back into the original will. Thus, the beneficiary takes the asset as legatee and acquires the assets at probate value (TCGA 1992, ss 62(4) and TCGA 1992, s 64(2)).

The result of this is somewhat surprising as the capital gains tax implications of an appointment prior to an assent or ascertainment of residue will be completely different from that of an appointment made after assent or ascertainment of the residue of the estate.

For example, where an asset has increased in value since the date of death, appointment of that asset following assent or ascertainment will result in a capital gains tax charge arising to the trustees on the appointment. Hold-over relief will only be available if the assets are business assets (see above).

However, if that asset were to be appointed to the beneficiary before assent or ascertainment, no chargeable gain will arise as the Revenue will treat the beneficiary as if he received the asset at probate value under the terms of the will (Revenue Capital Gains Manual CG31432). No chargeable gain will arise until the subsequent disposal of the asset by the beneficiary.

This distinction should be considered carefully by trustees wishing to appoint assets to beneficiaries as it may be important for capital gains tax purposes to exercise the power of appointment prior to assent or ascertainment of the residue if an unwanted tax charge is to be avoided.

Income tax

For income tax purposes the income arising under the discretionary trusts during the period from death to the exercise of the power will be taxed at the trust rate.

Conclusion

In spite of these disadvantages, most of which may be overcome by a little forward planning, the flexibility offered by discretionary wills is such that most clients with estates in excess of one million pounds should consider having wills in a discretionary form.

Types of gifts and legacies

[16.22] A testator should expressly state in his will where the inheritance tax on a specific bequest is to fall. If there is no express provision, the general principle is that the tax on UK unsettled property is a testamentary expense payable from the residue. When drafting a will, it is advisable that there be express provisions stating whether bequests are tax bearing or free of tax.

Free-of-tax legacies: grossing-up

[16.23] Under IHTA 1984, s 38, where the residue of an estate is exempt from inheritance tax because, for example, it passes either to the testator's spouse or to charity, then any legacies and bequests given in the will 'free-of-tax' will be grossed-up to determine the amount of tax chargeable which is in respect of those legacies, and payable out of residue. The gross sum which, after deduction of tax at the rate applicable to the chargeable value of the estate, will provide the amount required to meet the legacies and bequests, and inheritance tax is then charged on this grossed-up value. Where gifts have been made within 7 years of death, whether chargeable transfers or potentially exempt transfers, these will be aggregated with the value of the free-of-tax legacies and other chargeable property passing on the death to determine the rate at which tax is payable. Such lifetime transfers will have the benefit of the nil rate band in priority to the estate on death.

Where part of the residue is chargeable, and part is exempt, the grossing-up calculation involves a second stage in which the value of the chargeable residue as well as the value of the free-of-tax legacies (and the value of any transfers within seven years of the death) are included. If the calculated net value of the chargeable estate does not exceed the nil rate band at the death, grossing-up becomes irrelevant, and no tax is payable.

Grossing-up will be avoided if gifts to non-exempt beneficiaries are made subject to inheritance tax instead of free of it. This will result, however, in the non-exempt beneficiaries receiving a lower net sum which may not accord with the testator's wishes in every case. Of course, the testator could always increase the size of the legacy if the gift is to bear its own tax which will have a similar (if not identical) effect to the grossing-up provisions. Alternatively, if instead the legatees are given a share of residue to be divided between them, grossing-up will be avoided and some tax saved. However, such a gift is less precise, in that the sum which the legatee will receive often cannot be calculated accurately when the will is drawn up, but only on the distribution of the estate following the testator's death.

Where a will provides for half of the testator's estate to pass to an exempt beneficiary and the other half to a taxable beneficiary, will the estate be divided equally before inheritance tax or after it? In *Lockhart v Harker (re Benham's Will Trusts)* [1995] STC 210 (Ch D) the court decided that the division was after tax and therefore that the exempt beneficiary's after tax share was equal to the taxable beneficiary's. In *Holmes v McMullan (re Ratcliffe (dec'd))* [1999] STC 262 (Ch D) on similar facts the court decided that the division was before tax so that the exempt beneficiary received a larger net amount than the non-exempt beneficiary. The decision distinguished *Re Benham's Will Trusts* on the basis that no general principle was to be applied but rather the intentions of the particular testator were to be determined from the construction of the will.

Where a will provides for free-of-tax legacies and at the same time there are one or more separate funds (eg settlements in which the deceased had an interest in possession on 22 March 2006) also chargeable to tax on the deceased's death, then Revenue practice (reported in the Law Society's Gazette of 9 May 1990 on p14; see *Tolley's Yellow Tax Handbook* and HMRC Inheritance Tax Manual, para 26121) will operate to reduce the total amount of tax payable on the death. The Revenue accepts that the rate of tax applicable when grossing up free-of-tax legacies is that applicable to the free estate in isolation and not that applicable to the total value of all property chargeable on the deceased's death. This means that where, for example, a will contains free-of-tax legacies and provides for residue to pass to an exempt beneficiary (eg a surviving spouse or civil partner) and there is separately chargeable settled property, either there will be no grossing up if the legacies are less than the nil rate band or only one round of grossing up will be needed if the legacies are in excess of the nil rate band.

Incidence of tax: residue

[16.24] Whilst the tax attributable to any tax-free legacies will be borne by the whole of the testator's residuary estate (even if it includes exempt beneficiaries), the burden of tax on non-exempt residuary gifts cannot be shifted by the will on to exempt residuary gifts (IHTA 1984, s 41). Any such provision is void. Where residue is divided between exempt and non-exempt beneficiaries the tax payable on the estate and attributable to residue will be borne wholly by the non-exempt slice. However, the gifts contained in the will can reflect this fact: for example, instead of gifts of one half of residue to the spouse (exempt) and one half to the children (non-exempt) the will could contain gifts of one third of residue to the spouse and two thirds to the children.

Incidence of tax: land

[16.25] IHTA 1984, s 211 provides that inheritance tax is a testamentary expense payable from the residue if it is attributable to the value of UK property which vests in the deceased's personal representatives and was not comprised in a settlement immediately before the death, and so long as there is no contrary intention in the deceased's will. Therefore, to ensure that a legacy whether of land or other property bears its own tax, the will must state so expressly.

Gift of tax payable on potentially exempt transfers, etc

[16.26] A donor of a potentially exempt transfer who dies within seven years of the gift may leave the donee with a problem of funding the tax, for example, where the gift was of private company shares or other assets which are not easily realisable. To avoid this problem the donor may provide in his will that the tax due is to be paid out of his estate. This is the equivalent of a legacy to the donee of a sum equal to the amount of the tax. Such a legacy, if given free of tax, will have to be grossed-up as explained above. Personal representatives are under a secondary liability to pay the tax on a potentially exempt transfer under IHTA 1984, s 199. Therefore, where a legacy of the amount of the tax is given, rather than expressing this as a gift to the donee of the original gift, consideration should be given to coupling with it a power for the executors themselves to use the sum given to discharge the inheritance tax liability on the potentially exempt transfer (or even imposing a binding obligation on them to do so). This ensures that the gift is used for its intended purpose.

Similar considerations apply to chargeable lifetime gifts, where additional tax will be payable in the event of the donor's death within seven years, and to gifts where the deceased has reserved a benefit which are therefore taxable on his death as part of his estate. Legacies of the sum equivalent to the tax or additional tax which is payable need not be limited to one particular gift but could be expressed in general terms to cover all gifts by the testator during his lifetime which become chargeable, or give rise to tax payable, as a result of the death.

Annuities

[16.27] As a general rule, gifts by will of annuities are best avoided, because of their disadvantageous tax treatment.

For inheritance tax purposes, the setting aside of the annuity fund will be treated as a settlement and a charge to tax will arise on the death of the annuitant or on the termination of his or her interest in possession (IHTA 1984, s 50).

For income tax purposes, the whole of the annuity given by the will is taxable in the hands of the annuitant. An annuity payment under a purchased life annuity is charged to income tax as savings and investment income and not under the separate provision for annual payments generally (ITTOIA 2005, s 422). However, because an annuity payment contains an element of capital, the capital element is exempt from income tax provided the recipient makes a claim (ITTOIA 2005, s 717). Where, however, there is a direction in a will to purchase an annuity there is no exemption (ITTOIA 2005, s 718(2)(b)). A gift of a capital sum, calculated by reference to annuity rates, coupled with a non-binding suggestion to a legatee that it should be used to purchase an annuity is likely to be within the exemption. An annuity left to a spouse or civil partner may be advantageous because the transfer will benefit from the spouse exemption and over time the capital fund will reduce.

Precatory gifts

[16.28] It is common to give chattels by the will to a legatee or even to the executors with a non-binding condition that they are distributed in accordance with the testator's last known wishes as expressed in any note or memorandum left by the testator at his death (whether written before or after the date of the will). If the distribution is made within two years of the death it is treated as if it was made by the testator in his will and no additional charge to inheritance tax arises on that distribution (IHTA 1984, s 143).

A charge to capital gains tax could arise but in practice it is unlikely to do so. In the case of chattels, the exemption in TCGA 1992, s 262 will be available where the chattel is worth £6,000 or less, and marginal relief may apply where the value exceeds that sum.

The testator must appreciate that his wishes will not be legally binding on the legatee of the chattels, but assuming he is prepared to accept this risk, a 'memorandum of wishes' clause in a will provides a flexible and tax effective way of dealing with gifts of a large number of chattels to individual legatees. There is nothing in IHTA 1984, s 143 which limits the operation of the provision to chattels, although the use of the word 'bequeathed' may limit the operation of the section to personalty and not realty. It could equally well apply to cash, although generally testators are more prepared to put specific chattels at risk rather than sums of money.

Gifts for anatomical and therapeutic purposes

[16.29] At common law, a decedent has no ability to direct the disposition of their remains. The right to dispose of the remains passes to the next of kin. Directions in a will for the disposal of the body or organs are therefore only wishes of the testator. Nevertheless it is important for the spouse or next of kin to know whether the testator would be willing for his body and organs to be used for transplant purposes or for medical research. As very prompt action will be required if he would be willing for such use to be made of them, there will not be time to refer to the will. He should therefore record his wishes in writing and ensure that a copy is held by his doctor and his spouse.

Safe keeping and review of wills: personal assets log

[16.30] Once signed, a will should be kept safely where, following the death, it can be obtained easily. Banks will usually agree to release the will, following the death, to allow solicitors acting in the estate to make an application for probate. Those who will need to know of its existence should be informed of its location.

There is sometimes a tendency for a testator having made a will to forget about it. The testator should be encouraged to review it regularly and, in any event, following the introduction of any new tax legislation or a significant change in his personal or family circumstances or in the assets in his estate. Because of the large number of changes to inheritance tax legislation in the last few years, it is essential that wills are reviewed.

Small changes in a will can simply be made by a codicil. There is no requirement that a new will be made. Testators should, however, always bear in mind that after death a will and codicils are public documents and he or she may prefer to consolidate an earlier will as varied by subsequent changes into one document to avoid the testator's changing fortunes and/or whims being subject to public scrutiny. Because of the ease with which new documents may be created by word processing, codicils are now uncommon.

Executors often face a difficult task in locating a will, or a possible will, and share certificates and other documents of title. The testator should be encouraged to complete and to maintain a personal assets log. This should contain full details of

(a) assets;
(b) all insurance cover on the testator's life and assets;
(c) the names and addresses of his banks, building societies and professional advisers (eg solicitors, accountants and stock-brokers);
(d) the location of his will; and
(e) the lifetime transfers which he has made.

While it cannot be expected to contain details of every liability of the testator, it should at least record details of contingent liabilities under guarantees or indemnities, for example, knowledge of which may be crucial to the executors but which may otherwise be late in being drawn to their attention.

Variation of the will after death

[16.31] Whatever provision the testator may make in his will, his beneficiaries, if they are *sui juris*, may rearrange the distribution of the estate by means of a deed of variation or a disclaimer under IHTA 1984, s 142 or by an application to the court either under the Variation of Trusts Act 1958 or under the Inheritance (Provision for Family and Dependants) Act 1975. Any variation may result in different inheritance tax consequences. This should not prevent a testator making proper provision in his will as none of these routes can be relied upon to produce the result which the testator (and his beneficiaries) would wish and there is always a risk that those who survive him will be unwilling or unable to enter into a variation. In addition, any application to the court will inevitably deplete the value of the testator's estate. These matters are considered more fully in **CHAPTER 17 POST-DEATH ESTATE PLANNING**.

Death in service benefits and pension schemes

[16.32] For members of an approved death in service benefit scheme or pension scheme, it is important that any right of nomination or request in the form of a letter of wishes is exercised. These matters are considered fully in **CHAPTER 8 PENSIONS**.

Death-bed planning

[16.33] The scope for transferring assets only once it is clear that a person is dying is severely limited because there will be no mitigation of the inheritance tax payable on any lifetime gifts unless the donor survives for three years, when taper relief will commence (see **16.36** below). In addition, the benefit of the valuable capital gains tax base uplift on death will be lost. There are, however, some exercises which may be carried out.

(a) *The conversion of assets into excluded property.* Where persons are not domiciled in the UK and not deemed to be domiciled here, they can dispose of property situated in the UK in favour of property situated abroad. In the case of a person neither resident nor ordinarily resident in the UK any sterling bank accounts can be converted into foreign currency held in a qualifying bank account so that IHTA 1984, s 157 will apply. Alternatively, the purchase of exempt British government securities by persons non-resident and non-domiciled (any deemed domicile being ignored for this purpose) will be excluded property under IHTA 1984, s 6(2). While, for example, excluded property includes reversionary interests in settlements it will not include a reversion purchased for money or money's worth.
For individuals who are domiciled and resident in the UK the excluded property provisions do not offer tax planning opportunities.

(b) *Using up any unused lifetime exemptions such as the annual exemption and the small gifts exemption.*

(c) *Loans.* Where property which will qualify for business or agricultural property relief on a death is subject to a mortgage or charge to secure borrowings, the security should be transferred to non-qualifying property to ensure that the full advantage of the reliefs is taken. This is because the reliefs only apply on the value of property after it is reduced by the mortgage or charge. Alternatively, the borrowings could be repaid.

(d) *Assets pregnant with gains.* An individual should not make death-bed gifts of assets pregnant with gains because, as mentioned above, the valuable capital gains tax uplift on death will be lost. Where, however, the individual is married and his spouse or civil partner owns assets which are pregnant with gains, these assets could be transferred to the individual (free of capital gains tax) and then bequeathed back to the spouse or civil partner by will. The spouse or civil partner would then obtain a new base cost for the assets, ie their market value at the date of death. The pre-owned assets income tax charge will not apply in such a situation as any gift to a spouse or civil partner is an excluded transaction.

(e) *Joint bank accounts.* The conversion of bank accounts from sole to joint accounts and the transfer of property into joint names will assist in avoiding the need to obtain probate (see below). This will also assist with the funding of the payment of inheritance tax.

(f) *Charitable gifts.* Where an individual is intending to leave either a cash legacy or an interest in land to one or more charities, he could make the gifts whilst still alive so as to obtain an income tax advantage (see **Chapter 13 Gifts to Charities and Other Non-Profit Organisations**).

(g) *Heritage property.* Where a donor has heritage property qualifying for conditional exemption for inheritance tax purposes he could sell the heritage property to his children. The crystallised charge would be conditionally exempt provided the children are willing to give the requisite undertakings (see **Chapter 14 Gifts for National Purposes**).

(h) *Conversion of assets to relievable property.* Where there is a possibility that the individual may survive for the requisite two-year minimum ownership period, the acquisition of business or agricultural property will be effective in reducing the amount of inheritance tax payable on the death. Buying a farm or woodlands would qualify for 100% relief provided the 2-year period and the other criteria were satisfied. The acquisition of a balanced portfolio of securities dealt in on the Alternative Investment Market and qualifying for Business Property Relief would provide relief at 100% although the individual must be willing to accept the risks inherent in such an investment. There are also other strategies that might be followed where an existing interest is held which is eligible for 100% relief. The aim would be to enhance the level of relief available.

(i) *Maximise business property relief.* Although there is a two-year ownership period, it is not a requirement that the property must have been relevant business property throughout that period. It may be possible to convert an investment company into a trading company shortly before one of the shareholders die. There would need to be clear evidence of the change in the character of the business, there would need to be evidence of trading rather than an intention to trade.

    Assets which do not currently qualify for business property relief but would qualify if they were used in the business of a trading company could be transferred to the company. One would have to consider the capital gains tax implications of doing so but hold over relief under s 165 may be available. In addition, SDLT will need to be considered.

Funding the inheritance tax payable on death

The estate

[16.34] The personal representatives are accountable for the tax on the free estate passing on the death and must pay that tax on the application for the grant of probate or letters of administration. This is with the exception of instalments of tax which have not fallen due on any land or business property qualifying for the instalment option. This can create a number of difficulties as the personal representatives will often need to borrow from a bank to fund the tax. This problem is aggravated where the principal asset in the estate is a shareholding in a family company or some other asset which is not easily realisable. Borrowing from the bank to fund this tax, let alone the realisation of the asset to repay the bank loan, will be difficult. This burden of funding can be eased in a number of ways, for example, by the use of insurance policies held in trust or joint bank and building society accounts. Even joint shareholdings in quoted companies, all of which will pass to the survivor, can be realised before probate is granted. The survivor could then lend the proceeds to the personal representatives or purchase assets from the estate.

Funding through insurance

[16.35] Policies of insurance held in trust for the life assured's children are a useful vehicle for providing funds to pay the inheritance tax on death. In the case of a married couple where the sole or main inheritance tax charge will fall on the death of the survivor, the policy should be taken out on a joint life last survivor basis. The policy proceeds, will be paid to the trustees (or direct to the children if they are of age) on production of a death certificate only and will be available for loans to the personal representatives or for the purchase of estate assets. Ideally, the beneficial interests under the trusts should correspond to those under the will to avoid any question as to whether a loan by the trustees to the personal representatives will be in breach of trust.

Potentially exempt transfers and chargeable lifetime transfers

[16.36] In the event of the death of the donor within seven years of a lifetime chargeable transfer or a potentially exempt transfer, inheritance tax (which in the case of lifetime chargeable transfers will be additional inheritance tax) may be payable on that transfer. To determine the rate of tax payable on the death, the transfer will also be aggregated with the value of the donor's free estate at death and any other gifts made within the seven-year period. The donor's nil rate band will be applied to gifts within the seven-year period in the order in which they are made and any balance then remaining will be available in respect of his estate on death.

In addition to the nil rate band, potentially exempt transfers and chargeable lifetime transfers may have the benefit of taper relief. The relief (ranging from 20% where the death occurs in the fourth year following the gift to 80% where the death occurs in the seventh year following the gift) is given against the tax, and not against the value of the property, so that the full value of the gifts is aggregated with the estate throughout the seven-year period and the taper relief does not reduce the tax payable by the estate.

Tax on the gift

[16.37] Funding the tax on lifetime gifts which become taxable or subject to additional tax can cause problems for the donee, and for the personal representatives on whom a secondary liability falls. This is particularly the case if the subject matter of the gift is not easily realisable such as private company shares or land. The tax liability can be covered either by a seven-year decreasing term insurance policy effected by the donee on the life of the donor or by the donor effecting such a policy on his own life and assigning it to, or settling it in trust for, the donee. In the latter case any premium paid by the donor will be a gift but may be covered by the annual exemption or by the normal expenditure out of income exemption. Alternatively, the donor might pass funds to the trustees, which would be a potentially exempt transfer, leaving the trustees to pay the premiums themselves.

The cost of insurance will depend on the age, state of health of the donor and the sum insured. The decreasing sum payable under the policy in the fourth and subsequent years from the date of the gift should reflect the benefit of taper relief on the inheritance tax charge on the gift.

Additional tax on the estate

[16.38] Where the donor fails to survive for seven years after the potentially exempt transfer or a chargeable transfer is made, an increased charge to inheritance tax may arise on his estate. This is because the benefit of the nil rate band will be applied first to the chargeable lifetime gifts in the order in which they were made which may result in the estate paying a higher rate than would otherwise be the case. In addition, taper relief is only given against the tax on the gift and not against the value of the property given. Consequently, the risk of the higher amount of tax remains constant for the full seven-year term.

This additional tax can be funded by a seven-year term policy for a level sum rather than a decreasing one. The policy can be effected by the donor in trust for the beneficiaries of his estate or by the beneficiaries themselves. If the premiums are funded by the donor, such payments may again be covered by the annual exemption or normal expenditure out of income exemption, or may be potentially exempt.

If the policy is effected by the donor it should be written in trust for the beneficiaries. Otherwise, it will fall into the donor's estate and will be subject to inheritance tax on the death as part of that estate.

Methods of avoiding probate

[16.39] A grant of probate or letters of administration is necessary to prove the title of the executors or administrators to the assets of a person who has died in order that those assets may be collected in for the benefit of his estate. It is not required in respect of any assets where title automatically passes to someone else on the death. Where property is held in joint names the production of a death certificate will be sufficient. As a result considerable legal and other expenses may be saved.

There are other advantages as well. For example, in the case of a joint bank account, the survivor will have access to funds to meet immediate expenses and perhaps to meet some or all of the inheritance tax liability on the death.

Avoiding probate does not override the duty to submit an inheritance tax account of the property and to pay the relevant tax. Any liability to inheritance tax arising on the death will still have to be paid, even if all assets are in joint names and pass by survivorship. The duty to submit the account falls jointly upon the co-owner and the personal representatives and both are jointly liable for the tax although the incidence of tax falls on the deceased's share of the joint property (IHTA 1984, s 211(3)). Where, as often happens, the tax is borne by the estate in the first instance this can cause cash flow difficulties in the estate and this factor should not be overlooked.

Property held in joint names

[16.40] All property may be held in joint names. In the case of land, the maximum number of joint owners permitted by the Law of Property Act 1925, s 34(2) is four, and, in practice, a similar restriction is often applied to other types of property, for example, shares and bank and building society accounts. It should be remembered that because property is in joint names, and legal title passes to the survivor or survivors, the beneficial interest may not always pass in exactly the same way. The survivors may be holding as trustees. When property is first transferred into joint names some separate statement of the beneficial ownership will be desirable as evidence of the parties' intentions.

In the case of *Sillars v CIR* [2004] STC (SCD) 180 the issue arose as to whether the whole of a bank account in which the deceased owned a share as joint tenant was subject to inheritance tax on the basis that she had a general power to dispose of the entire account or, alternatively, whether she had made a gift subject to a reservation when she transferred the bank account into the joint names of herself and her daughters. The intention was to make an immediate gift to her daughters. All subsequent transfers into the account were made by, or derived from, the mother. Although the daughters operated the account on behalf of their mother when she was ill, it was held that they did not have a general power over the account. The mother and two daughters each included one third of the annual interest on the account in their respective income tax returns. The Special Commissioners held that a tenancy in common had not been established and that the deceased had a general power over the whole account by virtue of which, under IHTA 1984, s 5(2), the whole amount was liable to inheritance tax. In order to establish a tenancy in common, it was held that accounts should have been kept of who owned the funds and the parties would have needed an understanding of how deposits and withdrawals were dealt with. The joint account was plainly not settled property. There was no accounting procedures to see whether the deceased was taking more than her share. This case highlights the importance, when transferring property into joint names, of setting out clearly the shares of each joint owner and establishing whether a tenancy in common is intended.

In *Taylor v Revenue and Customs Comrs* [2008] STC SCD 1159 a widow, B inherited two building society accounts from her husband. She subsequently put the accounts in the joint names of herself and her brother-in-law, P. The withdrawals made from the accounts by B were to give presents to her family. B died in 2004 leaving all her property on trust for the benefit of her two nieces. The Revenue argued that B had been beneficially entitled to the moneys in these two accounts or alternatively the disposal was a gift of property subject to a reservation and so it was deemed to be property to which B had been beneficially entitled. B's executrix argued that B held the accounts as trustee and that the money belonged to P. The Special Commissioner held that B had not held the accounts as trustee and that B had a general power which enabled her to dispose of the whole of the accounts within the meaning of the Inheritance Tax Act 1984, s 5. She was therefore treated as having been beneficially entitled to the two accounts. If B had not required access to the accounts the problem could have been avoided if she had entered into a formal trust arrangement.

Benefits under death in service policies and pension schemes

[16.41] Such benefits can very often be paid to beneficiaries following production of a death certificate and without production of probate. This is the case where the trustees have a discretion to pay the proceeds among the dependants and are not required to pay them to the personal representatives. Where the proceeds are payable to personal representatives title must be proved by production of probate or letters of administration. The absence of a letter of wishes from the scheme member may lead to a delay and may tempt the trustees to avoid the issue of dividing the moneys between the dependants and to pay them to the personal representatives. In this case payment will be made when the grant is eventually produced some months later.

Care should be taken to ensure that the letter of wishes is lodged by the member with the scheme's trustees if this is required under the rules of the scheme or, if lodged elsewhere, can be obtained from safe custody and sent to the trustees without first having to obtain probate or letters of administration.

Insurance policies

[16.42] Life policies and personal accident policies can all be effected in trust for dependants and the proceeds paid to the named trustees on production of a death certificate and without production of probate. The Married Women's Property Act 1882 provides a relatively simple route for creating a trust over policies effected by one spouse on his life and expressed as for the benefit of a spouse and/or children. More elaborate trusts, and trusts for beneficiaries other than spouse and children, will require individual drafting, although most life offices can provide standard trust wordings on request.

Policy documents, if lodged at a bank or elsewhere in safe custody, should be held jointly to the order of the life assured and some other person, preferably the policy trustees or the beneficiary. If they are deposited in safe custody to the order of the assured alone, a grant of representation may be necessary to obtain the release of the policy document and therefore the policy proceeds cannot be used to fund inheritance tax payable before the grant is issued.

Assets worth less than £5,000

[16.43] Certain assets, if valued at less than £5,000 each, may be collected in by personal representatives, or intending personal representatives, without production of a grant. The Administration of Estates (Small Payments) Act 1965 authorises building societies, industrial and provident societies, trade unions and loan societies to pay over balances, etc held if less than £5,000 without production of a grant of representation. National Savings and Investments similarly permits balances on accounts, premium savings bonds, national savings certificates and government stock held on the department's register will usually to be released without production of a grant where the total invested is not more than £15,000, although the Department reserves its right to require production of the grant.

National savings investments

[16.44] Where these are required to meet the inheritance tax due on the death in order to obtain a grant of representation, there are procedures available through the Probate Registry and HMRC Inheritance Tax for most forms of national savings investments to be encashed prior to the grant being obtained.

Foreign assets

[16.45] Small holdings of directly owned foreign assets are usually best avoided in the absence of an overriding investment or recreational reason for acquiring such assets. Proving title to these assets on the death of the registered owner will often require the involvement of lawyers both in England and in the foreign country concerned as well as probate formalities (or the equivalent) in both countries because title in foreign countries will usually be established through title granted in the court of the place of domicile. Often the expenses involved do not justify collecting in an asset of modest value. Foreign death duties may be payable and foreign death duty returns will need to be submitted. There will usually be relief given against inheritance tax for foreign tax paid. In the case of land situated abroad, where there is a double tax treaty between the UK and the country where the land is situated, the credit is usually to be given in the overseas country for inheritance tax paid in the UK.

Ownership of foreign assets through offshore settlements or companies or through UK nominees may overcome difficult and expensive foreign probate requirements and may also avoid the payment of local death duties. These possibilities should be considered before a foreign asset is acquired, as should the disposal costs arising on death.

Where a testator is likely to die owning foreign realty consideration should be given to the succession implications of the law of the country in which the land is situated. The law of the jurisdiction may specify how the property is to devolve on the death regardless of any will left by the deceased. It may also be sensible to have a separate will dealing solely with that particular asset drawn up by a local lawyer under the local law.

Ownership of foreign assets is considered in more detail in **CHAPTER 18 UK DOMICILIARIES INVESTING ABROAD**.

Lloyd's underwriting interests

[16.46] A personal underwriting membership of Lloyd's terminates on death and therefore it should be discussed in conjunction with wills.

An interest in Lloyd's will form part of an individual's estate but business property relief may be available in respect of certain elements.

There are three distinct elements to the Lloyd's interest:

- the pipeline results of the open years of account together with the result of any closed year of account not distributed before death (open year run-off accounts also have to be valued);
- the value of assets held in a special reserve fund and in ancillary trust funds;
- the value of syndicate capacity.

A member of Lloyd's may be an individual member or a corporate member. The term 'corporate member' includes limited companies, Scottish limited partnerships and limited liability partnerships. The status of a member determines the amount of business property relief which is available.

Individual members

[16.47] In principle, ancillary trust fund assets and the value of assets and accumulated income and gains held in the special reserve fund attract full BPR. However, the total value of ancillary trust fund assets and other funds at Lloyds ('FAL') will only be eligible for 100% relief to the extent that those funds are, in the Revenue's words, 'commensurate with the amount of underwriting business that was being written by the Name' (Lloyd's Manual para 8290). The Revenue states that 'as a rule of thumb, [we] would not normally seek to restrict BPR if the value of FAL assets is not substantially greater than the minimum FAL requirement'.

As a general rule special reserve fund assets qualify for relief except in so far as they are used as funds at Lloyd's, in which case they are scrutinised in the same way as ancillary trust funds.

Relief is also available on the assets used to provide security for bank guarantees or letters of credit which form part of a Lloyd's deposit or reserve. The amount of relief 'cannot exceed the nominal value of the guarantee but will nevertheless be dependent on the market value of the collateral assets.

There is no restriction of relief by reference to the nature of the underlying assets supporting the guarantee or letter of credit, but the Revenue will treat the value of the underlying assets as reduced by the amount of the guarantee or letter of credit for the purpose of giving any other reliefs or exemptions' (Lloyd's Manual para 8290). Therefore, guarantees should not be secured against assets that would qualify for either business property relief or agricultural property relief.

In addition to business property relief, the investments and cash in the deposits and reserves are also discounted to reflect the fact that they are unavailable until the date pipeline profits are paid and the dates when FAL and special reserve funds assets are released to the estate. With business property relief at 100%, this further discount is not very important and is only likely to be relevant where the amount of deposits and reserves eligible for the relief is restricted (see above).

Corporate members

[16.48] SLPs and LLPs cannot benefit from the special reserve fund, but the rules stated above concerning the treatment of ancillary trust fund assets otherwise hold good for them.

Third party or interavailable ancillary trust fund assets, which support the underwriting of a company, have not qualified for business property relief since 31 December 2006. Owners wishing to maximise BPR should therefore seek to transfer the funds into the ownership of a corporate member or build them up within it from accumulated profits.

Individuals and members of SLPs and LLPs

[16.49] Profits or losses on the open years' accounts at death may be valued:

(a) on the Lloyd's audit basis, which is the strict legal basis and is adopted as the market value at date of death, usually producing a conservative result, or
(b) on the basis of the actual results of the open years. An election by the personal representatives to base the valuation on actual results must be made within 12 months of the grant of representation.

In either event the value will be discounted to reflect the fact that the profits will not have been available to the Name until after the accounts for the year have closed. Consequently, a member can use his underwriting property to make substantially larger gifts by will to children or other non-exempt beneficiaries at minimum tax cost, particularly if all or part of his nil rate band is available. In practice, the availability of 100% BPR means that the Lloyd's audit basis is invariably chosen and discounting is unnecessary.

Very often, the testator will be advised to take advantage of business property relief by giving his Lloyd's underwriting property to his children or other non-exempt beneficiary by his will. It should be borne in mind that some part of the underwriting property, including unpaid profits on a closed year of account which are simply debts due to the member, may not qualify for business property relief. If the will refers to underwriting property in general terms, but it is the testator's intention that only property which qualifies for business property relief is to be passed under that gift, it is necessary to use words of limitation to limit the gift and ensure that underwriting property which does not so qualify is excluded.

Where a member funds his Lloyd's deposit or underwriting reserves by a banker's letter of credit, the testator will have to consider whether the property held as security by the bank should be included in the gift. As mentioned above, the property so held by the bank will qualify for business property relief, up to the face value of the letter of credit.

Two other matters also need consideration.

(1) In the absence of express words in the will, a gift of Lloyd's underwriting profits will not carry the burden of income tax on those profits. If there are profits accruing to the estate, the executors will be liable to pay basic rate income tax, with the one exception of any amounts released from the special reserve fund, which is taxable as if it were income of the deceased's final period of assessment. It is therefore desirable that a gift of underwriting profits or gains should be made subject to payment out of that property of all attributable tax liabilities and similarly the gift should carry with it the benefit of income and capital gains tax repayments resulting from underwriting losses. Any income tax and capital gains tax repayments will not qualify for business property relief.

(2) It is desirable that an individual member is advised to effect an estate protection plan policy which on his death would protect his estate from underwriting losses and enable the executors to distribute assets without waiting until the open years have closed. Even so, the will should authorise the executors to reinsure the open years' underwriting at death or to effect stop-loss insurance, in case for any reason the estate protection plan policy is not kept in force by the testator or to cover any excess that the policy may not cover.

As membership of Lloyd's terminates on death for individuals the opportunity to utilise business property relief is only available on that occasion. There is no carrying on of the business after death so that relief will not be available on the death of a surviving spouse (unless he or she is also a member in his or her own right).

It used to be possible for the surviving spouse to apply to join Lloyd's and take over the deceased's underwriting capacity, but Lloyd's will not now allow new individual members. It is possible that it would allow the capacity of the deceased to be transferred to a SLP, LLP or company set up by the surviving spouse, but the spouse would have to apply for membership in her own right and provide her own ancillary trust funds, until those supporting the run-off of the unlimited accounts were released on their closure.

If the Lloyd's underwriting property is not given by the will to a child or other non-exempt beneficiary, consideration should be given to dealing with it in this way, if possible, in a deed of variation of the will. As NameCos and LLPs will not cease to be members on the death of a shareholder or designated member this issue does not arise for members of an LLP or a shareholder in a NameCo.

Chapter 17

Post-Death Estate Planning

Introduction

[17.1] Personal representatives do not have an easy task and the administration of an estate is made more complicated by the various options open to them and the beneficiaries of the deceased's estate, following the death, to mitigate the impact of inheritance tax and to take the estate planning steps which the deceased ought to have taken but failed (for whatever reason) to take during his lifetime. This is the case even where the deceased died intestate.

If the estate is subject to inheritance tax, it will be important to identify any property which may qualify for any of the available reliefs to reduce the amount of inheritance tax payable (such as relevant business property within the meaning of IHTA 1984, s 105 or agricultural property within the meaning of IHTA 1984, s 115) and to ascertain whether or not the relief will apply in the particular circumstances of the estate.

If the estate includes any assets such as works of art or land and buildings which are pre-eminent for national, scientific, historic or artistic interest, then a claim under IHTA 1984, s 31 may be made to the Treasury by the personal representatives to have the assets made exempt from tax. If the claim is allowed, an exemption will be granted, subject to various undertakings being given in relation to the preservation of the asset and the provision of public access to it. Therefore, no tax will be payable at death on the relevant assets but the exemption will be lost if there is a breach of one of the undertakings or if the asset is sold and so the tax will become payable at that stage. If an estate includes assets which might qualify for such relief, expert advice should be taken at an early stage to ascertain whether or not a claim should be made for an exemption and as to which assets should be included in the claim. (See **Chapter 14 Gifts for National Purposes** for a more detailed explanation of the rules.)

The personal representatives must also consider whether the inheritance tax may be paid by instalments; and must also establish upon whom the burden of the tax falls: for example, whether a legacy is to be paid subject to or free from inheritance tax.

The personal representatives should also consider that if any investments or land forming part of the deceased's estate are to be sold after the death and the values at the date of sale are less than the values at the date of death, then the sale price can be substituted for the value at death, provided that certain conditions are fulfilled. The timing of the sales is all important.

IHTA 1984, s 217 imposes an onerous duty of inquiry in relation not only to the deceased's estate at death but also in relation to lifetime chargeable transfers. These onerous duties are reflected in the form IHT 400 on which personal representatives make a return of the deceased's estate. Anybody, but especially professional advisers, should consider carefully before accepting an executorship in view of their personal liability for a failure to comply with these duties. Penalties are imposed for continuing failure to file an account or notify HMRC of the inheritance tax payable.

By far the most important estate planning consideration for personal representatives and the beneficiaries of the deceased's estate will be their ability to vary the dispositions effected by the will or by the applicable intestacy rules so as to redirect parts of the estate to different members of the family. Such rearrangements may be solely tax-driven or they may arise from other personal or family considerations. The personal representatives will wish to draw this possibility to the attention of the beneficiaries at as early a stage as possible.

Post-death estate planning must be undertaken within strict time limits in order to be tax effective, which may be during a particularly stressful and difficult period for the beneficiaries. An adviser will need to establish his clients' requirements with sensitivity and care but without delay.

A rearrangement can take many forms including a written variation by agreement, disclaimer, discretionary wills and precatory trusts, all of which are discussed in this chapter.

Reasons for a rearrangement

[17.2] In most cases the primary purpose of a rearrangement is to reduce the burden of inheritance tax. But there may be a secondary purpose which is to effect an equitable distribution of the deceased's assets between the beneficiaries and other members of the deceased's family.

There may be many personal or family reasons which prompt beneficiaries to surrender or redirect the whole or part of their entitlement under a will or on intestacy. It may be that a will does not provide adequately for a particular beneficiary. For example, a widow inheriting the whole of her late husband's estate may wish to make immediate provision for her children. Conversely, children who inherit under their father's will at the expense of their mother might wish to redirect part of their entitlement to her.

Occasionally, the personal representatives receive a claim under the Inheritance (Provision for Family and Dependants) Act 1975. This Act enables a person who was maintained by the deceased to make an application to the court for provision to be made for him out of the estate on the grounds that the deceased's will did not make reasonable financial provision for him. An order in favour of one or more members of the deceased's family and dependants will of necessity require rearrangement of the estate. If such a claim is anticipated, it might be preferable for the beneficiaries to reach an agreement with the potential claimants and to embody such an agreement in a written variation made within two years of the death without an application to the court.

Where the beneficiaries under a will are already wealthy, a generation might be missed out; this is known as 'generation skipping'. For example, a son of a deceased testator might wish to pass on a legacy bequeathed to him under his father's will to his own son. Once again, the desired result can be achieved by the testator's son entering into a written variation.

There are other non-tax motives which can sometimes prompt a rearrangement. For example, if a will is defective in some respect, perhaps because of a typing error or some mistake made by the testator in the description of an asset or beneficiary, it may be possible to avoid applying to the court for a remedy by rewriting that defective part of the will in the form of a variation which would save both time and expense.

Inheritance tax

Variations

General

[17.3] The provisions of IHTA 1984, s 142 enable the beneficiaries under a will or on an intestacy to alter the dispositions of the deceased's estate effected by the terms of the deceased's will or by the intestacy rules.

The popular notion that one is 'varying' the terms of a will is a misconception, since the terms of a will can never be varied once the testator has died. Section 142 speaks of 'varying' the dispositions of the deceased's estate effected by his will and is directed at cases where the recipient of property from the deceased chooses to redirect it to other persons whether by way of an outright gift or a declaration of trust or a settlement. If the provisions of s 142 are satisfied then the redirection will, for inheritance tax purposes, be treated as if it had been effected by the deceased on his death and tax will be charged accordingly. There is a similar back-dating provision for capital gains tax which is considered below. It must never be forgotten, however, that this retroactive effect is a fiction imposed for tax purposes — as a matter of strict law any redirection takes effect when the instrument effecting the redirection (be it a deed of gift, a stock transfer form or a declaration of trust) is entered into and not from the date of death. Thus, the redirection does not alter the income tax treatment of any income arising before the redirection is made. The charge to income tax on pre-owned assets, does not apply to a disposition made under a variation provided that the disposition is not treated for inheritance tax purposes (under IHTA 1984, s 17) as a transfer of value by that person (FA 2004, Sch 15 para 16).

Time limit for claim

[17.4] The variation must be made by an instrument in writing within 2 years of the death. There is no requirement that the variation be by deed as any instrument in writing which effectively transfers property, or an interest in property, will suffice (HMRC Inheritance Tax Manual, para 35022). Although in some cases, a deed may be necessary to transfer the property. The Revenue has published guidelines setting out the requirements that an instrument must satisfy (HMRC Inheritance Tax Manual, para 35021). The variation may be made not only in relation to the dispositions effected by a will but also in relation to those taking place under the intestacy rules. In addition, the section will apply to a redirection by a joint owner of the interest in property which automatically passes to him by survivorship on the other co-owner's death.

By virtue of IHTA 1984, s 142(5), an instrument of variation will not be effective for property comprised in a settlement in which the deceased had an interest in possession at his death. Thus, if the deceased had a life interest under a settlement and, under the terms of the settlement, his son takes an absolute interest therein on his death, his son cannot use the provisions of s 142 to redirect that interest in remainder elsewhere following the life tenant's death. Estate planning in relation to settlements therefore must be achieved during the life tenant's lifetime. There is nothing to prevent a variation being made in respect of a trust created by the will itself.

The subsection also ensures that property which is treated as forming part of the deceased's estate at the date of death because he has retained a benefit in it within the terms of FA 1986, s 102 (gifts with reservation) cannot be the subject matter of a post-death variation.

No consideration

[17.4A] For a variation to be effective the person entering into the variation must not receive any extraneous consideration for the variation as the provisions of IHTA 1984, s 142(1) do not apply to a 'variation . . . made for any consideration in money or money's worth other than consideration consisting of the making in respect of another of the dispositions, of a variation . . . to which [s 142(1)] applies' (s 142(3)). An indemnity given by one party to the variation to another in respect of tax liabilities or legal costs could amount to such extraneous consideration, if making the variation is conditional upon giving the indemnity, as the indemnity is given as part of a single transaction with the variation. It is understood that the Revenue seems to accept that a deed which is entered into solely to avoid or compromise a claim under the Inheritance (Provision for Family and Dependants) Act 1975 will not be regarded as a deed having been made for consideration in money or money's worth unless the deceased died domiciled outside the UK (HMRC Inheritance Tax Manual para 35100). The case of *Lau (executor of Lau dec'd) v Revenue and Customs Comrs* [2009] STC (SCD) 352 is an example of where it was held that consideration was given for a variation. In this case substantial cash gifts of £665,000 each made to the deceased's two daughters and step son were redirected to the surviving spouse. Subsequently, each legatee received £1m from their mother. The daughters accepted that s 142(3) applied. The son, however, argued that the £1m gift represented the honouring of an earlier promise that his mother would finance his business venture and also contained an element of a wedding present. This was rejected as being 'incredible' and 'unreliable'.

Parties to the arrangements

[17.4B] The persons entering into the variation must be of full age and capacity and willing to act. If minor or unborn beneficiaries are involved, it may be possible to apply on their behalf to the court under the Variation of Trusts Act 1958 for the court's consent (embodied in a court order). However, in those circumstances to be effective the court order must be made within the 2-year period.

Section 142 will automatically apply provided the document contains a statement made by all the relevant persons to the effect that s 142 should apply to the variation. Such a statement should include the appropriate statutory references, an example of the wording can be found in the HMRC's Inheritance Tax Manual, para 35028. In *Wills v Gibbs* [2007] EWHC 3361 (Ch) the statement had been omitted in the deed of variation and so an application for rectification was made. The High Court held that that rectification would be allowed as the deed did not give effect to the true agreement between the parties and the rectification was not solely intended to procure a beneficial tax consequence.

Section 142(2A) provides that the 'relevant persons' are:

(a) the person or persons making the instrument, and
(b) where the variation results in additional tax being payable, the personal representatives.

Personal representatives may decline to join in an election only if no, or no sufficient, assets are held by them in that capacity for discharging the additional tax.

This means that where additional tax is payable as a result of the variation, but the personal representatives are holding sufficient assets to discharge the liability, the personal representatives are necessary parties to the instrument and can be compelled to join in if they initially refuse to do so. However, where the personal representatives validly decline to join in the instrument, then IHTA 1984, s 142(1) will not apply to the variation, although it will be legally effective for all other purposes.

Where one of the beneficiaries (the 'second deceased') has died before a variation to a will is made, the Revenue has confirmed that the personal representatives of the beneficiary may enter into a deed (HMRC Inheritance Tax Manual, para 35042). Where the variation reduces the entitlement of the beneficiaries of the second deceased then they, as well as the personal representatives of the second deceased, must agree to the variation. The Revenue will require evidence of the consent of the beneficiaries of the second deceased, whether by signing the instrument or by other written means (Revenue Tax Bulletin issue 74, p 1069).

In cases where the deceased held an interest in jointly held assets which passed on death by survivorship, the Revenue has confirmed that s 142 will apply to a variation of that interest (HMRC Tax Bulletin October 1995, p 254). This means that a surviving joint owner may enter into a written variation to give the deceased's joint interest to someone else to which s 142 will apply provided that the necessary conditions are met. For both inheritance tax and capital gains tax the legislation provides that the rules apply not only to a disposition/inheritance arising under a will or the law of intestacy, but also to those effected 'otherwise' which includes jointly held assets passing by survivorship.

The Revenue states that a variation must be implemented 'in the real world' (CTO Newsletter December 2001 and HMRC Inheritance Tax Manual, para 35042). IHTA 1984, s 17 expressly provides that a variation or disclaimer within IHTA 1984, s 142(1) is not a transfer of value. The instrument in writing should be more than an empty piece of paper. An example is given where A leaves a life interest in property to B with remainder to C. On B's death (but within two years of A's death) C makes a deed of variation which purports to vary A's will by redirecting B's interest to C. The Revenue argues that, in the real world, B's interest does not exist at that time and there is nothing for the deed to do, so s 142 cannot apply. There has been much debate about this amongst commentators. Section 142 is artificial, in any event, as it retrospectively rewrites the will of the deceased and treats the retrospectively revised will as if the deceased had made different dispositions on his death to those he actually made. In the example given, the variation would not have been made by C alone. It would be made by B's executors and C. Certainly, there is no dispute that the executors can execute a deed of variation which itself makes the whole matter more artificial. However, that is the purpose of s 142. In the example, C is entitled to the assets both before and after the variation, the difference being the route by which he obtained them. One could argue that this was not an empty piece of paper because it could increase or decrease the amount of inheritance tax payable.

It is suggested that the deed of variation is ineffective under the general law, however, one must question the relevance of general law to this situation as s 142 is a deeming provision upon which a tax charge is based.

In their April/May 2002 Newsletter, the Revenue published its responses to two letters relating to the above.

> It would appear that in a situation where A dies leaving his estate outright to his widow B, who dies within two years leaving her estate to her children, your view is now that a deed of variation redirecting the estate to the children would be ineffective. Is this correct?
>
> The example you give is one where an absolute interest is given to the survivor. On the death of the survivor, the property inherited on the first death still exists in the survivor's estate and it is therefore possible, in the real world, for those inheriting on the second death to redirect the estate of the first to die. Contrast this with the example given in our Newsletter where, on the first death, the survivor is given a life interest in property. That interest is extinguished on the death of the survivor, so that when, in the real world, those inheriting on the second death come to consider a variation, there is nothing for the variation to bite on.
>
> You say that B's life interest does not exist because "there is nothing for the deed to bite upon". Surely:
>
> - The interest exists until the variation, and
> - It is a type of property which can be disposed of by B (or his personal representatives) at any time up to the deed of variation.

> As the variation was made after the death of the life tenant, there was then no life interest in existence. Whilst such an interest is capable of disposition by the life tenant, the fact that it ceases on his death means that it is not capable of being disposed of after that has occurred.

The Revenue's view has received some confirmation in the Special Commissioner's decision in *Souter's Executry v CIR* (SpC 325). In that case, under the will of Miss Souter, Miss Greenlees received a life interest in a property which had been the two ladies' residence. Miss Greenlees continued to live in the property after Miss Souter's death but died within two years of the death of Miss Souter. The executors and beneficiaries of Miss Souter's estate (including the executors of Miss Greenlees' estate) then entered into a deed under which they provided that Miss Souter's will was to take effect as if Miss Greenlees had not received the life interest. The Commissioners accepted the Revenue's contention that Miss Greenlees' executors could not have continued to enjoy the life interest after Miss Greenlees' death and therefore that they had nothing to vary. In order to satisfy s 142, the deed had to vary a disposition under Miss Souter's will and there could be no disposition following Miss Greenlees' death.

Compliance

[17.4C] Where a deed of variation is made which results in additional tax being payable, the relevant persons must submit a copy of the instrument and notify the Revenue of the amount of additional tax payable within six months of the instrument being executed (IHTA 1984, s 218A). A penalty of up to £3,000 may be charged where failure to comply continues after the six-month anniversary for delivery of the instrument and notification of the additional tax payable. The penalty will not be imposed where there is a reasonable excuse.

More than one variation?

[17.4D] There are occasions when it may be desirable for the beneficiaries to enter into more than one variation. Whilst this is clearly permissible with regard to different property in the estate, the Revenue takes the view that an instrument would not fall within IHTA 1984, s 142 if it further redirected any property or any part of any property that had already been redirected under an earlier instrument of variation (HMRC Inheritance Tax Manual, para 35082). The case of *Russell v CIR* [1988] STC 195, [1988] 2 All ER 405 (Ch D) confirmed this view. It is the Revenue's view that an election, once made, is irrevocable (HMRC Inheritance Tax Manual, para 35081).

Stamp Duty and Stamp Duty Land Tax

[17.4E] An instrument of variation relating to land is exempt from stamp duty land tax provided certain conditions are satisfied (FA 2003, Sch 3 para 4). A self-certificate form must be completed.

An instrument of variation relating to stock or marketable securities is exempt from stamp duty under the Stamp Duty (Exempt Instruments) Regulations 1987 (SI 1987 No 516) provided it contains the required certificate.

Rectification of deed of variation

[17.4F] It is possible for a deed of variation once executed to be varied but in limited circumstances. In *Lake v Lake* [1989] STC 565 it was held that a deed of variation can be rectified by the courts if the words mistakenly used mean that it does not give effect to the parties' joint intentions. It is immaterial that the rectification achieves a tax advantage or that it is made more than two years after the death. In *Wills v Gibbs* [2007] SWTI 1970, [2007] All ER (D) 509 the deed of variation did not contain the statement that it was intended by the parties that s 142 should apply. This of course meant that the provisions in the deed of variation would not be treated as being made by the will. An application for rectification was made. It was held that a deed could be rectified to achieve the correction of a voluntary settlement so as to enable any mistakes in the settlement as executed to accord with the settlor's true intention when he executed it. The court allowed the deed to be rectified to include the requisite statement because the parties although not aware of the formalities of s 142 knew of the consequences of making such a deed. In *Ashcroft v Barnsdale & Others* [2010] EWHC 1948 (Ch), [2010] 32 EG 61 (CS), [2010] SWTI 2514 the claim for rectification of a deed of variation was successful. The deed of variation had failed to give effect to the true agreement of the parties.

Disclaimers

Introduction

[17.5] A person cannot be made to accept a gift (whether lifetime or testamentary) if he does not wish to do so. He always has the right to decline the gift at any time before he expressly or impliedly accepts it but he will be treated as having accepted a gift once he takes any benefit from it or after a reasonable time has elapsed during which he could have disclaimed but failed to do so. A disclaimer is the refusal to accept a gift. It can be withdrawn but only if it has not been acted upon by any party relying upon it. While a legatee can accept one gift and refuse another, if they are separate and distinct, under the same will, he cannot in England and Wales accept only part of a gift and disclaim the remainder. (The law in Scotland is different.)

In the case of *Smith v Smith* [2001] 1 WLR 1937 the High Court held that a disclaimer in advance of the death of the relevant estate owner was not valid because, since the estate owner was alive at the date of the disclaimer and could vary her will, there was no real interest which could be disclaimed.

Effect

[17.5A] The effect of a disclaimer is that the original gift becomes void *ab initio*. Thus, if a legacy or other bequest or devise is disclaimed, it falls into the residue of the testator's estate and, if the residue is not effectively disposed of by will, it will pass under the intestacy rules. If a residuary gift is disclaimed, that part of the residuary estate disclaimed will pass as on intestacy. To be a genuine disclaimer, the person disclaiming must simply refuse to accept the benefit being disclaimed and must not have any ability to decide its ultimate destination. Thus, before contemplating a disclaimer, one should look to see to whom the benefit to be disclaimed will pass under the operative rules of law.

For example, if residue is left to A, B and C in equal shares and A disclaims his share, that share will pass as on the testator's intestacy and will not accrue to B's and C's shares. The disclaimer of a life interest in residue will either accelerate the vesting of subsequent interests or create a partial intestacy of income if the doctrine of acceleration is not applicable. However, if an interest in remainder is disclaimed, this will (unless there are subsequent remainders) result in the trust property passing on the partial intestacy of the testator. Where on an intestacy one of a class of beneficiaries disclaims, his or her share passes to the remaining members of the class. Care needs to be taken by anyone considering a disclaimer of an interest under an intestacy because the rules can operate so as to pass over closer relatives in favour of remoter ones.

IHTA 1984, s 142 applies to disclaimers and thus the effect of a disclaimer for inheritance tax purposes is that the ultimate beneficiary is treated as having received the benefit in question from the deceased and not from the person disclaiming.

Formalities

[17.5B] For s 142 to apply, the disclaimer must be in writing and made within 2 years of the deceased's death. However, there does not have to be an election or statement of intent to bring a disclaimer within the operation of s 142. Thus, in an appropriate case, where a disclaimer will achieve the desired result, it is a simple alternative to a written variation.

Stamp Duty and Stamp Duty Land Tax

[17.5C] A disclaimer is not liable to stamp duty nor stamp duty land tax, as it does not effect the transfer of any property.

Interests in settled property

Inheritance Tax Act 1984, s 93 provides that where a person who becomes entitled to an interest in settled property disclaims their interest, then provided the disclaimer is not made for money or money's worth, then the legislation applies as if he had not become entitled to that interest. Interestingly, there is no time limit in which a disclaimer should be made. Therefore, if the two-year time limit has passed and the beneficiary has taken no benefit from the assets, it may be possible to take advantage of s 93. However, where such time has passed it can be expected that the Revenue will examine the situation carefully.

Planning points

[17.6] The fact that a variation or disclaimer may be made within two years of a person's death should not be used as an excuse for not taking estate planning steps during his lifetime. IHTA 1984, s 142 does provide, however, a 2-year breathing space in which oversights may be corrected and account taken of changes in legislation since the will was made. The two-year period is also the appropriate time to review all the family's financial circumstances and in particular the needs of any surviving spouse or civil partner.

Use of nil rate band

[17.7] In the past, variations were often used to ensure that the nil rate band was utilised. It was used often where, for example, a widow who had inherited her husband's entire estate on death redirected sufficient sums to utilise her husband's nil rate band. With the ability to transfer nil rate bands between spouses and civil partners this will no longer be required as often as it was in the past.

Business and agricultural property relief

[17.8] Where property qualifying for business or agricultural property relief has been left to the surviving spouse or civil partner, consideration should be given as to whether it will still qualify as at the date of his or her death. If there is any prospect of the property not so qualifying (for example, if the property is likely to be sold) then the property might be redirected to non-exempt beneficiaries to ensure that the relief is not wasted. Any amount of property qualifying for 100% relief can be redirected at no tax cost. £650,000 of property qualifying for 50% relief may be redirected to children tax-free if the deceased died without having used any of the available nil rate band (see above). Where the surviving spouse requires the income from the property, consideration can be given to redirecting the property to a discretionary trust of which the survivor is a beneficiary. The income can be distributed to the widow. If she dies before the tenth anniversary, the trust can be terminated. However, an exit charge may arise because in calculating the inheritance tax on a capital distribution before the first decennial, the initial value of the trust fund is the unrelieved value. The exit charge based on current rates will not be more than 6% which must be compared with a possible 40% rate on unqualifying property in the spouse's estate on death.

Increase in asset value after death

[17.9] Where the deceased's estate has significantly risen in value during the two-year period a deed of variation can be used to pass the gain element on to the next generation free of inheritance tax.

Example

> Augustus leaves his entire estate worth £325,000 to his wife Abbie and 18 months after his death the estate has trebled in value.
>
> If Abbie declares in writing that she will hold the estate upon trust as if she had been left a legacy of £325,000 with the residue passing to her children, the inheritance tax provisions will operate so as to attribute the value of the estate at death (ie £325,000) wholly to the legacy (which is exempt from tax by virtue of the spouse exemption) with the result that the remaining £650,000 ((3 × £325,000) – £325,000) passes to the children tax-free.

Gifts with reservation

[17.10] The interaction of IHTA 1984, s 142 with the gifts with reservation provisions contained in FA 1986, s 102 could provide useful possibilities regarding the matrimonial home. For example, a widow inheriting her late husband's house may decide to redirect the gift so that the house passes to her children. However, her children may allow her as their licensee to continue to occupy the property. Provided the variation has been entered into within two years and a valid instrument has been delivered where relevant, it will fall within IHTA 1984, s 142(1). IHTA 1984, s 142 overrides FA 1986, s 102 thus preventing the gifts with reservation provisions applying, which they clearly would have done had the widow simply given the house to her children but continued to live there. HMRC Inheritance Tax accepts this interpretation (HMRC Inheritance Tax Manual, para 35151).

The pre-owned asset income tax charge will not apply to a disposition made under a deed of variation, provided that the disposition is not treated as a transfer of value by that person for inheritance tax purposes (FA 2004, Sch 15 para 16).

Potentially exempt transfers

[17.11] A gift qualifying as a potentially exempt transfer by a widow or other beneficiary should not be overlooked as an alternative to post-death variations of wills and other rearrangements. A potentially exempt transfer (of any amount or value) will be completely free from inheritance tax provided the transferor survives the transfer by seven years. Inheritance tax taper relief will apply if the transferor survives the gift by three years but not by the full seven. Thus, for example, a surviving spouse inheriting the deceased spouse's estate (free of inheritance tax) may wish to make lifetime gifts by way of potentially exempt transfers rather than become involved in varying the terms of the will especially if her life expectancy is greater than seven years.

HMRC Inheritance Tax Manual, para 35091 states that a variation should not be accepted as being within IHTA 1984, s 142 until any investigation in accordance with their instructions on exploitation has been satisfactorily concluded. Whether this is a prelude to an attack on the making of a potentially exempt transfer by the donee of property under a deed of variation by the application of the associated operations provisions contained in IHTA 1984, s 268 or on the basis that the dispositions under the will have not been varied, remains to be seen, but clearly an arrangement under which it is contemplated by all the parties that the beneficiary under a variation (eg a surviving spouse or civil partner) will return particular property by way of a potentially exempt transfer to the original legatee or beneficiary under a will (eg a child of the deceased) is vulnerable to an attack on these lines (HMRC Inheritance Tax Manual, para 35093). If the subject matters of the variation and the subsequent gift are different assets, then the transaction will be strengthened but may still be susceptible. Alternatively, the property could be settled on an interest in possession trust for the benefit of the surviving spouse, with their adult children having an interest in the remainder. The interest to the spouse would be an immediate post-death interest trust ('IPDI'). An IPDI will be subject to the old rules that used to apply to interest in possession trusts.

There will be no exit charge on property passing to a life tenant and there will be aggregation of the trust property with the beneficiary's free estate on death. Should the surviving spouse ultimately decide that she no longer requires the income, she could surrender her interest under the trust, thereby accelerating the interests of the children. The termination of her IPDI will be a potentially exempt transfer if the trust property is absolutely vested in her children. It is difficult, therefore, to envisage how the Revenue might seek to challenge this.

If the trust deed provided that the children would hold the property on trust for themselves then the tax implications would be quite different. The termination of the spouse's interest will not be a potentially exempt transfer because the children do not immediately take an absolute interest and the interest has not been terminated in favour of a trust for bereaved minors. Although the settlement is established by the will of the deceased parent and the age qualification is met there will still be a chargeable transfer.

The outlook for variations

[17.12] Over the years rumours have circulated about the abolition of variations and disclaimers but have not materialised. There is always the possibility that it will happen and so, whilst the opportunity remains, they are a useful tool which individuals should take advantage of.

Capital gains tax on variations

[17.13] TCGA 1992, s 62(1) provides that the assets of a deceased person's estate shall be deemed to be acquired on his death by his personal representatives for a consideration equal to their market value at the date of death but shall not be deemed to be disposed of by him on his death. Therefore, no capital gains tax is payable on the death.

The provisions of TCGA 1992, s 62(6)–(9) dealing with variations and disclaimers, correspond to those applicable to inheritance tax. Thus, TCGA 1992, s 62(6) provides that:

> where within the period of two years after a person's death any of the dispositions (whether effected by will, under the law relating to intestacy or otherwise) of the property of which he was competent to dispose are varied, or the benefit conferred by any of those dispositions is disclaimed, by an instrument in writing made by the persons or any of the persons who benefit or would benefit under the dispositions —
>
> (a) the variation or disclaimer shall not constitute a disposal for the purposes of this Act, and
>
> (b) this section shall apply as if the variation had been effected by the deceased or, as the case may be, the disclaimed benefit had never been conferred.

The above provisions apply only to property of which the deceased person was 'competent to dispose' as defined by TCGA 1992, s 62(10). Such property includes an interest under a joint tenancy but not property subject to a general power of appointment.

Section 62(6) will apply provided that the instrument contains a statement by the persons making the instrument that they intend that s 62(6) will apply to the variation. There is no longer a specified time period by which the instrument has to be submitted to the Revenue. This is because 'the Government . . . are content that the consequences of a variation should be considered, if necessary, by the Revenue only if and when they become relevant to the capital gains tax liabilities of the beneficiaries'.

In most cases the inclusion of the relevant statement stating the intention of the parties for s 62(6) to apply will in any event be appropriate, regardless of whether the administration of the estate has been completed or not. Where, however, the value of the relevant asset has increased since the date of death and any gain would fall within the donor beneficiary's annual exemption or within the exemption for chattels, then the advantage of not including such a statement is that the donee will acquire the asset at a higher base cost. The same point would arise where the original beneficiary can obtain a tax-free uplift because of principal private residence relief. Where, on the other hand, the asset has fallen in value, not to include a statement for the operation of s 62 will create a capital loss for the donor beneficiary, but if the donee is a 'connected person' within TCGA 1992, s 286 (and he often will be), such a loss can only be set against a gain on another disposal to the same donee (TCGA 1992, s 18), so little will be gained from not including a statement.

Where a statement to the effect that it is intended that s 62 should apply is included, it provides that 'section 62(6) shall apply as if the variation had been effected by the deceased'. There are special rules which apply where property becomes settled property as a result of the variation (TCGA 1992, s 68C). In such a case, the person making the variation will be treated as the settlor for capital gains tax purposes.

Example

> Marjorie leaves quoted shares worth £300,000 to Marian absolutely. As Marian does not need the money she decides to vary the will so that a discretionary trust is set up for the benefit of her grandchildren, Jasmine, Luke and Cory. Provided that s 62(6) applies, Marian will be treated as the settlor of the trust for capital gains tax purposes and not Marjorie.

Where property was already settled under the will or intestacy and then becomes comprised in another settlement as a result of the variation, the deceased person is treated as being the settlor and not the person making the variation.

Income tax on variations

[17.14] The income tax legislation does not provide the reliefs which are available in the case of inheritance tax and capital gains tax following a variation of beneficial interests in a deceased's estate. Income arising between the date of death and the date of the variation is generally taxed as though it were that of the beneficiary entitled prior to the variation. Disclaimers, because of their legal nature (and because they are not a fiction of fiscal legislation as is the case with variations), are treated differently and relate back to the date of death for income tax purposes.

Subject to the express terms of the will, a general legacy will normally bear interest from one year after the date of death if it still remains unpaid. The interest is payable when the legacy is paid. Where such a legacy is varied the interest paid on the legacy should only be taxable in the hands of the new beneficiary under the variation, even though it covers a period prior to the variation. This is because the liability to income tax depends on actual receipt of the income and not receivability.

The main exceptions to the above rule are contingent legacies, which do not bear interest until the contingencies are fulfilled unless they are set aside for the benefit of the legatee, and certain legacies to minors, which bear interest from the date of death. In practice, these types of legacies are rarely subject to any variation.

Income from property which is the subject of a specific legacy is taxed in the hands of the legatee from the date of death. Where the property is redirected to another person by way of variation, the original legatee will only be taxable on the income arising up to the date of the variation.

ITTOIA 2005, ss 649 and 654 provide for the taxation of income paid to beneficiaries with limited interests in residue during the course of the administration of the estate. Sums paid over to the beneficiary during the course of administration are taxed as the income of the beneficiary for the year of assessment in which they are paid. Any amount that remains payable in respect of the limited interest on the completion of administration of the estate is deemed to have been paid to the beneficiary as income of the year of assessment in which the administration period ended.

Where there is an absolute interest in residue the provisions of ITTOIA 2005, s 652 apply. The beneficiary is taxed on amounts he receives in any tax year to the extent that they do not exceed the residuary income for that year plus any residuary income of previous years on which he has not already been subject to tax. At the end of the administration period the residuary income for the whole period is aggregated and, where this aggregate exceeds the total amount on which he has already been taxed, the excess is treated as income paid to him immediately before the end of the administration period.

There are specific provisions (ITTOIA 2005, ss 671–675) dealing with successive interests in residue such as might arise where a residuary gift is varied. The overall effect of these provisions is to ensure that each beneficiary is taxed on the amount to which he is entitled.

An instrument of variation will be a settlement within ITTOIA 2005, Pt 5 Ch 5 whereas a disclaimer will not. As a result, any variation by a parent in favour of a relevant child will fall within ITTOIA 2005, s 629 and any income paid to or for the benefit of any relevant children will be taxed in his hands. A relevant child is defined as either an unmarried minor or a minor not in a civil partnership (ITTOIA 2005, s 629). In addition, any variation which involves the legatee resettling property upon trusts under which he retains an interest may be caught by ITTOIA 2005, s 624 and, if so, the income of the trust will remain taxable in his hands.

Instruments of variation should expressly deal with the right to income accrued up to the date of the instrument as between the donor and the donee. It is usually appropriate to provide that the income should belong to the person who would bear the burden of paying income tax on it and this will usually be the donor.

The charge to income tax on pre-owned assets, imposed by the Finance Act 2004, will not apply to a disposition made by a person in relation to an interest in the estate of a deceased person if, by virtue of IHTA 1984, s 17, the disposition is not treated as a transfer of value by that person for inheritance tax purposes. This means that any disposition made by variation or disclaimer and any disposition falling within IHTA 1984, s 143 (dispositions made in accordance with a testator's wishes within 2 years of the testator's death) will not be caught by the pre-owned assets rules. An election by a surviving spouse under Administration of Estates Act 1925, s 47A and a renunciation of a claim to legitim within the period mentioned in IHTA 1984, s 147(6) are also outside the scope of the pre-owned assets rules.

Discretionary wills

[17.15] As discussed in detail at **16.20**, some testators choose to execute discretionary wills conferring on their executors an overriding power of appointment drafted in wide terms which is exercisable over their entire estate in favour of a specified class of beneficiaries (relying on IHTA 1984, s 144). The power of appointment must be exercised within 2 years of the testator's death. Such a will usually contains provisions which the testator wishes to take effect in default of an appointment. The relief under s 144 will only be available where, in the period between the death and the variation, no IPDI or disabled person's interest has subsisted in the property.

It is essential that distributions from a discretionary trust are not made within 3 months of the death because s 144 only operates when there would otherwise be a charge to inheritance tax (IHTA 1984, s 144(1)). There is no inheritance tax charge on property leaving a discretionary trust within 3 months of its creation (IHTA 1984, s 68(2)) (see *Frankland v CIR* [1997] STC 1450 (CA)). FA 2006, Sch 20 provides that both pre and post 22 March 2006 appointments of IPDIs, TBMs and age 18–25 trusts may be made without a charge to inheritance tax and backdated to death.

Example

Malcolm died in January 2010 and on his death his will created a flexible trust. In June 2010 the trustees appointed property to a trust for a bereaved minor. No charge was imposed when property was transferred to the trust under IHTA 1984, s 71A. However, the appointment may be read back into the will.

A discretionary will offers considerable opportunities for estate planning, more so than relying on a variation which can usually only be made by adult beneficiaries acting unanimously. After the testator's death the executors and the family will have determined the assets in his estate and can then consider to what extent assets should be divided between the surviving spouse and subsequent generations. In addition they can consider whether there is scope to skip a generation. It should be remembered that unlike a variation, a discretionary will can also avoid the income tax disadvantages under ITTOIA 2005, s 629 of a parental settlement.

There is no provision in the capital gains tax legislation corresponding to IHTA 1984, s 144. TCGA 1992, s 62(6) has no application to an exercise of the overriding power of appointment, because the variation will not be made 'by the persons or any of the persons who benefit or would benefit under the disposition [made by the will]'. Consequently, if the power is exercised to make outright distributions of property to any beneficiary, a charge to capital gains tax may arise. There will usually only be a chargeable gain if the relevant assets have increased in value since the date of death because of the base cost uplift on the testator's death. Where a chargeable gain arises on business assets, it may be possible to make an election under TCGA 1992, s 165 to hold over the gain. Where the power is exercised before the administration of the estate is complete, the Revenue takes the view that the beneficiary acquires the asset as a legatee under the will and there is no disposal by the personal representatives and therefore no capital gain can arise.

This and other aspects of discretionary wills are considered in more detail in **Chapter 16 Planning for Death**.

Precatory trusts

[17.16] So-called precatory trusts are not in fact trusts at all. They are outright gifts coupled with an expression of preference by the donor as to how he would like the donee to exercise his ownership which is not enforceable against the donee. They are commonly used to deal with the distribution of chattels within a class of beneficiaries. For example, a testator may give a collection of paintings to one of his sons with the wish that he distribute the individual paintings between all the children of the testator in a fair and agreed manner. However, as a matter of law, the named beneficiary is the owner of the bequest. This might have caused inheritance tax problems if the named beneficiary then distributed the property comprised in the bequest to the intended recipients in accordance with the testator's wishes as this would *prima facie* be a transfer of value by him. However, IHTA 1984, s 143 provides that, if the legatee transfers any of the property bequeathed to him in accordance with the testator's wishes within the period of 2 years of the testator's death, IHTA 1984, s 143 will apply as if the property transferred had been bequeathed to the transferee by the testator. It is probable that this relief will not apply to real property as the reference in s 143 is to property 'bequeathed' and not 'devised' and a bequest is a disposition by will of personal and not real property.

In *Harding (Loveday's Executors) v CIR* [1997] STC (SCD) 321 the Special Commissioners held that s 143 did not apply to an appointment in exercise of a fiduciary power under a discretionary will trust, that is, one where there was no interest in possession between the deceased's death and the appointment. It is arguable whether s 143 applies to a distribution in exercise of a fiduciary power where there has been an interest in possession between the deceased's death and the exercise of the power, because one of the grounds for the decision in *Harding* was that, because an event within s 143 is expressly declared not to be a transfer of value (IHTA 1984, s 17), s 143 only applies to events which would be transfers of value apart from that provision. An appointment out of a discretionary trust is never a transfer of value, whereas the termination of an interest in possession to which a person became beneficially entitled to before 22 March 2006 is deemed to be a transfer of value (IHTA 1984, s 52(1)) Similarly, a disposition after 21 March 2006 of an interest in possession to which a person became beneficially entitled on or after 22 March 2006 and which is an IPDI, DPI, TSI or a section 5(1B) interest in possession is treated as a transfer of value.

There was no debate in *Harding* as to whether s 143 was confined to gifts of personalty, although land does seem to have been comprised in the residuary estate which was appointed, and it may therefore be that the argument that s 143 only applies to personalty was not a point taken by the Revenue.

Therefore, where it is intended that property disposed of by will should be distributed by the executors in accordance with the testator's wishes, at least where the property subject to such a gift will be valuable, it will be safer to provide that there is no interest in possession pending the executors' decision on how to distribute the property, so that s 144 can apply.

No special capital gains tax reliefs apply to precatory trusts, although the property concerned will often fall within the exemption for chattels valued at £6,000 or less (TCGA 1992, s 262).

Intestacy — redemption of surviving spouse's life interest

[17.17] On intestacy where the deceased leaves a surviving spouse and issue, the surviving spouse is entitled to the deceased's personal chattels, a statutory legacy of £250,000 (together with interest while unpaid) and a life interest in half the residue of the estate (Administration of Estates Act 1925, s 46(1).

The surviving spouse or civil partner under the Administration of Estates Act 1925, s 47A can elect to capitalise their life interest and to receive, instead of the income, part of the capital determined according to tables specified in the Intestate Succession (Interest and Capitalisation) (Amendment) Order 2008 (SI 2008/3162). If the surviving spouse or civil partner does so elect, IHTA 1984, ss 17(c) and 145 provide that the election is not a transfer of value and inheritance tax is charged as though the surviving spouse or civil partner had not been entitled to the life interest but had been entitled to the capital sum.

It should be noted that such an election, despite the advantage of giving the surviving spouse or civil partner capital, will reduce the property qualifying for the spouse exemption on the death and may thus increase the tax charge on the death. This is because, if the surviving spouse or civil partner had taken a life interest, the spouse exemption for inheritance tax purposes would have applied to the entire property in which the life interest subsisted.

Changes in value after death

[17.18] IHTA 1984, ss 178–198 provide relief for investments or land forming part of a deceased person's estate which are sold shortly after the date of death and have fallen in value. Although this section concentrates on personal representatives, it should always be borne in mind that these provisions will also apply to the trustees of a settlement following the death of a beneficiary entitled to a privileged interest.

Qualifying investments

Where an estate includes qualifying investments, such as quoted shares and securities and units in authorised unit trusts, which are sold within 12 months of the death for a sum less than the value at the date of death by the personal representatives or by the beneficiary if he is liable for the tax, they can apply to have the gross sale proceeds substituted for the value at the date of death for the purposes of inheritance tax. The lower value will be substituted for the probate value and the inheritance tax payable on the death will be recalculated accordingly. This relief also applies to situations where qualifying investments:

(a) are cancelled, without being replaced, within 12 months after the date of death. These must be held immediately before cancellation by the personal representatives or by the beneficiary if he is liable for the tax; or

(b) have their quotation on a recognised stock exchange suspended at the end of the 12-month period following the death and their value was at that time lower than at death. The investments must be held at the end of the 12-month period by either the personal representatives or by the beneficiary if he is liable for the tax.

These provisions deem qualifying investments within (*a*) above to have been sold for a nominal consideration of one pound and those within (*b*) to have been sold at their value at the end of the 12-month period following death. Guidance can be found on HMRC's website for the treatment of both Northern Rock and Bradford and Bingley shares.

It is important to note that where a claim is made all the investments sold within 12 months of the death have to be valued. The claim cannot be restricted to the investments which have fallen in value. Where some qualifying investments have risen in value since the date of death, but others have fallen, the personal representative should consider appropriating those that have risen in value to the relevant beneficiaries prior to selling the investments. This will enable a claim to be made only in relation to those investments which have fallen in value.

Land

A similar relief applies to land forming part of the deceased's estate which is sold within 3 years (or 4 years in certain circumstances, see below) after the date of death. The relief for land differs from that of qualifying investments in that in respect of sales within 3 years of death, a claim may be made even where the land has increased in value. In some circumstances this can be advantageous where the capital gains tax saving from making the election is greater than the increase in inheritance tax that results (for example, where the land is eligible for 50% business property relief reducing the effective inheritance tax rate to 20%). The claim must be made by the appropriate person, usually the personal representatives, or by the beneficiary if he is liable for the tax and, if there is more than one sale, the sale values must be substituted for all the sales of land and cannot be confined to one sale only.

In the case of *Stonor (Dickinson's Executors) v CIR* [2001] STC (SCD) 199 (SpC 288) the residuary estate was left to charities and the executors made a claim under IHTA 1984, s 191 so the higher property values on death could be used as base values for capital gains tax purposes. The legislation defines the 'appropriate person' as being the person liable for inheritance tax. The gifts to the charities were exempt transfers and no tax was chargeable on them. There was only a liability for tax which was actually payable. If there was no tax payable, there was no person liable to pay the tax and the executors claim was dismissed.

The relief for land will not apply if the sale price differs from the value at the date of death by less than £1,000 or 5% of the value on death, whichever is the lower. If the Revenue is of the opinion that the sale was for an under-value, it can substitute the best consideration that could reasonably have been obtained for it at the date of sale.

In certain circumstances, the relief is extended in relation to sales within 4 years of death. However, claims made in respect of sales in the fourth year following death are only valid where the sale value is less than the value on death, unlike claims made in the 3-year period. Therefore, the extension to the relief cannot be used to obtain an advantageous capital gains tax position as discussed below.

Date of sale

For the purpose of each relief, the date of sale is the date of the contract for sale provided that the contract proceeds to completion, see *Jones (Balls' Administrators) v CIR* [1997] STC 358 (Ch D). There are special rules in relation to sales pursuant to the exercise of options and under compulsory purchase powers. Where the sale or purchase results from the exercise of an option, if the option is exercised not more than 6 months after the grant of the option, the material date is the date of grant (IHTA 1984, s 198(2)). In the event that the sale follows a notice to treat under compulsory acquisition powers, the date of sale is generally the date on which compensation is agreed or otherwise determined or the date when the authority enters the land (if earlier) (IHTA 1984, s 198(3)). Where the sale is an acquisition under a general vesting declaration or a vesting order, the date of sale is then as stated in IHTA 1984, s 198(4).

It should be noted that the relief available for falls in value of qualifying investments and the relief for sales of land are entirely separate and are not aggregated for the purpose of the adjustment. Thus, a large gain on a sale of land will not reduce a loss on a sale of qualifying investments.

Anti-avoidance

The object of the provisions is to grant relief where assets have been sold to meet tax and other liabilities. For this reason there are anti-avoidance provisions which deny relief where investments or land are purchased within 2 or 4 months, respectively, of the last of the sales. Sales of land made in the fourth year after death are ignored for this purpose. However, a sale by the personal representatives followed by a cash distribution to the relevant beneficiary will enable that beneficiary to repurchase the investments sold without falling foul of these provisions.

If it is anticipated that qualifying investments or land which the personal representatives intend to sell in the course of administration, will have changed in value within the relevant period from the date of death, then it is essential that the sale of such assets is correctly timed to ensure that they receive the benefit of the relief provided for in these sections.

Capital gains tax

Under TCGA 1992, s 274, the value of an asset as determined for inheritance tax purposes in charging a deceased person's estate is deemed to be the market value on death for capital gains tax purposes. Thus, where the value of land is amended under the above provisions, it is the amended value that applies for capital gains tax purposes. This is why an advantageous capital gains tax position can be obtained on sales within 3 years of death at an increased value. If, however, the assets will not bear inheritance tax (because, for example, the estate is less than the nil rate band) it is understood that the Revenue's view is that no election can be made (this used to be stated in Capital Gains Tax Manual at CG 32461 and 32462, however, these paragraphs have now been deleted). (*Stonor (Dickinson's Executors) v CIR* [2001] STC (SCD) 199 (SpC 288)).

As regards qualifying investments, IHTA 1984, s 187 contains provisions for ascertaining the values for capital gains tax purposes of specific investments sold after death, which will usually be their respective sale values.

Where assets are sold after the death at a value lower than probate value and a claim for the relief is made, the result will be to reduce a capital loss for capital gains tax purposes. (There will still be a capital loss attributable to the difference (if any) between the gross sale proceeds and the net sale proceeds.)

Payment by instalments

[17.19] Tax chargeable on certain property passing on death may, while the property remains unsold, be paid in ten equal annual instalments (IHTA 1984, ss 227–229). The relief applies to:

(a) land wherever situated;
(b) unfelled timber (where exempt on death but later disposed of);
(c) a business or an interest in a business;
(d) controlling shareholdings; and
(e) unquoted shareholdings where either:
  (i) the Board are satisfied that the tax attributable to their value cannot be paid in one sum without undue hardship; or
  (ii) the tax payable on the shares represents not less than 20% of the tax payable by that person on the estate; or
  (iii) the value of the shares is over £20,000 and they form not less than 10% of the capital of the company.

The first instalment of tax will fall due for payment 6 months from the end of the month in which the death occurs.

Interest on unpaid tax

[17.20] Interest accrues on unpaid tax from six months from the end of the month in which the death occurs. To determine the current rate of interest reference should be made to HMRC's website. However, tax payable by instalments, other than where attributable to certain securities or to land (which is neither a business asset nor attracts agricultural property relief), is not chargeable to interest provided each instalment is paid on the due date (IHTA 1984, s 234). Therefore, if paid on time, tax on each instalment is interest-free.

Repayments of overpaid tax carry with them the benefit of interest supplement (IHTA 1984, s 235(1)). Interest paid on unpaid tax is not deductible from the income of the estate for income tax purposes so that the beneficiaries receive no income tax relief in respect of it. However, the interest supplement is not taxable in the hands of the personal representatives or the beneficiaries (IHTA 1984, s 235(2)).

Capital gains tax exemption and rates of tax

[17.21] Personal representatives have the same annual capital gains tax exemption as an individual (£10,100 for 2010/11) for the tax year in which the death occurs and for the following two tax years (TCGA 1992, s 3(7)). When deciding whether to sell an investment and distribute the proceeds to a beneficiary or whether to distribute the investment in specie allowing the beneficiary to use his own annual exemption on the sale the annual exemption should be considered.

Where the beneficiary is neither resident nor ordinarily resident in the UK, consideration should be given to distributing assets in specie rather than selling and distributing the proceeds as the beneficiary will not be chargeable to UK capital gains tax. Advice on the beneficiary's liability to tax in the jurisdiction where he is resident must be taken, however, to ensure that his overall position is not worsened.

Death benefits under insurance policies and pension schemes

[17.22] Death benefits under death-in-service benefit schemes and pension schemes often provide for the trustees of the scheme with a discretion as to the person to whom the payment is to be made. If the deceased has, by letter of wishes, nominated someone to receive the moneys then the trustees will normally follow those instructions. If no such nomination has been made then the trustees will usually either make payment to the next-of-kin or to the deceased's personal representatives, having first consulted the family. The opportunity should be taken to arrange for the payments to be made to specific members of the deceased's family with a view to satisfying immediate financial needs and to minimising the inheritance tax burden on subsequent deaths. For a more detailed discussion see **CHAPTER 7 INSURANCE** and **CHAPTER 8 PENSIONS**.

Chapter 18

UK Domiciliaries Investing Abroad

Introduction

[18.1] Increasing numbers of individuals cross national barriers in business, in the employment of multi-national companies or in pursuit of a better life and so often acquire assets situated outside the UK. Improved worldwide communications and the varying fortunes of national economies and governments encourage individuals, even if firmly domiciled and resident in the UK, to spread assets and risks by investing internationally.

The network of double taxation treaties has developed largely to encourage the international operations of business but also facilitates multi-national investment by individuals. The private international laws of national legal systems have also grown up in recognition of the increasing involvement of individuals in various legal jurisdictions. The development of the law of the European Union is increasingly affecting the direct taxation of member countries.

Foreign investments may be made and retained by an individual in his own name. However, direct ownership of those foreign assets can present disadvantages such as the obligation to comply with local administrative procedures and succession laws on death and the payment of gift or death duties imposed by the country in which the assets are situated. In these circumstances consideration may be given to other means of ownership of foreign assets.

By investing overseas an individual may also secure some measure of diversification against the threat of over-regulation of the United Kingdom economy.

The planning steps which may be taken by an individual who is moving to or from the UK and by a foreign domiciled and resident individual in relation to the ownership of assets in the UK are examined in **CHAPTER 19 THE INTERNATIONALLY MOBILE** and **CHAPTER 20 THE OVERSEAS CLIENT**. This chapter primarily considers the advantages and disadvantages of direct ownership of foreign assets by an individual domiciled and resident in the UK and the indirect ownership of those same assets through a nominee, a company or a trust.

Care must be taken to ensure that a charge does not arise under the pre-owned assets rules. For UK resident and domiciled individuals, the provisions will apply to their world-wide assets. Any tax or succession planning with overseas assets must be undertaken with care in order to avoid creating a continuing tax liability. These provisions are discussed in greater detail in **CHAPTER 2 LIFETIME PLANNING.**

It should be noted that these provisions do not allow deduction for overseas tax paid, although they do allow deductions for tax paid under certain charging provisions of ITA 2007 and TCGA 1992.

Direct ownership

[18.2] An individual may hold assets in a foreign country in his own name. As a UK resident and domiciled individual he will be liable to income tax on income arising from those assets, capital gains tax on gains realised on the disposal of those assets and potentially, inheritance tax on any gift (whether made during his lifetime or on his death) of those assets; in addition, he may also be liable to income tax on those assets in respect of a charge arising under the pre-owned assets rules. Similar taxes may also be imposed in the country in which the assets are located. The existence of a double taxation treaty may alleviate the position in one of two ways. Either the profit or gift which the tax system of the country in which the asset is situated and the UK tax system both seek to tax may be exempted from tax in one of those jurisdictions (or the liability may be reduced); or credit may be given in one country for tax suffered in the other. Even where no double tax treaty exists between the UK and the country in which the asset is situated relief may be given unilaterally by the UK. Relief may be given for tax suffered in the foreign jurisdiction against income tax or capital gains tax suffered on the same profits or for gift or death duties suffered in a foreign jurisdiction against inheritance tax chargeable in respect of the same assets.

Ownership of assets in a foreign jurisdiction will not only cause the UK individual to fall within that foreign country's tax net on his death but local administration procedures will apply. Title to the assets will have to be established by his personal representatives or beneficiaries. In some circumstances a UK grant of representation may be re-sealed by local authorities (as in, for example, most Commonwealth countries). In other jurisdictions (principally those governed by a civil code such as France and Spain) the concept of a personal representative is alien and it may be necessary to arrange for title to pass directly to the beneficiaries of the property.

In addition to the conflicting formalities in foreign jurisdictions relating to the transfer of property to an individual's heirs on his death, succession to that property may also be governed by the law of the foreign country.

Under the English doctrine of the conflict of laws, succession to immovable property (ie land) is governed by the law of the country in which that land is situated. Where a foreign country has particular rules relating to the devolution of a fixed portion of an individual's estate on death to his surviving spouse and/or children, any attempt to displace these rules by provision in his will, will be unsuccessful.

Even though succession to movable property (such as shares) situated abroad is usually governed (under the conflict rules of most foreign countries) by the law of the individual's country of domicile (or nationality) taxation difficulties may arise if the property is given by his will to his personal representatives to be held for others. These difficulties stem from the fact that many civil law jurisdictions do not recognise the role and duties of a personal representative in relation to the deceased's assets and those beneficiaries for whose benefit he holds and administers the deceased's property. Therefore, if a UK domiciled individual were to leave all his movable assets to his executors to be held by them for his widow, some foreign jurisdictions would attempt to impose death duties on his movable property situated there as though the deceased's gift had been an outright gift to the executors.

In many countries, death duties are imposed at rates determined according to the proximity of the relationship between the deceased and those who take his property on his death, the lowest rates usually being charged on gifts to widows, higher rates on gifts to children and grandchildren and the most punitive rates on gifts to unrelated individuals. This is particularly affected by the variations between states in the recognition of unions between individuals of the same sex. Some states do not give any legal recognition to such unions whilst, at the extreme, some allow individuals of the same sex to marry. Some, like the UK with its law of civil partnerships, have provided for a special legal status, separate from marriage, which yet receives many of the same privileges and is subject to similar duties.

Unless the foreign jurisdiction will accept that the 'gift' to the UK individual's executors is not a beneficial gift but, rather, an administrative measure, death duties may be imposed at the highest rates unless the deceased's executors are his close relations. The provisions of an applicable double tax treaty may alter this position but these problems require investigation at the outset. An individual owning assets abroad (in particular, land) should consider if there is any significant value in making a will (in the local language), in accordance with the applicable laws of each of those countries where his assets are situated, to ensure that he achieves the transfer of those assets to his chosen heirs at the lowest possible cost.

When dealing with more than one jurisdiction a timing issue may arise where there is a delay in concluding the tax liabilities in one country. In *Whittaker v CIR* [2001] STC (SCD) 61 (SpC 272) the Commissioners held that an executor could not validly appeal against an inheritance tax determination in respect of foreign property on the grounds that the Italian tax liabilities had not yet been concluded.

Where an individual wishes to invest in stocks and shares of companies in various foreign jurisdictions and intends that those investments will be bought and sold over a period of time, it is likely to be impractical, expensive and burdensome administratively for him to investigate the taxation and succession laws of each country and to make a will under the laws of those countries. In these circumstances, the individual may wish to simplify his affairs by making his investment through another medium situated in the UK, such as a unit trust or investment trust or a unit-linked life policy, which in turn invests in foreign companies. This will avoid any problems with foreign succession laws or taxes on his death.

Similarly, the enjoyment of foreign land may be achieved by participation in a 'time share' arrangement rather than by owning foreign property direct. The procedural and succession rules applying to the transfer of the individual's rights of occupation to his heirs will depend upon the nature of the time share structure and the terms of the individual's rights. However, if the occupation rights are conferred by a trustee holding land for the benefit of members of a time share club and permitting those members occupation of the property on specified terms the individual's asset may be his chose in action against the trustee (ie his entitlement to enforce his rights against the trustee). If this is so, the chose in action is likely to be situate in the jurisdiction of residence of the trustee to which the individual would have to go to enforce his rights. Frequently, the trustee of a time share arrangement will be resident in a jurisdiction other than that in which the property is held (and often in a tax haven such as Jersey or the Isle of Man) where procedural and succession rules on the death of the individual may be more akin to those of the UK than those of the countries in which the land is situate.

Ownership by a nominee and other possibilities

[18.3] It may be possible for the individual to avoid local succession procedures and laws by holding assets in the joint names of himself and another if the local law permits beneficial ownership to pass automatically to the survivor of joint owners. A problem may still arise, however, on the death of the surviving co-owner.

Alternatively, assets may be held in the names of corporate nominees which can exist indefinitely. An individual investing abroad could set up his own nominee company in the UK specifically for this purpose. On the death of the beneficial owner of the assets, his personal representatives need only direct the nominee to hold to the order of the beneficiary to whom the asset devolves under the will. There is no requirement for the legal ownership of the foreign assets to change.

This will avoid any local administrative procedures on death but may also, if the local law does not recognise the concept of a trust (which is what the nominee relationship is), avoid both local succession laws and local death duties. That would be the case if the local law treats the nominee as the absolute owner of the assets and does not recognise any changes in the underlying beneficial ownership.

If the local laws do not recognise beneficial ownership then it may be necessary to ensure that any foreign assets are purchased in the name of the nominee since to transfer foreign assets into the name of the nominee may result in a charge to local gift taxes. A liability to gift tax might also arise on a transfer of the assets by the nominee company to any new beneficial owner or owners and if the rates of tax depend upon the proximity of relationship between the transferor and the transferee, the highest rates are likely to apply.

Another potential problem is that if the nominee were to transfer assets into the names of the deceased's heirs shortly after the death it might constitute itself an 'executor de son tort' if the local law recognised such a concept, with a resulting exposure to death duties on the assets in the jurisdiction. The case of *CIR v Stype Investments (Jersey) Ltd* [1982] 3 All ER 419, [1982] 3 WLR 228 is a reverse illustration of this potential risk, where a foreign nominee owned UK situs assets.

In relation to the purchase of foreign stocks and shares many investment businesses have in-house nominee companies, in the name of which the investments are registered or which, in the case of bearer securities, hold the bearer certificate on behalf of the investors thereby saving the expense of registering each purchaser with the security or providing him with a separate bearer certificate.

In some countries (Switzerland, for example) it may be possible to give another person a power of attorney, valid under local law, to deal with the individual's assets in the event of his death. In such a situation, normally the attorney will acquire no beneficial interest in the assets but only the right to administer them. This may assist in relation to procedural matters but will not prevent the application of local succession laws or the imposition of local death duties.

Ownership by a company

[18.4] Ownership of foreign investments by a company, the shares of which are owned by the individual investor, may avoid local succession procedures and laws and duties on the death of the individual if that company is incorporated and resident outside the jurisdictions in which its investments are made. However, it will be necessary to arrange the transfer of the shares of the company itself to the heirs of the deceased who will inherit the company's shares. The ownership of the underlying investments will remain unchanged.

The cost-effectiveness of this arrangement as a means of holding foreign assets will depend upon the value of the investments to be acquired (in view of the costs of setting up and administering the company), the tax liability of that company in its country of residence and in the countries in which its investments are made and the UK tax liability of the shareholder. Overall, some simplification of the administration of the deceased's estate may be achieved.

An individual resident and domiciled in the UK would not, by holding his assets through a foreign resident company, save any UK income, capital gains or inheritance tax. If he held foreign assets directly he would be charged to income tax on his foreign income. Dividends received from a foreign resident company interposed between the individual and his investments would be charged to income tax as savings and investment income. Under ITA 2007, ss 736–742, however, where the income from the foreign assets is rolled-up in the offshore company and not distributed by way of dividend, such undistributed income would be deemed to be the individual investor's for all purposes (ITA 2007, ss 720 and 727) unless it was successfully claimed that the transfer of assets abroad was not to avoid any liability to UK tax. This charge is on a current year basis. The individual would, however, receive the benefit of any rebates or reliefs under any double taxation treaties between the UK and the country in which any investment is situated (ITA 2007, s 746(2)).

There was a concern for some time, reinforced by the decision in *R v Allen; R v Dimsey* [2002] 1 AC 509, [2001] 4 All ER 768, that a benefit in kind charge under ITEPA 2003, Ch 5 may be imposed on an individual who has a controlling interest in a non-resident company which holds, for example, a Spanish holiday home which the individual uses for his personal use (see **19.33**).

However, ITEPA 2003, ss 100A and 100B, specifically exempts certain living accommodation outside the United Kingdom from the benefit-in-kind charge which might otherwise apply. The living accommodation must have been provided by a company for a director or other officer of the company ('D') or a member of his family or household. It must have been provided by a company which is wholly owned by D solely or by D and other individuals. The exemption is available both in relation to direct holdings of interests in such accommodation and to holdings through wholly owned subsidiaries. In relation to direct holdings, the interest must be the company's main or only asset and the only activities undertaken by the company must be ones that are incidental to the ownership of the interest. In relation to holdings in a subsidiary, the subsidiary must be wholly owned by the company and must meet the conditions set out in relation to direct holdings. Various exceptions apply. Most importantly, there is an exception if the living accommodation is provided in pursuance of an arrangement the main purpose, or one of the main purposes, of which is the avoidance of income tax, corporation tax or national insurance contributions. There are also complex provisions relating to transactions with connected companies.

Whilst domiciled and resident in the UK, an individual will suffer capital gains tax on all gains realised on his worldwide assets. Even if assets are held beneficially by a non-resident company, gains realised by that company may be deemed to be his by virtue of TCGA 1992, s 13. Where the provision applies, its effect can be unduly harsh. Losses made by a non-resident company cannot be used to reduce its gain before apportionment, nor can the losses as such be apportioned except to the extent that a shareholder has had a gain apportioned to him in that tax year and the apportioned loss would reduce the gain. Unlike ITA 2007, ss 720, 727 and 731, there is no 'commercial' defence available to mitigate the charge to tax.

Any transfer *inter vivos* or on death of foreign assets or the shares of a foreign company through which foreign assets are held will be chargeable to inheritance tax provided the individual is domiciled in the UK (IHTA 1984, s 6).

In any situation where a company holds funds, one has to consider the issue of how to extract moneys in the most tax efficient manner. One possibility is that the company could be initially funded by way of a cash loan. This will enable capital to be subsequently extracted from the company tax-free by way of repayment of the loan. Alternatively, a special type of redeemable share capital could be used although that can cause difficulties with the rules concerning transactions in securities (ITA 2007, ss 682–685). Alternatively any income received by the company may be extracted by payment of a dividend. In practice, this may not give rise to an additional income tax charge for the investor if he has already been taxed on the income under ITA 2007, ss 720 and 727 (ITA 2007, s 743(4)). However, strictly speaking, the payment of the dividend represents an additional source of income. In such circumstances, ITA 2007, s 743 (no duplication of charge) may not help as like is not being compared to like. In practice, the Revenue does not appear to take the point, albeit that the risk of it so doing would increase where an offshore investment company retains income for a substantial period of time before paying a dividend.

Because of the UK tax consequences both for the company and for the individual, the holding of foreign investments through a UK resident company is unlikely to be attractive. In practice, the company will be incorporated and resident in an offshore tax haven.

Offshore settlements

[18.5] When considering the purchase of foreign investments, one might hold one's foreign investments through an offshore settlement. By transferring assets to trustees all of whom are resident outside the UK the settlor removes them from his control. The terms of the settlement should be such that neither he nor any other beneficiary can require the trustees to return assets to them. Nor should the settlor or any UK resident person have the power to appoint or remove the trustees or to direct how the trust fund should be invested.

Although no individual resident in the UK should be able, under the terms of the settlement, to enforce the distribution of assets from the settlement, whether to himself or others, it may be possible for the cautious settlor to retain some say in the running of the settlement if its terms provide that any distribution of assets from the settlement can only be made by the trustees with his consent. To reverse the balance and repose a power of appointment in the settlor but provide that it is exerciseable only with the trustees' consent, is more dangerous.

Forms of settlement

[18.6] Previously, the most common form of settlement has been one giving a life interest to the settlor (and his spouse or civil partner) under which the trustees have power to pay capital to the settlor at their discretion. Such settlements secure the division of ownership between settlor and trustees whilst leaving the settlor almost in the same position as if he owned the assets directly. For inheritance tax purposes, it used to be the case that, provided the settlement conferred an interest in possession on the settlor, no inheritance tax charge would arise on the transfer of assets to the trustees since he would be treated as remaining the beneficial owner of all the settled property in which his interest subsists (IHTA 1984, s 49).

However, where a UK domiciled settlor creates any trust (unless it is a privileged interest trust — see **Chapter 4 Creating Settlements**), he will suffer an inheritance tax charge unless an exemption or relief applies. When a settlor and beneficiaries are UK resident and domiciled there are no particular taxation advantages in holding assets including foreign property in a non-resident settlement during the settlor's lifetime.

Tax situation of trustees

[18.7] Trustees will be regarded as non-resident for UK income tax purposes (ITA 2007, s 475) and capital gains tax purposes (TCGA 1992, s 69) where a trust is created by a settlor who is resident, ordinarily resident and domiciled in the UK provided all the trustees are resident outside the UK. It should be remembered that a non-resident trustee will be deemed to be resident when he acts as a trustee in the course of a business which he carries on in the UK through a branch, agency or permanent establishment.

Where the income of a settlement is payable to, or applicable for the benefit of, the settlor or his wife or civil partner, that income will be treated for income tax purposes as the settlor's, and therefore will be subject to UK income tax. The UK resident settlor will, because of his interest in the settlement, be subject to capital gains tax on the gains realised by the trustees in the tax year they are realised (TCGA 1992, s 86, Sch 5).

For more detailed explanation of the taxation of non-resident settlements see **CHAPTER 6 OFFSHORE TRUSTS**.

Having said that, an individual may wish to create a non-resident trust because the holding of assets, situated in a number of foreign countries in one settlement, may centralise administration and may avoid the need to comply with local succession procedures, laws and taxes on the death of the settlor.

Considerations

[18.8] Before creating the settlement, the income and capital taxes position of the trustees in their country of residence should be considered, together with the applicability of double tax treaties between the country of residence of the trustees and those countries where their assets are situate. Treaties with those countries without a local law of trusts may not cover trusts and trustees.

It is usual to create a settlement in a tax haven which does not impose taxes on income or capital gains in the hands of the trustees or on a change of interests under the settlement or upon beneficiaries becoming absolutely entitled to the settled property. However, since there are also unlikely to be full double taxation treaties between those countries and the countries in which the trust assets are invested or those where the beneficiaries are resident, it may be difficult to secure relief for any foreign taxes paid.

If the intention behind creating a settlement is to ensure that the death of an individual does not give rise to charges to local death duties in the countries in which foreign assets are situated it may be advisable to ensure that the settlement is either discretionary or that, if the settlement is a life interest settlement, successive life interests are created so the property will continue to be held in the settlement for as long as possible. This is subject to such perpetuity restrictions upon the length of time for which assets may continue to be held in a settlement as may be imposed by the law governing the settlement. At the time when the settlement terminates and one or more individuals become absolutely entitled to the trust assets it will be necessary to comply with the formal requirements for transfer of the foreign assets laid down by the laws of the countries in which those assets are situated (unless the trustee continues to hold, as their nominee, the assets to which the individuals have become absolutely entitled or those individuals re-settle those assets).

Care should be taken where assets situated in a civil law country are to be held in a settlement. The ability of an individual to dispose of immovable property may be governed by the law of the country in which that property is situated. A transfer of that property to a settlement may contravene succession laws which reserve fixed portions of the individual's estate for his widow and children. Since succession to movable property will (in most cases) be governed by the law of the individual's domicile (ie that of the UK) such property may be transferred to a settlement. However, the transfer into the settlement may have extreme tax consequences in relation to gifts to personal representatives in those countries where the concept of a trust and the division of ownership of property between the legal owner and the equitable owners is not recognised or understood. The transfer of property to trustees may suffer gift duties at the highest rates in jurisdictions where such duties are charged at rates determined by the degree of relationship between donor and donee since the transferor and the trustee are likely to be unrelated. Similar consequences may arise when beneficiaries become absolutely entitled to the assets held in a settlement.

A number of civil law jurisdictions already recognise trusts established by foreigners to a varying degree, although it is fair to say that the vast majority still do not fully do so. Where civil law jurisdictions do not recognise a trust they will instead treat the trustee who is resident there as the absolute owner of the assets. If the trustee becomes bankrupt the trust assets may go to satisfy his creditors and if he breaches his trust few remedies will be available to the aggrieved beneficiaries. Even in those jurisdictions such as Switzerland, where trusts will, in certain circumstances, be recognised, it will be difficult to recover from a third party any trust property which has wrongly passed to him. Other jurisdictions still experience great difficulty in both recognising the concept, and taxing it in a satisfactory manner.

The Hague Convention on the recognition of trusts does not introduce the trust concept into the legal system of civil law states, but rather sets out the ground rules under which individual states will give legal recognition to trusts, in accordance with a system of common conflict of laws rules.

Even where a jurisdiction has incorporated the Hague Convention in its domestic law, it may have failed to make corresponding changes in its fiscal code. It is therefore advisable to take appropriate legal advice in the jurisdiction concerned to ensure that no legal or other difficulties will arise.

Chapter 19

The Internationally Mobile

Introduction

[19.1] This chapter deals with those who take up residence in the UK or cease to be resident in the UK either in the long or the short term. By far the greater part deals with the position of a person taking up residence in the UK.

The chapter does not address the immigration rules applied by the Home Office to individuals resident abroad wishing to come to the UK to live or to work or European Union law on the free movement of nationals of Member States. These aspects should be reviewed well in advance of the anticipated date of entry into the UK.

A brief summary of the concepts of domicile, residence and ordinary residence is given in this chapter. These concepts are taken from case law and so reference is made in this chapter to the relevant cases. The Revenue has published its practice in relation to these topics and their relevance for the purposes of UK taxation and so reference should be made to the Revenue explanatory pamphlet 'Residence, Domicile and the Remittance Basis' (HMRC 6). It should be remembered that this booklet contains the Revenue's view of the law and is not determinative of the law on these matters.

Domicile

[19.2] Domicile is of fundamental importance in estate planning. There are two types of domicile; domicile under the general English law and an artificial deemed domicile which applies specifically for inheritance tax purposes.

Actual domicile

[19.3] Under the law of England and Wales, every individual must at any time have a domicile in one specific country. There are three categories of domicile; those of origin, dependency and choice. Scotland also has a law of domicile which varies from the law of England and Wales in some aspects. The following is a description of the law in England and Wales.

Domicile of origin

An individual is born with a *domicile of origin*, which if he is legitimate, will be that of his father's at that time. Where an individual is actually born has little to do with his domicile. It is therefore important when a client is claiming to have a foreign domicile of origin to determine his parents situation both at the time of his birth and subsequently, bearing in mind that while under the age of 16 his domicile of origin will remain but if his father's domicile changes (while he is under that age) his domicile will follow that of his father's and will be a *domicile of dependence.*

Domicile of choice

Once an individual reaches the age of 16, he has the legal capacity to acquire an independent domicile in a different country — a *domicile of choice* (Domicile and Matrimonial Proceedings Act 1973, s 3). This is acquired both by actual physical presence in another country and by forming a definite intention (evidenced by all the circumstances surrounding the individual and his way of life) to make his home in that country permanently or indefinitely (*Udny v Udny* (1869) LR 1 SCD 441. In *Bell v Kennedy* [1868] LR 1 SCD 307 it was said that the question to be considered was whether the appellant had 'determined to make, and had made, [the new country] his home, with the intention of establishing himself and his family there, and ending his days in that country'. If he does not acquire a domicile of choice in this way, he will retain his domicile of dependence, and if he loses that without acquiring a domicile of choice, his domicile of origin will revive.

Change of domicile

An individual loses a domicile of choice (and a domicile of dependency) by leaving the country in question with the intention (supported by clear evidence) of ceasing to regard it as his permanent home. An individual may thereupon acquire a new domicile of choice, if the requirements mentioned below are met. If they are not, his domicile of origin will revive.

It is difficult to lose a domicile of origin. There must be clear and positive evidence that a change has been made. Going abroad for a period of years is unlikely to result in the acquisition of a domicile of choice. The intention to remain in the new country permanently or indefinitely has to be formed free of all external constraining factors. For example, in *F (Personal Representatives of F dec'd)* [2000] STC (SCD) 1 (SpC 219) above the deceased moved to the UK from Iran for various reasons including religious persecution. He had maintained a settled intention to return but was unwilling to do so immediately because an exit bar meant that if he had gone to Iran he might have been prevented from leaving again. It was held that he did not acquire a domicile of choice in a country of the United Kingdom. An individual may be taken to have acquired a new domicile of choice for a period even if he later changes his mind and returns to his previous country of domicile. In practice, however, the evidence of the necessary intention at the outset will have to be very strong to convince the Revenue that an individual has lost a domicile in a country of the United Kingdom and has acquired a domicile of choice in another country if he subsequently resumes residence in the UK. It has not been uncommon for Englishmen to spend many years in a foreign country (for example, in government service in India, or working in the Far East), with the intention of leaving that country eventually, either to retire to England or some other country. In those circumstances, the individual will not acquire a domicile of choice in the foreign country regardless of the length of the period he resides there. This approach was confirmed in *Civil Engineer v CIR* [2002] STC (SCD) 72 (SpC 299).

Where a person maintains more than one residence as was the case in *Gaines-Cooper v Revenue and Customs Comrs* [2008] STC 1665, he will have a domicile of choice in that country in which he has his chief residence.

In *Mark v Mark* [2005] UKHL 42 domicile was considered by the House of Lords in relation to divorce proceedings. Despite the leading text book stating that someone in the UK illegally could not acquire a domicile of choice here, Lady Hale, giving the leading judgment, held that domicile was a means of connecting an individual with a jurisdiction for certain purposes. Sometimes that connection would be to the individual's advantage and sometimes it would not. There was no reason why his residence in a country and his intentions should not determine his domicile in the normal way simply because that residence was illegal.

That a finding as to domicile requires a careful evaluation of all the facts was clearly demonstrated in *Cyganik v Agulian* [2005] EWHC 444. In that case the individual's unbroken 30-year residence in the UK was not conclusive of an acquisition of a domicile of choice.

In *Barlow Clowes International Ltd v Henwood* [2008] EWCA Civ 577, which was a non-tax case, the Court of Appeal considered the interaction of a domicile of origin with a domicile of choice.

The respondent Mr Henwood ('H') had a domicile of origin in England and Wales and later acquired a domicile of choice in the Isle of Man. In 1992, he left the Isle of Man and moved to Mauritius. He also spent significant periods in France. It was argued by H that his domicile of choice in the Isle of Man was replaced by a new domicile of choice in Mauritius. The Court of Appeal held that when H abandoned his domicile of choice in the Isle of Man he did not acquire a new domicile of choice. As a result H's domicile of origin revived and between then and 2005 H had not acquired a new domicile of choice. In the case Arden LJ held that when the court has to determine which of two jurisdictions represents an individual's chief residence, the court has to look at the quality of the residence in the two jurisdictions. It is not as simple as looking at which contains the individual's main home in terms of size or amenities or of the jurisdiction in which the individual spends most time. The key is to ascertain in which jurisdiction the individual intends to reside permanently.

The fact that an individual makes an application for naturalisation in another country does not of itself indicate a change of domicile (*Wahl v A-G* (1932) 147 LT 382 (HL) and *F (Personal Representatives of F dec'd) v CIR*.

Married women

It used to be the case that a woman on her marriage automatically took her husband's domicile as a domicile of dependence. Her domicile is now determined in the normal way (Domicile and Matrimonial Proceedings Act 1973, s 1). Where a woman already married on 1 January 1974 had acquired her husband's domicile as a domicile of dependence, that domicile is her domicile of choice until such time as she acquires a new domicile. A married woman can, therefore, have a different domicile to that of her husband. If an Englishwoman marries a man with a domicile of origin in New York and after the marriage the couple live in Europe for the time being (eg due to the husband's employment) she will not acquire a domicile of choice in New York. She will retain her English domicile. By way of further example, suppose a man with an English domicile of origin works for most of his life in Hong Kong. At the time of his retirement he marries a woman domiciled in California, and they decide to live in California for a while, but not necessarily permanently. His wife, having never lived in England and having no intention of doing so, remains domiciled in California, but the husband, at any rate initially, does not become domiciled in California. So they have different domiciles. The case of *CIR v Bullock* [1976] STC 409, [1976] 3 All ER 353 (CA) is authority for the proposition that a married couple (only one of whom already has an English domicile) may set up home in England on a permanent basis without the spouse with the foreign domicile necessarily thereby acquiring an English domicile of choice. If one spouse maintains links with his or her original country and demonstrates a clear intention (rather than 'a vague hope or aspiration') of returning there should he or she survive the other or in the event that the other were to agree to go and live in that original country, then that spouse will retain his or her domicile in that original country.

Deemed domicile

[19.4] For inheritance tax purposes a person who is not domiciled in the UK under the general law will be deemed to be domiciled here when a transfer of value is made if:

(a) he was domiciled in the UK under general English law within the period of three calendar years immediately preceding that time; or
(b) he was resident in the UK for income tax purposes in 17 of the 20 years of assessment ending with the year in which the relevant time falls (IHTA 1984, s 267).

In determining whether the individual is resident in any year for purposes of the rule, residence is determined as for income tax purposes (see **19.5** below).

Because of these rules, it is often the case that an individual is, under general principles, not domiciled in the UK but deemed to be domiciled in the UK for inheritance tax purposes. The deemed domicile rules may in certain situations be overridden (IHTA 1984, s 267(2)). If an individual is domiciled in a country which has a suitable double tax treaty with the UK, then assets held outside the UK will not be subject to UK inheritance tax provided they do not pass under a disposition governed by law of any part of Great Britain. Such countries include France, Italy, India and Pakistan.

Determining One's Domicile Status

[19.4A] Being able to plan one's future financial affairs may be dependant upon determining one's domicile status to a high degree of probability and yet, as we have seen, domicile is a complex concept which is determined by a detailed consideration of the factual background. One might have thought, therefore, that there would be a facility to obtain a ruling on one's domicile status from the Revenue. There has never been a formal statutory procedure but for many years, in practice, it was possible to obtain a ruling on which one could rely by submitting a DOM1 form to the Revenue. In recent years, the Revenue have only been willing to provide an opinion on a taxpayer's domicile status where the issue was relevant to determining a tax liability which had already arisen. The Revenue's current practice, set out in Revenue & Customs Brief 34/10, is that:

> ' . . . HMRC will consider opening an enquiry where domicile could be an issue, or making a determination of Inheritance Tax in such cases, only where there is a significant risk of loss of UK tax.
>
> The significance of the risk will be assessed by HMRC using a wide range of factors. The factors will depend very much on the individual case but will include, for example:
>
> - a review of the information available to HMRC about the individual on HMRC databases;
> - whether there is a significant amount of tax (all taxes and duties not just Inheritance Tax) at risk
>
> HMRC does not consider it appropriate to state an amount of tax that would be considered significant, as the amount of tax at stake is only one factor. It should be borne in mind that HMRC will take into account the potential costs involved in pursuing an enquiry, and also those of potential litigation should the enquiry not result in agreement between HMRC and the individual; clearly such costs can be substantial.
>
> Where HMRC does open an Inheritance Tax enquiry in any of these cases, it will keep the factors in view and may stop the enquiry at any stage if it considers the continuation of the enquiry is not cost effective. The outcome of such an enquiry may be that HMRC does not consider it appropriate to make a determination of the Inheritance Tax.
>
> Individuals should also bear in mind that enquiries into domicile involve a detailed inquiry into all of the relevant facts and HMRC is likely to require considerable personal information and extensive documentary evidence about the taxpayer and the taxpayer's close family.'

Residence

Statute

[19.5] There is no general statutory definition of 'residence' in tax legislation. The nearest that we get to a statutory definition are the provisions contained in ITA 2007, ss 829–835 which determine whether certain types of income are taxable in the UK. Because of the lack of a general definition, the meaning of residence has to be determined from the provisions of the Taxes Acts to the extent that they provide particular rules and from decisions of the courts. One then needs to take into account any relevant double tax treaty. Having done so, one needs to consider the Revenue's guidance which is now given in a booklet entitled HMRC6 which has superseded its previous explanatory booklet IR20. The guidance is both deliberately vague and, in parts, of doubtful accuracy. It is essential that an adviser identifies where the guidance differs from the law and ensures that their clients do not rely on inaccurate guidance in planning their affairs. The lack of a statutory residence test, the lacunae in the relevant case law and the inadequacy of the Revenue's published guidance creates great uncertainty in this area of Revenue Law.

Income tax

[19.6] ITA 2007, s 831 (with effect from 6 April 2008) provides that in determining an individual's income tax liability, an individual will be treated as non-resident where:

(a) he is in the UK for some temporary purpose only and with no intention of establishing his residence here; and
(b) he spends less than one hundred and eighty three days in the UK in any relevant tax year (the 'Temporary UK Purpose Rule').

The provisions in ITA 2007, ss 832–835 adopt this rule in relation to specific sources of income.

The statutory test does not cover the situation of a person who is in the UK for some purpose which is not temporary. In *Revenue and Customs Comrs v Grace* [2009] EWCA Civ 1082, [2009] STC 2707 Lewison J's observation in the High Court that the fact that the statutory test does not apply 'does not of itself assist HMRC to show that [an individual is] resident generally' was approved by Lloyd LJ in the Court of Appeal.

When determining whether the statutory test applies, any living accommodation available for the individual is ignored.

For the purposes of these limited statutory provisions concerning individuals who are in the UK for 'some temporary purpose' there is a special rule which determines when a day is spent in the UK (ITA 2007, s 831 and the equivalent provision in TCGA 1992, s 9(3)). An individual is treated as spending a day in the UK only if he is present in the UK at the end of the day. Presence in the UK in transit, however, will be disregarded providing the individual does not engage in activities that are to a substantial extent unrelated to his passage through the UK whilst in transit. HMRC has adopted this rule with effect from 6 April 2008 in applying its understanding of, and practice in relation to, the rules for determining residence. The meaning of temporary purpose has been considered by the courts and is discussed below.

Individuals who are resident and ordinarily resident in the UK are still treated as UK resident for the purposes of establishing any income tax liability if they leave for only occasional residence abroad (the 'Occasional Residence Rule') (ITA 2007, s 829). The meaning of occasional residence abroad was considered in *Reed v Clark* [1985] STC 323, 58 TC 528 (Ch D). That case illustrates that a person who:

(a) wishes to leave the UK for a period of one year;
(b) does not work full-time abroad

may become non-UK resident by spending a year out of the UK. Ideally, an individual should not spend any time in the UK in the relevant year.

The courts have created a rule by extrapolation from the statutory rule now found in ITA 2007, s 831 that a person who is in the UK for at least 183 days is resident for that year (the 183 Day Rule) (*Levene v IRC* [1928] AC 217, (1928) 13 TC 486, HL, *Lysaght v IRC* [1927] 2 KB 55, (1928) 13 TC 511, CA, *Wilkie v IRC* [1952] Ch 153, (1951) 32 TC 495). In *Levene v IRC* it was stated that:

> 'the residence which makes a person chargeable depends not on mere presence in the UK (unless that is for six months in all) but on the quality of the presence in relation to the objects and intentions of the person sought to be made chargeable.'

Capital Gains Tax

[19.7] TCGA 1992, s 9(1) provides that in the capital gains tax legislation 'resident' and 'ordinarily resident' have the same meanings as in the Income Tax Acts. In addition, TCGA 1992, s 9(3) contains a similar provision to that found in ITA 2007, ss 831 and 832 that an individual who is in the UK for a temporary purpose only and with no view or intent of establishing his residence in the UK shall only be chargeable to capital gains tax if he spends at least 183 days in the UK in any relevant tax year. As we have said above, the same day counting rules apply as those which apply for income tax.

Case Law

[19.8] Because neither 'residence' nor 'ordinary residence' is statutorily defined, it is necessary to consider in detail the decisions of the courts in cases concerning residence and ordinary residence. The case law is considerable but does not give expression to a consistent conceptual framework. It spans two centuries and because a great deal of it was decided before international travel became commonplace its application to modern conditions is difficult. In *IRC v Lysaght* [1928] AC 234, 13 TC 526 the House of Lords held that the question of residence is one of degree and therefore one of fact. Because residence is a question of fact the cases rarely involve the application of clear, general principles to simple facts. They are often inconsistent. As Lloyd LJ in the Court of Appeal said:

> 'Decided cases illustrate a great variety of examples, and the result of one case cannot normally be used as a guide to how another should be decided, even if the two have some factors in common.'

It is often difficult, therefore, for a person to determine with certainty whether he has been, is or will be resident in the UK.

In *Grace v Revenue & Customs Commissioners* [2009] EWCA Civ 1082 at para 3 Lloyd LJ cited with approval Lewison J's summary of a number of principles which have arisen from relevant case law in the following way:

> '(i) The word 'reside' is a familiar English word which means 'to dwell permanently or for a considerable time, to have one's settled or usual abode, to live in or at a particular place': *Levene v Commissioners of Inland Revenue* (1928) 13 TC 486, 505. This is the definition taken from the

Oxford English Dictionary in 1928, and is still the definition in the current on-line edition;

Physical presence in a particular place does not necessarily amount to residence in that place where, for example, a person's physical presence there is no more than a stop gap measure: *Goodwin v Curtis* (1998) 70 TC 478, 510;

In considering whether a person's presence in a particular place amounts to residence there, one must consider the amount of time that he spends in that place, the nature of his presence there and his connection with that place: *Commissioners of Inland Revenue v Zorab* (1926) 11 TC 289, 291;

Residence in a place connotes some degree of permanence, some degree of continuity or some expectation of continuity: *Fox v Stirk* [1970] 2 QB 463, 477; *Goodwin v Curtis* (1998) 70 TC 478, 510;

However, short but regular periods of physical presence may amount to residence, especially if they stem from performance of a continuous obligation (such as business obligations) and the sequence of visits excludes the elements of chance and of occasion: *Lysaght v Commissioners of Inland Revenue* (1928) 13 TC 511, 529;

Although a person can have only one domicile at a time, he may simultaneously reside in more than one place, or in more than one country: *Levene v Commissioners of Inland Revenue* (1928) 13 TC 486, 505;

"Ordinarily resident" refers to a person's abode in a particular place or country which he has adopted voluntarily and for settled purposes as part of the regular order of his life, whether of short or long duration: *R v Barnet LBC ex parte Shah* [1983] 2 AC 309, 343;

Just as a person may be resident in two countries at the same time, he may be ordinarily resident in two countries at the same time: *Re Norris* (1888) 4 TLR 452; *R v Barnet LBC ex parte Shah* [1983] 2 AC 309, 342;

It is wrong to conduct a search for the place where a person has his permanent base or centre adopted for general purposes; or, in other words to look for his 'real home': *R v Barnet LBC ex parte Shah* [1983] 2 AC 309, 345 and 348;

There are only two respects in which a person's state of mind is relevant in determining ordinary residence. First, the residence must be voluntarily adopted; and second, there must be a degree of settled purpose: *R v Barnet LBC ex parte Shah* [1983] 2 AC 309, 344;

Although residence must be voluntarily adopted, a residence dictated by the exigencies of business will count as voluntary residence: *Lysaght v Commissioners of Inland Revenue* (1928) 13 TC 511, 535;

The purpose, while settled, may be for a limited period; and the relevant purposes may include education, business or profession as well as a love of a place: *R v Barnet LBC ex parte Shah* [1983] 2 AC 309, 344;

Where a person has had his sole residence in the United Kingdom he is unlikely to be held to have ceased to reside in the United Kingdom (or to have "left" the United Kingdom) unless there has been a definite break in his pattern of life: *Re Combe* (1932) 17 TC 405, 411.'

Lloyd LJ also referred to the Special Commissioner's summary in *Shepherd v HMRC* (SpC 00484) [2005] STC (SCD) 644 and considered the following items to be 'worth quoting':

> '... that no duration is prescribed by statute and it is necessary to take into account all the facts of the case; the duration of an individual's presence in the United Kingdom and the regularity and frequency of visits are facts to be taken into account; also, birth, family and business ties, the nature of visits and the connections

> with this country, may all be relevant (*Zorab*; *IRC v Brown* (1926) 11 TC 292) . . . that in general the availability of living accommodation in the United Kingdom is a factor to be borne in mind in deciding if a person is resident here (*Cadwalader* (1904) 5 TC 101) (although that is now subject to s 336(3)). Next that the fact that an individual has a home elsewhere is of no consequence; a person may reside in two places but if one of those places is the United Kingdom he is chargeable to tax here (*Cadwalader* and *Levene*).'

In *Grace* the taxpayer was an airline pilot who made his home in Cape Town but retained a house in the UK which he used for rest periods in the UK. He had applied the rules which were then set out in the Revenue's explanatory booklet IR20. In IR20 it was stated that a person going abroad permanently would be treated as remaining resident and ordinarily resident in the UK if his visits averaged 91 days or more in the UK in a year. The average was calculated over the shorter of the total period after he had left the UK and four years. In determining how many days a person was in the UK, IR20 provided that days of arrival and departure were to be ignored. IR20, however, was no more than the Revenue's statement of their understanding of the law and their practice in applying it. It could not determine the law and the Special Commissioners and the courts decided the matter by reference to principles derived from case authority without reference to IR20. Mr Grace had averaged less than 91 days in the UK in the relevant periods if one ignored his days of arrival and departure (in accordance with IR20) but not if he was counted as present in the UK on any day when he was present here at midnight. The Special Commissioners found that he was not resident in the UK but their decision was reversed by the High Court. The Court of Appeal has recently remitted the matter back to the First-tier Tribunal having found as a matter of law that presence in the UK in order to fulfil duties under a permanent (or at least indefinite) contract of employment could not be described as casual or transitory.

In *Yugraneft v Abramovich* [2008] EWHC 2613 (Comm), [2008] All ER (D) 299 (Oct) which was not a case concerning taxation, it was held that Mr Abramovich was not resident in the UK for the relevant year despite the large number of days on which he was present in the UK and the fact that he owned a number of UK residences and Chelsea Football Club. Interestingly, he had spent more time in the UK in the relevant period than had Mr Grace. The case of *Gaines-Cooper v Revenue & Customs Comrs* [2007] EWHC 2617 (Ch), [2008] STC 1665 involved a taxpayer who was born in the UK where he lived until he began pursuing business ventures elsewhere. The case received a great deal of attention because it raised the question as to whether the taxpayer could rely on HMRC's statement in IR20 of their practice in determining residence and ordinary residence. The meaning of 'temporary purpose' was also considered in this case. The Special Commissioners relying on *Cooper (Surveyor of Taxes) v Cadwalader* 1904 5 TC 101 said that 'temporary purpose' means a casual purpose as distinguished from the case of a person who is here in pursuance of his regular habits of life. Temporary purpose means 'the opposite of continuous purpose.' The Special Commissioners did not consider that visiting a spouse and children was a purpose which lasted for limited time. It was a permanent and not a transient purpose. Neither was it a casual purpose, it was in pursuance of the regular habits of the appellant's life. The High Court confirmed the Special Commissioners' decision. An application for judicial review was made on the basis that the Revenue had failed to apply the rules set out in IR20 and that a taxpayer had a legitimate expectation that those rules would be applied. The Court of Appeal held that a taxpayer did indeed have a legitimate expectation that, for the period before its withdrawal, the Revenue would apply the provisions of IR20 but found that the Revenue had done so and that Mr Gaines-Cooper was indeed resident and ordinarily resident in the UK in the relevant years. It is understood that leave to appeal to the Supreme Court has been granted to Mr Gaines-Cooper.

In *Hankinson v HMRC* [2009] UKFTT 384 (TC), [2010] SWTI 1368, a case which was decided on a detailed examination of very particular facts, the taxpayer argued that the principles derived from case law, principally cases such as *Lysaght* and *Levene*, both decisions given in 1928, need to be applied ' . . . with due regard to the social and historical condition of the time with which they were concerned; a direct or inflexible approach might lead to a conclusion at odds with contemporary behaviour. A modern approach should be taken to the issues of residence and ordinary resident.' The Tribunal Judge commented ' . . . changing communications and social conditions have to be dealt with in the context of reviewing residence, occasional residence and ordinary residence, but there is no suggestion that the tests to be applied should be altered in any way to take account of such changes.' That makes explicit the approach taken in recent residence cases; the principles derived from established case authorities are to be applied to the very different conditions of modern life rather than being modified to take account of them.

Residence, and as we shall see below, ordinary residence, have continued to occupy the courts in 2010. In *Farquhar v Revenue and Customs Comrs* [2010] UKFTT 231 (TC), [2010] SWTI 2399 the taxpayer was a merchant seaman. His employers had dealt with HMRC South Wales on behalf of many of its merchant seaman employees over 30 years and had agreed with that office a method of calculating the average number of days in the UK spent by the taxpayers they represented. The appellant's tax return was dealt with by another office which applied a different method. The appellant contended that he had a legitimate expectation that the same method would be applied to his return as the Revenue applied to other taxpayers in his situation and so the South Wales working practice should have been adopted. The Tribunal accepted that the appellant had not been treated in the same way as other taxpayers in the same position. They recorded the fact that they would have 'found that the appellant had a legitimate expectation that he be treated as other taxpayers in his position' but declined to actually do so because 'whether this point can be taken by the Tribunal, and whether it should instead be raised in the High Court by way of judicial review, is due to be considered by the Tribunal in another case . . . ' Bizarrely, the Tribunal suggested 'the appellant consider referring his case to the Revenue Adjudicator.'

HMRC Practice: Background

[19.9] For many years the Revenue's practice was based on applying the principles set out in its booklet IR20 but in *Gaines-Cooper* the Revenue adopted a position which the appellant contended was incompatible with

IR20. As we have seen, in the lower courts HMRC contended that the courts were concerned only with the law and that IR20 was irrelevant to the question at issue. When the case was heard by the Court of Appeal, the court found that HMRC was bound to apply the practice set out in IR20 but that, contrary to the view of most informed commentators, it had actually done so. In response to the *Gaines-Cooper* case, HMRC replaced IR20 with Booklet HMRC6 'Residence, Domicile and the Remittance Basis' with effect from 6 April 2009. In that booklet it is specifically stated that:

> 'any practices associated with the IR20 –whether overtly expressed or not –will not apply from 6 April 2009, unless provided for outside the IR20 (in statute law, in case law, in published extra statutory concession, or in a guidance note).'

HMRC6 only offers 'general guidance on HMRC's view of how the rules apply and does not have legal effect. Whether [its] guidance applies in a particular case will depend on all the facts of that case.' HMRC6 (like its predecessor, IR20) adopts different rules depending upon whether someone is arriving in, or leaving, the UK.

The Revenue considers that where an individual spends 183 days or more in the UK they are UK resident and there is no exception to this. IR20 states that 'you will always be resident if you are here for 183 days or more in the tax year. There are no exceptions to this.' HMRC6 states that:

> 'in all cases when you are physically present in the UK for 183 days or more, you will be resident here in that tax year.'

HMRC6 says, correctly, that an individual can be UK resident even if he has spent less than 183 days in the UK. HMRC6 goes on to say that with 'one exception, [the 183 Day Rule], it is not simply a question of the number of days you are physically present in the UK during a tax year although this is an important consideration.' HMRC6 goes on to say that:

> 'Things [one] should consider would include what connections [an individual has] to the UK such as family, property, business and social connections. Just because [one] leave[s] the UK to live or work abroad does not necessarily prove that [one is] no longer resident here if, for example, you keep connections in the UK such as property, economic interests, available accommodation and social activities or if you have children in education here. For example, if you are someone who comes to the UK on a regular basis and have a settled lifestyle pattern connecting you to this country, you are likely to be resident here.'

For many years, HMRC have operated what was known as 'the 91 Day Rule'. This rule applied only to individuals leaving the UK and those visiting the UK on a regular basis.

From 2009/2010 if an individual comes to the UK to live here permanently or to remain here for three years or more, HMRC treat him as being resident and ordinarily resident from his date of arrival. 'Remain' in HMRC's view is:

> 'that [an individual is here] on a continuing basis – the only trips [he makes] outside the UK are when [he goes] abroad for holidays or short business trips.'

If he is not going to live here permanently or remain here for more than three years it may be that an individual is merely visiting. HMRC6 goes on to say, however, that someone is 'not simply visiting' if, when he arrives, he comes 'to the UK for a purpose which means that [he] will be remaining here for at least two years,' and the Revenue will treat him as resident from the date of arrival. If an individual is not within the 183 Day Rule, does not intend to remain for two years in the UK and can genuinely say that he has come only to visit the UK, then the guidance for visitors will apply. Two types of visitor are identified by HMRC, the short term and the longer term visitor. A short term visitor is one who is 'not going to remain in the UK for an extended period who will visit for limited periods in one or more tax years.' A longer term visitor is someone who has 'not come to the UK permanently but has come here indefinitely or for an extended period which might cover several tax years.'

Where an individual's visits average 91 days or more over a four year period, he will be resident and ordinarily resident from the fifth year. He *might*, however, become resident and ordinarily resident before the four year period if, when he starts visiting the UK, he knows his visits are going to be for an average of 91 days or more, in which case he will be resident and ordinarily resident from the 6 April of the tax year in which he first starts making his visits. The use of the word 'might' undermines the reliability of the guidance on when a visitor will be UK resident. The annual average of a taxpayer's visits is calculated as follows:

$$\frac{\text{Total days visiting the UK}}{\text{Tax years [the taxpayer concerned has] visited (in days)}} \times 365$$

HMRC6 states that it is possible for an individual to be resident and ordinarily resident before visiting for four years if:

- at the start of visiting he knows that his visits are going to be for an average of 91 days or more;
- he realises after starting to visit the UK regularly his visits are going to be for an average of 91 days or more.

It then goes on to say that a longer term visitor will be resident and ordinarily resident in the UK from the date of arrival if he has come here for at least two years.

Under IR20 it was the normal rule that days of arrival in and departure from the UK were ignored in counting the days spent in the UK. Days spent in the UK due to exceptional circumstances were also ignored. This practice changed from 6 April 2008. Under the Revenue's practice set out in HMRC6, the average number of visits to the UK is calculated as follows:

'If you need to calculate your annual average visits to the UK, you do so like this:

$$\frac{\text{Total days visiting the UK}}{\text{Tax years you have visited (in days)}} \times 365 = \text{annual average visits}$$

A day visiting the UK for this purpose is a day in which a taxpayer is physically present in the UK at midnight subject to a number of limited exceptions.'

Leaving the UK

[19.10] When an individual leaves the UK, when does he become non-UK resident? HMRC 6 para 8.1 says that in the case of an individual who has been resident and ordinarily resident in the UK, the act of leaving the UK to go abroad does not mean that he will automatically become non-resident. An individual's residence status will be affected by a number of factors which include:

- the reason he left the UK;
- what visits he makes to the UK after he has left;
- what connections he keeps in the UK such as family, property, business and social connections.

Whilst this is an accurate summary of the law it is hardly guidance which is of any use to an individual wishing to determine his residence status.

Ordinary Residence

[19.11] Ordinary residence is also not defined in tax legislation.

Case Law

[19.12] In *Thomson v Minister of National Revenue* [1946] SCR 206, [1946] 1 DLR 689 the Supreme Court of Canada ruled that residence is ordinary if it is habitual and in the course of the taxpayer's customary life. In *R v Barnet LBC exp Shah* [1983] AC 309 it was held that ordinary residence is 'a man's abode in a particular place or country which he has adopted voluntarily and for settled purposes as part of the regular order of his life for the time being, whether of short or long duration.' This has been cited with approval in subsequent cases, including *Genovese v Revenue and Customs Comrs* [2009] STC (SCD) 373 and *R (Davies), (James and Gaines-Cooper) v HMRC* [2010] EWCA Civ 83, [2010] STC 860.

It was pointed out in *Genovese* that the various cases cited did not involve an individual originating from outside the UK and the Commonwealth coming to the UK and therefore were of limited application to individuals who come from a non-commonwealth country. In that case, the Special Commissioner considered that Mr Genovese's presence in the UK because of employment, coupled with the presence of his family and the taking up of accommodation did amount to voluntarily adopting an abode in the UK. He concluded that there was no guidance as to the minimum period required to establish that such a person has become ordinarily resident in the UK. A pattern of two years was not considered habitual but a pattern of three years was. The taxpayer was held to have become ordinarily resident on the third anniversary of his arrival in the UK.

In the case of *Tuczka v Revenue and Customs Comrs* [2010] UKFTT 53 (TC), [2010] SWTI 1594 heard before the same Special Commissioner, now a Tribunal Judge, HMRC argued that *Genovese* had been wrongly decided and that no minimum period of physical presence was required to establish ordinary residence. A taxpayer can become ordinarily resident in the UK on first coming to the country if his coming here is voluntary and for a settled purpose. Peter Vaines, writing in 'Taxation Magazine' has commented that the ' . . . decision shows that there is a very narrow distinction (or perhaps no distinction at all) between residence and ordinary residence and that a person who becomes resident in the UK and takes up employment here voluntarily becomes ordinarily resident almost immediately on his arrival – even if his intention is not to stay for very long.'

Revenue Practice

[19.12A] In the Revenue's view, set out in HMRC6, ordinary residence has the following attributes:

- The person concerned has come to the UK voluntarily;
- His presence in the UK has a settled purpose;
- His presence in the UK forms part of the regular and habitual mode of his life for the time being.

Reform Of The Determination Of Domicile And Residence

[19.12B] Although the Income and Capital gains taxation of persons who are not domiciled but resident in the UK was extensively revised by the Finance Act 2008, the fundamental concepts of domicile, residence and ordinary residence remain largely unchanged. The only statutory changes of any significance made in recent years are to the method of determining the number of days that a person is physically present in the UK for a limited number of statutory purposes and the introduction of the remittance basis charge.

As we have said, the case law governing residence and ordinary residence is conceptually confused and does not allow the taxpayer to determine his residence and ordinary residence status with even reasonable probability. The replacement of IR20 by HMRC6 means that the taxpayer also cannot predict HMRC's practice with any certainty. An exhaustive statutory definition of residence and ordinary residence is desperately needed. The professional bodies have made detailed representations to government asking for such a definition and suggesting how it might be framed. Detailed discussions proceeded under the last government but it is not clear whether the new government accepts the urgent need for reform. In the new government's Budget Report on 22 June 2010 it was announced that the Government is to review the taxation of non-domiciled individuals to assess 'whether changes can be made to the current rules to ensure that non-domiciled individuals make a fair contribution to reducing the deficit, in return for greater certainty . . . especially for those bringing skills and investment to the UK.' Whether this review will include a review of the use of the concept of domicile in UK tax legislation generally and of the need for a statutory definition of residence and ordinary residence, is currently unclear.

Double Tax Treaties

[19.12C] It is possible for an individual to be resident in more than one country at the same time. As a result the OECD Model Tax Convention on Income and Capital contains a provision to determine in which of the contracting counties an individual will be treated as being resident for the purposes of the treaty concerned and all Double Tax Conventions contain some version of this provision. Because of the greater uncertainty introduced by HMRC6, double tax treaties ('DTTs') are now of more importance than in the past. DTTs have a clearer definition of residence than UK domestic legislation and provide relief from UK taxation in many circumstances.

The definition of residence under a Treaty, however, only applies for the purposes of the Treaty itself. It does not apply to determine a person's general tax status under UK tax law.

Overseas law

[19.13] For would-be immigrants to the UK it is important that they understand the extent to which they will continue to be affected by the revenue and other laws of their current country of residence when they come to the UK and how they will be taxed under UK law. Conversely, for those considering leaving the UK it is important for them to understand how they will be taxed under the law of their new country of residence and the extent to which they will continue to be effected by UK Revenue and other law. This applies to both long-term and short-term residents. The individual, depending on his circumstances, should consider these matters and take any necessary advice in the appropriate country before taking any irrevocable steps. For example, the Civil Partnership Act 2004 recognises overseas relationships as falling within the definition of a civil partnership, whereas other countries do not recognise a UK civil partnership. Therefore, civil partners directly owning property in say, France, would be subject to a French inheritance tax charge because they will not be eligible to the spouse exemption or its equivalent. Timing may be all-important, and the time to consider these matters is before departure, rather than when one is en route to the new country or on arrival.

Considerations for the long-term resident

[19.14] It is essential that an individual plans well in advance of his arrival. He should consider his position well before the UK tax year in which he plans to arrive, so that appropriate action may be taken before the start of that tax year.

In advising such an individual, the following factors should be taken into consideration:

(a) his age and the period for which he is coming to the UK;
(b) his domicile of origin and general background;
(c) his family circumstances;

(d) his employment or professional situation;
(e) the composition of his estate and his sources of income;
(f) his likely financial needs in the UK;
(g) the existence of any funds not required for actual expenditure in the UK;
(h) whether he has any intention of making gifts of capital assets to family members and others, the nature of those assets and the residence and circumstances of the donees;
(i) his intentions for his estate in the event of his death.

The following general points should be remembered.

(1) If a UK domicile is not acquired immediately upon, or within a short time after, arrival in the UK, any funds held abroad in the immigrant's personal ownership representing foreign source income or the realised gains of foreign assets, may be used outside the UK for expenditure as appropriate (eg for travel, holidays or maintenance of a property abroad), without involving a liability to UK income tax or capital gains tax because neither income nor capital will have been remitted to the UK.
(2) Wherever possible, an immigrant should, before arrival (and preferably in the tax year before arrival), sell and repurchase personally held capital assets to ensure new base costs for future UK capital gains tax purposes. The same applies to any trust property previously settled by him. This is to achieve a higher base cost for the trust assets before the trust comes within the scope of the capital payments charge (TCGA 1992, s 87) or the offshore settlor charge (TCGA 1992, s 86 and Sch 5).
(3) The would-be immigrant should ensure that accrued income is realised before he becomes UK resident. So for example, when the interest payment date on a bank account would fall after the change of residence, closing the account can ensure that the accrued interest is paid before the change.
(4) Any foreign income arising from new sources should be kept outside the UK as far as possible.
(5) An immigrant should make a new will. Probably, if he is going to be domiciled in the UK, this will should be written under English law. If, however, he retains real property abroad it may (subject to local advice) be appropriate for him to make a will under the local law to deal specifically with that property, leaving his new English will to deal with UK situated assets.

A long-term immigrant should always consider the risk that HMRC will argue that he has acquired, or reacquired, a domicile within the UK upon his arrival if he intends to reside in the UK for a long time. As discussed earlier, it may however, be that (following *CIR v Bullock* [1976] STC 409, [1976] 3 All ER 353), one spouse of a married couple may be able to retain a domicile in his or her home country. There may be circumstances where an individual will not acquire a UK domicile until he has been here for a few years. It may be possible to take advantage of his foreign domicile whilst resident in the UK by making gifts of foreign situated assets which will not be within the charge to inheritance tax. However, it is sensible that such gifts are made before his arrival in the UK.

A person who intends to reside permanently here will be treated as being resident and ordinarily resident in the UK from the date of his arrival. Where a person comes to the UK with a settled intention of residing in the UK on a permanent basis, he will become UK domiciled as soon as he arrives. Where the immigrant does not intend to settle in the UK permanently, it is possible that the issue of domicile will not be raised with or by the Revenue for a number of years after the individual's arrival, and in that event it may be that, depending on the evidence, he will not be treated as domiciled in the UK until some later date.

If a UK domicile is acquired upon or soon after arrival, UK income tax will be charged on the individual's income, wherever it arises, including income received from trusts of which he is a beneficiary (whether he is entitled to income or dependent on the trustee's discretion for income). If a UK domicile is not obtained, advantage can be taken of the remittance basis so as to avoid a charge on unremitted foreign source income and capital gains, subject to paying the £30,000 charge (see **19.15**). The use of non-resident trusts can achieve valuable tax savings, and not simply deferment, as will be seen later. During this period, gifts can be made of foreign assets without liability to inheritance tax. As indicated above however, it is dangerous to rely on the ability to do this, if there is any uncertainty as to his domicile status.

Remittance basis

[19.15] The Finance Act 2008 substantially changed the taxation of income and capital gains of individuals who are resident in the United Kingdom but are not domiciled in a country of the United Kingdom.

An individual who is resident in the UK but not domiciled here can claim to be taxed on the remittance basis. Where the remittance basis is available, an individual's relevant foreign earnings, foreign income and foreign chargeable gains are taxable only when they are remitted to the United Kingdom rather than when they arise. The intention of the legislation would seem to be that unless income or gains, loosely, are actually brought to or enjoyed in the UK, there is no tax charge. In fact, the new rules are of such complexity and have been so poorly drafted that it is quite possible to make a technical remittance in circumstances which, in ordinary usage, would not be described as a remittance.

The remittance basis may be claimed by an individual who is UK resident in the fiscal year but is either not domiciled or not ordinarily resident in the UK in that year. Where that individual is aged 18 or over in that year and has been UK resident for at least 7 of the 9 tax years immediately preceding the year, he will only be able to continue to benefit from the remittance basis if he pays the charge of £30,000. To benefit from the remittance basis an individual must make a claim through their self-assessment tax return (SA 109) except in two circumstances.

First, where the individual is not domiciled in the United Kingdom in that year or is not ordinarily resident in the year and his unremitted foreign income and gains for that year are less than £2,000. Second, where the individual is not domiciled in the United Kingdom or is not ordinarily resident in the UK in that year, he has no UK income or gains for the year, he has not remitted any relevant income or gains to the UK in the year and either:

(a) he has been UK resident is not more than 6 of the 9 tax years immediately preceding that year; or
(b) he is under the age of 18 throughout that year.

What is a remittance?

[19.16] What constitutes a remittance has been significantly extended by the provisions of ITA 2007, ss 809K–809Z6. The definition now includes circumstances where money or other property is brought to or received or used in the UK or any services provided in the UK where it derives from foreign income or gains. Where a chattel is purchased with foreign income or gains outside the UK and then brought to the UK, there is a remittance even though no money will have been brought to the UK. There are exemptions to the remittance rule (see ITA 2007, s 809X) which include exemptions for clothing, footwear, jewellery and watches if they meet the 'personal use rule', assets brought into the UK for repair, assets which are in the UK for less than nine months and property which satisfies the public access rule and for assets (or sets of assets) costing less than £1,000.

Where foreign income or gains are alienated by a transfer to a relevant person, there will be a remittance by the donor if the donee remits the money to the UK. A relevant person is defined in ITA 2007, s 809M, and does not include an adult child. Therefore, a father could make a gift of non-UK interest to his adult daughter outside the UK which his daughter could bring into the UK without any charge arising on the father provided he does not benefit from the money in the UK. Interestingly, a man and woman living together as husband and wife or two people of the same sex living together as if they were civil partners will be treated as if they were married or civil partners respectively. In relation to welfare benefits the Revenue identifies a number of factors used in determining whether two people are living together as husband and wife or civil partners (Applicant Compliance Guide para 9010). Where a UK resident but non-domiciled individual has a foreign loan for use in the UK, any repayments of the principal amount out of foreign income or gains will be treated as a remittance. In addition, the payment of interest on a foreign loan will now also be a taxable remittance. These rules will not apply where interest is paid on qualifying loans in place on 12 March 2008 which are secured on UK residential property provided that the terms of the loans are not varied, no further advances are made and that the loan continues to be secured on the same property.

Because of the very wide definition of a remittance, clients need to pay careful regard to these rules to avoid inadvertently making a remittance. Revenue guidance on the statutory provisions is contained in the Residence, Domicile and Remittances Manual.

Remittance basis claims are made on a year by year basis. Where the remittance basis is available only if an election is made, if no election is made the taxpayer will be taxable on a worldwide arising basis. Income or gains unremitted in a year in which the remittance basis applies which are subsequently remitted when the remittance basis is not claimed will be taxable in the UK.

It is therefore important for an individual to consider in advance (as far as he is able) any transactions and movement of funds or assets to minimise his overall tax liabilities.

The £30,000 charge

[19.17] Foreign domiciled individuals who have been resident in the UK for 7 out of the last 9 tax years who make a remittance basis election will pay an additional tax charge under ITA 2007, s 809H. When making a claim, an individual must nominate the income or chargeable gains to which the special charge (under s 809H(2)) is to apply. The income nominated to be charged is chargeable on an arising basis whether or not it is remitted. To the extent that the tax charged on the nominated income is less than £30,000, an additional amount of income is deemed to arise under s 809H(4) so ensuring that the combined charge under s 809H will always be £30,000.

Each year a decision will have to be made as to whether it is beneficial to pay £30,000 for the privilege of the remittance basis.

Segregated funds

[19.18] It is best practice for UK residents who are not domiciled in a country of the United Kingdom to segregate the proceeds of capital disposals, other capital and income. In practice, however, this does not always happen, hence the statutory rules which apply to mixed funds (ITA 2007, ss 809Q–809S). Segregating capital from income is the traditional technique of remitting capital to the UK without triggering a tax charge; it is still effective and is an important part of tax planning for a non-domiciliary.

Effect of remittance basis claim

[19.19] Where the remittance basis is claimed, but not where it applies automatically, various personal reliefs from income tax are not available to the claimant. These are the personal allowance, the blind person's allowance, the married couples allowance and the relief for payments of life insurance. Similarly, no annual exempt amount for capital gains tax is available.

In effect, the Finance Act 2008 has imposed a cost on claiming the benefit of the remittance basis which, in the case of those who have been resident for at least 6 of the 9 preceding tax years, is £30,000 plus the cost of being denied the various allowances listed.

Limited spouse exemption

[19.20] The inheritance tax exemption on transfers between spouses is limited to £55,000 if the transferee spouse or civil partner is not domiciled in the UK but the transferor spouse is. Under the last government, the then Paymaster General stated in a letter to Scottish Life International that the threshold will not be raised and she asserted that an increase 'could be seen as running counter to our commitment to tackling avoidance and encouraging a fairer tax system' [sic]. There is no similar limitation on the spouse exemption given in relation to the income tax charge on pre-owned assets. It should be noted that other inheritance tax exemptions may apply to such transfers, such as the exemption in relation to dispositions between spouses for the maintenance of the other party (IHTA 1984, s 11(1)). This maintenance exemption would not normally be available where the domiciled spouse gives an interest in a property (*Phizackerley (Personal Representative of Phizackerley (dec'd)) v Revenue and Customs Comrs* [2007] STC (SCD) 328) (but see *McKelvey (Personal Representatives of McKelvey Deceased) v HMRC* [2008] SSCD 944).

Excluded property trusts

[19.21] IHTA 1984, s 6(1) provides that non-UK situs property is excluded property if the beneficial owner is domiciled outside the UK. Excluded property is not included in a person's death estate nor taken into account in calculating any charges under the relevant property trust regime. However, it is taken into account when determining the quantum of charge on any relevant property within a trust.

Example

> Cory, a non-UK domiciled individual settles UK situs assets with a value equal to the then nil rate band and non-UK situs assets valued at £500,000 on a non-UK resident trust. The value of the UK situs assets in 2010/2011 is £325,000 and the non-UK situs assets are worth £1m as at the first decennial. Although no charges arise on the excluded property, the £325,000 of UK situs assets is charged at a rate of 3.64% because of the requirement to include excluded property when calculating the applicable rate for the purposes of the decennial charge under IHTA 1984, s 64.

There is also another trap when adding property to an excluded property trust. In HMRC's view, where additions are made after the settlor has become UK domiciled or deemed UK domiciled, the trust property added property and property deriving from it will not be excluded from property. The Revenue's vew is clearly incorrect but to avoid a dispute no additions should be made to existing trusts in such circumstances.

An individual not domiciled in the UK who wishes to avoid UK inheritance tax applying to his worldwide estate in the event that he should acquire a UK domicile should establish a non-UK resident trust-based structure to hold a substantial proportion of his personal wealth. If a suitable trust is established with non-UK situs assets by an individual who is not domiciled in the UK for inheritance tax purposes, no inheritance tax will be chargeable on the assets held in the trust (IHTA 1984, s 48(3)).

Section 48(3) excludes from charge non-UK property (eg the shares in a non-resident company) in a settlement made by an individual who was not domiciled in the UK at the date of settlement. This rule applies even if subsequently the settlor becomes actually domiciled or deemed domiciled in the UK and the position is unaffected by whether the settlor is also a beneficiary of the trust. Property is not excluded property where a person domiciled in the UK has acquired after 4 December 2005 an interest in possession in the property for a consideration in money or moneys worth (IHTA 1984, s 48(3B)). This provision was introduced to stop strategies which involved the sale of excluded property interests to UK domiciled individuals to mitigate inheritance tax.

Reservation of benefit

[19.22] Individuals who are not domiciled in the UK for inheritance tax purposes often establish discretionary trusts under which they retain a benefit. This occurs where the settlor is either a beneficiary or is capable of being subsequently added as one (*Gartside v CIR* [1968] 1 All ER 121, [1968] 2 WLR 277 (HL)).

How does the rule in IHTA 1984, s 48(3) that non-UK *situs* settled property is excluded property if the settlor is not domiciled in the UK at the time the settlement was made relate to the reservation of benefit rules? The Revenue's position seems to be a confused one. In correspondence published in the Law Society Gazette on 10 December 1986, the Revenue accepted that if a settlor settled property in which he reserved a benefit when he was not domiciled in the UK, and then died while domiciled in the UK, the settled property would be excluded from charge under IHTA 1984, s 48. The Revenue IHT Manual at para 14396, however, gives the following example:

> 'The donor, who is domiciled in Australia, puts foreign property into a discretionary trust under which he is a potential beneficiary. He dies five years later domiciled in the UK and without having released the reservation.
>
> The property is subject to a reservation and is therefore deemed to be part of the donor's death estate.
>
> Refer any cases where this is the situation to litigation.'

One has to be careful where either the settlor or his spouse has an initial interest in possession which is an IPDI or a DPI (see **CHAPTER 4**) (called a 'postponing interest') which is followed by an interest which is not a postponing interest. To ensure excluded property status, the individual must be both non-domiciled when the trust is created and on the termination of the postponing interest or the spouse's successive postponing interest.

Situs of assets

[19.23] When establishing an offshore structure, the inheritance tax rules as to *situs* should be considered subject to contrary provisions in double taxation treaties. Below is a brief outline of the rules.

(a) *Land.* Immovable property is situated where it is actually located (*Johnson v Baker* (1817) 4 Madd 474).

(b) *Registered shares and securities.* The general rule is that these are situated where they are registered or, if transferable upon more than one register, where they would normally be dealt with in the ordinary course of business.

(c) *Bearer shares and securities.* Such assets are transferable by delivery and are situated where the certificate or other document of title is kept (*A-G v Bouwens* (1838) 4 M & W 171).

(d) *Government securities.* Here the *situs* is determined by the place of registration or inscription or, if bearer securities, where the certificate is kept.

(e) *Specialty debts.* These are debts under a deed. The *situs* is determined by the place where the deed is kept and not, if different, by reference to the country in which the debtor resides. Different rules apply in Scotland.

The capital gains tax rules can be found in TCGA 1992, ss 275 and 275A which also applies for the purposes of ITA 2007, s 809W (consideration for certain services but not for the remittance basis generally).

Where a trust, established by a settlor who was not domiciled in the UK, holds UK *situs* assets, that property will be within the UK inheritance tax regime. However, the use of a non-UK incorporated holding company can change the *situs* of the underlying assets for inheritance tax purposes, even if that holding company is itself resident in the UK (although corporation tax, capital gains tax and income tax issues would, of course, have to be addressed). In addition, where an individual is not domiciled in the UK for inheritance tax purposes and owns shares in a UK private company it may be possible to arrange matters so that the *situs* of the asset is itself changed prior to inclusion in an offshore structure. Such steps require careful planning.

Location of the trust

[19.24] For inheritance tax purposes it is not necessary for the trustees to be resident outside the UK. A trust with trustees resident in the UK which contains trust property not situated in the UK will be as effective for inheritance tax purposes as a trust with trustees resident outside the UK. However, it is usual, to establish the trust outside the UK (ie with all the trustees being non-resident (TCGA 1992, s 69). This is to avoid capital gains tax being payable by the trustees in respect of their gains. It is important, however, to remember that, even though the foreign trustees may not be liable for capital gains tax, if the settlor later becomes domiciled and resident or ordinarily resident in the UK he will become taxable on all gains realised by the trustees if (broadly) either he or his spouse or civil partner or their children or their grandchildren or their spouses or civil partners are beneficially entitled under the trust (TCGA 1992, s 86 and Sch 5).

The capital payments charge imposed by TCGA 1992, s 87 will apply to all settlements regardless of the domicile of the settlor.

Normally, however, an individual will want to keep his trust completely offshore in the hope of avoiding future UK taxes. He will also be able to obtain the benefit of the remittance basis for income tax on foreign source income and gains subject to paying the remittance basis charge for as long as he can defer the acquisition of an actual domicile of choice in the UK under general law.

Advisers should review trust arrangements on a continuing basis to ensure that the trust does not inadvertently become UK resident particularly in family situations. In the majority of cases, however, where the trustee is an offshore trust company and all administration is done overseas, it will be clear that the trust is not resident in the UK.

Trustees and protectors

[19.25] For UK tax reasons, neither the settlor nor his spouse or civil partner should be a trustee. This can sometimes cause difficulty for the proposed settlor in the selection of the trustees of his settlement. He may not have any non-resident friends or relations whom it would be appropriate or fair to ask to act, and so usually professional trustees or a trustee organisation are appointed. The settlor will wish to appoint trustees whom he can trust and whose charges he finds acceptable. He may want to appoint a 'protector' to oversee in some respects the actions of the trustees. A protector is usually an individual or company, whose duty is to give or withhold consent to the exercise of certain powers by the trustees. A protector is appointed under the terms of the trust. Generally, the protector should take care that his appointment does not have any tax or other repercussions for him in his country of residence. Although the protector may give some comfort to the settlor over the running of the trust, care must be taken not to make his involvement too complicated, in order to avoid confusion and an unsatisfactory administration of the settlement in practice. For a more detailed treatment, see **CHAPTER 18 UK DOMICILIARIES INVESTING ABROAD**.

Form of the trust

[19.26] In the past, the type of trust settled by a settlor had a significant effect on its taxation treatment. For example, grandparents would often establish an accumulation and maintenance trust for the benefit of grandchildren rather than a discretionary trust. There is no longer any reason to establish an accumulation and maintenance trust rather than a discretionary trust because their tax treatment is now the same and the former type of trust is less flexible. In a situation where the settlor and his spouse or civil partner are to be excluded from benefitting, a discretionary trust is often the better choice. As, with careful planning, the trust will be outside the scope of IHT forever, the trust should be as long-lasting as possible and should not vest automatically at an early age or in the first generation.

Where a settlor and his spouse or civil partner are to be beneficiaries, a discretionary trust or interest in possession trust may be appropriate.

A discretionary trust should constitute excluded property during its life and on the settlor's death. A life interest for the settlor will not be a reserved benefit because the settlor's life interest is not a benefit reserved in any property given away but is an interest retained by the settlor, the remainder to which is the subject matter of the gift. Since the income tax and capital gains tax treatments of both types of trust are very similar in certain respects, it will almost always be better to use a discretionary trust so as to provide the greatest flexibility.

Capital gains tax

[19.27] The taxation of non-UK resident trusts established by a settlor who later becomes resident in the UK and then domiciled here is subject to a complex set of rules.

Gains realised by offshore trustees cannot be attributed to a settlor until the settlor becomes both resident or ordinarily resident *and* domiciled in the UK (TCGA 1992, s 86 (the 'offshore settlor charge')). However, beneficiaries can be subject to the capital payments charge under TCGA 1992, s 87 (the 'capital payments charge') regardless of the residence or domicile status of the settlor.

As we have seen, non-domiciled individuals who are resident in the UK can be assessed on their capital gains under the remittance basis. The remittance basis rules are adapted by TCGA 1992, s 87B to apply to gains treated as accruing under s 87.

For a settlor resident but not yet domiciled in the UK it is important that the trust assets be periodically rebased for capital gains tax purposes so that the base cost of the assets held are as high as possible prior to the settlor becoming domiciled in the UK. This is because, if the settlor has an interest in the settlement when he becomes domiciled in the UK, future gains will become immediately chargeable under the offshore settlor charge (TCGA 1992, s 86) rather than being chargeable under the capital payments charge (TCGA 1992, s 87) only when capital payments are made.

It is important to appreciate that the capital gains tax status of a trust can fluctuate over the course of time. Whilst the settlor is non-UK domiciled the trust is outside the offshore settlor charge. Once the settlor becomes both resident and domiciled in the UK the trust will be brought within that charge. After the settlor's death the trust will revert to being within the capital payments charge alone. Indeed, if the beneficiaries who receive capital payments are not resident in the UK, the trust gains may escape UK capital gains tax entirely. Yet it is still important to bear in mind that, irrespective of the trustees' residence status, they will be subject to UK capital gains tax where they hold assets used in a UK trade undertaken on their behalf through a branch or agency there. This situation would arise, for example, where the trustees own farmland which is run on their behalf by a manager. In practice, there are a number of ways round this, including ensuring that the land is held by one legal entity, whilst being farmed by another. Alternatively, the entire farming business could be incorporated.

Income tax

Settlement provisions

[19.28] The UK has a complex regime of anti-avoidance provisions aimed at nullifying any income tax advantages which might be obtained through a resident establishing a trust for his own benefit, or for his spouse or civil partner, or for his unmarried children under the age of 18 which are contained in ITTOIA 2005, Pt 5 Ch 5. Payments of income made to or for the benefit of a settlor's own unmarried infant child will be treated as the income of the settlor (ITTOIA 2005, s 629). The rule applies to settlements regardless of when they were made but where the total income paid to the child is less than £100 in any year it will not be treated as the settlor's income. If income is accumulated, the income is not treated as that of the settlor's until it is paid out. In addition, where during a settlor's life any property subject to a settlement, or any derived property, can become payable to or applicable for the benefit of, the settlor his spouse or civil partner, the income of the settlement is treated as the settlor's income for all income tax purposes (ITTOIA 2005, ss 624–628). A settlor who is taxed on the remittance basis cannot be taxed on foreign income accumulated overseas, even where he has an interest in the settlement. However, if that income is subsequently remitted to the UK in a tax year in which the settlor is UK resident, it will be treated as income arising in that year and chargeable to tax as the settlor's income (ITTOIA 2005, s 648). However, all UK source income will be assessed upon an arising basis.

In certain circumstances, the income tax charge on pre-owned assets will apply to UK-resident but non-UK domiciled individuals. Under FA 2004, Sch 15 para 12(4) an individual is treated as domiciled in the UK if he is deemed to be domiciled in the UK for the purposes of IHTA 1984. There are exemptions from the charge in relation to non-UK domiciled individuals where the property transferred is non-UK situs property or excluded property within IHTA 1984, s 48(3)(a).

The UK has a number of other anti-avoidance provisions which seek to nullify the income tax advantages to be derived from offshore trusts.

Transfer of assets abroad

[19.29] ITA 2007, ss 720–730 (previously ICTA 1988, s 739) are extremely widely drawn anti-avoidance provisions which seek to prevent the avoidance of income tax by individuals who are ordinarily resident in the UK and who establish offshore structures to shelter income. These provisions have a long legislative history but were rewritten under the Rewrite Project. In the following discussion, where a case has been decided in relation to a statutory provision we refer to the actual provision considered in that case. Elsewhere the references are to ITA 2007 unless otherwise stated. In general terms, the net effect of the provisions is to 'look through' any offshore arrangement, deeming the income received to be that of the settlor/beneficiary. The *quantum* of the assessable income is, in general, the gross income received by the trustees.

The scope of what was then charged under ICTA 1988, s 739, which has been rewritten in ITA 2007, s 720, came under detailed scrutiny by the House of Lords in the case of *CIR v Willoughby* [1997] STC 995, [1997] 4 All ER 65 which concerned the tax treatment of offshore personal portfolio bonds (see **Chapter 7 Insurance** under **7.5**). It was held that in order for the provision to apply, it was essential that the transfer of assets should be made by an individual who was UK ordinarily resident at that time. Such a finding was consistent with the House of Lord's decision in *Vestey v CIR* [1980] STC 10, [1979] 3 All ER 976, but at variance with the earlier decisions of *Congreve v CIR* [1948] 1 All ER 948, 30 TC 163 (HL), and *Herdman v CIR* (1969) 45 TC 394 (HL) which the court declined to follow.

In *R v Allen; R v Dimsey* [2001] STC 1537 it was argued unsuccessfully that, because the transfer of income abroad provisions deem the income of a transferee company to be the transferor's, it was therefore also deemed not to be the transferee company's income. The House of Lords held that on the true construction of ICTA 1988, s 739(2) a foreign transferee of assets was not relieved of liability to tax on income.

Where an individual makes a relevant transfer of assets and as a result of the transfer or of associated operations, income becomes payable to a person abroad and the transferor has either power to enjoy that income (ITA 2007, s 720) or to receive a capital sum (ITA 2007, s 727), the income of the person abroad is treated as that of the transferor. There must be a relevant transfer of assets by an individual. This means a transfer of property or rights of any kind and includes shares or obligations of any company to which assets have been transferred or obligations of any other person to whom assets have been transferred. Second, as a result of the transfer, either alone or together with associated operations, income must become payable to a person abroad (ITA 2007, s 716). A person abroad is defined as a person who is resident or domiciled outside the UK. A UK resident company which is incorporated overseas, trustees treated as non-resident under ITA 2007, s 475(3) and personal representatives treated as non-resident under ITA 2007, s 834(4) are treated as being non-resident for the purposes of the transfer of asset abroad rules (ITA 2007, s 718). An associated operation is widely defined in ITA 2007, s 719.

An individual has the power to enjoy income if one of the enjoyment conditions in ITA 2007, s 723 is satisfied. Those provisions utilise the term 'benefit'; a term which is not defined in the legislation. It will include benefits in kind, such as the interest foregone on an interest-free loan, as well as straightforward distributions of capital. The Revenue considers that the free use of property is a 'benefit'. There used to be much debate as to whether or not an interest-free loan repayable on demand conferred a benefit on the recipient. Interestingly, in *Billingham v Cooper; Edwards v Fisher* [2001] STC 1177 the Court of Appeal held that, for the purposes of the capital payments charge under TCGA 1992, s 87, an interest-free loan to the life tenant repayable on demand was a benefit and by conferring such a benefit, a capital payment had been made under TCGA 1992, s 97. (The Special Commissioners had held that the benefit of such a loan was nil.) The appointment of a life interest is not a benefit within the meaning of the section because it is not 'provided out of assets' as required by the provisions (Law Society: agreed note of meeting with the Board of Inland Revenue 1981). Tax is charged on the 'amount of income treated as arising in the tax year'. Section 721 appears to support the view that it is the same income and not an amount equal to it, which is treated as arising.

In calculating the income which is chargeable under ITA 2007, ss 720 and 727, the transferor is only entitled to such deductions and reliefs as he would have been allowed had he actually received the income (ITA 2007, s 746). Trust management expenses are generally not deductible. Relief for foreign taxes is allowable only to the extent that such taxes would have been paid if the income had been received by the individual himself (ITA 2007, s 746). No relief is given if the foreign tax arose because the income was diverted abroad rather than having arisen there itself. Where a foreign investment holding company, owned by an offshore trust, itself owns UK shares and securities, the transferor will be assessed under ITA 2007, s 720 on dividends paid by the UK company and will receive the applicable tax credit to set against his UK taxation liability on the dividends.

The remittance basis for non-UK domiciliaries who are taxable under s 720 is preserved by ITA 2007, s 726. Section 726 provides that a non-UK domiciliary is not chargeable 'in respect of any income . . . if he would not, by reason of his being so domiciled, have been chargeable to tax in respect of it if it had in fact been his income'. HMRC has issued guidance on the interaction of the remittance basis with the transfer of assets provisions which can be found on its website.

ITA 2007, s 727 applies where, in connection with a transfer of assets abroad, an individual receives or is entitled to receive any capital sum whether before or after the relevant transfer. A capital sum is defined as a sum paid or payable by way of loan or repayment of a loan or any other sum (not being income) which is paid or payable otherwise than for full consideration in money or money's worth.

Defences

There are two defences to these anti-avoidance provisions which are now contained in ITA 2007, ss 737–742. For transactions which took place before 5 December 2005, an individual had to satisfy an officer of HMRC that:

(a) the purpose of avoiding tax was not the purpose, or one of the purposes for which the transactions were undertaken; or
(b) the transfer and any associated operations were genuine commercial transactions and were not designed for the purpose of avoiding tax.

The *Willoughby* decision provided further insight into the operation of the defence available under what was then ICTA 1988, s 741(1)(a). The House of Lords held that as the offshore policies or bonds held by Professor Willoughby were themselves subject to a separate statutory charging regime the transfers had not been effected with a view to avoiding income tax. Accordingly, it was also held that Professor Willoughby could avail himself of the defence set out in ICTA 1988, s 741(1)(a), as the transaction itself was entirely commercial.

Where a transfer and any associated operations take place after 4 December 2005 the conditions which must be satisfied are that an officer of HMRC must be satisfied that:

(a) it would not be reasonable to draw the conclusion, from all the circumstances of the case, that the purpose of avoiding liability to tax was the purpose, or one of the purposes, for which the relevant transactions were effected (Condition A); or

(b) all the relevant transactions were genuine commercial transactions and it would not be reasonable to draw the conclusion from all the circumstances of the case, that any one or more of those transactions was more than incidentally designed for the purpose of avoiding liability (Condition B).

A relevant transaction will only be a commercial transaction if it is effected in the course of a trade or business and for its purpose or with a view to setting up and commencing a trade or business and for its purpose (ITA 2007, s 738). A commercial transaction must not be on terms other than those that would have been made between unconnected parties dealing at arms' length or be a transaction that would not have been entered into between such persons so dealing.

The making and managing of investments is not 'commercial' except to the extent that the persons by whom and for whom the activity is carried on are unconnected persons dealing at arm's length.

The revised test has widened the scope of those whose intentions must be taken into account in ascertaining whether tax avoidance was a purpose of any arrangements. Such persons are those who design or effect the relevant transactions or provide advice in relation to the relevant transactions or any of them. This will include a tax adviser.

It should be noted that where there are transactions some of which were implemented before 5 December 2005 and some after, special rules apply.

The Special Commissioners case of *Burns v Revenue and Customs Comrs* [2009] STC (SCD) 165 is an example of a case where the motive defence failed.

ITA 2007, s 731 applies where, as a result of a transfer of assets, income becomes payable to a person abroad, and an ordinarily resident individual receives a benefit provided out of those assets. The provisions apply regardless of the tax status of the settlor, but are only relevant where the UK beneficiary is not otherwise liable to income tax under ITA 2007, ss 720 and 727. As is the case under ITA 2007, ss 720 and 727, the rule will only apply where there is a UK tax avoidance motive which leads to the creation of the structure, and taxpayers can therefore rely upon the same defences outlined above. ITA 2007, ss 735 and 735A adopt the remittance basis rules to determine the benefits assessable under s 731.

The rationale behind the legislation is to negate any tax advantage in permitting gross funds to accumulate offshore. In essence, the rules apply a remittance basis with UK beneficiaries paying tax when the benefit is received. If the trustees confer a benefit on a beneficiary at a time when they have undistributed income which could be used to benefit him, he is liable to income tax on the value of that benefit to the extent of the undistributed income. Where there is insufficient relevant income to match the value of a benefit, future receipts of relevant income can be set against the unmatched element of any benefit and will result in a liability to income tax arising at that time. Tax credits on UK dividend income cannot be utilised.

Generally, there is transparency under ITTOIA 2005, s 624 and ITA 2007, ss 720 and 727 so that if income is segregated and kept offshore, the capital can then be remitted to the UK tax free. It is therefore essential that income and capital are kept separate at all times. It is generally safer to pay the income by way of dividend or an appointment to a non-resident beneficiary before any benefit is made available to a beneficiary resident in the UK. If this is not done, beneficiaries other than the settlor or his spouse may be subject to income tax under ITA 2007, s 731 if they receive a benefit.

Capital v income

[19.30] Where ITA 2007, ss 720 and 727 or the income tax settlement rules apply, as distinct from cases where ITA 2007, s 731 is in point, it is usually beneficial for offshore trusts established by non-domiciled individuals to realise capital rather than income related profits. Whilst the settlor retains his non-UK domicile, capital gains will not be assessable on an arising basis by virtue of TCGA 1992, s 86 but will be charged when matched with capital payments under s 87 and then only when remitted. Section 87B contains complex provisions applying the remittance rules to gains otherwise chargeable under s 87.

The offshore fund rules provide an instance of where an apparent capital profit has an income nature for UK tax purposes. The rules for taxing gains on offshore funds were changed with effect from 1 December 2009 and are now governed by the Offshore Funds (Tax) Regulations 2009 (SI 2009/3001).

A charge to tax arises following the disposal of an interest in an offshore fund which is a non-reporting fund and on reporting funds which have previous been non-reporting funds unless an election was made at the time of the conversion. An offshore insurance policy is not an offshore fund (Offshore Funds (Tax) Regulations 2009 (SI 2009/3001), reg 25). Transitional provisions apply in respect of interests held before 1 December 2002.

The family home

[19.31] One of the main considerations of a non-resident proposing to take up long-term residence in the UK will be where he is going to live in the UK. This will normally be settled (at least in principle) before he arrives, even though the purchase of an actual property may not be completed until after his arrival. It is unlikely that an individual and his family will want to live with relatives or friends or in rented accommodation or a hotel for any appreciable period of time.

The straightforward solution will be for the individual to purchase a property in his own name or in the joint names of his wife and himself. This means that the property will on his death (regardless of domicile because it is a UK situs asset) be wholly within the scope of inheritance tax. If he leaves the property under his will (or his share in it as a tenant in common) to his wife, or if he and his wife are joint tenants, there will be no inheritance tax liability on the property until the death of the survivor of them. However, there will only be a limited spouse exemption of £55,000 if the surviving spouse or civil partner is not domiciled in the UK but the deceased spouse or civil partner was (IHTA 1984, s 18(2)). In such circumstances the property will be subject to inheritance tax on the first spouse's death, subject to the exemption. It may therefore be preferable for the property to be bought in the name of the non-domiciled spouse or civil partner and left by will to the domiciled spouse or civil partner.

Owned by a company

[19.32] In the past, a wealthy, non-domiciled individual was usually advised that UK property should be acquired by a non-resident company, the shares in which should be owned by a trust established by the individual before he acquired a UK domicile. The trust would be created and funded before the individual took up residence in the UK. The property could be purchased afterwards. This arrangement was designed to convert the property into 'excluded property' for inheritance tax purposes under IHTA 1984, s 48(3) and therefore avoid inheritance tax. There are, however, a number of difficulties and uncertainties in such an arrangement.

Income tax charge

[19.33] Care must be taken to avoid (as far as is possible) the individual incurring a tax liability under ITEPA 2003, ss 97, 102. These provisions treat the value of any living accommodation provided for an employee (including a director of a company) or his family by his employer as a taxable emolument.

For some years the Revenue has held that, where an individual has a controlling shareholding in a non-resident company which holds a UK property in which the individual lives, an income tax charge on earnings from employment can arise. This is on the basis that the individual is a shadow director of the company and, as such, his employment is an employment for the purposes of the income tax earnings and benefits provisions (see HMRC Employment Income Manual para EIM11413).

In *R v Dimsey; R v Allen* [2001] STC 1537 (HL), it was argued by the defendant that because a shadow director has no 'actual emoluments' and no 'actual duties', he would not have an employment falling within the earnings from employment provisions. This argument was rejected. It was held that a shadow director is taxable on the benefit of living accommodation in the same way as a director under ICTA 1988, ss 145 and 154 (now ITEPA 2003, ss 97–113) which provided that the benefit was an emolument of the director's office. It is clear that all earnings from employment provisions apply to shadow directors.

In the non-tax case of *Secretary of State for Trade and Industry v Deverall* [2000] 2 WLR 987, it was suggested that the shadow director test was even wider than had been thought up until then. It was suggested that a person can be a shadow director if he simply made suggestions to the formal board which were followed through even if the suggestions did not cover the whole activities of the company. However, it would seem that the width of this principle has been restricted by *Ultraframe v Fielding* [2005] EWHC 1638. In that case it was held that for a person to be classified as a shadow director there must be some substantive course of influence or instruction given or exercised by the individual to the actual board of directors over a period of time regarding substantive matters.

The relief from the employment benefit charge provided in relation to foreign accommodation by ITEPA 2003, ss 100A and 100B does not apply to UK property.

Does that mean that using offshore companies to hold UK property for non-UK domiciled but resident individuals will necessarily result in an earnings from employment charge? No, it does not. *Dimsey* concerned a situation in which it had been found as a fact by the High Court that the defendants had centrally managed and controlled the offshore company in the UK. The defendants were, therefore, clearly shadow directors. There can be no assessment unless an individual resident in the UK is a person in accordance with whose instructions or directions the directors of the company are accustomed to act. Any reputable offshore company management business will ensure that they do not simply accept instructions from shareholders or follow their advice without independent thought or enquiry.

The taxpayer will have added protection on this point if the offshore company is in turn owned by an offshore trust in which he has only a limited interest. Even so, HMRC may still argue that the company's board acts in accordance with the taxpayer's instructions.

Provided the property is held in an excluded property trust, the pre-owned assets income tax charge cannot arise (however, see **19.36** below).

Use of loans

[19.34] As an alternative, a property could be purchased by an individual in his own name and financed by way of a 100% loan charged on the property. This will effectively reduce the initial value of the property to nil for inheritance tax purposes, although any increase in value in the property will be within the scope of the inheritance tax charge.

For a non-domiciled individual who currently occupies a UK property owned by an offshore company which in turn is owned by an offshore trust, the directors of the offshore company could sell the property to a new offshore bare trust for a promissory note in the form of a deed governed by an appropriate law. If the 'specialty' debt is kept outside the United Kingdom, it will have the effect of stripping out the initial value of the UK property and transferring it into the form of a foreign situs security. There are, however, a number of difficulties with such an arrangement.

The offshore company on selling the property to the new trust, will make a disposal for capital gains tax purposes and may realise a gain on the sale, as a result of which there will be a double-tiered gain in respect of the company shares in the trust. It is possible that these double gains will ultimately be distributed to UK-domiciled beneficiaries who will be taxed under TCGA

1992, s 87 and may also incur a supplementary charge. If the property is transferred back to the settlor for the settlor to settle the specialty debt on new offshore trusts, a pre-owned asset charge may arise. In the case of a person who is UK resident but non-UK domiciled, the pre-owned asset charge will apply if the property which has been transferred is land, chattels or intangible property situated in the UK. The charge does not apply, however, where the property in question is excluded property falling within IHTA 1984, s 48(3) (FA 2004, Sch 15 para 12). These measures are considered in more detail in **CHAPTER 20 THE OVERSEAS CLIENT**. The sale of the property to an offshore trust will result in a stamp duty land tax charge of up to 4% depending upon the amount of the consideration.

Where a UK property is purchased by a relevant property trust, a decennial charge may be triggered under the inheritance tax rules under IHTA 1984, Ch III. One might avoid the charge by transferring the property to an underlying offshore company for a short period before and after the decennial. This strategy, however, involves a transfer to a connected company and will create a stamp duty land tax charge of up to 4% and may create a benefit in kind charge. Consideration also needs to be given to the exit charge under IHTA 1984, s 65 and in particular to the provisions of subsection (7).

There was a concern that the transfer pricing rules in ICTA 1988, Sch 28AA could apply to such a structure. These rules apply where any provision in a transaction made between two different persons differs from what it would have been had the transaction been at arms' length, and results in a potential UK tax advantage to one of those persons. For the legislation to apply at the time of making the provision, one of the two persons must directly or indirectly control the other. One might consider that this condition would not be satisfied if a company is owned by overseas trustees. However, ICTA 1988, Sch 28AA para 4 provides that the rights and powers of connected persons can be taken into account and it is specifically stated that the trustees of the settlement are a connected person with the settlor. There is a potential UK tax advantage to the offshore company as, if the company had charged rent for the property, it would have a UK source of income and therefore be liable to UK income tax. The Revenue has stated however, that it will not take this point (Taxation, 1 April 1999, p 5).

Use of offshore funds

[19.35] Another possibility involves using an offshore fund. In such a situation, an individual could sell his UK property for a cash sum to an offshore fund to which he is not connected. The consideration would be satisfied by both a grant of a lease for life for the vendor in the property and units in the fund. Stamp duty land tax would be payable by the fund on the sale. The lease for life which is for full consideration is not a deemed settlement under IHTA 1984, s 43(3) and will cease on the death of the individual. The individual could then make a gift of the units to, say, his children which would be a PET. The value of the units would relate to the lease for life and would increase significantly on the client's death. It would appear that the pre-owned assets charge would not apply because of the full consideration exemption.

Income tax charge on pre-owned assets

[19.36] The income tax charge on pre-owned assets does not apply in relation to any person in any year of assessment during which he is not resident in the UK. In such a case a person's domicile is immaterial. The charge may still apply to a UK resident but non-domiciled person in certain circumstances, even if the individual has no other UK-source income. In that case the individual will be required to make an income tax return declaring the benefit. Where, however, such a person makes a transfer of property which is land or chattels or of intangible property comprised in a settlement which is not situated in the UK the charge will not apply.

Example

Bruce is UK-resident for the tax year 2009/10 but is not UK domiciled (or deemed domiciled). Bruce has given his house in Sydney, Australia to his son from which he derives a benefit. In 2001, Bruce gave his London flat to his daughter. He will be living in the flat in 2009 and intends paying rent to his daughter on an informal basis.

The pre-owned assets rules will not apply to the house in Sydney because the property is situated outside the UK. He will be subject to a charge to income tax on his occupation of the London flat from 6 April 2009 and subsequent fiscal years. As the rent paid by Bruce to his daughter is not under a formal agreement, it will not be deductible against the market rental value on which the income tax charge will be based.

There is a further exemption for property which is excluded property for the purposes of IHTA 1984, s 48(3)(a) in relation to the person making the transfer. There is some uncertainty as to whether an individual is subject to the pre-owned asset charge when he becomes deemed to be domiciled in the UK. The Revenue says that 'even if that person becomes domiciled in the United Kingdom at a later date his property will remain excluded from the charge' (Income Tax and Pre-Owned Asset Guidance).

Example

Xavier has been resident in the UK for 10 years and he retains his French domicile of origin. In 1998, Xavier established a family discretionary trust and an offshore company to hold his Spanish residence which he occupies.

In 2009/10 he will not be subject to any income tax charge because he is not domiciled or deemed domiciled in a country of the UK. When he becomes deemed UK domiciled, in the Revenue's view he will not be subject to an income tax charge on his occupation because the Spanish property is excluded from charge.

The charge to income tax has incorporated, for the purposes of the charge, the inheritance tax concept of deemed domicile. Many commentators have regarded the import of inheritance tax rules into the income tax legislation in this way as an undesirable and anomalous development.

The Short-term visitor

General points

[19.37] This section deals with the short-term visitor who becomes resident in the UK but does not acquire a UK domicile.

(a) He should ensure that his behaviour does not suggest that he is acquiring a domicile in the UK, otherwise he might be subjected to time consuming enquiries from HMRC.

(b) He should keep his assets in the UK to a minimum (ideally below the threshold for the actual payment of inheritance tax). For instance, his main bank account should be held abroad rather than in the UK.

(c) He may need to purchase accommodation in the UK. This can be arranged either through a non-UK resident trust structure, or through a direct purchase in his own name or in the joint names of himself and his wife by means of a non-UK loan charged on the property. The loan (plus any accrued interest) should be repaid in a fiscal year after he has ceased to be resident in the UK. He should not repay any principal or interest on the loan while he is resident in the UK. He may consider purchasing a property, in his own name or in joint names, and effect life assurance (outside the UK) to provide funds to meet any inheritance tax liability in respect of the property either on his death or, if the property is in joint names, or on the death of the survivor of him and his wife. The holding of UK situs assets through the medium of a non-resident company owned by the individual will be enough on its own to take the assets outside the scope of inheritance tax, but where the property is the individual's residence, the fact that no trust is interposed between the individual and the company may make it more difficult for him to counter an attack under ITEPA 2003, ss 97 and 102 — see under **19.33** above. This is because the individual will have a much greater connection with the company and its directors by reason of his ownership of the company's shares.

(d) Funds required in the UK should be obtained by remitting capital from abroad. Care should be taken, through separate capital and income bank accounts, to demonstrate that remittances have clearly been made from a capital source unless income can be remitted free of UK tax under a double tax treaty.

The short-term visitor is not within the inheritance tax regime except in relation to UK assets. Even then he may be protected under a double tax treaty. However, he will probably still be subject to the tax and succession laws of his home country in which case his scope for estate planning may well be governed by those laws. He should, therefore, take advice in that country, as well as in the UK, before taking any steps whilst in the UK.

The long-term emigrant

General points

[19.38] An individual leaving the UK is not in a position to make disposals of assets which are outside the scope of inheritance tax until he has lost his UK domicile and his deemed UK domicile. Even if he loses his domicile under the general law (ie he acquires an overseas domicile of choice) soon after leaving the UK, under IHTA 1984, s 267 he will have to wait for at least 3 calendar years (and, in most cases, three complete tax years) before his property will be excluded property. See under **19.4** above.

Even the transfer of non-UK *situs* assets will not avoid inheritance tax until the donor has ceased to be domiciled in the UK and three years have elapsed. However, the transfer of certain British Government securities ('exempt gilts') may be made free of inheritance tax by a person not domiciled in the UK under the general law even if he is deemed to be domiciled here under IHTA 1984, s 267(1). A way of reducing the value of assets after an individual has emigrated may be to borrow on the security of such assets and to invest the borrowed funds in exempt gilts. Alternatively, a possibly more cost effective solution would be to cover the inheritance tax liability which would arise if the emigrant died within the relevant three year period by entering into a term insurance policy written in trust for the benefit of his heirs.

A potentially exempt transfer made when the donor was domiciled in the UK will still be chargeable even if he is no longer domiciled in the UK at his death within the seven-year period.

A relevant question in planning for the emigrant is where the individual's heirs live. If they live in the UK estate planning will still be substantially affected by inheritance tax and other UK taxes, but generally it will be possible for a non-domiciled individual (ie an individual who has shed his UK domicile under the general law for at least three years) to give or bequeath non-UK property to his heirs who are resident in the UK, or to set up an offshore trust for them, without liability to inheritance tax.

It is very important for the emigrant to have a clear understanding of the tax regime of his new country before he leaves the UK. There may well be timing considerations and action might need to be taken before residence is taken up in the new country (for example, the creation of a discretionary trust to avoid taxes in that country). On the other hand, if such action is taken too soon it will involve an inheritance tax liability since the emigrant will not have shed his UK domicile. A temporary period in a 'third' country will probably not be helpful in that a domicile of choice will not be acquired there. It is often possible to devise an arrangement which has advantages in both the UK and the new country, but each case must be considered carefully on its precise facts.

If the emigrant is a beneficiary under a foreign trust, there could be timing problems in obtaining distributions of income or capital from the trust. Generally, from the UK tax viewpoint, distributions should be delayed until he becomes non-resident, but by then he may be resident in another country and the distributions subjected to tax in that country. Again, every case has to be examined on its own particular facts.

Where a person is considering emigrating, it is often advisable to defer the setting up of any settlements until the UK domicile is lost to retain complete flexibility and to avoid locking the trust assets into the UK tax net.

The short-term emigrant

General points

[19.39] A person who ceases to be resident or ordinarily resident in the UK for a period, for example, through full-time employment abroad which lasts for a period including a full tax year, is likely to remain domiciled in the UK and therefore subject to the inheritance tax regime in the same way as any UK domiciliary. Therefore, opportunities for estate planning generally are no greater than for a UK resident. It may be possible, however, for an individual working abroad and earning a large salary which is subject only to low local income tax to make substantial regular gifts out of his net income which would be exempt from inheritance tax under the 'normal expenditure' exemption (IHTA 1984, s 21). To take advantage of this exemption, it is advisable that the individual should not simply make regular voluntary gifts but instead create a commitment to do so (for example, by effecting life policies in trust involving regular premium payments or by entering into an agreement to make regular payments). However, consideration should be given to the individual's ability to continue to meet the payments when the individual returns to the UK and has a lower net surplus income.

Chapter 20

The Overseas Client

Introduction

[20.1] This chapter deals with a foreign individual who does not himself become resident or domiciled in the UK, but becomes involved with UK laws and with actual or potential liabilities to UK taxation through:

(a) the ownership of assets in the UK; or
(b) the wish to benefit persons resident in the UK.

It is assumed that the individual is and remains domiciled, resident and ordinarily resident outside the UK. For a consideration of the meaning of these terms, and the concept of 'deemed domicile' which applies only for inheritance tax purposes and for the purposes of the income tax charge on pre-owned assets, see **CHAPTER 19 THE INTERNATIONALLY MOBILE.**

Tax considerations

Inheritance tax

[20.2] Where a foreign individual directly owns an asset in the UK, there may be an inheritance tax charge where there is a lifetime transfer of the asset or in the event of the individual's death. Of course, one of the exemptions under IHTA 1984, Pt II may apply. Those exemptions include:

(a) transfers between spouses;
(b) the annual exemption;
(c) small gifts;
(d) normal expenditure out of income;
(e) gifts in consideration of marriage; and
(f) gifts to charities or political parties or for national purposes or public benefit.

An asset may also be eligible for business property relief, agricultural property relief or relief on woodlands under IHTA 1984, Pt V.

For example, if a foreign individual gives or bequeaths an asset to his spouse (wherever she is domiciled) or to a body recognised as a charity, the transfer will be exempt, and if he invests in agricultural or business property he may be eligible for the appropriate relief. For further details see **CHAPTER 2 LIFETIME PLANNING** (for exemptions), **CHAPTER 10 THE FAMILY BUSINESS, CHAPTER 11**

The Family Farm and **Chapter 12 Woodlands**. However, from a capital gains tax perspective, a capital gains tax charge can arise on disposals made by non-UK residents of UK sited trading-related assets (TCGA 1992, s 10) (see below).

A foreign individual may make a lifetime transfer of a UK asset by accident (for example, a sale at an undervalue) or without his realising the implications of a particular transfer. It will be more usual for him to die owning a UK asset. Very often he will have acquired the asset without much thought as to the possibility of UK inheritance tax being payable in the event of his death. Not all countries levy a charge to tax on death or, where they do, at rates as high as in the UK. Alternatively, foreign tax on death may operate as a true inheritance tax, under which it is the recipient of the bequeathed property who is charged to tax, rather than the estate.

Excluded property

[20.3] Certain property situated in the UK is excluded from the scope of inheritance tax.

(a) Under IHTA 1984, s 6(2), certain British Government securities (known as 'exempt gilts') are excluded property for inheritance tax purposes if they are in the beneficial ownership of a person ordinarily resident outside the UK. Domicile is irrelevant for this purpose. Gilts can be used by individuals to avoid inheritance tax on their assets in the event that they die within the three years of their departure from the UK (IHTA 1984, s 267(1), (2)).

(b) Under IHTA 1984, s 6(3) certain property owned by a person who is domiciled in the Channel Islands or the Isle of Man is exempt. The property so exempted consists of war savings certificates, national savings certificates, premium bonds, deposits with the National Savings Bank or a trustee savings bank and any certified SAYE savings arrangements within ITTOIA 2005, s 703(1).
Under IHTA 1984, s 6(1A), holdings in authorised unit trusts and shares in open-ended investment companies are excluded property, provided the person beneficially entitled to them is an individual domiciled outside the UK.

(c) Exemption from inheritance tax on death is given by IHTA 1984, s 157 to a qualifying foreign currency bank account, held at a bank or post office in the UK, which is owned by a person who immediately before his death was not domiciled, resident or ordinarily resident in the UK.

(d) Certain property owned in the UK by visiting forces and staff of allied headquarters (IHTA 1984, ss 6 and 155).

Capital gains tax

[20.4] The disposal of an asset situated in the UK by a foreign individual will not generally give rise to a capital gains tax liability. This is because a person is chargeable to capital gains tax in respect of chargeable gains accruing to him in a year of assessment during any part of which he is resident in the UK, or during which he is ordinarily resident in the UK (TCGA 1992, s 2(1)).

However, TCGA 1992, s 10 provides that a person who is neither resident nor ordinarily resident in the UK *will* be chargeable to capital gains tax on gains accruing to him on a disposal, at a time when he is carrying on a trade in the UK through a branch or agency, of:

(a) assets in the UK used in or for the purposes of the trade at or before that time;
(b) assets in the UK used or held for the purposes of the branch or agency; and
(c) assets acquired for use by or for the purposes of the branch or agency. It would seem that on a strict reading of the legislation this charge applies whether or not the asset is situated in the UK. The Revenue's view, however, appears to be that the charge applies only to UK-situated assets (Revenue Capital Gains Manual CG25520).

A chargeable gain can arise in respect of such assets where the non-resident person ceases to carry on the trade, profession or vocation through the branch or agency or the assets become situated outside the UK (TCGA 1992, s 25). In practice, it is possible to side-step these rules. Generally speaking, the trading entity should be kept apart from the entity which holds the valuable asset likely to generate the gain. Farming activities would represent a typical example where land could be held by an entity other than the one which is going to farm it.

TCGA 1992, s 10A provides that individuals who have acquired assets before they leave the UK for a period of residence abroad of less than five complete tax years will remain chargeable to capital gains tax on gains made on those assets while abroad. Gains made after the year of departure will be chargeable in the year of return. These provisions will apply if the following conditions are satisfied.

(i) The individual is a previous resident of the UK who is resuming tax residence in the UK.
(ii) The individual has been resident outside the UK for less than five complete tax years between the year of departure and the year of return.
(iii) The individual was resident or ordinarily resident in the UK for some part of at least four of the seven years preceding the year of departure.

Income tax

[20.5] A foreign individual will be liable to UK income tax on income arising from a source in the UK.

The income tax charge on pre-owned assets is only chargeable upon persons who are resident in the UK for the tax year in which the charge arises. Accordingly, a non-UK resident is outside the scope of the charge. The incidence of the charge on UK resident non-domiciliaries is discussed in further detail in **CHAPTER 19 THE INTERNATIONALLY MOBILE**.

Double tax agreements

[20.6] The liability of a foreign individual, or his estate, to inheritance tax, capital gains tax and income tax may be relieved or modified under a double tax agreement between the UK and his country of residence. For example, the provisions of TCGA 1992, s 10 (see above) do not apply to a person who under any relevant double tax agreement is exempt from income tax for the particular year of assessment in respect of his profits from the branch or agency. Nothing in the terms of any double tax agreement can be read as having effect to prevent a tax charge under TCGA 1992, s 10A. Relief will be given in the usual way in respect of any foreign tax paid in respect of any gains arising.

Generally, the small number of double tax agreements which cover inheritance tax, deal with its interaction with similar taxes in other jurisdictions by determining the domicile of an individual for the purposes of the agreement and allowing primary taxing rights to the country in which the individual is so domiciled. Certain old double taxation agreements contain their own rules for determining domicile and for resolving the issue where both countries claim domicile. HMRC accepts that domicile determined under these agreements override deemed domicile. The Revenue accepts this is the position when considering the double tax agreements with France, Italy, India and Pakistan, although if a person is domiciled under the general law in Italy, India or Pakistan, the deemed domicile rules can apply to chargeable lifetime transfers (HMRC Inheritance Tax Manual, para 13024). Charges on the basis of situs are usually restricted to land and business property. There are currently ten double tax agreements applying to, or capable of applying to, inheritance tax between the UK and the Irish Republic, France, India, Italy, the Netherlands, Pakistan, South Africa, Sweden, Switzerland and the United States of America. It should be noted that Pakistan has no tax on death and India has no effective inheritance tax. Therefore if the domicile of an individual is determined under the treaty with either Pakistan or India as being outside the UK, any property which is situated outside the UK will not be subject to UK inheritance tax and it will not be subject to an equivalent tax in Pakistan or India.

In the absence of a relevant double tax agreement, the Revenue will allow unilateral relief by way of credit for a foreign tax similar in character to inheritance tax which has been imposed on property upon a disposition or event on which inheritance tax is chargeable in respect of the same property (IHTA 1984, s 159).

Planning points

[20.7] It is now appropriate to consider whether it is possible to avoid any of the liabilities to UK taxation discussed above for a foreign individual who wishes, for whatever reason, to own assets in this country.

It is possible for inheritance tax to be avoided on a UK asset if it is owned by a company incorporated outside the UK rather than by a foreign individual directly. This arrangement ensures that the individual holds a non-UK asset (his shares in the foreign company) rather than the UK asset directly. The shares will be 'excluded property' (by virtue of IHTA 1984, s 6(1)). This will generally be sufficient protection against inheritance tax for a foreign individual who is never likely to become domiciled in the UK. Care should be taken when UK land is being transferred to a connected company as a stamp duty land tax charge based on market value can arise. This is discussed in more detail in **CHAPTER 19, THE INTERNATIONALLY MOBILE.**

Such a company structure runs the risk of the Revenue attempting to impose an income tax charge under ITEPA 2003, ss 97 and 102 where living accommodation owned by the company is provided to an individual. The possible impact of these provisions is discussed in detail in **CHAPTER 19 THE INTERNATIONALLY MOBILE** under **19.33**. There can be no charge under these sections where the individual is neither resident nor ordinarily resident in the UK, unless he performs any of his duties as a director or 'deemed director' in the UK. In the case of a 'deemed director' it is hard to see what duties he would be likely to perform in the UK and there would therefore seem to be little scope for the charge to bite. There used also to be a concern that the extension of the transfer pricing rules introduced by the Finance Act 1998 could apply to such a structure. The Revenue has, however, stated that it will not take this point. This is discussed in more detail in **CHAPTER 19 THE INTERNATIONALLY MOBILE.**

Another method of reducing exposure to inheritance tax on death in respect of a UK asset would be to borrow in the UK for the purposes of the investment so that on death the value of the loan could be deducted from the value of the UK assets (IHTA 1984, ss 5 and 162). A loan could also be taken out abroad, to reduce the net estate chargeable to inheritance tax but it would need to be secured by a charge on property situated in the UK (IHTA 1984, s 162(5)).

If the UK asset has already been bought, a loan secured by a charge on the asset could still be taken out and then the funds invested in excluded property, for example, in exempt gilts (see above).

Inheritance tax will not be payable on a UK asset owned by an individual who is not domiciled in the UK if it passes to his spouse on his death, either under his will or under the relevant succession laws or through the right of survivorship under a joint tenancy.

A foreign individual may consider it worthwhile to take out life assurance to provide funds to meet an inheritance tax liability in respect of UK assets in the event of his death. Any such policy should either be effected outside the UK or written in trust to avoid the proceeds being treated as part of his taxable estate in the UK.

Other considerations

Probate

[20.8] If an individual dies owning assets in the UK, it will usually be necessary for a grant of probate or letters of administration to be obtained in this country. This will normally be an ancillary grant to the administration of the deceased's estate in his home country, issued to the person(s) entitled to administer the deceased's estate under the law of his home country. The procedure involves submitting an account of the UK assets to the Revenue, together with a statement giving the reason why it is considered that the deceased died domiciled in a foreign country. No grant will be issued until all the tax due is paid. All this can involve time and expense, which may be disproportionate to the size of the UK estate. For example, the proceeds of a UK bank account will not be released by the bank without production of a UK grant of probate. It is also unwise for any UK assets to be disposed of or transferred abroad without production of a UK grant and without the tax position having been settled, since the person so disposing of or transferring the asset may be treated as an executor *de son tort* and accountable for any inheritance tax payable (*New York Breweries Co Ltd v A-G* [1899] AC 62).

A will in respect of which a grant of probate has been issued is a public document which can be inspected by anyone. Double tax agreements often permit the exchange of information between two Revenue authorities. The administration of the UK estate of a foreign individual can result in the exchange of information between the relevant authorities. Therefore, where UK assets are owned, consideration should be given to making a will governed by UK law dealing solely with those assets.

There are generally no ways of avoiding these considerations for a foreign individual who wishes to own UK assets beneficially himself. The use of a UK nominee to hold the assets on his behalf will not avoid the need to obtain a grant of probate (or letters of administration) nor the payment of UK taxes. The use of a foreign nominee may avoid the need for a grant of probate although the nominee may itself constitute an executor *de son tort* if it deals with the assets following the death (see *IRC v Stype Investments (Jersey) Ltd* [1982] Ch 456, [1982] 3 All ER 419; [1982] 3 WLR 228). This structure does not avoid the obligation to submit an account of the assets for inheritance tax purposes, and to pay the tax due.

Where the only UK asset is a joint bank account, on the death of one of the owners its ownership will automatically pass to the survivor. The bank will normally only want to see the death certificate and not a UK grant of probate. If, however, the survivor is not the deceased's spouse there will be a duty to submit an inheritance tax account and pay any liability due (unless the account is a qualifying foreign currency bank account which is exempt from inheritance tax, see under **20.3** above).

The safest way to avoid the need to obtain a UK grant of probate is for the foreign individual to incorporate a company outside the UK to own the property as discussed earlier in the chapter. In the event of the death of the owner of the company a grant of probate would not be necessary as the company's shares would not be UK *situs* assets.

For foreign investors wishing to invest in shares in UK companies, there are various types of offshore collective investment schemes which avoid the problems of directly owning assets located in the UK.

Benefitting persons resident in the UK

Outright gifts

[20.9] The simplest way in which a foreign individual can benefit a person resident in the UK is to make a gift to such a person of non-UK assets, eg foreign currency or foreign investments, which are subsequently remitted to the UK by the donee as desired. A gift made in this way will not involve any inheritance tax liability. For capital gains tax purposes, the donee will have acquired the asset given to him on the date of the gift at its market value on that date.

It is important to ensure that any gift of cash is made in a way which avoids the gift being of a UK asset and therefore liable to inheritance tax. A payment made from a bank account situated in the UK will be liable to inheritance tax as will a gift of the beneficial ownership of the whole or a part of the balance on the account. Conversely, a payment made from a bank account held outside the UK or the gift of the beneficial ownership of the whole or part of the balance on the account will not be so liable regardless of whether the account is denominated in sterling.

Offshore settlements

[20.10] If the foreign donor does not wish to make outright gifts to his beneficiaries in the UK, or his objective is to benefit his beneficiaries in the most tax efficient way, he may consider establishing a trust with trustees who are not resident or ordinarily resident, in the UK. Assuming that he settles non-UK assets, the creation of the trust will not involve any UK tax liability. During its life the trust will not usually attract any liability to inheritance tax, assuming that its funds continue to consist entirely of foreign assets. This applies regardless of the type of trust used. Disposals by the trustees resident outside the UK will not be liable to UK capital gains tax. However, the capital payments charge will apply where capital payments are made to beneficiaries who are both resident in the UK when the gain is deemed to accrue to them. (TCGA 1992, s 87), subject to the remittance basis.

If income is distributed to UK resident beneficiaries, they will be liable to income tax in the normal way, unless they are non-UK domiciled and the remittance basis applies. If benefits, which are not otherwise liable to income tax, are given by the trustees to a beneficiary ordinarily resident in the UK, he will be liable to income tax to the extent that the value of the benefit falls within the 'relevant income' of the trust, but only if UK tax avoidance is the motive for the transfer (ITA 2007, s 731). This is subject to relief being given for a non-domiciled beneficiary where there has been no remittance of the relevant income to, and the benefit was not received in, the UK. This will catch, for example, capital payments to a beneficiary ordinarily resident in the UK, if income has been accumulated in the trust (or in any underlying foreign company) rather than distributed.

With regard to the trustees, provided at least one trustee is resident outside the UK, *all* of them will be treated as resident outside the UK for income and capital gains tax purposes as the settlor is non-resident and non-domiciled in the UK (ITA 2007, s 475). Therefore they will only be liable to tax on UK source income.

UK settlements

[20.11] It may also be worth considering a trust with UK resident trustees. Inheritance tax may be avoided if non-UK assets are settled and retained throughout the life of the trust.

ITA 2007, s 731 has no application to a trust with UK resident trustees. However, the trustees will be liable to UK income tax on all trust income in the normal way. Income of most UK resident trusts will be liable to tax at 50% year by year, subject to the special rate of 42.5% on dividends. An offshore trust will not normally be so liable (assuming it does not have UK source income) but income tax liabilities may arise under ITA 2007, s 731. Care is required in particular where an offshore trust subject to ITA 2007, s 731 is imported into the UK. Whilst in general terms the trust will not normally generate 'fresh' relevant income, importation does not cause any previously retained income to cease to be 'relevant income'.

Conclusions

[20.12] For the wealthy foreign individual it may be appropriate to have both a trust in the UK and a trust abroad, both of which might include UK residents as beneficiaries. The former would be regarded as a 'spending' fund (ie the capital and income would be paid out to the beneficiaries as necessary), and the latter would be a 'roll-up' fund with neither capital nor income being remitted to the UK except in emergency situations.

The foreign individual who wishes to benefit beneficiaries resident in the UK should take advice in his home country regardless of the type of structure proposed to ensure that he is aware of the tax and other implications of his proposed action in that country as well as the UK.

The foreign individual who on his death wishes to benefit persons resident in the UK should also be advised to consider setting up, by his will, a continuing trust (probably outside the UK) rather than making outright bequests which would bring the property bequeathed into the UK tax net. The trust could either be contained in the will itself or be established by the individual during his lifetime, with his will simply directing the relevant assets into the trust.

Chapter 21

A Lifetime of Planning — A Case Study

In this chapter we provide an example of estate planning throughout an adult life. All statutory references are to IHTA 1984 unless otherwise stated. For the sake of simplicity it is assumed that tax legislation will remain unchanged over the period covered by the example and in particular that the nil rate band will remain at £325,000. Inflation is ignored. This assumption is of course unrealistic. Taking account of likely legislative changes and changes in the value of assets and of money is an important element of inheritance tax planning. In an example dealing with tax planning over the whole of an individual's adult life, however, it would be entirely artificial to attempt to guess at the legislative changes which will be made over that period.

Early adulthood

Family

[21.1] Henry Clerestory is the eldest son of David and Eleanor Clerestory. He was born on 30 June 1985. He has just completed a commission in the Guards after coming down from University and is about to start work in an environmental consultancy.

Henry's father, David, was born on 30 January 1935 and is therefore 75 years old. David is a widower and has two other children, Richard and Caroline who are one and two years younger than Henry respectively.

Assets

[21.2] Henry has no substantial assets of his own but he has an interest in a settlement.

Interests in settlements

David Clerestory's 18th birthday settlements

[21.3] As each of his children reached his or her 18th birthday, David Clerestory settled £100,000 on trusts giving the child concerned an interest in possession subject to a wide power of appointment exercisable by the trustees in favour of a beneficial class consisting of Henry, Richard, Caroline and their issue. Each settlement was named after the child concerned. Each child took out a unit linked whole of life policy on his or her life with Insco Plc paying a premium of £1,000 and immediately assigned the policy to the trustees in consideration of a payment of £1,000. The trustees then paid an additional premium of £99,000.

Each policy was in the conventional form. That is, it matured on the death of the life assured and could be surrendered, in whole or in part, at any time. The premiums paid under the policy were notionally invested in assets of Insco accounted for as 'units'. The surrender benefits were to be calculated as the amount which would be realised on a disposal of these units and the maturity benefit was 101% of the amount which would have been paid on a surrender taking place at the time of maturity. The contract provided that additional premiums could be paid by any person at any time up to the time of the maturity or final surrender of the policy.

The trusts made by David Clerestory are existing IIPs. David Clerestory is a very wealthy man and although he is in good health he is conscious that at the age of 75 his life expectancy is quite short. In fact based on actuarial tables he has a life expectancy of just under 10 years. He therefore wishes to make some transfers in favour of his children but he does not want them to have unfettered control of large amounts of money. He therefore pays an additional premium of £100,000 in respect of each of the three policies with Insco held on the trusts of the three settlements.

These payments are transfers of value by David Clerestory because they reduce his estate.

Each of the insurance contracts satisfies the conditions of s 46A, because:

(a) each settlement commenced before 22 March 2006;
(b) each contract of insurance was entered into before that day;
(c) each added premium is payable under the contract on or after 22 March 2006;
(d) immediately before 22 March 2006 and at all subsequent times up to the payment of the premium, there were rights under the insurance contract which were comprised in the settlement and those rights were settled property in which a transitionally protected interest subsisted. That was because the same person had had an interest in possession in the contract continuously since before 22 March 2006;
(e) enhanced rights under the contract have become comprised in the settlement by reference to the premium because the premium increases both the surrender and maturity benefits payable under the policy;
(f) there has been no variation of the contract, or if one argued that the payment of the premium was a variation, it was one that increased the benefits secured by the contract and was an allowed variation. That is, the payment of the premiums took place as a result of the exercise of rights conferred by provisions which formed part of the contract immediately before 22 March 2006.

Because s 46A applies to the insurance contract held by the settlement the payment of the premium does not prevent the rights under the contract from being treated for inheritance tax purposes as having become comprised in the settlement before 22 March 2006 and the beneficiary from being treated as having been entitled to his interest in possession since before 22 March 2006. The result of that, of course, is that the beneficiary's interest in the insurance contract is an existing IIP and therefore s 49 applies to it so that the beneficiary is treated as beneficially entitled to the contract. In turn, that results in David Clerestory's transfer of value being treated as a gift to another individual (by virtue of IHTA 1984, s 3A(2)) to the extent that, by virtue of the transfer, the estate of the beneficiary has been increased. That extends to the whole of the transfer of value because the premium immediately enhances the surrender value by an amount equal to the premium.

Henry makes a will

[21.4] Although Henry has no significant assets outside his trust interest he makes a will because he appreciates that he is likely to accumulate assets in the near future. As his parents would have no need of any assets which he had accumulated in the event that he were to die, he makes a simple will leaving his assets equally to Richard and Caroline. If he had had substantial assets he would have made a will creating flexible life interest trusts for his siblings. In the event of his death, those life interests would have been IPDIs and so the inheritance tax consequences of his death would have been the same as for outright gifts. The advantage of creating flexible life interest trusts, however, would have been to allow flexibility for the future.

Marriage

[21.5] On 20 July 2015, when he is 30 years old, Henry marries Polly who was born on 1 July 1992 and who is therefore, 23 years old.

Henry's career has progressed and his wealth increased

[21.6] Henry has been successful in his career and he is now a director of Caring for the Planet Inc. He has inherited a share portfolio from a bachelor uncle. His major assets and liabilities are:

	£000
Share ISAs	80
Other Shares	1,000
Flat in Wimbledon	500
Mortgage	<200>
Pension fund	100
Venture Capital Trust shares	200
Cash at bank	70
	1,750

The inheritance tax liability which would arise were he to die is:

	£000	£000
Assets	1,750	
Less: pension fund value written on discretionary trusts	<100>	
Free estate		1,650
Interest in possession in 'David Clerestory Insurance Settlement for Henry Clerestory'		429
Taxable estate		2,079
Nil rate band		325
Subject to inheritance tax at 40%		1,754
Inheritance tax thereon at 40%		£702

Pension fund death benefit

[21.7] The pension fund death benefit is held on discretionary trusts under the rules of the scheme. A scheme member can nominate any person or persons to be a member of the beneficial class other than himself. Once a nomination is made he can remove any person from the beneficial class provided that there shall always be at least one member of that class. In default of such a nomination the death benefit is held on trust for the member absolutely. Henry has nominated Richard and Caroline, any issue of his born during the trust period and any person who is at the time concerned his wife. He now gives the pension fund trustees a letter of wishes in which he asks them, in exercising their discretion, to take account of his wish that, if his wife survives him, he wishes her to benefit from the trust and not his siblings subject to whatever is appropriate for tax planning purposes.

Liability for the inheritance tax

[21.8] That amount of the total charge which is proportionate to the property held on the trusts of the David Clerestory Insurance Settlement in which he has an interest in possession would primarily be a liability of the trustees of the settlement concerned.

Henry makes a new will

[21.9] On Henry's marriage his will is revoked by operation of law. He therefore makes a new will under which he creates a flexible life interest trust for his wife and, subject to that, a broad discretionary trust for his issue, his brother and sister and their issue and his father. The trustees are to be his wife and an old friend, who is now his solicitor.

Although there is a large potential liability which would arise on Henry's death if he were to be predeceased by his wife, he is not particularly concerned about it. The life interest trust he establishes for his wife on his death would be an IPDI and therefore his estate would receive the spouse exemption if she were to survive him. He has no children or other dependants and Henry takes the attitude that, after their father's death, Richard and Caroline, who would be the principal beneficiaries of his discretionary will trust after his wife's death, are likely to be very well provided for and so he need not worry about any inheritance tax which would arise on the discretionary trust.

Henry insures his life

[21.10] Polly is currently working part time in an art gallery and does not have a large income. Henry is concerned that, if he were to die suddenly, Polly would not have a very high standard of living.

On 15 July 2015, therefore, he takes out whole of life assurance on his own life for a sum assured of £1m which he writes on discretionary trusts for a beneficial class consisting of Polly, his brother Richard, his sister Caroline, his issue, Richard's issue, Caroline's issue and any spouses of Richard or Caroline. The annual premium paid for this assurance is £14,000.

The assurance is constructed as a bundle of 100 separate policies.

In spite of the large sum assured the current market value of the policy is insignificant because it is not likely to mature for many years due to Henry's young age. The trustees of the policy are himself and his wife. He has a power of appointing new trustees and of requiring trustees to retire. He gives the trustees a letter of wishes in which he sets out his requests as to the principles which he would like to govern their exercise of their discretion under the settlement.

Henry will pay the premiums out of his income. So Henry's payment of the premiums will be exempt as normal expenditure out of income. The settlement will be a relevant property settlement but because of the insubstantial value of the property within the settlement and the fact that Henry has made no previous chargeable transfers it is likely that any decennial and exit charges in the early years would be at 0%.

His father makes a gift of £300,000 to help towards the purchase price of a house. This gift is a potentially exempt transfer. Henry sells his Wimbledon flat and half of his share portfolio, takes out a larger mortgage loan of £400,000 and buys a house in the same area for £1.7m.

Henry becomes a father

[21.11] In rapid succession Henry and Polly have three children, Simon, who is born on 31 March 2016, Charity who is born on 20 June 2017 and Prudence who is born on 15 November 2018.

Henry revises his will

[21.12] Henry makes a new will. Having considered whether it is necessary to do so in view of the transferrable nil rate band provisions of s 8A, he provides for a discretionary will trust over a legacy equal to the nil rate band at the time concerned less the aggregate chargeable transfers made in the 7 years before his death. The beneficial class of this trust includes his wife, his issue, his brother, sister and father. Now that he has children, he begins to worry about the inheritance tax liability which would arise if he and Polly were both to die prematurely.

Henry insures his life again

[21.13] On 30 April 2016, Henry takes out joint life last survivor policies on the lives of himself and his wife for a level sum assured of £1m written on similar trusts to those governing the previous policies. Although Henry is older than when he took out the previous policies, because the new policies are is written on a last survivor basis, the premiums are primarily determined by reference to Polly's life expectancy, which, because she is both female and considerably younger than Henry, is significantly longer than his. The annual premiums are, therefore, only £11,000 in aggregate. Again, Henry pays these premiums out of income and so they are covered by the normal expenditure out of income exemption. The settlement is a relevant property settlement but because of the low immediate value of the policies it is apparent that decennial and exit charges will not arise in the near future.

David Clerestory establishes further settlements

[21.14] With the birth of his third grandchild, David is keen to help Henry acquire a larger house in the country. Aware that many of his friends' children's marriages have broken down within a short period of children being born, however, he is reluctant to make outright gifts to Henry which could pass outside the family on divorce. He would like to settle funds on trust for this purpose but he is concerned to treat his three children equally and he doesn't want to trigger an immediate charge to inheritance tax. He has been in the habit of making gifts of £1,000 each to his three children, utilising his annual exemption, for a number of years but apart from these he has not made any further transfers. On successive days on 28, 29 and 30 November 2018 he makes three discretionary trusts earmarked for each of his three children and their families settling £1,000 in each trust. The trustees are himself and a family friend and the trust confers a broad discretion to apply income and capital for the benefit of a beneficial class consisting of Henry, Richard, Caroline and their issue. Both Richard and Caroline are married but as yet have no children.

David then adds £108,333 to each settlement on 15 December 2018. Because the settlements are made on successive days they are not related settlements and therefore, in calculating decennial and exit charges on each settlement the additions made to the other two settlements will not be taken into account. There is therefore plenty of room for future growth in the value of the assets.

David lends £390,667 to the settlement earmarked for Henry and that settlement in turn lends £500,000 to Henry interest free and repayable on demand.

Henry sells his house in Wimbledon for £2.0m, maintains his mortgage of £400,000 and buys a house in Sussex for £2.5m.

David Clerestory's death

David's taxable estate

[21.15] David Clerestory died on 20 December 2025 when he was 90 years old. Under his will £1m is to be divided between the Prayer Book Society and four other Anglican charities and the residue of his estate is to be divided equally between Henry, Richard and Caroline. His estate at death was as follows:

	£000
Clerestory Court	8,000
Clerestory Farm qualifying for agricultural property relief	12,000
Shares in Clerestory's Ecclesiastical Outfitters Ltd ('CEO Ltd'), qualifying for business property relief	5,000
Share portfolio	2,025
Cash at bank	3,000
Loan due from 28 November 2017 Settlement for Henry Clerestory	391
	30,416
Less agricultural and business property relief (Clerestory Farm and shares in CEO Ltd)	<17,000>
Total taxable estate	13,416
Charitable legacy	(1,000)
	12,416
Nil rate band	<325>
	12,091
Tax thereon at 40%	£4,836
Tax rate on estate 15.9%	

It will be seen that tax is chargeable on his gross estate at an average rate of only 15.9% because a large amount of the property in David Clerestory's estate qualifies for business and agricultural property relief or is bequeathed to charity.

Division of David's estate

[21.16] Henry and Richard are executors of their father's will. Richard is now managing director of Clerestory's Ecclesiastical Outfitters Ltd and he wishes to take all of the shares in that company. Caroline is anxious to make as clean a break as possible between her affairs and the family's.

It is agreed, however, that they should avoid selling the farmland if possible. Clerestory Court is surrounded by grounds of 30 acres. The house and grounds are surrounded by Clerestory Farm which has been let to a variety of tenants for many years. Although the land is let and an agent is engaged to manage the lettings, the land requires the owner to be involved on a regular basis in a variety of decisions. Henry has been very successful financially over the last few years and so he is able to agree to take Clerestory Court with the farmland being held equally between the three siblings on bare trusts under which he is to be responsible for the management decisions in relation to the land for as long as the property is held in trust. The trustees' decisions in relation to the land, other than in relation to its management, are to be taken unanimously. In this way, the land could not be sold without Henry's consent and, until it is sold, he would be in a position to take the day to day management decisions in relation to it with the help and advice of the family land agent.

Henry considers making an application for National Heritage Property Relief on Clerestory Court (an outstanding Grade I listed Jacobean house) but decides that the public access requirements are likely to be too onerous.

Henry repays the loan of £500,000 which was made to him by the trustees of 28 November 2018 Settlement and the trustees in turn repay to the executors the loan of £390,667 which had been made to it by David Clerestory.

Henry sells his family home for £4.5m and repays the £400,000 mortgage on it. His gain on the sale of the home is exempt from capital gains tax as it is the sale of his principle private residence. Although the home has garden and grounds of five acres the whole of the gain relating to this area is exempt because the whole of the garden and grounds are required for the reasonable enjoyment of the dwelling house.

After his father's death Henry takes stock

[21.17] After the death of his father, when he is 40 years old, Henry takes stock of his financial position. His free estate now consists of the following.

	£000
A shareholding in EnviroEthics Group Plc	5,000
ISAs	250
Share portfolio	2,500
Venture Capital Trust shares	2,500
Portfolio of shares qualifying for EIS relief which are listed on the Alternative Investment Market and which are business property for inheritance tax purposes	1,500
Cash at bank	500
Clerestory Court	8,000
One third interest in Clerestory Farm	4,000
	24,250

Interests in settlements:

	£000
Existing life interest in insurance policies held by David Clerestory Settlement. The fund value is:	510

	£000
Discretionary object of settlement made by David Clerestory on 28 November 2018 earmarked for Henry Clerestory. The fund value is:	100
Pension fund	1,000
In addition the following settlements hold assets on discretionary trusts for beneficial classes including his wife Polly and their children—	
The Henry Clerestory Insurance Trust No 1	
Holds whole of life policies on Henry Clerestory's life for a level sum assured of £1m for annual premiums of £14,000. These policies have an insignificant market value	0
The Henry Clerestory Insurance Trust No 2	
Holds joint life, last survivor policies on the lives of himself and his wife for a level sum assured £1m for annual premiums of £11,000. These policies have an insignificant market value	0

Henry has the following income:

	£000
Net dividend income from free estate (a small proportion of dividends are not subject to income tax)	200
Interest income	25
Director's emoluments	1,000
Share of rents from share of Clerestory Farm	50
	1,275

His annual expenditure is £850,000. This total includes taxation but excludes his regular investments which are deductible from income for taxation purposes (VCTs, pension contributions and EIS shares) and his payments of life insurance premiums.

The inheritance tax liability which would arise if he were to die immediately, followed shortly by the death of his wife Polly, would be as follows:

	£000
Free estate	24,250
Interests in existing IIPs	510
	24,760
Property qualifying for BPR: EIS portfolio	<1,500>
Property qualifying for APR: Interest in Clerestory Farm	<4,000>
Nil rate band utilised by Henry's legacy on discretionary trusts	<325>
Nil rate band utilised on Polly's death	<325>
Subject to inheritance tax at 40%	18,610
Inheritance tax thereon at 40%	7,444

Henry's pension fund death benefit has continued to be held on discretionary trusts. Although his pension fund is £1m the value of the death benefit is very low. This is both because Henry is still a comparatively young man in good health and because, when Henry reaches the age of 55, he will have the ability to deplete the fund (and thus the death benefit) by opting to take his pension.

Henry is alarmed at the size of the potential inheritance tax liability on Polly's death. He therefore decides to take two courses of action.

First, he settles six discretionary trusts on successive days on the first six days of February 2026, settling £500 on each (thus using his annual exemption). The beneficial classes of these trusts are exactly the same and consist of Henry's issue, any spouses of his issue and any charity. They are divided into three groups of two trusts earmarked informally for a particular child. During his children's minorities (or until their earlier marriage or their entering into a civil partnership) if any income is paid to a beneficiary or applied to his benefit, that income will be treated as Henry's.

On 28 February 2026, Henry adds £54,666 to each settlement. The trustees, Henry and Polly, invest the capital of each settlement in capital redemption bonds maturing in 99 years time but surrenderable at will. In this way the administration of the trust is very much simplified because no capital gains will arise in the trust and no income will arise until the bonds are encashed. In each of the next six years Henry intends to add £500 to each trust thus utilising his annual exemption. These additions will be used by the trustees to pay additional premiums under the capital redemption policies.

Because the settlements are not related settlements, in calculating the decennial charges arising in each settlement the additions made to the others will not be taken into account. Because the initial settled fund is exempted by the annual exemption and Henry has made no other chargeable transfers in the seven years before the settlements are made each settlement's assets may grow in value by £266,667 (£325,000 - £58,333) before a decennial charge (and therefore before an exit charge) can arise. Even with the six annual additions of £500 such a growth in value is likely to take a very long time. After the seventh anniversary of the last of the six large additions, Henry will repeat the process settling six new trusts on successive days and making an addition shortly thereafter followed by six annual additions of £500 per settlement. He will repeat this pattern after each seventh anniversary of the previous large additions.

He is conscious, however, that the gifts into these settlements are not going to make a significant inroad in reducing his taxable estate of £19m. He therefore decides that he will also make regular additional gifts out of income in favour of his children. Although these gifts out of income will not be immediately chargeable, gifts into relevant property trusts of a significant size would create inheritance tax charges on the decennials of the trusts. He therefore decides that he will make gifts on bare trusts for his three children absolutely. He has no wish, however, to place large amounts of money into the hands of his children on their 18th birthday.

He therefore takes out with an insurance company a group of 100 identical policies written on the joint lives of himself and Polly on a last survivor basis so that the policies will mature on the death of the last of them to die.

An unusual feature of the policies is that they have no surrender value. In that way they do not offer the immediate ability to realise spendable cash. The policies are not, however, a complete answer to the problem of giving beneficial ownership of assets to children at an age before they are fully financially responsible. Immediately on reaching an 18th birthday, the beneficiary of the bare trust could require the trustees to pass the trust property to him and, even though the insurance policies could not be surrendered, they could be sold for a capital sum or used to secure borrowing. Accepting these drawbacks, Henry enters into the policies.

He will pay aggregate annual premiums of £400,000; that is £4,000 per policy per year, being the surplus of his income over his annual expenditure and the premiums which he pays in respect of the insurance policies which he has previously taken out (£1,275,000 - £850,000 - £14,000 - £11,000).

The premiums under the policies are payable for a minimum of ten years. After ten years the policies can be made paid up at any time in which case no further premiums would be payable. Because of this, the policies will be qualifying policies which, therefore, will not, in most circumstances, give rise to chargeable event gains. The yield on the policies will therefore escape higher rate tax.

From age 40 to age 60

[21.18] Between the ages of 40 and 60 Henry continues the pattern of transfers that he has established. There are also the following significant developments.

Henry requests the trustees of his pension fund death benefit to exercise their discretionary powers to hold the death benefit for his three children in equal shares absolutely. That is the occasion of an exit charge but because the value of the death benefit was less than the nil rate band at the last decennial, the rate of charge is 0%.

Henry continues to prosper, becoming the Chief Executive of EnviroEthics Group Plc and subsequently its chairman.

As Henry's, Richard's and Caroline's lives develop, Richard and Caroline become increasingly dissatisfied at having a substantial amount of capital tied up in Clerestory Farm which produces a very low income and which enhances Henry's enjoyment of Clerestory Court but does not similarly benefit them. Henry therefore buys their interests at their current market value of £6m each.

As each of his children comes down from university, he buys that child a flat for £500,000. When each reaches his or her 25th birthday he makes a gift to that child of £250,000 to provide an investment fund for them. All of these gifts are PETs.

Henry reaches 60 and retires

[21.19] When Henry reaches his 60th birthday he retires after a long and profitable career in environmental lobbying and consultancy. He feels that it is time once again to take stock of his position. Simon is engaged to be married, although Charity and Prudence are showing no particular signs of settling down.

Disinvestment from EnviroEthics Group Plc

[21.20] His shareholding in EnviroEthics Group Plc has continued to increase in value significantly, although he has been making regular sales of shares accepting the capital gains tax charge which arises on the sale at an effective rate of 28%.

Assets and income

[21.21] In spite of the substantial gifts he has made, his assets have increased significantly and his wife Polly has inherited assets from her father. Their joint estates are now as follows:

	Henry	Polly	Total
	£000	£000	£000
ISAs	1,300	100	1,400
Pension fund	0	0	0
VCTs	5,000	0	5,000
Portfolio of shares qualifying for EIS Relief which are listed on the Alternative Investment Market and which are Business Property for inheritance tax purposes	4,500	400	4,900
Cash at bank	1,000	200	1,200
Clerestory Court	24,000	0	24,000
Clerestory Farm	18,000	0	18,000
Portfolio of shares, bonds and gilts	20,000	1,000	21,000
	73,800	1,700	75,500

Henry's pension fund is now valued at £1,500,000. He is very conscious that, now that he has retired, his income will have reduced substantially. He estimates that his and his wife's incomes will now be:

	Henry	Polly	Total
	£000	£000	£000
Dividends from ISAs	30	3	33
Dividends on VCT and EIS shares	50	4	54
Bank interest	40	10	50
Rents from Clerestory Farm	160	0	160
Other net dividends	330	10	240

	Henry	Polly	Total
	£000	£000	£000
Other interest	200	23	223
	810	50	860

Henry has not drawn down his pension and does not intend to do so in the near future.

Henry and Polly estimate their annual expenditure including taxation but excluding his payment of annual premiums on life assurance policies at £560,000 per annum.

Annual insurance premiums

[21.22] Henry realises that he can no longer pay all of the insurance premiums which he has been paying out of his surplus income which is now only £250,000 (£810,000 - £560,000). He decides to continue to pay the premiums on the policies held by the Henry Clerestory Insurance No 1 and No 2 Trusts amounting to £25,000 per annum. Of the 100 policies taken out in 2026 he makes 44 paid up so that the annual premiums on these policies reduce from £400,000 per annum to £224,000; an amount which he can afford to pay from his surplus.

Potential inheritance tax on Henry's and Polly's estates

[21.23] The inheritance tax liability which would arise if he were to die immediately followed shortly afterwards by his wife, Polly, would be as follows:

	£000
Aggregate free estate of Henry and Polly	75,500
Interests in existing IIP's David Clerestory Settlement for Henry	1,100
	76,600
Property qualifying for BPR: EIS shares	(4,500)
Property qualifying for APR: Clerestory Farm	(18,000)
Nil rate band utilised by Henry's legacy on discretionary trusts	(325)
Nil rate band utilised on Polly's death	(325)
Subject to inheritance tax on Polly's death at 40%	53,450
Inheritance tax thereon at 40%	21,380

Henry is once again appalled at the idea of so much of the family wealth being expropriated by the Government.

Simon has just obtained an appointment in New York with Carbon Trading Credits Plc which he will take up immediately after his honeymoon. He will be out of the country for at least 2 years and expects to be non-resident.

The trustees of the David Clerestory Settlement have made no withdrawals from the policies on the life of Henry which were taken out at the time the settlement was made. If the policies were to be encashed by the trustees, who are now Henry and Polly, the trustees would be chargeable on substantial chargeable event gains. The trustees decide to advance the policies to Simon. That is a potentially exempt transfer and is not a chargeable event for the purposes of ITTOIA 2005, Pt 4 Ch 9. If Simon were to surrender the policies whilst he was not resident in the United Kingdom, the chargeable event gain would be realised free of taxation. Simon subsequently does so receiving £1,100,000.

Henry reaches his 70th birthday

[21.24] By 2055 when Henry reaches his 70th birthday, Simon is married to Emma and has three children, James, John and Julia. Charity is married to Fergus and has one child, Angus. Prudence has been married, is divorced and is childless.

Gift of Clerestory Court

[21.25] Henry has reorganised his investments reducing his holdings in VCTs and increasing his investments in Enterprise Investment Scheme companies qualifying for business property relief.

Simon is now settled in this country and, although he continues to travel internationally on business, he thinks it is unlikely that he will again reside for long periods abroad. It is agreed that Simon and his family will occupy Clerestory House with Henry and Polly and that Henry will give a 99% interest in the house, which is now worth £35m, to Simon. In the hope of preventing a reservation of benefit arising Henry will pay his proportionate share of the expenses of the house.

Simon takes on the burden of managing Clerestory Farm relieving Henry of the responsibility.

Hope of development on Clerestory Farm

[21.26] A change of planning criteria has had the result that it is now hoped that an area of some 50 acres (the 'Ciborium Land') of Clerestory Farm, which is situated near Ciborium village and which forms that part of the farm which is furthest away from Clerestory Court, will be zoned for development. It is hoped that subsequently it will be possible to obtain planning permission for its development. Simon decides that he will instigate a policy of bringing the Ciborium Land in hand employing a professional farm manager. He does this for two reasons.

First, so that the land will qualify for business property relief. Although it already qualifies for agricultural property relief, any excess of its value over its agricultural value would not receive APR. Second, because any purchaser of the land for development will require vacant possession as a condition of the sale.

Henry's pension fund

[21.27] Henry is aware that when he reaches the age of 77 he will have to take an annual pension from his pension fund. Annuity rates seem particularly good at the time he reaches his 70th birthday. He decides that his pension fund should purchase an annuity. The result of this is that on his death there will be no assets remaining in his fund.

Henry's charitable donation

[21.28] Henry wished to make a substantial charitable donation to the Prayer Book Society (registered charity number 1099295). He was considering making this donation under his will but decided that he could maximise the tax relief on it by making annual gift aid donations. He therefore made an interest free loan to the Society of £1m and determined to make payments under gift aid of £50,000 per year which the Society would apply in reducing the loan. He makes a new will providing that the balance of the loan outstanding at his death should be written off. At the same time he provided that Polly and Simon should be the executors of his will.

The death of Henry

[21.29] Henry died on 30 June 2070 when he was aged 85. The only chargeable transfer he had made in the seven years before his death was a transfer of £325,000 in total into six settlements made in February 2068 under the pattern of settlement which he had first established in 2026. All of the other transfers he had made within seven years of death were either covered by the annual exemption or by the exemption for ordinary expenditure out of income. His estate on death and Polly's estate on that date were as follows:

	Henry's estate on death	Polly's estate
	£000	£000
ISAs	4,100	275
1% interest in Clerestory Court	640	0
Portfolio of shares on which EIS relief was given and qualifying as business property	10,000	1,000
Cash at bank	1,000	200
Clerestory Farm excluding the Ciborium Land	10,000	0
Ciborium Land	50,000	0
Portfolio of shares	27,000	0
Gilts and bonds	27,000	3,000
	119,740	4,475

The Ciborium Land

[21.30] Simon had been successful in freeing the Ciborium Land from the tenancies to which it had been subject and the land was now farmed in hand. Planning permission had been obtained on the land in 2068 and a number of offers from property development companies had been received for the land since that time. Henry had been in poor health for the last two years of his life and he had therefore determined to reject these offers so as to obtain the uplift to market value in the value of the land on his death for his children.

The land qualified for business property relief.

No discretionary will trust

[21.31] Henry had not changed his will since 2055. He had, however, reviewed it regularly.

As we have seen, his will provided for a legacy on discretionary trusts of an amount equal to the nil rate band less the amount of any lifetime transfers within seven years of his death. Because Henry had last made a chargeable trust of £325,000 by settling property on discretionary trusts in 2068, the discretionary legacy was reduced to nil.

Charitable legacy to the Prayer Book Society

[21.32] David had made 15 annual gift aid payments of £50,000 each to the Prayer Book Society with the result that the outstanding balance on the loan he had made to it was £250,000. The writing off of this outstanding balance under the terms of his will was a charitable donation which was exempt from inheritance tax. By making gifts of £750,000 under gift aid David had, in effect, received tax relief at 70%. He had received 50% income tax relief on his gift aid donations and, because, had he not made those donations, his net income would have increased his estate at death, he had received a further 40% inheritance tax relief on the net payments after 50% income tax relief. Had he made the donation under his will, the tax benefit would have been only 40%. By making lifetime gifts, therefore, he had increased the tax relief on the gifts from 40% to an effective 70%.

No inheritance tax chargeable on Henry's estate

[21.33] The EIS shares and the Ciborium Land received 100% business property relief. Clerestory Farm, excluding the Ciborium Land, received 100% agricultural property relief. The will trust arising under Henry's will conferring an interest in possession on Polly was an immediate post death interest with the result that IHTA 1984, s 49 applied to it. The bequests and devises to the trust were therefore relieved from inheritance tax by virtue of being transfers to a spouse.

The advance from the will trust

[21.34] Polly decided that her own personal assets were sufficient to meet her living expenses and so it was decided to advance the assets arising under Henry's will trust to Simon, Charity and Prudence in equal shares. The Ciborium Land was advanced jointly to Simon, Charity and Prudence and the trustees appropriated the 1% interest in Clerestory Court and remaining Clerestory Farm land to Simon in part satisfaction of his remaining share. The EIS shares and the Ciborium Land again received 100% business property relief. Clerestory Farm again received 100% agricultural property relief. The advance of the remaining trust assets was a potentially exempt transfer by Polly which would only become chargeable if she were to die within seven years of the advance.

Sale of the Ciborium Land

[21.35] Simon, Charity and Prudence sold the Ciborium Land for a price roughly equal to its probate value to developers a few months after Henry's death. The land having passed free of inheritance tax on Henry's death, no chargeable gain was now realised on the disposal of the land because of the uplift of its base cost to market value on Henry's death. The effect of the sale was that business property relief would not be available on the trustees' previous advance of the land if Polly were to die within 7 years of the advance so that her potentially exempt transfer would, in that event, become chargeable.

Relevant property settlements; planning for the decennial charges

[21.36] Henry had been either the settlor or a beneficial object of various relevant property settlements. They had been dealt with by the trustees in the following ways.

At Henry's death, in addition to the settlements Henry had made in 2026 and thereafter, there are three relevant property settlements in existence, the assets of which are earmarked for Henry's family. They are the settlement made by David Clerestory on 28 November 2018, the insurance trust which Henry made on 15 July 2015 and the further insurance trust which he made on 30 April 2016.

In calculating decennial charges, one posits a hypothetical transfer by a transferor who has aggregate chargeable transfers equal to the chargeable transfers made by the settlor in the seven years preceding the settlement and the amounts on which exit charges had been made in the ten years preceding the decennial. Therefore, exits made in the ten years before the decennial will increase the rate of tax charged on that decennial. In order to minimise decennial and later exit charges therefore, trustees need to anticipate the growth in value of the trust assets not only to the next decennial but to the following one as well. The trustees of these three settlements have done so, carefully advancing amounts to the beneficiaries so as to ensure that the decennial charges arising on each decennial are at 0%.

Groups of relevant property trusts made at seven-year intervals from 2026

[21.37] By the time of his death in 2070 at the age of 85, Henry had made seven groups of six discretionary settlements under the pattern of settlement which he had established in 2026. These settlements contained assets with a total value of £3,053,000. The trust property of each of the trusts made in 2026 was valued at £82,000 and of course the value of the property in each trust settled in later years was very much less than this. Henry had therefore, by means of these settlements, managed to move a substantial amount of property out of his estate and to keep it for a long period of time in an inheritance tax free environment. What is more it was possible to continue to hold this property in the settlements so that it would continue to grow in an IHT free environment.

The death of Polly

[21.38] Polly lived a further 11 years to the age of 89 and so the potentially exempt transfer resulting from the exercise by the trustees of Henry's will trust of their discretion to advance assets to Simon, Charity and Prudence absolutely proved not to be a chargeable transfer.

After Henry's death the group of whole of life last survivor life insurance policies written on bare trusts for his children which commenced in 2025 were made paid up. On Polly's death the insurance policies matured. The aggregate maturity value of the policies at that time was £72m, premiums of £15.36m in total having been paid over the life of the policies.

Over his lifetime, and on his death, the following advances, gifts, devises and bequests had been made from the property which either did, or was deemed to, form part of Henry's estate for inheritance tax purposes without any inheritance tax being payable whatsoever.

Year	Event	Comment
2015	Henry takes out whole of life assurance on his life for a level sum assured written on discretionary trusts for his family and paying annual premiums of £14,000.	The trustees advance 25 policies each to Simon, Charity and Prudence during Henry's life. On his death £250,000 is received by the discretionary trust and £250,000 each is received by his children.
2016	Henry takes out life assurance on the joint lives of himself and Polly on a last survivor basis written on discretionary trusts for his family and paying annual premiums of £11,000.	The trustees advance 25 policies each to Simon, Charity and Prudence during Henry's life. On his death £250,000 is received by the discretionary trust and £250,000 each is received by his children.

Year	Event	Comment
2026 and there-after	Henry makes groups of discretionary settlements equal to the nil rate band every seven years with annual additions equal to the annual exemption.	No inheritance tax arises on the settlement of the trusts or whilst they continue. At Henry's death the trust assets have a total value of £3.1m.
2026	Henry takes out a group of policies on bare trusts for his children paying annual premiums out of income which initially amount to £400,000 per year.	On Polly's death Henry's children share £72m between them premiums of £15.4m having been paid under the policies.
2037-2039	Henry gives each of his three children a flat worth £500,000 and money to invest of £250,000 so that he makes gifts of £2.25m in all.	These gifts are PETS.
2045	The trustees of the David Clerestory Settlement defeat Henry's life interest in the fund advancing the settlement assets to Simon absolutely.	Simon surrenders the capital redemption bonds advanced to him whilst he is non-resident realising £1.1m.
2055	Henry gives a 99% interest in Clerestory Court which is now worth £35m to Simon absolutely.	This is a PET.
2055–2070	Henry makes charitable donations totalling £750,000 under gift aid.	These are exempt transfers and receive income tax relief under Gift Aid.
2070	On his death, Henry makes a charitable donation of £250,000.	This is an exempt transfer.
2070	The trustees of Henry's Will Trust advance assets with a value of £120m to the children.	This transfer receives APR and BPR of £71m and is a potentially exempt transfer as to the balance. The potentially exempt transfer does not become chargeable.

Index

D

E

F

O

P

U

V

W